EXPERIENCE AND IDENTITY

A Historical Account of Class, Caste, and Gender among the Cashew Workers of Kerala, 1930-2000

ANNA LINDBERG

MANOHAR

2023

First published by
Lund University in 2001

Reprinted 2021, 2023

© Anna Lindberg, 2001

ISBN 978-93-90729-91-3

Published by
Ajay Kumar Jain *for*
Manohar Publishers & Distributors
4753/23 Ansari Road, Daryaganj
New Delhi 110 002

Printed at
Replika Press Pvt. Ltd.

CONTENTS

Tables   ix
Figures   x
Abbreviations   x
Glossary   xi
Note on the Spelling of Indian Names   xii
Map of Kerala   xiii
Acknowledgements   xiv

I INTRODUCTION   1
Meeting at the Factory   1
Positioning the Study   4
Why Kerala?   10
A Brief Historical Overview of Kerala   12
    Travancore   12
    Matrilineal society   13
    The caste hierarchy   16
    Social movements   21
    Radical policy and the present crises   23
The Significance of Research on the Cashew Workers   25
Aims and Objectives   27
Structure of the Study   29

II CONCEPTS AND METHODOLOGY   30
Introduction   30
Housewifization   30
Ideology and Discourse   35
Consciousness, Experience, and Identity   41
Caste and Class   46
Adding Gender to the Caste and Class   51
The Field of Research   54
A Multiplicity of Methods and Sources   60
Field Work and the "Outsider"   62
Interviews and the Oral History   66
Interviewing Procedures   68
Interpreters in the Field   70
Summary of Main Theoretical Concepts and Methodologies   71

III A HISTORY OF THE CASHEW FACTORIES 73
The Dawn of the Cashew Factories in South India 73
Concentration of Cashew Factories in Quilon 78
Dependency on Imported Raw Cashew Nuts 83
From Perennial to Seasonal Factories 85
State Interventions in the Cashew Industry 89
KSCDC and CAPEX 91
Balancing Between Two States 94
Summary 99

IV GENDER IN THE WORKPLACE 101
Introduction 101
Work Processes 104
  Roasting 104
  Shelling 108
  Drying 109
  Peeling 110
  Grading 110
  Packing 111
  The work process—a summary 112
Masculinity and Femininity in the Cashew Factories 113
  Work for able-bodied men? 113
  Patient women with nimble fingers? 122
Conclusion 130

V CASTE IN THE WORKPLACE 132
Introduction 132
Caste Division of Labor 133
Recruitment of Laborers in the Early Days 138
Cashew Workers on Caste 148
  The creation of a caste division of labor 149
  Overcoming caste barriers 156
  The persistence of the caste division of labor 163
  The meaning of caste 170
Conclusion 176

VI WAGES AND GENDER DISCOURSES 178
Introduction 178
The Model of Male Breadwinners 179
The Male Breadwinner Model in India 181

Representation of Women Workers in the 1940s 183
   Factory owners 183
   Civil servants 185
   Trade union leaders 187
The Institutionalization of Male Breadwinners 187
Stipulated Minimum Wages in the Cashew Factories 191
   Gender discourse in the report of 1953 194
   The Minimum Wage Committee of 1959 200
   Revisions of minimum wages in 1967 and 1975 202
   The committees in 1989 and 1998 204
Female Cashew Workers as Breadwinners 208
Conclusion 214

VII TRADE UNIONS 217
Introduction 217
Early Mobilizations and Successes: 1937–1954 222
Institutionalization of Trade Unions: ca. 1955–ca. 1975 229
Crises and Declined Militancy: ca. 1975–2000 237
Labor Laws at the Factory Level 240
   Wages and other financial benefits 241
   Tools, working clothes, and protective measures 243
   Unpaid work 245
Kudivarappus, Class Consciousness, and Trade Union Loyalty 251
Illiterate and Ignorant—Exploited for Political Purposes? 265
Relationship to the Leaders 271
Exceptions in the Labor Movement: "the Others" 273
Conclusion 280

VIII MARRIAGE, CASTE, AND GENDER 285
Introduction 285
Central Concepts 287
Theoretical Approaches 289
Marriage Payment in Travancore and Kerala 292
Cashew Workers and Marriage Payment 294
   Bridegroom price: the legitimacy of dowries 300
   Earned welfare benefits turn into dowries 305
   Inter-caste marriages and love-marriages 308
   Unstable marriage patterns and divorces 312
   The importance of marriage, motherhood, and work 315
Conclusion 319

IX CONCLUSION 323
Main Themes 323
Gender Division of Labor 326
Trade Unions Participation 329
Class Consciousness and Class Identity 331
Caste Identities 334
Dowry and the Male Breadwinner 336
The Process of Effeminization 338
Theoretical Implications 340

EPILOGUE 343

APPENDIX 347

BIBLIOGRAPHY 352

Tables

3.1 Number of registered cashew factories and employment in
    Kerala, 1958–2000 88
4.1 Distribution of workers by category in Kerala cashew factories,
    1965 and 1977 113
4.2 Composition of workers in Travancore cashew factories,
    1936–1939 114
4.3 Composition of workers in Kerala cashew factories,
    1952–1994 116
5.1 Caste and gender composition among Vijayalakshmi
    Cashew Factory 134
5.2 Caste and gender composition in KSCDC Factory No. 1 135
5.3 Daily wages in different departments of Musaliar's factories,
    1932 and 1939 154
6.1 Estimated average daily wages according to the stipulated
    minimum wages for cashew workers 192
6.2 Wages demanded by unions on 15 April 1966 203
6.3 Estimated contributions of female cashew workers to
    households in January 1998 211
7.1 The cashew workers' earliest leaflet of demands, 1937 225
7.2 Labor rights introduced for cashew workers, 1945–1953 229
7.3 Trade unions among cashew workers in Kerala 230
7.4 Social welfare schemes for cashew workers, 1963–1975 233
8.1 Number of marriages with dowries paid and received
    among Scheduled Castes, 1940–1999 295
8.2 Number of marriages with dowries paid and received
    among Ezhavas and other middle castes, 1940–1999 295
8.3 Number of marriages with dowries paid and received
    among Nairs, 1940–1999 296
8.4 Amount of dowry paid or received 1960–1999 among
    Scheduled Castes 297
8.5 Amount of dowry paid or received 1960–1999 among
    Ezhavas and other middle castes 297
8.6 Amount of dowry paid or received 1940–1999 among Nairs ... 298
8.7 Percent of love-marriages among cashew workers of different
    communities, 1930–1999 311
9.1 Schematic overview of important results 325
9.2 Various attributes related to gender 333

Figures

Figure 7.1 Structure of the formal and informal sector
of the Kerala cashew industry 256

Abbreviations

AITUC	All-India Trade Union Council
ARA	Arbetarrörelsens Arkiv, Stockholm
ASI	Annual Survey of Industries
CAPEX	Kerala State Cashew Workers Apex Industrial Cooperative Society, Ltd.
CEPC	Cashew Export Promotion Council
CCI	Cashew Corporation of India
CITU	Centre of Indian Trade Unions
CPI	Communist Party of India
CPI-M	Communist Party of India, Marxist
CWM	Council for World Mission
ESI	Employees State Insurance Scheme
ILO	International Labour Organisation
INC	Indian National Congress
INTUC	Indian Trade Union Congress
KSA	Kerala State Archive, Nalanda, Trivandrum
KSCDC	Kerala State Cashew Development Corporation
NRC	North Record Cellar, Secretariat, Government of Kerala, Trivandrum
PF	Provident Fund
RCFW	Report of the Committee on Fair Wages
RCLI	Royal Commission on Labour in India
RSP	Revolutionary Socialist Party
SC	Scheduled Castes
SICMA	South Indian Cashew Factory Manufacturers Association
SOAS	School of Oriental and African Studies
SRC	South Record Cellar, Secretariat, Government of Kerala, Trivandrum
ST	Scheduled Tribes
UTUC	United Trade Union Congress

Glossary

Avarna	Hindus not belonging to any of the four varnas
Ayah	children's nurse in factories
Borma	oven for drying cashew nuts
Brahmins	priests and religious teachers in the *varna* system
Casu	Travancore coin: 1 casu = 1/16 chuckram
Cent	area, 1/100 of an acre
Chitti	savings fund
Chuckram	Travancore coin: 28.5 chuckrams = one British Rupee
Dewan	former title of prime minister in Indian states
Dharma	Hindu concept for cosmic principle, divine standard of conduct
Dhoti	loin-cloth
Ezhavas, Izhavas	caste in Travancore and Kerala, traditionally related to work with coconut trees, here defined as a middle-caste
Harijans	"children of God", concept introduced by Gandhi for "untouchables"
Janmi	landlord
Jati	"birth", an endogamous group (caste), earlier associated with distinct occupations
Kanji	rice soup (often with vegetables and ghee)
Karanavan	elder, male head of a *taravad*
Kshatriyas	category in the varna system associated with rulers and warriors
Kudivarappu	clandestine, illegal processing of cashew nuts
Kuravas	an *avarna*, former slave caste in Travancore and Kerala. Traditionally they were agricultural workers. Registered as a Scheduled Caste.
Lakh	100,000
Marumakkathayam	matrilineal system of kinship and inheritance
Moopan	recruiter, intermediary
Mycaud	casual worker
Nairs, Nayars	caste in Travancore and Kerala, traditionally landowners, here defined as high-caste
Nambuthiri Brahmins	caste in Travancore and Kerala, traditionally landowners and priests. They were considered the highest in the caste hierarchy.
Onam	important festival in August or September
Parayans	an *avarna*, former slave caste in Travancore and Kerala. Traditionally they were agricultural workers. Registered as a Scheduled Caste.

Pavan	unit of weight, 8 grams
Pulayas	*avarna*, former slave caste in Travancore and Kerala. Traditionally they were agricultural workers. Registered as a Scheduled Caste.
Purampokke land	"nobody's land, outside land", often land close to rivers, roads, and railroads, owned by the state
Purdah	"screen, veil", female seclusion
Sanskritization	emulation of cultural behavior of a higher caste in order to raise one's ritual status
Satyagraha	civil unrest, protest
Savarna	Hindus belonging to one of the four *varnas*
Scheduled Castes	administrative concept to identify unprivileged groups. In reality the Scheduled Castes are identical with former untouchables.
Shudras	category in the *varna* system associated with peasants and servants.
Sovereign	unit of weight, 8 grams
Stridhanam	"women's wealth", dowry controlled and owned by the bride
Taluk	administrative area
Taravad	house and property of the matrilineal Nairs
Thali	marriage symbol for women
Untouchables	castes outside the *varna* system, considered to be particularly polluted
Vaishyas	category in the *varna* system, associated with trade and handicraft
Varna	"color", hierarchical categories in the Hindu caste system. The four *varnas* are Brahmins, Kshatriyas, Vaishyas, and Shudras

Note on the Spelling of Indian Names

In the late 1990s, the names of many Indian places were changed to their pre-British pronunciations. The British versions will be employed as they were most common in printed material and references during the years studied. Hence, "Quilon", "Alleppey", and "Travancore", although in some quotations the forms "Kollam", "Allapuzha", and "Tiruvitamkur" occur.

Map of Kerala

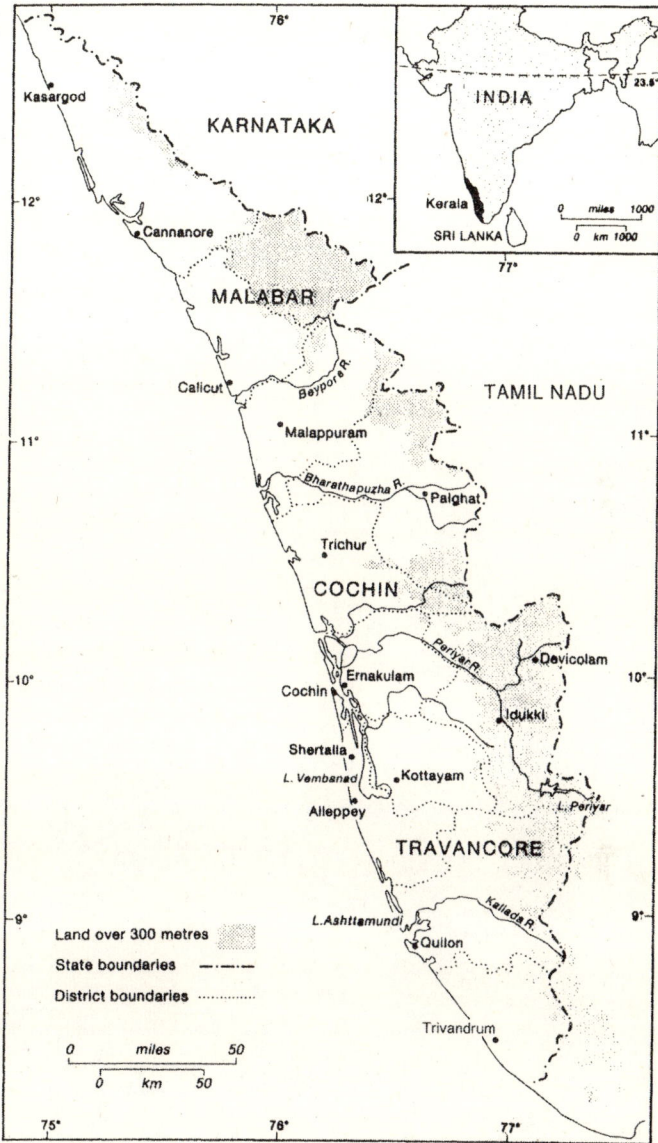

Land over 300 metres

State boundaries — · — · —

District boundaries ··········

Kasargod

KARNATAKA

INDIA

23.6°

12°

12°

Kerala

SRI LANKA

Cannanore

miles 1000

km 1000

MALABAR

Calicut

Beypore R.

TAMIL NADU

11°

Malappuram

11°

Bharathapuzha R.

Palghat

Trichur

COCHIN

10°

Periyar R.

Devicolam

Ernakulam

10°

Cochin

Idukki

Shertalla

L. Vembanad

Kottayam

Alleppey

L. Periyar

TRAVANCORE

9°

L. Ashttamundi

Kallada R.

9°

Quilon

Trivandrum

0   miles   50

0   km   50

75°

76°

77°

xiii

Acknowledgements

For several years I have been a research scholar at the Department of History at Lund University. These years have been among the best I have ever had and so it is with mixed feelings I realize they are drawing to a close. The academic as well as the social environment in Lund has been most inspiring. I would like to record my gratitude to all who have helped me carry forward this thesis, although words are inadequate to express my indebtedness.

Professor Lars Olsson, my supervisor and long-time friend, has been a neverending source of encouragement. Not only your scholarly knowledge, but your tolerance and patience over the years has been admirable. Without your help and support, I would never have dared continue. Thank you for this, Lars, and also for always reading my drafts with such thoroughness.

My sincere thanks to Professor Eva Österberg. Despite my topic being far from your own field of research, you were a perfect guide. You have always drawn upon your rich field of knowledge to give me the most valuable academic advice and intellectual inspiration. A heavy workload never hindered you from making the time to carefully read and discuss my drafts with me. Your encouraging words gave me confidence to believe in this project. Without your help, I would never have brought it to completion.

Dr. Diana Mulinari, who entered the process at a critical moment, helped me to find my way out of the jungle of feminist theories in which I was lost. I always looked forward to our stimulating meetings. Thank you for your wonderful determination to guide and assist me, no matter when it was. You made me believe I had the capacity to finish the project, and were instrumental in nurturing that feeling in me.

Several seminars have contributed to this dissertation in many ways. In particular, I would like to express my gratitude to all the members of Professor Österberg's doctoral seminar in the Department of History at Lund University. The seminar for labor historians in Lund has also served as a great source of inspiration. To the Center for Gender Studies in Lund, with its wonderful library, dedicated members, and stimulating seminars, I would like to express my thanks. Professor Staffan Lindberg of the Department of Sociology at Lund University has been a principal source of motivation for my research in India. Participating in the Development Study Seminar which he has led has been fruitful in many ways. Thank you, Staffan, and thanks to all "Third World Sociologists" in Lund.

At an early stage, Dr. Ingrid Millbourn's criticism and advice was a turning point for me. From the depth of my heart, thank you! To Dr. Torvald Olsson, many thanks for generously letting me use your library and for our long discussions on the topic of caste in South India. Our conversations have guided and inspired me. My dialogues with Cecilia Persson were important for my work. Thank you for reading my drafts and for encouraging me. Thanks also to Carola Nordbäck, who read some chapters and gave me fruitful comments. Monica Erwér, I will always remember our intellectually stimulating, but also humorous, conversations when we both were doing research in Kerala. Thank you for good advice and encouragement. Sincere thanks also to Dr. Dianne Jennett for valuable support and for sharing a house with me in Kerala.

Drs. Monika Edgren, Christina Carlsson-Wetterberg, and Professor Kim Salomon were kind enough to read parts of the manuscript. Sincere thanks for all of your valuable comments and suggestions for improvement.

Every word in this thesis has crossed the Atlantic through cyberspace more than once, to and from Washington, D.C., where Teddy Primack worked miracles with the language to make my English readable. Teddy, you became much more than a linguistic reviser: a meticulous and critical reader, English teacher, and true friend. If there are still some linguistic mistakes, they are not yours but mine.

Several individuals and institutions in India have made this work possible. First, I would like to thank Dr. Leela Gulati, who introduced me to the topic and to the Centre for Development Studies (CDS) in Trivandrum. During the four years I worked in India, I was affiliated with CDS. My gratitude for this opportunity knows no bounds. Sincere thanks, also, to Dr. I.S. Gulati, who, in spite of "ruling the country", made time to discuss my small problems and guide me in the early phase of this study. Dr. Thomas Isaac, my formal supervisor in Kerala, was always most helpful. Despite being one of the busiest politicians in Kerala, you always managed to spare a few minutes for me, and always helped me with good advice and provided me with valuable contacts in my research area of Quilon. I would also like to thank Drs. K.P. Kannan, Michael Tharakan, and K.T. Rammohan—all of them active at CDS—for generously giving of their time in talking with me. Many thanks also to Drs. K. Saradamoni, S. Radha, and Professor Uma S. Devi for advising and assisting me with academic as well as practical things. I should also like to thank Xavier and Naazu Romero, my wonderful neighbors in Kerala, for everything you have done for me. Ms. Chitra T. Nair translated a great deal of material from Malayalam into English. I should like to thank her for her excellent work. Without the help of Ms. Renu Henry, my interpreter and research assistant, this study could never have been carried out. Thank you, Renu, for being so patient, for everything you taught me, and for working so hard together with me during all these years!

Several others have assisted me with matters small and large. Among those are Mr. Sam Nathaniel, Mr. K. Sivan, Mr. A.A. Azeez, Mr. J. Chitharanjan, Mr. Sukumaran Nair, Mr. Antoni Das, and the many trade union leaders, politicians, factory owners, managers, and civil servants who gave of their valuable time in interviews, or helped me obtain documents and information in other ways. Thank you, all of you!

The staff at the CDS library deserves special mention for their unfailing assistance. I would also like to thank the following libraries and archives in Trivandrum for their great help: the CPI Library, the Legislative Library at the Secretariat, the University Library, the Loyola College Library, the Kerala State Archive, the AKG-center Archive and Library, the Departments of Sociology, History, and Demography and Population Studies at Kerala University, and the South and North Record Cellar at the Secretariat. Special thanks also to the Rajagiri College of Social Sciences in Kalamassery, Scott Christian College in Nagercoil, and the Institute of Social Sciences in New Delhi.

I have had the privilege of receiving several financial grants to carry out this study. Swedish Agency for Research Cooperation with Developing Countries (SAREC) has underwritten the major portion. I am most grateful for their support. Craafordska Stiftelsen in Lund, Stiftelsen Fil Dr. Uno Otterstedts Fond, the Swedish Institute, the Lund Zonta Club, and Knut och Alice Wallenbergs Stiftelse have provided the means for me to complete this thesis. My sincere thanks for this!

During the last four or five years, I have been shuttling between three worlds: the world of the cashew workers in Kerala, the academic world at Lund University, and the world of a loving family in what my sons call "the most boring little fishing village in the world". Daniel and Isak, you mostly saw your mother's back while she faced the computer. If I was not sitting in front of my computer, I either was in Kerala alone, or dragged you with me to India, while I pursued my research project. Perhaps it was not always a wonderful adventure, with all the difficulties you had to go through. You have been so courageous and patient—I cannot imagine better sons than you. Börje, with your wisdom and calm, you saved me from going mad at my most exasperated and exhausted moments. Thank you for always helping me keep my feet on the ground. No words suffice to thank my wonderful family for the support they have given me. A sincere thanks also to my dear neighbors and friends, my sister, mother, and late father, for always being understanding and supportive.

Kavitha, Gomathi, Sarojini, Geetha, and all your "sisters": I admire your power and strength. I dedicate this work to you, the cashew workers of Kerala, who generously have shared your experiences and your time, patiently answered the questions I posed over and over, and who showed neverending friendliness. It has been a privilege to know you, each and every one. The gifts you have given me cannot be measured. Many times, I was beset by doubts about the relevance of carrying out this research, feeling it utterly ridiculous and *unethical* to be engaged in academic hair-splitting while you were struggling for survival. It has been said that human beings cannot aspire to happiness, but can only hope to be worthy of happiness. You have merited that, and deserve the best of lives in your beautiful country!

Baskemölla, Trivandrum, and Washington D.C., August 2001

Anna Lindberg

I   Introduction

Meeting at the Factory

Kavitha and Vijayamma were born in the southern Indian state of Travancore before it became part of the new state of Kerala in 1956.[1] Kavitha, a low-caste woman, was about seventy-seven at the time of the interview.

> I do not know when I was born, but it was in the time of the Travancore king. I have never been to school. When I was a child I lived with my parents, brothers, sisters, and grandmother in a small hut in the landlord's field. We did not have any land of our own. Everybody in the house worked in the paddy field and I went there with my parents and helped to weed. We got rice as payment in kind from the landlord—he gave us extra rice sometimes when our bellies were crying too loud, but we have been starving a lot. I remember the hard times when I was a child and my parents could not get work every day.
>
> One day—I think I was seven years old—my mother took me to the cashew nut factory. We had to walk a long distance [eight kilometers] every morning and night. Women, children, and some men from the surroundings came along with us. It was a huge place with hundreds of people working there. Most of the people belonged to our caste or to the Pulayas. I sat next to my mother, who shelled the nuts. She taught me how to do it and I shelled the whole day, but now and then I had to comfort my younger brother, who lay on a sack on the floor beside my mother, just like my children would do later on. My sisters worked as shellers and they still do; my brother became a roaster. A foreigner owned the first factory where I worked. I did not like that factory, because the discipline and punishments were very hard. Once, when I was hungry, I could not resist to eat a cashew kernel. I was being beaten by one of the owner's men and dragged out of the factory, and during the two following weeks I had to wait for my mother outside the factory. Our wages were low, but we got cash money in contrast to when we worked in the paddy field. Moreover, we got work every day— for a long time we worked on Sundays as well. We had no specific working times; we just worked from early morning to night. It was always dark when we walked back home and we used to light torches made of coconut leaves.

---

[1] For an account of Travancore and Kerala history, see A. Sreedhara Menon, *A Survey of Kerala History* (Madras, 1984).

Later on, after the trade unions had shown their power, we worked from eight o'clock in the morning to six in the afternoon. Like most of the Kuravas, I joined the communist trade union after some years of work. My husband did not object, even though he was not a member of the Communist Party. It was during the rule of the dewan, C.P. Ramaswamy Ayyar. He was here to agitate for an American model of ruling the country, so that he could retain his power; but the people here were much against him.

Later on I shifted to another factory, right here in Kottiyam—it was the same year E.M.S. was dismissed.[2] Early in the morning the factory bell is ringing; I think it is to wake us up, and then it rings again, and the third time we have to be there. I still work in the same factory, I still do the same job—I think I will work until I die. Now there is no landlord to give us rice when there is no work. We are still poor, even if things are not as bad as in the old days. But nowadays we cannot get full-time employment in the cashew factories as in my youth.

I have three daughters and two sons. They were all born in this house and I had to bring them to the factory when they were babies. My daughters are shellers, one son is a roaster, and the other son is an agricultural laborer. My granddaughters are shellers. Here in our area it is as if we are born with the cashew mallets in our hands.

—Kavitha , woman of Kurava caste, sheller, born around 1920[3]

I was born in the Kollam year of 1095.[4] I went to school for four years, but when I was about twelve years old I started to work in the cashew nut factory. The factory was located near our house. My father did not have any employment, but we had a small plot of land which my mother had inherited from her mother. My parents had some income from that land, but it was not enough for making a living. My grandmother owned a lot of land in the past. The family sold some of it and the rest was given to their children. The original land had been divided in so many plots, since there were eight or nine children. My mother got such a plot, on which my father built a house. We had become poor—that is why my mother, my sisters, and I had to go to work in a factory.

We worked in the grading section. This was in the time when the caste system with untouchability was prevalent. It was very odd for women of our caste to go to places like this. It was a place for low-caste people and it was a shame for us to work like that, but we had to. The 1930s was the decade of

---

[2] E.M.S. Namboodiripad was chief minister in Kerala 1957-58.
[3] Interview 11 March 1997.
[4] This calendar, which meant the beginning of the so called "Kollam Era", was founded by a ruler, Udaya Mart'handa Varma, in 825 A.D. See T.K. Velu Pillai, *Travancore State Manual*, Vol. II (Trivandrum, 1940), pp. 51-52.

starvation and poverty. Most Nair women worked at home with different things like coir and sewing. It was the custom at that time for women of our caste to remain in the house. Poverty drove us to the factory, but it was very difficult. Maybe not so difficult for my sisters and me—we were still young—but for my mother I think it was painful.

The trade unions were agitating very hard during these years, when the dewan, C.P. Ayyar, ruled. The leaders used to visit the houses of the workers, but we never joined the union at that time. My father did not like the communists. My parents arranged my marriage. My husband was a casual agricultural worker and soon he became a communist, so after my marriage I joined the union. My husband did all kinds of work, but mostly he could only get work a few days a week. For long periods we were totally dependent on my income. We had two sons and two daughters.

After the 1960s it was even harder for us to survive, because the factory where I worked closed down for long periods and unemployment was an affliction for my husband, too. To survive we had to pawn some gold ornaments and we had to receive help from our relatives. About twenty years ago, my youngest son went to the Gulf—Bahrein—to work, and he is still there. My daughters work in the cashew factory, and so does one of my granddaughters. But my grandchildren are able to live a better life than I did. Kerala has developed so much. My mother would not recognize this world any longer. People are educated and modern, and the traditional caste society is completely abolished. So much has changed—so much!
—Vijayamma, woman of Nair caste, grader, born in 1920[5]

Kavitha belonged to the former slave caste, and Vijayamma to the traditional landowning caste, two communities which usually did not interact. These women had met in the cashew nut factory, which represented an utterly new kind of workplace in Travancore—especially for women. The society which Kavitha and Vijayamma were born into was a traditional society in the sense that it was mainly based on an agricultural economy.[6] As characterized by Kavitha's story, the relationship between the agricultural workers and the landlord may be described as feudal.[7] The workers lived on the property of the landlord (the so-called *janmi*), they worked his

[5] Interview 5 December 1997.
[6] The terms "traditional" and "modern" have been defined in various way. A "modernization", for example, of the military system, land settlement, administration, education, health care, communication, trade, and commerce had started already in the eighteenth century. See K. Saradamoni, *Matriliny Transformed* (New Delhi, 1999), pp. 29-56.
[7] It has been debated whether pre-capitalist India should be denoted "feudal" or not. Marx chose to call it the Asiatic mode of production. See Daniel Thorner, "Marx on India and the Asiatic Mode of Production", *Contributions to Indian Sociology*, No. 9 (1966), pp. 33-66.

fields, and they were paid in kind with some extra rice now and then—a situation which reinforced dependency on the goodwill of the landlord and the patriarchal character of his relations with the workers.

Vijayamma spoke in terms of caste and stressed the shame of working beside low-caste people. Her story illustrates the powerful and extremely rigid caste system which formed the basis of the social hierarchy. Religious leaders had tremendous power and there was little individualism possible in terms of mobility and freedom.[8]

This study concerns women like Kavitha and Vijayamma, as well as their children and grandchildren—their experiences and identities. There are thousands of women with similar life stories. It is their situation in the workplace, their participation in trade unions, the importance of marriage, and the effects those experiences and surrounding ideologies and discourses have had on their consciousness and identity that are the main interests of this investigation. It covers a period from 1930 to 2000, a time when Kerala underwent great social and economic change—from feudalism to a welfare state. The purpose of my research was to study these changes and their consequences for women in the globalized cashew factories. However, although such material issues as wages and working conditions are analyzed, the primary focus remains the identity of female workers.

Positioning the Study

The writing of history requires choosing perspectives and selecting phenomena to analyze, since the idea of writing "total history"—grasping the whole multiplicity and complexity of human life—is hardly achievable.[9] This is a study in the field of social gender history. Its perspective comes

---

[8] Menon, *A Survey of Kerala History*, pp. 317-321.

[9] The effort of writing "total history" has mainly been ascribed to the French Annales School. See, for example, Fernand Braudel, *La Méditerranée sous la régime de Philippe* (Paris, 1947). To come closer to the goal of writing total history, the Annales historians produced local studies as the dissolution of traditional barriers between different research fields, i.e., religion, politics, and economy may easier be transcended by focussing on a limited geographic area. See, for example, Le Roy Laduries, *Les Paysans de Languedoc* (Paris, 1966). For a criticism of these efforts, see Jack H. Hexter, *On Historians: Reappraisals of Some of the Makers of Modern History* (Cambridge, 1979), pp. 132-140. The effort to write a more integrated history was also expressed by the Marxist historian, Eric Hobsbawn, who pleaded for a turn away from social history to history of society, thereby indicating that social history must not be isolated from economic and political history, or the history of ideas. Eric Hobsbawn, "From Social History to the History of Society", in Eric Hobsbawn, *On History* (London, 1997), pp. 71-93. For a criticism of efforts to write "total history" and social history, see Patrick Joyce, "The End of Social History?", *Social History*, 20:1 (1995), pp. 73-91.

"from below", trying to give voice to people who usually do not leave written records behind.[10] It is an effort to analyze multiple dimensions of the lives of female factory workers, although many aspects must go unobserved. Avoidance of a fragmented perspective can better be done if one limits the study to a demarcated and well-defined group, which is the reason for pursuing a case study of the female cashew workers of Kerala. This approach inevitably requires an interdisciplinary point of departure in order to attain a long-term perspective while also focusing on different aspects of the lives of these workers.

Labor historians writing on India have often considered the year 1947 to be a watershed, after which the study of Indian society becomes the property of such other scholars as economists and social scientists. The implication is that research on working people after Independence often treats only short periods, and does not consider broader changes. Development researchers, too, with their future-oriented perspective, mainly focus on their immediate world. The present study bridges the line between colonial India and contemporary society, thereby encompassing disciplines other than history.

This investigation was carried out in the 1990s, a decade when postmodernism, poststructuralism, and postcolonialism deeply challenged earlier theories (especially Marxist), methodologies, and epistemologies. Although not rooted in the postmodern tradition, the research here presented, both with regard to theory and methodology, is not unaffected by "the cultural and linguistic turn". This study situates itself in the crossroads of labor history, a sub-field of social history, sociology, and anthropology, and is affected by feminist theories and, to some extent, postmodern criticism.

Social history, especially that with a structural and non-cultural perspective, has recently been criticized by postmodern scholars and has been called outdated, reductive, deterministic, and "totalizing". One critic even declared "the end of social history."[11] Social history has also been characterized as belonging to the meta-narratives (more specifically, Marxism) which conceive of human progress as directed toward a specific higher goal, a position which has been fiercely denounced.[12] In the West, the debate between those with a more postmodern perspective, and those adhering to a basically materialist view of history, has been lively and sometimes rigid

---

[10] For an overview of the development of social history, see John Tosh, *The Pursuit of History: Aims, Methods and New Directions in the Study of Modern History* (London, 1999), pp. 83-90.

[11] Joyce, "The End of Social History?". See also William H. Sewell, Jr., "Towards a Post-materialist Rhetoric for Labour History", in Leonard R. Berlanstein (ed.), *Rethinking Labour History: Essays on Discourse and Class Analysis* (Urbana, 1993), pp. 15-38.

[12] See, for example, Jean-Francois Lyotard, *The Postmodern Condition* (Manchester, 1984).

and hostile.[13] Defense of social history and efforts to take a broader perspective (one approaching total history) have been castigated as sectarian, severely reductive, and "old social history at its worst".[14]

In India, a similar debate has been going on, mainly centered around the group of historians belonging to the school of Subaltern Studies. In 1982, these researchers published their first volume, whose purpose was writing the history of the "subalterns." Greatly inspired by Antoni Gramsci and E.P. Thompson, they declared their rejection of the elitist writings of colonialist and nationalist historiographies.[15] The term "subaltern" is borrowed from Gramsci and implies the existence of independent forms of consciousness and culture among non-elite groups. The scholars of Subaltern Studies took as their point of departure "history from below", in the spirit of Thompson, stressing the non-elite (peasants, industrial workers, tribes, and other subaltern groups) as being agents in history, and not merely passive victims of oppressive structures.

However, Subaltern Studies no longer adheres to the views of Thompson, but rather to postmodern or, more specifically, postcolonial theories. Some Indian Marxists have brutally dismissed Subaltern Studies, accusing it of having a culturally reductionist perspective and ignoring oppressive structures of capitalism and imperialism.[16] Critiques concerning the absence of gender perspectives have only surfaced very recently.[17]

The main interest of Western postmodern researchers does not seem to be in empirical, traditional, historical sources; rather, influenced by Edwaid Said and his followers, they analyze literature and discourses (especially the representation of "the Others"). The scholars of Subaltern Studies have done likewise, according to Sumit Sarkar. He objects that the Subaltern School has degenerated from a genuine interest in "the subalterns" to becoming an elitist project, neglecting empirical research, and seeking, instead, a position at the center of postmodernist historical writing.[18] Sarkar also regrets that such scholars seem to have given up their initial aim to

---

[13] Examples from academic journals during the early 1990s are reprinted in Keith Jenkins (ed.), *The Postmodern History Reader* (London, 1997). With regard to social history, see especially pp. 315-384.

[14] Joyce, "The End of Social History?", p. 78.

[15] Guha Ranajith. "On Some Aspects of the Historiography of Colonial India", in Ranajith Guha (ed.), *Subaltern Studies I: Writings on South Asian History and Society* (New Delhi, 1982), pp. 1-8.

[16] Ramachandra Guha, "Subaltern and Bhadralok Studies", *Economic and Political Weekly*, 30:33 (1995), pp. 2056-2058; Vinay Bahl, "Relevance (or Irrelevance) of Subaltern Studies", *Economic and Political Weekly*, 32:23 (1997), pp. 1333-1345.

[17] Himani Bannerji, "Projects of Hegemony: Towards a Critique of Subaltern Studies' 'Resolution of the Women's Question'", *Economic and Political Weekly*, 35:11 (2000), pp. 902-920.

[18] Sumit Sarkar, *Writing Social History* (New Delhi, 1999), p. 103.

produce research for emancipation. He points out that the number of essays concerning underprivileged groups has declined: from being the entire
first two volumes of Subaltern Studies, it comprises hardly one-third of the
later volumes.[19] In addition, the tendency of Subaltern historians to study
discourses of dominant elite groups has been criticized for depriving the
non-elite groups of agency.[20]

Social history built on empirical fieldwork, archival research and, above
all, oral history forms the basis of the present investigation. It is the intention of this study to explore the lives of the subalterns from *their* perspective, not as colonial rulers and Westerners have represented them. Such
representations have had little impact on the daily lives of workers or on
their perceptions of themselves.[21] However, female workers probably *have*
been affected by what people in their everyday world (e.g., factory bosses
and trade union leaders) have said or written about them, and how they
have been treated. Their sense of identity must also have been influenced
by memories and stories related to their own experience that have survived,
the reality of their daily lives in the factories, and how marriage and the
reproductive sphere have been shaped.

Reappraising social history need neither be an adherence to orthodox
Marxist analysis, with its frequently economic reductionist perspective; nor
need it uncritically adopt Thompson's more cultural approach, which has
itself been criticized for its gender bias.[22] Thompson's basic assumptions,
however, his perspective from below, concern with material "realities",
stress on the ability of unprivileged groups to achieve agency, and his vision
of emancipating people, have been adopted.

Although postmodern theories of society may be criticized for focusing
excessively on language and discourses, there are aspects of postmodernism
which are relevant for the study of gender relations and identities—two
central concepts in this examination. Gender relations are explored from
several perspectives: gender as practice, as discourse and ideology, and as
identity. It may, therefore, be said to be a "thick description" of gender
relations,[23] although far from a total description, as certain gendered as-

---

[19] Sarkar, *Writing Social History*, p. 82.
[20] Richard M. Eaton, "(Re)imag(in)ing Otherness: A Postmortem for the Postmodern in
India", *Journal of World History*, 11:1 (2000), pp. 57-78; Rosalind O'Hanlon and David
Washbrook, "After Orientalism: Culture, Criticism, and Politics in the Third World",
Contemporary Studies in Society and History, 34:1 (1992), pp. 141-167; Guha, "Subaltern
and Bhadralok Studies", p. 2056; Dilip M. Menon, "Review of Subaltern Studies III",
The Indian Economic and Social History Review, 32:3 (1995), pp. 392-394.
[21] Clifford Geertz has stressed the drawbacks of an approach with "the describer's descriptions, not those of the described" in his *Works and Lives: The Anthropologist as Author*
(Cambridge, 1988), p. 144.
[22] Joan W. Scott, *Gender and the Politics of History* (New York, 1988), pp. 68-90.
[23] The concept of "thick description" was developed by anthropologist Clifford Geertz.

pects of social life have been excluded (for example, the education of children, religion, and leisure time).[24] I adopt the definition of the British sociologist Harriet Bradley: "Gender relations are those by means of which sexual divisions and definitions of masculinity and femininity are constructed, organized, and maintained."[25]

With an interpretative approach, the study aims at understanding the lives of poor, working class women, and analyzing continuity and change from their perspective. The experience and identity-creating processes of female cashew workers based on class, caste, and gender are primary concerns. Such processes cannot, however, be analyzed outside the context of the lives of female workers, that is, working conditions at the factories, the overall structure of the industry, participation in trade unions, the importance of marriage, and relationships with male family members. It is a study of people which takes their daily lives and problems as its point of departure. A problem-oriented and explorative methodology yields an interdisciplinary approach, as "reality" does not make its appearance in demarcated disciplines. *Interdisciplinary* is here used to indicate establishing a topic for study by drawing upon several disciplines which, although they may interact, have their own distinct theoretical and methodological frameworks. The aim is to embrace a wider social context than is usually available within strict disciplinary boundaries, in order to include a diversity of aspects which have had an impact on people's lives and identities.[26]

Efforts to transcend circumscribed disciplines have always been a central tenet of feminist theory, which provided the main source of inspiration for this study. Feminist studies have gone through a substantial shift since

---

See *The Interpretation of Cultures*, Chapter 1 (New York, 1973). Geertz was mainly interested in symbols giving cultural meaning, and less with power-relations, which is the concern here. However, he also stressed a perspective from below, as he wanted to study culture from the actors' point of view. See Clifford Geertz, "On the Nature of Anthropological Understanding", *American Scientist*, 63:1 (1975), pp. 47-53.

[24] For an indication of the multiplicity of aspects of social life which are gendered, see Harriet Bradley, *Fractured Identities: Changing Patterns of Inequality* (Cambridge, 1997), pp. 19-20.

[25] Bradley, *Fractured Identities*, p. 19.

[26] For a recent discussion on the rigidity of established disciplines and the necessity of transcending disciplinary barriers for individual researchers, see *Open the Social Sciences. Report of the Gulbenkian Commission on the Restructuring of the Social Sciences* (Stanford, 1996). The sociologist, André Béteille, rejects the dividing line between sociology and anthropology, stressing the irony in that, when we study other cultures, we call it anthropology, but when the same kind of study is carried out in our own society, it is called sociology. The sharp division between the two should be seen as a remnant of the time when the Orient was constructed as the "unknown, exotic, and traditional other", which contrasted with the "developed and modern" West. See André Béteille, *Society and Politics in India. Essays in Comparative Perspective* (London, 1991), pp. 3 ff.

the 1970s. It is a transformation which Michèle Barrett has called a shift from "things" to "words", from material realities (e.g., low pay, rape, female feticide) to discourses; from social structures to symbols and representations; from patriarchy and women's equality to cultural meaning and difference.[27] The shift is part of the general postmodern criticism against meta-narratives built on *essentialism* and *reductionism*. More specific, behind the deconstruction of categories in feminist theory lies outspoken criticism stemming from women who did not fit into the norm of white, middle-class Western women—the focus of feminist studies and theory of the 1970s and early 1980s.[28] The pioneering work of the feminist historian and theorist, Joan Wallace Scott, has advocated deconstruction methodology which seeks to disclose how discourses of masculinity and femininity (thereby *power*) are constructed.[29]

Mainstream feminist writing seem to have welcomed this "cultural and linguistic turn", although warnings have been raised that a dissolution of the category "woman" will de-politicize feminist studies.[30] Some scholars, in fact, hold that the aforementioned category be reserved for strategic, rather than analytical, purposes.[31]

Warnings that social and economic factors, such as poverty, inequality, and deprivation, fail to be considered by postmodern approaches which reject thinking in terms of capitalism or patriarchy, are heard from some scholars who have not castigated earlier theories. The risk that postmodernism, with its focus on differences within categories, leads to relativism and the abandonment of theories has also been pointed out by feminist scholars.[32]

---

[27] Michèle Barrett, "Words and Things: Materialism and Method in Contemporary Feminist Analysis", in Michèle Barrett and Anne Phillips, *Destabilizing Theory: Contemporary Feminist Debates* (Cambridge, 1992), pp. 201-219.

[28] See H. Carby, "White Woman Listen! Black Feminism and the Boundaries of Sisterhood", in Centre for Contemporary Cultural Studies (eds), *The Empire Strikes Back* (London, 1982); bell hooks, *Ain't I a Woman? Black Women and Feminism* (London, 1982); F. Anthias and N. Yuval-Davis, "Contextualizing Feminism: Gender, Ethnic, and Class divisions", *Feminist Review*, 15 (1983), pp. 62-75.

[29] Scott, *Gender and the Politics of History*.

[30] Tania Modleski, *Feminism Without Women: Culture and Criticism in a 'Postfeminist' Age* (New York, 1991), p. 15; Nancy Hartsock, "Foucault on Power: A Theory for Women?", in Linda J. Nicholson (ed.), *Feminism/Postmodernism* (New York, 1990), pp. 157-175.

[31] Denise Riley, *'Am I that Name?': Feminism and the Category of 'Women' in History* (London, 1988), p. 113.

[32] Sandra Harding, "Feminism, Science, and the Anti-Enlightenment Critiques", in Nicholson (ed.), *Feminism/Postmodernism*, pp. 83-106; Seyla Benhabib, "Epistemologies of Postmodernism: A Rejoinder to Jean-Francois Lyotard", in Nicholson, ibid, pp. 107-130; Susan Bordo, "Feminism, Postmodernism, and Gender-Scepticism", in Nicholson, ibid, pp. 133-156; Hartsock, "Foucault on Power", pp.157-175; Sylvia Walby, "Post-Post-Modernism? Theorizing Social Complexity", in Barrett and Phillips (eds), *Destabilizing Theory*, pp. 31-52.

In the debate between either Marxist or socialist, and postmodern feminists, this study takes a position similar to that advocated by Barbara Marshall and Harriet Bradley: it is not necessary to abandon modernist or materialist feminist theory. One should, rather, improve upon it and appropriate the best insights of postmodern feminism.[33]

The concept of materialist feminism rose out of Marxist theories in the 1970s. The term was favored over "Marxist feminism" in order to stress that Marxism had failed to address women's oppression in an adequate way.[34] Recently, Rosemary Hennessy and Chrys Ingaham declared that postmodern feminism has suppressed research on the forces of capitalism and their gender consequences. Hennessy and Ingaham express the need to reclaim an anti-capitalist feminist theory and to return to a focus on what people require to produce their means of subsistence, i.e., to survive.[35] Hennessy has favored such a perspective, but with the adoption of some postmodern insights. She sees materialist feminism as a synthesis of materialism and postmodernism.[36]

Following Hennessy, this thesis argues for a pluralist perspective. The position is taken that it is possible to cross-fertilize a materialist feminist perspective with postmodern insights when producing history, without abandoning concrete, lived experiences, and without being trapped in a theoretical paradox.

Why Kerala?

This research arose out of a fascination with the historical development in Kerala, which seems to provide hope for other regions where people live in poverty and deprivation. In the 1970s, a new concept, "The Kerala Model", emerged among development researchers.[37] Achievements which had taken place despite a lower GNP per capita than in

[33] Barbara L. Marshall, *Engendering Modernity: Feminism, Social Theory and Social Change* (Cambridge, 1994); Bradley, *Fractured Identities*.
[34] For a criticism of the synthesis of Marxism and feminism, see Lydia Sargeant (ed.), *Women and Revolution: A Discussion of the Unhappy Marriage of Marxism and Feminism* (Boston, 1981).
[35] Rosemary Hennessy and Chrys Ingaham (eds), *Materialist Feminism: A Reader in Class, Difference and Women's Lives* (London, 1997), Introduction, pp. 1-16.
[36] Rosemary Hennessy, *Materialist Feminism and the Politics of Discourse* (New York, 1993).
[37] For a discussion of the Kerala Model, see *Economic and Political Weekly*, 25:35-36 (1990), pp. 1951-2019, 2053-2107; Robin Jeffrey, *Politics, Women and Well Being: How Kerala Became 'A Model'* (New Delhi, 1993); "The Kerala Model of Development: A Debate, Part 1 and 2", *Bulletin of Concerned Asian Scholars*, 30 (1998), No. 3, pp. 25-36, No. 4, pp. 35-52; Monica Erwér, "Development Beyond the 'Status of Women': The Kerala Model from a Gender Perspective" (M.Phil., Göteborg University, Depart-

other parts of India, and in the absence of industrialization, were documented in 1975 when a group of scholars drew the conclusion that Kerala "has certainly some lessons for similar societies seeking social and economic advance".[38] They especially emphasized the successes in the areas of health and education. Since then, Kerala's positive achievements in human development have been documented. Social indicators for Kerala have been compared with India as a whole; with other countries in the poorer parts of the world; and with the so-called rich world. With regard to standards like literacy, infant mortality, life expectancy, and birth rate, Kerala is far above low-income countries, and can even be compared favorably with some of the countries in the West.[39] Amartya Sen has shown that survival chances are better for Keralites than for black Americans.[40]

With regard to the status of women (e.g., literacy, health, demographic factors), Kerala has been described as far more advanced than the rest of India.[41] Moreover, Kerala is the only state in India with a sex ratio (i.e., the proportion of females to males) favorable to women.[42] It has also been asserted that caste-related problems are less pronounced in Kerala than in other states of India.[43]

To explain Kerala's development, the particular history of the region, dating back to the nineteenth century, has been singled out,[44] but achieve-

---

ment of Peace and Development Research, 1998); M.A. Oommen (ed.), *Kerala's Development Experience*, 2 vols (New Delhi, 1999); Govindan Parayil (ed.), *Kerala, The Development Experience: Reflections on Sustainability and Replicability* (New York, 2000). However, there seems to be a consensus that the development in Kerala is not a "model" which can be applied in other regions, as each place has its own specific culture and history.

[38] *Poverty, Unemployment and Development Policy: A Case Study of Selected Issues with Reference to Kerala*, United Nations (New York, 1975), p. 154.

[39] Richard Franke and Barbara Chasin, *Kerala: Radical Reform As Development in an Indian State* (San Francisco, 1989), pp. 10 ff.; M.D. Morris, *Measuring the Condition of the World's Poor: the Physical Quality of Life Index* (New York, 1979), pp. xi, 64, 138-145; V.K. Ramachandran, "On Kerala's Development Achievements", in Jean Drèze and Amartya Sen (eds), *Indian Development: Selected Regional Perspectives* (Oxford, 1996), pp. 221 ff.; Amartya Sen, *Development as Freedom* (New Delhi, 2000), pp. 21-23, 46-47, 199, 221-222.

[40] Sen, *Development as Freedom*, pp. 21-22.

[41] Ramachandran, "On Kerala's Development", pp. 221 ff.; Erwér, "Development Beyond the 'Status of Women'", pp. 43-45.

[42] Monica Erwér has asserted that a gender paradox in Kerala implies the high human development indicators for women do not correspond to their participation in the political and public arena. Erwér, "Development Beyond the 'Status of Women'".

[43] Oliver Mendelsohn and Marika Vicziany, *The Untouchables: Subordination, Poverty and the State in Modern India* (Cambridge, 1998), p. 39.

[44] Jeffrey, *Politics, Women and Well Being*; P.K.M. Tharakan, "Socio-Economic Factors in Educational Development: Case of Nineteenth Century Travancore", *Economic and Political Weekly*, 20:46 (1985), pp. 1959-1967.

CHAPTER 1

ments have also been attributed to a leftist policy with a radical strategy of redistribution. In the late 1980s, Richard Franke and Barbara Chasin described Kerala as follows:

> Kerala is more than a tiny subtropical segment of the world's second most populous country. It is a region in which radical reforms over the past several decades have brought about some of the world's highest levels of health, education, and social justice. Kerala is an experiment in radical reform as a modern development strategy.[45]

Vijayamma, one of the women cited at the beginning of this chapter, stressed the rapid changes that she had experienced in her village. But she and Kavitha (the low-caste woman) particularly recalled the extreme poverty suffered by a large percentage of the population in the 1930s and 1940s, and blamed the caste system. The rigid and inhuman caste rules in Travancore induced the Indian religious leader, Swami Vivekananda, who visited the princely state in 1892, to call it "a madhouse of caste and communities".[46] In the 1930s high-caste people still measured the distance from which they had seen an "untouchable" person with extreme exactitude in order to determine whether or not they had to undergo the ritual of purification.[47]

The transformation of Kerala in the last seventy years, and its far-reaching, rapid development, serves as a background for the different generations of women who are the focus of this study. Before framing the research task within a theoretical and methodological discussion, a brief historical overview will set the context.

A Brief Historical Overview of Kerala

Travancore

Travancore, located in the southwest of the Indian subcontinent, was never part of British India, but had always remained an independent, so-called "princely" state. It was created in the eighteenth century when seven small kingdoms were annexed by the king, Martama Varna, after a war. In 1949, the state of Cochin was integrated in its administrative territory, and the

---

[45] Franke and Chasin, *Kerala: Radical Reform*, pp. 10 ff.
[46] Louise Ouwerkerk, *No Elephants for the Maharaja* (New Delhi, 1994), pp. 43 ff.
[47] Interview 19 December 1997 with K. Bhanu, male former journalist, born 1913, Quilon district; Interview 14 September 1999 with K. Chellappan, male former trade union leader, born 1914, Quilon district.

region was then named the state of Travancore-Cochin. The present state, Kerala, was formed on linguistic grounds in 1956, as part of an all-Indian policy of assembling people with a common language in the same state. A region of the old Madras presidency was added to the state, and another part, Kanyakumari, in the south, where people spoke Tamil, was transferred from Travancore to Tamil Nadu.[48] The people in Kerala speak Malayalam, a Dravidian language, hence they are called Malayalees.

The old state of Travancore, in spite of being a small kingdom with its own monarchy, was ruled de facto by the British, who first took control of the economy of the state early in the eighteenth century. They soon afterward gained political control of the country by entering into various treaties with local rulers, the first of which was signed in 1723. From that time onward, Travancore had no possibility of sovereignty or controlling its own policy, as all decisions had to be approved by the British, and the state had to pay tribute to the colonial overlords.[49]

One of the most decisive changes during the British period, which lasted up to 1947, was the thorough transformation of the country into a capitalist cash economy.[50] This took place gradually from the second half of the nineteenth century to about 1940. Land became a commodity, crops were grown commercially, large-scale agri-processing industries began to appear, foreign trade grew dramatically, and the country's infrastructure was modernized to adapt to the expanding trade.[51] Social changes in the society led to the creation of a rural proletariat.[52] Agricultural laborers, such as Kavitha and her family, who formerly had lived and worked on their landlord's fields, faced widespread unemployment during the late 1920s and 1930s, and, as a result, some began to work in the newly-established cashew factories.

Matrilineal society

Friedrich Engels introduced the theory that, as a society develops towards capitalism, commodifying land and other resources while priva-

---

[48] George Matthew, *Communal Road to a Secular Kerala* (New Delhi, 1989), p. 20. In the interest of simplicity, the term Kerala will be used throughout, except when referring only to the period prior to 1949 (Travancore), or only to the period 1949-1956 (Travancore-Cochin).

[49] Menon, *A Survey of Kerala History*, pp. 207 ff.

[50] Robin Jeffrey, *The Decline of Nair Dominance* (New Delhi, 1976), pp. 79-90; K.P. Kannan, *Of Rural Proletarian Struggles: Mobilization and Organization of Rural Workers in South-West India* (Bombay, 1988), pp. 38-71; Jeffrey, *Politics, Women and Well Being*, pp. 72 ff.

[51] Kannan, *Of Rural Proletarian Struggles*, pp. 35-88.

[52] Ibid., passim.

CHAPTER 1

tizing property, a transition in the reproductive sphere occurs as well. According to Engels, the inheritance of private property by the next generation requires the control of women's sexuality, with the most appropriate system for this purpose being monogamous nuclear families.[53] The anthropologist, Marion den Uyl, stresses that Engels' theory conforms well with the development of Kerala, where a matrilineal system of inheritance and kinship (implying joint families with shared ownership of property, and polyandry as well as polygyny) was widespread in the nineteenth century.[54] The abrogation of this system is considered to have been decisive in thoroughly transforming Kerala in a rapid and determined process which many leaders in Travancore called "modernization".[55] Matriliny, however, never totally dominated Travancore. The historian, Robin Jeffrey, asserts that about 56% of the population followed a matrilineal system, whereas den Uyl is of the opinion that this figure must be adjusted upward, claiming that several lower castes have mistakenly been considered patrilineal.[56]

The most extensively-documented community in Travancore is probably the Nairs.[57] The important position they held among the matrilineal castes derives from their being great landowners. The matrilineal system of Travancore was called *marumakkathayam*. Property was collectively owned by the members of a joint family, a so-called *taravad*. It was not possible for an individual to claim his or her share of the property. A *taravad* consisted of men and women with a common ancestress. Kinship was traced on the female side, and children always stayed in their mother's *taravad*—even after marriage. Although inheritance followed the female line and most land was registered in the names of females, *marumakkathayam* did not imply that women controlled property.[58] The *taravad* was headed by the

[53] Friedrich Engels, *The Origin of the Family, Private Property and the State* (London, 1972) [1884].
[54] Marion den Uyl, *Invisible Barriers: Gender, Caste and Kinship in a Southern Indian Village* (Utrecht, 1995), p. 30. Also anthropologist Kathleen Gough links the transformed reproductive system to capitalism. See Kathleen Gough, "Changing Households in Kerala", in D. Narain (ed.), *Explorations in the Family and Other Essays* (Bombay, 1973), pp. 218-276. This standpoint has been challenged. See C. J. Fuller, *The Nayars Today* (Cambridge, 1976).
[55] A. Sreedhara Menon, *Kerala and Freedom Struggle* (Kottayam, 1997), pp. 64; Menon, *Cultural Heritage of Kerala* (Madras, 1996), pp. 284-301; Jeffrey, *The Decline of Nair Dominance*; Jeffrey, *Politics, Women and Well Being* ; Saradamoni, *Matriliny Transformed*, pp. 97-98, 110.
[56] den Uyl, *Invisible Barriers*, pp. 89 ff.
[57] See Kathleen Gough, "Nayar: North Kerala", "Nayar: Central Kerala", and "Tiyyar: North Kerala", in D. Schneider and K. Gough (eds), *Matrilineal Kinship* (Berkeley, 1961), pp. 298-442; Joan Mencher, "The Nairs of South Malabar", in M.N. Nimkoff (ed.), *Comparative Family Systems* (Boston, 1965), pp. 162-191; Fuller, *The Nayars Today*; Jeffrey, *The Decline of the Nayars*.

14

eldest male, the so-called *karanavan*, who controlled the resources.

Marriages have been described as loose and unstable for large groups of both men and women in Travancore.[59] A woman had stronger ties with her brothers than with her husbands, and a man bore more responsibility for his sister's children than for those whose biological father he was.[60]

Characteristic of this society was the fact that a woman was not identified through a man (i.e., her father or husband), but through belonging to a particular *taravad*, designated by its female ancestor. This influenced a woman's self-identity, and belonging to the *taravad* gave her a lifelong right to security and autonomy, as well.[61]

The abandonment of the matrilineal system has been described as a reform necessary in a "progressive" and "civilized" society.[62] The initiative for the abolition of matriliny emanated from educated, young men of the upper classes, who took a stand against the power of male elders in the *taravad*, and who were influenced by ideas of what they called "modern Western family systems". The disintegration of matriliny can be traced in the legislation which successively loosened up the strict rules of joint ownership after 1896, the most important laws being instituted in 1925. These laws gave individuals belonging to joint families the right to demand their share of the property.[63] This happened in the case of Vijayamma and her family, who spoke of her grandmother's land being partitioned into small, individual plots. Many Nairs could not make a living on their small plots; as a consequence they sold them, and started to seek other ways of maintaining themselves.[64] Obviously, they went through a process of proletarization. Enormous parcels of land were transferred from matrilineal joint families (mainly Nairs) to people of other castes or religious groups.[65]

The final blow to the *marumakkathayam* came in 1976, when a new law stipulated that property could not be owned jointly, but had to be individualized. By that time, however, most joint families had already dissolved. According to Jeffrey, the matrilineal system with *taravads* was abandoned by the end of World War II.[66]

---

[58] Saradamoni, *Matriliny Transformed*, pp. 71, 90.
[59] Saradamoni has shown that stabile, monogamous marriages among the Nairs were common in the late nineteenth century. See *Matriliny Transformed*, p. 16, n. 6.
[60] den Uyl, p. 73. Saradamoni has opposed this view and pointed out that one can find many cases where husbands did take economic responsibility for their wives and biological children. See *Matriliny Transformed*, p. 67.
[61] Saradamoni, *Matriliny Transformed*, p. 68.
[62] Menon, A. Sreedhara, *Social and Cultural History of Kerala* (New Delhi, 1979), p. 92.
[63] Jeffrey, *Politics, Women and Well Being*, pp. 34-53.
[64] Ibid., pp. 47 ff.
[65] Ibid.
[66] Ibid., pp. 33, 44-47.

CHAPTER 1

For some Nair women, the best—perhaps the only—solution was to get married and become dependent on a single man, instead of their mother's *taravad*. The abandonment of *marumakkathayam* implied monogamous marriages. The new kind of nuclear families imposed duties on men to provide for a wife and children—a situation quite unfamiliar to many of them.[67]

The Travancore matrilineal system included unique features other than inheritance, such as kinship organization, ceremonies, and rituals; and it offered identity and security to women. As a result, the women of Travancore were often described as freer and possessing of more authority than women in other parts of India.[68] According to the Malayalee scholar, K. Saradamoni, the matrilineal system implied some autonomy to women in comparison to patrilineal systems, but we must not be led to believe that women held power over men.[69] The authority the male *karanavan* had and restrictions imposed upon women has been stressed.[70]

Earlier matrilineal traditions have not completely disappeared in Kerala. Saradamoni asserts that several features of *marumakkathayam*, such as strong relations between brothers and sisters, brothers supporting their sister's children, women owning houses and property, and children keeping their mother's name as a surname, still continued into the late 1990s.[71]

For groups such as the lowest castes who did not own any land (or many belongings), the question of a system of inheritance may be considered irrelevant. However, *marumakkathayam* was much more than this, and matrilineal customs other than those connected to inheritance were followed among some of the poorer families. Saradamoni found the lower castes adhering to the traditions of their masters, although it was not precisely the same among all castes, and several mixed forms existed.[72]

The caste hierarchy

Travancore was constrained by an extremely inhumane caste hierarchy. The system there was more rigid than in the rest of India and penetrated all aspects of life.[73]

---

[67] Saradamoni, *Matriliny Transformed*, pp. 97-98, 158.
[68] Govt. of Travancore, *Travancore Administration Report* 1103 ME/1927-28 AD, p. 3.
[69] Saradamoni, *Matriliny Transformed*, p. 71.
[70] D. Renjini, *Nayar Women Today: Disintegration of Matrilineal System and the Status of Nayar Women in Kerala* (New Delhi, 2000), pp. 78-84.
[71] Saradamoni, *Matriliny Transformed*, pp. 61, 158-159. Also, Marion den Uyl stresses reminiscences of the *marumakkathayam*, especially among Scheduled Castes. See den Uyl, *Invisible Barriers*.
[72] Saradamoni, *Matriliny Transformed*, p. 59.
[73] Jeffrey, *Politics, Women and Well Being*, pp. 19 ff; Richard Franke, *Life is a Little Better: Redistribution as a Development Strategy in Nadur Village, Kerala* (New Delhi, 1996), pp. 70-71; Ouwerkerk, *No Elephants*, pp. 43-47.

The word *caste* originates from the Portuguese *casta*, meaning family or lineage, but the term is hardly used among Indians in everyday life. In Sanskrit literature, the term *varna*, literally "color", is associated with particular social occupations. The four *varnas,* hierarchically arranged, are the *Brahmins* (priests and religious teachers), *Kshatriyas* (rulers and warriors), *Vaishyas* (merchants), and *Shudras* (peasants and servants). The arrangement was based on the dichotomy of ritual purity and pollution, whereby the Brahmins, in their own view, were considered the purest.[74] Three principal signs of purity are a vegetarian diet, abstinence from alcohol, and constraints on women, such as *purdah* (female seclusion), restrictions on divorce, and the issue of the remarriage of widows.[75]

Some communities were considered below the *varna* system. They were seen as especially polluted because they carried out the dirtiest work, such as removing dead animals or cleaning excrement. Certain agricultural workers were also categorized in this way. People of higher castes had to undergo ritual cleansing after having come in contact with "untouchable" persons or their belongings. As several scholars have pointed out, the *varna* system has never been a social reality, and should rather be considered the construct of an "ideal" society.[76] Nevertheless, the notion of *varna* is widespread throughout India. Even if sociologists claim it does not represent a social reality, it is widely used as a model to describe Indian society. The Indian sociologist, M.N. Srinivas, is of the opinion that the *varna* system has created an incorrect and distorted image of the social hierarchy; on the other hand it has provided a common social language to which people all over India can refer.[77]

Jati (Sanskrit "birth") is the term the Indians use to refer to the community they are born into. There are thousands of *jatis* throughout India, but they are not comparable. Each linguistic region has its own system of *jatis*, and the hierarchy is much more obscure and disputed than that of the *varna* system. Moreover, most *jatis* have a system of sub-groups whose hier-

---

[74] Luis Dumont, *Homo Hierarchus* (Chicago, 1970). Torvald Olsson has pointed out that the relation between the four *varnas* is not explicit in the Rig-Veda, and did not become so until the second century in an interpretation of *Dharma Shastra* known as *Manu Smriti* (The Law of Manu). See Torvald Olsson, *Folkökning, fattigdom, religion* (Lund, 1988), pp. 249 ff. The dichotomy purity versus pollution has been contested by Declan Quigley, who asserts that some Brahmins also carried out "polluting" work, which is why they were both pure and polluted. See Declan Quiley, "Is a Theory of Caste Still Possible?", in Mary Searle Chatterjee and Ursula Sharma (eds), *Contextualising Caste: Post-Dumontian Approaches* (Oxford, 1994).
[75] M.N. Srinivas, *Caste in Modern India and Other Essays* (London, 1962), pp. 42-62. The relation between caste and gender will be discussed in Chapter 2.
[76] See K.M. Pannikar, *Hindu Society at the Cross Roads* (Bombay, 1956), p. 7.
[77] M.N. Srinivas, "Varna and Caste", in Dipankar Gupta (ed.), *Social Stratification* (New Delhi, 1996), pp. 28 ff.

archies are equally unclear. According to André Béteille, the distinction between the terms *varna* and *jati* can be described, on the one hand, as a model, and, on the other, to represent social groups or categories. He asserts that they should be understood as two different but related systems that have co-existed for at least 2000 years.[78]

Jatis are generally considered to belong to one of the four *varnas*. The so-called "untouchables" are organized in *jatis* but are not included in the *varna* system, which is why they have been referred to as "outcastes" (*avarna*), in contrast to "caste Hindus" (*savarna*). Henceforth, when the word caste is used it refers to *jati*.

The traditional four-fold division of society was not applicable to Travancore. In fact, in 1931, the census officer of Travancore asserted that the system of four *varnas* had never existed in Travancore and that the large majority were "stamped as Shudras".[79] The Kshatriyas were represented only by a minor group and the Vaishyas did not exist at all in Travancore. Foreign traders, such as Jews, Muslims, Brahmins from Madras Presidency, and Christians performed the functions of the Vaishyas, (viz., trade).[80]

Even if the *varna* affiliation of Travancore castes was questionable, four major groups with a strict hierarchical order did exist, namely the Brahmins, Nairs, Ezhavas, and the former slave castes—among which Pulayas, Parayans, and Kuravas were the most numerically important.[81] A feature of the caste (i.e., *jati*) system in Travancore, was a large number of groupings—on average seventeen to a village.[82] Complicating matters further, there was a large group of Christians and Muslims who were likewise ranged in the societal hierarchy. The present study concentrates on four Hindu communities—Nairs, Ezhavas, Kuravas, and Pulayas—whose members dominate the workforce of the cashew factories (although most castes and religious groups, except Brahmins, are represented there).[83]

In 1936, the British included all "untouchable" communities in an official list of so-called Scheduled Castes, a quasi-legal concept which served to

---

[78] Béteille, *Society and Politics*, p. 44.
[79] Govt. of India, *Census of India 1931*, Vol. XXVIII, Travancore, Part I, Report, p. 364.
[80] Jayadeva D. Das, "Genesis of Trade Union Movement in Travancore", *Journal of Kerala Studies*, 7:1-4 (1980), p. 102; K. Saradamoni, *Emergence of a Slave Caste* (New Delhi, 1977), p. 7.
[81] This was the Brahmanic view of this order, which may have been contested by others.
[82] McKim Marriot, *Caste Ranking and Community Structure in Five Regions of India and Pakistan* (Poona, 1960), pp. 26-31.
[83] For a discussion of the Christian population in Kerala, see C.J. Fuller, "Kerala Christians and the Caste System", in Gupta (ed.), *Social Stratification*, pp. 195-212. Christians in the cashew factories consisted of recently converted Hindus, and they just as the Muslims, were placed in the caste hierarchy above Scheduled Castes, but below Nairs (i.e., at the same level as the Ezhavas).

identify unprivileged groups that were entitled to certain quotas in parliament, education, and employment. In Travancore, all former slave-castes were placed among the Scheduled Castes, whereas Ezhavas were considered to be too privileged to be placed on this list, despite having suffered from being treated as strict untouchables in the past. As it is less degrading than "untouchables", the term Scheduled Castes will be used here.[84]

At the beginning of the twentieth century, the Brahmins constituted less than 2% of the total population, but they had the economic and spiritual power and occupied the uppermost social rank. The Brahmins, however, were divided into many sub-castes. The most influential Brahmins were the *Nambuthiris,* who controlled the bulk of the land. The Nambuthiris were the highest authorities in religious matters, and in the nineteenth century were generally considered to be conservative and resistant to the influence of "Western civilization".[85] Their system of kinship and inheritance was strictly patriarchal, and the Brahmin women were held in *purdah.*

It is notable that the Brahmins never tried to impose their cultural system on the lower castes; in fact, they conspicuously prevented it, leaving space for alternative systems of kinship and inheritance to co-exist alongside theirs.[86] When sons of Brahmin families married Nair women, which occurred often, they encouraged the matrilineal system of the Nairs. To keep family property undivided, only the oldest son in a Nambuthiri family was permitted to marry a Brahmin woman, and thereby receive his inheritance. The acceptance of the family system among Nairs was a means of giving sexual access to the younger Brahmin sons, who were not held responsible for their biological children. Thus, the *caste* system and its marriage rules supported the *class* hierarchy and maintained the social structure with regard to landowning.

The Nairs, like the Ezhavas, were a fairly large group and represented almost 20% of the population of Travancore in the early twentieth century. They were an influential caste of landowners and tenants who held slaves. But in spite of their power, they were regarded as Shudras by the Brahmins.[87] It has been questioned whether they should be regarded as a caste at

---

[84] The term "untouchable" is highly derogatory, which is why Mahatma Gandhi introduced a new term in 1933, *Harijans,* which may be translated as "people of God". But this term is contested as well, and for many people (especially leftists) it stands as an acknowledgement of the caste system and, therefore, denotes a non-radical policy. The term "Dalit" is used by some groups to indicate a radical policy with regard to the untouchables". See Mendelsohn and Vicziany, *The Untouchables,* pp. 3-5.

[85] Govt. of India, *Census of India 1901,* Vol. XXVI, Travancore, Part I, Report, p. 364.

[86] Joanna Liddle and Rama Joshi, *Daughters of Independence* (London, 1986), p. 58.

[87] In the Census of 1901, they were classified as Shudras. However, this classification was declared erroneous by the census officer in 1931, who maintained that there was no evidence of the Nairs ever having been Shudras. See Govt. of India, *Census of India 1931,* Vol. XXVIII, Travancore, Part 1, Report, pp. 376-377.

all. The Keralite historian, K.M. Pannikar, asserts that "Nayars were not a caste, they were a race. Every kind of caste with varying social pretensions existed among them."[88]

All the groups below the Nairs were considered to be outcastes. The Ezhavas were placed between the former slaves, Pulayas and Parayans, and the *savarnas* in the caste hierarchy. The position of the Ezhavas was quite unclear at this time, and their community, which comprised about 17% of the population, was not homogenous.[89] Traditionally, the Ezhavas had been engaged in occupations linked to the processing and trading of coconut products, but in the early twentieth century they were divided into classes with differing economic status. They were no longer simply a group of workers, but for some time had been well-organized, had run their own newspapers and educational institutions, and had led the struggle against caste discrimination.[90]

The hierarchy and rigid caste rules of Travancore can be illustrated by the so-called "distance" regulations that existed between different castes. The Pulayas and other former slaves, such as the Parayas and Kuravas, were victims of the most oppressive and rigid caste rules. They were not only regarded as untouchable, but even "unseeable": the mere sight of them was considered to pollute higher castes. Distinct rules existed regarding the degree to which proximity to different castes polluted a Brahmin. A Nair could approach a Brahmin, but not touch him; an Ezhava could not come closer than twenty-four feet, but a Pulaya had to remain at a distance of seventy-two feet.[91] Even with regard to criminal law, the caste affiliation of the victim as well as the perpetrator was of decisive importance when it came to determining punishment. Brahmins enjoyed immunity from the death penalty.[92]

In addition to the rigid rules of distance, several other rules existed that humiliated the lowest castes, reminded them of their "pollution", and eliminated the possibility of upward mobility.[93] They were forbidden to enter temples, public markets, and roads near the temples. Several re-

---

[88] K.M. Pannikar, *A History of Kerala* (Annamalai, 1960), p. 10.
[89] Govt. of India, *Census of India 1901*, Vol. XXVI, Travancore, Part I, Report, pp. 279 ff.
[90] Ouwerkerk, *No Elephants*, p. 43; Thomas Isaac, "Class Struggle and Structural Changes in the Coir Industry in Kerala" (Ph.D., University of Kerala, 1983), p. 82.
[91] Mencher, "The Nairs", p. 167; Fuller, *The Nayars Today*, p. 35. Different sources give different figures regarding the actual distance rules; however, there is consensus about the relationship between the communities. See also Gough, "Nayar: Central Kerala", p. 313; L.A.K. Iyer, *The Tribes and Castes of Cochin* (Madras, 1909), pp. 120-121.
[92] Menon, *Cultural Heritage*, pp. 270-273.
[93] Unni Raman, "Sources of Agricultural Labour in Kerala: Some Social Perspectives", in Balakrishna Nair (ed.), *Culture and Society: A Festschrift to Dr. A. Aiyappan* (New Delhi, 1975), p. 231.

strictions on clothes, hairstyles, ornaments, and other externals existed. Moreover, they were even forbidden to wear clean clothes and had to speak about themselves and their belongings in a most degrading manner.[94] Thus, the notion of ritual pollution was extended to include material and linguistic "uncleanliness", which further demeaned their self-identity. Connected to the concept of pollution was a strict rule prohibiting inter-caste dining and all inter-caste marriage except those between Brahmin men and Nair women.[95]

Social movements

Jeffrey gives an expressive picture of the changes that took place in Travancore since the 1920s when describing how low-caste people would use their hands. In the 1920s, they held them over their mouth for fear that they would pollute the air of higher castes with their breath. Thirty years later, the fists of low-caste men and "increasingly women, too" were raised over their heads when they chanted "victory to revolution".[96]

The society of the 1930s has been described as segmented and closed, but one in which strong forces which boded far-reaching changes were emerging.[97] Effective social movements[98], initially led by religious leaders, promoted mass-education, the abandonment of untouchability, the dismantling of the hierarchical social order, and an end to the *marumakkathayam*.[99]

The first community to start a caste-based emancipatory association was the Ezhavas, whose leader, Sree Narayana Guru, formed a powerful social movement in 1903. The aim was to liberate, modernize, and uplift the Ezhava community. One part of the struggle was directed towards the rulers of the country and the dominant castes. It aimed at giving Ezhavas the legal right to enter any temple and street, to worship the Brahmin dei-

---

[94] See Fuller, *The Nayars Today*; Iyer, *The Tribes and Castes*; Joseph Mathew, *Ideology, Protest and Social Mobility: Case Study of Mahars and Pulayas* (New Delhi, 1986); Joan Mencher, "On Being an Untouchable in India: A Materialist Perspective", in Eric B. Ross (ed.), *Beyond the Myths of Culture. Essays in Cultural Materialism* (New York, 1980); Saradamoni, *Emergence of a Slave Caste*.

[95] A marriage between a Brahmin man and a Nair woman was possible (and common), although the husband had to undergo ritual purification after the couple had sexual relations and they could not dine together.

[96] Jeffrey, *Politics, Women and Well Being*, p. 1.

[97] Ibid., pp. 1-2.

[98] I use the concept of social movement here with the meaning "collective action based on religion, caste, or class", and not in the sense of more recent so-called "new social movements", to which a large body of theory is linked. For an introduction to theories of new social movements, see *Social Research*, 52:4 (1985).

[99] Menon, *Cultural Heritage*, pp. 284-305; Menon, *Kerala and Freedom Struggle*, pp. 55-64.

ties, to have access to proper education, and to secure employment in the state administration. Their strength in numbers, their education, and their charismatic leaders made the Ezhavas an influential community—especially after the successful struggle for the right to enter all temples and roads was won in 1936.[100] This represented, in essence, the legal abolition of untouchability. A special organization with the intention of promoting inter-caste dining had been formed in 1917 by another Ezhava leader, K. Ayyappan, who also modified and radicalized Sree Narayana Guru's slogan "One caste, one religion, one God" to "No caste, no religion, no God"![101]

Another part of the struggle was spearheaded towards the people in their own community, as it was said, "to uplift them". The movement was modeled on the Brahmins with regard to religious rituals and the abolition of drinking alcohol.[102] Srinivas introduced the term *Sanskritization* for the process of trying to raise the status of a caste through the imitating of castes which were considered higher in the social hierarchy.[103] We will return to this concept when dealing with gender and caste in the following chapter.

In 1907, the Pulaya leader, Ayyankali, formed an organization for his caste after the model of the Ezhavas.[104] The abolition of caste restrictions with their inhumane rules (which affected the Pulayas even worse than the Ezhavas) was the main issue for Ayyankali and his followers. But the right to education was also one of the pressing questions for the Pulayas, and Ayyankali instructed his caste fellows to refuse to work for the Nairs until the children of the workers were permitted to enter schools.[105] The putting an end to *marumakkathayam* also had a high priority for Ayyankali.

Higher castes, such as the Nairs and Brahmins, also formed caste-based organizations in the early 1910s. The Nairs were also greatly interested in promoting the abandonment of *marumakkathayam*. The Brahmins, too, focussed on reforming marriage customs. To them it was important that younger brothers were allowed to marry within the caste and not be compelled to seek brides among Nair women. Such marriages were often unstable and easy to dissolve. Moreover, polyandry as well as polygamy existed.[106] In fact, all the caste-based organizations strongly promoted nuclear families and the dismantling of the *marumakkattayam* system of inheritance. No voices seem to have been raised in defense of the matrilineal system.

---

[100] Menon, *Cultural Heritage*, pp. 291-293.

[101] Menon, *Kerala and Freedom Struggle*, p. 59.

[102] Georg Jacob, *Religious Life of the Ilavas of Kerala: Change and Continuity* (New Delhi, 1995), pp. 53.

[103] M.N. Srinivas, *Social Change in Modern India* (Berkeley, 1966), pp. 1-46.

[104] Menon, *Cultural Heritage*, p. 288.

[105] Jacob, *Religious Life*, p. 41.

[106] Menon, *Cultural Heritage*, p. 290.

Very soon the struggle for social reform was complemented by opposition to the rule of the dewan—and directed against the British, all of which was greatly inspired by Mahatma Gandhi and the Congress Party of India.[107] Such social movements, originally taking issue with religion and caste, were the beginning of the strong civil society, mainly based on political parties, that has characterized Kerala for the last four or five decades.[108] The struggle for the abolition of caste rules became a class struggle. In the 1930s, there was a correlation between economic hierarchy (class) and ritual hierarchy (caste), although they were never totally in accord with each other.[109]

Radical policy and the present crises

Social movements, active trade unions, and strong parties of the left have long been significant features of Kerala. In 1939, as part of the struggle for independence and against the policy of the dewan (both of which had begun in the early twentieth century), a branch of the Communist Party of India (CPI) was formed in Travancore. The CPI had started in 1934 as the socialist wing of the Indian National Congress, Congress Socialist Party. In the 1920s and early 1930s there were no organized communists in Travancore, but since literacy already was better than in most other parts of India, and there were unusually many newspapers, political ideas could easily spread. The fight for freedom resulted in the large-scale imprisonment and victimization of the people involved: they were followed, harassed, and tortured for their political involvement. Agricultural laborers, as well as factory workers, participated in the struggle, and the mobilization of the masses in trade unions and political groups was successful.[110]

In 1956, E.M.S. Namboodiripad, one of the leaders of CPI and an extremely influential ideologist of the so-called Kerala Model, became chief minister after the election of the Kerala Legislative Assembly. Since then, Kerala's government has typically pursued a radical policy which includes far-reaching land reforms, large-scale public expenditures on education and health, and a system of redistribution of resources through, for example, so-called "fair-price" shops.[111]

Several leftist parties have been functioning in Kerala, and the political

---

[107] Menon, *Kerala and Freedom Struggle*, pp. 42-55, 97-108.
[108] Olle Törnquist, *The Next Left? Democratisation and Attempts to Renew the Radical Political Development Project. The Case of Kerala* (Copenhagen, 1995), pp. 23 ff.
[109] P. Sivanandan, "Caste, Class and Economic Opportunity in Kerala: An Empirical Analysis", *Economic and Political Weekly*, 14:7-8 (1979), pp. 475-480.
[110] Kannan, *Of Rural Proletarian Struggles*.
[111] Franke, *Life is a Little Better*.

landscape has been characterized by coalitions between parties on the left, although there have been fierce conflicts and rivalries between the two main communist parties, Communist Party of India (CPI), and Communist Party of India, Marxist (CPI-M). In spite of a political situation in which nearly every second government has been led by non-leftist politicians, the political climate may be described as radical. Kerala has also been depicted as a welfare state, having a strong civil society with a high degree of political participation among its inhabitants. Since the 1960s, the political arena has been dominated by different parties in two coalitions: the United Democratic Front (UDF) under leadership of the Congress party, and the Left Democratic Front (LDF) led by the CPI-M. The two coalitions included different parties at different times and alternated to keep the majority in the State Assembly.[112]

In the late 1970s and 1980s, the state underwent a severe crisis involving economic stagnation and extreme unemployment.[113] The policy of creating a public industrial sector has not been very successful, as many of the companies run at a loss.[114] Kerala has also not managed to retain investments of private capital, the flight of capital to neighboring states being remarkable.[115]

Unemployment has induced many Malayalees to migrate to the countries of the Persian Gulf and, in fact, remittances from these workers have grown to be the biggest source of Kerala's foreign currency, mounting to between 25% and 40% of the state domestic product.[116] This makes the economy extremely vulnerable, as was experienced during the war in Kuweit, when thousands of Malayalees had to return home.

There is a consensus that Kerala faces a crisis at the moment, although different scholars give different explanations for this. The most negative voices assert that crisis is built into the Kerala Model, with its priority on social development and redistribution, and with economic growth only as a second goal.[117] Others are more inclined to seek an explanation in Kerala's dependence on a global capitalist system, structural adjustment programs,

---

[112] K. Raman Pillai, "Coalition Politics: The Kerala Experience", in Oommen (ed.), *Kerala's Development Experience*, vol I, pp. 99-110.
[113] See, for example, B.A. Prakash, "Kerala's Economy: An Overview", in B.A. Prakash (ed.), *Kerala's Economy: Performance, Problems, Prospects* (New Delhi, 1994), pp. 15-39.
[114] P. Mohanen Pillai, "Performance of State Sector Enterprises in Kerala", in Prakash (ed.), *Kerala's Economy*, pp. 259-278.
[115] M.A. Oommen, *Inter State Shifting of Industries: A Case Study of Selected Industries in Kerala, Tamil Nadu and Karnataka* (Trichur, 1979).
[116] M.P. Parameswaran, "Kerala 'Model'—What Does It Signify?", *Bulletin of Concerned Asian Scholars*, 30:4 (1998), p. 41.
[117] Joseph Tharamangalam, "The Perils of Social Development without Economic Growth: The Development Debacle of Kerala, India", *Bulletin of Concerned Asian Scholars*, 30:1 (1998), pp. 23-34.

a new liberal economic order, and a growing culture of consumerism.[118]

In the 1990s, Kerala emerged on the world map once again—this time because of a serious attempt from above to decentralize power and strengthen civil society by the ruling parties of the left.[119] In spite of the crisis, there is no doubt that people in Kerala live closer to a welfare state than in other parts of India, and they are more engaged in politics. With regard to the participation of women in social and political movements, a leading female politician has stated that in Kerala, one sees working women—not intellectual feminists—in the public arena.[120] Working women such as these, employed within the cashew industry, are the focus of this study.

The Significance of Research on the Cashew Workers

The economic and political importance of the cashew industry is based on the great number of workers it employs and the amount of foreign currency it brings into the country. From its inception in the mid-1920s, the industry grew very quickly, and in 1941 cashew workers accounted for 45% of the registered factory workforce in Travancore.[121] Since then, this number has fluctuated, reaching 60% at its highest, but never declining below 32%.[122] In 1998 there were more than 200,000 registered cashew workers.[123]

A registered factory denotes a workplace covered by the Factory Act and, thereby, a workplace in the so-called formal sector regulated by labor laws.[124] That an overwhelming majority of all cashew workers are women (about 95%, since 1960) is remarkable, as most female workers in India have only found employment in agriculture or in the informal sector. In no other state in India do we find such a large proportion of women in registered factories as in Kerala.[125]

---

[118] Richard W. Franke and Barbara H. Chasin, "Is the Kerala Model Sustainable? Lessons from the Past, Prospects for the Future", in Parayil (ed.), *Kerala, The Development Experience*, pp. 16-39.

[119] Olle Törnquist, "The New Popular Politics of Development: Kerala's Experience", in Parayil (ed.), *Kerala, The Development Experience*, pp. 116-138.

[120] Jeffrey, *Politics, Women and Well Being*, pp. 215-216.

[121] Govt. of India, *Large Industrial Establishments 1941* (Simla, 1943).

[122] Govt. of Kerala, *Economic Review,* various issues 1960-1998. In 1947 it reached 60%, its highest point. See Govt. of India, *Large Industrial Establishments 1947* (Simla, 1949).

[123] List with registered factories obtained from Special Officer of Cashew Industry, Quilon, January 1998.

[124] The dichotomy "formal and informal" sector will be discussed in Chapter VII.

[125] The proportion of women in registered factories at an all-India level has been fairly constant, except for a small decrease during the post-colonial era. In 1946 women were at 11.7% and nearly fifty years later it remained around 10.7%. See Govt. of India, *Statistical Profile on Women Labor 1983* (Simla, 1985), p. 33; Govt. of India, *Statistical Profile on Women Labor 1998* (Simla, 1999), p. 23.

During the last fifty years, the industry's share of earned foreign currency (measured as the value of total exports from Kerala) has ranged between 19% and 33%.[126] This has led the state government of Kerala, as well as the Indian central government, to intervene by either regulating trade, or by running the factories themself.

Cashew workers have been organized in trade unions since 1939. With regard to strike activity, the cashew workers have been extremely militant—especially up to the mid-1970s, as reflected in official statistics.[127]

The cashew workers of Kerala show great potential for power, in contrast to the stereotype of Third World[128] women, who are often portrayed as illiterate, powerless victims.[129] Nevertheless, it was recently stated that 75% to 90% of all cashew workers are living below the poverty line, a figure some three times greater than that of the general population in Kerala.[130]

Previous research on the cashew industry has almost exclusively been carried out by economists.[131] K.P. Kannan, whose research on this topic was done during the 1970s, provides a useful and detailed study on the

---

[126] Thomas Isaac, "The Trend and Pattern of External Trade of Kerala", in Prakash (ed.), *Kerala's Economy*, pp. 371 ff.

[127] K. Balan Pillai, "The Economic Impact of Collective Bargaining on Cashew Industry in Kerala" (Ph.D., Department of Economics, University of Kerala, Trivandrum, 1986), p. 158.

[128] The concept of Third World belongs to those categories that are non-essential constructions. Lately, there also seems to be a consensus about its inadequacy as an analytical category. The criticism of the concept has its roots in Edward Said's *Orientalism* (New York, 1978). See alsoPeter Worsley, *The Three Worlds: Culture and World Development* (London, 1984); Stuart Hall, "The West and the Rest: Discourse and Power", in S. Hall and B. Gieben (eds), *Formations of Modernity* (Cambridge, 1993), pp. 276-320. It has been stressed that the relationship between the so-called First World and Third World is complex and that, for example, some women in the First World live under conditions resembling those in the Third World. See Swasti Mitter, *Common Fate, Common Bond: Women in the Global Economy* (London, 1986), p. 80.

[129] Chandra Talpade Mohanty, "Under Western Eyes: Feminist Scholarship and Colonial Discourse", in Chandra Talpade Mohanty, Ann Russo, and Lourdes Torres (eds), *Third World Women and the Politics of Feminism* (Bloomington, 1991), pp. 51-80. For discussions on Third World Women, see Haleh Afshar and Bina Agarwal (eds), *Women, Poverty and Ideology in Asia* (London, 1989); Hilary Standing, "Employment", in Lise Östergaard (ed.), *Gender and Development: A Practical Guide* (London, 1992), pp. 57-75; Janet Momsen Henshall, *Women and Development in The Third World* (London, 1991), pp. 44-92.

[130] The Kerala Cashew Workers Welfare Board in Quilon estimated this in 2000 (interview with the chairman of the board, A.A. Azeez, January 2000). For Kerala in general, see M. Mohandas, "Poverty in Kerala", in Prakash (ed.), *Kerala's Economy*, pp. 78-94, 87-88. See also K.P. Kannan, "Poverty Alleviation as Advancing Basic Human Capabilities", in Parayil (ed.), *Kerala, The Development Experience*, pp. 40-65.

[131] Minor field studies have been carried out by students of social science. Although they ordinarily have not been very comprehensive, they may serve as a source of primary data.

trends of cashew cultivation and trade. His concern was with government policy and its effects on trade and labor.[132] He interviewed union leaders and outlined the strategies of trade unions in the cashew factories. He also analyzed statistics on wages and working days, and briefly surveyed working conditions.[133] Kannan's study on trade and policy is quite detailed, but his two papers dealing with working conditions, trade unions, and wages are less comprehensive. Kannan's research is, with small exceptions, an example of a study with a macro-perspective that frequently invokes official statistics.[134]

In the mid-1980s, an economist at the University of Kerala, K. Balan Pillai, carried out a study intented to explore whether trade union activities and collective bargaining could be held responsible for the crisis which the cashew industry had suffered since the 1960s.[135] Like Kannan, he primarily used census and official statistics for the analysis.

Neither of these studies give us any insight into the reactions of female workers. The historical perspective is restricted to the period from about 1960. For the most part the past is presented without analyses of ideologies, values, and perceptions, except for the ideology of factory owners to maximize profits, which is an intrinsic logic of capitalism.

Aims and Objectives

The picture of the cashew worker we get from Kannan and Pillai is that of a low-caste, submissive, poor, illiterate, ignorant, exploited woman. On the other hand, the ideas of a "Kerala Model" have implied a relatively positive picture of women's situation in recent decades, without however analyzing the female cashew workers in particular. The reading of Kannan's and Pillai's studies gave me impetus to meet the cashew workers, to try to reconstruct their profile in a historical perspective, and to grasp their ideas, val-

---

[132] K.P. Kannan, *Cashew Development in India, Potentialities and Constraints* (Trivandrum, 1981).

[133] K.P. Kannan, "Employment, Wages and Conditions of Work in the Cashew Processing Industry" (Working Paper No. 77, Centre for Development Studies, Trivandrum, 1978); K.P. Kannan, "Evolution of Unionisation and Changes in Labor Process under Lower Forms of Capitalist Production" (Working Paper No. 128, Centre for Development Studies, Trivandrum, 1981). A version of this paper is published in Arvind Das et al. (eds), *Worker and the Working Class* (New Delhi, 1984), pp. 45-61.

[134] One has to be cautious in drawing conclusions largely based on macro-material such as this, especially when dealing with changes. Very often different methods of data collecting, setting categories, and definiting concepts have been used in different historical settings. Instead of giving a reliable picture, statistics on the cashew industry often give contradictory results. It is also a problem that long series often are incomplete.

[135] Pillai, "The Economic Impact".

ues, and life experiences. Except for a few very short extracts from interviews, earlier studies are mainly based on quantitative methods. We are given no sense of how the lives of the workers have evolved, the consequences for their children and grandchildren, or their understanding of their own situation. I wished to explore the dynamics of the workplace and the changes there which have affected their lives. How did the meeting of Kavitha and Vijayamma at the cashew factory take place when the effect of untouchability remained in Travancore? How was the factory work organized with regard to gender and caste? What did it mean to them and how did it change? My concern was directed not only to achievements resulting from trade union activities (which according to Kannan and Pillai have been quite meager), but how the organizing of women into unions has shaped their view of their own lives. Have the trade unions created a class identity among the cashew workers? How have marriage and motherhood influenced their identities as workers?

At a theoretical level the aim is to study both "things" and "words", as well as their interconnection. Which ideologies and discourses can we discern and what impact have they had on the women's lives? My intention is to analyze how elements in three spheres: factories, trade unions, and marriage, have interacted in the formation of identities based on *class, caste, and gender*, and how tensions between ideologies or discourses and social practices have intertwined to create complexities and paradoxes.

The extensiveness of the subject matter has made a circumscription of the topic necessary. As a result, certain aspects of the caste system (such as rituals, cultural patterns, and traditional interactions with other castes) could not be treated in depth. In addition, only the four castes which predominate among cashew factory workers have been included, although others exist. Minority groups (whether Hindu, Christian, or Muslim) are also not considered. Finally, when discussing changed identities, the lowest castes (the former so-called "untouchables"), whose members comprised those who first entered the factories on a large scale, are the main focus of the analysis. It is the identity of women which is stressed, although male voices have not been excluded. However, systematic in-depth interviews among male workers have not been carried out for reasons of time and the textual limitations of the thesis.

The main purpose of this study (i.e., to analyze the formation of identities based on class, caste, and gender among a certain group of female cashew workers) led to a selection of a few themes to focus on. The themes chosen affect the everyday life of these women at a material level, but also at a discursive and ideological level. Both of these levels are decisive in the construction of peoples' identities.

Structure of the Study

The following chapter presents theories and concepts. It also includes an overview of prior work in the field, an account of the methodology employed, and a discussion of oral history and other sources.

Chapter III analyzes the development of cashew factories in Kerala from their inception in the mid-1920s up to the year 2000. This is one of two empirical chapters in which voices of workers will *not* be used as sources. Rather, the cashew industry will be viewed from outside and above, in order to illuminate the arena in which the cashew workers have worked. It views the context of their lives, but also analyzes the power of capitalism.

The next two chapters explore the nature of work, and changes and continuities in two major divisions of work: gender and caste division of labor. The testimony of workers, trade union leaders, and factory owners, will figure in this analysis. Power structures, such as a patriarchy, but also the power of tradition, will be considered.

Chapter VI also has a perspective from outside and above. It analyses wages, and the gender discourses that have been guiding people who held the power to decide wages. The chapter provides an example of the impact of Western concepts, and the power and consequences of the introduction of a collective bargaining system.

Chapter VII examines the social struggles, methods, and chief questions advanced at different times by the trade unions. It especially focuses on the union activity of women and their identity-shaping processes. The quality of women's participation in unions and the relations between them and union leaders are major concerns. Finally it analyzes how trade union leaders have represented female cashew workers.

Chapter VIII turns to the reproductive sphere and analyzes the role of marriage. The main concern is women's own perception of the importance of marriage, rather than marriage ceremonies. Again, the consequences of everyday life and the identity of women are stressed.

In Chapter IX, the results are summarized and reviewed as a whole.

II   Concepts and Methodology

Introduction

Much research on women's work has focused either on capitalist or patriarchal structures, or on questions of people's agency and identity within these structures. My aim is to link these two approaches. How have the women who are the focus of this study adapted, resisted, or negotiated within oppressive structures? Have their interests been obscured under a "false consciousness"—and are those interests based on caste, class, or gender? Have dominant ideologies been able to mystify or blur their consciousness? Or have they been aware of oppressive structures and of their collective interests, while constrained by poverty and material circumstances? Should we rather see their agency as the confrontation with a hegemonic discourse and ideology, or as the negotiation of an agreement? Another possibility is that certain orders into which one is born are taken for granted as natural, and therefore never contested. This chapter will consider several concepts which are central to an analysis of women's agency, consciousness, and identity.

Housewifization

Three German feminists, Claudia von Werlhof, Veronika Bennholdt-Thomsen, and Maria Mies, became well-known in the 1980s when they asserted that women of the Third World had gone through a process of domestication as a result of the development of global capitalism.[1] Howev-

---

[1] Maria Mies, Veronika Bennholdt-Thomsen, and Claudia von Werlhof, *Women: The Last Colony* (New Delhi, 1988); Maria Mies, *Patriarchy and Accumulation on a World Scale. Women in the International Division of Labour* (London, 1986). The transformation of women from producers in a pre-industrial society into dependent housewives with the emergence of capitalism, and the succeeding division of the public and private spheres, have been common themes for scholars in the West, although there has not been any consensus on the consequences with regard to power relations between the sexes. Alice Clark was a pioneer in this direction, arguing that relations between men and women were more egalitarian in pre industrial England, and that women's economic contributions gave them more independence and higher status than in industrialized society. Alice Clark, *Working Life of Women in the Seventeenth Century* (London, 1919). Edward Shorter

er, Mies and her colleagues castigated traditional Marxist economic theory and broke with dependency theorists by not giving class priority over gender.[2] Their main criticism concerned Marxism's neglect of power structures (by which they primary meant patriarchal ones) other than those of class. Not only capital, but men of all classes have benefited from women being defined as housewives and having been excluded from adequately remunerative work.[3]

The aforementioned authors were highly influenced by Rosa Luxemburg's early work on the accumulation of capital. Whereas classical Marxist imperialist theories (Lenin's, for example), did not sufficiently consider the so-called undeveloped world, Rosa Luxemburg took it into account. Her main thesis was that in the capital accumulation of the world, non-capitalist forms of production, e.g., the domestic production of peasants and household production, are a necessity for subsidizing capitalism and supporting its eternal expansion.[4] To the plight of such half-proletarianized groups as subsistence peasants in the West and in the colonies, one could add the domestic labor of women, unpaid or underpaid small peasants, and subsistence producers (such as street vendors, day laborers, petty traders, beggars), along with others who are not fully proletarianized. Those who are only half-proletarianized, i.e., who are not considered to be totally dependent on wages for their survival, can more easily be underpaid. In the case of women, the myth is that they are supposed to be cared for by their husbands. In contrast to Rosa Luxemburg, who labeled these groups "non-capitalist strata", Bennholdt-Thomsen is of the opinion that "capital itself

---

has argued against Clark, holding that patriarchy was stronger prior to industrialization. Edward Shorter, "Women's Work: What Difference did Capitalism Make?", *Theory and Society*, Vol. 3,4 (1976), pp. 513 ff. For a discussion of the impact of industrialization in Western countries on women's status, see Harriet Bradley, *Men's Work, Women's Work: A Sociological History of the Sexual Division of Labor in Employment* (Cambridge, 1989), pp. 33-49. With regard to the Third World, Ester Boserup and Barbara Rogers came to the conclusion that with modernization women were excluded from development. Rogers introduced the concept of *domestication* of women and stressed Western ideological forces in defining women as housewives. Barbara Rogers, *The Domestication of Women: Discrimination in Developing Countries* (London, 1980); Ester Boserup, *Women's Role in Economic Development* (New York, 1970). For a case study of the Maasai society in Tanzania, see Aud Talle, *Women at a Loss: Changes in Maasai Pastoralism and Their Effects on Gender* (Stockholm, 1988). See also Bina Agarwal, *A Field of One's Own: Gender and Land Rights in South Asia* (Cambridge, 1994).

[2] For a discussion of the dependency school, see P.W. Preston, *Development Theory: An Introduction* (Oxford, 1996), pp. 153-233.

[3] Mies, Bennholdt-Thomsen, and von Werlhof, *Women: The Last Colony*; Mies, *Patriarchy and Accumulation*.

[4] Rosa Luxemburg, *Die Akkumulation des Kapital, Ein Beitrag zur ökonomischen Erklärung des Kapitalismus* (Berlin, 1923). Several scholars belonging to (or inspired by) the dependency school followed her line of reasoning. See, for example, Andre Gunder Frank, *Capitalism and Underdevelopment in Latin America* (New York, 1969).

reproduces its own 'non-capitalist' surroundings in the imperialist as well as in the dependent countries".[5]

A central concept for Mies, who mainly bases her discussion on fieldwork in India, is what she calls *housewifization*, "a process in which women are socially defined as housewives, dependent for their sustenance on the income of a husband, irrespective of whether they are de facto housewives or not".[6] Thus, it is a process of creating a "non-capitalist strata". Mies suggests, along with dependency theorists, a de-linking of women's work from global production, since years of lace work for export had aggravated—not alleviated—their poverty.[7]

Chandra Mohanty cites Mies' work on lace makers as an exception in the stereotyping of Third World women.[8] However, several writers have criticized Mies' concept of "housewifization". One set of critics has voiced concerns over the absence of agency among women and the depiction of them as passive victims. The Norwegian scholar, Halldis Valestrand, has argued that an active strategy of women can be precisely that of becoming housewives and that this should not necessarily be seen as a coercive process imposed upon them from the side of capital and/or patriarchy. Using data from her fieldwork in Costa Rica, Valestrand has shown that the majority of the women in her sample affirmed a new order, implying that men (to a higher degree than earlier) provided for their families by working for wages, whereas women withdrew from wage labor and, thereby, were left with more time for domestic duties.[9] The criticism that women in Mies' perspective suffer from victimization and that she rejects women's own agency and choice is a reaction to her strong emphasis on monolithic, overarching structures.[10]

It is evident that to a poor woman, used to toiling sixteen to eighteen

---

[5] Veronika Bennholdt-Thomsen, "Subsistence Reproduction and Extended Production: A Contribution to the Discussion about Modes of Production", in K. Young et al. (eds), *Of Marriage and the Market* (London, 1981), p. 24. The view that subsistence production is part of a capitalist world economy was also expressed by Immanuel Wallerstein, *A Capitalist Agriculture and the Origins of the European World-Economy in the Sixteenth Century* (New York, 1974).

[6] Maria Mies, *The Lace Makers of Narsapur. Indian Housewives Produce for the World Market* (London, 1982), p. 180, n. 2.

[7] In a later book, Mies and Bennholdt-Thomsen forcefully argue for subsistence production for poor women in order to improve their situation and empower them. Maria Mies and Veronika Bennholdt-Thomsen, *The Subsistence Perspective Beyond the Globalised Economy* (London, 1999).

[8] Mohanty, "Under Western Eyes", pp. 64-65.

[9] Halldis Valestrand, "Housewifization of Peasant Women in Costa Rica", in Kristi Stölen and Mariken Vaa (eds). *Gender and Change in Developing Countries* (Drammen, 1991).

[10] See also Naila Kabeer, *Reversed Realities: Gender Hierarchies in Development Thought* (London, 1994), pp. 50-53.

hours a day for little or no pay, it must have been an attractive prospect to be spared from some of this work—something which could materialize by shunning remunerative labor. In other contexts in the West, many working-class women subscribed to the ideology of housewives and contributed to this ideology gaining a foothold within their class in the early twentieth century.[11]

The position of a housewife must not necessarily be viewed as a negative exclusion from paid work, but can be seen as the *right* of being supported in exchange for domestic work. In this view, it is seen more as a negotiation of gender relations and the outcome of a contract. Structurally, however, the duty of husbands to provide for their families implies female dependence on males and relegates females to an inferior position within a gendered power relation—if, in fact, there is a husband in the picture at all. In most places, there must have been widows, single mothers, runaway fathers, drunkards, unemployed men, disabled or sick husbands, unhappy marriages, and other "anomalies". For women who did not fit into the dominant gender ideology of a nuclear family with a present husband who had both the will and the capacity to provide for wife and children, life must have been far more difficult. But even in cases where such a will and capacity existed, these could be used to exert power in the household, and did not necessarily create harmonious households containing empowered individuals. The tendency to stress agency and to reject the writing of "misery history" must not lead us to shy away from the existence of oppressive structures in an effort, however benevolent, to ascribe power and dignity to subaltern people.

Valestrand appears to consider the concept of "housewifization" quite literally. However, the concept is not simply to be taken as 'becoming a housewife' in the Western sense, i.e., a label for a woman who carries out unpaid reproductive work in her home. "Housewifization" is, instead, the process of ideologically defining women as dependent housewives, and this need not mean *de facto* that they work in their homes. The sense, rather, is that they must carry out whatever work they are called upon to do, at any time or place, unpaid or underpaid, and that all this is due to women being considered materially dependent on a man—whether or not such a man exists, or whether he is capable of maintaining her or not.[12]

Another kind of criticism directed towards Mies is her definition of essential categories such as men, women, white men, colonies, and global

---

[11] Christina Carlsson, *Kvinnosyn och Kvinnopolitik: En studie av svensk socialdemokrati 1880-1910* (Lund, 1986), pp. 261-264.

[12] For a similar discussion, see Veronika Bennholdt-Thomsen, "Why do Housewives Continue to be Created in the Third World, too?", in Mies et al. (eds), *Women: The Last Colony*, pp. 166 ff, p. 357.

patriarchy. These, according to Naila Kabeer, are a simplification of reality which leads Mies to see all men as "monsters", and all women as "victims".[13] Mies is over-esteeming female characteristics here—something even more evident in her later writings.[14] Her theory is, in fact, based on antagonism between men and women. Mies has also been criticized for having reduced and presented empirically wrong generalizations of the past.[15]

The thesis of "housewifization", as exemplified in Mies' analysis of the lace makers, in some ways is self-evident. Although the female lace makers were important wage earners, they were not working outside their homes—something they did in earlier times. It would seem that Mies ascribes to women working in their homes a decisive role, her conception only being applicable to that category of women. In a later work, Mies widens "housewifization" to cover women who are employed in the formal sector full-time and who are their families' main breadwinners. In such cases, "housewifization" is manifested by low wages, legitimized by defining women solely as supplementary providers.[16]

My point of departure is that the ideology of women as dependent housewives has broad significance. The main concern should not be to investigate whether women have been homeworkers or not. For those women who de facto are full-time workers outside the home, who are even registered as workers and perhaps organized into trade unions, the ideology of housewives may nevertheless have had a strong impact. Mies shows that in India there has been a decline of registered female workers in the formal sector, and holds that women have been pushed out into the informal sector through the process of "housewifization".[17] My concern here is with those women who have remained in the formal, registered factories.

In Mies' investigation of the lace makers she asserts that the women whom she studied lacked insight into the exploitative nature of the trade they were in and did not understand the necessity of forming unions. Thus, she gives us the impression that the lace makers suffered from a "false consciousness", both with regard to class and gender. Mies generalizes starkly, and although her examples are full of empirical data (the women's low wages, their confinement to their homes, the burden of their household), the question of *how* the ideology of housewives has been spread remains obscure.

---

[13] Kabeer, *Reversed Realities*, pp. 50-53.

[14] Mies and Bennholdt-Thomsen, *The Subsistence Perspective*, p. 34.

[15] Sylvia Walby, *Theorizing Patriarchy* (Oxford, 1990), pp. 46-49.

[16] Mies and Bennholdt-Thomsen, *The Subsistence Perspective*, p. 34.

[17] Maria Mies, "Capitalist Development Production" , in Mies et al. (eds), *Women: The Last Colony*, pp. 27-63.

When using concepts like "housewifization" and "ideology of male breadwinners" in specific historical contexts, it becomes necessary to ask such questions as: how has this ideology emerged? how, why, and by whom has it been upheld? who are the different agents? how have women reacted to it? These are questions which shall be addressed in the specific context of the cashew workers.

A theoretical point of departure in this study is that people, however suppressed, poor, or "unimportant", have always had the capability of thinking, describing, and analyzing their own situation. Although discourses may operate on several levels—some of them influencing people beyond their consciousness—people are also active in supporting or contesting ideologies and creating their own identity. This is not a polemic against influential power structures, but an expression of the human ability to negotiate within such structures. This standpoint makes it relevant to discuss the concepts of ideology and discourse, identity and consciousness.

Ideology and Discourse

The concept of ideology may be roughly distinguished in two basic senses. The first is when the concept is taken broadly to mean a system of different ideas and thoughts about society, as held by various groups. This would be basically a neutral and descriptive use. A second sense originates with Marx and amounts to a critical definition which views ideologies as means to maintain power and considers the knowledge included in an ideology as a distortion of truth.[18] According to classical Marxism, the concept is closely linked to "mystification" and politics, and is thus based on a distinction between *science*, which has a material basis (i.e., true statements about the world) and *ideology*, which betokens false statements. From this latter perspective, an ideology is never neutral. As Marx and Engels wrote:

> The ideas of the ruling class are, in every epoch, the ruling ideas: i.e., the class which is ruling the material forces of society is, at the same time, its ruling intellectual force. The class which has the means of material production at its disposal has control, at the same time, over the means of mental production, so that thereby (generally speaking) the ideas of those who lack the means of mental production are subject to it.[19]

---

[18] For a discussion of the concept of ideology, see Jorge Larrain, *The Concept of Ideology* (London, 1979), and John B. Thompson, *Studies in the Theory of Ideology* (Berkeley, 1984).

[19] Karl Marx and Friedrich Engels, *The German Ideology* (London, 1965), p. 61.

Ideology is seen as related to the mode of production, implying a system of ideas which are produced by the ruling class. This approach has been interpreted as a situation in which the ruling class imposes its ideas on oppressed classes, who thereby may be seen as suffering from "false consciousness". Such false statements about reality may be disclosed by "ideology critique", a central concept and methodological approach in Marxist writing.

The concept of "false consciousness" has been fiercely criticized.[20] Using poor peasants in a Malaysian village to illustrate his thesis, James Scott asserts that it is not at the level of ideological domination that people are prevented from resisting oppression, but rather at the level of material power structures.[21] Stuart Hall, along with the group identified as "Cultural Studies", points out that the concept of "false consciousness" indicates an elitist view of humanity, as it is only "others" who suffer from such a consciousness.[22] In defense of the classical conception of ideology as a critical notion—in contrast to that of a neutral concept—it has been asserted that the meaning of "false consciousness" has been distorted, and that Marx never intended to say the working class was brainwashed or that only a minority understood society.[23]

Socialist feminists of the 1970s applied the Marxist definition of ideology to patriarchy, arguing that this ideology offered a false image of women's material position and lived experiences and, thus, contributed to women's false consciousness.[24] This view was later criticized by Veronica Beechey, among others.[25]

Hall emphasizes that by doubting whether ideologies were "true" or "false", Louis Althusser introduced not only a rejection of "false consciousness", but also a dialectical view which questioned economic reductionism. The "subject" was considered to be constitutive of *all* ideologies, which

---

[20] See, for example, M. Mann, "The Social Cohesion of Liberal Democracy", *American Sociological Review*, 35 (1970), pp. 423-439.

[21] James C. Scott, *Weapons of the Weak: Everyday Form of Peasant Resistance* (New Haven, 1985). For a view of absence of resistance as a recognition of structural constraints, see Pierre Bourdieu, "The Social Space and the Genesis of Groups", *Theory and Society*, 14 (1985), pp. 723-744.

[22] Stuart Hall, "The Problem of Ideology: Marxism Without Guarantees", in David Morley and Kuan-Hsin Chen (eds), *Stuart Hall: Critical Dialogues in Cultural Studies* (London, 1996), pp. 31-32. See also Mann, "The Social Cohesion of Liberal Democracy".

[23] Jorge Larrain, "Stuart Hall and the Marxist Concept of Ideology", in Morley and Chen (eds), *Stuart Hall: Critical Dialogues*, pp. 58 ff.

[24] Ann Foreman, *Femininity and Alienation: Women and the Family in Marxism and Psychoanalysis* (London, 1977). The term "socialist feminism" was favored over "Marxist feminism" to indicate that class must not necessarily dominate other social relations, e.g., gender.

[25] Veronica Beechey, "Studies on Women's Employment", *Waged Work: A Reader* (London, 1986), pp. 151 ff. For a defense of the concept of "false consciousness", see Sabina Lovibond, "Feminism and Postmodernism", *New Left Review*, 178 (1989), pp. 5-28.

were not seen as merely a reflection of productive relations.[26] In the following, Hall's definition of ideology, which is broader than that of classical Marxism, will be employed.

> By ideology I mean the mental frameworks—the languages, the concepts, categories, imagery of thought, and the systems of representation—which different classes and social groups deploy in order to make sense of, define, figure out, and render intelligible the ways society works....In this, more politicized perspective, the theory of ideology helps us to analyze how a particular set of ideas comes to dominate the social thinking of a historical bloc.[27]

Ideologies, in this view, are not necessarily class-based and can be applied to other social categories (gender and caste, for example), and even transcend those categories.[28] Hall's definition implies forms of knowledge which are neither true nor false. He does assert, however, that ideologies *are* politicized. Hall does not see ideology in the negative way Marx had, but argues that the degree and nature of "distortions" remain open, and that the two ways of approaching ideology are not contradictory. Although, in Hall's view, the concept of ideology does not strictly signal falseness, it is inadequate, as only one side (i.e., the economic relations) of the totality is considered. It may, in that sense, be considered false or, rather, a partial truth.[29] Hall rejects the notion that ideologies are fixed and stable, seeing instead several elements of discourses combining with each other in constant variation. Analyses of ideologies must therefore be done in more concrete situations and always historicized.

Drawing on Antonio Gramsci, Hall asserts that ideologies cannot be assigned a certain class position, although they "do arise from and may reflect the material conditions in which social groups and classes exist".[30] With this view, Hall still maintains a materialist perspective, stressing the dialectical relationship between ideology and materiality.

Postmodern theory places stress on the power of language, the concept of *ideology* dwindling in much social and human science to give way to *discourse*.[31] The two concepts are often seen as incompatible. They are con-

---

[26] Hall, "The Problem of Ideology ", pp. 30 ff.
[27] Ibid., p. 26. For a criticism of Hall's use of ideology, see Larrain, "Stuart Hall and the Marxist Concept of Ideology", pp. 47-70.
[28] Hall, "The Problem of Ideology", p. 40. See also Stuart Hall, "The Toad in the Garden: Thatcherism among the Theorists", in Cary Nelson and Lawrence Grossberg (eds), *Marxism and the Interpretation of Culture* (Houndmills, 1988).
[29] Hall, "The Problem of Ideology", pp. 36-40.
[30] Ibid., p. 42.
[31] For an introduction to the concept of discourse, see Sara Mills, *Discourse* (London, 1997).

sidered to belong to different theoretical traditions and based on opposite epistemological grounds. Although analyses of discourses show numerous approaches, a widely-accepted definition would be the one offered by Hall.

> Discourses are ways of talking, thinking or representing a particular subject or topic. They produce meaningful knowledge about that subject. This knowledge influences social practices, and so has real consequences and effects. Discourses are not reducible to class-interests, but always operate in relation to power—they are part of the way power circulates and is contested. The question whether a discourse is true or false is less important than whether it is effective in practice.[32]

Discourses are linked to linguistics. Specifically, to study discourses is to study the *meaning* conveyed by language. This concept has its roots in Foucault's writing. His main objection against classical Marxist theory on ideology is that it reduces power relations to those between economic classes. Advocating the use of the concept of discourse in favor of ideology may be considered a rejection of a materialist perspective. However, it is, in addition, a rejection of the need—or rather the possibility—of discovering the "truth". The knowledge about society that we can obtain is seen as power-related and a product of the way we categorize "reality". In this view, truth is something *produced*, which indicates a rejection of essentialist categories.

Adopting the concept of discourse instead of ideology also has consequences on one's view of power and resistance. In the discourse perspective of Foucault, power is more difficult to locate, define, and thereby resist. This has an impact on an individual's capability to take action against power: people are seen to negotiate power-relations, rather than to resist them.[33] A discourse-theory perspective tends to see people less as victims of oppressive structures at the level of mind and consciousness than as being engaged in the process of shaping their own consciousness and identity. In this way, the concept of discourse has similarities with some of the interpretations of Antonio Gramsci's *hegemony*.[34]

The concept of discourse has been used in various ways by different scholars. On the one hand, discourses are seen as totally constituting the human subject and social 'reality'; on the other, discourses are considered as reflections of social practice. In the first view, as followed by Foucault,

---

[32] Hall, "The West and the Rest", p. 295.

[33] Mills, *Discourse*, pp. 38-39.

[34] For a discussion of Gramsci's concept of hegemony, see Raymond Williams, *Problems in Materialism and Culture* (New York, 1980), pp. 37-40. See also Marion Leffler, *Böcker, bildning, makt: Arbetare, borgare och bildningens roll i klassformeringen i Lund och Helsingborg 1860-1901* (Malmö, 1999), pp. 52-63.

Ernest Laclau, and Chantal Mouffe, the concept of ideology has no relevance, as there is no "truth" to be disclosed, and such a thing as "distorted knowledge" does not exist. There are only discursive practices, and social practices are considered the equivalent of the discourses.[35] We only have access to "reality" via discursive structures which give us meaning.

At the other extreme of the scale would be the view that discourses are reflections of other social practices—for example, the economic base. A historical materialist perspective would fall here, but such a theory does not need the methodology of discourse analysis, because it is more relevant to explore what has caused the discourses (as, in the case of historical materialism, the economic structure).[36]

Several scholars have tried to find ways between both extremes and thereby bridge the concepts, by combining two theoretical perspectives. That is also the aim of this study. Hall employs the concept of ideology, but says he wants to give it a more discursive understanding, one "which mediates the link between ideas and social forces through language and representation". Drawing examples from the Thatcher era in Britain, he shows that a struggle over the meaning of words—the discursive level—was decisive in the formation of ideologies. He also shows that these ideologies were not simply class-based: what was at issue was a struggle within the ruling class, too.[37]

Hall does not reject Marxism, but asserts that "I keep the notion of classes, capital/labour contradiction, social relations of production—I just don't want to think them reductively".[38] My point of departure is also that discourses are used to convey ideologies, and that classes and capital/labor relations are decisive in social relations, but I would add a pronounced gender perspective, which is absent from Hall's point of view.

This study employs the concepts of ideology and discourse as defined by Hall above, including the view that discourses constitute other social practices only to a degree. A discourse may be ideological in its essence, but it is not identical with that ideology; rather, a discourse is a tool to express, mediate, and uphold ideologies, but they both operate at the same level— that of conveying meaning. The power of discourse also lies in the fact that it sometimes operates at the unconscious level and appears to be "true".

[35] Michel Foucault, *The Archeology of Knowledge* (London, 1989) and *Diskursens ordning* (Stockholm, 1993); Ernesto Laclau and Chantal Mouffe, "Post-marxism without Apologies", in Ernesto Laclau, *New Reflections on the Revolution of Our Time* (London, 1990). For a detailed analysis of different approaches to the concept of discourse, see Marianne Winther-Jörgensen and Louise Phillips, *Diskursanalys som teori och metod* (Lund, 2000).
[36] Winther-Jörgensen and Phillips, *Diskursanalys*, p. 26.
[37] Hall, "The Toad in the Garden", p. 73.
[38] Ibid., p. 72.

Those who produce the discourse have the power to *make it true*.[39] As I interpret Hall, this more open and discursive approach to ideologies does not imply a total abandonment of their critical dimension. It only signifies that ideology critique may be extended to include competing discourses, putting less emphasis on distorted knowledge, but more on agency and the constitution of competing and multiple subjectivities. The major difference between ideologies and discourses is that ideologies are normative and more consciously formulated, whereas discourses operate at a more subtle level and are not necessarily seen as value-laden, but appear to be "true".

The media-researcher, Norman Fairclough, has an even more pluralistic view than Hall. He considers discourses (although not *all* discourses) to be ideological, i.e., to convey meaning that contributes to create, preserve, or transform power relations, which a critical analysis may disclose. Thus, like Hall, he does not abandon the Marxist tradition. In his own work, Fairclough primarily engages in discourse analyses of texts, but he forcefully indicates that these are not enough to investigate social phenomena. The discursive practice is an integral part of a dialectical interplay with other social practices. Fairclough advocates that a multiplicity of analytical tools and methods be used because some social phenomena have a logic other than that of discourses (economic logic, for example, or the institutionalization of certain kinds of social activity).[40]

This study adheres to Fairclough's theoretical principle that interdisciplinary approaches are necessary to analyze social and cultural processes and structures. His model for discourse analysis will not be used, however, as it is too focused on texts for the present purpose; but his view that speeches, and stories *in everyday social interaction* contribute to social and cultural changes, as well as to the formation of identities, has been integrated into what follows. It is the everyday consciousness, or—to use the vocabulary of Gramsci—the "common sense", which is the focus here, rather than any theoretical ideology or Gramscian "philosophy". The concern in the following pages is how subalterns have rendered their everyday life intelligible.

The critical dimension of ideology has been retained by many feminists, often with additional emphasis on "lived" experiences (i.e., everyday practice, as Althusser had done), rather than placing stress on ideas alone.[41] However, several feminists have come to similar conclusions as Hall with regard to the concepts of ideology and discourse. One of them, Rosemary Hennessy, defining herself as a materialist feminist, advocates a conceptualizing of discourses as ideologies when analyzing constructions of "subjects",

---

[39] Hall, "The West and the Rest", p. 295.
[40] Norman Fairclough, *Discourse and Social Change* (Cambridge, 1992); *Critical Discourse Analysis* (London, 1995).
[41] Louis Althusser, *Lenin and Philosophy and Other Essays* (London, 1977).

e.g., the category "woman".[42] These scholars also recommend a two-fold approach: "materiality and meaning",[43] which is also the stand taken in this study. They, therefore, suggest that there is no contradiction in combining the two theoretical perspectives which see social phenomena as social constructions *and* objective "realities", as long as the relationship between these aspects is acknowledged.[44]

Like Hall, Hennessy finds a way to reconcile materialism with postmodern ideas. Hall, however, seems less bothered about the rigidity of the category of class and thereby retains much of Marxist theory. Hennessy follows the feminist tradition with a rejection of essentialist categories such as women and men, and a gender neutral concept of class.[45] Her analysis is mainly philosophical and, in contrast to Hall's, does not offer guidance with regard to which methodological tools to employ in an analysis of society. For both, however, the agency of subalterns is crucial.

Consciousness, Experience, and Identity

A major concern in this study is understanding the construction of masculinity and femininity, and the power relations in this process. Central to its theme is the consciousness and identity of female workers, and their own agency or passivity in processes of constructing those identities.

Labor historians have commonly taken E.P. Thompson's *The Making of the English Working Class* as a point of departure in exploring the concept of class consciousness and class formation. The importance of Thompson's work may be said to lie primarily in its rejection of structural determinism and its emphasis on agency "from below". His narrative is a story about the road from "class in itself" to "class for itself", i.e., the way to a *class consciousness*—one of his central concepts.

Class, for Thompson, is neither a structure nor a category, but something that *happens*. It is to be understood as a process in which the concept of *experience* is central. He asserts that people's daily and shared experiences, shaped by productive relations, led them to identify common interests. Thompson rejects purely economic relations in the formation of class consciousness and asserts that "class-consciousness is the way in which these experiences are handled in cultural terms: em-

---

[42] Hennessy, *Materialist Feminism*. For similar views, see Bradley, *Fractured Identities*; Marshall, *Engendering Modernity*; Anita Göransson, "Meaning and Materiality: An Attempt to Synthesize or a Reconciliation of Realist and Poststructuralist Positions?" (Paper presented at the Nordic Thought Conference at the University of Oslo, March 1994).
[43] The expression is borrowed from Bradley, *Fractured Identities*, p. 9.
[44] Ibid., p. 8.

bodied in traditions, value-systems, ideas, institutional forms".[46]

However, it is obvious that people's experiences in productive relations are considered to be the most decisive in the process of shaping people's consciousness. He thereby follows classical Marxist theory in saying that people's economic class position affects their consciousness. Marx asserted that "life is not determined by consciousness, but consciousness by life."[47] For Thompson, the awareness of capitalist oppression and the necessity to collectively combat it has emerged from shared economic, political, and social experiences—and from collective memories of oppression: it was the cultural expression of past experience.

Thompson does not distinguish between class identity and class consciousness. (The first concept was hardly discussed either by him or other labor historians at the time). It seems as if the two were equivalent concepts for Thompson and many of his followers.

A central point of departure in the present study of the Kerala cashew workers is the separation of class identity and class consciousness. Class consciousness is here defined as 'awareness of capitalist oppressive relations and the need to challenge them by class struggle', but it does not necessarily mean that the subjects *totally* identify themselves with a given class. Other identities may be of as great or greater importance than that of class.

The view that consciousness is dependent on material conditions (part of a more general doctrine about economic relations as dominant) has been denounced by post-structuralists. For Foucault, the constructing of people's thoughts and consciousness is primarily conveyed by language. This is not to say that language is only an expression for meaning, but that meaning is constructed by language.[48] The implication of Foucault's perspective is that a study of people's consciousness is best done by studying discourses.

Joan Scott, greatly inspired by Foucault, has criticized Thompson's work. She argues that by using concepts of class formulated by the labor movement of the nineteenth century, Thompson (in *The Making of the British Working Class*) reproduced a gendered definition of the working class. Women were constantly linked to domesticity, even when they were unquestionably workers; they were described as "loyal" instead of "political", and derided as romantic reactionaries when they favored past social systems, such as pre-capitalist society. Men, in Thompson's work, were seen as radical and critical towards capitalism if they favored a pre-capitalist society. Women's strategies were considered related to religious and expressive movements, contrasting the "rational" class consciousness of males.[49]

---

[45] See Hennessy, *Materialist Feminism*, pp. 112 ff., for a discussion of gender and class.

[46] E.P. Thompson, *The Making of the English Working Class* (London, 1963), p. 9.

[47] Marx and Engels, *The German Ideology*, p. 47.

[48] Foucault, *The Archeology of Knowledge*, passim.

Thompson's extensive narrative is, in Scott's view, not a "true" story, but a creation of political identities through representations of sexual difference in a highly gendered language. "As such, it can be read as a double historical document: it gathers rich evidence about how class was understood in the past, and it incorporates those meanings into its own construction of working-class history."[50]

Thompson defines experience as the "lived realities of social life", which includes both ideas and feelings. Thus, he adds a subjective, psychological dimension to the structural, i.e., experience is viewed both as an internal and external issue.[51] The structural dimension must also be viewed as an objective and neutral experience that comes into being not only when it is thought of or spoken about. Scott has criticized Thompson for only considering experience shaped by relations of production and overlooking other social arrangements. He thereby gives essential identities to people (as the notion of experience is closely related to identity) based only on class. Scott suggests that a solution for avoiding the construction of essentialist identities is to historicize experience and trace the processes of discourses which affect people's identities. Scott illustrates this by citing Hall's observation that people in Jamaica have always been black, but did not speak of themselves as such until about 1970, when discourses which promoted black identity affected the Jamaicans. To analyze these discourses "is to historicize the 'experience' of blackness".[52]

Scott denies that to consider experience as a linguistic event is to adhere to linguistic determinism, arguing that we should rather consider experience as inseparable from language, i.e., it is a part of everyday language: experience has a discursive nature and it is this production of knowledge that should be our focus for analysis.[53] In this, she subscribes to Foucault's opinion that there is no "dumb reality".[54]

Scott has been of great importance to scholars interested in gender studies by identifying the way gender discourses were constructed through a language of dichotomies relating to masculinity and femininity. This is especially true of her methodology of deconstruction. Her main contribution in feminist studies has been to convincingly argue that *women* does not simply indicate a group to be studied, but the core issue is the representation of women—how they have been defined and, thus, how gender rela-

---

[49] Scott, *Gender and the Politics*, pp. 68-90.
[50] Ibid., p. 71.
[51] Joan W. Scott, "Experience", in Judith Butler and Joan W. Scott (eds), *Feminists Theorize the Political* (New York, 1992), pp. 22-40.
[52] Scott, "Experience", pp. 33-34.
[53] Ibid., pp. 34-38.
[54] Foucault, *The Archeology of Knowledge*, p. 49.

tions were constructed. Scott's analysis offers excellent insights into how women have been silenced. Nevertheless, to grasp the complexity of people's rationality and construction of identities, women's own voices need to be heard, and the link between dominant discourses and 'the subalterns' must be analyzed.

Along with Scott, I find Thompson's study to have a narrow focus on economy and class. A wider definition of experience would avoid a reductive perspective. On the other hand, people do have silent experiences which are *not* linguistic events. Hunger, poverty, oppression, division of labor (e.g., gender, class, or ethnic), violence, rape, and sexual harassment exist, no matter what we call them. The forces of capitalism operate in an exploitive manner, whether we speak about them or not. In accordance with the discussion above, these are structural and objective experiences; they affect the way people think about and identify themselves. Discourses do not change these experiences; they may, however, change people's understanding of them. Although of great importance, discourses *alone* are not responsible for meaning and identity-creating processes. Objective experiences, which are interpreted by people themselves, are also decisive in such processes. Thus, identities are shaped and constituted in the intersection of 'lived realities' and ideologies and discourses.

It is important to distinguish between experience which stems from an individual's biography, and experience as a social relation. It is the latter which is of interest here: it refers to collective experience and history, and how groups are positioned in society. The concept of "women's experience" has rightly been criticized on the ground that there is no homogeneous category *women*.[55] However, when analyzing the experience of female cashew workers in factories and family life, the homogeneity was striking—which would justify the use of collective experience for this particular group.

The concept of identity introduced earlier needs further elaboration. Kathryn Woodward defines identity in the following way: "Identity gives us an idea of who we are and of how we relate to others and to the world in which we live. Identity marks the way in which we are the same as others who share that position, and the ways in which we are different from those who do not".[56] We here exclude personal identities, which are highly individualized and unique, and incorporate far more facets and complexities relating to an individual's life experiences than that of *social identity*. The latter concept refers to how people locate themselves in society in relation

---

[55] For a defense of the concept of women's experience, see Diana Mulinari and Kerstin Sandell, "Exploring the Notion of Experience in Feminist Thought", *Acta Sociologica*, 42 (1999), pp. 287-297. Others have argued that the concept "women's experience" should be kept for moral and strategic reasons. See, for example, Rilay, *Am I That Name?*

[56] Kathryn Woodward (ed.), *Identity and Difference* (London, 1997), pp. 1-2.

to other perceived groups and institutions.[57] Social identity—people's sense of societal belonging—is also complex and exists on several levels, since individuals have overlapping, fragmented, and sometimes conflicting identities.[58]

Interest in "identity" rose out of extensive criticism of analyses of social inequality, which mainly concentrated on class and neglected other categories such as gender, ethnicity, sexuality, and race. The result of this earlier neglect has been the recent stream of research on identities other than that of class. If it previously was common with research on class and class consciousness, the tendency during the last two decades has been a neglect of class aspects—something criticized by those who oppose postmodern theories.[59]

The postmodern approach to identity may well be used in other societies than contemporary Western. It is not a postindustrial or postmodern phenomenon for people to have multiple identities—neither in the West nor in other parts of the world. People have always simultaneously been workers, husbands, or wives; women or men; Indians, Westerners; gays, lesbians, or heterosexuals; neighbors, friends, or parents.

The definition of identity followed here is more in line with postmodern interpretations than classical modernist theories, whether those allude to class, gender, or other social categories. The concept of identity may be viewed as essentialist or non-essentialist.[60] The former implies a perception of identities as either a result of biological qualities or as built on other "truths", such as kinship or a shared history. It also would see identity as fixed and transhistorical. Such an approach has long been contested by feminist scholars and those focusing on the question of race and ethnicity.[61] Many others concerned with the identity of caste in India have rejected an essential view and considered caste a social construction.[62] Central to the postmodern approach to the concept of identity is that identities are fluid and contingent, rather than fixed and persistent.

---

[57] Bradley, *Fractured Identities*, pp. 24-25; see also Sheila Allen, "Race, Ethnicity and Nationality: Some Questions of Identity", in Haleh Afshar and Mary Maynard (eds), *The Dynamics of 'Race' and Gender: Some Feminist Interventions* (London, 1994), pp. 85-105.
[58] For a discussion of the concept of identity, see Bradley, *Fractured Identities*, pp. 23-27 and 202-214.
[59] See, for example, the contributions in Ellen Meikins Wood and John Bellamy Foster (eds), *In Defense of History: Marxism and the Postmodern Agenda* (New York, 1997).
[60] Kathryn Woodward, "Concepts of Identity and Difference", in Kathryn Woodward (ed.), *Identity and Difference*, pp. 8-50.
[61] See, for example, Kum-Kum Bhavnani and Ann Phoenix (eds), *Shifting Identities. Shifting Racisms: A Feminism and Psychology Reader* (London, 1994); Afshar and Maynard (eds), *The Dynamics of 'Race' and Gender*.
[62] See, for example, C.J. Fuller, *Caste Today* (Bombay, 1996); Mary Searle-Chatterjee and Ursula Sharma (eds), *Contextualising Caste: Post-Dumontian Approaches* (Oxford, 1994).

People have multiple identities which are changeable, fragmented, overlapping, dynamic, ambiguous, and sometimes conflicting. It may, for example, conflict to be of high caste and yet belong to the working class; to be a woman and a worker; to be a mother and a trade union leader. Identities are historically and culturally formed, i.e., they are non-essential and cannot be derived from an external referent.

Harriet Bradley has conceptualized different forms of social identity in a useful way by identifying three levels on which they may work: passive, active, and politicized.

Having a *passive identity* means that a person or social group does not particularly think about their identity. It is in a sense a potential identity, only being activated when specific events occur. Bradley suggests that in contemporary British society, class is a passive identity for many people who, although they do not deny belonging to a class and recognize the existence of class inequalities, do so without thinking much of their own place within that social order.

An *active identity* has reached the consciousness of individuals who are, for the most part, aware of belonging to a specific, identified group— whether that is a class, gender, ethnicity, or any other group. According to Bradley, active identities are promoted by the experience of discrimination. Race, class, ethnicity, or gender may occasion such identity-shaping crises. For example, a black person's identity as "black" is activated when addressed in a derogating way because of the color of his or her skin; a woman's identity as "woman" becomes manifest when being sexually harassed.

An identity becomes *politicized* when it is a basis for action and results in collective organizing. A number of contemporary movements may be given as examples of politicized identities. Bradley mentions two instances from the West: feminism, and the gay and lesbian movement, but to this could be added ethnic, environmental, religious, and traditional political movements.[63]

A politicized identity belongs, of course, to the active categories. Several identities may also compete and overlap, making active and politicized identities more complex and even contradictory. To the politicized identity we may add a further dimension: *central or peripherical* identity, in the sense of having the feeling either of one's own powerful activity, or of being led.

Caste and Class

The Indian caste system is an area of research which has generated an enormous literature in the field of anthropology, religion, history, and sociology.

---

[63] Bradley, *Fractured Identities*, pp. 25-26.

Any discussion of the caste system runs the risk of being a grave simplification. The aim here is not to investigate all the ramifications of the caste system among the workers who are the focus of this study. The discussion below is restricted to certain aspects of the caste system—the relation between caste and class, and the complications of gender. The focus is on social rather than religious issues: the social interaction of different castes in the factories, and views held by the cashew workers regarding the meaning and importance of the caste system as a nexus of social interaction.

Researchers have dealt with the caste system from both a cultural/religious and from a materialist perspective; rarely have the two been integrated. A number of scholars have asserted that caste and class belong to different social systems, caste being based on social and ritual status, and class on economics. Max Weber offered a *cultural interpretation* of the caste system, implying that it had no analytical relevance for the economic structure of Indian society.[64] A similar view was advanced by the French anthropologist, Louis Dumont, and has been especially influential since the 1960s. Dumont's main thesis is that Indian society is characterized by cultural consensus on the caste system which, in turn, is legitimized by the Hindu *dharma* concept and the dichotomy of purity and pollution.[65] Dumont claims that the caste system has, for the most part, remained intact during the twentieth century. His thesis is founded on a belief that lower-caste groups suffer from *false consciousness*, having simply accepted the Brahmin values and representations of the lower castes. Dumont sees this not as connected to the power of the economic ruling classes to define an ideology, but to the elite in the *ritual* hierarchy.[66] He is of the opinion that people are socialized into the caste system from childhood on. The identity of caste is seen as primordial, therefore unquestioned as natural and decisive for an individual's social identity. Dumont's stance with regard to cultural consensus has been contested, both by those with a materialist orientation and those who prefer to interpret castes as cultural phenomena.[67] As Mary Searle-Chatterjee stresses, gender, and often class, is as primordial as caste,

[64] Max Weber, *The Religion of India* (Glencoe, 1958).
[65] Dumont, *Homo Hierarchus*. Hinduism is based on the concept of *dharma*, from the verb *dhri*, 'support', 'make firm'. It means foundation and is seen as a cosmic principle. In the field of ethics it manifests itself as the Karma doctrine: as a man sows, so will he reap in a future existence. See Helmer Ringgren and Åke V. Ström, *Religions of Mankind: Today and Yesterday* (Philadelphia, 1967), pp. 350-351. Dharma implies the idea of an eternally fixed and divine standard of conduct, a sacred law which is never to be altered, but only to be interpreted by legislation or by social reform. See A.L. Basham, "Hinduism", in R.C. Zaehner (ed.), *The Concise Encyclopedia of Living Faiths* (Boston, 1959), p 253.
[66] Dumont, *Homo Hierarchus*.
[67] See, for example, the contributions in the anthology by Searle-Chatterjee and Sharma (eds), *Contextualising Caste*.

and may be as dominant.[68] Several studies show that lower castes do not share the opinion of higher caste people that there exists a scale of purity which applies to different groups of people, or that the caste system has been upheld by consensus rather than power.[69]

Writers with a Marxist perspective, whose aim is to integrate caste into a theoretical framework in which class is the central analytical category, have often stressed that excess focus on caste as the main hierarchical order in India has distorted reality and neglected the analysis of class in a devastating way.[70] Their perspective rejects the notion, engendered by the cultural interpretation of caste, that India is *completely different* in its social structures, as compared to the West.

Partha Chatterjee, a member of the Subaltern School in Calcutta, holds that the materialist position may be further subdivided into two strands. The first sees caste as part of an ideological superstructure. According to this view, caste is a system which reflects economic, material, productive relations. Indian sociologists commonly show how changed relations of production have led to changes in the caste system. Chatterjee considers such an approach, which maintains the distinction between base and superstructure, as functionalist.[71]

For others, caste is the Indian form of social reality, having a material base—not only a superstructure linked to a particular mode of production. Researchers of this school speak of a caste-feudal society in India in the pre-British period. The castes were the feudal classes. With the British colonialization and the transformed relations of production towards capitalism, caste and class began to be separated.[72] Such a view draws heavily on the traditional link between caste and occupation.

---

[68] Mary Searle-Chatterjee, "Caste, Religion and Other Identities", in Searle-Chatterjee and Sharma (eds), *Contextualising Caste*, p. 149.

[69] Pauline Mahar Kolenda, "Religious Anxiety and Hindu Fate", *Journal of Asian Studies*, 23 (1964), pp. 71-82; Gerald D. Berreman, *Caste and Other Inequities: Essays on Inequality* (Meerut, 1979); Gerald D. Berreman, "The Brahmanical View of Caste", *Contributions to Indian Sociology*, No. 5 (1971), pp. 16-25; Rosalind O'Hanlon, *Caste, Conflict and Ideology* (Cambridge, 1985); Robert DelLège, "Caste without a System: a Study of South Indian Harijans", in Searle and Chatterjee (eds), *Contextualising Caste*, pp. 122-145; Mencher, "On Being an Untouchable in India"; Joan P. Mencher, "The Caste System Upside Down", in Dipankar Gupta, *Social Stratification* (Oxford, 1996), pp. 93-109; Gail Omvedt, "Class, Caste and Land in India: an Introductory Essay", in Gail Omvedt (ed.), *Land, Caste, and Politics in Indian States* (Delhi, 1982); Karin Kapadia, *Siva and Her Sisters: Gender, Caste and Class in Rural South India* (Boulder and Oxford, 1995).

[70] See, for example, André Béteille, *Social Inequality: Selected Writings* (Harmondsworth, 1970), p. 138; Mencher, "The Caste System Upside Down".

[71] Partha Chatterjee, "Caste and Subaltern Consciousness", in Ranajit Guha (ed.), *Subaltern Studies VI: Writings on South Asian History and Society* (Oxford, 1989), pp. 169-209.

[72] Omvedt, "Class, Caste and Land in India", pp. 15 ff.

Chatterjee criticizes both of these materialist approaches and argues that to understand people's consciousness we cannot work with the concepts used in class analyses, which presuppose a "legal framework of bourgeois freedom and equality".[73] Here Chatterjee positions himself among post-colonial scholars who have objected to transferring concepts from the (Western) Enlightenment to the Indian context.[74] On the other hand, Chatterjee also criticizes Dumont and his followers for focusing too much on the dominant religious ideology of *dharma*. He dismisses the earlier views and argues that to grasp the subaltern's consciousness, we have to start *at the level of concrete social life and practical activity*. This is also the position taken in the present study of the cashew workers of Kerala.

Chatterjee employs Gramsci's division of "common sense" in a dual and contradictory consciousness as a theoretical tool to explain the consciousness of subalterns in India. In his *Prison Notebooks*, he discusses the relation between religion, science, and consciousness, asserting that ordinary workers have two theoretical consciousness: one which emerges from his [!] activities at work and cooperation with other workers, i.e., from "his" experiences, and another, more verbal one, uncritically inherited from the past—an ideological submission. In this view, the consciousness of workers are two-fold and conflicting: one autonomous, and one borrowed, both trying to intersect in a realm of "common sense".[75] The relation between the two sides of the consciousness is not fixed and may change with time. The consciousness of subaltern groups, in this perspective, is more contradictory, fragmented, and multiple than in classical Marxism or in Dumont's perspective. Gramsci seems to view religious ideology as having less scope for negotiation than other ideologies. Religion, as he explicitly writes, has been "uncritically absorbed".[76]

Another member of the Subaltern School, Dipesh Chakrabarty, takes a position similar to Chatterjee in his highly regarded study of jute mill workers in Calcutta from 1890 to 1940. Chakrabarty asks why jute workers, in spite of some militant action, have rarely organized into trade unions. Previous explanations stressed the state's oppression of left-oriented trade unions, the linguistic heterogeneity of the workers, ignorance, lack of awareness, or rural background. Another reason given is that they were never fully proletarianized, because they could—at least during certain pe-

---

[73] Chatterjee, "Caste and Subaltern Consciousness", p. 207.

[74] See, for example, D. Chakrabarty, "Radical Histories and Questions of Enlightenment Rationalism", *Economic and Political Weekly*, 30:14 (1995), pp. 751-759.

[75] Quintin Hoare and Geoffrey Nowell Smith (eds), *Antonio Gramsci: Selections from the Prison Notebooks* (Chennai, 2000), pp. 333 ff. See Chatterjee, "Caste and Subaltern Consciousness" , pp. 170 ff.

[76] Hoare and Smith, *Antonio Gramsci*, p. 333.

riods—revert to their home villages for survival. Chakrabarty finds it problematic to view organizing in trade unions only as matter of literacy and self-awareness, stressing that such issues as culture and consciousness, or authority and power, cannot be ignored. He makes a distinction between ideology (a number of conscious ideas) and culture (a system through which a social order is mediated, reproduced, experienced, and investigated). He further argues that although, ideologically, trade unions of the left were based on democracy, there was a distinct hierarchy evident in daily culture. Power relations that were culturally driven were built into the unions: the theory of democracy was replaced by the practice of loyalty. Thus, democratic ideology was not strong enough to eradicate power relations, which were culturally coded.

Chakrabarty, too, stresses that Western ideals from the Enlightenment, such as bourgeois freedom, equality, and citizenship, were necessary cultural entities for successful and democratic trade unions—ideals that were lacking in Indian culture.[77] He has been criticized for this by historians who advocate an economic, structural perspective, i.e., the traditional historical-materialists—precisely those whom Chakrabarty challenges in his book by castigating the categories "bourgeois", "pre-capital", and "capital" used in their analyses.[78] Chakrabarty earnestly challenges the dogmatic, unreflective application of standard categories to Indian society. However, his study is problematic in three aspects: employing official reports to analyze workers' consciousness;[79] focusing perhaps overmuch on culture and religion to the neglect of material "realities" when analyzing aspects of identities; and failing to link gender to the question of work and identity. The fact that Chakrabarty does not address gender at all is remarkable when one considers that approximately 20% of the jute mill workers around 1900 were women, strikes have been conducted solely by women, and the jute workers have had a powerful female trade union leader. Although Chakrabarty does not go into this, the fact that the female-led trade union wing was dissolved warrants further consideration from a gender perspective. On several occasions Chakrabarty documents conflicts in which women's honor was at issue. Such situations could have occasioned an analysis of gender relations, but Chakrabarty sees such matters as solely religious issues, since they also involved antagonistic Muslims and Hindus.

---

[77] Dipesh Chakrabarty, *Rethinking Working-Class History* (New Delhi, 1989).
[78] Ranajith Das Gupta, "Indian Working Class and Some Recent Historiographical Issues", *Economic and Political Weekly*, 31:8 (1996), pp. L27-31; Bahl, "Relevance (or Irrelevance) of Subaltern Studies", pp. 1333-1343.
[79] This has also been stressed by Amiya Kumar Bagchi, "Working Class Consciousness", *Economic and Political Weekly*, 25:30 (1990), pp. PE54-60.

Chakrabarty's conclusion—that the undemocratic culture of traditional India has been a major obstacle to developing class consciousness among workers—does not deviate from earlier, discredited interpretations of this issue, although his theoretical discussion is new. In essence, he views failures to unionize or develop class consciousness as strongly linked to cultural inheritances from the past.[80] From a gender perspective, however, such arguments are flawed, and the polarization "traditional vs. modern" appears as inadequate.[81]

Adding Gender to the Caste and Class

Joanna Liddle and Rama Joshi note that the relationship between caste and gender in India was considered by several authors in the 1960s, but none of them gave this link any theoretical explanation. The higher a caste was placed in the social hierarchy, the more regulations were imposed upon women. Prominent among them were child marriage, prohibition of divorce or remarriage of widows, and *purdah*, i.e., issues controlling women's sexuality.[82] A loss of freedom by women became conspicuous when a caste tried to rise in the social hierarchy.[83] M.N. Srinivas discusses this phenomenon and concludes that it was part of the process of *Sanskritization*, defined as the process by which a lower caste changes its customs in a direction of a higher caste—although he does not see this as a problem requiring analysis.[84] It must be stressed that a process of Sanskritization does not necessarily imply imitating Brahmins, but may equally be the emulation of any dominant caste.

Restrictions on women of higher castes, mainly Brahmins, included disinheritance of land. Instead, a dowry was given to a women at marriage. Liddle and Joshi stress the material basis for the relationship between caste and gender—the more property involved, the more important it was to restrict women's sexuality. In India the freedom of low-caste women, and the inability of men to control their women, were part of the circle of behavior that made the whole caste impure. Hence, gender ideology legitimized and reinforced the caste system. Liddle and Joshi assert that the so-

---

[80] For a similar criticism, see Leela Fernandes, *Producing Workers: The Politics of Gender, Class, and Culture in the Calcutta Jute Mills* (Chicago, 1997), pp. 15-16.
[81] See note 102.
[82] Liddle and Joshi, *Daughters of Independence*, pp. 57-69.
[83] Srinivas, *Caste in Modern India*, p. 46; J.H. Hutton, *Caste in India: Its Nature, Function and Origins* (Bombay, 1963), p. 129, cited in Liddle and Joshi, *Daughters of Independence*, pp. 59 ff.
[84] Srinivas, *Social Change in Modern India*, p. 6.

cial processes that promoted male dominance in the class system were similar to those operating in the caste system. They were only modified to include aspects other than sexual purity.

Liddle and Joshi take a very long-term perspective, beginning with the Aryan invasion during the second pre-Christian millennium. Geographically, the analysis of the authors is mainly based on North Indian circumstances.

As discussed in Chapter I, Travancore was unique, having a matrilineal system which flourished among at least half of the population up to the 1940s. Only Travancore's small Brahmin community held its women in *purdah*, thus preventing them from being employed for wages.[85] According to the Travancore census of 1931, the proportion of women in the labor force decreased markedly when higher castes were tabulated.[86] Sources from the beginning of the twentieth century give evidence that low-caste women (Scheduled Castes in particular) were often agricultural workers. Their high divorce rate, the remarriage of widows, and greater mobility were also documented.[87]

In a study on Pulayas in four different regions in Kerala in the 1960s, K.C. Alexander convincingly demonstrates that the link between gender and caste still remained decisive. In two villages, he found that gender relations had not changed much, compared to the situation earlier in the century. However, in Trivandrum, the capital of Kerala, and in one village dominated by Syrian Christians, he observed that families were *more stable* and *divorce rates were down*. The husbands had greater responsibility for the financial maintenance of the family, while their wives were more bound to household work. The custom of "bride price" had become a dowry and women held lower status than their husbands.[88] Wives were more respectful and obedient towards their spouses.[89]

In two of the villages, Punnapra and Kunnathunadu, such changes had not occurred. Alexander describes the situation in the following way:

---

[85] If a Brahmin woman was suspected of unchastity, she had to undergo a humiliating investigation organized by the caste association, with "no consideration of personal affection or public policy intervening." Govt. of India, *Census of India 1901*, Vol. XXVI, Travancore, Part I, Report, p. 311. For a discussion of the centrality of women's sexual purity in the upholding of the purity of the caste among Brahmins, see Uma Chakravarty, "Conceptualising Brahmanical Patriarchy in Early India: Gender, Caste, Class and State", *Economic and Political Weekly*, 28:14 (1993), pp. 579-586; and Uma Chakravarty, "Gender, Caste and Labour: Ideological and Material Structure of Widowhood", *Economic and Political Weekly*, 30:36 (1995), pp. 2248-2256.
[86] Govt. of India, *Census of India 1931*, Vol. XXVIII, Travancore, Part I, Report, pp. 269 ff.
[87] Ibid., p. 385; Govt. of India, *Census of India 1901*, Vol. XXVI, Travancore, Part I, Report, p. 343.
[88] The institution of bride-price and dowry will be discussed in Chapter VIII.
[89] K.C. Alexander, *Social Mobility in Kerala* (Poona, 1968).

The husband-wife relationship continues to be what it was without much change. The husband is the head of the family and important decisions affecting the family and its members are taken by him. But the authority of the husband is seriously impaired with the relative self-orientation in the behavioural pattern of other members of the family—wife and children. It was found that the wife did not conceive her role as entirely subordinate to that of her husband. The wife enjoyed a status more or less equal to that of the husband and equality between them was revealed in a number of behavioural patterns, similar to those we have seen from Punnapra, such as the husband and wife eating together from the same plate, the wife not getting up from the seat when the husband is entering the house, the wife opposing the husband in public, etc. This is clearly an area in which the Pulayas have to assimilate much of the value of the higher castes and modify behaviour accordingly in order to be on par with the higher castes.[90]

Alexander attributes the changed pattern to caste mobility, rather than class, seeing the process as one of Sanskritization. It is also noteworthy that he does not view the process of stricter control on women as a problem and he does not try to give it a theoretical explanation, considering it rather a so-called normal development.

Another process, Westernization[91], which concept includes the adoption of Western education, secularization, and lifestyle (including consumerism), has especially been noted among the urban population. For some educated, professional women, upward mobility in the class system has permitted them to break out of caste and gender constraints, and their professionalism has been received—even by their husbands—as a means of improving their own class status.[92] The two processes, Sanskritization and Westernization, thus strive in opposite directions with regard to gender. But being influenced by the West should also be seen in terms of a variety of outcomes concerning gender, depending on which particular class is under consideration. With Westernization, such organizations as trade unions, and institutionalization of labor laws and wages, have a decisive impact, as this study will attempt to show. Westernization might bring about higher education and more freedom for some women, but it might also occasion greater stress on the nuclear family, with the woman strictly relegated to the role of housewife. Upward (class) mobility, for example, where a husband is improving his economic status, may similarly result in a withdrawal of the wife from public life, as some studies of Indian working

---

[90] Ibid., p. 146.
[91] For a discussion on Westernization, see Srinivas, *Caste in Modern India*, p. 55, and Srinivas, *Social Change in Modern India*, pp. 46-88.
[92] Liddle and Joshi, *Daughters of Independence*, pp. 109-111.

women suggest.[93] Class, caste, and gender are thus interrelated in ways that are a bit unclear and certainly complex.

Liddle and Joshi find it misleading to hold that the Western impact on gender relations, a consequence of British colonialism, was liberating for Indian women. In the authors' view the final and overarching reason for the inferior position of Indian women vis-à-vis men is one of international capitalism and cultural imperialism. The West's economic exploitation of India is bound up with an interest in maintaining both a gender division of labor and an image of Western superiority in gender relations. The portrayal of Indian women as submissive is seen as a Western strategy for continuing the patriarchal attitude of colonial times.[94]

The Field of Research

Such questions as poverty, political resistance, work, and empowerment in contemporary society have been essential issues for gender research in the so-called Third World.[95] The discussion here is restricted to a review of a few central studies on women's work, and on other studies which raise the question of class, caste, and gender identities in India.

For a long time women's work in India was primarily the concern of economists or sociologists, rather than labor historians. Most of their studies had a quantitative and structural approach, considering mainly the productive sphere and neglecting cultural aspects; rarely were the voices of women themselves heard. The question of women's identities was not posed, and most often caste, too, was neglected in those analyses.[96] The study by Maria Mies cited earlier is an important exception.[97] Its long historical perspective focuses on the analysis of change. It is a detailed micro-level study, which takes class, caste, and gender into consideration and tries

---

[93] See, for example, Maria Mies, "Capitalist Development Production", in Mies et al. (eds), *Women: The Last Colony*, pp. 40-45.

[94] Liddle and Joshi, *Daughters of Independence*, pp. 237-240.

[95] These are questions shared by Third World researchers. To give an overview of such a vast field is hardly possible. A few studies on women's work during the last three decades have been central: F. Fröbel, J. Kreye, and O. Heinrich, *The New International Division of Labour* (Cambridge, 1980); Swasti Mitter, *Common Fate, Common Bond;* Guy Standing, "Global Feminization through Flexible Labor", *World Development*, 17:7 (1989), pp. 1077-1096; Cynthia Enloe, "Silicon Tricks and the Two Dollar Woman", *New Internationalist*, January (1992), pp. 12-14.

[96] See, for example, Nirmala Banerjee (ed.), *Indian Women in a Changing Industrial Scenario* (New Delhi, 1991); Alakh N. Sharma and Seema Singh (eds), *Women and Work: Changing Scenario in India* (New Delhi, 1992); U. Kalpagam, *Labour and Gender: Survival in Urban India* (New Delhi, 1994).

[97] Mies, *The Lace Makers*.

to offer a theoretical framework for them—although, as discussed earlier, it is not immune to criticism. There are, however, other studies which offer important insights, as well.

A group of researchers carried out a number of local investigations of female industrial workers in India in the early 1980s.[98] These centered on the textile industry in Tamil Nadu, the garment industry in New Delhi, garment and electronic industries in Maharashstra, and a number of prawn processing, leather, silk yarn, and electronic industries in West Bengal. The contributors to the resulting anthology show that women are not in the periphery of the labor force, but at the heart of production. The authors, therefore, dismiss the Marxist concept of a reserve army of labor, as does the present study of cashew workers.[99] The various essays show that, in spite of large differences in culture, there was a remarkable similarity in the working and living conditions of female industrial laborers. In all of the studies, women had a weak position in trade unions, were often seasonal employees paid by piece work, and were seldom allowed to use machines or advanced technology. Female workers always held inferior status vis-à-vis male workers. The authors account for this by citing the ideology of the superior male worker, an ideology supported and maintained by such institutions as the family, religion, and the state. They thereby differ with writers who assert that women's subordinate position in Indian industries is largely a result of capitalist strategies. According to Nirmala Banerjee, none of the employers in their study were particularly powerful, nor would have had the possibility to influence structures working against women.[100] The reason for women's weak position at work, as compared to men's, should rather be sought in patriarchal structures in such powerful social institutions as the family, religion, and the state.[101] However, it would be reductionist to seek a single explanation for oppression. The fact that an employer appears to have little influence, or employs only a limited number of workers, need not imply that he does not actively participate in the creation or maintenance of a suppressive structure.

If studies of women's labor have often failed to encompass broader time periods, social changes, and the importance of caste, many anthropologists have employed a historical perspective when studying social relations— including class, caste, and gender. Their focus is primarily on kinship and marriage patterns, rather than on workplaces or work processes. Several

---

[98] Banerjee (ed.), *Indian Women*.

[99] Nirmala Banerjee, "Introduction", in Banerjee (ed.), *Indian Women* pp. 23-24. For a discussion of the concept of the reserve army of labor, see also Kalpagam, *Labour and Gender*, pp. 120-145, and Bradley, *Men's Work, Women's Work*, pp. 66-67.

[100] Nirmala Banerjee, "Introduction", pp. 23-24, in Banerjee (ed.), *Indian Women*, p. 27.

[101] Nirmala Banerjee, "Conclusion", in Banerjee (ed.), *Indian Women*, p. 307.

recent studies in anthropology have addressed the question of the complex relations between caste and gender, or class, caste, and gender, in changing societies in South India, and have especially focused on low-caste women. These studies, although having different points of departures, draw similar conclusions: caste or class emancipation during the twentieth century has resulted in declining status for certain groups of women. Feminist researchers in the fields of history, development studies, and political science have also highlighted the failure of earlier analyses of caste and class identities to include gender. It has been stressed that interconnections and boundaries between these categories are complex and contested, and that the construction of categories itself is an act of exerting power.[102] The argument regarding the impact of ideologies of female domesticity and hegemonic discourses in the construction of identities has been forcefully developed by Samita Sen with regard to colonial India, and Leela Fernandes and Karin Kapadia with regard to contemporary India.[103]

In a detailed study of the cultural aspects of the former matrilineal system, Marion den Uyl focuses on Kerala from the perspective of low-caste women. She asserts that the twentieth century has implied new gender ideologies and new roles for women as well as men. Den Uyl holds that Kerala offers a gender paradox in its development process and that so-called Harijans have become "civilized" by emulating higher castes, a process which Alexander had also described. To adopt the values of a higher caste also means the adoption of increasing inequality between men and women. The new ideology identifies men as responsible breadwinners, and women more and more as unproductive and passive housewives. Women have experienced increased ideological stress on their roles as mothers, wives, and housewives, and a stricter control of their sexuality. At the same time, certain formerly positive attributes of being a woman have disappeared, as well as several traditional rights—mostly linked to the matrilineal system. Den Uyl explains this historical process as emancipation from caste oppression, although the consequence of capitalist development is also considered.[104]

---

[102] Kapadia, *Siva and her Sisters*; Fernandes, *Producing Workers;* Amrita Chhachhi and Renée Pittin, "Multiple Identities and Multiple Strategies: Confronting State, Capital and Patriarchy", in Ronaldo Munck and Peter Waterman (eds), *Labour Worldwide in the Era of Globalization: Alternative Union Models in the New World Order* (New York, 1999), pp. 64-79; Kalpana Ram, *Mukkuvar Women: Gender, Hegemony and Capitalist Transformation in a South Indian Fishing Community* (New Delhi, 1992).

[103] Samita Sen, *Women and Labour in Late Colonial India: The Bengal Jute Industry* (Cambridge, 1999); Fernandes, *Producing Workers*; Karin Kapadia, "Gender Ideologies and the Formation of Rural Industrial Classes in South India Today", in Jonathan P. Parry, Jan Breman, and Karin Kapadia (eds), *The Worlds of Indian Industrial Labour* (New Delhi, 1999), pp. 329-352.

[104] den Uyl, *Invisible Barriers*, passim.

A similar perspective is employed by Kalpana Ram in a study of a fishing community in the Kanyakumari district in Tamil Nadu, close by the border of Kerala. It examines capitalist transformation, but focuses on culture and sexuality more than work or labor processes. Ram also links other social changes, such as marriage patterns and household formations, to this development. Economic processes are interconnected to cultural ones, and within the latter, symbolic and religious aspects are strongly emphasized. Ram rejects both Marxist economist theories and solely cultural interpretations of Indian society, such as Louis Dumont's perspective. In Ram's view, culture is an arena of conflicting interest and power contestation between different groups. She shows that cultural constructions of sexuality were important to support new gender relations under capitalism: a new gender division of labor was introduced, in which women both gained and lost power. However, the twentieth century also saw a process of widening the gap between men's and women's activities in Tamil Nadu, where there was no tradition of a matrilineal society. In contrast to den Uyl, Ram gives great importance to the capitalist development of the changed work tasks for men and women, arguing that capitalist productive relations have narrowed the horizons of (fisher)women's lives.[105]

In a more labor-oriented study which focuses on the last thirty years, the anthropologist, Karin Kapadia, shows that a de-skilling and feminization of labor has occurred in the mid-1970s in the informal sector that produces gems in Tamil Nadu. A new category of workers was recruited among women of a higher caste than the former male workers. This was done to establish a specific female working class more constrained by discourses of domestication and submissiveness than low-caste women, who were regarded more as equals of male workers. Kapadia's study highlights the interrelation of class, caste, and gender in ways that may be paradoxical.[106]

Indian labor history was long restricted to the biographies of nationalists and trade union organizers. A few studies focused on the working process or trade union movements, mainly taking a structuralist perspective from above, with little concern for other identities than that of class.[107] Since the 1970s and 80s, several micro-level studies have been carried

---

[105] Ram, *Mukkuvar Women*.

[106] Kapadia, "Gender Ideologies and the Formation of Rural Industrial Classes in South India Today". The interrelation between class, caste, and gender is also elaborated in a detailed study of kinship, rituals, and work among five castes in contemporary Tamil Nadu. See Kapadia, *Siva and her Sisters*.

[107] See, for example, G.K. Sharma, *Labour Movement in India* (New Delhi, 1963); C. Revri, *Indian Trade Union Movement: An Outline History 1880-1947* (New Delhi, 1972); Sukumal Sen, *Working Class in India: History of Emergence and Movement, 1830-1970* (Calcutta, 1977); Panchanan Saha, *History of the Working Class Movement in Bengal* (New Delhi, 1978).

out—certain of them from a cultural perspective influenced by E.P. Thompson. Most often they draw attention only to male workers and lack gender perspective, even if they do mention female workers now and then.[108]

Lately a few labor studies with a pronounced gender perspective have been published. Samita Sen treats the same workers and the same period as Chakrabarty—Calcutta jute workers during the first half of the twentieth century. However, in contrast to Chakrabarty, Sen's explicit gender perspective may reflect the fact that, around 1900, 20% of all jute workers were women, and then their proportion dwindled considerably during the following fifty years. Sen argues that exclusion of women from city factories was linked to new perceptions of femininity and patriarchal family ideologies in society at large, especially in the rural areas where their labor was recruited. She points out that Chakrabarty's study of the jute workers in Calcutta, which stresses the lingering traditional Indian hierarchies in the factories, implies that existing gender ideologies were sustaining hierarchies of wages and status in the factories (although Chakrabarty does not discuss gender division of labor). Sen's study repudiates such a view and illustrates that unequal gender relations are also built into the capitalist system.[109]

Within the confines of the present study of the cashew workers of Kerala, it may be argued that unequal gender relations were less marked in traditional society among certain communities, but were strengthened with capitalist work organization and the institutionalization of trade unions. Sen has shown that mill owners used prevailing gender ideologies to devaluate women's work and to place women in jobs with low status, as well as systematically replace them with male workers. In this process, the ideology of female domesticity and docility, emerging from the "elite discourse of femininity", and including stricter controls over women, played a decisive role.[110] It manifested itself outside the workplace in the increasing practice of paying dowries in favor of bride-prices.[111] Female jute workers

[108] Satya Brata Datta, *Capital Accumulation and Workers' Struggle in Indian Industrialisation: The Case of Tata Iron and Steel Company 1910-1970* (Stockholm, 1986); Vinay Bahl, *The Making of the Indian Working Class: A Case Study of the Tata Iron Steel Company* (London, 1995); Janaki Nair, *Miners and Millhands: Work, Culture and Politics in Princely Mysore* (New Delhi, 1998). One of the few studies on women's activities in trade unions in India was carried out by Chhaya Datar. However it is a sociological rather than a historical study and covers only the period from 1970 to 1985. Chhaya Datar, *Waging Change: Women Tobacco Workers in Nipani Organize* (New Delhi, 1989).
[109] Sen, *Women and Labour*, p. 8.
[110] Sen seems to allude to both caste and class with this expression. Sen, *Women and Labour*, pp. 9, 56-65.
[111] Sen, *Women and Labour*, p. 85.

themselves contested the conception of women as domestic and docile and became militant workers—although often outside of trade unions because their leaders did not address specific female issues. Sen's study thus underlines women's resistance to hegemonic gender ideology.

Why would mill owners have so strongly supported a discourse of femininity, categorizing women as housewives or supplementary providers, if they only intended to fire women? Would not such an ideology have been more understandable if the goal were to *hire* women, and thereby keep wages low, because affirming the ideology of dependent housewives means lending support to the concept of male breadwinners? Most workers in the jute mills were migrants. The reasons women were not recruited in greater numbers were two-fold, according to Sen: a) the new perceptions of female seclusion which became current around 1900, and b) the state's support of a patriarchal gender ideology by introducing a law which protected men and children from women who wanted to "escape" them. Married women could not migrate without their husbands, and therefore the recruitment of women for the mills had to be directed towards widows or abandoned women, and those individuals were not so easily found in large numbers. The savings in wages that could be realized by hiring such women were less than the cost of recruiting them. Seeing to it that the families of male workers would remain living in their native areas was part of the strategy of the factory owners. In this way, when those workers were seasonally dismissed, they would have a home to return to, enabling their employers to evade responsibility for providing for them year around.[112]

Sen's explanation of the reasons for substituting women for men in the labor force is thus built on a belief in economic rationality on the part of the mill owners. However, as this study will hope to show, a change in the gender composition of labor is not primarily built on economic rationality, but rather on a complex and contradictory web of economic factors, gender ideologies, and discourses—and the institutionalization of these.

The jute industry in Calcutta has also been studied from a gender perspective by a political scientist, Leela Fernandes, who focuses on the entire postcolonial period. In contrast to Sen, Fernandes' concern is with identities and the politics of categories. She draws inspiration from Joan Scott and other postmodern writers, contesting the perception of clearly defined identities and strict boundaries between social categories and identities, and asserting that the important thing is to analyze how such boundaries are constructed in consequence of power and political processes. One conclusion Fernandes draws is that trade unions and the state have generated a discourse leading to class being seen as a monolithic unity, and in which

---

[112] Ibid., pp. 48-52.

differences and hierarchies based on gender, religion, language, or caste are not addressed.[113]

Fernandes' study has an interdisciplinary approach wherein ethnography and history serve as complementary disciplines to the science of politics. Although Fernandes asserts that her analysis covers the period 1950 to 2000, it falls short of being a systematic historical analysis, and does not treat the way changes are initiated and effected. It is more a study of the present situation than of historical processes.

Sen and Fernandes differ in their theoretical approaches. Sen is more inclined toward a structural perspective, using concepts like patriarchy and capitalism to explain changes in ideologies and identities. Fernandes, on the other hand, does not regard such overall oppressive systems, but sees identities as discursively-constructed constituents of political and economic structures. It would seem preferable to take a two-fold approach, examining the dialectical interplay between discourses and ideologies on the one hand, and social practices and oppressive structures on the other, in the shaping of people's identity and consciousness.

As proposed in the Introduction, the major dividing line between labor historians and other writers who deal with factory workers in India is often simply the periods studied, i.e., colonial or independent India. The studies of Sen and Fernandes exemplify this.[114] The sharp division between the two disciplines with regard to the epoch under consideration has had negative consequences: rather than observing and analyzing transformations that have occurred across those eras, important changes may have been overlooked. This study of the cashew workers attempts to fill that gap.

A Multiplicity of Methods and Sources

My concern with material aspects as well as with ideologies and discourses necessitates a variety of analytical tools, methods, and sources. These include:

1. Printed and written sources.
2. Interviews with different agents in various institutions.
3. In-depth interviews with workers and trade union leaders.

---

[113] Fernandes, *Producing Workers*.

[114] However, in a later article, Samita Sen complements her previous research on jute workers in colonial times with a discussion of more recent developments, thus taking long-term changes into consideration. Samita Sen, "Women Workers in the Bengal Jute Industry", in Parry, Breman, and Kapadia (eds), *The Worlds of Indian Industrial Labour*, pp. 239-269.

The sources include archival documents, such as correspondence between factory owners, trade union leaders, and representatives of the government; government and academic reports on wages and working conditions among cashew workers; and trade union historical accounts, biographies, and newspaper articles.

Printed material is utilized to establish a social and material context, but some of the sources are employed to analyze how women and men have been represented. In this way more importance is given to the language and form, i.e., the implied meaning and discourses, than to its content. Joan Scott has stressed that historians must analyze how historical sources (especially categories) have been produced, and that content is less important than their form of presentation.[115]

Some sources, however, are useful for the more "traditional" purpose of determining such "hard facts" as gender or caste composition in the work force, wages, numbers of factories and workers, work processes, and state interventions.

Discursive practices have been studied in three areas:

1. How influential people in the immediate surrounding of the workers, i.e., trade union leaders, politicians, and factory owners, have represented female workers.
2. How women workers have been represented in contexts where wages and other working conditions have been discussed and institutionalized .
3. The voices and memories of women themselves.

Interviews were carried out with trade union leaders, representatives of the government, and factory managers—but especially with cashew workers.[116] Oral sources have not been used in the absence of other forms of documentation, but to solicit answers that only the cashew workers themselves could provide through their remembrances and reflections on the meaning of their own past.[117] Certainly, many stories purport to describe what "actually" has happened in years gone by, but people may also "lie sometimes, forget a little, exaggerate, become confused, get things wrong.

---

[115] Scott, *Gender and the Politics of History*, especially Chapter 6, pp. 113-138.

[116] Interviews with factory owners, managers, civil servants, politicians, and trade union leaders at higher levels were usually conducted in English, whereas interviews with workers were carried out in collaboration with an interpreter. My knowledge of the local language did not enable me to converse more than superficially, but I learned enough to create an entree for my efforts (and to amuse people with my mistakes).

[117] For a discussion of the tendency to use oral history when "real" or "better" sources are lacking, see Joan Sangster, "Telling our Stories: Feminist Debates and the Use of Oral History", in Robert Perks and Alistar Thomson (eds), *The Oral History Reader* (London, 1988), p. 88.

Yet they are revealing truths."[118] These "truths" will disclose how they interpret the past and how they explain who they are, and how they see themselves in society.

Field Work and the "Outsider"

Who is an outsider in the context of poor, Indian working class women in the State of Kerala? Men? The middle and upper class? Non-Indians? Westerners? All non-Keralites? (In such a case—how do we define a Keralite?) Anyone who interprets other people's lives is an outsider, more or less, depending on gender, ethnicity, class, religion, age, education, or family background—to which may also be added language, ideology, worldly experience, and sympathetic understanding.

Chandra Mohanty has forcefully argued that a construction of Third World Women has been made by researchers from the West and from the Third World who employ Western theories and concepts. Mohanty has issued a powerful critique against Western feminism for portraying contemporary women of the Third World in a stereotypical and homogeneous way without considering, for example, class and ethnicity. Such women are persistently seen as the negative counterpart of the secular, liberated, modern, educated women of the West. Third World women are represented in terms of an "average woman", who is depicted as ignorant, poor, tradition-bound, domestic, family-oriented, and victimized. She is so different that she is *the Other*. Mohanty finds this way of representing women of the Third World the persistence of a colonialist mode of representation, and thereby an act of wielding power.[119] Mohanty is situated among postcolonial theorists, who also have criticized locating the cultural dimension outside the domain of the history of colonialism.[120]

Mohanty's important criticism need not be restricted to the Third World. Within the West there is no such thing as a homogeneous entity called women, nor is there any homogeneous culture, history, or economy. The neglecting of differences among women in feminist theories (the exclusion of women of color and working-class women, for example) is true

---

[118] Personal Narratives Group (eds), *Interpreting Women's Lives: Feminist Theory and Personal Narratives* (Bloomington, 1989), p. 261.
[119] Mohanty, "Under Western Eyes".
[120] The application of Western theories in regions without the characteristics of the West has also been opposed by historians dealing with colonial times. The meta-narratives stemming from thoughts and ideas of the European Enlightenment have especially been mentioned as distorting theories concerning non-Western countries by failing to consider the difference. See, for example, Dipesh Chakrabarty, "Marx after Marxism: History, Subalternity and Difference", *Meanjin*, 52:3 (1993), pp. 421-434.

of several academic works on Western women as well, so perhaps it is unavoidable in the emergence of a young discipline.[121] Theories like those emanating from Western feminism are not static, but undergoing continuous development, improvement, and adaptation to new insights.

One must also reflect upon how much the language of Western feminism influences the everyday life of women in what has been called the Third World. Although perhaps not having an immediate impact on their lives, such representations may influence the *theories* employed in various development projects and long-term planning.

There is a certain contradiction or ambivalence in Mohanty's criticism. On the one hand it points out the risk of neglecting differences and the faulty application of Western theoretical concepts and categories. On the other hand, the error of viewing Third World women as *too different* is stressed.[122] Hence, there seems to be a call for a balanced use of general social and historical theories, and their sensitive application to specific, local circumstances and conditions.

Maria Lugones and Elizabeth Spelman have written of the dilemma of Westerners seeking to interpret "women of colour", and in particular the asymmetry in power between the white academic woman and the non-white informant.[123] They point out the necessity for the white researcher to weigh her motives for the involvement with "women of colour" and to carefully "learn the text". My own motives for venturing into the world of poor women in Kerala were numerous. I admired the social achievements of the state and wished to attain a deeper understanding of its history. I also had a strong sense of solidarity with the struggling female workers I met, and the closer I came to them, the stronger I felt their friendship—something Lugones and Spelman cite as a necessity if Westerners are to study a non-Western culture. One should not exaggerate the differences between Westerners and Third World women. Other barriers, such as class or gender, may be equally powerful. A sympathetic attitude on the part of the researcher toward the subject being studied is, of course, a precondition for any careful investigation—whether carried out by a Westerner or not, whether in the West or in the Third World.

Donna Haraway has introduced the useful concept, "situated knowledge", to contrast universal knowledge with knowledge that is contextual.

---

[121] It has been stressed that Western feminism has focused on white, middle-class women. Denis Riley, *Am I That Name?*; Maria C. Lugones and Elizabeth Spelman, "Have We Got a Theory for You! Feminist Theory, Cultural Imperialism and the Demand for 'The Woman's Voice'", *Women Studies International Forum*, 6:6 (1983), pp. 573-581.

[122] This has also been highlighted by Maria Baaz-Ericson, "Bortom likhet och särart", *Feministiskt Perspektiv*, No. 4 (1998), pp. 7-11.

[123] Lugones and Spelman, "Have We Got a Theory for You!", pp. 573-581.

According to this perspective, our position with regard to 'how we see things' (depending on our political standpoint, family tradition, and personality) is more important than factors such as from which geographical region we come, our experiences as women, or other essential categories. "Situated knowledge" is not total and universal; it is partial, and specific to a given context. It also highlights power relations between the researcher and the researched.[124]

In 1983, Maria Mies called for a research methodology which sharply contrasted to value-free and neutral research, urging the replacement of indifference by *conscious partiality* (not to be confused with *subjectivity*): the view from above must be replaced by a systematic *view from below*, with the conscious goal of *changing the status quo*[125] —declarations that still have great value. Several feminists (postmodern and others) have subsequently held that so-called value-free objectivity, which they ascribe to a typical male research tradition, obscures subjectivity and power relations under the guise of "science".[126]

However, although the researcher sympathizes with the subjects of the study, hierarchical power relations will never be equalized to the extent that one could create a "sisterhood". Such a sisterhood as Ann Oakley has argued for can hardly exist: the researcher will eventually return to the academy.[127] The researcher's control over perspective, the interpretation of the material, and the power of inclusion or exclusion cannot be overestimated.[128] Personnally, the feeling of being an outsider, a Westerner, a stranger, or even an exploiter, required a lot of effort to overcome. The fact that some people told me my endeavor was impossible, as I had not been born and bred into the Keralite culture, distressed me, but then became a strong motivation for carrying out this study.

After several short visits during the early 1990s, each lasting a month or two, I returned to Kerala in 1997 for longer stays. For the past four years, Kerala has been my second home. I have lived there for almost two years

---

[124] Donna Haraway, "Situated Knowledge: The Science Question in Feminism and the Privilege of Partial Perspective", *Feminist Studies*, 14:3 (1988), pp. 575-597.

[125] Maria Mies, "Towards a Methodology for Feminist Research", in Gloria Bowles and Renate Duelli Klein (eds), *Theories of Women's Studies* (London, 1983), pp. 117-139.

[126] Sandra Harding, *Whose Science? Whose Knowledge? Thinking from Women's Lives* (Buckingham, 1991), pp. 156-161; Donna Haraway, "Situated Knowledge"; Hilary Rose, *Love, Power and Knowledge: Towards a Feminist Transformation of the Sciences* (Cambridge, 1994).

[127] Ann Oakley, "Interviewing Women: A Contradiction in Terms", in H. Roberts (ed.), *Doing Feminist Research* (London, 1981). For an opposite view, see J. Stacey, "Can there be a Feminist Ethnography?", *Women's Studies International Forum*, 11:1 (1991), pp. 21-27.

[128] For discussions of power relations between the researcher and the people studied, see Joan Acker et al. (eds), "Objectivity and Truth. Problems in Doing Feminist Research", *Women's Studies International Forum*, 6:4, pp. 423-435, and Sandra Harding, *Whose Science?*

altogether, initially in 1997, together with my husband and two children. Living a so-called normal life, including visiting the local shops, traveling on buses, going to the market, and having a lot of contact with local people, was a way to slowly learn the context. Being a mother helped to become accepted and was a key to opening up conversations with women workers. The children sometimes would come with me when I visited cashew workers in their homes.[129]

Close collaboration with an indigenous research assistant and friend made me overcome my initial trepidation, and I began to see that, in fact, being an outsider in some ways put me in an advantageous situation, since I could ask questions which would have been impossible for a local person to pose. Nevertheless, both perspectives—Insider and Outsider—have limitations and advantages which need to be taken into account in each situation, an issue anthropologists have long discussed.[130] I came to realize that there were indigenous researchers who, because of their class, caste, or gender, were actually greater outsiders than I. One illustration of the distortions class position can occasion is Jayati Lal. She returned home to India, where she had been born, spent her childhood, and gone to the university. However, in coming back from the West as a researcher to study relations between factory workers and owners, her privileged class position acted as a hindrance.[131] As a foreigner who was not part of the social hierarchy, I found my class position less of a burden than Jayati Lal did. It may well be that, unless we are writing our own autobiography, we are always outsiders because of such factors as the epoch we live in, our class, education, gender, ethnicity, religion, generation, and many other elements. Kirin Narayan has called for discarding the dichotomy outsider/insider, and focusing instead on "the quality of relations with the people we seek to represent in our texts".[132] It seems clear that being born in the West does not necessarily mean you have to think and act as the stereotype of a Westerner.

As a foreigner accompanied by a sensitive interpreter with a great social gift for interacting with the rural poor, I had the opportunity of discussing everything from the most obvious and trivial to the most forbidden issues.

---

[129] For a discussion of the positive impact of bringing children to "the field" when interviewing Third World women, see Diana Mulinari, *Motherwork and Politics in Revolutionary Nicaragua* (Lund, 1995), pp. 49-52.

[130] See, for example, Robert Merton, "Insiders and Outsiders: A Chapter in the Sociology of Knowledge", *American Journal of Sociology*, 78:1 (1972), pp. 9-47.

[131] Jayati Lal, "Situating Locations: The Politics of Self, Identity, and 'Other' in Living and Writing the Text", in Dianne Wolf (ed.), *Feminist Dilemmas in Field Work* (New York, 1996), pp. 185-214.

[132] Kirin Narayan, "How Native Is a 'Native' Anthropologist?", in Louise Lamphere, Helena Ragoné, and Patricia Zavella (eds), *Situated Lives: Gender and Culture in Everyday Life* (New York, 1997), pp. 23-39.

Since I had no power, I was not a threat—neither in the trade unions nor among factory owners; nor was I considered someone in any way involved in their society. I could, therefore, pose the most awkward questions about caste, sexuality, or other sensitive matters—subjects people do not usually discuss. Instead of inquiring, "Is there (or Why is there) a caste division of labor in the factories?", I would ask, "Could you explain to me the caste system, which is totally unknown in the part of the world where I live? What did your parents teach you about it? In what ways has it changed during your lifetime?"

Interviews and the Oral History

My research methodology is close to ethnography, which Shulamith Reinharz has defined as a "multimethod research [that] usually includes observation, participation, archival analysis, and interviewing".[133] This study may, to some extent, be said to be based on participatory observation, as I visited numerous cashew factories, trade union offices, and union meetings, and spent much time in the dwellings of cashew workers, where I was received as a familiar person. However, the observation and participation was rather to "learn the context and culture" than to actually analyze what I registered. Although my concern extended to the present, it was more with the past, which is why I mainly consider my field methodology to be oral history.

British social historians have been developing the methodology of oral history since the 1960s. To interview and thereby give voice to people who usually do not leave written sources behind is a democratic alternative which challenges the monopoly of an academic elite in producing history.[134] Oral history in this context is often used to provide eye-witnesses to the past and is subject to such traditional criticism of sources as distance in time, motives for obscuring facts or forgetting, and the influence of others, among other reasons for not telling 'truths'.

Feminist researchers have often interviewed women as part of the feminist research methodology described above, asserting that discourses on the 'objectivity' of traditional research methodologies and science obscure both racism and sexism when producing 'facts'.[135]

---

[133] Shulamit Reinharz, *Feminist Methods in Social Research* (Oxford, 1992), p. 46.
[134] Paul Thompson, *The Voice of the Past* (Oxford, 1978), *passim*. For an anthology including more recent debates, see Perks and Alistair (eds), *The Oral History Reader*.
[135] S. Geiger, "What's So Feminist about Women's Oral History?", *Journal of Women's History*, 2:1 (1990), pp. 169-170; Sara Goodman and Diana Mulinari (eds), *Feminist Interventions in Discourses on Gender and Development* (Lund, 1999), p. 10.

Joan Sangster points out that the utility of hegemonic ideologies in analyzing narratives was already elaborated in the 1970s by oral historians whose concerns were very similar to later postmodernists.[136] Recently, the postmodern use of oral history has tried to explore the *form* of narratives in order to analyze how identities are constructed. Margaret Somers identifies four kinds of narratives which are decisive for the constitution of identities: ontological narratives are the personal stories of individuals; public narratives are the official stories of institutions, such as the church, trade unions, the government, the family, or the workplace; analytical narratives are explanations given by academics; and meta-narratives are the master narratives in which we all are embedded and from which our theories and concepts stem (e.g., Enlightenment, Industrialization, Liberalism, Nationalism).[137] In the case of Kerala, an obvious meta-narrative would be "from a traditional society to modernization". Among official narratives, the trade unions and various governments behind the successful "Kerala Model" are obvious public stories.

Discussing the relation between "the discourses of the West and the possibility of speaking of (or for) the subaltern women", Gayatra Spivak has asserted that cultural discourses determine oral narratives. She answers her provocative question "Can the Subaltern Speak?" in the negative: "Subaltern women will be as mute as ever".[138] Spivak grounds her reply on a belief that the researcher can never step outside of cultural, political, and economic conditions, all of which limit the kind of questions that can be posed. According to her, nobody will be able to represent subalterns in an adequate way. This also implies that others cannot be represented either, leading to a conclusion that we are not able to produce any meaningful history.

Another debate circles around whether narratives are best presented in their original form, or if the researcher with greater theoretical tools should have the right (or obligation) to interpret the stories.[139] The risk of imposing our own interpretation on an interviewee's narrative was illustrated by Kathrin Borland, who advocates a dialectical relationship with mutual learning between the interviewer and the interviewee.[140]

Arguing for less sophisticated interpretation on the part of the researcher and more stress on the interviewees' own interpretation of their past

---

[136] R. Grele, *Envelopes of Sound* (Chicago, 1975), quoted in Sangster, "Telling Our Stories", pp. 89-90.

[137] Margaret Somers, "Deconstructing and Reconstructing Class Formation Theory: Narrativity, Relational Analysis, and Social Theory", in John R. Hall (ed.), *Reworking Class* (New York, 1997), pp. 73-105.

[138] Gayatri Chakravorty Spivak, "Can the Subaltern Speak?", in Patrick Williams and Laura Chrisman (eds), *Colonial Discourse and Post-Colonial Theory* (New York, 1993), p. 90.

[139] For a discussion of this debate, see Reinharz, *Feminist Methods*, pp. 134-140.

[140] Katherine Borland, "That's Not What I Said: Interpretive Conflict in Oral Narrative Research", in Perks and Thomson, *The Oral History Reader*, pp. 320-332.

must not be confused with an uncritical attitude, but rather expresses trust in the subject's intellect. This is of decisive importance when analyzing identities. Ultimately, however, as Shulamith Reinharz has stressed, the researcher chooses what will be published, giving her the preferential right of interpretation.[141] These may be unavoidable problems, but awareness of them may improve the quality of our interviews.

Diana Mulinari and Kerstin Sandell have argued that postmodern theory has legitimized a shift in the focus of research from political subjects with collective experiences to the analysis of individuals and their subjective identities. As a consequence, two central weapons of oppressed groups—collective memories and oral testimonies—are withheld from sociological analyses because they do not provide true versions of lived experiences. Mulinari and Sandell plead for a re-appraisal of the concept of experience, while cautioning that this means going back to "homogenizing" women. They suggest "disentangling experience from conflation with identity and political commitment, while still seeing their interconnections".[142] A similar stand is taken by Sangster, who proposes that interviews for the purpose of oral history may be interpreted at many levels. We may study the subjectivity and the form of narratives, but then must tie that back to the level of collective experience which allows women to "name their own lives", thus giving oral narratives a firm grounding in their material and social contexts.[143] Such a methodology has guided this analysis.

Interviewing Procedures

Before scheduling interviews in the homes of factory workers, I visited several cashew factories to get an idea of the present situation with regard to such issues as work processes, labor composition, and working conditions.[144] I gained admittance to cashew factories by permission of the Kerala Government. My interpreter and I joined the labor commissioner on his inspection tours, and we also visited state-owned factories without the labor commissioner.[145] We visited some private factories, too, again without the labor commissioner. During these tours I had the opportunity to interview workers, staff, and management. I also met with trade union

---

[141] Reinharz, *Feminist Methods*, p. 137

[142] Mulinari and Sandell, "Exploring the Notion of Experience", pp. 291-292, 296.

[143] Sangster, "Telling Our Stories", pp. 94-97.

[144] The factories are listed in the Appendix.

[145] I am deeply grateful to Mr. Sam Nathaniel, Quilon Labour Commissioner, who spent a great deal of his own time guiding me, and who also arranged for me to revisit some of the factories.

leaders and representatives of the Kerala Government. These initial and rather short and unstructured pilot interviews, combined with various historical sources, gave me some idea of the issues to focus upon. Interviews with workers and certain trade union leaders were accomplished with the help of an interpreter (see below), whereas most of the other interviews were conducted in English.

Using a structured questionnaire along with a few unstructured questions, a quantitative survey was administrated to every tenth worker in each section of a large, private factory. In those departments with very few workers, everyone could be interviewed. Almost 100 workers were questioned in all. This resulted in a fairly clear picture of the present situation with regard to wages, the caste and gender division of labor, education, family situation, economic and social conditions, as well as historical facts about the living and working conditions of the parents or grandparents of the cashew workers.

Forty-five in-depth interviews among different generations of cashew workers (belonging to the four predominant castes mentioned in Chapter I) were conducted in their homes.[146] Each family was visited at least twice, and in most cases three to six times (or more). This proved to be a fruitful approach, since new memories and insights were constantly emerging. Frequent visits obviously also led to mutual trust and understanding. I prepared for these interviews by having a semi-structured questionnaire, but the interviews always began with a free conversation, since that resulted in the most spontaneous stories and allowed the interviewees to direct the course of the conversation. The questionnaire, as it turned out, served more as a list of checkpoints.

The interviews were used in three different ways: a) As *eye-witness* depictions of different events, which were corroborated in printed sources or by the testimony of several interviewees; b) In a more *quantitative* way to determine empirical patterns; and c) As *life-stories* with the interviewees' interpretations of historical developments, their own roles, and the roles of others.

The first two kinds of interviews represented a more traditional way of oral history in stressing the content of the stories and not their form. These interviews were linked to an analysis of the material sphere, particularly social conditions. In the life-story interviews, more stress was laid on individual identity-creating processes. Life history can be seen as a dialectical process in which oral accounts provide the impetus to explore other sources, and vice versa. Institutional and social changes were also reflected in the life stories of the cashew workers.

---

[146] The different castes are the Pulayas, Kuravas, Ezhavas, and the Nairs. See the Appendix for a list of interviewees.

The advantages of having living sources are obvious. We could return to the interviewees and correct our transcriptions when we suspected misunderstandings. We could ask the same question, but put it another way, and we could come back and pose new questions. Most interviews lasted from two to three hours, a time frame which we found optimal. Most of the women were busy with household chores and children, and two hours (or occasionally three) seemed to be the maximum amount of time they could spare and still concentrate. A second, third, or fourth interview often proved more informative than the first one. Establishing friendship with the workers promoted an open atmosphere: most often our meetings were like informal conversations interrupted by domestic work, nursing of babies, and visits from neighbors. Rather than disrupt the interviews, these events reinforced the friendship and trust which had built up. With a few exceptions, all interviews were taped, translated, and transcribed.[147] Some workers expressed fear that their opinions would come to the attention of factory owners or union leaders, so we agreed to keep the identity of all workers anonymous and use pseudonyms.

Interpreters in the Field

The problems of working through an interpreter have been discussed by several scholars.[148] Within the confines of a single tongue, ideas are already distorted by being more-or-less inexactly put into words by the speaker, then received as similar but unidentical thoughts conditioned by the ambiguities of language and colored by the subjectivity of the listener.[149] When a second language and a third person intervene between two interlocutors, the potential for distortion can be magnified exponentially. Absent native fluency in the local language on the part of the researcher, this is a problem which cannot be circumvented, although it may be mitigated by finding and establishing a good relationship with the appropriate interpreter.

To locate a person both well-suited to the job and a good fit with the

---

[147] The reason for sometimes not taping a session was that the interviewee asked me not to record the conversation. This, however, only happened when managers or trade union leaders were to be interviewed.

[148] For other Westerners who have enlisted the aide of interpreters to carry out in-depth interviews in India and South Africa, respectively, see Clare L. Tanner, "Class, Caste and Gender in Collective Action: Agricultural Labour Unions in Two Indian Villages", *The Journal of Peasant Studies*, 22:4 (1995), pp. 672-698, and Belinda Bozzoli, *Women of Phokeng: Consciousness, Life Strategy and Migrancy in South Africa 1900-1983* (London, 1991).

[149] For a discussion on translation, see Gayatri Chakravorty Spivak, "The Politics of Translation", in Barrett and Phillips (eds), *Destabilizing Theory*, pp. 177-200.

interviewer may take considerable trial and error. The ideal interpreter must be accurate, unbiased (either by their own or another's class, caste, or gender), hardy, and freely available to the interviewer. Above all they should be interested in the work at hand and temperamentally suited to facilitate exchanges between interviewer and interviewee.

It was my great good fortune to have found such a person in Renu, an Indian Christian woman of about thirty, after having given up on four previous interpreters for such deficiencies as are alluded to above. Whomever we interviewed, they were always eager to share their life stories and opinions with Renu, and thereby also with me. Renu and I became close friends, learned to know each other's personalities very well, and shared many important ideological positions. The fact that Renu is a Christian, although these groups are ranked in the social hierarchy as well, mitigated such biases as might occur when Hindu women of low caste meet with high caste women. Renu and I worked together for four years, cooperating in trust and friendship. In this case, I would argue, the relationship between a white woman from the West and a "Third World woman" was based on equality and deep friendship. For long periods we spent both days and nights together, as we lived in the same house. In the evenings we transcribed and translated the interviews and discussed the individual words, expressions, and body language we had experienced from the workers during the day. Renu not only taught me some Malayalam, but also certain Keralite cultural codes which would have been impossible for someone to learn without an indigenous teacher.

Summary of Main Theoretical Concepts and Methodologies

I have tried to position my study by a discourse on Marxist, Subaltern, postmodern, and feminist scholars. Most of all, I have made explicit my views on certain important concepts such as discourse, ideology, consciousness, and identity.

The experiences which have shaped the lives of women in the cashew factories—matters such as working conditions, wages, social struggles in trade unions, and marriage—will be the principal focus, as they have contributed to the shaping of people's identities.

However, identities are also influenced by *ideologies* and *discourses*. A central tenet in this study is that ideologies and discourses are viewed as correlated with one another, instead of belonging to antagonistic theoretical positions. They both operate at the level of creating meaning for people, although ideologies are more conscious, explicit, and normative, whereas discourses often are less value-impregnated (at least explicitly) and may have the appearance of being 'true'. Discourses and ideologies may also be conflicting or even contradictory.

The view taken here is that it is useful to separate the concepts of identity and consciousness. Consciousness is herein defined as "awareness" (as, for example, the awareness of oppressive structures based on class, caste, or gender); identity, on the other hand is the sense of belonging to a particular social group, and therefore more complex, dynamic, fragmented, and ambiguous. Consequently we may speak of identities existing on three levels: passive, active, and politicized (with the latter further subdivided into central and peripheral).

In analyzing the situation of women in India, two additional concepts were especially useful: *housewifization* and *Sanskritization*. The first is mainly related to gender, the second to caste, but they are interrelated to a considerable extent, and both involve a class aspect. *Housewifization* is the process of women being represented as housewives, whereas *Sanskritization* is the emulation of the culture of higher castes in order to raise one's social status.

The theoretical point of departure here has been an interdisciplinary approach, which requires drawing upon a multiplicity of sources to analyze social and cultural phenomena. Many different printed and written source materials, such as archival documents, newspapers, historical accounts, and official reports, as well as in-depth personal interviews, have been incorporated. From a theoretical perspective, oral narratives are taken into consideration both as testimonies of collective memories and at the level of subjective identities. Without denying the difficulties and extreme inequality of power relations when a researcher from the West meets subaltern women in the Third World, being an outsider may include some positive aspects when interviewing. The researcher's position and the quality of the relationship should be stressed, rather than essential differences with regard to ethnicity or other matters.

III   A History of the Cashew Factories

A great foreigner came one day;
He stood silent for some time.
Nuts are hit.
Kernels are sent to the next section.
(They just find fault, find fault.)

Here we have spices and ginger,
ganja[1] , camphor, palode payasam[2] ,
betel and sugar cane.
Whatever you want is here.
(It's a crime, a big crime.)

If necessary, lies are there.
Cashew kernels disappear in a horse cart,
The cash is gone,
Only empty boxes remain—
Boxes which can store gold and silver,
(Big enough for a child to sleep in.)

—Song sung by the cashew nut workers in the 1930s in Quilon [3]

The Dawn of the Cashew Factories in South India

The Portuguese introduced the cashew tree into southern India in the seventeenth century because they hoped its extensive root system would help prevent soil erosion. Cashew cultivation was taken up on a small scale in family gardens, but the trees soon flourished quite extensively in the wild. The latter were the source of the emerging cashew industry in the 1920s and 1930s.[4] Raw nuts were also imported from Africa, since the domestic

---

[1] Word for Indian marijuana.
[2] Sweet dessert.
[3] Interview 11 March 1997 with Chirutha, woman of Kurava caste, born 1919.
[4] Pillai, *Travancore State Manual*, Vol. III, p. 361; Govt. of India, *Report on the Marketing of Cashew Nuts in India*, Agricultural Marketing in India, Marketing Series No. 47 (Calcutta, 1944), p. 1; John Thomas Chirayath, *A Study on the Cashew Industry in Kerala*, Labour and Industrial Bureau, Government of Kerala (Trivandrum, 1965), p. 1.

crop in southern India was often never enough to meet the growing demand of the region's processing factories.[5] It was not until the 1940s that the tree was systematically cultivated on a commercial scale.[6]

Before the cashew kernel became an export product, locals had gathered raw cashew nuts and roasted them in open pans. This caused the outer shell to become brittle, making it easier to remove the kernel. Cashew nuts were often sold at local markets.[7] They were considered a health food because of their vitamin content and high nutritional value, and were fed to people who were weak or ill.[8] But by 1940, the price of cashew kernels had risen so high that growers and villagers could hardly afford to eat cashew nuts themselves, although they had been doing so for a long time.[9] Now about 75% of all processed kernels were destined for export, consumption being confined to the wealthy classes in urban areas.[10]

One of the pioneers in the exportation of cashew kernels was the British firm of Peirce Leslie & Co., considered one of the most important companies in transforming Travancore into a capitalist economy.[11] The company, which was founded in 1862, originally dealt in the export of colonial merchandise for the European and American markets, including coffee, tea, rubber, spices, and coir fibers. They were attracted to the possibilities of exporting the cashew nut sometime around 1920. Cashews were destined to become one of the company's most profitable business ventures in the years that followed.[12]

Other foreign companies were also attracted to the marketing potential of cashew kernels. Shortly after World War I, the American corporate giant, General Foods, instructed their agents in India to be on the lookout for new export commodities. General Foods, too, became instrumental in the development of the cashew industry in India. In cooperation with a local firm in the city of Mangalore (in Madras Presidency of British India, just north of Travancore), General Foods set up one of the earliest cashew facto-

---

[5] Govt. of India, *Report on the Marketing of Cashew Nuts in India*, p. 4.

[6] Ibid., p. 1; Pillai, *Travancore State Manual*, Vol. III, p. 361. The systematic cultivation has, however, been limited. In 1969, it was asserted that "only in recent times systematic cultivation of cashew on plantation scale has been undertaken". Govt. of Kerala, *Cashew Industry in Kerala*, State Planning Board (Trivandrum, 1969), p. 2.

[7] W.K.M. Langley, *Century in Malabar, The History of Peirce Leslie & Co., Ltd. 1862-1962* (Madras, 1962), pp. 55 ff.

[8] Chirayath, *A Study on the Cashew Industry*, p. 5.

[9] Govt. of India, *Report on the Marketing of Cashew Nuts in India*, p. 3.

[10] Ibid., pp. 7-9.

[11] Raman Mahadevan, "Industrial Entrepreneurship in Princely Travancore: 1930-47", in Bhattacharya (ed.), *The South Indian Economy: Agrarian Change, Industrial Structure, and State Policy c. 1914-1947* (New Delhi, 1991), p. 165; Isaac, *Class Struggle and Industrial Structure*, p. 27.

[12] Langley, *Century in Malabar*, pp. 55 ff.

ries. The combined venture was successful since General Foods knew the American consumer market, and also had well-established commercial relationships with other countries in the West. General Foods soon became actively involved in the development of more efficient methods of producing and packaging cashew nuts, which made possible the exportation of cashews on a large scale.[13]

During the mid-1920s, the interest of General Foods was directed to the area of Quilon,[14] and in 1927 the first cashew kernels from this city reached the U.S. market.[15] In subsequent years, cashew nut processing in the Quilon region expanded tremendously, whereas it stagnated in the region around Mangalore, after several factory owners left British India in order to relocate across the border in Travancore.[16] One of these was Swaminathan, who cooperated with an American, W.T. Anderson (probably the man alluded to in the song which prefaced this chapter), to establish a new firm known as the Indian Nut Company.[17] For a short period of time, the cashew trade in Quilon and elsewhere in southern India was entirely in the hands of foreign companies or foreign agents who registered with the government as cashew traders, but never became factory owners.[18] Large European companies which had previously been involved in other business ventures now emerged as exporters of cashew kernels.[19]

During the first few decades of the twentieth century, cashews were exported almost exclusively to the U.S. In 1925 alone, fifty tons arrived from India. This figure increased to 3,000 tons five years later, and by 1941

---

[13] Ibid.; J.G. Ohler, *Cashew*, Department of Agricultural Research (Amsterdam, 1979), pp. 16-17.

[14] Langley, *Century in Malabar*, p. 58.

[15] Govt. of Travancore, *Statistics of Travancore*, 8th issue 1102 ME/1926-27 AD (Trivandrum, 1928), p. 243.

[16] Mahadevan, "Industrial Entrepreneurship", p. 181. The owners of Urban Stanislaus Cashew Factory, Hindustan Cashew Factory, Ganesh Naik Cashew Factory, and Swaminathan Cashew Factory have been mentioned by local inhabitants as such persons. A foreigner named Periera was also mentioned as a pioneer in cashew trading in the 1920s. Interview 19 December 1997 with K. Bhanu, male journalist, born 1913. Interview 10 December 1997 with K. Bhaskaran, tinfiller, born 1924; See also Govt. of Travancore-Cochin, *Report of the Minimum Wages Committee for Cashew Industry 1953* (Trivandrum, 1953), p. 41; K.C. Govindan, *Memoires of an Early Trade Unionist* (Trivandrum, 1986), pp. 58-59.

[17] K.T. Rammohan, "Material Processes and Developmentalism: Interpreting Economic Change in Colonial Tiruvitamkur, 1800 to 1945" (Ph.D., Centre for Development Studies, Trivandrum 1996), p. 153.

[18] Rammohan, "Material Processes and Developmentalism", p. 153. John Michael Casey from the USA arrived in 1936 and was registered as a cashew trader. His address coincided with that of some other American men in Quilon. (KSA, General files 1936, 8813/855). There are indications that he later on became the manager of Indian Nut Company (See Govindan, *Memoires*, p. 71).

[19] Rammohan, "Material Processes and Developmentalism", p. 153.

it had risen to 18,000 tons.[20] Ninety-five percent of cashew exports in 1940 were bound for the U.S., 4% for Canada, and 1% for England.[21] In those early years, General Foods was the sole distributor of cashews in the United States, enjoying a monopoly which allowed them to set prices and control the market. Cashew processing was also quite profitable for native factory owners in India, and the lucrative gains they realized were talked about as the 'road to riches' in the 1930s and 1940s.[22]

Cashew nuts were Travancore's second largest food export commodity in 1938, representing 15% of that country's total exports.[23] Because of the importance of cashew kernels as a source of generating foreign currency, the government of Travancore supported cashew traders with loans and such other benefits as reduced shipping tariffs.[24] In 1940, a government review of the previous year concluded that "Travancore maintained its dominant position as the exporter of larger quantities of cashew nut than any other part of India".[25] This suggests that cashew nut processing for export was well underway in the 1930s, after foreign companies such as General Foods had given impetus to the field.[26]

The cashew trade continued to flourish during the depression of the 1930s and huge profits were realized. The demand for cashews to satisfy the U.S. market seemed limitless. During the period from 1926 to 1936, cashew exports increased more than four-fold, with prices rising a startling 2,500%![27] Since cashews were one of the few products that could be exported profitably during the depression, many companies that had depended on trading in coir fiber and other cash crops were saved by the cashew nut.[28]

Thousands of men and women walked to work in the cashew factories

[20] Govt. of India, *Report on the Marketing of Cashew Nuts in India*, p. 1.
[21] Pillai, *Travancore State Manual*, Vol. II, p. 631.
[22] Interview 26 October 1997 with K. Gopinathan Nair, owner of several cashew factories in Quilon.
[23] Govt. of Travancore, *Statistics of Travancore*, 19th issue 1113 ME/ 1937-1938 AD (Trivandrum, 1939), p. 290.
[24] KSA, Dev. Files No. 113/1494 1930, Letter from Economic Development Board, Trivandrum to Chief Secretary to Government, Trivandrum, dated 28 June 1930; KSA, Dev. files No. 352/166 1946, Letter from SICMA to Government of India, Commerce Dept, dated 23 sept 1944.
[25] Govt. of Travancore, *Travancore Administration Report 1115 ME/1939-40 AD* (Trivandrum, 1941), p. 18.
[26] Others have located the growth to the 1940s. See, Rammohan, "Material Processes and Developmentalism", pp. 153 ff, and Mahadevan, "Industrial Entrepreneurship", p. 162. This may be an error due to reliance only upon sources in *Large Industrial Establishments*, Government of India 1937-1949. They show a misleading increase in the 1940s, since most cashew factories were not registered in the 1930s.
[27] Rammohan, "Material Processes and Developmentalism", pp. 148-149.
[28] Govt. of India, *Census of India 1931*, Vol. XXVIII, Travancore, Part I, Report, pp. 249 ff.

each day. Although statistics in the cashew industry have been criticized as unreliable, they may give some indication of growth. In 1933, government records indicate that there were two factories (although the informants I spoke with claimed there were many more than two at the time) employing a total of 3,990 workers. By 1938, this figure had risen to 40 factories employing 22,121 workers. Ten years later, there were 117 factories and 35,247 workers.[29] As these factories were labor intensive and did not require an extensive outlay of capital, it was possible for native men without access to large amounts of money to establish cashew factories and advance in the social hierarchy. Many indigenous men began to buy raw nuts on a small scale and then send them out for processing on consignment. They then sold the shelled nuts to factories for further processing and packing. Later they were able to centralize the processing operations and open their own factories.[30]

The various cashew factory owners were quite heterogeneous with regard to caste and religious community: there were Muslims, Syrian Christians, Ezhavas, and Nairs among the owners in Quilon.[31] The only individuals not encountered among the ranks of the cashew factory owners were members of the extreme poles of the social hierarchy: Brahmins and Scheduled Castes.

In contrast to many other export trades, the cashew industry came increasingly under the control of native entrepreneurs,[32] with a few families dominating the field. In the 1940s, such families employed more than 50% percent of the total workforce in the Travancore plants, and the pattern has since continued.[33] The political and economic power of these fam-

---

[29] Govt. of Travancore, *Statistics of Travancore*, 14th issue 1108 ME /1932-1933 AD (Trivandrum, 1934), pp. 134-135; Govt. of Travancore, *Statistics of Travancore*, 19th issue 1113 ME/1937-1938 AD, pp. 160-169; Govt. of India, *Large Industrial Establishments in India 1947* (Simla, 1951), pp. 99-100.

[30] One such entrepreneur, Thangal Kunju Musaliar, owned eight cashew factories by 1940. Over the next ten years, the number of his factories rose to 26, and he employed more than 15,000 workers. Musaliar also accumulated holdings in the brick, timber, and metal industries. To this day, he is referred to as "the Cashew King" in and around Quilon, and the name Musaliar can be found on everything from computer companies to colleges and charitable institutions. Although in a patriarchal way, he was revered as a benefactor of laborers, distributing rice and even land to them. See Yoonus Kayamkulam, *Thangal Kunju Musaliar Biography* (Quilon, 1997) (in Malayalam), Chapter 3, pp. 23 ff; Govindan, *Memoires*, p. 59; KSA, Development Files 1955, File No. 25/157; Interview 14 November 1997 with Sreedharan Pillai, clerk, cashew factory, born 1922; Interview 14 September 1999 with K. Chellappan, trade union leader, born 1914; Interview 13 March 1997 with Ravindran Nathan Nair, factory owner, VLC, Cashew factories, son of Krishna Pillai, who started a factory in 1932.

[31] Rammohan, "Material Processes and Developmentalism", p. 155.

[32] Ibid., p. 153.

[33] Mahadevan, "Industrial Entrepreneurship", pp. 182 ff; The same statement was made in 1953. See Govt. of Travancore-Cochin, *Report of the Minimum Wages Committee for Cashew Industry 1953* (Trivandrum, 1953), p. 9.

ilies is well-known in Kerala. Two concerns, V.L.C. and K.P.P., are the largest processors of cashew kernels in the world, each having more than 20,000 employees. Both are owned by descendants of the pioneers of the 1920s.[34] Their owners are also engaged in other enterprises, such as hotels, shipping, and entertainment, and are reputedly powerful political lobbyists. Some are known for their charitable and philanthropic activities.[35] Such cashew industrialists as these are reported to be extremely wealthy and continue to be referred to by the locals in Quilon as "cashew-kings", "cashew-magnates," and "cashew-barons".[36]

Concentration of Cashew Factories in Quilon

Due to the growth of its cashew factories in the 1930s, the city of Quilon in Travancore became the center of the cashew industry. By the early 1950s, more than 75% of India's cashew workers were situated there.[37] A decade later, the concentration had increased even more, and Quilon still is the cashew processing center *par excellence* of India. This has given the city and its environs a unique character. The smell of roasting cashew shells is present everywhere. One grows accustomed to the sight of thousands of workers shuffling off to the factories in the morning and winding their way back each evening. Things in Quilon have been this way for many years. On the other hand, unemployment, lock-outs, and strikes, have a profound effect on the entire area. When cashew workers in Quilon are deprived of income, their impoverishment spreads to others—the fish-vendors, tea shop owners, and provisions merchants. It has been stated that the entire city of Quilon becomes depressed—even paralyzed—during such periods.[38]

The pronounced concentration of cashew factories in Quilon has gen-

---

[34] Interview 13 March 1997 with Ravindran Nathan Nair, owner of several cashew factories and son of the founder of Danalaxsmi Cashew factory in 1932, Krishna Pillai; Interview 14 March 1997 with K.P. Ramachandran Nair, general manager, Lakshman & Co, Kilikilloor.

[35] SICMA Office, Quilon, *SICMA Souvenir 1967* (Quilon, 1968).

[36] By examining industrial statistics, K.P. Kannan has also concluded that the cashew sector is characterized by very high profits. See Kannan, *Employment, Wages and Conditions of Work*, pp. 1-2. Kannan has used data from official statistics published in the *Annual Survey of Industries*, Govt. of India (ASI). We must be aware that it is not possible to arrive at an absolutely correct figure of the profit, as the reliability of the accounts given to ASI is limited. The cashew factories have also been known for having imperfect bookkeeping and it is likely that the profitability far exceeds the data given to the authorities.

[37] Govt. of India, *Report on an Enquiry into Conditions of Labour in the Cashewnut Processing Industry in India*, Labour Bureau (Simla, 1954), p. 8.

[38] See, for example, *Jennajugham*, 18 July 1967, p. 4.

erally been accredited to the area's infrastructure and easy access to cheap labor.[39] Proximity to the supply of raw nuts has been cited as another reason, as well as the enterprising spirit of the pioneers.[40] But are these interpretations valid? Do they, in fact, suffice to account for Quilon—and more generally the Princely State of Travancore—becoming the cashew center of all India?

Access to raw cashew nuts can hardly have been the main reason for the growth of processing factories in Travancore. During the 1920s, there was no large-scale systematic cultivation of cashew trees in Travancore. Not until the trade in cashews became established did such agricultural endeavors begin. In 1940, the author of the Travancore State Manual cited only a few *taluks* where the cultivation of cashew nuts had begun. Quilon was not one of them: only a single *taluk* in its vicinity, Kottarakara, along the railroad line about 50 kilometers from Quilon, was mentioned.[41] In 1942, it was estimated that more than 50% of the cashew nuts grown in India were harvested in Madras Presidency, and only about 20% in Travancore.[42] However, Travancore *processed* more than 75% of India's export of cashew kernels.[43] Obviously raw nuts were being brought into the factories from places outside the Princely State of Travancore.[44] Why, then, did W.T. Anderson and others like him come to Travancore to establish their processing plants, when the main areas where cashew grew were elsewhere?

To explain the growth of cashew factories in Travancore, and particularly the immigration of entrepreneurs from British India into Travancore, we have to consider the situation of workers in the cashew factories and the labor laws affecting them. It should be realized that the phenomenon of factories relocating to areas outside British India was not unique to Travancore. Raman Mahadevan points out that other autonomous Princely States saw factories moving in from British India. He suggests that lower costs of

---

[39] Pillai, "The Economic Impact", p. 30; Oommen, *Inter State Shifting*, pp. 67 ff.; Chirayath, *A Study on the Cashew Industry in Kerala*, p. 17; K.P. Kannan, "Evolution of Unionisation and Changes in Labour Processes under Lower Forms of Capitalist Production", in Das et al. (ed.), *Worker and the Working Class*, p. 46; Michael Tharakan and Thomas Isaac, "Historical roots of industrial backwardness of Kerala" (Working Paper No. 215, Centre for Development Studies, Trivandrum, 1986), p. 14.

[40] Pillai, "The Economic Impact", p. 30; Oommen, *Inter State Shifting*, p. 67; Chirayath, *A Study on the Cashew Industry in Kerala*, p. 17.

[41] Pillai, *Travancore State Manual*, Vol. III, p. 361.

[42] Govt. of India, *Report on the Marketing of Cashew Nuts in India*, p. 2.

[43] Ibid., p. 3.

[44] It was estimated that in 1945 only about one-third of the production of kernels in Travancore was of locally grown nuts. Twenty-five percent of the raw nuts were imported to Travancore from South Canara and Malabar and the rest from East Africa. KSA, Development department, Vol. I, part A, 1947, series 48, file No. 50, "A Note on the Cashewnut Industry in Travancore", p. 13.

production (a consequence of depressed wages), different tax policies, and more liberal labor legislation were decisive in this process.[45]

Factory owners in British India are on record as complaining that unless the regulations under which they were required to operate were made similar to those in the principalities, they would have difficulty competing with those operations.[46] They were specifically referring to the absence of protective legislation for factory workers in other jurisdictions—the non-existence of child labor laws, for example, which had been in effect in British India since 1881. In fact, it has been argued that the Factory Act of 1881, which regulated child labor and working hours for the first time, was primarily implemented in India after pressure from British textile interests who decried the absence of labor laws as unfair competition.[47]

In the specific case of the cashew factories, where women constituted the majority of the labor force, the absence of a law providing maternity benefits was of great financial significance to the owners and the workers. In addition, the cashew manufacturers considered cashew processing quite suitable for children, and so they made strenuous efforts to prevent the introduction of laws against child labor.[48]

The first national investigation of the cashew industry was ordered by the Indian Government in 1952 at the request of the Cashewnut Workers' Union in Mangalore.[49] Twenty-five cashew factories in four different areas were visited by investigators for the purpose of comparing their production methods, wages, and working conditions. The areas investigated were Travancore, South Canara, Bombay, and Madras. The latter two had only a small number of factories, all of which employed relatively few workers, but South Canara, in what was formerly British India, was a major industrial center.

Employers in South Canara had a policy of paying half-wages for cashew kernels broken during processing. In Travancore there was no compensation for broken nuts. Piece rates were also different for African and Indian raw cashew nuts in South Canara. Workers there were paid more per piece for the imported cashew nuts because African nuts were smaller and took a considerably longer amount of time to process. In Travancore, the same rate was paid for either kind of nut.[50]

---

[45] Mahadevan, "Industrial Entrepreneurship", pp. 189 ff.

[46] G. Ramanujam, *Indian Labour Movement* (New Delhi, 1990), p. 71.

[47] Mark Holmström, *Industry and Inequality: The Social Anthropology of Indian Labour* (Cambridge, 1984), p. 50.

[48] KSA, Development Files, No. 341/2093, Feb 1945, "Exemption of the Cashew Factories from the Operation of Factory Act".

[49] Govt. of India, *Report on an Enquiry into the Conditions of Labour in the Cashewnut Processing Industry in India*, p. 2.

[50] Ibid., p. 26.

Factory workers in South Canara labored under substantially better working conditions than their colleagues in Travancore, even receiving bonuses. Investigators reported from South Canara that laws governing the treatment of employees seemed to be honored in the factories there. Among other fringe benefits, workers in South Canara received one day of vacation per twenty days of work, as stipulated in the factory labor laws. Those workers who requested maternity compensation had received it—something hardly the case in Travancore.[51]

Wages were between 15% and 50% higher in the cashew factories of South Canara. Child labor was more prevalent in Travancore, where more than 13% of the total workforce consisted of children. The corresponding figure for South Canara was only a few percent.[52]

Although the investigation of 1952 does not give us any information regarding conditions ten or twenty years earlier, it is reasonable to believe that the great disparities uncovered in 1952 had also existed in the 1940s—and quite probably as far back as the 1930s. In 1945, the Travancore labor leader, M.N. Govindan Nair, declared that, in contrast to those in Travancore, cashew workers in British India were "not denied the benefits of any of the labor legislation there".[53] Although Govindan Nair may have had an interest in exaggerating the differences between the two regions, A.D. Bolland, the manager of the Travancore factory of Peirce Leslie & Co., was also of the opinion that workers in British India had been paid better and worked under stricter and better enforced labor legislation than in Travancore.[54]

For women to work in Travancore's factories during the 1920s was uncommon. Only between 9% and 14% of all factory workers in Travancore during that period were women. Even the percentage of children employed in the factories was larger—between 13% and 18%.[55] British India was similar to Travancore with regard to the employment of female factory workers. The proportion fluctuated from 11% to 16% between 1920 and 1930. Travancore did, however, have the dubious distinction of employing greater numbers of children in its factories than was the case across the border in British India. According to official sources, the extent of child labor in registered factories in British India was about 5% in the 1920s but

[51] Ibid., pp. 33.
[52] Ibid., p. 13.
[53] KSA, Development Files 1946, file No. 507, Letter from M.N. Govindan Nair to the dewan of Travancore, 1946.
[54] Interview 12 June 1998 with A.D. Bolland, former managing director, Peirce Leslie & Co.
[55] Govt. of Travancore, *Travancore Administration Report 1926-27*, p. 120; *1927-28*, p. 133; *1928-29*, p. 148; *1929-30*, p. 149.

had dropped to 1% during the 1930s.[56] In contrast, the census of 1931 shows that *nearly one-third* of the labor force in the organized industrial sector of Travancore consisted of children! By that time, 24% of all factory workers were women, and the remaining 45% adult men.[57] The increase in female factory workers was due to the establishment of cashew factories. In 1937, the proportion of female factory workers had grown to about 48%.[58] Although the majority of the children traditionally worked on plantations, in places with a large child labor force, their presence in the *cashew factories* was specifically mentioned in the census.[59] Prior to 1946, employers in Travancore could hire children of any age for work in their cashew factories and not break any laws. The fact that the cashew industry expanded in Travancore and other Princely States, while stagnating in British India, may be due to the undeveloped state of labor legislation outside of British India—especially with regard to the employment of children.

Why, then, did Quilon become the city where all the early factories were situated, despite its principal rival, Alleppey (70 kilometers distant), having a well-developed infrastructure, the beginnings of industrial activity, and more factory workers in the mid-1920s? For all their workers, a labor shortage did arise in Alleppey, because of traditional migrations for seasonal employment, leaving Quilon (with the greater availability of its lower-caste population) a more attractive site. In Alleppey, Thomas Isaac found this shortage due to lower caste workers leaving for jobs in the nearby rice cultivation region of Kuttanad.[60] Although there was somewhat of a shortage of cheap, low-caste labor in Quilon, it was less pronounced than in Alleppey. Other districts, such as South Canara in British India, had an ample supply of workers, which we can understand from their seasonal migration to coffee and cardamom plantations.[61]

It is significant for its commercial development that Travancore's financial system (including its banking system) had been modernized after

[56] Govt. of India, *Indian Labour Investigation Committee, Main Report 1946*, p. 13.
[57] Govt. of India, *Census of India 1931*, Vol. XXVIII, Travancore, Part I, Report, p. 254.
[58] Govt. of Travancore, *Travancore Administration Report 1937-38*, p. 142; *1938-39*, p. 145.
[59] Govt. of India, *Census of India 1931*, Vol. XXVIII, Travancore, Part I, Report, p. 254.
[60] Isaac, *Class Struggle and Industrial Structure*, p. 78. It has also been noted that in Alleppey, Pulayas and Parayas were held as attached, indebted laborers up to 1943. This prevented them from taking up factory work. See George Alex, "Social and Economic Aspect of Attached Labourers in Kuttanad Agriculture", *Economic and Political Weekly*, 22:5 (1987), pp. A141-150.
[61] Govt. of Mysore, *Report of the Administration of Mysore for the Year 1921-22*, p. 31; *1925-26*, pp. 36 ff.; *1927-28*, p. 45; *1928-29*, p. 42; *1929-30*, p. 36; *1930-31*, p. 32; *1931-32*, p. 35; *1932-33*, p. 67; *1934-35*, p. 82; *1939-40*, pp. 93 ff.
[62] Govt. of Travancore, *Report of the Banking Enquiry Committee Travancore 1929*, pp. 196, 200.

World War I, along British, Canadian, and American lines.[62] Native entre-preneurs, who had been praised in pre-capitalistic times, were now criti-cized by a government committee for their lack of productivity and for not knowing how to invest surplus capital in effective ways, in contrast to ex-amples of more modern, foreign businessmen.[63] The new banking system was vital in transforming the region's economy from a pre-capitalist society dominated by a land-owning class to a thoroughly capitalistic one. Banking grew phenomenally in Travancore after 1918, the number of banks orga-nized as joint-stock companies increasing from eight in 1918 to 258 in 1929.[64] One of these was the Quilon Bank, established in 1919. The founder of the bank, C.P. Matthen, summed up its primary business activ-ity in a few words: "From 1925 onwards the main business of our bank was the financing of the business in these [cashew] nuts."[65]

The presence of the Quilon Bank also stimulated the development of the cashew industry in the region—not only by cooperating with General Foods, but by assisting domestic merchants with loans which enabled them to process and export cashew nuts. [66]

Banking in Quilon continued to play a crucial role in the local infra-structure until 1938, when, after a trying conflict, the Quilon Bank went into liquidation.[67] By this time, however, cashew processing was firmly established as a major export industry in Quilon.

The growth of cashew factories in the Quilon region, rather than at some other location in Travancore, may be explained by a combination of factors: access to labor, modern economic infrastructure, and the pioneer-ing efforts of enterprising individuals. However, places such as Calicut in British India could offer features at least as good as Travancore (and even better access to raw material); but Travancore had the advantage of supply-ing cheap labor in a market unfettered by restrictive labor legislation.

Dependency on Imported Raw Cashew Nuts

It is estimated that only one-third of the cashews processed in Travancore in 1945 were grown locally. Twenty-five percent of the raw nuts were import-ed from South Canara and Malabar, and the rest came from East Africa.[68]

---

[63] Ibid., p. 101.
[64] Ibid., p. 31.
[65] C.P. Matthen, *I Have Borne Much* (Madras, 1951), p. 37.
[66] Ibid., p. 37.
[67] Ouwerkerk, *No Elephants for the Maharaja*, pp. 145 ff.; Matthen, *I Have Borne Much*, pp. 60 ff.
[68] KSA, Development department Vol. I part A 1947, series 48, file No. 50, "A Note on the Cashewnut Industry in Travancore", p. 13.

The import of raw cashew nuts, however, had been a feature of the cashew factories from their very beginning. As early as 1925, raw nuts were being imported.[69] Then, toward the end of the 1950s, the first large-scale factory was established in East Africa, marking the gradual decline in the availability of raw African cashews for export to India. With the aid of the World Bank and European companies, fully-mechanized cashew nut processing systems were eventually set up in East Africa.[70] India had held a monopoly on the export of cashew kernels until shortly after 1960, when competition from other countries arose. Recently, other raw nut exporting countries like Vietnam have begun to encourage domestic processing.[71] But, in contrast to most other places in the world, cashew processing in India has never been mechanized, and the low wages which prevail there have been attributed to this fact.[72]

Recent years have seen severe competition for raw nuts in the global arena. Poorer countries in Africa, Latin-America, and Asia have realized the potential value of the cashew nut for generating foreign currency.[73] Such efforts may be described as a peripheral country's striving to raise itself to semi-peripheral status.[74] India's position in the cashew trade has become one of a semi-peripheral country, buying raw nuts from the periphery, and selling in bulk to the rich core-countries.

In response to declining imports of raw nuts from East Africa and the scarcity of raw nuts overall, the Directorate of Cashewnut Development was established in 1966 as a subordinate office of the Union Ministry of Agriculture of the Government of India. The main purpose of this organization was to promote domestic cultivation of cashew nuts.[75] As a result, the production of raw cashew has increased threefold within India since

---

[69] Govt. of India, *Report on the Marketing of Cashew Nuts in India*, p. 4.

[70] Kannan, *Cashew Development in India*, p. 39, n. 5; The World Bank, India Staff Appraisal Report, Cashewnut Project, Confidential Report No. 2437-IN, 1979 p. 2; Roger J. Wilson, *The Market for Cashew-nut Kernels and Cashew-nut Shell Liquid*, Tropical Products Institute (London, 1975), p. 20; Obituary Notice for D.C. Russell, *The Times* 31.1.1991, London.

[71] René Véron, "State Interventions in the Cashew Sector in Kerala, India" (Paper presented at the 14th European Conference on Modern South Asian Studies, Copenhagen, 21-25 August 1996), p. 6.

[72] Ohler, *Cashew*, p. 48; Ezriel Brook, *Cashew-nuts: Review and Outlook*, Economic Analysis and Projections Department. World Bank, Commodity Note No. 5, June 1978, pp. i, 3; *Cashew Marketing*, International Trade Centre, Unctad, Gatt (Geneva, 1968), p, 11.

[73] Kannan, *Cashew Development in India*, pp. 33-38.

[74] Immanuel Wallerstein, *Historical Capitalism* (New York, 1974); Terence K. Hopkins and Immanual Wallerstein (eds), *World-systems Analysis* (Beverly Hills, 1982); Immanuel Wallerstein, "World-systems Analysis", in A. Giddens and J.H. Turner (eds), *Social Theory Today* (Cambridge, 1987), pp. 309 324.

[75] Véron, "State Interventions in the Cashew Sector in Kerala", p. 9; Govt. of Kerala, *Cashew Industry in Kerala*, pp. 5 ff.

1966. Still, this has not been enough to cover the loss of imported raw nuts or supply what appears to be an inexhaustible market demand for the cashews.[76]

The dependency on imported raw nuts is a characteristic of the cashew nut industry in India, and one which makes it vulnerable to international market factors and other circumstances out of the control of Indian producers or politicians. Kerala's cashew factories are now part of a highly globalized world, in which prices and the flow of raw materials are set by economic forces in the West. The final processing, i.e., consumer packaging, adding salt, and mixing cashews with other nuts, remains largely undeveloped in India. This more profitable aspect of production is carried out in the cashew-consuming countries of Europe and the US.[77] In 1996, even after more than three-quarters of a century, 99.8% of India's cashews were still exported in bulk tins to over seventy Western countries.[78] The reason is probably not a lack of know-how or capital, but a reluctance to make long-term investments in the machinery necessary to modernize production.

Since 1990, the shortage of raw nuts within India seems to have reversed. Consequently, an upward surge in Indian export of bulk-packaged cashew kernels can be noted. From the perspective of factory owners, and judging by national export statistics, we may even speak of a period of recovery in the 1990s.[79]

From Perennial to Seasonal Factories

In the 1930s and 1940s, the cashew nut factories in Quilon were running six or seven days a week for most of the year.[80] Up to 1947, all factories in India were officially designated "seasonal" or "perennial", depending on their annual operations; the cashew industry was classified as "perennial".[81] This classification became a costly issue in 1947 with the implementation of the Industrial Disputes Act, because employers were required

---

[76] Véron, "State Interventions in the Cashew Sector in Kerala", p. 9.
[77] *Cashew Bulletin* 1995, No. 5, p. 14.
[78] SICMA Office, Quilon, "Note Attached to a Call for the 378th Meeting of the Committee of Administration of the Cashew Export Promotion Council", dated 18 Dec 1996.
[79] For a discussion of this, see Véron, "State Interventions in the Cashew Sector".
[80] Interview 5 January 1997 with Ponni, female sheller, born around 1920; Interview 11 March 1997 with Kavitha, female sheller, born around 1920; Interview 19 December 1997 with K. Bhanu, former journalist, man born 1913, Quilon district; Interview 14 September 1999 with K. Chellappan, former trade union leader, man born 1914, Quilon district.
[81] Govt. of India, *Large Industrial Establishments*, Ministry of Labour, 1931-1947.

to provide workers in perennial factories with unemployment compensation. The Employees State Insurance Act of 1948 further exacerbated the situation, as it exempted owners of seasonal industries from its provisions. The Central Government, in trying to reach a uniform policy for all India, had declared the criterion for a seasonal factory to be its dependency on natural forces (such as the harvest cycle or weather conditions) for its raw materials.[82] The cashew factory owners in Travancore-Cochin, for obvious financial reasons, fought through the early 1950s to have their industry declared "seasonal".

The labor commissioner, however, argued that although cashew factories were in part dependent on the seasonal crop of indigenous raw nuts, the gap could be filled with imported raw nuts. He showed that from 1950 to 1952, most of the 155 cashew nut factories in Travancore-Cochin were in operation for more than ten months a year, with a large number of them running almost continuously (i.e., six days a week, 52 weeks a year) during the period surveyed.[83]

The Central Government of India now sided with the cashew manufacturers, in opposition to the state governments of Madras and Travancore-Cochin, which sought to protect the right of their workers to claim certain benefits.[84]

Meanwhile, trade unions were growing stronger, and with their influence, the factories came under the law of minimum wages in 1953. This exacerbated the question for the plant owners, who balked at extending such entitlements as paid sick leave, unemployment compensation, and maternity benefits to all factory workers. In 1956, after years of discussion, the cashew factories were definitively declared "perennial" by the government of Travancore-Cochin.[85] The outcome was an important victory for cashew factory workers.

In response, the owners continued a strategy begun in 1945, cyclically shutting down operations in one place and opening them in another, thus artificially creating a "seasonal" workforce, and thereby depriving workers in both factories of benefits given to perennial employees.[86] Both the trade union leader, M.N. Govindan, and the labor commissioner held the view that unless this problem was solved, "lengthening periods of unemployment will become the recurring lot of the [cashew] workers".[87]

---

[82] KSA, Development department (labour) 1954, File No. 35-419, "Declaration of cashew-nut factories as seasonal".
[83] Ibid., pp. 19 ff.
[84] Ibid., p. 5.
[85] KSA, Development department (labour) 1954, File No. 35-419, "Declaration of Cashew-nut Factories as Seasonal", Notification No. L2-15660/56/DD, dated the 31ˢᵗ of July 1956.
[86] KSA, Development files 1946, No. 507, Letter from M.N. Govindan Nair to The Dewan of Travancore.

The historical record shows that these fears became a reality. Whereas employment in the cashew factories amounted to year-round work in the early 1950s, the number of annual work days gradually dwindled to slightly over 100 by 1970. All the while, the total number of workers employed "seasonally" steadily increased.[88]

The reason given by factory owners for the "seasonalization" of the cashew factories has been the lack of raw nuts. In 1983, however, in a study on the trade and processing of cashew nuts conducted by staff from the government of India, it was concluded that the decreasing working days in the cashew factories were not to be attributed to a lack of raw nuts. In fact, the investigators noticed that the supply of raw nuts increased considerably in the 1960s and 1970s, both from indigenous sources and imports. The number of working days in most factories had fallen simply because factory owners resorted to the employment of more and more workers for shorter and shorter periods.[89] The investigators concluded that the intentional creation of a seasonal labor force was artificial, and that the number of factories and workers far exceeded the capacity of the industry.[90] It is true, however, that import of raw nuts decreased considerably after mid-1970.[91] In spite of this, the number of factories, as well as the number of seasonal workers, increased.

Employers have also wielded the argument that it is not possible to store raw nuts for a long period in a tropical climate—something which they say justifies hiring a lot of workers for short periods.[92] Specialists in the field, however, have pointed out that long-term storage is possible, although it requires some investment in buildings.[93] Rather than tie up their capital in this way, factory owners found it unnecessary to begin storing raw nuts, as long as labor was readily available for seasonal work. The seasonal character of the cashew factories has, thus, greatly affected conditions

---

[87] KSA, Development files 1946, No. 507, Memorandum of the Travancore Cashewnut Workers' Union. Report of the Labour Commissioner.

[88] Govt. of India, *Annual Survey of Industries*, cited in Oommen, *Inter State Shifting*, p. 99.

[89] Govt. of India, *Report on the Cashew Industry*, The Cashew Corporation of India Ltd. (New Delhi, 1983) p. 6.

[90] Ibid., p. 12.

[91] CEPC, *Cashew Statistics; Indian Cashews: Facts and Figures; Indian Cashew Statistics 1991-1996.*

[92] KSA, Development file, 1955 No. 10397, "Memorandum Submitted by the South India Cashewnut Manufacturers' Association, Quilon", dated 20th April 1955, p. 3.

[93] D.C. Russell, *Cashew-nut Processing*, Food and Agriculture Organization of the United Nations (Rome, 1969), pp. 14-16; Interview 12 June 1998 with A.D. Bolland, former managing director, Peirce Leslie & Co. The same conclusion was drawn by the Industrial Tribunal in Trivandrum in 1951. See RSP Office, Quilon, Thrivananthapuram Industrial Tribunal, Labour Conflict No. 15/1951, paragraph 13.

for the laborers, since many labor laws continue to stipulate that they need to be employed for a minimum number of working days annually to be eligible for benefits.

As applied to the cashew industry, "casualization" differs from the definition given by scholars focusing on female workers after 1970 in the so-called export processing zones—areas where labor laws and trade unions are excluded in order to attract foreign capital.[94] Swasti Mitter explains the general term as follows: "Casualisation means a shift away from full-time, state-regulated and often unionized labour, reducing job rights and disorganising labor."[95] In the cashew industry, on the other hand, casualization was deliberately aimed at keeping females as part-time workers, deprived of benefits. It existed despite the presence of unions or state labor laws. Any effort to limit the proliferation of factories was soon abandoned. The Industries Development and Regulation Act, which was intended to restrict

Table 3.1 Number of registered cashew factories and workers in Kerala, 1958–2000

Year	Number of cashew factories	Number of workers in cashew factories	Cashew workers as % of total workers
1958	n.a	67,278	41%
1960	181	69,249	41%
1963	197	78,695	45%
1967	241	96,867	48%
1971	266	99,050	48%
1975	267	122,465	46%
1978	243	122,029	45%
1981	260	127,550	42%
1984	243	104,727	36%
1987	264	107,067	36%
1996	379	180,598	44%
2000	400	200,000	not available

Sources: Govt. of Kerala, *Economic Review*, various issues (Trivandrum, 1958-1997). The figures for 2000 are approximate and are based on an interview 9 January 2001 with A.A. Azeez, trade union leader, politician (RSP), and president of the Kerala Cashew Workers Welfare Organisation, Quilon.

[94] See, for example, the contributions in Sheila Rowbotham and Swasti Mitter (eds), *Dignity and Daily Bread. New Forms of Economic Organising Among Poor Women in the Third World and the First* (London, 1994).
[95] Swasti Mitter, "On Organising Women in Casualised Work: a Global Overview", in Rowbotham and Mitter, *Dignity and Daily Bread*, pp. 14-52.

new factories from opening, was relaxed, permitting the number of factories to continue to grow.[96] Table 3.1 shows the growth of registered factories and workers in Kerala.

State Interventions in the Cashew Industry

State interventions in connection with women's work in the Third World have mainly been seen in the so-called world market factories and export-processing zones which first emerged in the late 1960s. Such interventions, by providing exemptions from import-export regulations, tax laws, and labor legislation, have served to increase exports.[97] Scholars have remarked upon the oppressive nature of these interventions, finding that such actions have served the interests of entrepreneurs while worsening the plight of females working in such factories.[98]

The first state intervention occurred in Travancore in 1946, when plants there were brought under the Factory Act after severe agitation from the trade unions. The concern of the central government of India has mainly been to protect the Indian export trade, whereas the state government of Kerala has had a double aim: to stimulate export, but to also serve the interests of the workers. There has been a great degree of state involvement in Kerala cashew factories during the whole period under consideration. Often it has reflected the competition in raw nuts. In the post-colonial period, the central government restricted the import of cashews twice: in 1954 and 1970. Then, in 1970, the import and distribution of raw cashew nuts was monopolized by the government of India through the Cashew Corporation of India (CCI).[99] Politicians and trade unionists in Kerala fiercely denounced this agency for unfair distribution practices and for allotting raw nuts to

---

[96] RSP, office, Quilon, *Confidential Report of the Central Team on Cashew Industry in Kerala State*, Decisions taken at the meeting of the all-party delegation from Kerala and the Prime-Minister of India on 13th May 1971, chairman R.V Raman, 13 May 1971, p. 6.

[97] Diane Elson and Ruth Pearson, "The Subordination of Women and the Internationalisation of Factory Production", in Kate Young, Carol Wolkowitz, and Roslyn McCullagh (eds), *Of Market and the Market: Women's Subordination in International Perspective* (London, 1981), pp. 144-166; Fröbel et al., *The New International Division of Labour*; Swasti Mitter, *Common Fate, Common Bond: Women in the Global Economy* (London, 1986), pp. 25-64; Standing, "Global Feminization through Flexible Labor"; Cynthia Enloe, *Bananas, Bases and Beaches: Making Feminist Sense of International Politics* (London, 1990).

[98] Linda Lim has argued against a "stereotypical view of women workers", finding that women have benefited from factory work, too. See Linda Lim, "Women's Work in Export Factories: The Politics of a Cause", in Irene Tinker (ed.), *Persistent Inequalities: Women and World Development* (New York, 1990), pp. 101-119. For an answer to Linda Lim's essay, see Ruth Pearson, "Industrialization and Women's Subordination: A Reappraisal", in Valentine M. Moghadam (ed), *Patriarchy and Economic Development. Women's Positions at the End of the Twentieth Century* (New York, 1996), pp. 169-183.

factories that were in violation of labor laws.[100] The CCI was also said to encourage factories that employed a large number of workers for short periods, instead of those giving a smaller group full-time jobs.[101] After years of criticism, the central government partly liberalized the import of raw cashew nuts in 1981, and three years later dropped all restrictions.[102]

The Kerala government introduced its own "state-monopoly procurement" in 1976, as a means of stimulating employment in Kerala and preventing factories there from migrating to other states. Raw nuts were declared an essential article and trade in raw cashews to other states was made illegal. Fixed prices on indigenous raw nuts were set by the Kerala government and an allotment of raw nuts could only be distributed to factories registered under state organizations.[103] The "monopoly procurement" policy has been a contested political question, disliked by cashew growers (who asserted that the prices fixed by the government were too low)[104] and by private factory owners (who held that the monopoly was created to secure cheap raw nuts for the state-owned factories).[105] In 1995, the law was finally declared incompatible with the Constitution of India.[106] Private cashew factory owners considered this a great victory in the struggle for free trade, seeing it as part of a new era with a liberalized economy.[107]

An objective announced by politicians of the left and trade unionists since the mid-1950s was the formation of a state-owned public sector in the cashew factory area.[108] In 1969, this demand materialized. The call for state-owned factories was a logical outcome of the then prevailing development strategy.

---

[99] KSA, Development Files 1954 No. 1187/10967, "Rehabilitation of the Cashew Industry. Official Memorandum"; Kannan, *Cashew Development in India*, pp. 41-47.

[100] *Jennajugham*, 29 November 1971, p. 2; 2 February 1972, p. 1; 9 February 1972, p. 2; 23 February 1972, p. 1.

[101] Govt. of India, *Report on the Cashew Industry*, CCI (New Delhi, 1983), p. 19.

[102] Veron, "State Interventions in the Cashew Sector in Kerala", p. 10.

[103] René Veron. "Markets Environment and Development in South India. Cultivating and Marketing of Pineapple and Cashew in Kerala" (Ph.D., University of Zurich, 1997), Chapter 6.

[104] For a general discussion of farmers' movement in contemporary India, see Staffan Lindberg, "Farmers' Movements and Agricultural Development in India", in Staffan Lindberg and Árni Sverrisson (eds), *Social Movements in Development: The Challenge of Globalization and Democratization* (Basinstoke, 1997), pp. 101-125.

[105] However, there is no obvious correlation between the average number of working days in the public sector and restrictions on import and purchase of raw-nuts. (List with average number of working days obtained from Antoni Das, personnel director, KSCDC, 15 January 1999).

[106] "Judgement, "The Kerala Raw Cashew-nuts (Procurement and Distribution) Act 1981 declared as ultra vires the constitution of India", in *Cashew Bulletin*, 33:11 (1996).

[107] *Cashew Bulletin*, 32:5 (1995), p. 2; Interview 14 March 1997 with K.P. Ramachandran Nair, general manager Lakshman & Co, Kilikilloor.

[108] *Jennajugham*, 27 June 1956, p. 2; 29 September 1956, p. 4; 19 March 1958, p. 1.

KSCDC and CAPEX

The introduction of minimum wages in the 1950s had led to an expansion of *kudivarappu*, which literally means "cottage processing". *Kudivarappus* are clandestine factories where labor laws are ignored and wages are lower than the stipulated minimum. Very often, the owners of the *kudivarappus* were the same individuals managing the registered factories. Registered factories closed down and *kudivarappus* opened up in a strategy of decentralization of production in order to avoid labor laws. In 1967, the Kerala government implemented a law banning non-registered factories, which, according to Kannan, had reached their peak in that year. With factory after factory in the registered sector closed down, a public sector was formed in the cashew industry to improve working conditions and secure employment in Kerala.[109] Thus, the government's aim was to set up model factories.

In 1969, the Kerala State Cashew Development Corporation (KSCDC) was formed with the intention of purchasing and processing raw cashew nuts and marketing cashew kernels. The corporation opened one factory in 1971, the year which marks the beginning of an era of state capitalism in the cashew field. Gradually KSCDC took over private factories, either by lease or by purchase and, by 1975 thirty-four factories, with a workforce of about 30,000 workers, were under the KSCDC.[110] The year before, the Kerala Government had introduced a law which gave the state the authority to take over cashew factories that either violated labor laws, neglected to process raw nuts allotted to them (in order to prevent the shifting of raw nuts to *kudivarappus* or other plants), or had large-scale unemployment beyond that caused by natural lay-offs or down-sizing.[111] This law was never put into effect until 1988.

In 1988, monopoly procurement of raw nuts by the state was again introduced by the leftist Government in order to assure the availability of raw nuts and, thereby, employment for the laborers. In response, many of the factory owners closed their plants and refused to purchase the raw nuts allotted to them, considering their price unrealistically high.[112] The

---

[109] Kannan, *Cashew Development in India*, pp. 125-131.

[110] R. Sundaresan, "State Intervention in Support of Traditional Industries—Case of the Kerala State Cashew Development Corporation" (University of Kerala, Centre F.M.N. College, Quilon, 1994), p. 59; Govt. of Kerala, *Economic Review 1971*, pp. 35-36; *1972*, p. 56, *1973*, p. 91; *1974*, p. 108; *1976*, p. 61.

[111] SICMA Office, Quilon, In the Supreme Court of India, Civil Original Jurisdiction, Writ Petition (C), No. 415 of 1988.

[112] SICMA Office, Quilon, Note submitted to Shri Kamaluddin Ahmed, Hon'ble Minister of State for Commerce, Govt. of India, New Delhi, p. 5.

CHAPTER 3

Kerala Government then declared itself prepared to implement the law of 1974 and assume control of certain cashew factories. It informed the owners of thirty-six factories of its intention and, with the aid of police, these factories were taken over at midnight on July 7, 1988. The government had promulgated an order dated July 6 which gave them the legal right to take over closed-down cashew factories (which they termed "sick units"). Prior to July 6, the KSCDC had thirty-four factories under its control. With nationalization, thirty-six more factories were taken over, making a total of seventy. Workers employed by the state corporation almost doubled overnight, from 29,860 to 54,860, and the KSCDC became the largest cashew employer and processor in Kerala.[113]

Meanwhile, the private owners had filed a petition with the Supreme Court. The matter was pending at the time of the government takeover.[114] After a protracted process, the Supreme Court issued its decision in May 1994, in which it declared the nationalization of the cashew factories unconstitutional and nullified the Kerala Cashew Factories Acquisition Act of twenty years before. The court ordered the factories returned to their original owners within two weeks.[115] Demands were then raised by owners of plants taken over by KSCDC prior to 1988 that the first group of thirty-four KSCDC factories also be returned, this time as a logical extension of the 1990 policy declaration on privatization and liberalization issued by the Government of India.[116]

In the beginning of the 1970s, there had been a great deal of optimism among those who favored a public sector. KSCDC could pride itself on having proven it was possible to run cashew factories at a profit while paying the legal minimum wage and providing fringe benefits.[117] However, the situation has since changed, and in recent years the cashew factories have only been able to remain open for three or four months a year, due to changing world-wide logistics of cashew production and the resulting competition for raw nuts in India. Factories have generally been running at a loss; in 1995, this cumulative loss exceeded US$ 37,000,000.[118] In addition, the directors of KSCDC were accused of mismanagement and cor-

---

[113] Govt. of Kerala, *Economic Review 1988*, p. 53.

[114] SICMA Office, Quilon, Report of the Committee of Administration on the Proceedings of the Committee and on the Activities of the Council for the Year ended 31st March 1992, Cashew Export Promotion.

[115] SICMA Office, Quilon, In the Supreme Court of India, Civil Original Jurisdiction, Writ Petition (C), No. 415 of 1988.

[116] *Cashew Bulletin*, 32:2 (1995), p. 2,

[117] Govt. of Kerala, *Economic Review 1971*, p. 36, 1975, p. 150.

[118] Sundaresan, "State Intervention in Support of Traditional Industries", pp. 70-73; *Indian Express*, 4 June 1995, cited in Véron, "State Interventions in the Cashew Sector in Kerala", p. 12.

ruption, and 56,000,000 rupees (about US$ 1,250,000) were declared missing.[119]

In certain years, the management of KSCDC has not been able to buy raw nuts at all. As a result, the number of annual working days in the KSCDC factories in 1993 and 1995 were only thirteen. Since then, the number has slightly increased.

In 1984, with the Congress Party in power and filling the post of Chief Minister in Kerala, a new organization aimed at solving the problem of closed factories, unemployment, and starvation among cashew workers was established: the Kerala State Cashew Workers Apex Industrial Cooperative Society, Ltd. (CAPEX). The goal of CAPEX was very much in line with that announced when KSCDC was founded fifteen years earlier, i.e., to organize the cashew industry on a commercial basis and to procure and process raw nuts for the national and international market. The establishment of a new organization was the result of a political struggle between the Congress-led Ministry and the leftist opposition, which had established the KSCDC. Representatives of the Left Front accused the Congress of establishing CAPEX for the sole purpose of undermining the KSCDC.[120] By the end of 1985-86, eight factories, numbering 4,145 workers, were members of CAPEX.[121] In 1998 the number of factories had risen to ten, employing about 5,100 workers.[122] The average number of annual working days in the CAPEX factories has only been slightly higher than that of the KSCDC factories. During the fifteen years that CAPEX has been in existence, only two years have been profitable. As in the case of KSCDC, the cumulative result has been a loss,[123] and the management of CAPEX has also been accused of corruption and conspiring with private factory owners.[124] In October 2000, debts and accusations of mismanagement grew to a level which led the Kerala Government to discuss the closing down of CAPEX.[125]

Representatives of KSCDC and CAPEX have asserted that the reason for their failure has been the existence of private factories whose owners pay higher prices for raw cashew nuts, but then balance this by exploiting workers. The result is that the public sector has suffered from a shortage of

---

[119] *Jennajugham*, 11 February 1989, p. 6; see also *The Hindu*, 1 August 1995 and *Indian Express*, 4 June 1995, both cited in Véron, "State Interventions in the Cashew Sector in Kerala", p. 12.

[120] *Jennajugham*, 7 January 1985, p. 4.

[121] Govt. of Kerala, *Economic Review 1986*, p. 57.

[122] Information received from the managing director of CAPEX, V.N. Giri, 15 September 1999.

[123] Interview 15 September 1999 with the managing director of CAPEX, V.N. Giri.

[124] *Deshabhimani*, 10 May 1994, p. 6.

[125] *The Hindu*, 14 October 2000, p. 5.

raw nuts.[126] Nevertheless, even in periods of monopoly procurement of raw nuts, annual working days have been far from enough to give the workers full-time employment in the state-owned sector. Representatives of the private sector maintain that heads of the public factories are unprofessional and lack management experience.[127]

There has been a fierce struggle between the leftist government of Kerala and the private cashew factory owners. To this has been added the struggle between Congress-led ministries, which have pleaded for a less regulated economy, and ministries of the left, with their policy of nationalization and strict state intervention. Such has been the political battlefield which has constituted the arena for cashew workers since the mid-1950s. At the same time another struggle has been taking place between Kerala and its nearest neighbor, Tamil Nadu—a struggle to attract and keep cashew factories within their respective states.

Balancing Between Two States

The first entrepreneurs who migrated from British India to the city of Quilon in the princely state of Travancore to start cashew factories (from the late 1920s to the mid-1940s) were attracted by the prospect of cheap labor and the absence of laws governing employment. To start a cashew business in the early days did not require much capital, since no machines, hardly any buildings, and no electricity was necessary.[128] The only start-up capital needed was for buying raw nuts. Even in later times, the cashew industry has typically been characterized by low capital investment.[129] Employers have extensively used the factor of a cashew processing operation's mobility as a weapon against workers.[130] The threat of relocation to other regions where labor laws and wages are more favorable, workers less militant, or civil servants less stringent in implementing the law was intended to keep employees and unions dependent on the owner's conditions.[131]

---

[126] Interview 15 September 1999 with the managing director of CAPEX, V.N. Giri.
[127] Interview 13 March 1997 with Ravindran Nathan Nair, factory owner, VLC, Cashew factories; Interview 14 March 1997 with K.P. Ramachandran Nair, general manager, Lakshman & Co, Kilikilloor.
[128] Govt. of India, *Report on an Enquiry into Conditions of Labour in the Cashewnut Processing Industry in India 1954*, p. 4.
[129] Kannan, *Cashew Development in India*, pp. 110 ff.
[130] Oommen, *Inter State Shifting.*
[131] Such threats were often articulated in discussions between labor, capital, and the state. See, for example, Govt. of Travancore-Cochin, *Report of the Minimum Wages Committee*

Although the threats had already started in the 1950s, it was first in the 1960s and 1970s that they materialized, with severe consequences for the workers. A mass shift of cashew production from Kerala to the neighboring state of Tamil Nadu resulted in a tremendous reduction in the number of annual working days for cashew workers in Kerala. Most cashew factory owners in Tamil Nadu also have factories in Kerala.[132]

Entrepreneurs who owned cashew factories in both Kerala (Quilon) and Tamil Nadu met to found an organization called the Tamil Nadu Cashew Manufacturers' Association in Kollam.[133] The only information available about this organization is limited and fragmentary, since its activities are unofficial and more or less clandestine. Even the date of its founding is unclear. It has no office and its name seems never to have appeared in any of the largest newspapers in Kerala, which usually give extensive coverage to questions concerning the cashew industry.[134] Trade union leaders whom I interviewed in Kerala had not even heard of this association.

In 1979, the South Indian Cashew Manufacturers Association, SICMA, presented a memorandum to the Minister of Labor in Tamil Nadu, in which the factory owners asked for special treatment in the future with regard to the Factory Act.[135] It reads:

> This infant industry in the District of Kanyakumari deserves parental care at the hands of the State Government. We, therefore, pray that suitable protective measures be taken to encourage industry, to prevent all actions which may have a tendency to stifle the industry, by issuing suitable directives to the officers concerned to avoid unnecessary harassment of processors by vigorous and blind implementation of the Factories Act and Rules made thereunder and allied enactments at least until such time as this industry takes deep root and stands on its own legs.[136]

---

for Cashew Industry 1953, Dissenting note of Sri P. Krishna Pillai and Janab A. Thangal Kunju Musaliar, pp. 41-42; SICMA Office, Quilon, Quilon, "Memorandum of Objections submitted by the South India Cashewnut Manufacturers' Association, Kollam, and the Kerala Cashew Manufacturers Association, Kollam, to the Secretary to the Government of Kerala, Health and Labour Department", dated 12th September 1966, p. 1.
[132] Oommen, *Inter State Shifting*, pp. 79-90; letter to the author from T.K. Rangarajan, General Secretary, CITU—Tamil Nadu State Committee, Chennai, November 1999.
[133] SICMA Office, Quilon, "Memorandum submitted by Tamil Nadu Manufacturers Association. Before the Honourable Minister for Labour, Govt. of Tamil Nadu". Dated 18th March 1983; SICMA Office, Quilon, List of Cashew Factories in Tamil Nadu 1981.
[134] I have excerpted three daily newspapers: *Jennajugham* (ceased 1993), *Kerala Kaumudi*, and *The Hindu* from 1950 to 1999.
[135] SICMA Office, Quilon, Memorandum submitted by the South India Cashewnuts Manufacturers' Association, Kollam, Kerala State, "To the Honourable Minister for Labour, Tamil Nadu", dated 3 November 1979, signed by K. Gopinathan Nair, Secretary of SICMA , p. 1.
[136] Ibid., p. 6.

This line of argument was exactly the same as that put to the Travancore Government about thirty-five years earlier by another representative of SICMA, when cashew factories were about to be included in the Factory Act. SICMA then asked for exemption from the Factory Act on the grounds that the factories needed time to establish themselves.[137] The letter clearly demonstrates the intention of intimidating the government. We do not know anything further about the willingness of the minister to "issue the suitable directives", or his motives for acting or not acting in this matter, but a frequent comment heard in the 1980s in connection with the reports of the implementation of minimum wages in different states in India was "Tamil Nadu has no inspection machinery".[138] The political will to implement and control labor laws was then lacking in Tamil Nadu. A similar situation prevailed during the late 1960s.[139]

The same threat made to the Kerala Government, i.e., the loss of foreign currency and large-scale unemployment, was also put forward in Tamil Nadu. In 1983, the cashew factory owners wrote a memorandum to the Labor Minister of Tamil Nadu, as follows:

> To the utter surprise of the undersigned, the Government of Tamil Nadu have promulgated a notification G.O. MS 327 Labour and Employment Department dated 8.2.1983 fixing minimum wages for the various categories of employment engaged in the cashew industry with effect from 21.2.1983.... In Kerala, large number of Kudils (units which do not conform to rules and regulations inclusive of Labour Legislation) are operating. Cashewnuts are being processed in Kudils at much lower cost than could be done in Tamil Nadu Units, even at the existing wage rates, since notified minimum wages are not being paid there at all.... The average cost of processing one bag of rawnuts (80kgs) in a kudil works out to Rs. 40 only. Whereas the cost of production, even at the agreed and existing wage rates works out to Rs. 57 in Tamil Nadu. Many of the employers who run regular factories in Kerala are getting their rawnuts processed in these kudils.... It is in this context that the new structures of Minimum Wages has been notified, introducing a steep and sudden increase from 18 to 30 % in respect of various categories. This will only add to the difficulties which may have the cumulative effect of undermining the very existence of the industry in Tamil

---

[137] KSA, Development file No. 341/2093, Feb 1945, "Exemption of the Cashew Factories from the Operation of Factory Act".

[138] Govt. of India, *Report on the Working of Minimum Wages Act for the Year 1982* (Simla, 1986), p. 150; Govt. of India, *Report on the Working of Minimum Wages Act for the Year 1983* (Simla, 1988), p. 135.

[139] Govt. of India, *Report on the Working of the Minimum Wages Act, 1948, During the Years 1968 & 1969* (Simla, 1973), p. 194.

Nadu. *This will pave the way of its re-migration (for the very reason for which the industry migrated to Tamil Nadu) to Kerala* [italics added], in view of the better advantages in Kerala, throwing large number of workers into unemployment and poverty in Tamil Nadu. <u>It is submitted in this connection that about 250 factories operating in K.K. District employ more than a lakh of workers.</u>[140]

The *Kudils* mentioned in the letter are identical to the previously mentioned *Kudivarappus* in Kerala. In referring to clandestine factories which pay wages far below the already very depressed wages in Tamil Nadu, the threat of re-migration was reinforced. In underlining the last sentence, the authors wanted to stress the importance of the cashew industry for the region. A future scenario with more than 100,000 persons unemployed, in a region where starvation and unemployment already was the main problem, certainly exerted an influence upon the authorities of Tamil Nadu.

The taint of corruption is even more evident in some handbills distributed to the managers of cashew factories in Tamil Nadu. They emanated from the Tamil Nadu Cashew Manufacturers Association in Kollam, were signed by a cashew factory owner from Quilon, and bore the organizational seal of SICMA. They were distributed in 1985 and 1986, but it is probable that those were not the only two occasions.

In essence, the circulars asked that each factory in Tamil Nadu hand over a certain sum of money to the bearer of the letter. In 1985, the amount requested was 250 rupees. This was to establish a sum of cash which would be taken by a representative of the factory owners to a meeting with government authorities in Madras. The aim of this bribe was to evade compliance with the minimum wage law. The circular of 1985 was accompanied by a list of seventeen factory owners in Kerala, and the number of factories each of them had operating in Tamil Nadu.[141] Below is an extract from one of the circulars:

> In several cashew factories in Tamilnadu the DY. [Deputy] Chief Inspector of Factories, Tirunelvelli, after inspection, has recently issued show-cause notices and threatened with prosecution proceedings for certain defects

---

[140] SICMA Office, Quilon, "Memorandum submitted by Tamil Nadu Manufacturers Association. Before the Honourable Minister for Labour, Govt. of Tamil Nadu", dated 18th March 1983. (K.K. District is short for Kanyakumari District in Tamil Nadu. One lakh is 100,000).

[141] SICMA Office, Quilon, Tamilnadu Cashew Manufacturers' Association, Kollam. Circular with heading "Implementation of Minimum Wages in Tamilnadu Cashew Factories", dated 21st July 1986 and circular with the heading "Contribution for the initial expenses of handling Tamilnadu Minimum Wages case", dated 21st May 1985.

found in the implementation of minimum wages, among so many other matters also. As it is well known, if such prosecution materializes, it may result in disastrous consequences in cashew industry in Tamilnadu. To forestall such an eventuality it is proposed certain representatives of the cashew industry in Tamilnadu may forth-with proceed to Madras and take up the matter with concerned authorities.

In order to defray the expenses that may be involved it is decided to collect at the rate of Rs. 500/- (Rupees - Five hundred only) per cashew factory operated by different cashew processors. It is requested that your contribution may kindly be handed over through the bearer of this letter in cash so that the trip can be undertaken positively tomorrow to avoid the least possible delay. The matter is so urgent that your kind co-operation is solicited.[142]

According to handwritten annotations on the list, 11,500 rupees was collected in all. In the following year the request per factory had risen to 500 rupees. Assuming the same number of factories contributed as in the previous year, 23,000 rupees must have been collected for "the approach" to the government official.[143] By way of comparison, the monthly base salary of a supervisor in a cashew factory was then between 420 and 530 rupees.[144] It may be pointed out that round-trip transportation and a good hotel cannot have cost more than 1,000 rupees, leaving between 10,000 and 22,000 rupees unaccounted for.

We do not know if the SICMA representative ever met with the Labor Minister, nor do we know when these trips to Madras started, or when they ended. The memorandums and circulars demonstrate the methods the factory owners were prepared to resort to. According to laborers, trade unionists, and state civil servants only a small number of private "model factories" were not involved in the evasion of labor laws during the period.[145]

---

[142] SICMA Office, Quilon, Tamilnadu Cashew Manufacturers' Association, Kollam. Circular with heading "Implementation of Minimum Wages in Tamilnadu Cashew Factories", dated 21st July 1986.
[143] SICMA Office, Quilon, Tamilnadu Cashew Manufacturers' Association, Kollam. Circular with heading "Implementation of Minimum Wages in Tamilnadu Cashew Factories", dated 21st July 1986, and circular with the heading "Contribution for the initial expenses of handling Tamilnadu Minimum Wages Case," dated 21st May 1985.
[144] KSCDC Office, Quilon, *The Kerala State Cashew Development Corporation Ltd., Quilon, Details of Revision of Pay Scales 1.1. 1987.* To the basic salary was added a part (the so-called dearness allowance) intended to compensate for inflation.
[145] Interview 14 September 1999 with K. Chellappan, trade union leader, born 1914; Interview 21 November 1997 with Labour Commissioner Sam Nathaniel, Quilon; Interview 13 August 1998 with R.S. Unni, trade union leader born in the late 1920s; Interview 20 December 1997 with Velu, male sheller, born 1923, worked at Peirce Leslie & Co. in Kundara for 23 years, 1940-1963.

The cashew factory owners, since they had plants in Kerala and Tamil Nadu, were able to play the two state governments against each other. The economic climate in Kerala and Tamil Nadu has been optimal from the perspective of the factory owners. Both governments fear mass unemployment and mass starvation. On both sides of the state borders, thousands upon thousands of poor workers and their families remain dependent on the pittance they receive from work in the cashew factories for their survival. The companies do not actually have to move—it is sufficient for owners to threaten to move their factory to chasten workers in both states.

Summary

This chapter has focused on the global and competitive nature of capitalism, and its continuous attempt to minimize costs of production. The search for profitable export commodities by Western companies was decisive for the emergence of cashew factories in India during the 1920s. These factories came to be concentrated in Travancore, mainly because management was unrestrained by the presence of labor legislation. Soon indigenous proprietors came to dominate the ranks of the factory owners. Cashew workers became the largest group of factory workers in the state, and have remained so up to present date, with about 200,000 registered cashew workers—most of them female.

In the global arena international competition for the valuable raw cashew nut emerged, creating a dependency on imports and often a lack of raw nuts in India. The ensuing sporadic supply of raw nuts was embraced by factory owners as the justification for running their factories on a seasonal basis, something which would enable them to evade labor laws entirely because of an exemption afforded to "seasonal industries". In point of fact, however, the number of cashew workers has increased steadily, although technically this huge force continues to be considered seasonal labor. Another strategy of management in seeking to bypass labor laws has been the decentralization of production in non-registered factories which are established in locations beyond the purview of trade unions or government oversight.

Since about 1960, the same quest for a cheap and compliant labor force which originally brought the cashew factories to Travancore has been responsible for the relocation of plants from Kerala to the neighboring state of Tamil Nadu, where trade unions have been weak and wages lower. Owners with factories in both states have played the two areas against each other; as a result they have kept wages and working conditions substandard in both places.

In Kerala, the nationalization of the cashew industry has been a goal since 1970, although this objective has not been able to stem the seasonal closings and willful relocation of factories. A liberal economic policy has prevailed in India since 1990, resulting in the deregulation of the industry and the return of many state-owned factories to their former owners.

The arena of cashew production has been characterized by struggle. This has occurred on the global level among nations competing for market share; at the state level between Kerala and Tamil Nadu; on the bureaucratic level between the national and state governments; and on the local level between different political factions in Kerala.

IV   Gender in the Workplace

The rich products of that Garden of Eden, the Malabar Coast, can surely never run dry. Indeed, weighed in the scale of values, no sooner did general produce fall off than we saw the dawn of a great new industry, the preparation, packing and shipping of the fruit of the Cashew tree....Malabar has no monopoly of this tree, which is indigenous to Brazil and grows more extensively in East Africa; but what Malabar does possess above all others are the nimble fingers and unrivalled skill of its beautiful women, who alone make its benefits available to the markets of the world.
—W.K.M. Langley, *Century in Malabar, The History of Peirce Leslie & Co., Ltd. 1862-1962* (Madras, 1962), p. 54.

Introduction

Materialist feminists' concern with the issue of labor processes and their gender codes rests on a presumption that a gender division of labor reflects the broader social relations of gender,[1] a view also taken here. In India most research focusing on gender division of labor has been carried out by sociologists and is based on contemporary local case studies. A result of such studies is that, in spite of large regional, cultural, and traditional diversity, there are pointed similarities in working conditions. Female industrial workers are mainly employed doing labor intensive serial production with a low input of capital per worker and are often paid by piece-rate.[2] The suitability of women in the Third World for monotonous serial production has been linked to an ideology that women are naturally endowed with manual dexterity.[3] These studies often focus on the development of world market

---

[1] See, for example, Cynthia Cockburn, *Brothers: Male Dominance and Technological Change* (London, 1983); Ruth Milkman, *The Dynamics of Job Segregation by Sex during World War* II (Urbana, 1987); Miriam Glucksmann, *Women Assemble: Women Workers and the New Industries in Inter-war Britain* (London, 1990); Ava Baron (ed.), *Work Engendered: Toward a New History of American Labor* (New York, 1991).

[2] See, for example, Banerjee (ed.), *Indian Women in a Changing Industrial Scenario*. This anthology includes case studies of the textile, garment, electronic, prawn, and leather industries in India.

[3] Diane Elson and Ruth Pearson, "'Nimble Fingers Make Cheap Workers': An Analysis of Women's Employment in Third World Export Manufacturing", *Feminist Review*, No. 7 (1981), pp. 87-107.

factories based on exportation which emerged in Southeast Asia around 1970 in the era of the so-called *new international division of labor*. They do not, however, address the question of when and how women were first deemed best suited for labor-intensive tasks, and thus suffer from a lack of historical perspective. The women in these factories are most often young and unmarried[4], which distinguishes them from the general Indian female workforce of predominantly married women.[5] Nevertheless, they, too, are considered to be especially well-equipped for meticulous and labor-intensive work. An important question for us to consider is whether or not this is an opinion inherited from a traditional society.

Closely related to the issue of the gender division of labor are the implications of changes in technology.[6] Historians in India have addressed the question of the introduction of machines, and their conclusion is that changes in the labor process brought about by mechanization inevitably seem to have been followed by an exclusion of female workers. In traditional industries (i.e., jute, textile, and mining), the proportion of women workers has been reduced drastically as a result of mechanization.[7] Radha Kumar has shown that mechanization in the 1920s in the Bombay cotton textile industry led to the dismissal of women.[8] Another example of the same process is the block printing industry.[9] In Bengal, rice husking, a traditionally female occupation, was transformed into a male occupation when machines were introduced.[10] In the agricultural sector, too, it has been shown that mechanization has led to a decrease in women's participa-

---

[4] Fröbel et al., *The New International Division of Labour*.

[5] Banerjee (ed.), *Indian Women in a Changing Industrial Scenario*, p. 303.

[6] Cynthia Cockburn has shown that male workers excluded women from the work tasks with the highest status in the printing industry in England under the pretext of women's unsuitability for handling machines. Cockburn, *Brothers: Male Dominance and Technological Change*.

[7] Uma Ramaswamy, "Women and Development", in Sharma and Singh (eds.), *Women and Work*, pp. 323-337; Govt. of India, *Towards Equality, Report of the National Committee on the Status of Women in India* (New Delhi, 1974), p. 201. For the jute industry, see Dagmar Engels, "The Changing Role of Women in Bengal, c.1890-c.1930, with special Reference to British and Bengali Discourse on Gender" (Ph.D., SOAS, University of London, 1987).

[8] Radha Kumar, "Family and Factory: Women in the Bombay Cotton Textile Industry, 1919-1939", in J. Krishnamurty (ed.), *Women in Colonial India: Essays on Survival, Work and the State* (Delhi, 1989), pp. 133-162.

[9] Devaki Jain, "Displacement of Women Workers in Traditional Industries—Three examples: Cotton Handlooms, Woolen Cottage Industry and Handblock Printing" (Paper Submitted to the Second National Conference on Women's Studies, Trivandrum, April 1984); Kalpagam, *Labour and Gender*, pp. 137 ff.

[10] Mukul Mukherjee, "Impact of Modernisation on Women's Occupations: A Case Study of the Rice Husking Industry of Bengal", in Krishnamurty (ed.), *Women in Colonial India*, pp. 180-198.

tion in such work.[11] In 1974, the authors of the report *Towards Equality* attributed the decline of women in the organized sector to a lack of preparedness when new technology was introduced. They asserted that management as well as trade unions, contrary to what they were doing for male workers, overlooked the need to train women: "The main impact of modernisation and new technology thus falls on the women who become dispensable. Senior executives of important industries admit practicing a policy of 'replacing women by men or machines'".[12] Samita Sen has argued that male-dominated trade unions in Bengal encouraged the myth that women were unable to handle machines.[13] The possibility of a connection between women and machines seems to very strongly have collided with the dominating discourse of femininity in India.[14] Cynthia Cockburn has shown how gender is constructed through technology at work.[15] The point of departure in this thesis is also that workplaces are important sites where people construct identities.

The following will partly focus on the consequences of the introduction of machines. My primary aim, however, is to analyze the gender composition of the factories and offer a longer historical perspective on this issue than previous studies have done. The first part of this chapter explores the work processes involved in the cashew industries, the disposition of workers in different operations, and historical changes that have occurred.

A second concern is how the gender coding of different work tasks has been culturally and ideologically legitimized—an overarching question running through the entire study, and further dealt with in Chapter VI in the context of the question of wages. In this chapter arguments raised by

---

[11] For the case of Punjab, see Martin, H. Billings and Arjan Singh, "Mechanisation and the Wheat Revolution—Effects on Female Labour in Punjab", *Economic and Political Weekly*, 5:52 (1970), pp. A169-174. For the case of Bihar see Sinha, S.P. "Technological Change in Agriculture and Women Workers in Rural Bihar: A Case Study", in Sharma and Singh (eds.), *Women and Work*, pp. 209-218.

[12] Govt. of India, *Towards Equality*, 1974, p. 200.

[13] Samita Sen, "Women Workers in the Bengal Jute Industry, 1890-1940: Migration, Motherhood and Militancy" (Ph.D., Cambridge University, 1992).

[14] In the Swedish context the correlation between gender and mechanization of a work task has not been obvious. Historians have shown that a shift in the gender typing of a work task often implied that men took over when the work task was less heavy or tedious. In contrast to the Indian case, technological change and the introduction of machines did not have an unequivocal gender implication. Sometimes mechanization led to a feminization of a work task, sometimes to a masculinization. The unambiguous result, however, was that the status of the work always was gendered in disfavor of women. See Lynn Karlsson and Ulla Wikander, *Kvinnoarbete och könssegregering i svensk industri 1870-1950: Tre uppsatser*, Uppsala Papers in Economic History, Research Report No. 9 (Uppsala, 1985).

[15] Cynthia Cockburn, *Machinery of Dominance: Women, Men and Technical Know-How* (London, 1985).

employers' representatives, civil servants, and male trade union leaders will be analyzed. The voices of workers will also be heard.

The focus is not solely on learning about the gender division of labor, but also on understanding how historical narratives are constructed, so that we may thereby grasp cultural perceptions of gender. In this analysis a wide range of sources will be used, including contemporary records by former officials, and academic articles published at the time. Later historical accounts and oral narratives which have described the period in retrospect (and, thus, should rather be seen as memories or narratives of the past) have also been scrutinized.

Work Processes

Roasting

Producing the final product (the cashew kernel) involves six principal manufacturing operations: roasting, shelling, drying, peeling, grading, and packing. The purpose of roasting the raw nut is to make the thick, outer shell brittle, thereby facilitating the extraction of the inner kernel. Roasting has generally been described as an extremely dirty and unpleasant job. In the early factories, the roasters often had to start work at three or four o'clock in the morning, to have the nuts ready when the shellers arrived after sunrise. In the earliest or "open-pan" method, the raw nuts were roasted in a shallow, perforated iron pan over an open fire. After about two minutes of heating and burning under continuous stirring to achieve uniform roasting and prevent charring, the pan was tilted and the burning nuts cast on the ground. Water was sprinkled over the raw nuts to cool them and afterwards they were scrubbed with mud or ash so that the cashew nut shell oil would be absorbed.[16] The extracted cashew oil took fire, causing a very harsh and irritating smoke.[17] The danger of being hurt by the burning raw nuts and the sputtering oil was obvious. There was also the risk of over-roasting, which made the kernels brownish and not saleable for export.[18] A variation of the pan-roasting method employing small mud vessels was mentioned in a description from 1944. It was stressed that the method was no longer in use.[19] A few people in the area where the inter-

---

[16] Pillai, *Travancore State Manual*, Vol. III, pp. 527-528; Govt. of India, *Report on the Marketing of Cashew Nuts in India*, p. 10; Ohler, *Cashew*, pp. 201 ff.; Russell, *Cashew-nut Processing*, pp. 28 ff.; Chirayath, A *Study on the Cashew Industry in Kerala*, p. 7.

[17] Ohler, *Cashew*, p. 203; Chirayath, A *Study on the Cashew Industry in Kerala*, p. 7.

[18] Pillai, *Travancore State Manual*, Vol. III, p. 528.

[19] Govt. of India, *Report on the Marketing of Cashew Nuts in India*, p. 10.

views were conducted could remember these small earthen pots, which were mainly used in homes and for small-scale processing for market.[20]

The earliest shipments of cashew kernels sent abroad were neither peeled nor graded. The pioneer exporters used to buy the kernels from the local markets, dry, pack, and then ship them.[21] The exporter's role was that of a trading company, using the existing system of production. With the expansion of the export market in the 1920s and 1930s, these companies introduced a cottage industry system of production.[22] Their reason was probably the need for larger quantities and a continuous flow of the product. The raw nuts were distributed under a contract to cottagers, who returned the roasted and shelled nuts to the factory for further processing. In Mangalore, in British India, the contracted roasters were obliged to carry out their work in special areas far from the town, since the smoke was such a nuisance that town councils legislated against processing in populated areas.[23] These special sites for roasting and shelling were called "establishments", and in 1931 Peirce Leslie & Co. had seventeen such places in the vicinity of Mangalore.[24] Travancore, having more lenient legislation, differed from Mangalore because it allowed pan roasting in the factories in the densely populated areas. The resulting smoke was experienced as a general health problem by people living nearby. In letters to the authorities, they complained about the fumes and the generally unhealthy conditions (the lack of latrines, to give one example).[25] However, no legislation against the roasting of nuts was introduced until implementation of the Factory Act of 1948. No government permission had ever been required to set up cashew nut factories in Travancore.[26] Thus, it was not only labor laws that were weaker in the Princely State than in British India, but other regulations, as well.

In 1932, the open pan method was abandoned in Mangalore when at Peirce Leslie an engineer named Jefferies invented a new machine for roast-

---

[20] Interview 10 December 1997 with K. Bhanu, male former journalist, born 1913; Interview 19 December 1997 with K. Bhaskaran, born 1921, male former tinfiller at a cashew factory; Interview 15 December 1997 with Ponni, female sheller, born 1920.
[21] Langley, *Century in Malabar*, p. 56.
[22] Rammohan, "Material Processes and Developmentalism", p. 148; Langley, *Century in Malabar*, p. 56.
[23] Russell, *Cashew-nut Processing*, p. 30; Langley, *Century in Malabar*, p. 56.
[24] Langley, *Century in Malabar*, p. 56.
[25] KSA, Development files, Vol. IV, 344/2486, 1946, "Establishment of a Cashew Factory"; KSA, Development files, Vol. IV, 367/1607, 1946, "Complaint against a Cashewnut Factory"; KSA, Development files, Vol. IV, 362/1269, 1946, "Cashewnut Factory near Temple".
[26] KSA, Development files, Vol. IV, 362/1244, 1946, "Starting of Cashewnut Factory"; SRC, "Revision of the Wages for Employment in the Cashew Industry", Health and Labour Department 1960, G.O No. MS 282/60/H&L, Appendix III, p. xxiii.

ing—the drum roaster.[27] The drum roasting process rests on the same principle as the pan roasting method, but without the nuisance of the copious smoke, since fumes are lead up large chimneys into the atmosphere.[28] The first drum roaster required six persons to operate and consisted of a cylindrical iron drum manually rotated on an axle.[29] At one end, two men fed the slightly tilted drum with raw nuts, while another man rotated it from the other end. A fourth man attended a furnace in which cashew shells were used as fuel under the drum. One person then removed the roasted raw nuts, by tilting them out after a few minutes. The sixth man in the crew managed a water barrel that sprinkled water to cool down the roasted raw nuts.[30]

Management considered the old "establishments" beyond the town limits as a problem, since "supervision was limited to short visits to each contractor from time to time."[31] Pan roasting also presented a problem, in that the quality varied and a considerable number of kernels became scorched because they were kept in proximity with the heat for too long.[32]

Drum roasting was inaugurated in Travancore much later than in British India; in 1940 the open pan roasting method was still the most prevalent type.[33] The fact that the newer procedure was not introduced in Travancore, where the open pan method was conducted in centralized factories, suggests that the main reason for installing drum roasters was to control the work process, not to increase the output per worker. However, the economic incitement for introducing drum roasting may not have been totally absent: in 1944 it was asserted that there was a saving in wages to be had when roasters used the drum method.[34] In a publication on cashew processing printed in 1954, the open pan-roasting method was no longer mentioned,[35] and obviously the majority of the factories in Travancore had switched over, pan roasting having been banned in 1948.[36]

During the first few decades of the twentieth century, the roasting

---

[27] Langley, *Century in Malabar*, p. 56.
[28] Russell, *Cashew-nut Processing*, p. 30.
[29] Govt. of India, *Report on the Marketing of Cashew Nuts in India*, p. 10.
[30] Ibid. See also Govt. of India, *Census of India 1961*, Vol. VII, Kerala, Part VI E, Village Survey Monographs, Quilon District, p. 99; Chirayath, A *Study on the Cashew Industry in Kerala*, p. 8; Russell, *Cashew Nut Processing*, pp. 30 ff.
[31] Russell, *Cashew Nut Processing*, p. 30.
[32] Ibid., p. 30.
[33] Pillai, *Travancore State Manual*, Vol. III, pp. 527 ff.
[34] Govt. of India, *Report on the Marketing of Cashew Nuts in India*, p. 10.
[35] Govt. of India, *Report on an Enquiry into Conditions of Labour in the Cashewnut Processing Industry in India*, p. 5.
[36] KSA, CS files 1948, No. 16/147, "Travancore Factory Act 1948".

and shelling of cashew nuts went from a small-scale family enterprise, where the producers controlled everything—raw material, equipment and working time—to a cottage system where the processing was farmed out, and finally to a factory system in which the means of production were totally under capitalist control. In most cases, the same course in European countries required a considerably longer time span. This is not, however, to say that the roasters and shellers were a powerful group in the early days. They were much too poor and the profit was far too small for that. But with increasing demand for cashew kernels, the trade became so lucrative that the exporters wanted to control the entire process themselves. The Swedish historian, Per Nyström, has identified three main areas of control in connection with the shift from handicraft production to a capitalist manufacturing system: control over production (aiming at a homogeneous product); control over working efficiency, with the intention of achieving production without disturbances and interruptions; and, finally, control over property.[37] In the case of cashew production, the "property" was the precious raw nuts distributed to contractors in the cottage system. The risk that the roasters and shellers might spoil, or even steal, the raw nuts and thereby waste the capital of the exporters must have been conspicuous, and the invention of the drum roaster, followed by the centralization of production in factories, must have been welcomed by cashew exporters. In Travancore, where no restrictions against pan roasting were implemented prior to 1948, the introduction of drum roasting was delayed until the law put an end to the old method. Thus, it was possible for factory owners to exercise the desired control and centralize production without investing in new machinery.

The drum roaster was, and still is, a very simple machine and does not require electrical power, a fact pointed out by cashew manufacturers as being of great economic advantage.[38] In most factories, the same type of drum roaster was still in use in the late 1990s.[39]

---

[37] Per Nyström, *Stadsindustrins arbetare före 1800-talet* (Stockholm, 1955), pp. 18 ff.

[38] Interview 26 October 1997 with K. Gopinathan Nair, man born in the 1920s, cashew factory owner; Interview 13 March 1997 with Ravindranathan Nair, man born in the 1920s, cashew factory owner.

[39] Another method of roasting involving a more advanced machine was already introduced at Peirce Leslie & Co. in the second half of the 1930s. This method, called the oil bath process, safeguards the valuable cashew nut shell liquid (CNSL), but up 1992 only about 15% of the factories in India had installed this machinery. See R.C. Mandal, *Cashew Production and Processing Technology* (New Delhi, 1992), p. 148. The main field of application of CNSL is in brake linings of motor vehicles, but it has also a variety of possible use (for example, in paints and varnishes). Ohler, *Cashew*, p. 18; Chirayath, A *Study on the Cashew Industry in Kerala,* pp. 13 ff.

Shelling

The object of shelling is to produce a clean, whole kernel. Like roasting, which leaves the raw nuts black and coated with the sticky, corrosive oil, shelling has often been described as extremely dirty and unpleasant. Workers squat on the floor with a wooden mallet in one hand and a block of wood between their feet. Every raw nut is placed on the piece of wood, where it is held between the thumb and the middle finger, with the line of cleavage facing the sheller. Three or four deft strikes are delivered with the wooden mallet while the sheller rotates the nut with the aid of the index finger. The roasted nut ordinarily splits open along the line of cleavage and the kernel is extracted. To protect the palms from the corrosive cashew shell oil, workers continuously dust their hands with wood ash from a tin beside them. This is the method which has almost exclusively been in use in India since the very beginning of the production of cashew kernels, and was still in use in the late 1990s. Shelling is highly monotonous and stressful work.

Efforts have been made to speed up the shelling process. In the 1940s, General Foods invented a machine (a hand and foot driven semi-mechanized tool) called a *cracker*, but it was reported to be not very successful.[40] The cracker was tried in a few factories in Bombay and in one factory in Mangalore.[41] It consisted of two knives shaped like the contour of half a nut and placed opposite each other in a manner resembling a pair of scissors. The machine was operated by two people. One operated the knives with one foot and one hand, and cut the raw nut. The other person then picked it up and separated the shell from the kernel.[42] General Foods patented the machine, but the method was discontinued after some years.[43] There may have been several reasons for abandoning it. For one thing, the variety in size of the raw nuts rendered the process difficult. It could only be used for Indian nuts, as the imported raw nuts were too small. As India became more and more dependent on imported raw nuts, the machine lost its significance. In addition, it had not increased productivity, and the quantity of broken kernels far exceeded the number resulting from the manual method.[44]

---

[40] Govt. of India, *Report on the Marketing of Cashew Nuts in India*, p. 11.

[41] Ibid., p. 11; Govt. of India, *Report on an Enquiry into Conditions of Labour in the Cashewnut Processing Industry in India*, pp. 5, 12.

[42] See Ohler, *Cashew*, p. 206, for a description of a similar machine used in Brazil.

[43] The cracker has not appeared in the sources from 1954 to the late 1990s. See Govt. of Kerala, *Report of the Delegation Committee for the Revision of the Minimum Wages of Cashew Workers 1998*, Labour Department, Trivandrum 1998, p. 19. (Copy received from the chairman, P. Madhavan.)

[44] Interview 13 March 1997 with Ravindranathan Nair, man born in the 1920s, cashew factory owner; Wilson, *The Market for Cashew-nut Kernels*, p. 20.

It would have been possible to improve the machine so that varieties other than Indian nuts could be processed. In the 1960s, semi-mechanized shelling machines were used in such parts of the world as Brazil, Mozambique, and Tanzania.[45] More than thirty years later, semi-mechanized shelling machines were introduced in a few of the larger private factories in Kerala.

The process of using a semi-mechanized machine is called *cutting*. The newly introduced cutting tools are very similar to the old crackers of the 1940s. They are said to increase worker productivity, a strong argument in support of this method. There is also a fear that it will become more and more difficult to get labor for the manual shelling process because of the dirty and unpleasant nature of the work. However, the new method does require steam to soften the shell, whereas roasted raw nuts generate a much higher percentage of broken nuts. The main reason for the factory owners not investing in cutting machines and the ancillary equipment for steam processing has been said to be the fact that it is only profitable for large-scale, permanent factories, since it involves a considerable amount of capital investment.[46] In countries other than India, advanced, fully-mechanized shelling machines were introduced in the 1960s.[47] Thus, on the *world-market*, the shellers of India do compete with machines, as labor costs must be controlled whereever mechanized factories yield higher profits.

Drying

Before peeling the shelled kernels, it is necessary to dry them. This process reduces the moisture and shrinks the kernel so that the surrounding thin, brown skin can easily be removed. The earliest and most primitive way of drying the kernels was to sun-dry them. In Travancore, this method prevailed up to the 1940s, when ovens were introduced in almost every factory. In the first of Peirce Leslie's cashew factories in Mangalore, the flues of the factory boiler were used to dry the nuts by putting the nuts on racks inside the flue. (This factory had a boiler, since it also processed coffee.[48]) Very soon, an oven for drying the kernels became common. It was a simple steel chamber containing a rack on which ten to twenty trays with cashew

---

[45] Wilson, *The Market for Cashew-nut Kernels*, p. 20; Mandal, *Cashew Production and Processing Technology*, p. 149.

[46] Interview 26 October 1997 with K. Gopinathan Nair, man born in the 1920s, cashew factory owner; Interview 13 March 1997 with Ravindranathan Nair, man born in the 1920s, cashew factory owner.

[47] Russell, *Cashew-nut Processing*, pp. 46 ff.

[48] Langley, *Century in Malabar*, p. 56.

kernels could be spread out. Below the steel chamber was a fire that was fed with cashew nut shells. Workers had to move the trays from the bottom to the top every thirty minutes to avoid scorching the kernels while they dried for six to eight hours. These ovens in India are called *bormas*.[49] Usually only a few individuals in any given factory work this process, which has undergone marginal changes during the last fifty years. A few of the larger factories in Kerala use electric bormas to facilitate the control of temperature.[50]

Peeling

After being cooled, the kernels are peeled—a process which has always been conducted the same way everywhere in India. The thin brownish skin covering the kernel is manually removed with fingernails or with the help of a small knife.[51] The pre-graded kernels have to be further graded by size and color by peelers after they have removed the thin skin. These workers have several baskets at their work station. The number of different grades vary in different factories, the smaller factories having less.[52] The peeling operation has the same characteristics as the shelling process, viz., it is monotonous and stressful.

Grading

The final grading, like shelling and peeling, is a totally manual process. Early shipments of cashews were not graded, but very soon American firms, who were the main buyers, demanded that kernels be graded and checked for quality. They returned considerable amounts of cashew kernels when the quality was considered to be poor.[53] In the later part of the 1940s, a system of grading, the so-called "American standard of quality",

---

[49] Mandal, *Cashew Production and Processing Technology*, p. 150; Russell, *Cashew-nut Processing*, pp. 51 ff.; Ohler, *Cashew*, pp. 207 ff.; Chirayath, A *Study on the Cashew Industry in Kerala*, p. 9.

[50] Interview 26 October 1997 with K. Gopinathan Nair, man born in the 1920s, cashew factory owner; Interview 13 March 1997 with Ravindranathan Nair, man born in the 1920s, cashew factory owner.

[51] The kernels to be peeled are of varying quality and can be divided into three main categories: whole kernels, pieces, and so-called *kattals*. Kattals literally means "unpeelable" and consist of scorched and damaged pieces of kernels which are very difficult to peel.

[52] According to interviews with managers and workers, the number has varied between six and eight grades. Govt. of Kerala, *Report of the Minimum Wages Advisory Committee for Cashew Industry 1959* (Trivandrum, 1959), p. 18; Interview with Bharathiamma, Nair woman, born 1912, peeler 1925-1975.

[53] Govt. of Travancore, *Travancore Information and Listener*, 4:12 (1944), p. 7.

was adopted by most of the exporters.[54] It was further strengthened in 1963 when the Government of India implemented compulsory quality control on all exported kernels.[55] The evaluation system recognizes six main grades and twenty-four subcategories based on size and color. Each worker is only responsible for one or two main groups, since the pre-graded kernels normally have to be separated into four to eight different kinds. The workers have to train their eyes to estimate size quickly to sort the nuts with considerable speed. The process of grading cashew kernels has remained the same since the introduction of the new grading system in the 1940s.[56]

Packing

Cashews were originally exported in mango-wood cases, but very soon more uniform, better-protected kernels came to foreign markets.[57] The problem of infestation by weevils was serious and several methods of improving the packing were tried.[58] One satisfactory system was to pack the kernels in vacuum-sealed tins of 25 lbs (11.34 kg) each, which kept the kernels sound for about a year.[59] In the 1920s the General Foods Corporation invented a new method of packing, the so-called *Vitapack-method*. This involved removing the air in the tin and substituting carbon dioxide gas by means of an electrically operated machine. A lid placed on the bung-hole of the tin was manually sealed with solder. The method was patented by General Foods and only their contractors in Travancore and Mangalore were allowed to use it.[60] The method was highly coveted by others, who had to pay a royalty of 5% of the gross value of goods exported in carbon dioxide to the United States. Some exporters tried to evade the royalty by using a small hand-driven machine to inject the gas. In 1932 firms using the latter method were prosecuted.[61] Only after expiration of the patent in 1950 was the method adopted by a majority of the factories.[62] Many

[54] Interview with Kousalya, Nair woman, grader 1940-1990, born 1928; Interview 13 March 1997 with Ravindranathan Nair, man born in the 1920s, cashew factory owner.
[55] "Indian Cashews", Leaflet from Cashew Export Promotion Council, Cochin.
[56] Interview 13 March 1997 with Ravindranathan Nair, man born in the 1920s, cashew factory owner.
[57] Langley, *Century in Malabar*, p. 55.
[58] Pillai, *Travancore State Manual*, Vol. III, pp. 529; Langley, *Century in Malabar*, pp. 55 ff.
[59] Ohler, *Cashew*, p. 213.
[60] Pillai, *Travancore State Manual*, Vol. III, p. 529; Langley, *Century in Malabar* p. 55.
[61] Pillai, *Travancore State Manual*, Vol. III, p. 529; Rammohan, "Material Processes and Developmentalism", p. 154.
[62] Langley, *Century in Malabar*, p. 59; Interview 13 March 1997 with Ravindranathan Nair, man born in the 1920s, cashew factory owner.

processors send their kernels to special packing centers. The same type of tins are still used for export, and only after 1990 have some of the larger factories started to pack cashew kernels in consumer packages.[63] Tins continue to be filled by hand or by machine.

The work process—a summary

The work process has not changed very much during the period under consideration. It is worth noting that only very small technological improvements have occurred since the industry's inception. It is still, by and large, a manual, labor intensive process. The main innovation in the field was the drum roaster, invented in 1932 and introduced into most factories during the 1940s. Two of the work tasks, shelling and roasting, are especially hazardous and unpleasant due to the corrosive nature of cashew shell oil. It has not been possible to find quantitative information on the distribution of workers in different processing operations for the period prior to 1952. The fact that processing of cashew nuts has remained essentially unchanged suggests a similar pattern during the early decades of the industry, a fact which has been corroborated by interviews with factory owners and trade union leaders active in the 1940s.[64] In 1952 a survey of forty-two cashew factories showed that more than 94% of all workers were engaged in shelling, peeling, or grading[65], a phenomenon which was substantiated in the following two decades. The results in table 4.1 are drawn from studies of thirty factories in 1965 and seventeen factories in 1977.

---

[63] Interview 11 August 1998 with P. Rajeendran, chairman, Kerala State Cashew Development Corporation; Peirce Leslie India, Calicut, "Random Thoughts from a Century and a Half in Malabar of a British Firm". In the 1980s consumer packing was practiced on a small scale at Peirce Leslie India, but in the mid-1990s the company decided to extend the export of consumer packing. See Peirce Leslie India, Calicut, various Annual Reports, 1980-1995.

[64] Interview 13 March 1997 with Ravindranathan Nair, man born in the 1920s, cashew factory owner; Interview 14 September 1999 with K. Chellappan, male trade union leader in Kilikolloor, born 1914.

[65] Govt. of India, *Report on an Enquiry into the Conditions of Labour in the Cashewnut Processing Industry in India*, p. 9.

Table 4.1. Distribution of workers by category in Kerala cashew factories, 1965 and 1977

Category	1965	1977
Shellers	42%	42%
Peelers	46%	42%
Graders	8%	10%
Roasters, Borma-workers, packers, etc.	4%	6%
Total	100%	100%
Total number of workers:*	12,030	6,715

Sources: Chirayath, A *Study on the Cashew Industry in Kerala*, p. 36 (for 1965); Kannan, "Employment, Wages and Conditions of Work in the Cashew Processing Industry", p. 7 (for 1977).

* Estimated by multiplying the average number of workers per factory as reported in 1965 and 1977 with the number of factories in the sample.

All the factories visited during the period 1997 to 2000 had a pattern in almost total accord with the above, and thus seem to have been relatively constant in their distribution of workers over the last five decades.[66] It is apparent that the two most labor intensive processes are shelling and peeling, with grading third.

Masculinity and Femininity in the Cashew Factories

Work for able-bodied men?

Having obtained a background knowledge of the period from various printed sources (most of them dating beyond the 1940s), I began to explore the gender composition of the cashew factories from a historical perspective. My initial method was to interview employers, civil servants, and trade union leaders who were currently engaged in the cashew business. All of them were men with rather high status in Indian society. Most of them firmly stated that no more than 5% of all those employed in the cashew industry were ever men, and that shelling, peeling, and grading were operations that had always been done by women. I was confused since the printed sources which I had consulted on the early cashew factories presented a picture at variance with their statements. The table below shows that more than one-fourth of the work force in the latter half of the 1930s was male.

[66] The information was given by the management in each factory. The factories visited are listed in the Appendix.

Table 4.2. Composition of workers in Travancore cashew factories, 1936–1939

Year	Males	Females	Factories surveyed
1936–37	27%	73%	32
1937–38	26%	74%	39
1938–39	27%	73%	41

Sources: Govt. of Travancore, *Statistics of Travancore*, 18th issue, 1112 ME/1936-1937 AD, pp. 147 ff.; *Statistics of Travancore*, 19th issue 1113 ME/1937-1938 AD, pp. 160 ff.; *Statistics of Travancore*, 20th issue, 1114 ME/1938-39 AD, pp. 151 ff.

In our conversations, I referred to the statistics above, insisting that a substantial number of men clearly had been involved in the cashew production in the early factories. Not all of them, I pointed out, could have been roasters or borma-men, unless the work process had changed dramatically since then—something of which I could find no indication. I remarked that it rather appeared as if men had been involved in tasks which today are exclusively performed by women. The answers I received, a few of which are cited below, illustrate a gender discourse patently linked to the specific work task and to characteristics attributed to the workers. I heard remarks like:

> No, no, there have never been any men in the shelling, peeling, or grading section. They do not have the patience—they are absolutely unfit for such a job. It must be wrong data you have. Men have only been engaged in roasting, drying, and head-loading.[67] No woman ever worked these tasks, because it is heavy work.
>
> —A.P. Udayabhanu, chairman of the Minimum Wage Committee for Cashew Workers in 1953[68]

A union official expressed himself this way:

> No, there has never been any men in those sections—only some very young boys who came there with their mothers. That must be the reason for the statistics you found. Nowadays we have no child labor any more, so those boys have disappeared. The roasters have always been men and they still are—it is dangerous work. Women do the shelling, peeling and grading—work which demands patience and nimble fingers. Men can't do that.
>
> —R.S. Unni, trade union leader and politician, active since the 1950s[69]

---

[67] A head-loader normally conducts all kind of work which involve carrying of sacks and tins.
[68] Interview 29 August 1998.
[69] Interview 13 August 1998.

Another, younger trade union activist told me thus:

> Perhaps there were some men in the shelling sections, but if so, they were very old, sick, or handicapped. Some young boys also worked there in the old days, but no men have worked there ever since. Men have always done the heavy, hot, and unpleasant work, like roasting and drying.
> —P. Prakasan, trade union leader, active since the 1960s[70]

A relatively young factory director concurred, insisting:

> No, men never worked with tasks like shelling, peeling, or grading. Maybe a few, but it would have been very rare. Maybe if they were sick or disabled in one way or another. No able-bodied men have ever been there. They have always been roasters, borma-men, tin-fillers, and head-load workers—heavy work tasks which are not suitable for women.
> —K.P. Ramachandran Nair, managing director, born in the 1950s[71]

The voices above all belong to men who entered the scene after 1950, so they did not actually witness the period I asked them about. Their remarks must be taken as a reflection of the practice at the time when they entered the field. Perhaps even more so they mirror dominating ideas of gender and work. These ideas are also apparent in various historical accounts of the cashew factories written by trade union leaders.[72] The suggestion of the trade union leader, R.S. Unni, that many boys joined their mothers in factory work, appears to explain the figures to some extent. However, as we shall see, it cannot fully explain the substantial numbers of male workers.

The authors of the first report on minimum wages in the cashew factories stated in 1953 that "the small percentage of men employed in the industry do the hard jobs like bag carrying, roasting, etc."[73] Almost exactly the same words can be found in later government reports, as well as in academic writing.[74] What actually constitutes a hard job has not been defined, and the correlation between male and "hard" has been taken for granted. As shown in Table 4.3, the proportion of male cashew workers has stabilized around a few percent since the 1960s.

---

[70] Interview 12 March 1997.
[71] Interview 14 March 1997.
[72] See, for example, T.M. Majeed, *The Strike History of the Cashew-nut Workers* (Kollam, 2000), p. 75 (in Malayalam).
[73] Govt. of Travancore-Cochin, *Report of the Minimum Wages Committee for Cashew Industry 1953*, p. 11.
[74] Govt. of Kerala, *Cashew Industry in Kerala*, p. 31; Kannan, "Employment, Wages and Conditions of Work in the Cashew Processing Industry", p. 7.

Table 4.3. Composition of workers in Kerala cashew factories, 1952-1994

	Males	Females	Children
	%	%	%
1952	14	73	13
1964	7	93	
1969	5	95	
1978-79	6	94	
1983-84	5	95	
1989-90	6	94	
1993-94	3	97	

Sources: Govt. of India, *Report on an Enquiry into Conditions of Labour in the Cashew-nut Processing Industry in India*, p. 14; Govt. of India, *Annual Survey of Industries (ASI)* 1964, Vol. II, p. 131; *ASI* 1969, Census sector, Vol. II, p. 179; *ASI* 1978-79, Factory sector, Vol. II, p. 256; *ASI* 1983-84, Factory sector, Vol. II, p. 130; *ASI* 1989-90, Factory sector, Vol. III, p. 191; *ASI* 1993-94, Factory sector, Vol. III, p. 181.

The figures for 1952 are based on a survey of seventeen factories in Travancore. They illustrate that some adult men must have been working in shelling, peeling, or grading, since the same inquiry found that 94% of the workers belonged to these sections, but only 86% of the work force were women and children.[75]

In printed sources from 1953 and beyond describing the cashew processing, it is presupposed that roasting has always been a man's job, whereas shelling, peeling, and grading were tasks suited for women and children. This view has been expressed in official government reports, articles, pamphlets, and books coming from politicians, academics, and trade union leaders who have written descriptive accounts of the processing.[76] Specifically, these documents give no indication that women had

---

[75] Govt. of India, *Report on an Enquiry into Conditions of Labour in the Cashewnut Processing Industry in India*, pp. 9, 14.

[76] Govt. of Travancore.Cochin, *Report of the Minimum Wages Committee for Cashew Industry 1953*; Govt. of India, *Report on an Enquiry into Conditions of Labour in the Cashewnut Processing Industry in India*; Govt. of Kerala, *Report of the Minimum Wages Advisory Committee for Cashew Industry 1959*; Chirayath, *A Study on the Cashew Industry in Kerala*; N. Sreekantan Nair, *Memories of the Past, II* (Kottayam, 1976), chapter 44, (in Malayalam); Govindan, *Memoires of an Early Trade Unionist*; Pillai, "The Economic Impact"; M.N. Govindan Nair, *Autobiography of M.N., Part II* (Trivandrum, 1988) (in Malayalam); G.L. Deepa, "Industrial Crisis and Women Workers, A Study of Cashew Processing Industry in Kerala" (M.Phil., Centre for Development Studies, Trivandrum, 1994); Kesavan Nair, "The Strike History of the Cashew Workers, part 1-29", *CITU Sandesam*, Vol. 17-19, 1993-1996 (in Malayalam); Majeed, *The Strike History of the Cashew-nut Workers*. Kannan's study is one exception in that he briefly mentions that 15% to 20% of the workers were male in the beginning. See Kannan, *Evolution of Unionisation and Changes*, p. 7 (However, his own reference, viz. official statistics, shows 14%-27%).

ever been involved in roasting. Nevertheless, a photo in a publication from 1969 puzzled me, as it showed a woman and a man working together, roasting cashew nuts. The author did not comment on this, but only noted that the method they used was no longer practiced.[77] In a report printed in 1944, I found another description of the cashew roasting process. Three methods of roasting were described: pan roasting, rotary cylinders (drum roasting), and oil bath roasting. Regarding the oldest method, pan roasting, it was asserted that "generally one man and one woman work at each oven".[78] A method using earthen vessels was also mentioned, followed by the statement that *this method was used only by women.*[79]

Several old people gave me a description which served to clarify some of my confusion. One of the retired shellers I met in Kilikolloor recounted her childhood in the 1940s:

When I was a child, we processed the cashew nuts on the roadside or in the backyards here in Kilikolloor. It was done on a commission basis. The workers got the raw nuts in sacks from the exporters. They made a furnace with mud and then they roasted the nuts in a shallow open iron pan, stirring the nuts all the time. It was hot, smoky, and dangerous work. When after some minutes the nuts were ready, the roasters tilted the pan and spilled them on the ground. Water was poured over the nuts to cool them, and then they were covered with ash and scrubbed to absorb their oil. I was a ten-year-old child when I started to work and I could not do the roasting, so I shelled. But many women roasted the nuts. They were dressed in long-sleeved dresses to protect themselves from the splashing, burning, and corrosive oil, and their hands were wrapped in sacks. I think that about half of the roasters on this street were women. At that time, women did all kinds of work. Sometimes a man and a woman worked together, sometimes only men or only women handled the roasting. The shelling was done by women and men, girls and boys. Some roasters had to employ shellers to be able to finish the work in time, but in many cases it was a family who worked together. After the prohibition of the pan method, it continued to be done at night to escape the eyes of the civil servants. Today nobody knows how to roast that way. But in the early factories the method was used, and both women and men did their work that way, although most of them were men. When the machines came, women were no longer employed

---

[77] Russell, *Cashew-nut Processing*, p. 29.
[78] Govt. of India, *Report on the Marketing of Cashew Nuts in India*, p. 10.
[79] Ibid., p. 10.

as roasters and nobody questioned it. Women themselves did not want to be considered as carrying out men's job.

— Gomathi, woman of Ezhava caste, sheller, born 1930[80]

In 1962, a reporter from the daily newspaper *Jennajugham* in Quilon interviewed three female cashew workers. Two of them had been roasters in the 1920s, 1930s, and 1940s, but had switched over to other processing operations after some time. One of them, Kalyani, explained that she had been working with cashews for the last forty-five years, that is, since 1917. In the beginning, she was a roaster and worked in three different factories. One of them was the Swaminathan factory, where Kavitha also worked. Whether she worked as a self-employed roaster prior to her factory years is unclear, although it seems likely that she did, since factories probably did not exist as early as 1917. As a roaster, Kalyani performed all kinds of tasks related to roasting, including carrying the sacks with raw nuts. "I can still feel what it was like to carry those sacks", she remembered in 1962. Quite astonishingly, Kalyani informed the newspaper reporter that, when she was a roaster, she had employed several shellers. Kalyani searched for shellers in the countryside and brought them to her property, where twenty-five huts were built for the shellers to live in. In the article there is no mention of any husband, and Kalyani described the land as her own. One cannot be sure, but the article gives the impression that she alone had been responsible for the bringing up of her children and that her work as a roaster demanded a great deal of enterprising spirit. When asked what advantages forty-five years of work with cashews had given her, she replied, "I managed to bring up my seven children and feed them. What else might I expect?" She said she stopped working as a roaster because children—especially the factory owner's children—started to abuse her, shouting "*Edi, Podi*" after her. [81] This was in 1949 and Kalyani managed to find another job, still in a cashew factory. Most probably she was one of the last female roasters. Since then she worked as an *ayah*—an occupation for a woman more in accordance with the dominating gender discourse. [82]

The supervisors from Peirce Leslie have characterized the sites where roasting was going on by the pan method as "something resembling a stage setting for Dante's Inferno."[83] The horror of those working conditions

---

[80] Interview 30 August 1998. Others, too, remembered female roasters. Interview 14 September 1999 with K. Chellappan, male trade union leader, born 1914; Interview 19 December 1997 with K. Bhanu, journalist, born 1913.

[81] "Edi Podi" is a very disrespectful way to ask a person to leave in Malayalam.

[82] Thengamam Balakrishnan, "Life and Strikes in the Middle of Smoke and Coal Dust", *Jennajugham*, 2 August 1962, pp. 2,3 (in Malayalam).

[83] Langley, *Century in Malabar*, p. 56.

comes out in the stories told about this work, in government reports with a historic perspective, and in booklets and articles published by the trade unions.[84] Remarkably, the fact that women were also doing this work has been omitted from the stories. This is not to say that roasting had been a female-dominated task, although the early mud pan method, as asserted by the author of the report from 1944, may have been. Rather, it is likely that the gender composition of the factories varied considerable in the different regions, so that we may find places where female roasters never existed. Still, the stories referred to above indicate that a considerable percentage of the early roasters in some factories, and perhaps even more so in the cottage processing, were incontrovertibly women—a fact which has largely been consigned to oblivion. It is ironic that when the drum roasting method was introduced and working conditions became a little better, those women roasters who still remained were transferred to the shelling section or, as in the case of Kalyani, to other work considered more suitable for women, i.e., taking care of the children in the factory crèche.[85]

It would be logical to assume, as Marx did, that employers, in order to minimize labor costs, would seek to substitute men for women to greatest degree possible. However, this did not happen with roasters, even though women were obviously able to carry out this factory operation. Instead, women ceased to be engaged in this task. Several potential legal reasons for this emerged simultaneously. In 1946, the cashew factories were declared to be covered by the Factory Act, which stipulated that women were not allowed to work from 6 p.m. to 8 a.m.[86] Two years later, pan roasting was banned and, as we have seen, was followed by a change to a new technology—the drum roasters. In 1957 the Kerala Government, after pressure from the trade unions, declared roasting and shelling to be "hazardous occupations", basing this decision on a finding that cashew shell oil had a negative effect on workers' health. These processes thus became the focus of

---

[84] Govt. of Travancore-Cochin, *Report of the Minimum Wages Committee for Cashew Industry 1953*; Govt. of India, *Report on an Enquiry into Conditions of Labour in the Cashewnut Processing Industry in India*; Govt. of Kerala, *Report of the Minimum Wages Advisory Committee for Cashew Industry 1959*; Chirayath, *A Study on the Cashew Industry in Kerala*; Sreekantan Nair, *Memories of the Past, II*, chapter 44; Govindan, *Memoires of an Early Trade Unionist*; Pillai, "The Economic Impact"; Govindan, *Autobiography of M.N.*; Nair, "The Strike History of the Cashew Workers, part 1-29"; Majeed, *The Strike History of the Cashew-nut Workers*.

[85] Swedish historians have given several examples of masculinization of work tasks, which at the same time there was an improvement of working conditions. "There was no wish to spare women from heavy or unpleasant work tasks" is the conclusion drawn by the economic historians, Lynn Karlsson and Ulla Wikander. See *Kvinnoarbete och könssegregering i svensk industri 1870-1950*, p. 15 [my translation].

[86] KSA, Development Files 1945 No. 341/2093, "Exemption of the Cashew Factories from the Operation of Factory Act", p. 13.

specific restrictions.[87] A remarkable outcome of this legislation was that women and adolescents were banned from carrying out roasting, but not shelling.[88]

The prohibition on women working at night probably did not have an immediate impact on the cashew factories. According to an official inquiry in 1953, most labor laws were flagrantly violated in the majority of the cashew factories in Quilon[89], so it is doubtful this particular law should have been an exception. Moreover, the practice of roasting early in the morning was increasingly abandoned after 1950.[90] The number of roasters in the cashew factories was small, and if any women were dismissed from roasting, it cannot have been a substantial number. They probably could all have switched over to the shelling section or to other work tasks, as Kalyani and her friend did. The issue probably was not of great importance at the time. Discussions of the elimination of women from certain factory operations in India have suggested two different kinds of explanations: introduction of gender specific protective legislation, and such changes in the work process as the introduction of machines.[91] The veteran sheller and trade union convener, Gomathi, was of the opinion that women ceased working as roasters because machines were introduced, a view also held by the trade union leader, K. Chellappan, who confirmed my finding about female roasters in the early days. The *rationale* for withdrawing women from roasting was that women were incapable of handling the machines. The issue was not disputed because the link between machines and men was regarded as self-evident.[92] Kalyani was not forced to leave her job as a roaster in 1949, but the cultural gender codes which also encompassed the factory owner (just as his children had abused Kalyani for not being feminine) made

---

[87] Interview 14 September 1999 with K. Chellappan, male trade union leader in Kilikolloor, born 1914; See also Govt. of Kerala, *The Kerala Factories Rules 1957* (Ernakulam, 1989), pp. 177-178.

[88] Ibid., p. 177.

[89] Govt. of India, *Report on an Enquiry into Conditions of Labour in the Cashewnut Processing Industry in India*, pp. 19-20, 31.

[90] Ibid., p. 19.

[91] For example, Morris D. Morris held the view that the decline of women in the Bombay cotton textile industry was a result of legislation, viz, the passage of the Maternity Benefit Act and the Prohibition of Night Work Act. Morris D. Morris, *The Emergence of an Industrial Labour Force in India: A Study of the Bombay Cotton Mills, 1854-1957* (Bombay, 1965). This view has been contested by Radha Kumar, who rather stressed the change of production technology as a plausible explanation for the exclusion of women in certain jobs, but she also maintained that the process was a result of attempts to reform the working class family and include a male breadwinner. Kumar, "Family and Factory: Women in the Bombay Cotton Textile Industry, 1919–1939", *passim*.

[92] Interview 15 December 1997 with Ponni, sheller, born 1920; Interview 18 January 1998 with Gomathi, sheller, born 1930; Interview 14 September 1999 with K. Chellappan, male trade union leader in Kilikolloor, born 1914.

her voluntarily choose to change work tasks. She did not mention the introduction of machines, and it would appear that an ideology of gender segregation in the workplace acted as strongly as the mechanization per se.

The male dominated trade unions pleaded for legislation against female roasters, and this may have had a twofold aim. There probably was a sincere wish to protect women from heavy, dirty, and dangerous operations.[93] Another likely aim, however, was a preventive measure intended to secure job opportunities for male workers. Specifically, roasting was a job which yielded higher wages than other work tasks in the cashew factories.[94] The ban on female roasters in 1957 was introduced a bit late to be the reason for their disappearance in the plants. In the first report on minimum wages (1953), the possibility of a female roaster was not even considered.[95] None of my informants could remember the existence of female roasters as late as 1957. Cultural perceptions of gender had probably strongly influenced factory life already. Employers did not try to hire female roasters in order to keep wages low, and obviously they, too, were surrounded by the more rigid gender ideology. It was also in their interest to stress gender differences to legitimize having only women carry out shelling.

Radha Kumar has argued that the introduction of gender specific protective legislation and the dismissal of women as a result of mechanization in India in the 1930s should be seen as symptomatic of another phenomenon, viz., a reforming of the working class family into a unit centered on a male breadwinner.[96] Such a view explains the decline of female work participation, but only partly clarifies the reason for constructing workplaces

---

[93] The need for gender specific protective legislation was less disputed in India than in many countries in the West. In Western countries an organization named Open Door International was formed in the late 1920s. One of its main programs was to oppose all specific protective legislation for women, on the ground that it discriminated against them on the labor market. See Anna Lindberg, "Class-collaboration and Gender Struggle" (paper presented at Department of History, Lund 1996). Women's India Organization (WIO), founded by Annie Besant in 1917, held a view in line with the Open Door International and in 1931 the representatives of WIO demanded the deletion of a resolution delivered by the Indian National Congress in which protective laws for women were included; but their position was not sympathetically received. See Janaki Nair, *Women and Law in Colonial India: A Social History* (New Delhi, 1996), pp. 116-118. The standpoint of WIO was probably not widespread among other women's organizations. For example, the organization, All India Women's Conference, founded in 1926, had gender specific labor protective laws on its program. See Radha Kumar, *The History of Doing* (New Delhi, 1993), pp. 68.

[94] This will be further elaborated in Chapter VI.

[95] Govt. of Travancore-Cochin, *Report of Minimum Wages Committee for Cashew Industry 1953*, p. 10.

[96] Kumar, "Family and Factory: Women in the Bombay Cotton Textile Industry, 1919-1939".

with predominantly full-time women employees, and the resultant increasingly stricter gender division of labor. An old woman, Ponni, told me that the recruiter from the cashew factory who came to her village, first and foremost, wanted women workers.[97] It seems as if men served as a reserve labor force when women could not be hired in sufficient numbers. The few other machines which were introduced into the cashew factories, such as the Vita-packs and the electric bormas, seem never to have been run by women. Women in the packing sections have always filled tins manually, whereas men handle the Vita-pack machines used to seal the tins. However, the newly-introduced cutting tools which have supplanted the manual shelling operations are regarded as the province of women. This work process is still very labor intensive, and the possibility that men might be employed to do this task has never been considered.

Patient women with nimble fingers?

Three of the main work processes—shelling, peeling, and grading—are, in present-day Kerala, unconditionally defined as female occupations. As previously noted, the consensus among civil servants, trade unionists, and factory owners is that shelling, peeling, and grading can only be carried out by women. Their view may stem from a "biological" assumption about the nature of women, namely, that they embody patience and manual dexterity. Women workers have been defined as the antithesis to able-bodied, machine-oriented male workers, and often they have been merged into a single group: "women and children". The classification of women and children into one category further stresses the status of women as "non-workers". In the 1940s, cashew factory owners repeatedly stressed how well-suited women and children were for cashew processing. The fact that no machinery was employed was given as a strong argument for the feminine nature of the work. Cashew factory owners have always attributed certain characteristics to women (i.e., deftness, nimble fingers, and patience) to justify the fact that the majority of these workers were women. Physical strength and aptitude for machines have been defined as male characteristics, as has the capability of conducting dangerous, responsible, or difficult factory operations. In 1945, the representative of the cashew employers in Quilon wrote:

> There is no machinery employed at any stage of the cashew nut manufacturing process and as such none of the labour employed has at any time to remain in constant attention on any machinery....There is no item of work

---

[97] Interview 15 December 1997 with Ponni, female sheller, born around 1920.

in the manufacture of cashew nuts which involves any appreciable bodily exertion....What is actually required in the various stages of manufacture such as shelling, peeling and selection is only deftness of fingers. It is thus clear that work in the cashew nut factory has no harmful effect whatever on the health of even children.[98]

In most sources the argument regarding the employment of children disappeared in Kerala after the 1940s, but the same argument has recently been used in Tamil Nadu. A civil servant exposed child labor in one factory in the 1960s and, according to the report which followed the inspection, the factory owner defended this violation of the labor law as follows:

The reason given by the management for the employment of children, who were all females, was the same as in the case of women labour, viz., they were found to be efficient in the work of shelling and peeling of cashewnuts which requires finger dexterity.[99]

Since the 1960s, we find no defense of child labor in the cashew factories in Kerala, but the suitability of women for monotonous, manual work has been repeated with impunity by employers.

The predominant employment of women in the industry is, according to the employers, due to the repetitive nature of the job which requires a lot of patience and speed which are special qualities of women workers.[100]

The view that women are suitable for the work in cashew factories because of their dexterity has become so firmly rooted in the society that even academics researching the cashew factories have taken it for granted.[101] During my visits to different cashew factories and to the housing areas where cashew workers live, I came across a few men who were still actively engaged in shelling, and several old men who were former shellers. In agreement with Gomathi's story earlier, several other informants held the view that a long time ago (i.e., about 1925-1945), shelling was done in many

---

[98] KSA, Development files No. 341/2093, p. 3, "Exemption of the Cashew Factories from the Operation of Factory Act", Letter from Cashewnut Manufacturer's Association to the dewan of Travancore, dated 6th February 1945.
[99] Govt. of India, *Report on Survey of Labour Conditions in Cashewnut Factories in India 1965-66*, Labour bureau (Simla, 1969), p. 8.
[100] Govt. of India, *Report on the Working and Living Conditions of Workers in the Cashewnut Processing Industry in Kerala 1982*, Labour bureau (Chandigarh, 1983), p. 2.
[101] Pillai, "The Economic Impact", p. 286.

poor families by *men, women, and children.*[102] It was not gender-typed in
the rigid way it came to be later. In some of the early factories, males continued to do the work they knew best—shelling. The proportion of male
shellers varied from factory to factory. When we study the statistics available from the 1930s, the picture is varied. Some factories had hardly any
male workers at all, whereas others had a large number. Among forty factories during 1937-1938, there is a weak correlation between the proportion
of men and the proportion of children and adolescents, suggesting that
some workers classified as males were in reality boys, as the trade union
leader, R.S. Unni, had stated. However, this correlation was not absolute,
and we find many cases where the number of adult men must have been
considerable—in some cases above 40% of the total workforce.[103] By way
of example, in the Vadakkevila region, males amounted to between 25%
and 40% of the cashew workers in the seven factories from which information is available. The average proportion of males in these was 37%, a statis-
tic which cannot be explained in terms of male workers being children,
since only 8% of those employed in these factories were children or adolescents.[104]

In addition to the factory owner quoted earlier, accounts given by older
people living near the factories, by workers, and by trade union leaders
provided evidence that in certain factories many adult men actually had
been employed as shellers, and some as peelers, during the early epoch of
cashew processing. This would confirm the data in Table 4.2 that one of
my informants had dismissed as unreliable. The majority of those interviewed estimated the proportion of male shellers to total shellers to be
about 25%, but estimates have ranged from 5% to 50%. According to
A.D. Bolland, former managing director of Peirce Leslie at Kundara, about
half of the workers in the shelling section were adult men in the mid-
1940s.[105] The relatively large proportion of male shellers was also confirmed by a male worker in the same factory:

> I started to work as a sheller in 1939 in a small cashew factory. I was 16 years
> old and I came with my parents. I had learned how to shell at home, since
> my parents used to conduct the work on a commission basis. A lot of men

---

[102] Interview 23 August 1998 with Kavitha, female sheller, born around 1920; Interview
18 January 1998 with Velu, male sheller, born 1923; Interview 11 March 1997 with
Chirutha, female sheller, born 1919; Interview 14 September 1999 with K. Chellappan,
male trade union leader in Kilikolloor, born 1914.
[103] Govt. of Travancore, *Statistics of Travancore*, 19th issue, 1113 ME/1937-1938 AD, pp. 160 ff.
[104] Ibid., p. 167.
[105] Interview 12 June 1998 with A.D. Bolland, manager at Peirce Leslie cashewnut factory
in Kundara in the mid-1940s.
[106] Interview 18 January 1998.

worked in the shelling section in that factory. In 1945, when I was 22 years old, I started to work at the Peirce Leslie cashew factory in Kundara. I think that about one-fourth of the shellers were men—maybe more. In the grading and peeling section there were only a few adult men—twelve or thirteen as far as I can remember. I worked in this factory for a couple of years and then at the KMK cashew factory. I stopped working in 1983. When the KMK factory closed down for periods of time, I could never get job in the other cashew factories, as my wife and other women could. The watchmen wouldn't even open the gate for me and the other men. We were accused of starting unions. During these periods, my wife and daughters were the only earners in our family. There was never any problem of men and women cooperating inside the factory, but people outside used to scold us. Shellers and roasters were chided for being dirty, and later on male shellers were rebuked for doing women's work.

—Velu, man of Kurava caste, former sheller, born 1923[106]

Another man, who still was active as a sheller when I met him in 1997, expressed himself similarly:

For the last forty years I have been working in this factory as a sheller. Both my parents were shellers. There used to be more men in this section. According to my parents, about half the shellers were men a long time ago. In the early 1960s maybe twenty-five out of a hundred were men, but then the factory was closed for some years, and when it reopened only very few men were employed. During the years when the factory was closed, I could not get a job as a sheller in any other cashew factory, although my wife could. It was impossible for male shellers to get a job. The factory owners did not even let us inside the gate. The same thing happened everywhere. When my factory opened again, only four male shellers were reemployed. I have nothing against working with all the women. Inside the factory there is no problem. I would prefer another job—this one is not well paid—but I have no choice.

—Kuttan, man of Kurava caste, sheller, born 1938[107]

As shown in Table 4.3, the proportion of male workers to the total workforce stabilized between 3% and 6% after the 1960s, and obviously male shellers ceased to be present in the factories. Two brothers, both born in the 1920s and both the owners of several cashew factories which they inherited from their father (one of the pioneers in Quilon) give different explanations of why male shellers have hardly been seen since the 1950s.

---

[107] Interview 21 November 1997.

Formerly, men worked with shelling and, to some extent, with peeling as well. In my father's time, maybe 15% to 25% of the shellers and peelers were men. I think there were more men in the shelling section. These men disappeared around 1960. People were not keen to employ them because they were trouble makers: they organized the workers. The men could do the work as well as the women—maybe even better. But women are more patient. It is in their nature and that is why they are more suitable for this kind of work.

—Ravindranathan Nair, cashew factory owner[108]

Curiously, the first brother, Ravindranathan Nair, quoted above, a man with more than sixty years of experience in the field, contradicted himself to some extent when he spoke about work and gender and asserted that *men worked as well as women, but that women were more suitable by nature.*

The other brother held a slightly different view with regard to the disappearance of men from the cashew factories.

Yes, in the beginning there were men in all sections—maybe not in grading, but in shelling there was a considerable proportion of adult men. Fewer were in the peeling section and these were mainly young boys. The men did not like the job. They are not patient and lack the finger dexterity. They worked because they were poor, but quit as soon as they could. I think they disappeared in the mid-1950s, maybe the end of the 50s.

—K. Gopinathan Nair, cashew factory owner[109]

His view implies that with economic development men could withdraw from the lowest paid jobs like shelling. Velu, Kuttan, and several other men were prepared to continue with their work, but from around 1950 onward they seemed to have been barred from participation in shelling by the factory owners. Several other workers have testified to the difficulty of men finding employment as shellers after the 1950s.[110] Factories closed, and when they reopened they no longer employed men. In the daily newspaper of Quilon, *Jennajugham*, such a case was reported in 1958. A factory was leased out and the new entrepreneur refused to give work to the twenty-six male shellers who had been working there for a long time.[111]

---

[108] Interview 13 March 1997.

[109] Interview 26 October 1997.

[110] Interview 25 August 1998 with Aiyyan, male sheller, born 1930; Interview 10 September 1998 with Arangan, male sheller, born 1931; Interview 15 December 1997 with Ponni, sheller, born 1920; Interview 14 September 1999 with K. Chellappan, male trade union leader in Kilikolloor, born 1914; Interview 18 December 1997 with Venu, male sheller and roaster, born 1930.

[111] *Jennajugham*, 27 February 1958, pp. 1-2.

After listening to the workers and reading the article in *Jennajugham*, inclines one to agree with the first brother, Ravindranathan Nair. However, the reasons for not wanting to employ male workers as *shellers* may have been manifold. The view just cited, i.e., that men were trouble-makers, may have been a valid argument, but even a few radical male *roasters* would have been able to create a lot of trouble for the factory owners if they organized the workers. Another strong reason might have been to introduce a strict gender division of labor at a time when trade unions were emerging and wages were becoming standardized. If a considerable number of the shellers had been men, it would have been more difficult to justify the low wages.

The period from the end of World War II until approximately 1960 saw the dismissal of male shellers from the cashew factories. The process of shelling, like roasting, was declared hazardous to a worker's health because of the presence of corrosive oil, but was never invoked as a prohibition for female workers. Women were obviously needed as full-time workers, but only in certain operations. Scholars in the West have observed a similar phenomenon with the construction of jobs in the 1930s and 1940s, when certain jobs became coded as female and typically had such characteristics as labor-intensity, piece-work remuneration, and assembly line processing.[112]

Was the second owner wrong when he asserted that male workers no longer wanted to do shelling? We have seen that Velu and Kuttan would have continued to work as shellers if they had had the opportunity. But, in addition, the social pressure for male shellers to act in line with the prevailing discourse of masculinity must have been a powerful force driving them to find other work. In a sense, the owner may have had a point when he asserted that men did not want to continue doing this work. However, the aversion to shelling among men seems to have emanated from the factory owners' overt strategy in transforming that section into a workplace totally dominated by women. Men were certainly also repelled by the low wages. As we shall see in Chapter VI, the strict gender division of labor became institutionalized when minimum wages were introduced. The strategy of the trade unions in trying to "rescue" the honor of the remaining men was to try to place them in other factory occupations considered more respectable work tasks for males.

"Inside the factory there is no problem", Kuttan had said when discussing the issue of working with women, thereby indicating that there *was* a problem outside the factory. "We were chided for doing women's work",

---

[112] See, for example, Milkman, *The Dynamics of Job Segregation*; Glucksmann, *Women Assemble*.

Velu had stated. Several others have testified to the increasing social pressure and changed attitude regarding what a proper male or female work task would be. Gomathi, the sheller, declared that "when male shellers became less common in the factories, the remaining men used to be called disdainfully 'those who only mingle with women' by other men".[113]

In 1949, Kalyani, the female roaster, prudently searched and found more suitable work after being harassed by children. The words of the children most probably reflected the opinions of the adults around them: a woman could not be a cashew roaster because it had a male connotation. Her new choice of work, looking after children, was much more in keeping with her gender. The other female roaster interviewed in 1962 had also changed her work task in the factory and had become a sheller.

The idea of appropriate work for women and men was becoming deeply entrenched among shellers and roasters in the 1940s and 1950s. It was an idea which had not been particularly strong among them twenty years earlier. The men who remained in the female-dominated shelling and peeling sections did work which now was considered incompatible with masculinity and, thus, they were defined as "non-men". As illustrated by the voices above, such men were considered sick, weak, or handicapped in some way—either not able-bodied, or belonging to an age-group (i.e., very old or youngsters) which could not be defined as "able-bodied men".[114] They were almost viewed as the antithesis of men, and were rather seen more like women. The very few men who were not actually dismissed and who opted to stay in the predominantly female sections were too poor and too depressed to be able to assert their own masculinity, and had not been able to find other jobs.

It is paradoxical that male shellers have been given these epithets, since they contrast so greatly with the epithets given to women who were doing the same work. These women, as we have seen, have been called "dexterous", "nimble", "patient" and, in some instances, also "skilled".[115] The male shellers did not believe that a specifically feminine patience or that nimble fingers were necessary for this particular work. Velu told me with pride that there was a time when he was one of the best shellers, and could shell up to a maximum of eleven kilos in an eight hour day—something which was far above average. Neither men nor women of his generation attributed special gender characteristics to the shellers. Among the women interviewed, it was obvious that those females who did not belong to the older generation

---

[113] Interview 23 August 1998 with Gomathi, sheller, born 1930.
[114] For an example of old men conducting work which were coded for women, see Haleh Afshar (ed.), *Women, Work, and Ideology in the Third World* (New York, 1985), p. xii.
[115] Anna Lindberg, "The Concept of Skill and the Kerala Cashew Workers" (Paper presented at Department of History, University of Lund, 1999).

had adapted a strong view of work tasks suitable for men, as opposed to women. None of the shellers born in the 1940s or later would send their sons to shell, as their mothers or grandmothers had done before them. I asked if they or their daughters could conceive of being a roaster. Sarojini's reply is representative of the twelve shellers who responded to this question:

> I would never send my son to the shelling section or any other of the sections where women work. He would probably not have been accepted by the manager, but he would never have gone there either—even if we were starving. Boys don't have patience and dexterity like girls and they are just not suitable for this kind of work. Shelling—it is a woman's job. How could a boy work there? About the roasting—I would do it if I had to for survival but, really, it is difficult to imagine women at such a post.
> —Sarojini, woman of Pulaya caste, sheller, born 1954[116]

Thus, we see that the opinion of what is appropriate work for men and women has become firmly rooted among workers themselves. This was not so earlier. The ideological transformation is reflected in the choices of individuals.

The majority of the workers in these three sections—shelling, peeling, and grading—have long been women. The cashew factories have here followed a pattern noted in other industries in India, strongly linking the degree of labor intensity of a task with gender.[117] It seems obvious, however, that in the early period (about 1925-1945) there was a less strict gender division of labor with regard to the processes of roasting and shelling—two processes that had existed prior to the export boom and prior to the processing of cashew nuts in factories. It was not envisioned that the cashew factories would become totally female-dominated; there was no clear original gender tradition in the work process. Women as well as men were engaged in both roasting and shelling. During this period, the shellers were not given epithets like "nimble" or "patient", these being constructions formed later to legitimize the dismissal of male shellers and the establishment of a rigid gender division. In fact, with regard to other work tasks, too, social anthropologists in the early twentieth century observed that low-caste men and women often worked together at agricultural jobs.[118]

---

[116] Interview 29 August 1998.

[117] For other examples of such correlation, see Banerjee (ed.), *Indian Women in a Changing Industrial Scenario.*

[118] Edgar Thurston, *Castes and Tribes of Southern India,* Vol. VII (Madras, 1909), p. 21; L.A.K. Iyer, *The Tribes and Castes of Cochin,* Vol. I (Madras, 1909), p. 117; L.A.K. Iyer, *The Travancore Tribes and Castes,* Vol. II (Trivandrum, 1939), p. 141.

CHAPTER 4

Conclusion

We have seen that in the early phase of the cashew factories, the gender division of labor was less rigid than it came to be later. Beginning with 25% to 30% male workers in the 1930s, the number of males has declined to a minimum. In an effort to create work places with solely women, factory owners argued emphatically that the labor intensive work operations in the cashew factories were only suitable for women, and consequently male shellers were dismissed. Women who earlier had been carrying out roasting ceased to perform this task in the late 1940s—mainly a result of their own choice. However, it was a choice which followed after a more dichotomized gender discourse took root among low-caste men and women, leading female roasters to feel masculine and uncomfortable.

The *less rigid gender division of labor* in the early years has been neglected in accounts of the history of the cashew nut factories, and it has been omitted from narratives about the cashew workers. The writing of history is an endeavor in the present and reflects the prevailing contemporary discourse. Most probably the authors of reports or books with a historical perspective on the cashew workers never concerned themselves with questions of whether men or women were exclusively assigned certain work tasks. The issue was considered self-evident, just as speakers cited earlier revealed in their utterances. Those informants neither lied, nor had they forgotten. They recounted the past as they had heard it from the narratives of others or learned it from historical accounts; neither the informants nor the printed sources need be viewed as having a conscious bias.[119] More likely, the reason that certain narratives survive can be attributed to an unquestioning perception of a gender ideology. None of the authors of the governmental reports or the historical accounts of the trade unions express any doubt regarding the rigid gender division of labor. In the words of Rosemary Hennessy, "understanding history as ideology implies that no matter how covert, the narrativity of history always issues from a set of values that support or disrupt a particular social order".[120] The 'support of a particular social order' may not be conscious, but rather based on an unquestioned assumption and, therefore, looked upon as natural.

The undisputed social order of the 1950s involved an even stricter gender division of labor than before. This was legitimized and mediated

---

[119] The historian Patrick Joyce has seen the link between the present and the past as problematical when institutions like trade unions write their own history, creating their own language and norms, their own discourse, in an effort to exert an influence on people's apprehension of the past. Patrick Joyce, *Visions of the People: Industrial England and the Question of Class 1848–1914* (Cambridge, 1991).
[120] Hennessy, *Materialist Feminism*, p. 102.

through dichotomous thinking and the language of femininity and masculinity. Thus, female and male characteristics among the workers engaged in roasting and shelling began to be a very conscious issue among a group of people who thus far certainly had not identified themselves in those terms as rigidly as they began to do. Such gendered language, that is, a linguistic usage which is conditioned by differences—real or presumed—between males and females, but not openly pejorative, was expressed by factory owners, civil servants, and trade union leaders. As we shall see in Chapter VI, the rigid gender division of labor was also institutionalized in contracts when minimum wages were introduced. The workers themselves, who were actual eye-witnesses of the less rigid gender division of labor in roasting and shelling, had not forgotten the existence of male shellers and female roasters, but it was not an issue they mentioned until they were asked about it directly. Probably it was not important to them. Maybe it even reflected a shameful past, when women were considered less feminine and men were seen as not masculine.

Kalpana Ram has observed a development in a direction towards "being more feminine" among female fish traders in Tamil Nadu. Young women, whose mothers traded fish, started to look down upon this work as being "masculine".[121] When speaking about the past, the cashew workers found it much more important to talk about poverty, marriage, children, exploitation in employment, caste oppression, or trade union activities—topics they continually raised, whether asked about them or not—than about gender differences. This speaks for the relatively stronger importance of these issues than gender equality or the lack thereof.

Prior to the large scale processing of cashew nuts in factories, peeling and grading were unknown occupations. When these jobs came into existence in the early factories, strictly gender-coded work tasks appear to have been a reality from the outset.

However, yet another pervasive division of labor existed in the cashew factories: the caste division, to which we must now turn.

By way of introduction, I recall meeting one of those denigrated former shellers, a man named Velu, who was about seventy-five at the time. He was still very "able-bodied" and strong, and I could not conceive of him or any of the other male shellers I met as sick, disabled, or weak. Neither they themselves nor their families considered them as such. However, they all had one thing in common: they belonged to either the Pulaya or the Kurava caste.

---

[121] Ram, *Mukkuvar Women*, p. 222.

V   Caste in the Workplace

Kadheeja with the veil, Mary with the tail dhoti,
Sarawathy Amma, Chinna, and Kotha,
Processing cashew nuts, working together.
Sharing their sorrows as they sit toiling,
Joining in "Sunnath" at the house of Khadeeja,
Tying the thread at a birth—Kotha's child.
Now eating together and joking as one.
Laying the ground for revolutionary changes.
The success that social reformers had dreamed of
These cashew workers themselves had achieved.[1]

Introduction

In 1996, the Quilon based trade union leader, Kesavan Nair, wrote these
lines in an account of the history of the cashew workers.[2] His message is
clear: Muslims, Christians, and Hindus of different castes came together in
the factory, where old traditional barriers were broken as workers joined
against the forces of capitalism. It traces a story about the transition from a
traditional to a modern, capitalist society; from caste identity to class identity—a common way development has been represented in India.[3] This
kind of meta-narrative has been opposed, mainly by historians belonging
to the so-called "Subaltern Studies", who instead have stressed continuity

---

[1] Kadheeja is a Muslim name, Mary a Christian name. A tail dhoti is a dress traditionally
worn by Christians in Kerala. The name Saraswathy Amma signals a high caste woman;
Chinna and Kotha are names common among women of lower castes. The Sunnith festi-
val is a Muslim celebration, whereas the thread tying ritual is performed in Hindu families (belonging to the three highest Varnas) when a child is born.
[2] Kesavan Nair, "The Strike History of the Cashew Workers, part 29. The Social Revolution by the Cashew Workers", *CITU Sandesam*, 19:11(1996), p. 22 (in Malayalam).
[3] Marx predicted that industrialization in India would lead to the dissolution of the caste system. See Shlomo, Avineri (ed.). *Karl Marx on Colonialism and Modernisation, his Dispatches
and Other Writings in China, India, Mexico, the Middle East and North Africa* (New York,
1968), pp. 132-139; Karl Marx and Friedrich Engels, *On Colonialism* (Moscow, 1968), p.
85. For scholars who have stressed the shift from caste to class, see, for example, André
Béteille, *Caste, Class and Power: Changing Patterns of Stratification in a Tanjore Village* (Berkeley, 1965); Anil Bhatt, *Caste, Class and Politics* (New Delhi, 1975); Mark Holmström,
"Caste and Status in an Indian City", *Economic and Political Weekly*, 7 (1972), pp. 769-774;
Stephen A. Barnett, "Approaches to Changes in Caste Ideology in South India", in Burton,
Stein (ed.), *Essays on South India* (New Delhi, 1975); David F. Pocock, "Sociologies: Urban
and Rural", *Contributions to Indian Sociology*, 4 (1960), pp. 63-81.

with a hierarchical past when analyzing the identity of the subalterns.[4]

A common method of exploring the question of workers' identity has been to examine their class or caste solidarity at moments of crisis, such as riots, or strikes.[5] There are limitations in such an approach, and one should consider not only workers' loyalty in those situations, but also take into account the importance of caste in daily life. To only analyze exceptional instances of caste alliances (e.g., in strikes) restricts one to a consideration of *moments* when caste identities have been weakened. One way of approaching the connection of everyday activities to caste is to explore caste relations in the factory. When interviewing cashew workers in 1997, I was quite surprised to find that the tasks involved in cashew nut processing seemed to be not only highly gender coded, but caste coded as well.

Caste Division of Labor

Very few detailed studies on the caste composition of the factories have been carried out in India and none of them bridges a very long time span. In a study of the cotton textile industry in Coimbatore, Southern India, in the late 1970s, Uma Ramaswamy asserted that factory work had contributed to the breakdown of caste barriers. She did not find any particular caste division of labor and concluded that the close interaction on the shop floor had led to the overcoming of traditional barriers. Over time, jobs in mills had gradually gained in prestige, but simultaneously the proportion of Scheduled Castes in the factory had decreased. This group had traditionally been discriminated against in the labor market, but once they entered the factory, they were not channeled into jobs with lower wages or a lower sense of dignity than higher caste individuals.[6] Other studies on the same theme, however, noted a caste division of labor, with the lowest castes in less prestigious, lower paying tasks. These writers all concluded the reason was not hostility between different castes, but was rather to be explained in meritocratic terms or as job competition. For example, M.D. Morris found it conspicuous that Scheduled Castes were excluded from the highest paid department in the mills at Bombay in the 1940s. He concluded that this was a means of preserving economic advantages for a small group, more than a caste phenomenon in terms of hostility or prejudice.[7] In a study of

[4] See, for example, Dipesh Chakrabarty, "Marx after Marxism: A Subaltern Historian's Perspective", *Economic and Political Weekly*, 28 (1993), pp. 1094-1096.
[5] See, for example, S. Bhattacharya, "Capital and Labour in Bombay City, 1928-29", *Economic and Political Weekly*, 16: 42-43 (1981), pp. PE35-44; Bahl, *The Making of the Indian Working Class*.
[6] Uma Ramaswamy, *Work, Union and Community: Industrial Man in South India* (New Delhi, 1983), pp. 105-106, 122-125.

CHAPTER 5

factory workers in Bangalore published in 1976, Mark Holmström noted the marked correlation between traditional high castes and skilled or managerial jobs, and between Scheduled Castes and unskilled jobs such as sweepers and watchmen. Meanwhile, middle castes were found everywhere, except among those who cleaned. Holmström also accredited this phenomenon to meritocratic principles and asserted that caste was not decisive in securing a particular factory position.[8]

To verify the impression I obtained during my earliest discussions with cashew workers, I examined the caste division of labor in 1998 in two factories—one private and one state-owned. In the private cashew factory, I interviewed every tenth female worker in the three main departments. Since the others were few in number, the caste affiliation of packers, male workers, and staff could be easily ascertained individually. Although a number of castes were represented among the workers, it became obvious that a few castes were dominant, which is why the four categories below sufficed:

    I. Higher castes (mainly Nairs)
    II. Middle castes (mainly Ezhavas)
    III. Scheduled Castes (SC) (mainly Pulayas and Kuravas)
    IV. Others (Christians and Muslims)

Table 5.1. Caste and gender composition of the Vijayalakshmi Cashew Factory (Chandanathoope, January 1998)

Section	Higher castes	Middle castes	SC	Others	Total in the sample	Total in the department	Percentage of women
Shelling	2	11	22	2	37	370	100
Peeling	13	11	1	9	34	340	100
Grading	7	2	0	1	10	100	100
Packing	4	2	1	2	9	10	45
Roasting	0	2	5	0	7	7	0
Borma*	1	3	0	1	5	5	0
Others	1	2	2	1	6	6	0
Staff	4	2	0	0	6	6	17
Totals	32	35	31	16	114	844	97
%	28	31	27	14	100		

Sources: Interviews carried out in January 1998

* Drying of roasted and shelled cashews

[7] Morris, *The Emergence of an Industrial Labour Force in India.*
[8] Mark Holmström, *South Indian Factory Workers: Their Life and their World* (Cambridge, 1976). For similar conclusions, see N.R. Sheth, *The Social Frame Work of an Indian Factory* (New Delhi, 1981).

The most striking sight was in the shelling section where female workers of the Scheduled Castes were clustered. The majority of the women of higher castes belonged to the peeling division, where members of various castes worked together but the Scheduled Castes were hardly represented. The Nairs held a near-monopoly in the grading department; not a single person from a Scheduled Caste was found in this section. The middle castes seemed to carry out all different work tasks, but predominated in peeling and shelling. The pattern for Christians and Muslims was also over-representation in the peeling section, similar to the higher castes.

As the number of male workers was small, one cannot draw strong conclusions, but the tendency of roasters belonging to Scheduled Castes seems to be clear, whereas the categories of "bormamen" and "others" were more mixed with regard to caste affiliation.

In the state-owned cashew factory, it was possible to obtain data on caste from the rolls of all the workers and staff. A closer look into KSCDC Factory No. 1 in Kottiyam yielded findings similar to the private factory. A small variance with regard to female workers was that the grading section was more mixed, but still contained very few individuals from the Scheduled Castes. Male workers also showed a pattern similar to that in the private factory. In both cases it was obvious that higher castes were over-represented among the staff and supervisors, who were almost exclusively male.

Table 5.2. Caste and gender composition in KSCDC Factory No. 1 (Kottiyam, August 1998)

Section	Higher castes	Middle castes	SC	Others	Total	Percentage of Women
Shelling	9	59	110	9	187	100
Peeling	75	68	2	18	163	100
Grading	16	24	7	12	59	100
Packing	3	6	2	1	12	50
Roasting	0	2	6	0	8	0
Borma	1	2	1	0	4	0
Others*	4	25	13	2	44	0
Staff	5	1	1	0	7	0
Totals	113	187	142	42	484	
%	23	39	29	9	100	

Source: K. Anirudhan, Personnel Clerk, KSCDC Factory No. 1, 21 August 1998

* The KSCDC factory included a sheet metal department and manufactured tin containers in which the cashew nuts were packed, employing 24 men—which explains the high number of males in this row.

What we see in the three main departments is largely a caste division of labor, with a correlation between rank in the traditional caste hierarchy and the degree of cleanliness of the task—from the oily, black, and corrosive raw nuts in the shelling section, through the peeling section where the nuts are still covered with brown skins, to the white kernels in the grading section.[9]

The following principal questions form the basis of our inquiry: What is the historical reason for the caste division of labor, and to what extent has it changed? How and why has the caste division of labor been upheld in a society which has developed in such a radical direction as Kerala? What has the caste division among workers meant at different periods?

There is little printed evidence of caste composition in the early period of the industry. The first written source mentioning caste in connection with cashew factories is a police report from 1939. There it was stated that *a large number of Kuravas* were employed in the cashew nut factories and that it should be the task of the local police to "wean them off from joining the Labour Union".[10] The police report illustrates the importance of caste in the society at that time. Caste affiliation was the established way of describing a group of people. They were not characterized as workers, laborers, or poor people, but as Kuravas. The report also suggests that the Kuravas constituted the majority of the cashew workers.

In his memoirs, the trade union leader, K.C. Govindan, who was active among cashew workers in the 1940s, gives us evidence of a rigid division based on caste in those days: "Ninety-five percent of the workers engaged in this work [shelling] were Harijans [Scheduled Castes]....The women workers in the peeling and passing [grading] sections were mostly from the relatively higher castes such as the Ezhavas."[11] Although Govindan wrote his memoirs in the 1980s, there is no reason to doubt his observations, even if the percentage he gives is not to be taken literally. Another trade union leader, N. Sreekantan Nair, also active in the 1940s, wrote his memoirs in 1976 and commented that only Harijans carried out shelling and peeling.[12] In the Minimum Wage Report of 1953 it was mentioned that

---

[9] In the discussion below, I exclude Christians and Muslims. None of the Christians in the cashew factory belonged to the so-called Syrian Christians, but to those newly converted. As discussed in Chapter I, these Christians and the Muslims were traditionally included in the caste hierarchy, as well, and they were placed somewhere above the Ezhavas. The inclusion of these groups in the following would have introduced extraneous complications into this study.

[10] KSA, Confidential file 48/238, Letter from Police Inspector Karim Sahib to the Chief Secretary, Govt. of Travancore, Trivandrum, 11 May, 1939.

[11] Govindan, *Memoires of an Early Trade Unionist*, pp. 67-68.

[12] Sreekantan Nair, *Memories of the Past*, Chapter 44.

[13] Govt. of Travancore-Cochin, *Report of the Minimum Wages Committee for Cashew Industry 1953*, p. 11.

shellers and roasters were mostly "drawn from the agricultural classes".[13] It is obvious that what was called "agricultural class" coincided in the main with Scheduled Castes.[14] In the 1950s caste was no longer the term used to identify a certain group of people, officials choosing to express themselves in terms of class instead. The educated civil servant's choice of words was probably not accidental, but may be interpreted as a rejection of the old traditional society and its strict caste system. This was also reflected in the census of 1951, the first time caste was largely abandoned when categorizing people (the category Scheduled Castes was kept).

Later, micro-studies were conducted about various cashew factories by sociologists and economists in Kerala. They noted the same caste division of labor and gave quantitative evidence. The first of these studies was carried out in 1958, and the most recent in 1994; they all point in the same direction—to a rigid caste division of labor. This is especially pronounced with regard to the Scheduled Castes, who have been relegated to the shelling section in glaring disproportion. The grading section, on the other hand, was dominated by Nairs, and the peeling section by groups which traditionally were placed between the Nairs and the Scheduled Castes on the hierarchical social ladder. However, no efforts have been made to explain this caste division of labor, nor has it even been stated as a problem.[15]

Following the studies of Morris and Holmström, cited earlier, we could expect that wages were lowest and required skills a minimum in the shelling section. However, there has not been any deviation in either the stipulated daily minimum wages or the requirements of formal training in the three main departments of the cashew factories.[16] Thus, meritocratic or economic ex-

---

[14] P. Sivanandan, "Caste, Class and Economic Opportunity in Kerala: An Empirical Analysis", *Economic and Political Weekly*, 14:7-8 (1979), pp. 477-478.

[15] See, for example, S.H. Faria, "A Study of the Socio-economic Conditions of the Cashew Labourers with Special Reference to the Women Workers at Dhanalakshmi Vilasam, Quilon" (M. Phil., Rajagiri College of Social Sciences, Kalamassery, Cochin 1958), p. 5; A.J. Eman Beevi, "Impact of Minimum Wage Legislation on Cashew Industry" (M.Phil., Jawaharlal Nehru University, New Delhi, 1978), p. 21; N.K. Aravindakshan Nair and P.N. Varughese, "Women Workers in the Cashew Industry in Kerala" (Indian Institute for Regional Development Studies, Kottayam, 1979), pp. 50-51; Kannan, "Evolution of Unionisation and Changes in Labour Processes", p. 173; Pillai, "The Economic Impact", p. 177; Deepa, "Industrial Crisis and Women Workers", pp. 61 ff. Deepa's study is an exception in that she asserted that the caste division of labor called for further research.

[16] Govt. of Travancore-Cochin, *Report of the Minimum Wages Committee for Cashew Industry 1953*, pp. 21 ff.; Govt. of Kerala, *Report of the Minimum Wages Advisory Committee for Cashew Industry 1959*, pp. 9-19, 19-26; NRC, Govt. of Kerala, *Report of the Minimum Wages Committee for Cashew Industry 1989*, Go. No. 3218/90/LBR. RT; Govt. of Kerala, *The Report of the Delegatory Committee for the Revision of the Minimum Wages of Cashew Workers 1998*, copy received from P. Madhavan, chairman of the Committee for the Revision of the Minimum Wages of Cashew Workers 1998, Trivandrum.

planations, including higher wages for higher castes, such as one finds in previous research on the caste division of labor, is not applicable in the case of the cashew factories, and others have to be sought. To trace the historical roots of the caste structure in the cashew factories, we need to examine the way in which workers were recruited in the earliest days.

Recruitment of Laborers in the Early Days

There seems to have been an abundance of laborers willing to carry out the dirtiest operations for low wages in the pioneering cashew nut factories. The tremendous growth of the plants, however, soon led to a shortage of labor and it may have surprised foreign owners that not everybody, in spite of poverty, was willing to work in their factories.

The population of Travancore had relatively high hopes for the future with the "boom prices" of 1925-1928. This optimism, however, quickly changed during 1929 and 1930.[17] The price of exports dropped dramatically—often by 40% or more—and this was followed by a great shortage of cash throughout the country, reduced wages, and increased unemployment.[18] The situation was especially precarious in central and northern Travancore, where "*lakhs* [one lakh =100,000] of unemployed people" were found.[19] In spite of this, it was difficult to locate sufficient workers for the growing number of cashew factories, especially in the 1940s.[20]

Small-scale farmers, who were dependent on export crops for their survival, were seriously affected by the depression.[21] In 1931, more than 30% of the Ezhavas were registered as agriculturalists, but most often they did not work their own land.[22] As stated in the census of 1931, the "gentleman farmer", among whom were many Ezhavas or Nairs, did not want to soil his hands, no matter how poor he was—which is why most of the manual work was done by Pulayas, Parayans, and Kuravas.[23] Yet, certain manual work in agriculture was done by Ezhavas as well, especially the cultivation

---

[17] Govt. of Travancore, *Report of the Economic Depression Enquiry Committee 1931* (Trivandrum, 1932), p. 18.

[18] Ibid., p. 19; Govt. of India, *Census of India 1931*, Vol. XXVIII, Travancore, Part I, Report, p. 26.

[19] Govt. of Travancore, *Report of the Economic Depression Enquiry Committee 1931*, p. 20.

[20] KSA, Development files, No. 352-166, *Export of Cashew to USA*, "Letter from South India Cashew Manufacturer's Association to Government of India", dated 23 November 1944.

[21] Govt. of Travancore, *Report of the Economic Depression Enquiry Committee 1931*, p. 20.

[22] Govt. of India, *Census of India 1931*, Vol. XXVIII, Travancore, Part I, Report, p. 238-39.

[23] Ibid., p. 245.

of coconuts and other "dry land" crops.[24] In 1931, about 16% of the Ezhavas who were classified as workers were agricultural workers, although most often they were assigned other work tasks than the lower castes.[25]

The resistance of individuals other than members of the lowest castes in carrying out certain manual tasks and dirty work continued for a long time. In the early 1950s, an official comparison of the labor supply in the cashew factories in different parts of India was carried out. It was established that the workers were plentiful in most places, except for shellers in the area around Quilon. "Recruitment is at the factory gate and there is usually no difficulty in obtaining the required complement. In some places, however, particularly in factories located near about Quilon, it is difficult to get adequate number of shellers, as shelling work is considered *infra dig*".[26]

Although the investigation does not provide information about the 1930s, it would be unrealistic to believe that shelling work was considered unworthy only in the 1950s. In fact, the same perception existed in the 1930s and 1940s, making the supply of Pulayas, Parayas, Kuruvas, and other low-caste individuals mandatory, as others would deem such work beneath their station. The most powerful motive for the employment of these castes in the 1920s and 1930s was, of course, that they were the cheapest labor force available. Most of them were occupied as landless agricultural workers. In addition, a system involving payment in kind was still prevalent in the 1930s. The amount of rice doled out to these workers as wages was just enough to meet their daily needs for survival.[27]

The shortage of labor was reflected in the payment routines which existed in the cashew factories. Part of a worker's daily income was obligatorily reserved for a savings fund, a so-called *chitti*. The fund money was distributed during the yearly harvest holiday, *Onam*, which takes place in August or September. However, only workers *who had not worked in other factories during the year* could receive money from the fund.[28] By 1940, the

---

[24] Dry land crops are distinguished from wet land crops, such as rice, which has to be cultivated in water and requires that laborers stand in the water while working.

[25] Govt. of India, *Census of India 1931*, Vol. XXVIII, Travancore, Part I, Report, p. 269. The division with Ezhavas on the dry land and former slave castes working the wet land was especially pronounced among male workers. Alex, "Social and Economic Aspects of Attached Labourers in Kuttanad Agriculture", pp. A141-150.

[26] Govt. of India, *Report on an Enquiry into Conditions of Labour in the Cashewnut Processing Industry in India*, pp. 12, 27.

[27] Das, "Genesis of Trade Union Movement in Travancore", pp. 122-123. For accounts of the deplorable conditions among agricultural laborers in the 1930s, see also Saradamoni, *Emergence of a Slave Caste,* and Joseph Tharamangalam, *Agrarian Class Conflict: The Political Mobilization of Agricultural Labourers in Kuttanad, South India* (Vancouver, 1981).

[28] Govindan, *Memoires of an Early Trade Unionist*, p. 68; Interview 12 January 1998 with Chirutha, sheller, born 1919; Interview 18 December 1997 with Kotha, sheller, born 1919; Interview 17 August 1998 with Vijayamma, peeler, grader, born 1920.

amount in this fund was one *chuckram* per day per worker.[29] According to official statistics, the average wage for a woman working in a cashew factory at this time was between four and seven *chuckrams*.[30] The forced saving of 15% to 25% of one's wages represented a considerable sum.

According to colonial civil servants, a general problem for factory owners in India in the early twentieth century was their dependency on the infrastructure of the cities. They, therefore, would profit by localizing the factories there. On the other hand, the greatest proportion of the laborers lived in the countryside, so that cities often suffered from a shortage of labor. A means to secure labor from rural areas was the institution of intermediaries or jobbers (different names were used in different parts of India).

In most cases, the intermediary was a man with a good relationship to the factory owner; apart from being a recruiting agent, he generally was employed in the factory as a supervisor, engineer, or in another position with a considerable amount of responsibility.[31] Often the jobber went out into the countryside to recruit workers. He acted as a buffer between workers and management and usually had the authority to hire and fire. The intermediary system might also be based on a contract, in which it was the responsibility of the jobber to perform a stipulated amount of work for a certain compensation. The intermediary determined wages, and management never had to discuss this matter directly with the workers. Nor did management take responsibility for the workers' welfare.[32]

Some have linked the labor shortage to the migrant workers' ties with their home villages. It is said that this involved a high rate of absenteeism, desertion, and lack of industrial discipline. This view, the so-called "lack of commitment thesis", which holds that traditional institutions such as the caste system and village communities have obstructed industrialism, was predominant among colonial civil servants and researchers in the 1940s and 1950s.[33] It has not remained unchallenged and several scholars have, in fact, rejected it. By way of example, Morris, in his studies of the cotton mills of Bombay and the steel industry in Jamshedpur, showed that workers from rural areas were not incapable of cutting their ties with their villages. He concluded that there had never been difficulties in recruiting labor,

---

[29] *Chuckram* was a coin in the Princely State of Travancore. 28.5 *chuckrams* was equivalent to one British Rupee. Govindan, *Memoires of an Early Trade Unionist*, p. 68.
[30] Govt. of Travancore, *Statistics of Travancore*, 19th issue, 1113 ME/1937-1938 AD, pp. 160 ff.
[31] Govt. of India, *Report of the Royal Commission on Labour in India* (Calcutta, 1931), pp. 23 ff.
[32] Govt. of India, *Indian Labour Investigation Committee*, Main Report 1946, p. 79.
[33] For a discussion and overview of this issue, see Jan Breman, "The Study of Industrial Labour in Post-colonial India—The Formal Sector: An Introductory Review", in Parry, Breman, and Karin Kapadia (eds), *The Worlds of Indian Industrial Labour*, pp. 4-17.

but that the primary reason for hiring people from distant places was to obtain cheap, submissive laborers.[34]

During the 1920s, the system of intermediaries was widespread among factories in Travancore, such as those in the city of Alleppey, where coir was processed. In Travancore, these intermediaries were usually called *moopans*.[35] The so-called "moopan system" differed slightly from the contract system, but the differences were minimal. In the *moopan system*, a person would recruit workers, and the employer would pay him a commission on the workers' wages, as well as a fixed monthly salary. Workers in this system would be directly responsible to management and not to the *moopan*. In the contract system, on the other hand, the management paid the intermediary, who then paid the workers. Differences between the two systems decreased in time, as management tended to give the *moopan* a fairly free hand. Desirable workers were tempted with big advances. It was also still common to pay in kind.[36]

There were such intermediaries in the cashew factories, too. A contract system was prevalent during the early phase of the industry. Roasters were contractually employed by exporters to deliver pre-shelled cashew nuts. In these cases, the roaster had to pay the shellers. Kalyani, the female roaster mentioned in the previous chapter, recounted a contract system in which she had made such payments.[37] Others have borne witness to a system where the *moopan* was apparently responsible for factory discipline and was entitled to extract a fee from the workers' wages. In the cashew factories, the amount which the workers had to pay the *moopan* consisted of about 5% of what they made.[38]

The search for cheap labor from the lowest castes led to the companies sending agents—usually foremen or roasters— into the countryside to recruit shellers from what was considered to be the bottom of the social hierarchy. The newly-hired workers would be put up in simple sheds, which either the cashew manufacturers or the contractors built for them. As the case of Kalyani illustrates, a female roaster could also act as a contractor and build dwellings on her own land for the shellers. Kalyani stated explicitly that it was the roasters duty to recruit the shellers.[39] During the 1930s, hundreds of such sheds were built in the vicinity of the factories around Quilon. Mainly women

[34] Breman, "The Study of Industrial Labour in Post-colonial India—The Formal Sector", pp. 7-12.
[35] The Malayalam word *moopan* can be translated as foreman.
[36] Govindan, *Memoires of an Early Trade Unionist*, pp. 13 ff.
[37] Balakrishnan, "Life and Strikes in the Midst of Smoke and Coal Dust", p. 2.
[38] Apart from this, the workers had to pay an additional 20% for such fees as drinking water and tool rental! Interview 14 September 1999 with K. Chellappan, male trade union leader in Kilikolloor, born 1914; Kannan, "Evolution of Unionisation and Changes in Labour Processes ", p. 60 n. 10.

CHAPTER 5

would live there, although most of them arrived with a male relative. A man worker often came with his wife, his sisters, his wife's sisters, and perhaps other female relatives—all of these belonged to the Scheduled Castes.[40] The aim was to recruit women, but it was difficult to hire only women, because people were probably reluctant to split up families. This recruiting system may have contributed to the fact that there was a larger proportion of men in the factories in Travancore than in British India, where labor quarters of this kind seem not to have existed in connection with cashew plants. To attract low-caste women to the factories, the cashew manufacturers were forced to accept a few men into the bargain.

In other parts of India, recruiting agents have been described as powerful, authoritarian men, and it has also been argued that their power was built upon the use of violence.[41] This view has been contested by Arjan de Haan, whose area of study was the jute mills of Calcutta.[42] In the Travancore cashew factories, it does not seem as if recruiters were always powerful men with close ties to the factory owners. Often they were ordinary workers, who could optain certain benefits by providing the owner with more workers. Male shellers were commonly promoted to roasters or foremen if they were able to recruit a stipulated number of shellers.[43] Samita Sen has argued that it was more difficult to recruit women for the jute mills in Calcutta because patriarchal values in the rural areas did not permit any women to migrate. The women who arrived at the mills were often widows, or abandoned by their husbands, or themselves runaways from husbands or oppressive family relations, which made it difficult to return back to the village. Such women were more economically drained than other migrants, and also more vulnerable, because they had no family who could support them when unemployed. In that sense, these women were more proletarianized than a male migrant, who often could return to the village where his wife and other family members worked in agriculture.[44]

In the late 1930s, in one cashew factory, a young boy (actually his job was to look after the babies—another case which confirms the less rigid gender roles at that time) had eaten a cashew nut. The owner discovered this and his response was to dismiss a supervisor, whose job was to control

[39] Balakrishnan, "Life and Strikes in the Midst of Smoke and Coal Dust", p. 2.
[40] Interview 14 September 1999 with K. Chellappan, male trade union leader in Kilikolloor, born 1914; Interview 15 December 1997 with Ponni, sheller, born 1920.
[41] Chakrabarty, *Rethinking Working-Class History*, pp. 106-114.
[42] Arjan de Haan, *Unsettled Settlers; Migrant Workers and Industrial Capitalism in Calcutta* (Rotterdam, 1994), pp. 73 ff.
[43] Interview 14 September 1999 with K. Chellappan, male trade union leader in Kilikolloor, born 1914; Interview 18 January 1998 with Velu, male former sheller, born 1923.
[44] Samita Sen, "Women Workers in the Bengal Jute Industry", pp. 249-255.

the workers. Obviously this man had chosen to close his eyes to the boy's "crime". The dismissal resulted in a spontaneous strike that lasted until the supervisor was taken back.[45] At this factory the relation between the workers and the supervisor, who most probably also was a recruiter, seemed to be amiable, which further supports the thesis that the *moopans* could be men with the same social background as the workers.

Poverty prevented the inhabitants of the sheds around the cashew factories from leaving. They were frequently in debt to the employer or the *moopan* and some could not go home because of that.[46] Many of the older inhabitants of areas surrounding Quilon testified to the difficulty of life in these sheds. Despite their male relatives, whom not every woman had, women were very vulnerable and different kinds of harassment were common. The social status of the low-caste men who accompanied the women did not allow them to intervene when the foremen and the so-called *rowdies*[47] attacked the women.[48] The harassment could take the form of actual rape, or the factory owners might pick out beautiful girls to help them "entertain" when they had guests. The girls were not actually forced into this and they did receive payment or gifts, but it was difficult for them not to cooperate, as it could lead to dismissal.[49] This can be compared to the situation of women in the jute industry in Bengal, where male workers, agents, and manufacturers looked upon lonely women as prostitutes.[50] An old woman related a telling story:

> I cannot say how often this happened, but I witnessed it several times—this was in the old days when the *dewan* ruled. I remember one young Pulaya girl, who was extremely beautiful. She lived with her sister, who was slightly retarded, in one of the sheds here in this village. When the *moopan* came to look for nice girls, she used to look down to the floor, but they always chose her. We could all see that she suffered, but she stayed silent. What can a poor girl do? One day she and her sister had left—nobody knew where, but we

[45] Balakrishnan, "Life and Strikes in the Midst of Smoke and Coal Dust", pp. 2-3.
[46] Interview 14 September 1999 with K. Chellappan, male trade union leader in Kilikolloor, born 1914; Interview 15 December 1997 with Ponni, female sheller, born 1920.
[47] Rowdies were men who may be described as hoodlums, employed by factory owners to prevent workers from joining the growing trade unions, sometimes called goonies or goons in British slang.
[48] Interview 14 September 1999 with K. Chellappan, male trade union leader in Kilikolloor, born 1914; Interview 15 December 1997 with Ponni, female sheller, born 1920.
[49] Interview 14 March 1997 with Devaki, female sheller, born 1918; Interview 15 December 1997 with Ponni, female sheller, born 1920.
[50] Dagmar Engels, "The Myth of the Family Unit: *Adivasi* Women in Coal-Mines and Tea Plantations in Early Twentieth-Century Bengal", in Peter Robb (ed.), *Dalit Movements and the Meanings of Labour in India* (New Delhi, 1993), pp. 225-244.

understood why. Maybe she was even pregnant. Things like this don't happen anymore.
—Devaki, woman of Ezhava caste, sheller, born 1918[51]

Joseph Tharamangalam, who did fieldwork among agricultural laborers in Kerala in the 1970s, heard old people tell stories of sexual exploitation of Pulaya women by the high-caste landlords in the 1930s and 1940s.[52] It appears as if this right of men from higher castes to exploit low-caste women sexually was present in the sheds of the cashew workers as well.

A similar recruitment system existed in the plantations of South India. Barbara Evans has pointed out that those who were not fit for work, such as very young children and old people, were left in the villages when people were recruited for plantations in Nilgiri, on the borderland between the present Kerala and Tamil Nadu. Thus, the real cost for reproducing labor was paid by the villages, not by the plantations.[53] The same phenomenon seems to have been prevalent in the cashew factories. It has not been possible to accurately determine the age and gender composition of those dwelling in the sheds, but there was a consensus among old people interviewed that the majority of the workers housed there were able-bodied women or children, and a significant number of men.[54]

One old worker, Ponni, belonged to the earliest batch of workers who came from a rural area to work in the cashew factory of Musaliar in Kilikolloor:

> In my childhood we lived in Mavelikara, in a hut in the landlord's field. There was my mother, one younger sister, two younger brothers, and me. My father had left to work somewhere else. We all worked in the paddy fields, except for my youngest brother. He was either sleeping near the field or looked after by me or my sister. One day when I was about ten years old, my mother told me that we were going to leave. They were bad times and poverty drove us away. We walked all the way to Kilikolloor. My uncle came with us, along with several other workers from the paddy field. I don't know how many we were, but it was a crowd—women, men, and children—and I think that all of us belonged to the Kurava caste, although maybe there were some Pulayas. It was a long way to walk, so the old or sick people were left back home, and

---

[51] Interview 14 March 1997.
[52] Tharamangalam, *Agrarian Class Conflict*, p. 58.
[53] Barbara Evans, "Constructing a Plantation Labour Force: The Plantation-village Nexus in South India", *The Indian Economic and Social History Review*, 32: 2 (1995), pp. 167 ff.
[54] Interview 15 December 1997 with Ponni, female sheller, born 1920; Interview 19 December 1997 with K. Bhanu, former journalist in Kilikolloor, born 1913; Interview 14 September 1999 with K. Chellappan, male trade union leader in Kilikolloor, born 1914.

many women came alone because, first and foremost, women workers were wanted. Some people left the youngest children with grandparents or other relatives in Mavelikara, but later on the children were brought to them. We did not have much to carry—a basket, and two or three pots…I don't remember exactly. We had no more clothes than those on our bodies.

One man from Kilikolloor (I think his name was Kannan) led us to a place where we would live. He was the one who came to our village to show the way. It was a huge shed made of bamboo leaves and sticks. We were all hungry. The people who came to the shed were all very poor people of low caste. We had been starving a lot. We got some *kanja* when we arrived. We got a corner for ourselves in the shed, and later on we screened off that corner with a cloth to get some privacy. The next day we started to work shelling nuts. It was not a factory like today. It was an open area with many fireplaces for roasting and shellers sitting all around. Later on, a shed was put up where people—mainly women of other castes—were employed to peel and grade the cashew nuts. Then the shellers got a shed, as well. We lived in this place for many years—maybe fifteen or more. We never went back to our old village. Hardly anybody did. Some women went back to get their children, but except for them, I do not know of anybody who went back. What was there to go back to?

—Ponni, woman of Pulaya caste, sheller, born 1920[55]

In addition to recruiting laborers from surrounding areas and offering them shelter in or near the city of Quilon, the reverse phenomenon (i.e., removing the factories to the rural areas) occurred. Gradually, many factory owners expanded their business by setting up factories in the countryside near Quilon, since it was easier to find cheap labor there than in the city. In the early 1950s, at least fifty additional factories had opened in the rural neighborhood of Quilon.[56] Apparently, it was profitable to pay the high cost of transportation, a consequence which the factories situated outside the cities must have borne. The cashew factories continue to be mainly in the rural areas outside the city of Quilon. The strategy of locating the factories there dates back to the early 1940s, and, therefore, the general discussion on workers' ties to the village versus their commitment to factory work has limited relevance for the cashew factories. The recruiters mainly operated in the 1930s and 1940s, and the people recruited in this way were nearly always shellers.

There were also certain difficulties finding labor in the countryside. In

---

[55] Interview 15 December 1997.
[56] Govt. of Travancore-Cochin, *Report of the Minimum Wages Committee for Cashew Industry 1953*, p. 8.

his autobiography, M.N. Govindan, the early trade union leader among cashew workers, wrote about the competition between cashew factory owners and landlords in the 1940s.[57] In 1944, some landlords from Kunnathoor Taluk (in the vicinity of Quilon) came to see him. They wanted his help in closing down a newly established cashew factory. Agricultural workers who had been employed by these landlords for generations had now started to work in the cashew factory without their consent. As a trade union leader, Govindan was, of course, considered the natural enemy of the factory owners, which was why the landlords hoped for joint action against the management of the plant. Govindan stated, "This is not the story of Kunnathur alone. It happened in all the villages where the industry penetrated". Govindan rejected their proposal and replied that he would even join the factory owners and fight against the rights of the landlords.[58]

Legally, slavery was abolished in 1855, but as Alex George points out, it survived in a veiled form for a long time. Former slaves became bonded fieldworkers with a system of advance payment, a situation which was extremely difficult for them to avoid. Opportunities in society were very few for such individuals, since they were prevented from leasing land and the old social rules of pollution were still powerful barriers to prevent them from entering into occupations that demanded contact with higher castes.[59] The reason former slaves like Pulayas, Parayas, and Kuruvas were sought after as bonded labor in agriculture was their utility in labor-intensive tasks in wetland paddy cultivation—tasks that were rejected by Ezhavas, even if they, too, were mainly a laboring caste.[60] For the cashew factories, the clash between the two groups representing different systems of production was obvious, pitting the landlords, on the one hand, against the emerging industrial capitalists, on the other. It was a struggle for cheap labor to do work of the lowest status.

As reflected in their wages, these workers asked for and received little. Former slaves had never been able to raise claims for much. The story of Ponni illustrates the hunger and lack of personal belongings of a poor agricultural worker. Her plight suggests that the cashew factory had, in fact, saved them from starvation. She also rejects the thesis that migrant labor had strong ties with their home villages, since, as she indicates, there was nothing to go back to. They had no land, and their relatives may have dispersed, since they were dependent on the landlords. It is also likely that

---

[57] Govindan Nair, *Autobiography of M.N.*, Chapter 34, pp. 147 ff.

[58] Ibid., p. 147.

[59] Alex, "Social and Economic Aspects of Attached Labourers in Kuttanad Agriculture", pp. A141-42.

[60] Ibid. , pp. A141 ff.

many of them were women, as discussed earlier, who had no family to return to. M.N. Govindan's memories of how poor agricultural laborers chose the cashew factory in preference to the paddy field confirms the fact that the cashew factory offered some advantages, however small, over the life of an agricultural laborer.

In 1953, accommodation sheds for the shellers in Quilon still existed in four out of seventeen factories investigated. Although there was one plant where about hundred workers lived in such sheds, the number of migrant workers was low.[61] The accommodation sheds gradually disappeared during the 1950s and early 1960s. The reasons for this may have been manifold. First, the shortage of workers was no more, mainly as a result of a growing population, decreasing work days in agricultural work, and the willingness of groups other than the Scheduled Castes (mainly Ezhavas) to carry out the shelling. According to several old Ezhava women, the increased wages in 1953 enticed them to overcome the objection to doing unclean work which had always been relegated to people of the Scheduled Castes, implying that the early caste barrier also had an economic dimension.[62] The expressed shortage of labor, thus, was more than a caste phenomenon. It was also a question of the unwillingness of factory owners to pay reasonable wages. Second, the industry became more and more seasonal, so that having a workforce living on one's land would tend to disturb and be inconvenient for factory owners. Then again the strategy of locating factories where the Scheduled Castes and other low-paid workers lived had developed. Finally, a general amelioration in the standard of living and the new radical policy in Kerala had its impact. Some workers moved to the Harijan Colonies provided by the government, some managed to buy some land and build their own huts, and some built them illegally.[63] In Kilikolloor, Musaliar, the "cashew-king", felt the winds of change and distributed land to his workers so that they could build their own private dwellings.[64]

The hordes of low-caste people who came to work in the cashew factories in the 1930s and 1940s have been described as half-starving, miserable,

---

[61] Govt. of India, *Report on an Enquiry into Conditions of Labour in the Cashewnut Processing Industry in India*, p. 36.

[62] Interview 9 February 1998 with Sujatha, Ezhava woman, born 1925, peeler; Interview 10 December 1997 with Seethu, Ezhava woman, born 1938, peeler, sheller.

[63] Interview 14 September 1999 with K. Chellappan, male trade union leader in Kilikolloor, born 1914; Interview 15 December 1997 with Ponni, sheller, born 1920. The policy of giving land and houses to the Scheduled Castes in special colonies had begun prior to 1947, but expanded in the following decades. See Saradamoni, *Emergence of a Slave Caste*, p. 203.

[64] Interview 14 September 1999 with K. Chellappan, male trade union leader in Kilikolloor, born 1914.

and extremely dirty—the poorest of the poor.[65] These low-caste immigrants living in the cashew sheds constituted a social group which was decried and even feared by many inhabitants in the surrounding areas.[66] Because such impoverished masses were always associated with the cashew factories, others who placed themselves socially above these migrant workers were deterred from working there.

Cashew Workers on Caste

To achieve a deeper understanding of the caste division of labor, its preservation, and the related question of the meaning and importance of caste among different groups, the cashew workers from different castes and generations must be heard—especially with regard to their contact with other castes. There are methodological problems with this approach, as caste attitudes today are condemned as traditional and backward, and it is unlikely that people want to depict themselves as such—neither in the past, and especially not in the present. However, some informants were extremely open about their own caste prejudices, especially with regard to the past. As a strategy, I found that comprehensive information on caste relations could be obtained by asking for *their parents' opinion* about other castes.

I interviewed forty-five female cashew workers of all ages and different castes, and generally the discussions were very long and intense. I have selected the most significant portions of our conversations and have chosen about one-third of their voices as representative of Nairs, Ezhavas, Kuravas, and Pulayas, extending over three different generations. I let the women select what they themselves wished to stress, in a rather free dialogue, but first I introduced the issue by asking a few general questions on caste, such as: "What do you know about the origin of caste? How has the caste system changed during your lifetime? Why has it changed? Tell me something about caste in the cashew factory." During the conversation, I introduced more direct questions, like: "Were there or are there conceptions like impurity in connection with caste, and if so, what does it mean? Has it changed? What has it meant to you to work in the department where you have been? What were your parents' opinion about other castes with regard to association, eating together, working together, or

---

[65] Interview 19 December 1997 with K. Bhanu, male former journalist in Kilikolloor, born 1913; Interview 14 September 1999 with K. Chellappan, male trade union leader in Kilikolloor, born 1914.
[66] Interview 19 December 1997 with K. Bhanu, male former journalist in Kilikolloor, born 1913.

visiting each other's houses? Have your parents changed their opinion? Have you? Why?"

The women's narratives are integrated in the following analysis under four different themes: the creation of a caste division, overcoming of certain barriers, persistence of caste division, and meaning of caste.

The creation of a caste division of labor

A common opinion among older workers was that a shift in caste composition had occurred in the cashew factories since the 1930s, when most cashew workers had belonged to the lowest castes. Two elderly women of a Scheduled Caste expressed themselves thus:

> We did not mix with higher castes in my childhood—at least not with Brahmins and Nairs—but in the paddy field some Ezhava women worked. It was in the cashew factory that I met Nairs. Almost only Kuravas and Pulayas worked in the cashew factories in the 1930s—also in the peeling section, but not in the grading section. Later on, more workers from other castes came to the cashew factories. The wages were low, but at least it was something, and we were not the only caste that was starving. When the Ezhavas saw the wages we held in our hands, they came, too. Later on, the Nairs came to the peeling section as well. But for a long time roasters and shellers were exclusively Kuravas and Pulayas, and to a great extent it is still the case.
> —Kotha, Pulaya caste, born 1919, sheller since the late 1920s[67]

> In the early factories there were hardly any castes other than Kuravas and Pulayas; we were the poorest at that time. Most Kuravas were poor and were often starving. Gradually other castes entered the factory—first the Ezhavas and then the Nairs.
> —Kavitha, Kurava caste, born around 1920, sheller since the late 1920s[68]

Other informants of the same generation recalled larger numbers of Ezhavas and Nairs entering the factories during the 1940s and 1950s. They also stated that in the earliest cashew factories there were more Scheduled Castes in the peeling section, and more Ezhavas in the grading section, than in later years.[69]

---

[67] Interview 16 August 1998.

[68] Interview 23 August 1998.

[69] Interview 30 January 1998 with Chirutha, woman of Kuruva caste, born 1919, sheller since the late 1920s; Interview 19 December 1998 with Chakki, woman of Pulaya caste, born 1927, sheller since 1935; Interview 22 December 1998 with Devaki, woman of Ezhava caste, born 1918, sheller since about 1930; Interview 5 December 1997 with Bharathiamma, woman of Nair caste, born 1912, peeler 1925-1975.

Many Ezhava women were engaged in the production of coir yarn in the 1920s and 1930s. Coir processing was principally organized as a cottage industry with its center in Alleppey, although many women in the Quilon district were also engaged in this occupation.[70] Many of the older women interviewed (especially the Ezhavas) said that their mothers or grandmothers produced coir yarn in cottages in the 1920s.

After 1928, the prices of export products related to coir declined steadily, bringing down wages as much as 70%. There was also a reduction in the hours of each worker. This was also the case in the coconut gardens, where Ezhava women were also employed.[71] The depression forced some of the poorest Ezhavas to search for jobs in the cashew factories, and in the 1940s they flocked there in even larger numbers. K.C. Govindan, the trade unionist, stated in his memoirs that many Ezhavas were found in the peeling and grading sections in the 1940s[72], but he made no mention of the Nairs, probably because the latter had not yet entered the cashew factories in large numbers.

The Nairs went through a process of impoverishment after 1925, when a new law permitted the partition of jointly-owned property. The resultant smaller landholdings were not enough for survival and many individual owners sold them and tried other occupations, or joined the ranks of the unemployed.[73] Bharathiamma, who recounted how her family had sold their land, belonged to such a family:

> My mother took me to the cashew factory. We had to start working there because our family had become poor. We had to sell most of our land. It was not common for Nairs to work in the factories at that time, and in the section where I worked most women were Ezhavas. At the outset, there was no grading at the factory, but after some time such a section was inaugurated and more Nairs came to the factory. Today there are a lot of them. I do not know what it was like in the shelling section, because we never mingled with them very much—not when I started to work, and not in the 1970s when I stopped. We could not work with the lowest castes—that was not even to be considered. I joined the union later on, but my mother never did: that was below her dignity, as most union members were Scheduled Castes.
>
> —Bharathiamma, Nair caste, born 1912, peeler 1925-1975[74]

---

[70] Pillai, *The Travancore State Manual*, Vol. IV, pp. 682, 667.
[71] Isaac, *Class Struggle and Industrial Structure*, pp. 94 ff.
[72] Govindan, *Memoires of an Early Trade Unionist*, p. 68.
[73] Govt. of India, *Census of India 1931*, Vol. XXVIII, Travancore, Part I, Report, p. 244. For an account of this process, see Jeffrey, *Politics, Women and Well Being*, pp. 41-49.
[74] Interview 5 December 1997.

In spite of abject poverty and unemployment, many Nair women avoided the cashew factories, if they had a choice. Bhaggerathi Amma's mother, was in agony because she sent her daughter to the cashew factory. As her daughter relates:

> We had become poor and my mother sent me to the factory, but she did not go herself. I think that would have been too much for her and she suffered a lot in sending me there. Besides, I had a younger sister and brother who needed attention. Women of our caste were not supposed to go to work for wages outside their houses. I came with a neighbor, a Nair girl. We were sent to the grading section, and there was never any discussion of where to work: we were just placed there. I was quite nervous because I was a bit afraid to work with Pulayas, Kuravas, or other low-caste people. We had never mingled with them before. But I knew that other Nairs worked in the factory, so I hoped to work with them—and I did. Most of the Nairs belonged to the grading section, but a few Ezhavas were there, as well. We felt that we could work with the Ezhavas, but not with the Scheduled Castes.
> —Bhaggerathi Amma, Nair caste, born 1926, grader 1940-1990[75]

It is not difficult to imagine the aversion of a Nair woman to seeking employment in the cashew factories in the 1930s and 1940s. Several elderly Nair women have testified that it was utterly shameful for them to work there for many reasons. First, as expressed by Bhaggerathi Amma, the gender ideology prevailing among the Nairs prescribed that women should stay at home. Secondly, and probably more decisively, many Nairs of the previous generation had owned considerable amounts of land in areas where agricultural laborers (mostly of Scheduled Castes, but also some Ezhavas) worked.[76] It was probably even more difficult to work together with former agricultural laborers of the lowest castes than to break the gender ideology. It was reported in the early 1930s that Nair women were employed in the government administration on a large scale because they were well-educated.[77] Such work was considered acceptable, whereas factory work was different. One way to cope with the humiliation of factory work was to be shielded from the dirtiest work (the shelling) and to be separated from the lower castes. We remember that Bharathiamma said that it was below her mother's dignity to join the union, as most of its members were Scheduled Castes. Thus, the caste division of labor was favorable to the Nairs: it could, at least, save them from being on an equal footing with the former slave castes—people that their parents had taught them to avoid, such as the

---

[75] Interview 3 January 1998.
[76] Jeffrey, *Politics, Women and Well Being*, pp. 41-49.
[77] Govt. of India, *Census of India 1931*, Vol. XXVIII, Travancore, Part I, Report, p. 241.

workers in the dwelling sheds near the cashew factories.

Among the Ezhava women of the oldest generation, a difference of opinion regarding working with the lower castes was very marked, as illustrated by Sarasu and Gomathi:

> In the beginning, it was difficult to work with them [Scheduled Castes], but not later on. I worked in the shelling section, so most of my co-workers were Scheduled Castes. I would have preferred to do the peeling, but I had no choice. I felt that I was not like them—I belonged to a nice family! Anyhow, I got used to them after some years. We were, after all, in the same situation.
> —Sarasu, Ezhava caste, born 1925, sheller since 1937[78]

> For me, there has never been any problem with caste. I became a trade union convener in the 1940s. The unions did so much to abolish the caste system at that time! My father was involved in communist politics and had some friends from the lowest castes, so his behavior taught me that the caste system was nonsense.
> —Gomathi, Ezhava caste, born 1930, sheller since 1940[79]

As pointed out earlier, the Ezhavas were a heterogeneous group with regard to their economic position in the 1930s and 1940s. Some Ezhavas had raised themselves up both economically and socially, while the status of others was not distinct from that of the Scheduled Castes, in that they carried out similar tasks. Gomathi, with a father who was active in the Communist Party and with friends among lower castes, could easily work together with Scheduled Castes, whereas the other Ezhava woman, Sarasu, who clearly expressed her negative feelings and her difficulty in having to work with Scheduled Castes, took a long time to accommodate to such a situation. The difference between Sarasu and Gomathi could be attributed to class position, but probably Gomathi's experience of her father as a communist politician, and her own trade union activity, enabled her to work with Scheduled Castes without any problems.

Another woman, Thankamoni, told how she differed from her parents with regard to associating with lower castes:

> I never had anything against working with Scheduled Castes, but my parents disliked all connections with them. But gradually they changed a little.

---

[78] Interview 1 February 1998.
[79] Interview 30 August 1998.
[80] Interview 14 August 1998.

I came to the peeling section since my mother worked there. When I started to work in the cashew factory, there were some Nairs and Ezhavas who did not like to be associated with Scheduled Castes, but they never said anything—they just kept to themselves.

—Thankamoni, Ezhava caste, born 1946, peeler since 1958[80]

Thankamoni's mother, who was born in the early 1920s, obviously had difficulty in relating to Scheduled Castes for a long time, whereas Thankamoni herself was able to accept working with them in the 1950s. However, several Ezhava women, such as Sarasu, indicated how uncomfortable it was for her to be associated with Scheduled Castes when she asserted that *she* belonged to a "nice family". Not only Nairs, but also many Ezhava women were active in trying to establish and maintain a caste division of labor, even though some of them had to work with Scheduled Castes.

The decreasing proportion of Scheduled Castes in the cashew factories was mainly due to the single circumstance that women belonging to castes *which traditionally did not work outside the home* were forced to seek their livelihood in the cashew factories. In my interviews with women of different castes, all of whom were born in the 1920s or 1930s, the majority of the mothers of Nair women were either housewives or worked producing something at home, whereas the mothers of Scheduled Caste women, without exception, worked outside the home as agricultural laborers, cashew workers, sweepers, or domestic servants. It became apparent that the higher in the caste hierarchy one goes, the more dominant the gender ideology which prescribes that women remain housewives—something also noticed in 1931 by the author of the Travancore Census.[81]

When Scheduled Caste women met upper-caste women (such as Nairs) in the cashew factories, historic overtones conditioned their encounter. On the side of the Nairs, who had lived mainly on the income from their land, it represented a humiliating process of proletarization and caste interaction. For the lower castes, who were used to working as bonded laborers under a landlord with whom they were in a relationship similar to that of master and slave, work in the cashew factory—although conditions there have been described as slavish—was an improvement.

In the 1930s, wages in the cashew factories did not appear linked to caste in the three main processing areas. In fact, wages in the less desirable shelling section were even slightly higher than in the peeling and grading sections. During this period, only the wage rates in Musaliar's factories are

---

[81] Govt. of India, *Census of India 1931*, Vol. XXVIII, Travancore, Part I, Report, p. 241.

known for certain, although it is likely that they did not differ much in the other factories. Wages in the shelling and peeling departments were based on a piece rate. Although we cannot presume that workers were actually paid the wages listed, the official rates are worth noting, as they must have been calculated with some ideas of the relative value of work in different sections.

Table 5.3. Daily wages in different departments of Musaliar's factories, 1932 and 1939*

	1932	1939
Shelling	112 casu	140 casu
Peeling	88 casu	110 casu
Grading	96 casu	112 casu

Source: RSP, Office, Quilon, "Wage Rates in the cashew industry 1932 and 1939" (dated 1939). This table is based on calculations of piece-rate wages for shelling and peeling. I estimate a daily output of 7 and 5.5 kilos respectively for shelling and peeling, which was an estimated average in 1952.

*I have converted monetary units from *chuckrams* to *casu* to facilitate comparison. *Chuckrams* and *casu* were the coins of Travancore. One *chuckram* was equal to 16 *casu*. One British rupee was 28.5 *chuckrams*.

Higher wages for shelling reflected the difficulty of getting enough workers in this section. One of Musaliar's main concerns in 1953, when minimum wages were about to be introduced, was to keep the wages of the peelers down; otherwise "no worker can be had for the shelling section".[82] We may conclude that employers had nothing to gain from a caste division of labor. Until trade unions became active in 1939, it appears that the division of labor based on caste was, to a great extent, a phenomenon which reflected Travancore society outside the factory. The laborers themselves—mainly those castes who stood above the Scheduled Castes—kept up a caste division of labor. Employers and managers must have also had the same caste prejudices as their workers and supported the caste division of labor for cultural reasons.

When trade unions started their activities, there was evident benefit for the employers in maintaining the split between workers. The lower castes in the shelling section were the ones who first had organized on a large scale.[83]

[82] Govt. of Travancore-Cochin, *Report of the Minimum Wages Committee for Cashew Industry 1953*, p. 45.
[83] KSA, Confidential file 48/238, Letter from Police Inspector Karim Sahib to Chief Secretary, Government of Travancore in Trivandrum, dated 11th May 1939; Interview 14 September 1999 with K. Chellappan, male trade union leader, born 1914; Interview 30 January 1998 with Kotha, woman of Pulaya caste, born 1919, sheller since the late 1920s; Interview 19 December 1998 with Chakki, woman of Pulaya caste, born 1927, sheller since 1935; Interview 5 December 1997 with Bharathiamma, woman of Nair caste, born 1912, peeler 1925-1975.

In the 1940s, one reason for the employers to segregate different castes was to prevent workers from joining the unions. Thus, the employers used and encouraged an existing social order for strategic purposes, as pointed out by M.N. Govindan Nair.[84] A trade union leader, J. Chitharanjan, who was active among the cashew workers in the late 1940s and early 1950s, remembered how difficult it was to organize Nair women, but also recalled their reluctance to work alongside lower castes—an observation very much in line with the workers' own statements.[85]

The women who did not belong to the Scheduled Castes were convinced by their employers to abstain from joining the union. They were told that it was beneath their dignity to join in a common organization for it would imply involvement with foreign, low-caste men.[86] I continually heard stories of husbands being pressured by representatives of the factory owners to control their women. To Govindan's statement that the employers "harped on caste and religion", we might add that they underscored gender as well, in order to create divisiveness among the workers. Several women of Nair and Ezhava caste, including Bhaggerathi Amma and Sarasu (see below), recalled that the factory owner's men had told their husbands to prevent their wives from joining the union.

> In the 1940s my husband told me several times not to join the union, because it could be dangerous and also because only Pulayas and Kuravas—men and women—were members. People from the factory came to our house to talk with my husband about these things. But finally I joined, like many other Ezhavas, and my husband agreed after the leaders of the union came to our house.
> —Sarasu, Ezhava caste, born 1925, sheller since 1937[87]

> In the 1950s, I joined the union, the communists, but first my husband told me to be careful, since most of the trade union members were Kuravas. He did not like them; that's why I did not join in the first place. Moreover, he had been warned by the supervisor of the factory. Later on, he became a member himself, and then I joined, too.
> —Bhaggerathi Amma, Nair caste, born 1926, grader 1940-1990[88]

Some Nairs were quite reluctant to join the union in the 1940s and early 1950s, but were gradually convinced of their common class interest as

---

[84] Govindan Nair, *Autobiography of M.N.*, Chapter 30, pp. 122-127.
[85] Interview 7 August 1998 with J. Chitharanjan, male trade union leader, politician.
[86] Ibid.
[87] Interview 1 February 1998.
[88] Interview 3 January 1998.

workers with the lower castes. However, before this rapprochement could occur, Nair women needed the approval of their husbands—an illustration of the deference and submissiveness of a "good" wife. Their husbands held the power to keep them from joining the union. Not only would they be coming into contact with Scheduled Castes, but with *men* of those castes.

On the other hand, Kavitha, the Kurava woman, joined the union without her husband's consent and even against his will, exemplifying the relative independence vis-à-vis their husbands enjoyed by low-caste women.

> The Kuravas were the first to join the union. I became a member of the communist union at the time of the Travancore king. My husband objected a little, but when he met the leaders he realized that I had done the right thing.
> —Kavitha, Kurava caste, born around 1920, sheller since the late 1920s[89]

In 1968, K.C. Alexander, in a study of Pulayas in Kerala, noted that low-caste women were documented as opposing their husbands in public, a behavior unknown among higher caste women.[90] Kavitha's mentioning of her husband's opinion indicates that—at least today—it could be considered a bit unusual, perhaps even suspicious, to act against a husband's will. However, several other elderly low-caste women told me that they joined the union in the 1940s and 1950s without asking their husbands for permission.[91]

Overcoming caste barriers

Central to the caste system were the rules of pollution in connection with food. Traditionally, caste rules restricted the acceptance of food from members of lower castes, and regulated with whom a person could share a meal.[92] In 1918, the social reformer of the Ezhava caste, K. Aiyappan, organized a lunch for 5,000 persons of different castes to break the taboo of inter-dining.[93] Inter-dining with lower castes like Pulayas was, however,

---

[89] Interview 12 August 1998.

[90] Alexander, *Social Mobility in Kerala*, p. 68.

[91] Interview 30 January 1998 with Kotha, Pulaya woman, born 1919; Interview 12 January 1998 with Chirutha, Kurava woman, born 1919; Interview 29 December 1998 with Theye, Kurava woman, born 1922; Interview 18 January 1999 with Kunji, Pulaya woman, born around 1920.

[92] The relationsship depended upon the ritual status of the persons concerned, but also upon the ritual purity and type of food given or received. *Kachcha* food, i.e., food cooked in water, such as rice, was considered to be highly pollutable, hence the rules involved with this kind of food were stricter. *Pakka* food is cooked in oil or *ghee*, e.g., vegetables, and was regarded as less pollutable. See Ahuja Ram, *Indian Social System* (Jaipur, 1993), pp. 304 ff.

[93] Genevieve Lemercinier, *Religion and Ideology in Kerala* (Trivandrum, 1994), p. 197.

not welcomed by all Ezhavas and it is reported that Aiyappan was "beaten up by izhava [Ezhava] leaders, who were ardent followers of Sri Narayana Guru".[94] In the following decades, inter-caste dining programs became an important part of the workers' struggle.[95] In 1938, the young communist, K. Damodaran, "shocked his Nair family" by inviting people of different castes, including a Pulaya, to eat at their house.[96] Damodaran's narrative helps us understand the deep-rooted mentality and strength of the caste rules that continued to thrive even after the Temple Entry Proclamation of 1936, which legally abolished untouchability.

The Factory Act of 1948 encompassed the cashew factories in Travancore-Cochin and declared that workers should be provided with such amenities of human welfare as restrooms and child-care. Factories in which more than 250 workers were employed should provide a canteen. Some of the cashew factory employers asserted that "caste prejudices would militate [against] the successful working of canteens".[97] In 1953, civil servants from the labor department expressed the tacit opinion that the reason for the lack of canteens was not to be found in caste prejudice. Noting that no factory in their sample had tried a canteen, these investigators blamed the factory owners for trying to avoid compliance with the Factory Act on the *pretext* of caste barriers among the workers.[98]

In theory, caste prejudice may have prevented the success of canteens in the early 1950s, but, in fact, most of the workers did not eat at all during their working day. In 1949 and 1950, Sarademma, a female trade union activist connected with the Communist Party, took a job in a cashew factory with the intention of organizing the workers there. She recalled that workers hardly had any money to buy even a cup of tea.[99] The trade union leader, J. Chitharanjan, who lived underground with the cashew workers in 1949 and 1950, also witnessed their poverty. "I was shocked. Most of them cooked only once a day—in the evening. They worked all day without eating at all. They just drank some water".[100] However, there were some workers who could afford to eat, as the Nair woman, Bhaggerathi Amma, related:

---

[94] Saradamoni, *Emergence of a Slave Caste*, p. 146.
[95] Meera Velayudhan, "Caste, Class and Political Organisation of Women in Travancore", *Social Scientist*, 19:5-6 (1991), p. 64; Kathleen Gough, "Palakkara: Social and Religious Change in Central Kerala", in K. Ishwaran (ed.), *Change and Continuity in India's Villages* (New York, 1970), p. 149.
[96] Robin Jeffrey interviewed K. Damodaran in 1975. See Jeffrey, *Politics, Women and Well Being*, p. 126.
[97] Govt. of India, *Report on an Enquiry into Conditions of Labour in the Cashewnut Processing Industry in India*, pp. 36-37.
[98] Ibid.
[99] Interview 19 November 1997 with J. Sarademma, female trade union activist, born 1933.
[100] Interview 12 January 1998 with J. Chitharanjan, male trade union leader, politician.

> Pulayas are a bit higher than Kuravas, but there is not much difference. Even if it was hard to mingle with them, we did not say anything. During lunch, those who felt that it was difficult to eat near to them sat a bit away—silent—they never said anything. People did not eat together before. It was like an unwritten law, just like the rule that low-caste people were not allowed to go inside the house of high-caste people.
>
> —Bhaggerathi Amma, Nair caste, born 1926, grader 1940-1990[101]

Some of the Ezhavas had similar feelings, although perhaps on a lesser scale.

> In my family, when I was young, we never let low-caste people come inside our house. And I would never take food from them—not even water. I would not touch it! They can eat our food and we can accept food from the Nairs, but not from them, the Scheduled Castes. My children would not do that either; we are from a nice family. At lunch break, we sat outside the shelling shed and ate, but I always brought my own food.
>
> —Sarasu, Ezhava caste, born 1925, sheller since 1937[102]

There were far fewer graders than shellers and peelers, and the Nairs were, in fact, a minority in the factories, so even if they had refused to visit the canteen, more than 80% of the workers still might. The reason for the "failure" of the dining-room in the only factory which did have a canteen in the early 1950s was probably attributable to the extreme poverty of the workers, and not primarily to caste barriers.[103]

The interviewees unanimously felt that trade union leaders were decisive in breaking caste barriers in the 1940s and 1950s.

> There was no caste problem in the factory, but most of the higher castes did not eat with us or speak to us. In the beginning they did not join the union. But after some years, when we had been fighting through the trade unions and they saw the help we got, they joined, too. But at home we seldom met. The leaders at that time, Sreekantan Nair, M.N. Govindan Nair, and K. Chellappan, did so much to make people overcome the old caste feelings. The leaders even slept in the houses of Pulayas themselves. Everybody knows that one of the famous leaders, a Nair, has two children with a sheller, a Pulaya woman. He did not live with them, but he paid for education and everything for them.
>
> —Kotha, Pulaya caste, born 1919, sheller since the late 1920s[104]

---

[101] Interview 3 January 1998.
[102] Interview 1 February 1998.
[103] Govt. of Travancore-Cochin, *Report of the Minimum Wages Committee for Cashew Industry 1953*, p. 43.
[104] Interview 16 August 1998.

In the 1940s, the union leaders talked a lot about caste and inter-caste dining and things like that. They even organized such dinners here in our village. I went to such a dinner; it was exciting and unusual, but there were no
problems at all.
—Kavitha, Kurava caste, born around 1920, sheller since the late 1920s[105]

With regard to cooperation between different castes, I would say that the
factory has been a better place than outside. At the factory, we became all
alike, especially after the trade unions had agitated so much during the years
before we got minimum wages and other benefits. The communists did so
much to change the minds of the people with regard to caste. They were
most active in the abolition of caste prejudices.
—Gomathi, Ezhava caste, born 1930, sheller since 1940[106]

As many women verified in their stories, the trade union leaders made great
efforts in the 1940s and 1950s to spread the message about overcoming
caste barriers. Meetings were held and discussions were initiated outside
the factories. Trade union leaders visited workers of all castes in their homes
and tried to convince them of the importance of giving class priority over
caste.[107] The agitation coincided with declarations that some unions were
unlawful, and several leaders—mainly Nairs and Ezhavas—hid among the
cashew workers. The statement from Kotha, the elderly Pulaya woman,
that union leaders of the Nair caste "even slept in the houses of Pulayas"
illustrates how extraordinary such an action was considered. It was with
some pride that she recounted the higher-caste trade union leader's willingness to pay for the children of the Pulaya woman whose biological father he
was, suggesting that this was not a matter of course.

The trade union leader, M.N. Govindan, was of the opinion that female cashew workers broke caste as well as religious barriers, a phenomenon which surprised the politicians at the time, since rural women, in general, were considered to be more conservative than men when it came to
religious and caste restrictions. Govindan did not specify which castes he
was alluding to, but he seemed to be referring to the Ezhavas and the
former agricultural slave castes, i.e., Pulayas, Parayans, and Kuravas. Otherwise, his statement contrasts with that of two contemporary trade union

---

[105] Interview 25 August 1998.
[106] Interview 30 August 1998.
[107] Govindan Nair, *Autobiography of M.N.*, Chapters 32 and 40; Interview 19 December
1997 with K. Bhanu, former journalist in Kilikolloor, born 1913; Interview 14 September 1999 with K. Chellappan, male trade union leader in Kilikolloor, born 1914; Interview 23 August 1998 with Gomathi, sheller, born 1930; Interview 7 August 1998 with J.
Chitharanjan, male trade union leader, politician.

leaders (K.C. Govindan and Sreekantan Nair), who witnessed the rigid caste division of labor and the lack of Nair women among the cashew workers, and also differs with the words of my informants.[108]

Georg Alex has shown that in the rice cultivating region of Kuttanad in the 1920s and 1930s the caste division of labor among women of the Ezhavas and the Scheduled Castes was not nearly as pronounced as among male workers.[109] As the old Pulaya woman, Kotha, had stated, in the rural area where the cashew factories were located, some Ezhava women had already worked in the paddy fields with women of Scheduled Castes, which facilitated their working side by side with them in the factories. Perhaps the Ezhavas who first began to work in the shelling section were those who were used to working with Scheduled Castes or others who were active in trade unions, such as Gomathi.

The Ezhavas who began in the cashew factories in the Quilon area did not openly show any caste prejudice in the 1930s and 1940s. Still, many of them preferred to work in sections other than shelling. For some of them, however, there was no choice. With poverty the motivating force, there was no scope for caste prejudice, as Gomathi expressed:

> I have seen some Ezhavas and Nairs who have had severe problems in cooperating with the Pulayas and Kuravas, but in the factory the majority just accepted the situation. How could we care about caste when our children were starving? Everybody needed every *paisa* [1/100 of a rupee]. They, too, had hungry children and did not want to create problems, and gradually they changed.
>
> —Gomathi, Ezhava caste, born 1930, sheller since 1940[110]

From such stories one sees that the caste problem was an internal process in the workers' minds, and that clashes or overt problems hardly existed inside the factories. The strategy of the higher castes was rather to remain silently aloof, avoid joining the union, and refrain from showing any antagonism. They were too dependent on their small incomes to object, and the proclamations of unity by trade unions probably hampered direct caste clashes, as well. Elsewhere, as among some Ezhavas of the Christian faith, the same harmony did not prevail. The British missionary, Bishop Leggs, complained in 1953 that some groups of Ezhavas did not have the correct Christian spirit. They were accused of separating themselves from the lower castes and showing a superior attitude towards those communities. The

---

[108] Govindan, *Memoires of an Early Trade Unionist*, p. 68; Sreekantan Nair, *Memories of the Past*, Chapter 44.

[109] Alex, "Social and Economic Aspects", pp. A141-142.

[110] Interview 30 August 1998.

bishop asserted that some Ezhavas impeded low-caste Christians from church activity and "prevented their success".[111]

Without exception, those cashew workers interviewed were of the opinion that the factory was a better place than outside. Gomathi alluded to this when she recalled caste restrictions of the 1940s and 1950s. The shared experience of poverty among cashew workers was decisive in the breaking of caste barriers. In addition, one should not underestimate the propaganda of trade union leaders during his period. There was a strong consensus among the workers interviewed that this agitation contributed to the breaking of caste barriers. Over and over again, the leaders spoke out against caste hierarchy and also broke barriers in practice when they hid among cashew workers and lived in their houses. However, their efforts seem to have been restricted to mobilizing workers of different castes into trade unions for joint actions against the factory owners, and failed to address the caste division of labor. None of the workers interviewed remembered any efforts on the part of trade union leaders to deal with this issue.

> We didn't see each other much in the factory, but when there was a problem we could cooperate. But nobody ever spoke about working more together. You just went to the division where you were placed—nobody has questioned that. We, the Kuravas and Pulayas, who were the shellers, were always in the forefront of the unions. Others were more scared than us. It is still a little bit like that.
>
> —Kavitha, Kurava caste, born around 1920, sheller since the late 1920s[112]

> My parents would never have entered the house of a Pulaya—maybe of Ezhavas, but never a house of the Scheduled Castes. I was taught that way, but gradually I changed my mind. We worked in different sections, but we could join together when there was a problem. But I did not want to work with shelling. It is far too dirty.
>
> —Bhaggerathi Amma, Nair caste, born 1926, grader 1940-1990[113]

Similar statements were voiced in several interviews. Thus, caste barriers were only broken on particular occasions in order to fight against capital, but less so in daily life. The workers interviewed unanimously declared that agitation against caste prejudice initiated by trade union leaders fizzled out and was discontinued in the first half of the 1960s, by which time most workers were already organized into unions.

---

[111] SOAS, CWM Archives, Indian Correspondence 1951-60, Box No. IN/4-B, Letter from A.H. Leggs to Mr. Craig, CWM Office in London, dated the 8 September 1953.
[112] Interview 25 August 1998.
[113] Interview 3 January 1998.

It is conspicuous that in their historical accounts of Kerala, trade unions stress their own role in the process of changing caste identity to class identity.[114] The link between the trade unions and the process "from caste to class" was expressed by the Ezhava woman, Gomathi, who explained her own ability to cooperate with Scheduled Castes as early as the 1940s by her activity in the trade union. Such accounts are part of the official story and the leftist discourse which such women have absorbed. This, however, is not to say that these women just repeated what they had been taught. Union leaders were most probably extremely active in agitating against caste hierarchies, and their role was important in the abandonment of prejudice—something the women interviewed remembered. But the discourse seems to have determined how "abolition of the caste system" should be defined:

> The caste system disappeared about twenty years ago or maybe thirty. It belongs to the past—now people are modern and don't accept being treated like that.
> —Sarasu, Ezhava caste, born 1925, sheller since 1937[115]

> My parents could not accept food from lower castes, but today we do. Old rules like that disappeared with time, maybe thirty years ago. If someone brings rice to the factory, we eat from the same plate. The caste system is no more.
> —Thankamoni, Ezhava caste, born 1946, peeler since 1958[116]

> My parents had some difficulties associating with low-caste people, but gradually they changed. The caste system disappeared more than twenty years ago! But I still prefer to eat only my own food—it has nothing to do with caste. I don't take food from anyone.
> —Raji, Ezhava caste, born 1957, trade union convener, sheller since 1968[117]

> The caste system is nothing to speak about today—it was abandoned maybe thirty years ago. But at the time when I started to work, it was very pronounced.
> —Bharathiamma, Nair caste, born 1912, peeler 1925-1975[118]

---

[114] Azeez, "The Great Organisation of Cashew Workers"; Majeed, *The Strike History*; Kesavan Nair, "A Brief History of Trade Union Movement among Cashew Workers" (Paper presented at the Conference on Development in Kerala, AKG-Centre, Trivandrum 1994); Kesavan Nair, "The Strike History of the Cashew Workers, part 1-29", *CITU Sandesam*, Vol. 17-19 (1993–1996) (in Malayalam).

[115] Interview 1 February 1998.

[116] Interview 22 February 1999.

[117] Interview 7 February 1999.

[118] Interview 8 December 1997.

When I was a child some people did not let us into their houses or let us use the wells. I also remember that my father, just before he left us fifteen years ago, was pushed into a ditch by a Nair for not moving when they met at the patch, but I never hear about things like that today. Every day I take water from this well, which belongs to a Nair family, and there is no problem. The *ayah* (she was an Ezhava, in the factory where I worked) refused to touch the Pulaya children, especially if they were wet, so we always had to come and wash them ourselves. She stopped working there a couple of years ago, and the next *ayah* was different. But that evil *ayah*, she was exceptional: she even protected her hands with a piece of paper when she had to touch our children. But usually things like that disappeared ten or maybe twenty years ago.
—Geetha, Pulaya caste, born 1973, sheller since 1987[119]

In the stories above, several women were in agreement that the caste system disappeared twenty to thirty years ago. They seem to have meant that the most conspicuous features of the caste system, such as derogatory treatment of lower castes, inability to eat together, untouchability, or lack of social interaction among different castes, were dismantled. Many aspects, however, like the caste division of labor and endogamous marriages, were left unchallenged and unchanged.

The persistence of the caste division of labor

The main dividing line among workers in the cashew factories has been that between the Scheduled Castes and the Nairs. The Ezhavas move on both sides of this division, whereas the Scheduled Castes show a remarkable continuity in the shelling section. State-owned factories present the same historical pattern. They took over existing plants where work assignments were already stratified, thus accounting for the persistence of caste composition in certain departments. Moreover, when new workers were recruited, they were already trained and skilled by working in other factories or *kudivarappus*, another reason for the continuity of caste division in the work place.

It is very difficult to determine whether higher caste women are reluctant to work in the shelling section nowadays because of an unwillingness to mix with Scheduled Castes, or because of the nature of the work—or both. The interviews suggest that a shift from an aversion to ritual impurity toward a more materialist concern with uncleanliness has occurred.[120]

---

[119] Interview 18 January 1998.
[120] For similar results, see Ramaswamy, *Work, Union and Community*, p. 107.

> When the owner needed graders there were always women who brought
> their daughters or some other relatives to the factory. That was how we got
> work in that section all the time. After some time we got used to the lower
> castes and I did not mind eating with them—if they were clean.
> —Bhaggerathi Amma, Nair caste, born 1926, grader 1940-1990[121]

> I can't remember my parents having any difficulties mingling with Sched-
> uled Castes—at least not with those who behaved in a nice way and were
> clean. As I told you—my father was a communist politician, so he was fight-
> ing against caste hierarchy!
> —Gomathi, Ezhava caste, born 1930, sheller since 1940[122]

> In my mother's house, they did not even let low-caste people into the yard. I
> have nothing against low-caste people, as long as they are clean.
> —Thankamoni, Ezhava caste, born 1946, peeler since 1958[123]

In the 1930s and 1940s many Nair women, such as Bhaggerathi Amma's
mother and Bharathiamma, refused to work with Scheduled Castes, however clean they were. For them it probably was a fear of ritual impurity. In
the 1930s, Bhaggerathi Amma found it easier to work with Ezhavas than
Scheduled Castes; but gradually she grew accustomed to them and accepted them "as long as they were clean"—an expression often used by younger
Nair women interviewed, when they speak about Scheduled Castes. Leela
is a typical example:

> I got the job in the grading section in the cashew factory when my mother
> introduced me there. After the cashew factory was closed down for some
> time, I could not get a job as a grader. I was offered shelling. I did not want
> to, because I did not know that job, so I would lose income. I also disliked
> the dirt in that section. Anyhow, I had to go there. They had started to wear
> gloves to protect their hands, so I agreed to go. We were only a few Nairs in
> that section. I never had anything against the Pulayas and other low-caste
> women, as long as they were clean, but maybe my parents had. They would
> not have taken any food from them, but I never thought that way. But I
> think my parents changed a bit with time.
> —Leela, Nair caste, born 1950, grader 1968-1980, sheller since 1982[124]

Younger Nairs found it acceptable to do shelling, because they could wear
gloves, which may have enabled them to believe that the nature of the work

---

[121] Interview 3 January 1998.
[122] Interview 30 August 1998.
[123] Interview 14 August 1998.
[124] Interview 3 March 1998.

had created their aversion to shelling, not the caste of their coworkers.

On the other hand, old attitudes regarding caste were still manifest among Nairs in the late 1990s. Most of the workers interviewed testified to the fact that close friendships between Scheduled Castes and Nairs outside the factory were rare. Moreover, negative caste-related incidents continue to recur in comparatively recent times, as when Geetha's father was pushed into the ditch for reasons connected to his caste in the mid-1980s, or when the *ayah* refused to touch the children of the Pulayas. The statements below illustrate how young Nair women often think in hierarchical terms with regard to caste:

> I wanted to do grading—it is cleaner and some of my friends work there—but it was not possible. Most of the peelers are Ezhavas, but there are also many Nairs. I would not like to go into the shelling section, even if I was paid better. It is so dirty—almost only Scheduled Castes work there. They are used to doing that work—we are not—which is not to say that they are bad. I have nothing against them.
> —Chitra, Nair born 1968, peeler since 1986[125]

> Anyhow, neither I nor my parents mingled very much with Scheduled Castes. We never did, but I do have some close friends of the Ezhava caste—they are a bit higher than Scheduled Castes.
> —Leela, Nair caste, born 1950, grader 1968-1980, sheller since 1982[126]

In turn, Scheduled Castes and Ezhavas, held the view that the Nairs in the cashew factory were better than other Nairs—"less snooty", as Raji, the Ezhava woman, expressed it.

> The Ezhavas started to work with us early on, but the Nairs—they don't want to soil their hands. They are a little bit like that, a little bit higher than others. Still they will not come to our houses.
> —Kavitha, Kurava caste, born around 1920, sheller since the late 1920s[127]

> We can work together, but when it comes to close interaction, things may be different. And still some people do not accept eating food prepared by lower castes—but I suppose they are few. For some people the caste feeling is there, deep in their minds. Externally, they show friendliness, but in their hearts they are not reconciled.
> —Gomathi, Ezhava caste, born 1930, sheller since 1940[128]

---

[125] Interview 24 August 1998.
[126] Interview 3 March 1998.
[127] Interview 25 August 1998.
[128] Interview 30 August 1998.

I learned to shell with my mother when I was a child. I used to come to the factory and sit next to her—that is how I started to shell. But it is difficult for us [Pulayas] to go to the grading or peeling section; the jobs there are for relatives of the Nairs, Christians, and Muslims. When there is a vacant place, it will be filled immediately—mostly by their young daughters with "clean hands". We have no chance.

—Sarojini, Pulaya caste, born 1954, sheller since 1966[129]

I started to work when I was ten years old and I have always been working with Scheduled Castes. The Nairs are all right, too. Those in the factory are less snooty than some others. In the factory there has never been any problem—it is just that they don't want to touch the dirty raw nuts. Some people talk about low-caste people being dirty and bad, but I'll tell you what: only those who speak like that are dirty in their minds.

—Raji, Ezhava caste, born 1957, trade union convener, sheller since 1968[130]

When I came to the factory, I was placed in shelling because I was trained a bit in that work. I had worked with my mother in a small factory before, so I knew that work. The Nairs don't come to that section; you know they are a bit "finer and higher" than us and they are afraid of soiling their hands. But the Nair girls in the factory are better than most other Nairs.

—Geetha, Pulaya caste, born 1973, sheller since 1987[131]

Most of my informants shared the view that caste restrictions connected to food disappeared around 1970. In 1965, almost 80% of the factories under statutory obligation to provide canteens had fulfilled their duty.[132] From around that time on, caste arguments for not having canteens disappear from official inquiries regarding the cashew factories, and it becomes no longer acceptable to speak in terms of caste in public.[133] The canteen system was put into practice during the 1960s, but deteriorated in the late 1970s and 1980s. Outsiders primarily ran the canteens on a contract basis in those factories which had them. With the decline in the number of working days in the factories, there was no longer any motivation for the contractors who ran the canteens to keep them up. A research team that interviewed 8,000 cashew

---

[129] Interview 29 August 1998.
[130] Interview 7 February 1999.
[131] Interview 2 September 1998.
[132] Govt. of India, *Report on Survey of Labour Conditions in Cashewnut Factories in India 1965-66*, pp. 22 ff.
[133] Chirayath, *A Study on the Cashew Industry in Kerala 1965*; Govt. of India, *Report on the Working and Living Conditions of Workers in the Cashewnut Processing Industry in Kerala 1982*.

workers in 1989 found hardly any canteens in evidence. However, in view of their poverty, many workers "did not care much about this aspect of welfare", as most of them could not afford to buy lunch[134]—just as in the 1950s. In the late 1990s, canteens were very rare, even in state-owned factories, despite legislation mandating them. Instead, workers would sit outside the sheds where they worked and eat their lunch, suggesting that the Scheduled Castes still only mingled with the Nairs to a very limited extent. In 1998, the author of an official report interpreted this as a caste phenomenon.[135] Most Nairs and Ezhavas, however, deny that such prejudices still exist.

One can never be sure of the purport of Raji's statement that "she only eats food cooked by herself". Is the reason that she is not reconciled in her heart, as suggested by Gomathi in an interview cited earlier? Or is Thankamoni correct in stating that different castes can eat together today—even from the same plate? For most informants it seems as if eating their own home-cooked food together with other castes was only problematic long ago—i.e., in the 1930s and 1940s, and less so in the 1950s. Even Sarasu, the Ezhava woman who openly expressed her negative feelings toward Scheduled Castes and asserted that she would still not even touch food cooked by Pulayas, told us that eating near them did not disturb her, as long as the food *she* ate was cooked in her own house. The observation, in 1998, that different castes ate at different places in the factory was probably more due to social familiarity with one's closest fellow-workers than to caste prejudice about inter-dining.

In her study of a factory in the 1970s, Uma Ramaswamy found that women were more conservative and would observe pollution taboos to a greater extent than male workers.[136] The proportion of men in the cashew factories is small, and the evidence we have for this is meager. My findings indicate that the caste division of labor which has existed in female-dominated sections was also prevalent (and continues to this day) among male cashew workers. In the roasting section, Scheduled Castes still dominate, and the apprehension that unclean work is *infra dig* and appropriate only for Scheduled Castes seems to be valid for both genders. That there were female roasters and male shellers in the early cashew factories has already been discussed. I have never found any indication of adult male graders and have encountered very few peelers. It appears that the possibility of men and women

---

[134] R. Gopalakrishnan Nair and T.S. Thomas, "Socio-Economic Conditions of Working Women in Cashew Industry in Quilon District, Kerala" (Loyola College of Social Sciences, Trivandrum, 1989), p. 67.

[135] S. Krishnakumar, "Women in Workforce—The Cashewnut Labourers in the State of Kerala" (Report, Centre for Education and Communication, New Delhi, 1998). During the period from 1997 to 2000, I visited twelve cashew factories, only one of which had a canteen.

CHAPTER 5

carrying out the same kind of work only came into consideration for Scheduled Castes.

We saw earlier that the growing unemployment and poverty of the 1930s and 1940s, which included a proletarianization of many Nair families, was a decisive reason for women of higher castes to enter the cashew factories for the first time, and thereby break down caste barriers to some extent. Later, however, unemployment served as a force to *preserve* the caste division of labor.

Unemployment, among women as well as among men, has steadily increased since the 1950s.[137] Agricultural work might have been an alternative for the women in the cashew factories, especially for the Scheduled Castes and the Ezhavas. However, the women I interviewed all agreed it has become increasingly difficult for them, as well as for the male members of their families, to find work in the agricultural sector during the past five decades—a phenomenon which has been well documented elsewhere, too.[138]

Since about 1960, due to growing unemployment and the seasonal nature of work in the plants (see Chapter III), employment in the cashew factories has become very competitive. Workers have secured their daughters and relatives a place in the factory to such an extent that employers need never look for new workers when they are needed. In eighty-five interviews with female workers at the Viyalalaksmi Cashew factory in January 1998, I found that 80% of them obtained their jobs as shellers, peelers, or graders through their mothers. This was further confirmed through the in-depth interviews I conducted. The majority of these women testified to being part of a labor tradition which placed several generations of women in the same occupation. The reason for the persisting caste division of labor can, therefore, also be understood in terms of competition for jobs. The skill of the workers is also a contributing factor. Workers learn such skills from their mothers, whether at home or in the factory; later very few of them want to shift to another section, as it could mean a decrease in piece-work wages due to their inexperience. It is, however, important to note that there is not any difference in *formal* training or stipulated daily minimum wages between the three female-dominated departments.

The declining proportion of Scheduled Castes in the cashew industry, a

[136] Ramaswamy, *Work, Union and Community*, p 105.
[137] P.P. Pillai, *Kerala Economy Four Decades of Development* (Thrissur, 1994), pp. 166-176.
[138] Govt. of Kerala, *Report of the Survey on Socio-Economic Conditions of Agricultural and other Rural Labourers in Kerala, 1983-1984* (Trivandrum, 1985); Joan Mencher, "The Lessons and Non-Lessons of Kerala: Agricultural Labourers and Poverty", *Economic and Political Weekly*, 15 (1980), pp. 1781-1802; Tharamangalam, *Agrarian Class Conflict*, pp. 59-65.

trend which began in the 1940s, has further accelerated lately—at least in the state-owned factories. In these, the proportion of Scheduled Castes has declined from about 45% in 1970 to 30% in 1998.[139] Employment in the KSCDC factories are coveted since it ensures workers certain fringe benefits often denied to their counterparts in the private factories.[140] Scheduled Caste women seem to have had difficulty in maintaining their dominance in the cashew factories. Uma Ramaswamy, in researching the cotton industry in Coimbatore, came to a similar conclusion.[141] It appears as if Scheduled Castes have been discriminated against when applying for jobs, something which may be ascribed to growing unemployment. In contrast to the situation in the cotton industry in Coimbatore, however, the Scheduled Castes have been clustered in a department with lower dignity. Old concepts of ritual pollution have gradually stopped being given as a reason for preserving the caste division of labor. Caste ceased to be a category in the census of 1951. Leftist politicians and union leaders declared that their work had led to the abandonment of caste, so civil servants started to use the category "class" instead when referring to certain groups. As a result of this new and "modern" discourse which gradually took shape after 1950, people of different castes have been able to work together and eat together during the past three or four decades without any overt display of caste prejudice.

Nevertheless, there still exists an unexpressed hierarchy in the three sections of the cashew factories. As this hierarchy is based on cleanliness, it could be related to concepts like pollution and purity, and position in the social hierarchy. The factory has, to some extent, been a site where caste prejudices were overcome, especially during the first half of the period studied—a time when, it should be remembered, caste discrimination outside the factory was pronounced. On the other hand, such caste division as has survived in the workplace has served to reinforce old conceptions of caste values. Visiting cashew factories in 1997-2000, I noted that the degree of cleanliness, healthy environment, and worker comforts followed the caste hierarchy. This, in turn, diminished the already low dignity of the Scheduled Castes still further. In some studies of cashew factories, it has been observed that the worst working conditions are to be found in the shelling section, beginning with its mud floor. Fans and proper lighting have been lacking, and space per worker has generally been smaller than in the other departments. By contrast, the best work-

---

[139] Information from KSCDC, Office, Quilon, provided 15 August 1998 by Antoni Das, personnel secretary, KSCDC.
[140] The violation of labor laws will be further discussed in Chapter VII.
[141] Ramaswamy, *Work, Union and Community*, pp. 107, 122.

ing environment is seen in the grading section, which is often brighter and cleaner than the peeling section. Tables, stools, or chairs, have only been provided in some of the factories, and never in the shelling section.[142] In this matter, the state-owned factories have not differed from the private ones and, in fact, in 1998 an official observer concluded that they were far from the model factories promised when they were established in 1970.[143] The cashew factories, therefore, have not only contributed to *break down* caste barriers, but also to *keep up* caste identity and the association of Scheduled Castes with dirty work.

The meaning of caste

All the women interviewed, regardless of generation, expressed themselves very vaguely on the origin of the caste system. I did not find any indication of cultural consensus on the Brahmanic view of caste, contrary to Dumont's claim that there is such a consensus.[144]

> I do not know much about the origin of the caste system, but I was taught by my mother and father that it is man-made. God would never create such a thing. Men created it and men abolished it. When I was a child, the caste system was very pronounced. We could not walk around where we wanted—there were so many restrictions—and I don't think my parents would have recognized this village today. Now we can walk everywhere and nobody disturbs us.
> —Kotha, Pulaya caste, born 1919, sheller since the late 1920s[145]

> I don't know much about the caste system, but my parents said that it was created because there was a lack of food. But why don't you ask the Brahmins or the Nairs? They made it up. A long time ago we were their slaves and

---

[142] Govt. of India, *Report on an Enquiry into Conditions of Labour in the Cashewnut Processing Industry in India*, p. 39; Govt. of Travancore-Cochin, *Report of the Minimum Wages Advisory Committee for Cashew Industry 1959*, p. 9; Govt. of Kerala, *Report of the Delegation Committee for the Revision of the Minimum Wages of Cashew Workers 1998*, pp. 18 ff. (copy provided by the chairman of the committee, P. Madhavan); Govt. of Kerala, *Cashew Sector and Women Labourers*, Preliminary Report, Department of Industries (Trivandrum, 1998), p. 6 (copy received from L. Radhakrishnan, Department of Industries, Trivandrum).

[143] Govt. of Kerala, *Cashew Sector and Women Labourers*, Preliminary Report, p. 2.

[144] Dumont, *Homo Hierarchus*, passim. Several other scholars who have studied lower castes have also rejected Dumont's consensus theory. See, for example, Kolenda, "Religious Anxiety and Hindu Fate", pp. 71-82; Berreman, "The Brahmanical View of Caste", pp. 16-23; O'Hanlon, *Caste, Conflict and Ideology*; Deliège, "Caste Without a System"; Mencher, "The Caste System Upside Down", pp. 93-109.

[145] Interview 16 August 1998.

we had to do all the unpleasant work. We had no choice. Of course, they were cleaner than us, they wore white clothes, they had shoes and umbrellas, but our hearts are as clean as theirs. That was what my mother taught me—but nothing else about the caste system.
—Kavitha, Kurava caste, born around 1920, sheller since the late 1920s[146]

Ezhavas and Nairs are at the same level in the caste ranking system—maybe like the Brahmins. Anyhow, the caste system was created by people when a scarcity of food came about. Some people wanted to secure food for themselves.
—Sarasu, Ezhava caste, born 1925, sheller since 1937[147]

I am not sure about the origin of the caste system, but my father told me that the caste system was created a long time ago, when the food was not enough for everyone, so the higher castes refused to share their meals with the lower.
—Gomathi, Ezhava caste, born 1930, sheller since 1940[148]

The caste system started because of struggling over resources, and the prejudices against the lower castes went very deep into the minds of the people.
—Thankamoni, Ezhava caste, born 1946, peeler since 1958[149]

Don't ask me about the origin of caste. I don't know. On top you find the Nairs and the Brahmins—they are the same. Then come the Ezhavas, and finally Pulayas and Kuravas. I think Pulayas are higher than Kuravas, but we are both Scheduled Castes. Most other castes have treated us nicely all the time.
—Sarojini, Pulaya caste, born 1954, sheller since 1966[150]

I do not know anything about the caste system. You have to ask those who are educated. They know—they made it all up! I have never heard of people being more or less pure. Of course, there is nothing like that! People do not have impure blood—all blood is red. We have only different blood-groups, like A and B, don't you know that? It is not difficult to work with Pulayas and Kuravas. They are the best workers—they are hard working.
—Raji, Ezhava caste, born 1957, trade union convener, sheller since 1968[151]

---

[146] Interview 25 August 1998.
[147] Interview 1 February 1998.
[148] Interview 29 January 1999.
[149] Interview 14 August 1998.
[150] Interview 4 September 1998.
[151] Interview 7 February 1999.

> I don't know anything about the origin of caste. My parents never spoke
> about it, but it is sometimes on our minds anyhow.
> —Indira, Ezhava caste, born 1980, peeler[152]

The elderly low-caste woman, Kavitha, recalled her mother teaching her
that the Kuravas' hearts and souls were as good as Brahmins and Nairs. This
demonstrates that the rejection of the Brahmanic view among the Kuravas
is of earlier origin than the 1930s. To women of Scheduled Castes, Brahmins and Nairs were equal in the social order—something a Brahmin
would hardly agree with. In the interviews, women of low and middle caste
showed a very materialist view of the origin of caste as man-made, and a
result of a struggle for power and resources (especially food). The idea that
one's caste affiliation is linked to *dharma* did not affect them. From the
stories of the two low-caste women, Kotha and Kavitha, who stated that
their parents had taught them that "men created it" for reasons connected
with "lack of food" or "struggling over resources", it seems as if this were
true for the previous generation as well. Kavitha, the old Kurava woman,
even suggested I would get better information if I asked those who "made it
up"—the Brahmins or Nairs, as did Raji, the middle-aged Ezhava woman,
who showed indignation over such questions about caste and similarly
asked me to pose them to "those who are educated and made it up". This
contrasts to Sheth's findings in his study of a factory in Gujarat in the
1970s, where workers are reported to have told him that the manager's
position was due to deeds in a previous life.[153] A plausible explanation for
this difference of opinion is the influence of non-religious communist egalitarian ideology on workers in Kerala. However, Kavitha's mother had
probably not heard of the communists in the early 1930s when she told
Kavitha that she was as clean in her heart as a high-caste girl.

Perhaps social reformers like Sree Narayana Guru, Aiyappan, Ayyankali, and others who taught equality of humankind—all of whom were active
in Travancore—expressed themselves in similar terms. Perhaps Kavitha's
grandmother taught her daughter this, or perhaps Kavitha's mother figured
out such a "natural truth" for herself. We only know for certain that the
Brahmanic explanation of the caste hierarchy was not accepted by her in
the 1920s and 1930s, and probably not by other low caste individuals in
her neighborhood either. Many low and middle caste women referred to
old stories that the caste system was created because of lack of food. Some
of the interviewees heard these in the early 1930s, so it is likely that they
existed before left-oriented parties influenced discourses on caste.

---

[152] Interview 6 September 1998.
[153] Sheth, *The Social Frame Work of an Indian Factory*, p. 101.

If the ideas of the caste system's origin, as well as its hierarchy, seem blurred, the placement of the Scheduled Castes is not. Sarasu, the Ezhava woman, located her own caste on the top of the social ladder and at the same level as the Nairs, something hardly corresponding to the traditional ranking system. At the other end of the spectrum, she showed strong caste prejudice against the Scheduled Castes. She thus applied a double standard, not acknowledging her own caste to be inferior to the Nairs, but clearly declaring Scheduled Castes below her station. The majority of women of middle or high caste had appropriated caste rules without reflecting on them, or, as they often expressed it, "I was taught like that".

> The origin of the caste system has to do with some people's will to rule others, but I was taught by my parents not to have anything to do with lower castes—especially not with the Scheduled Castes. But they never spoke about the reason—it was just like that. But all that changed with time and it was completely gone about twenty years ago.
> —Bhaggerathi Amma, Nair caste, born 1926, grader 1940-1990[154]

> My parents did not speak much about caste, but they avoided lower castes, so that was how we understood we should act as well. I have never experienced any caste problems.
> —Leela, Nair caste, born 1950, grader 1968-1980, sheller since 1982[155]

> My parents never showed any negative feelings towards the Scheduled Castes, and they never explained the origin of caste system to me. Some old people talk very badly about Pulayas and Kuravas, but in my generation we don't believe in those things any longer. And my husband and I live next to a Pulaya family and there is absolutely no problem at all; but most of the Scheduled Castes live in the Harijan Colony.
> —Chitra, Nair born 1968, peeler since 1986[156]

None of the Nair's interviewed could remember any stories about the origin of the caste system—perhaps because their elevated position in the caste hierarchy made such explanations less glorious, and perhaps an embarrassment, in the context of Kerala's radical history.

The stories of younger women reveal that people are still identified by caste, and hierarchical thinking continues to exist, although barely ac-

---

[154] Interview 3 January 1998.
[155] Interview 9 March 1998.
[156] Interview 24 August 1998.

knowledged. Young Nair women asserted that the Scheduled Castes were more accustomed to doing *dirty work*, but they often followed this with a remark that their view of the Scheduled Caste's job function should not be taken to mean that they thought such people lower in a social hierarchy. The Scheduled Castes still ridicule the higher castes as somewhat "snooty" or "higher and finer", although it is often done with a smile on their faces. I interpreted these smiles as their excuse for expressing an attitude which was considered to be a bit prejudiced, although ridiculing the behavior of higher castes may also be a kind of resistance because of a feeling of inferiority. All castes and generations were aware of the negative connotations of the traditional caste hierarchy and tried to belittle the importance of caste. However, all of my informants saw caste as an essential category to indicate groups with different habits and cultures, and hardly any of the interviewees spoke about dissolving those groups.

In the 1970s, Joan Mencher observed serious prejudice expressed and practiced by higher castes in Kerala with the deliberate intention of offending members of the Scheduled Castes. They apparently forced them to "take their meals sitting on the road outside the employer's compound" and excluded them from entering temples. She also found members of Scheduled Castes referring to themselves as "slave" instead of "I" in front of higher caste persons, as had been the custom in the nineteenth century.[157] Such overt caste hostility appears to have almost entirely disappeared during the past two or three decades in the area under consideration. One conclusion which may be drawn is that caste barriers are still present to some degree in the social life outside the factory, as is reflected in the workers' assertions that Nairs and Scheduled Castes are seldom in contact with each other. It is still common for Scheduled Castes to live in separate areas. The frequently-heard view that the cashew factory has become a better place with regard to caste barriers indicates those barriers do exist to a greater degree in the world outside the workplace. This corresponds with Uma Ramaswamy's findings in her study of Coimbatore mill workers.[158]

Caste still acts as a strong identity, but it has another meaning today than in the 1930s and 1940s. At that time, caste affiliation was related to one's economic position in an overt way. For the Scheduled Castes, this affiliation served as an explanation for their poverty, as illustrated by Kavitha saying, "We were the poorest at that time. Most Kuravas were poor and we were often starving", or in Kotha's words:

[157] Mencher, "On Being An Untouchable in India", p. 271.
[158] Ramaswamy, *Work, Union and Community*, p. 144.

In the old days, we were dependent on the higher castes—they gave us work, shelter, and food. People of our caste were all poor: there was no chance to escape poverty for the Pulayas.

—Kotha, Pulaya caste, born 1919, sheller since the late 1920s[159]

The poverty of a Nair woman like Bhaggerathi Amma or Bharathiamma was explained as their family's bad luck: "We had *become* poor" or "We had *lost* our land". To them, their low economic position was exceptional, considering their caste. It was not thought of as "normal" that a Nair woman should have had to work in a factory.

Factory work is still seen as undignified by many Nair women. I observed that women in the grading sections of the factories (i.e., mainly Nairs) were very hard to distinguish in appearance from government workers, teachers, or nurses. In fact, this was something they themselves often stressed. Their work is "light and clean" and they were dressed in saris and wore jewelry, in contrast to workers in the shelling section, who wore simpler dresses—*dhotis*, blouses, or plain towels instead of shawls over their shoulders. Many Nair women compensate for their loss of ritual status by repudiating unclean work (not in a ritual Brahmanic meaning, but in a more physical sense). However, it is discernable that the belief in a link between unclean work and Scheduled Caste still persists, and the tendency to consider lower castes as different and less sensitive to hard and dirty work was clearly expressed by such Nairs as Chitra, among many others. The difference in outlook between graders and shellers continues to delineate the caste hierarchy in a tangible way.

Although a fairly evident caste hierarchy still exists, a discourse has evolved which excludes the language of caste, and especially such concepts as purity and hierarchy, which are seen as suspect and almost "forbidden" to talk about in the context of a modern, radical society. Low-caste young women did not know such stories of the origin of the caste system as their mothers did, and often they simply said that caste belongs to the past or that they did not care about it.

I have no idea where the caste system came from. My mother never talked much about caste, but most of our neighbors and friends belong to the Kuravas or Pulayas. I never believed in the caste system, and I don't know anything about it. Maybe the Kuravas are higher than us—I have no idea... I don't care.

—Geetha, Pulaya caste, born 1973, sheller since 1987[160]

---

[159] Interview 16 August 1998.
[160] Interview 2 September 1998.

This may be interpreted as a wish to leave traditional society behind. Perhaps such women learned what abolition of the caste system actually is from leftist politicians and union leaders. In the face of such a dominant discourse, caste hierarchies become more hidden and difficult to criticize. As the Nair woman, Bharathia, said: "the caste system is nothing to talk about today".

Conclusion

The integration of the caste system into an industrial setting where the traditional link between caste and job task became unimportant was a characteristic of the early cashew factories. The caste division of labor that was a reflection of the society outside the cashew factory was upheld by employers for reasons connected with the rise of labor unions.

The early caste division of labor in the cashew factories was bound up with taboos, that is, the perception that a caste was either unclean or not. In spite of denials that the caste system has any relevance today, the caste division of labor continues in place after more than sixty years. To some extent this may be attributed to intense competition for jobs, which causes women to secure positions for their daughters or relatives, as well as teach them a particular job skill, such as shelling, peeling, or grading. This is not to be understood as the kind of meritocratic explanation other studies have given, as there is no formal training or education linked to the status of a work task. Furthermore, the present investigation shows that there was no relation between caste and wages, in contrast to findings of earlier studies on the caste division of labor.[161]

Traditional caste values have not totally crumbled, however; the link between low caste and unclean work has shown remarkable longevity, despite the fact that it is no longer clearly expressed, and has been, in part, overcome. Among male workers in the cashew factories there is a similar link between caste and work task, and so the dirtiest work—roasting— has remained a job for men of Scheduled Castes.

The factory owners instigated the reestablishment of the traditional social system in order to curb the growth of trade unions. However, agitation by trade union leaders in the 1940s and 1950s led workers of different castes to join the union and overcome caste barriers in the class struggle. The identity of caste was temporarily set aside. Obviously, there were women of higher castes who were amenable to the idea of class struggle through

---

[161] Morris, *The Emergence of an Industrial Labour Force in India*; Holmström, *South Indian Factory Workers*; Sheth, *The Social Frame Work of an Indian Factory*.

trade unions, but their stories demonstrate that their actions were dependent upon the permission of their husbands. The women of Scheduled Castes seemed to be less reliant on their husbands' views. We have noted earlier that the only men who worked in female-dominated sections of the cashew factory were of the Scheduled Castes. Taken together, these examples typify the difference between the Scheduled Castes and the higher castes: gender dichotomy has proven to be less pronounced among the Scheduled Castes.

Stories about the origin of the caste system among the lowest castes show that these groups did not see the caste hierarchy as natural, and did not give their assent to the Brahmanic view; rather, they had a materialist view of its origin. Although all interviewees denied that caste is of any significance to them, caste seems to have remained a vibrant part of their identity. The greatest importance of caste, however, lies in the reproductive sphere, to which we shall turn in a subsequent chapter. The idea of caste-class nexus has dwindled, and for the individual it can no longer serve as the sole explanation for one's impoverishment or wealth, as was the case in former generations. However, castes are still seen as essential groups which most people do not wish to dissolve. The dominating discourse does not condemn the caste system of today because, in effect, it is considered to have been abandoned. Those who had the power to define the "abolition of caste" have also made it become "true".

VI   Wages and Gender Discourses

> When the cashew factories close down, women [employees] are taken care
> of by their husbands. They are *only* housewives.
> —Ben Morris, male politician for Congress party in Kerala[1]

Introduction

A statement that was made in 1901 to the effect that "each Pulaya woman
is an earning member, and no great burden is felt by the husband in maintaining them"[2], was verified in the census of 1931. At that time investigators established that women of the lowest castes were, for the most part,
wage-earners who provided for themselves.[3] We have seen how, in the earliest phase of the cashew factories, cashew workers were mainly drawn from
the lowest castes. Thus, it must have seemed quite "normal" in the 1930s
that these women were primarily *workers* in the sense that they earned their
own living by selling their labor. This chapter explores ways in which cashew workers have been represented and defined by employers, civil servants,
and trade union leaders in discussions concerning certain labor laws and
stipulated minimum wages. Its purpose is to trace historical changes in the
representation of female cashew workers in order to find out how these
women have been viewed on a scale from housewives to workers. A necessary preliminary is a consideration of the model of male breadwinner wages
which has been central in discussions concerning wages. Not must only the
ideological and discursive level be taken into account but, actual wages
which resulted from the negotiations as well. This has only been possible
for the years following 1953. This was the year when the regulation of
wages in the cashew factories by the Minimum Wages Act was introduced,
in consequence of which a specific kind of historical source material has
been generated in the reports of the committees on minimum wages. For
the period prior to 1953, whatever correspondence exists between SICMA,
trade union leaders, and the Travancore Government has been systematically excerpted at the Kerala State Archive. Other sources, which deal with
female cashew workers' actual economic contributions to the household,
will also be examined.

---

[1] Interview 12 January 1997
[2] Govt. of India, *Census of India 1901*, Vol. XXVI, Travancore, Part I, Report, p. 343.
[3] Govt. of India, *Census of India 1931*, Vol. XXVIII, Travancore, Part I, Report, p. 241.

The Model of Male Breadwinners

The model of the male breadwinner emerged in Western societies with the dawn of industrialization.[4] Thus, it does not belong to traditional society, but rather developed with "modernization". Implied is a gender division of labor in society, with men earning sufficient wages to maintain a family, and women considered as dependents. However, this rarely corresponded to the reality—and especially not among the poorest classes.[5] Nevertheless, the ideal of the family wage system represents the formalization of human reproduction in a capitalist society, a model intended to preserve the family and maintain the stability of society.[6] This ideal has had profound consequences for power relations between men and women, for it defined work in a new way. Only work tasks which were remunerated with wages were defined as work per se, whereas traditional domestic subsistence work, such as small scale farming, small animal husbandry, running a household, and caring for elders and children, was ascribed a decreased value.

The model of male breadwinners and female caregivers was transformed during the latter part of the twentieth century in almost all Western countries, although this transformation has taken many forms. Rosemary Crompton has sketched the variety of possible arrangements with regard to waged work and caring for children along a continuum from "traditional " to "less traditional" societies. In a traditional (Western) country with unequal gender relations, the male breadwinner model is dominant. At the extreme of less traditional gender relations, Crompton sees a society in which men and women take equal responsibility for bringing home income and caring for dependents.[7]

The options between the two poles need not be seen as a necessary development, but as varieties arising in different geographic, cultural, and societal contexts. It may be noted that in socialist societies with dual wage-

---

[4] Martha May, "Bread before Roses", in Ruth Milkman (ed.), *Women, Work, and Protest: A Century of U.S. Women's Labor History* (London, 1991), pp. 1-22; Alice Kessler-Harris, *A Woman's Wage: Historical Meanings and Social Consequences* (Lexington, KY, 1990), pp. 9 ff.

[5] For a short overview of research concerning the male breadwinner system, see Angélique Janssens, "The Rise and Decline of the Male Breadwinner Family? An Overview of the Debate", in Angélique Janssens (ed.), *The Rise and Decline of the Male Breadwinner Family?* (New York, 1998), pp. 1-23.

[6] D.F. Bryceson and U. Vuorela, "Outside the Domestic Labour Debate: Towards a Materialist Theory of Modes of Human Reproduction", *Review of Radical Political Economics*, 16: 2-3 (1984), pp. 137-166; Jane Lewis, *Women in England 1870-1950* (Brighton, 1984), pp. 45-52.

[7] Rosemary Crompton (ed.), *Restructuring Gender Relations and Employment: The Decline of the Male Breadwinner* (Oxford, 1999), pp. 203-207.

earners and state caregivers, gender relations have not been characterized as equal. This has been attributed to a lack of change in the "gender culture", although there has been a considerable change in the economic sphere.[8]

In the early twentieth century, the labor movement in the West generally promoted the policy of male family providers.[9] There are three main interpretations of this position. One stresses the mutual interest among women and men of the working class in organizing their daily lives in an optimal manner. A family wage would then be a means to respond to the forces of capitalist production, which exploited whole families (including children), and kept wages low for all of them. From this perspective the demand for family wages may be seen as a class-strategy which benefited men, women, and children of the working class.[10] Others have asserted that patriarchal interests led males (who were better organized) to exclude women from paid outside work, while exploiting women's unpaid labor in the household. This approach, known as a dual-system theory, implies an alliance between the forces of capital and the male-dominated labor movement. In this case, the strategy of exclusion was chosen for more selfish and patriarchal reasons.[11] The third view rejects the simplistic interpretations of the two previous theories, and claims a more complex reality, emphasizing the conflicting interests among different groups in the working class.[12]

These three perspectives all assume that the working class (whether males alone or men and women jointly) has had the power to exert influence over employers and the state. This in turn presupposes that the working class is well-organized—in trade unions, for example—to be able to raise a common voice and, further, that this voice can be heard: the working class must be numerous enough or have other means of claiming power. In Europe the industrial workforce has been extremely dominant in the labor market, comprising as much as half of the total workforce. In many Third World countries (India included) circumstances are totally different,

---

[8] Crompton, *Restructuring Gender Relations*, pp. 205-206.

[9] Lewis, *Women in England 1870-1950*, pp. 49 ff.; May, "Bread before Roses", pp. 3 ff.

[10] Louise Tilly and Joan Scott, *Women, Work, and Family* (New York, 1987); Jane Humphries, "Class Struggle and the Persistence of the Working-Class Family", in Alice Amsden (ed.), *The Economics of Women and Work* (New York, 1980), pp. 140-165. For a discussion of the three perspectives, see Carlsson, *Kvinnosyn och kvinnopolitik*, pp. 24-31, 51-55.

[11] Heidi Hartmann, "The Unhappy Marriage of Marxism and Feminism: Towards a More Progressive Union", in Lydia Sargent (ed.), *The Unhappy Marriage of Marxism and Feminism: A Debate on Class and Patriarchy* (London, 1981), pp. 1-41; Helen I. Safa, *The Myth of the Male Breadwinner: Women and Industrialization in the Caribbean* (Boulder, 1995).

[12] Richard J. Evans, "Politics and the Family: Social Democracy and the Working Class Family in Theory and Practice before 1914", in Evans and Lee (eds), *The German Family* (London, 1981), pp. 256-280. See also Carlsson, *Kvinnosyn och kvinnopolitik*, pp. 259-264.

with only a small minority of the workforce engaged in factories, or in the organized sector at all.[13] But the Third World is not homogeneous, and India has its unique features, including parliamentary democracy and labor laws that were enacted rather early.

It has been pointed out that India differs from Western countries in that many labor laws were implemented during the colonial period without having been preceded by labor struggles. At least this was true prior to 1917, when the first trade union was formed in India—something attributed to the pressure applied to the British government by English mill owners who sought to hamper the competitive advantages Indian textile mills enjoyed. The scarcity of labor in the early industrial factories has also been cited as an explanation for the introduction of labor laws: better labor protection would be a means of attracting labor from the agricultural sector.[14] The labor laws introduced were, therefore, often more or less copies of laws formulated in the West, and many of the demands of the Indian trade unions were inspired by such Western ideals as breadwinner wages— reminding us of the international nature of the labor movement.

The Male Breadwinner Model in India

Radha Kumar has noted that in the 1930s large numbers of women were being dismissed from industrial plants in India. The bourgeois ideology of motherhood and domesticity was extended to include working class women en[15]—a phenomenon which seemed to have been almost global during the depression of the 1930s. In the West, the male breadwinner model has often been accompanied by a welfare system, such as a child allowance, encouraging women to retain their roles as housewives and mothers.[16] Such allowances, except for three months of maternity leave, have not been introduced in India: child allowances would go against government efforts toward controlling population growth.

The concept of the male breadwinner does not appear in official Indian sources prior to the 1930s. Earlier reports on wages and working class families presumed that women as well as men contributed to the maintenance

---

[13] Inga Brandell (ed.), *Workers in Third-World Industrialization* (London, 1991), Introduction, pp. 1-27.
[14] Radha Iyer D'Souza, "Industrialization, Labour Policies, and the Labour Movement", in T.V. Sathyamurthy (ed.), *Class Formation and Political Transformation in Post-colonial India* (Delhi, 1996), pp. 108-110.
[15] Kumar, *The History of Doing*, p. 71.
[16] A.F. Robertson, *Beyond the Family: The Social Organization of Human Reproduction* (Cambridge, 1991), pp. 1-5.

of the family. This did not imply equal wages, but only that a working class woman was expected to support herself. In 1932, a report on the budgets of working class families in Bombay made explicit for the first time the notion of a family wage,[17] thereby characterizing the ideal working class woman as a dependent housewife. Such household budget surveys as the Bombay Labour Office conducted beginning in the 1920s were based on Western models.[18] Surveys were not carried out in Travancore prior to the implementation of minimum wages. Thus, discussions concerning family wages are not seen in any historical documents from Travancore before 1948.[19]

A few labor laws were enacted in Travancore in the 1930s, but ten years later there was still no machinery for their enforcement, or for negotiating wages, despite the fact that trade unions had been established several years before. The influential George Committee, which included representatives of labor, management, and government, gave its recommendations for social legislation in Travancore in 1939. Travancore was encouraged to promulgate minimum wage legislation, along with the means for its implementation, in line with the British Trade Boards Acts of 1909 and 1918.[20] In 1943, a civil servant from Trivandrum, V.K. Velayudhan, was sent to the United Kingdom to study labor welfare and organization, and on his return to Travancore a separate labor department was formed.[21] This labor department and the bureaucratic system for implementing and controlling labor laws, and for institutionalizing industrial relations, was therefore shaped after the British model.

At the time of the initial growth of the cashew factories, the landless agricultural workers employed there were accustomed to being paid in kind for agricultural work.[22] Although one early twentieth century observer noted that some low-caste male and female agricultural workers were paid equal wages,[23] that seems to have been the exception. Wages in cash, as well as payment in kind, were often so construed that a woman received three-

---

[17] Kumar, "Family and Factory", p. 138.

[18] In England, surveys on working class families budgets started around World War I. See May, "Bread before Roses", p. 10.

[19] The subject of minimum wages for industrial labor was noted in India in 1928 when the ILO passed the Minimum Wage Regulating Machinery Convention, but it took twenty years for the Minimum Wages Bill of 1948 to be passed by the legislative assembly in India. See Govt. of India, *Report on the Working of the Minimum Wages Act of 1948* (Simla, 1955).

[20] Govt. of Travancore, *Travancore Information and Listener*, 6:11 (July 1946), pp. 37, 40.

[21] Govt. of Travancore, *Travancore Administration Report* 1120 ME/1944-45 AD, p. 100.

[22] Govt. of Travancore, *Report of the Banking Enquiry Committee Travancore 1929*, p. 13. Even as late as the mid-1950s some agricultural workers received wages in kind. See L. Thara Bhai, "Caste Stratification in South Travancore Region", *Journal of Kerala Studies*, 5, Parts III and IV (December 1978), p. 497.

[23] Iyer, *The Travancore Tribes and Castes*, II, p. 141.

quarters as much as a man[24], although a figure of two-thirds has also been cited.[25] In most of the early factories in Travancore, a similar wage structure was introduced when workers were paid in cash.[26] In the early cashew factories, however, all workers were paid by the piece—without consideration of gender.[27]

Representation of Women Workers in the 1940s

Factory owners

The earliest sources in which Travancore cashew factory owners referred to their workers in public were written shortly after 1940, when the cashew factories were under scrutiny because of the newly instituted Travancore Factory Act of 1939. Although so-called "factories" which did not use power were excluded, it did give the state government the right to declare such workplaces within the purview of the new law. This was a highly contested question in 1943 and 1944. In January 1945, the Travancore Government finally declared all cashew factories covered by the act, which prompted a number of petitions from the owners who, for various reasons, sought an exemption.[28] The inclusion of the cashew factories under the Factory Act meant, above all, that child labor would have to be abolished. Another important issue was the distinction between seasonal and non-seasonal factories, as people were allowed to work more hours per day and per week if they only worked for a short season.[29] It became common for many factory owners to have their factories declared seasonal, not only in order to maximize the legal daily and weekly working hours, but also because the Maternity Benefit Act of 1943 granted an exclusion to seasonal factories.[30]

The cashew factory owners, through their organization, the South India Cashew Manufacturers Association (SICMA), pressured the government to exempt them entirely from the Factory Act. Their arguments with

[24] Pillai, *Travancore State Manual*, III, p. 57.
[25] Tharamangalam, *Agrarian Class Conflict*, p. 61. See also Iyer, *The Cochin Tribes and Castes*, I, p. 92.
[26] Pillai, *Travancore State Manual*, III, p. 96; Govt. of India, *Census of India 1931*, Vol. XXVIII, Travancore, Part I, Report, p. 498.
[27] Interview 18 January 1998 with Kotha, sheller, born around 1920; Interview 23 August 1998 with Gomathi, sheller, born 1930; Interview 14 September 1999 with K. Chellappan, male trade union leader, born 1914.
[28] KSA, Development files, No. 341/2093, "Exemption of the Cashew Factories from the Operation of the Factory Act".
[29] Govt. of Travancore, *Travancore Information and Listener*, 6:11 (July 1946), p. 38.
[30] Ibid., p. 39.

regard to adult workers were based on contradictory statements. On the one hand, they asserted that the restrictions of the act "may tend towards the decline of the industry", resulting in serious economic problems for the workers. It was stated that "thousands of them will literally have to starve", since no other work was to be found in region around the cashew factories.[31] It is important to note that one consequence of these statements was that women were, in effect, defined as workers. On the other hand, employers also argued that it was impractical to restrict working hours, as women only came to work at times which suited them and which could be conveniently coordinated with their *main duties*, viz., domestic work. "Their earnings from the cashewnut factories are therefore virtually the earnings of their spare hours".[32] A strong argument was thus made for not regarding women as *true* workers, and it was urged that their incomes should only be seen as complementary to their households.

The appeal was unsuccessful and the cashew factories were declared covered by the Factory Act—mainly as a result of trade union activity, but also because of avowals by the chief inspector of factories and the labor commissioner that working conditions in the factories were inhumane.[33]

In a new petition shortly thereafter, SICMA demanded exemption from some of the paragraphs of the law, viz., those concerning child labor, crèches, minimum working space for each individual, sanitary facilities (such as providing water and latrines), the keeping of registers, and the regulation of working times. Reference to the dependency of workers on income from the cashew factories was now culled from the employers' pleadings. Instead in an effort to convince the dewan of Travancore to mitigate the legal restrictions, arguments were used which mainly referred to gender. It was asserted that "insistence on definite time for commencement and closing of work will work serious hardship to the labour and will upset the routine of their domestic life."[34] The petition, in another reference to gender, pointed out that no machinery was used, that no hard or dangerous work tasks were involved, and that only deftness of hand was required. It was even claimed that the cashew factories virtually should

---

[31] KSA, Development files, No. 341/2093, "Exemption of the Cashew Factories from the Operation of the Factory Act", Letter from South India Cashewnut Manufacturers Association to the Government of Travancore, 21 October 1943, pp. 17-18.

[32] Ibid., p. 17.

[33] KSA, Development files, No. 341/2093, "Exemption of the Cashew Factories from the Operation of the Factory Act", Letter from Chief Inspector of Factories to the Director of Industries, Trivandrum, 1945. See also pp. 13-15, 25-26, 39; KSA, Development Dept, 1946, No. 507, "Memorandum from the Cashewnut Workers", pp. 47-49.

[34] KSA, Development files, No. 341/2093, "Exemption of the Cashew Factories from the Operation of the Factory Act", Letter from South India Cashewnut Manufacturers Association to the Government of Travancore, 6 February 1945, p. 2.

not be regarded as factories at all: SICMA argued that the work could as well have been conducted as cottage processing, i.e., in the workers' homes[35] —which was another way to define the women as "non-workers". Probably the representatives of SICMA believed that they would be more successful in their appeal to the authorities if they used the same arguments as the legislators of Travancore themselves had lately used when they legislated against night work for women by invoking "domestic duties".

Civil servants

The Travancore Factory act of 1939 was equivalent to the British-Indian Factory Act of 1934, with one important exception: working hours for women in Travancore were set at 7 a.m. to 5 p.m. (as compared to British India, where it was 6 a.m. to 7 p.m.). The reason given by the legislative assembly in Travancore for cutting back on evening hours was to give women workers *sufficient time to attend to domestic duties.* This was considered a progressive aspect of the law, and the Travancore Government prided itself on it.[36]

How, then, did civil servants in the labor department respond to SICMA's efforts to define women employed in the factories as housewives who only worked in their spare time and, thus, should not be equated with *workers,* who were dependent on their wages for survival? Those handling the issue of labor laws in the cashew factories in the 1940s recognized that these women were *both* workers and housewives. The director of industries, I.E. Chacko, held that the argument of the factory owners for resisting the regulation of working hours (intended so that women could come and go in accordance with their need to coordinate factory work with their household duties) was based on a false premise. He pointed out that nothing prevented the factory owners from allowing their workers to work less than the stipulated maximum of nine hours per day.[37] The director of industries had visited several cashew factories and had observed women working eleven or twelve hours at a stretch because poverty compelled them to do so.[38] He, therefore, acknowledged them as workers who were not provided for by others.

[35] Ibid., p. 1.
[36] Govt. of Travancore, *Travancore Information and Listener,* 6:11 (July 1946), p. 38.
[37] KSA, Development files, No. 341/2093, "Exemption of the Cashew Factories from the Operation of the Factory Act", Remarks on the Memorial submitted by South India Cashewnut Manufactures Association to the Government of Travancore, 21 October 1943 by the Director of Industries, pp. 13-18.
[38] Ibid., pp. 31-35.

On the other hand, it was also very clear that women workers had a particular position in the eyes of legislators and of such officials as the director of industries. Their uniqueness was made apparent in the prohibition against night work for women. The law, which was introduced in many countries (under pressure from the ILO and the international labor movement), was designed to protect women from long working days. However, large groups of women found the law discriminatory, excluding them from certain jobs.[39] In Travancore, other arguments for the limitation of women's working hours were also launched. The expressed purpose was primarily to enable female workers to attend to their domestic work, which was unquestionably regarded as their *duty*. The second aim, according to the director of industries, was to enable women to leave and return home during daylight hours, thereby *protecting* them from the dangers of night.[40] The international convention of 1919 against women's night work had exempted those women working with highly perishable raw materials in the food industries from the night work prohibition.[41] This practice was followed in Kerala in processing fish, fruit, and vegetables. However, a clause stipulated that employers should provide adequate protection for women workers during nightime hours, and also supply them with transportation to and from work.[42] International practice had accommodated itself to a gender discourse which emphatically represented women as in need of protection—including dangers outside the workplace.

From the sources available, it is not possible to state why legislators were of the opinion that women should have protection when walking to and from work at night. Perhaps they believed women needed safeguarding from male violence and abuse for their own well-being, comfort, and honor. Alternatively, it may have been a way of controlling their sexuality and preserving both the new family norms and the role of the biological father (that is, it would support the nuclear family by shielding monogamous relations and faithful spouses). Probably a combination of the two views influenced the legislators.

---

[39] For Sweden, see Carlsson, *Kvinnosyn och kvinnopolitik*, p. 226. For England, see ARA, *International Conference of Women Trade Unionists held on the 7th July 1936 in London*, pp. 368 ff.

[40] KSA, Development files, No. 341/2093, "Exemption of the Cashew Factories from the Operation of the Factory Act", Remarks on the Memorial submitted by South India Cashewnut Manufactures Association to the Government of Travancore, 21 October 1943 by the Director of Industries, pp. 31-35.

[41] *Internationella Arbetsorganisationen II: Arbetskonferensens första femte sammanträden 1919-1923* (Stockholm, 1930), p. 77.

[42] NRC, File No. LBR/MS/74/77, "Permission for Women to Work at Night".

Trade union leaders

In the correspondence of trade union leaders from the 1940s and in their public appearances and speeches when representing the cashew workers, there are hardly any indications that these workers were mainly women.[43] Letters to the Travancore Government refer to them as *workers*, and they were, in fact, characterized as dependent on their wages, not as "house-wives" who only supplemented the family income. On several occasions, trade union leaders stressed that these workers were unemployed for about two months every year, and during the 1940s and 1950s, unemployment compensation was a frequent demand of trade union leaders[44], buttressing their acknowledgement of women as workers, and not merely as supplementary providers. Rarely can we discern in the texts that the workers they referred to were women. When for example, the president of the All-Travancore Cashewnut Workers' Union, M.N. Govindan Nair, wrote to the dewan of Travancore, he described the cashew workers as a group who had been tolerating the most deplorable working conditions without complaining, stating that that "the main bulk of workers comprise [sic] of our women-folk, well-known for their capacity for silent suffering".[45] The belief in a specific female mentality, i.e., *docility*, stressed the need for having male spokesmen and protectors.

The Institutionalization of Male Breadwinners

In 1948, a minimum wage act was enacted in India. This act did not make it clear whether the individual or the family was to be the basis for calculating minimum wages. This confusion was probably the reason a Committee on Fair Wages was soon formed.

A tripartite committee was appointed by the Government of India to equally represent employers, laborers, and the government. Its members were either leading businessmen, key labor leaders, or ministers of the na-

---

[43] KSA, Confidential files 1949, CS No. 132-4248, "Labour Resolution in Quilon", Travancore Cashew Workers Union: Appeal to Public, signed by M.N. Govindan Nair, dated 30-3-1120 (1945).

[44] KSA, Development department 1946, No. 507, "Memorandum from the Cashewnut Workers", Letter from M.N. Govindan Nair to the Dewan of Travancore, dated the 21st of Mithunam 1120 (1945), p. 2; Govt. of Travancore-Cochin, *Kerala Report of the Minimum Wages Committee for Cashew Industry 1953*, p. 56; *Jennajugham*, 3 November 1955, p. 3; *Jennajugham*, 19 October 1956, p. 13.

[45] KSA, Development files 1946, File No. 507, "Memorandum from the Cashewnut Workers", Letter from The Travancore Cashewnut Workers' Union to the Dewan of Travancore, 9 July 1945, signed by M.N. Govindan Nair, p. 1.

tional government, although state governments, chambers of commerce, and influential organizations of workers and employers from all over India were also consulted.

The recommendations of the committee were issued in the Report of the Committee on Fair Wages (RCFW). The main features of that report were the following:

a) A fair wage must be sufficient to meet the requirements of a standard family consisting of three consumption units: husband, wife, and two children (earnings of dependents being ignored).

b) Workers must be compensated for rises in the cost of living by means of a special compensation ("dearness allowance").[46]

c) There should be no difference in the wages paid to men and women doing the same type of work.

d) Wage differentials should be based on a scientific appraisal of skill, experience, and training required for a particular job. Strain, fatigue, hazards, and the disagreeable nature of certain work tasks should be taken into account.

e) The lowest wage must be a minimum subsistence wage. The upper limit is a wage upon which one can live reasonably, i.e., a "living wage". Between the minimum wage and the living wage, a fair wage should be fixed, depending upon the capacity of the industry to afford it. *An industry which is incapable of paying minimum wages has no right to exist.*[47]

On the one hand, it was asserted that women and men doing the same type of work ought to receive equal wages; on the other, the method of calculating minimum wages by using a standard family (or "natural unit") as the point of departure, led the committee to establish "the calculations of a woman's wage is defined in a different manner from that of an adult male".[48] The definition of a nuclear family as consisting of four individuals (a husband, a dependent wife, and two children), was hardly the reality for the majority of Indian households, which generally included several more members—a fact well-known to the authors of the report.[49] The construction of this nuclear family was based, rather, on Western ideals, and the report made reference to countries like Australia, New Zealand, and the United Kingdom.[50]

---

[46] Akin to the American term COLA (cost of living allowance).

[47] Govt. of India, *Report of the Committee on Fair Wages*, passim.

[48] Ibid., p. 21.

[49] Ibid., pp. 40-41.

[50] Ibid., pp. 16-17. In many Western countries family size was set at two adults and three children. The presumptive lower number of family members in India was probably a way to keep the estimated family wage at a low level.

It was argued that if a wife had to work for wages, it must be because of the absence of a providing husband: she must be either a widow, divorced, or unmarried. At any rate, she must not be expected to support a husband, even though she may have other dependents. A fair wage for a woman would, therefore, be based on two consumption units, and her wage should amount to two-thirds as much as a male worker's wage.[51] When it became obvious that women were doing identical work as men, and doing it as well as men, it was recommended that this principle not be put into practice, since it would lead to "unequal competition between men and women workers", i.e., if women were only to receive two-thirds as much as male workers and could do the work as well as men, employers would dismiss men and only employ female workers.[52] Thus, it became a main concern to avoid replacing male workers by females.

The committee's recommendations were a synthesis of discussions which had being going on for over fifty years in England. The idea of family wages had been strongly promoted by British trade unions since the latter part of the nineteenth century. The notion of equal pay for equal jobs was introduced during World War I.[53] In spite of international discussions on equal pay for men and women, the organization of production and reproduction among working class families based on male family wages first took hold in Northwestern Europe in the 1950s.[54] Similar discussions on equal wages went on in Travancore-Cochin in the 1950s.[55]

In 1958, India ratified the ILO Convention on Equal Pay. It lasted eighteen years, until the Indian parliament passed the Equal Remuneration Act. Nevertheless, the question of equal wages had already been on the agenda at the time of Independence and, in fact, was secured in the Indian Constitution of 1948.[56] The ILO Convention of 1958 differed from the Indian Constitution by stressing that equal wages should not only be paid for *equal* work, but also for work which requires *similar* skills, levels of responsibility, and exertion.

In many countries, bills were enacted in the 1960s and 1970s which prohibited different wages for women and men doing work requiring equal skill, effort, and responsibility.[57] Such bills were the outcome of

---

[51] Ibid., p. 20.
[52] Ibid., p. 22.
[53] Lewis, *Women in England* , pp. 49 ff., 202 ff.
[54] Wally Seccombe, *Weathering the Storm: Working Class Families from the Industrial Revolution to the Fertility Decline* (London, 1993).
[55] *Jennajugham*, 15 February 1956, p. 2.
[56] M.J. Antony, *Women's Rights* (New Delhi, 1989) , pp. 8-9.
[57] In the US it was enacted in 1963. See Kessler-Harris, *A Woman's Wage*, p. 81. Great Britain enacted it in 1975. See Lewis, *Women in England 1870-1950*, p. 80.

protests against discriminatory wages for women, and bolstered the ideology of every individual's right and responsibility to provide for her or himself. The government of India's Equal Remuneration Act, similar to Western legislation intended to curb gender discrimination in the workplace, was enacted in 1976.[58] The question had been hotly debated in the legislative assembly in Kerala in 1964, when a committee was appointed to study women workers, their wages, and the general working conditions in Kerala. The debate shows widespread awareness of the fact that women were discriminated against—cashew workers being specifically mentioned as such a group. The proceedings reveal several politicians of the opinion that male work, as it was considered "heavy", should be better compensated than "light" women's work.[59]

The two models—*male breadwinners* (with a disregard for women's waged work) and *equal wages for men and women* (which meant a denial of women's structural dependency on men) were ideologically incompatible. The only solution to the dilemma was a strict gender division of labor. The importance of the RCFW cannot be overestimated: fifty years after the committee was established, reference continues to be made to this report whenever minimum wages are discussed in Kerala.[60] It is not an exaggeration to claim that the RCFW institutionalized the ideology of the male breadwinner in India *and* the strict gender division of labor as the only solution to the incompatible recommendations in the report. Although the RCFW clearly based these on Western ideals, and even referred to Western countries as modern models to emulate, it would be false to conclude that the ideology of women as housewives comes solely from the West. The notion that women should be confined to the home was widespread among the higher castes in traditional Indian society. In some instances this resulted in their total seclusion.[61] The family-wage strategy of the international labor movement, and its institutionalization in India, was nurtured by an old, upper-caste ideology.

---

[58] D.P. Jain, *Industrial and Labour Laws* (New Delhi, 1996), p. 373.
[59] Govt. of Kerala, *Proceedings of the Kerala Legislative Assembly*, First Session 1964, 13 March 1964, XVIII, No. 25, "Resolution 3, Women Workers in Kerala", pp. 2211-2225 (in Malayalam).
[60] See, for example, Govt. of Kerala, *The Report of the Delegatory Committee for the Revision of the Minimum Wages of Cashew Workers 1998*, Order No. G.O. (RT) 2473/96 LBR, Trivandrum (in Malayalam). Copy provided by Labour Department, Trivandrum.
[61] Liddle and Joshi, *Daughters of Independence*, p. 59, 89-93.

Stipulated Minimum Wages in the Cashew Factories

In 1948, minimum wages were introduced in several industries in Travancore. The cashew sector, however, was not among them. During the early 1950s, trade union activities were strongly oriented toward including the cashew factories in the minimum wage scheme and, in 1952, the unions succeeded in having the first minimum wage committee for the cashew industry convened.[62]

Four committees were appointed between 1952 and 1998, and the minimum wage was revised twice, during that period without such committees.[63] The Minimum Wages Committee consisted of employers, employees, and a chairman.

Without exception, those who represented the workers were male trade union leaders and politicians. The chairman was nominated by the government and supposed to be neutral in conflicts between employers and employees. The language of the deliberations was to be framed in a neutral way so as not to offend any of the parties. The reports also had to take into consideration existing laws and other concurrent recommendations, but in a way that did not appear backward or old-fashioned. One may argue that the reports mirror official discourses and in the following it is the official *gender discourse* which we will focus upon. We can expect the reports to say what it was permissible to say or think about men, women, and their wages at the time.

It is important to separate the discursive level from the material. Before we turn to the arguments and language used in the reports, it may be helpful to consider the practical outcome of the negotiations. The annual wage of each cashew worker, male or female, is comparatively low and it has, moreover, steadily decreased in comparison with other factory workers in Kerala. This is both a result of low daily wages and dwindling annual working days. In 1962, a cashew worker earned 26% the annual salary of an average factory worker. Two decades later, this figure had decreased to 12%.[64] The wages in the cashew factories over several decades are shown in Table 6.1.

---

[62] Govt. of Travancore-Cochin, *Kerala Report of the Minimum Wages Committee for Cashew Industry 1953*, p. 54.

[63] According to the Minimum Wage Act of 1948, two methods of fixing minimum wages can be used: either a committee is appointed which makes the necessary inquiries and drafts a proposal which the government then revises by posting a notification in the official Gazette, or the government may publish its proposals without a committee.

[64] Govt. of Kerala, *Report on Annual Survey of Industries*, Department of Economics and Statistics, Trivandrum 1963-64, p. 31; 1973-74, pp. 14 ff.; 1974-75, pp. 30 ff.; 1976-77, p. 10; 1978-79, pp. 28-32; 1984-85, pp. 31-36.

Table 6.1. Estimated average daily wages according to the stipulated minimum wages for cashew workers 1953, 1960, 1967, 1975, 1990, and 1999.* (mw = monthly wages, ss = separate settlements)

	1953	1959	1967	1975	1990	1999
Females, piece work						
Shellers	1.25	1.60	3.24	8.00	24.23	63.02
Peelers	1.24	1.59	3.14	7.85	24.00	63.01
Females, daily wage earner						
Graders	1.25	1.56	2.92	7.43	24.65	65.00
Others**		1.56	2.92	7.43	24.65	66.00
Males, daily wage earner						
All workers	1.88					
Casual worker		2.21	3.72	9.18	28.40	75.00
Scrubber		2.31	4.02	mw	mw	mw
Roaster		2.76	4.28	mw	mw	mw
Fireman		2.76	4.28	11.38	32.60	80.00
Tinker		2.76	4.28	mw	mw	mw
Stenciller		2.61	4.02	9.83	31.05	75.00
Packer		2.61	4.02	mw	mw	mw
Bag carrier		2.56	4.02	9.83	31.05	80.00
Oilbath roaster		2.46	4.28	mw	mw	mw
Sizer	-	-	-	-	28.40	75.00
Others†	-	-	-	-	34.75	85.00
Monthly wage earners						
Males						
Borma-worker		2.66	4.34	10.70	ss	ss
Roaster, scrubber				10.70	ss	ss
Oilbath roaster				10.70	ss	ss
Tinker, packer				10.70	ss	ss
Females						
Crèche nurse, kernel checker	-	-	-	ss	ss
Female/male††	0.66	0.67	0.73	0.74	0.79	0.82

Sources: RSP Office, Quilon, Minimum wages for cashew workers and lists with dearness allowances for the years 1953, 1959, 1967, 1975, 1990, and 1999.

* In reviewing the results of the revisions of the minimum wages since 1953, it must be noted that, from 1960 onwards, wages were safeguarded from inflation. The figures here include this so-called dearness allowance. The gap between the wages stipulated at the time of revision compared to their prior rate is smaller than this table shows because the dearness allowance (which was regulated each year) has led to an annual increase. The estimated average daily output for shellers is 7 kilos and for peelers 5.5 kilos. See, for example, Govt. of Kerala, *Report of the Minimum Wages Advisory Committee for Cashew Industry 1959*, p. 17; NRC, Go No. 3218/90/LBR RT, "Report of the Minimum Wages Committee for Cashew Industry 1989", p. 24.

** Tinfillers, mycauds (casual workers), and lap-checkers (persons who search workers to insure that no kernels are hidden under their clothes

† Carpenters, blacksmiths, and mechanics

†† Estimated average wage for women divided by the average wage rate for men. Note that for the last two revisions (1990 and 1998) the majority of male workers are not included in this calculation, since they are paid monthly wages.

In the 1930s and 1940s, most cashew factories paid all their workers (including roasters) by the piece. Table 6.1 shows that after 1953 male workers (except for those who remained in female-dominated sections) were paid daily wages. The argument was that the various methods of roasting made it difficult to fix a reasonable daily output. Among women workers, however, only graders got daily wages, and for them a minimum daily quota was required to get the stipulated daily wage. [65] It was thus a combination of the two wage systems.

A striking feature of the wage system over this period is its strict gender division, and the equalizing of women's wages. Male workers, however, soon were differentiated into categories, with some more privileged than others. The first step in this direction occurred in 1959 when several new job classifications were introduced, and one of these, the borma-workers, started to receive monthly payments. Since then there has been a clear tendency to move an increasing number of male workers from the daily wage category and pay them monthly. In consequence of this change, men are being paid full or reduced salaries when the factories close down during slack seasons.

Shortly after the start of state-run factories, a new system of separate settlements for fixing monthly wages by means of industrial relations committees was introduced among some workers. [66] It has been in effect since the early 1970s and means considerably higher salaries, i.e., wages closer to a "living wage" or a family wage than the monthly wages regulated by the Minimum Wages Act. The first individuals to benefit from this system were those working in the state-owned factories.[67] As table 6.1 shows, most of the workers under this bargaining system are male.

Looking to daily wage earners only, we find the differences in income between male and female cashew factory workers appears to have decreased. But if we also consider those workers paid on a monthly basis (under the Minimum Wages Act or another system of fixing wages), a calculation of annual income discloses that the earnings gap has, in fact, widened considerably.[68] There is, in addition, a fundamental difference in the capital-labor relationship between male and female workers. Workers paid on a monthly basis receive salaries which (at least in theory) cover the costs of reproducing labor (i.e., suffice for feeding children or supporting them-

[65] Govt. of Travancore-Cochin, *Report of the Minimum Wages Committee for Cashew Industry 1953*, p. 54.
[66] SRC, LBR MS Series Go No. (p) 65/80/LBR , "Administration Report for 1978-1979, Special Officer for Cashew Industry, Quilon".
[67] Records from the Personnel Department, KSCDC, Quilon, received 15 January 1999 from personnel director, Antoni Das.
[68] This statement is also based on information from the Personnel Department, KSCDC, Quilon.

Chapter 6

selves in sickness and old age), whereas those on daily wages or piece work can hardly meet their daily subsistence needs. This can be illustrated by the situation of Chamally and her husband, Prabhakaran. They both had worked in the same registered factory for many years. She was a peeler and he a roaster. The two estimated that Chamally's annual wages for 1998 only amounted to about one-third that of her husband, despite the fact that she worked every day that he did. When the factory closed down, Chamally went to work in a *kudivarappu* for half the wages, whereas her husband received unemployment compensation.[69]

Gender discourse in the report of 1953

As in the West, the family was viewed as the most important unit for stability in Indian society, as was clearly expressed by the Minimum Wage Committee for Cashew Workers in 1953. The committee considered the nuclear family (with male breadwinners) a force that encouraged a work ethic, as each man became responsible for a family (in contrast to circumstances in a joint family). The benefits of the family in promoting the accumulation of capital was openly proclaimed:

> Family is considered to be the unit in our social life and the incentive and initiative to earn more is a direct result of the family responsibility on the worker. Therefore a proper approach to the wage question would be to consider the worker not as a unit by himself but as one with family obligations and liabilities.[70]

Such an approach, however, was seen as clashing with circumstances in the cashew factories, since most of the workers there were women. Here the members of the Minimum Wages Committee rejected the provisions of the RCFW, arguing that they were only applicable to male workers. Although the Minimum Wage Committee considered it their duty to standardize wages for women, they did not feel bound by the recommendations of the RCFW in this regard.[71]

A dilemma existed, in that paying different wages to men and women for the same work could not be justified. Although the majority of the members of the Minimum Wage Committee were in favor of gendered wages, they were aware that such a policy contradicted the recommendations of the RCFW, and possibly they feared criticism on the grounds of

---

[69] Interview 11 January 1999 with Chamally, Ezhava woman, peeler, born in 1955, and Prabhakaran, Ezhava man, roaster, born in 1950.
[70] Govt. of Travancore-Cochin, *Report of the Minimum Wages Committee for Cashew Industry 1953*, p. 19.
[71] Ibid., p. 20.

unfairness. Not only would they be disregarding the demand for equal wages for men and women; gendered wages would also clash with the Indian constitution. Seeking a solution, they took refuge in a Western book, *Industrial Democracy*, by Beatrice and Sidney Webb, in which it was claimed that a strict gender division of labor was the norm in England, and that different wages for men and women do not contradict the principle of equal pay for equal work.[72] The committee argued that if a "modern" country like England could practice a gender division of labor (i.e., certain jobs were relegated to women at lower wages), then Travancore-Cochin could do so as well.[73] The following quotation from the committee's report illustrates how the gender division of labor was used to legitimize the discrepancy between men's and women's wages. It is especially noteworthy for stating openly what may often have been thought, but seldom articulated:

> Since the men and women were employed differently in different sections, it can be argued that if minimum wages is [sic] to be calculated on the requirements of the worker and his family, there is justification for rating the standard family at a lower number of consumption [units] in the case of women, since they are not expected to maintain at least their husbands. The committee decided to fix different wages for different sections on the basis of the sections being "male" or "female", the female section being allotted a lesser wage, regard being had to the above considerations.[74]

When the committee was trying to set wages, they consulted a report which had surveyed 1,222 cashew worker families. The committee members then estimated the needs of a family, based on what they considered scientific methods. They determined that the average family consisted of 6.13 members, of whom 2.91 had an income; thus, about 110 rupees per month were needed for survival.[75] Instead of conforming to the internationally-proposed model for a working class family (i.e., men providing for their wives and children), they estimated need according to what was for them "reality". In most cases this reality was far from that of the nuclear family of husband, wife, and two children. Therefore, in contrast to the recommendations of the RCFW, financial contributions of all "dependents" (e.g., children, youth, and old people) were considered. Since women of all ages contributed about 40% of the family's income, the committee

---

[72] Beatrice and Sidney Webb, *Industrial Democracy* (London, 1920).
[73] Govt. of Travancore-Cochin, *Report of the Minimum Wages Committee for Cashew Industry 1953*, p. 20.
[74] Ibid., p. 20.
[75] Ibid., p. 27.

reasoned that wages for women should be set at about 40% of the total family income.

Men's wages were also set below the recommended family wage, the argument being that female household members already worked for wages. The committee intended for men to receive wages in the amount of 60% of their family's upkeep. However, since every family had an average of 1.32 working men, these wages could be lowered even further. Thus, 1.32 men should earn 60% of the income necessary for a family, just as 1.59 women (the average number of women per family) should earn 40% of the family's needs. The final results meant that a man was supposed to have a monthly income of about forty-seven rupees; a woman about thirty-one rupees, and the recommended proportion of men's to women's wages was to be kept at a tidy 3:2.[76]

With this reasoning, a system was legitimatized that not only lowered women's wages, but also lowered men's wages within the cashew industry to a level that was below the prevailing ideal of a man as sole provider for his family.

Naturally, the average family the investigators based their arguments on did not really exist. The same committee noted that families had a considerable surplus of women between the ages of 15-54. This situation may be attributed to a large number of divorced, separated, widowed, or deserted women (although this does not appear to have been considered by the investigators). The committee concluded that such women were probably relatives from other regions who had come to work in the factories. Considering the recruitment system described in Chapter V, this seemed to be a reasonable interpretation. Calculations were based on the assumption that the lodgers contributed to providing care for small children in the household. If these children were not the offspring of the migrant workers, the earnings of the workers were more likely to be sent back to their villages, where they might have other children of their own, or disabled parents, or other living relatives. In all likelihood there were certain families in which many adults were *unemployed*, as well as families in which women were the sole providers. However, ideological arguments holding that women should *not* provide for men, and that a family wage was *not* a male worker's *right* (although an admirable goal), justified lower wages for everyone.

By way of objection, the chairman, K.J.M. Tharakan (a professor of economics), in a 1952 minimum wage report about the equally female-dominated coir industry, stated forthrightly:

---

[76] Ibid., pp. 27 ff. The exact recommendations were 47 rupees and 4 annas for male workers and 31 rupees and 8 annas for female workers.

> In this connection we have to point out that we do not agree with the rec-
> ommendation of the Committee on Fair Wages that "the standard family
> should be taken as one requiring three consumption units and providing
> one wage earner". This may be a good ideal, but we feel that Indian econo-
> my at present is still not so advanced for the adoption of this, as a general
> standard for the working classes....We have therefore decided to take the
> actual numbers of earners in the average family for computing the family
> income.[77]

Tharakan's remarks indicate that he considered India neither advanced nor
modern, but he expressed hope that things would progress along the lines
of Western countries, i.e., towards nuclear families with male breadwinners
and female dependents.[78]

The only distinction among cashew workers that members of the Minimum Wage Committee recognized in 1953 was that of gender. The mental
and physical requirements of different work tasks, as had been recommended
in the RCFW, were not considered. A main concern was standardizing all
women's wages so that at the end of the business day, the piecework rate for
shelling and peeling would correspond to the daily wage for graders.

With the Minimum Wage Committee report of 1953, the gender division of labor was established in such a way that it would be difficult to
change in the future. The report endorsed the dichotomous language of
femininity and masculinity, which now, for the first time, embraced low-
caste men and women (see Chapter IV).

In the same report, employers defined cashew workers as agricultural
laborers—cashew work being viewed as a supplemental source of income.
They claimed, for example, that workers were often absent from the factories during harvest time and, therefore, were mainly agricultural workers.[79]
This was probably a strategy of transferring responsibility for the workers'
reproduction to landlords, while also claiming that cashew factory work
was only occasional employment. These views were in contrast to the dominant gender ideology, which had recently started to include all women.
Even low-caste women, who formerly cared for themselves and could even
be put to work at male tasks, slowly began to be included in the "housewife" ideology.

An investigation in 1952 revealed that only a very small number of
female cashew workers actually had incomes from sources other than the

---

[77] Govt. of Travancore-Cochin, *Report of the Minimum Wages Committee for the Manufacture of Coir 1952* (Trivandrum, 1959), p. 35.
[78] See also Mies, *The Lace Makers of Narsapur*, p. 180, n. 2.
[79] Govt. of Travancore-Cochin, *Report of the Minimum Wages Committee for Cashew Industry 1953*, p. 41.

cashew industry: more than 90% of their earnings came from cashew work.[80] These people, therefore, cannot have been mainly agricultural workers. In fact, female absenteeism might better be attributed to exhaustion! Children had the most absences, men the least. Women's absence was probably connected with motherhood and the need to take care of children who were sick and could not be brought to work. The workers interviewed stated that agricultural labor was only their recourse when the factories were closed, and even then, it was difficult to get such work. Moreover, wages were slightly higher in the cashew factories than in agricultural employment.[81] The surplus of able-bodied women in cashew workers' families (due to the arrival of relatives who had come to live with them from rural areas) further underscores the fact that people migrated *to* the cashew factories from the hinterlands, rather than the reverse.

Two union leaders, T.K. Divakaran and M.N. Govindan Nair, opposed the maneuver by which work in the cashew factories had intentionally been turned into a seasonal industry by the manufacturers. Wages had beer set under the assumption that there was only work twenty-five days per month. In reality, the cashew workers were only employed for an average of twenty days per month. According to the union leaders, this was because factories closed down and moved to other locations—often in the countryside—as soon as union activities became too intensive.[82] Union leaders also objected to the notion that cashew workers were mainly agricultural laborers—an argument which, according to the union, acted to lower wages. Instead, the union leaders pointed out that for these women, factory work was their only source of income.[83]

It is striking that union leaders barely addressed either the fact that female wages were lower than male's, or the rigid gender division of labor. In a dissenting note, T.K. Divakaran made no mention of it, although the other trade union leader, Govindan Nair, did. It was not Govindan Nair's most important objection, but in a subordinate clause he did question the committee's acceptance of the existing ratio between the earnings of male and female workers.[84] Thus, it seems clear that it was not the trade union leaders who launched the idea of a gender ratio of 3:2. Nevertheless, perhaps their relative silence on this matter reflected ambivalence with regard to the two incompatible strategies: male breadwinner wages versus equal

---

[80] Ibid., p. 15. The same report is referred to in Govt. of India, *Report on an Enquiry into the Conditions of Labour in the Cashew Processing Industry in India*, p. 30.

[81] Interview 20 January 1998 with Theye, Kurava woman, born 1922; Interview 4 March 1998 with Kotha, Pulaya woman, born 1919.

[82] Govt. of Travancore-Cochin, *Report of the Minimum Wages Committee for Cashew Industry 1953*, pp. 49 ff.

[83] Ibid.

wages for men and women. Govindan Nair was a staunch communist and in all probability well-acquainted with the gender ideology in the Soviet Union. Equal wages for women and men were declared there in 1917. Women, at least officially, were considered to have the same responsibilities as men. They were to participate in the advancement of society, a cause in which family wages were considered representative of petit-bourgeois values.[85] On the other hand, Govindan Nair had to take the Report of Fair Wage Committee seriously, as its recommendations were unanimously approved by the members of the committee, including such prominent trade union leaders, as the communist, V.B. Karnik.[86] The only logical outcome of the fallacy inherent in the recommendations was to condone gendered wages and to promote a strict gender division of labor.

There is no doubt that the two trade union leaders on the Minimum Wage Committee viewed women as workers and providers for their families. Govindan Nair asserted that "to deny them wages on any of the twenty-five days of the month can only be a direct blow to the rice bowl. And unemployment for a few months leaves them no other alternative than utter starvation".[87] On only one occasion did Govindan Nair remark that women workers should be considered in a different way than male workers. He asserted that housing conditions were terrible and workers were huddled together in overcrowded sheds like cattle—something especially deplorable *as the workers were women.*[88] Women were considered less able to endure such conditions. Probably Govindan Nair's intention in portraying women as weak was not to belittle their role as workers, but to call attention to the country's shameful treatment of its women, who were deserving of better protection. By alluding to a more general gender discourse which included a view of women as *weak and requiring protection*, he probably hoped to be more successful in justifying an alternative way of calculating their needs.

---

[84] Ibid., p. 56.

[85] Eric D. Weitz, "The Heroic Man and the Ever-Changing Woman: Gender and Politics in European Communism, 1917-1950", in Laura L. Farder and Sonya O. Rose (eds), *Gender and Class in Modern Europe* (New York, 1996), p. 311. The communist equality ideal of men and women should, however, not be overestimated.

[86] Ramanujan, *Indian Labour Movement*, p. 67; Govt. of India, *Report of the Committee on Fair Wages*, p. 2. None of the trade union leaders presented dissenting notes to the RCFW.

[87] Govt. of Travancore-Cochin, *Report of the Minimum Wages Committee for Cashew Industry 1953*, p. 56.

[88] Ibid., p. 55.

The Minimum Wage Committee of 1959

Prior to 1959, as we have seen, women had been represented as agricultural laborers who worked in the cashew factory for extra income, or as women (not necessarily housewives) who had lesser needs than men. In the 1959 report, employers argued for the first time that women were *mainly* housewives "whose earnings only were supplementary to the male members of their families", and hence were provided for by their husbands.[89]

The revision of the minimum wages in 1959 entailed a crucial improvement for workers and a concession from employers: from now on wages were safeguarded from inflation with the introduction of the so-called "dearness allowance" (d.a.) for all workers, male and female alike. When discussing the new wages, however, the committee based their recommendations on the same theoretical assumption made in 1953, namely, the ratio of wages between male and female workers should be 3:2. Just as in 1953, they presumed a strict gender division of labor.[90] The principle of family wages, which, according to the committee chairman, was the *right* of workers in all *civilized* countries, was taken up, but the committee concluded that, in reality, Travancore did not have nuclear families with male breadwinners, so neither men nor women were awarded such a wage.[91]

Most of the discussions revolved around the conditions of the *male* workers and, as a result, male workers were classified into different groups. The old division of workers into female and male was abandoned, although the norm of a rigid gender division of labor and gendered wages remained uncontested: all female workers, irrespective of job assignment, were still seen as homogenous workers, all of whom should be paid equal wages. Males were divided into workers who were paid monthly and those who were paid daily, and these paid workers were, in turn, arranged in a wage hierarchy, as shown in Table 6.1. In contrast to 1953, the recommendations expressed in the RCFW, i.e., taking into account the mental and physical requirements of different work tasks, were now weighed—but only for male workers. The chairman, K.J.M. Tharakan, wrote in the final report: "After careful consideration the Committee came to the conclusion that apart from the differentiation between men's jobs and women's jobs, at

---

[89] SRC, Health and Labour Department 1960, G.O. No. MS 282/60/H&L, "Revision of Wages for Employment in the Cashew Industry", Vol. I, Memorandum from South Indian Cashew Manufacturers Association and Kerala Cashew Manufacturers Association to the Labour Department, Trivandrum, 5 December 1959, pp. 235 ff.

[90] Govt. of Kerala, *Report of the Minimum Wages Advisory Committee for Cashew Industry 1959*, pp. 25-26.

[91] Ibid., p. 20.

least in the case of men's jobs, it is necessary to fix separate rates of minimum wages for each category of workers." He declared that this was a matter of justice. [92] Skilled, dangerous, hard, dirty, or heavy work should be rewarded, although only men's work fell under such categories. Shelling, peeling, grading, and other tasks that were stereotyped as female occupations were relegated to an amorphous category of "women's work". We may recall that only two years earlier the Kerala Government had declared roasting and shelling hazardous tasks, a characteristic which the RCFW held should entitle workers to augmented wages. However, only the roasters were singled out for extra remuneration because of the unpleasant nature of the work they were assigned.

A job which had formerly been done by men or women was carrying tins filled with cashew nuts. This was done by so-called *mycauds* or casual workers. It was now ruled that only men would be recruited for this work, as was also the case with tin-filling.[93] Women were now excluded from tasks which they had thus far performed along with men. The women who previously did this work had been paid about two-thirds as much as their male co-workers. This was no longer considered compatible with the norms for setting wages. Instead of raising the wages of these women, those jobs were taken away from them. The last instances of men and women performing the same operations were now deliberately discontinued in order to avoid a conflict between the irreconcilable principles of equal wages for equal work versus female wages which had been legislated to be two-thirds those of males.

The impression one gets from reading the report is that union leaders were quite satisfied with the results of the negotiations, since, even after an urgent request from the chairman, they refrained from appending a dissenting note.[94] During the negotiations, the labor representatives had demanded that the gap between male and female wages decrease, but, as the report states, "...after careful consideration the Committee has decided that it would be better to retain the ratio devised by the previous Committee as an approximate basis".[95]

We do not know exactly what was said by the different principals, how the committee reached their conclusion, or why trade union leaders approved the result. Perhaps M.N. Govindan tempered his communist ideals and endorsed the recommendations of the RCFW on such issues

---

[92] Ibid., pp. 25-26
[93] Ibid., p. 18.
[94] SRC, Health and Labour Department 1960, G.O. No. MS 282/60/H&L, "Revision of Wages for Employment in the Cashew Industry", Vol. I, Appendix No. X, pp. xxxviii.
[95] Govt. of Kerala, *Report of the Minimum Wages Advisory Committee for Cashew Industry 1959*, p. 23.

as family wages and gendered wages, recommendations which had been unanimously adopted in 1957 at the 15th session of the tripartite Indian Labour Conference, where representatives of employers, workers, and the Indian government came together. The conference has been described as a landmark in the history of the Indian working class movement.[96] The stance adopted by the trade union leaders in Kerala was therefore only logical. Probably they were also being careful not to jeopardize the results they had achieved (such as the d.a. for all workers and the introduction of different male work categories—creating a lighter workload for many, and monthly pay for some male workers). The employers' representatives probably acquiesced in the achievements of the minority male workers as the price for social peace. After all, it was in the labor-intensive female dominated sections of the factory that owners incurred their greatest expenses.

Revisions of minimum wages in 1967 and 1975

After the Minimum Wage Committee concluded its work in 1959, it took thirty years until the next committee was convened. In between, the government proclaimed new minimum wages twice—in 1967 and 1975, after trade unions demanded higher wages and unemployment compensation at 50% of their wages. Although these two revisions did raise most wages considerably, a wide gap still existed between wages for males and females. Once again, after great pressure from the unions, a few more male jobs were placed under the category of those paid monthly. In 1966, a joint outcry from the main trade unions demanded all male workers be paid on a monthly basis since, it was said, they did the "vital work and that it was reasonable to pay them a high salary", i.e., a family wage.[97] However, it took several years for this reform to take hold.

It may be argued that such gains point to benefits that were *possible* to obtain, just as asserted in 1959 by the chairman when he said that since male workers were in the minority, higher wages would not cost employers a great deal. Viewed in this light, the demands were not transparently sexist, but were, rather, related to the labor intensity in the factories. In 1966, gender was clearly the watershed in all of the unions' demands.

There were very few casual female workers, yet union leaders continued to exclude them from efforts to secure monthly wages for males in the same category. Thus, the demands of the trade unions were not based on an economic rationale, i.e., whether a department was labor-intensive or not,

---

[96] Ramanujam, *Indian Labour Movement*, pp. 114-115.
[97] *Jennajugham*, 18 August 1966, p. 2.

Table 6.2. Wages demanded by the unions on 15 April 1966

Shellers	20 paisa/500 gram	Rs 2.80/day
Peelers	30 paisa/500 gram	Rs 3.00/day
Graders		Rs 2.75/day
Casual worker/female		Rs 2.75/day
Casual worker/male		Rs 75.00/month
Stenciller, packer		Rs 75.00/month
Roaster, kernel checker		Rs 80.00/month
Bormamen		Rs 90.00/month

Source: SICMA, Office, Quilon, "Charter of Demands of the Cashewnut Workers Action Council, dated the 15ᵗʰ of April 1966"

but on gender. Such a gendered way of thinking was also reflected in a 1967 decision of the Government of Kerala to financially support cashew workers who were starving because the factories were shut down. In this instance, women workers received only three-fourths the allowance of men.[98]

Reports of minimum wage discussions in the cashew industry are lacking for the period 1959–1989. To understand the reasoning by officials regarding family wages at that time, I examined a discussion on minimum wages in the fish canning industry, which has several similarities to the cashew industry: it is export oriented, female-dominated, labor intensive, and low paid. In fact, several members of the minimum wage committee for the fish industry were the same individuals who were on the 1959 committee for cashew workers, including the chairman, K.J.M. Tharakan, and some of the labor representatives.[99]

In the 1950s, the model of a family wage in the cashew industries was rejected with the argument that the country was neither "modern" nor "advanced". By 1970, as seen in the report of minimum wages for the fish industry, the official argument for not adopting the family wage model (which was suddenly described as obsolete) was quite the opposite: "Their concept [family wage] is a little old-fashioned and in any case does not correspond to the realities of the situation in this industry, where 45 percent of the family income is contributed by women workers".[100] The result, however, was exactly the same as in the 1950s, that is, the legitimization of lower wages for women, again justified by the gender division of labor. Another result was the rejection of family wages for male workers, which

---

[98] *Jennajugham*, 1 August 1967, p. 1.
[99] Another such person was the UTUC leader, R.S. Unni. See Govt. of Kerala, *Report of the Minimum Wages Committee for Employment in Fish Canning, Freezing, Peeling and Exporting Seafood and Frogs Legs in Kerala State* (1970-73) (Ernakulam, 1973).
[100] Ibid., p. 17.

led to the de facto acceptance of a situation in which several family members, young and old, had to contribute financially to the household.[101] In the 1950s, such a family had been considered old-fashioned; by the 1970s it was called "modern", the implication being that women were liberated now and it was the duty of each citizen to support themself. However, this appears to have been a purely rhetorical attempt to defend the status quo among poor families, many of which were headed by females.[102] To talk about households with single "modern, liberated" women earning their own livelihood is very eurocentric and Western. One can hardly call poor women in India struggling for survival "modern". The same official gender discourse which was heard in the fish industry reflected the handling of cashew workers as well.

The committees in 1989 and 1998

Fifteen years passed without any revision of minimum wages for cashew workers, in spite of the fact that it was obligatory for the Government of Kerala to do so every fifth year. Finally, in 1989, a committee was appointed for this purpose.[103] Nine years later a similar committee was constituted.[104] It is apparent that a different way of arguing was used by the committees of 1989 and 1998 than by their predecessors, but there were similarities. Again the point of departure was the 15th Indian Labour Conference and the RCFW, with emphasis on family wages and the assumption that a normal household consists of a nuclear family of two adults and two children.[105]

In both the minimum wages report of 1989 and 1998, the word *male* family-provider is no longer mentioned. Instead, the reports are character-

---

[101] Ibid., p. 17.

[102] Madhu Kishwar has pointed out that, in Indian society, the option for a female to live as a single woman, as in the West, has never been considered compatible with Indian culture. Madhu Kishwar, "Why I Do Not Call Myself a Feminist", *Manushi*, No. 61 (1990), pp. 2-8.

[103] NRC, Go No. 3218/90/LBR RT, "Report of the Minimum Wages Committee for Cashew Industry 1989", Report pp. 1-4.

[104] Govt. of Kerala, G.O. (R.T) 2473/96, *Report of the Delegation Committee for the Revision of the Minimum Wages of Cashew Workers 1998*, Labour Department (Trivandrum, 1998) (in Malayalam). Copy received from the chairman, P. Madhavan.

[105] NRC, Go. No. 3218/90/LBR RT, "Report of the Minimum Wages Committee for Cashew Industry 1989", p. 21. It appears never to have been argued in the West that women should receive family wages. The concept of family wages disappeared as an increasing number of women joined the labor market and the stabilization of the idea of "equal wages for equal work" gained acceptance. It must be emphasized that neither of the two systems corresponds to the reality in the West, where few working class men have been able to maintain the family and where equal wages is still a utopian idea.

ized by an avoidance of statements in terms of gender. In fact, the cashew workers were referred to as males throughout, except in the introduction, where it was expressly remarked that women work in the cashew factories. The new line of reasoning held that cashew workers, including females (although not explicitly stated), could be the family breadwinners. It was no longer assumed that other family members, such as youngsters or the elderly, should contribute financially to the household. In the 1989 report, after an analysis of the price of food, fuel, rent, etc., the committee came to the conclusion that "the monthly requirement for a cashew worker to maintain *him and his family* in a reasonable way comes to Rs 661.50 [emphasis added]".[106] Quite astonishingly (since the low number of annual working days was well-known), the committee assumed that there were on average twenty-six working days in a month.[107]

However, in contrast to the prediction of 1959 that cashew workers would soon find employment twelve months a year, the situation in the late 1980s was catastrophic—something passed over in silence by the report. For the more than 50,000 workers employed in the KSCDC, for whom there had only been forty-two working days in all during a in 1985-86 (the highest number seen in thirteen years; there were 125 in 1988-89),[108] the situation was urgent. In addition, the CAPEX factories, with more than 5,000 workers, had been in operation only a couple of months a year.[109] In the private sector, the number of working days varied in the different factories, but according to official statistics it had averaged around 58 in 1988, or less than five days a month.[110]

In 1998 the committee members came to the conclusion that a nuclear family of four would need eighty rupees per day to maintain the quality of life suggested by the 15th Labour Conference.[111] However, in their final recommendations, wages were set considerably lower, the argument being that wage increases for the majority of workers who previously earned about forty-five rupees a day would jeopardize the cashew industry for several reasons:

---

[106] NRC, Go. No. 3218/90/LBR RT, "Report of the Minimum Wages Committee for Cashew Industry 1989", p. 22.

[107] Thus a worker should earn a daily wage of 25.40 rupees (i.e., 661.50 rupees per month divided by 26 working days).

[108] Govt. of Kerala, *Economic Review* 1989, p. 68. Primary data concerning KSCDC provided by L. Radhakrishnan, Secretary of Industries, Government of Kerala.

[109] Primary data concerning CAPEX provided by managing director, V.N. Giri, 15 September 1999.

[110] Govt. of India, *Annual Survey of Industries*, C.S.O, Factory Sector, Vol. III, 1989-1990, p. 188.

[111] Govt. of Kerala, *The Report of the Delegatory Committee for the Revision of the Minimum Wages of Cashew Workers 1998*, Order No. G.O. (RT) 2473/96 LBR, chapter 4, pp. 11 ff. (in Malalayam). Copy provided by Labor Department, Trivandrum.

1. It would encourage private factory owners to relocate their factories to neighboring states.
2. The existence of the already ill-functioning KSCDC and CAPEX would be endangered.
3. Factory owners would be driven to violate the conditions in the Minimum Wage Law.
4. Problems would be created for other traditional industries in the state.[112]

In spite of the official acknowledgement that women were (or could be) breadwinners, they were not recognized as such in when it came to employment. The Equal Remuneration Act of 1976 was also not considered. First the power of the factory owners needed to be taken into account. The threat of relocating the cashew factories to other states was still real in 1998, just as was the owners' practice of breaking the laws. A new argument had emerged, however, and that was the profitability of the state-owned factories. The old declaration by the **RCFW**, that an industry which was not able to pay minimum wages had no right to exist, was forgotten—or at least disregarded. The Kerala State, through KSCDC and CAPEX, had become an employer and now had to balance the welfare of its workers and the profit derived from their work. In the minimum wage committees, KSCDC and CAPEX had their representatives sitting side-by-side with the other employers, but we must remember that trade union leaders were also politicians interested in the survival of KSCDC and CAPEX. Kerala State's role in the cashew industry may be seen as a paradoxical one, aiming to protect workers from exploitation, while being driven to increase exports of this extremely important commodity for its value earning foreign exchange on the competitive global market.[113]

It will be recalled that the structure of other traditional industries (such as coir), resembled that of the cashew factories. Therefore, if the cashew workers were to be acknowledged as "workers" in the sense of being important family providers, turmoil may have been created among large groups of female workers. That this was a real consideration may be realized by the extent of the coir industry. In 1988, it was estimated that coir manufacturing employed almost 400,000 people and, although declining as a source of foreign currency, its importance was still felt.[114]

---

[112] Ibid., chapter 4, pp. 13-14.
[113] During the last fifty years, their proportion in the value of the total exports from Kerala has fluctuated between 19% and 33%. Isaac, "The Trend and Pattern of External Trade of Kerala", pp. 371 ff. It was recently stated that cashew was the most important earner of foreign exchange among the agricultural products of India. See Govt. of Kerala, *Economic Review* (1995), p. 100; *Cashew Bulletin*, No. 8 (1995), p. 1.
[114] Pillai, *Kerala Economy: Four Decades of Development*, p. 134.

The final recommendation was that the majority of workers (i.e., the women) should get between 60 and 66 rupees per day, or about 75% of the recommended minimum needed to support a family. The outcome of the discussions was that all male workers would achieve a wage level about 20% higher than female workers, yet male workers were, by and large, excluded from the discussions, since they belonged to a separate negotiating system which presupposed higher salaries.

In spite of the avoidance of gendered language in the reports, the practical outcome of the committee's deliberations exemplifies the persistence of this way of thinking about wage relations. Letters from the trade union leaders to the chairman of the Minimum Wage Committees and to SICMA show a similar orientation. In contrast to M.N. Govindan's tacit demand in the early 1950s that the gap between male and female wages be decreased, the wage gap itself was no longer questioned. In their appeals to the commission, the unions reveal a gendered way of thinking, but in contrast to the final reports, their letters were not intended for publication and they did not represent an official viewpoint. In 1989, trade unions differentiated between female and male workers, and implied that a female worker should receive 70% to 80% as much as the lowest paid male worker.[115] The same pattern can be seen in 1998. By way of example, the president of the Kerala Cashew Worker's Centre, CITU (CPI-M) wrote at the time: "Renew the wages for women workers in shelling, peeling and grading to Rs 80 and for the male workers to Rs 110."[116] Similarly, the general secretary of Cashew Nut Workers Central Council, AITUC (CPI), wrote: "The wages for the female workers should be revised to Rs 75 to 80 per day and for the male workers it should be Rs 90 to 100".[117]

It would be tempting to state that the minimum wage reports cited above reflect changed attitudes towards female cashew workers, but it is, rather, only their language and arguments that reflect a shift toward what was politically correct at the time. It was no longer possible to openly calculate wages on the basis of gender, since this attitude was considered out of line with a modern society. Arguments and language had changed considerably in the 1980s and 1990s, as compared to the 1950s. We may speak of a new discourse—at least at the rhetorical level. Two gender discourses may

---

[115] SICMA Office, Quilon, "Demands of Minimum Wages for Cashew Workers", signed by Kadakkal Syndharesan, General Secretary, CITU 12 December 1989; "INTUC Recommendation for Minimum Wages", signed by M. Sreedharan Pillai, 12 December 1989; "UTUC, Recommendation for Minimum Wages", signed by A.A. Azeez, 1 December 1989.
[116] Letter from E. Kasim, CITU, to chairman for Cashew Minimum Wages Committee 1998. Copy provided by Labour Department, Govt. of Kerala, Trivandrum.
[117] Letter from K.P. Chandran to chairman for Cashew Minimum Wages Committee 1998. Copy provided by Labour Department, Govt. of Kerala, Trivandrum.

be discerned: one in the official language, and another unofficial—more silent and discrete, but nevertheless stronger.

The two latest reports are characterized by less antagonism between representatives of the employers and the workers. Discussions on such contested issues from the 1950s as the role of women as either workers or housewives are absent. Demands for unemployment compensation were dropped, and probably would not have been realistic, since both the number of workers and the yearly days of unemployment had increased greatly. Nevertheless, the silence of trade union leaders on these issues reflects resignation (if not acceptance) of the fact that women are low-paid, seasonal, and supplementary workers. As we have noted above, two of the expressed reasons for not suggesting higher wages were the threat of moving factories to other states and the risk of encouraging the violation of the agreed minimum wages. The fact that the trade unions did not object to the low wages and seasonal character of women's work reveals the unequal balance of power between unions and capital; it also reflects a lack of dedication and concern for the welfare of female workers.

Female Cashew Workers as Breadwinners

While visiting several cashew factories in the late 1990s, I asked the managers and staff how workers (i.e., females) survived during periods of plant closure. Without hesitation, they all gave similar answers: "They are being provided for by their husbands; they only supplement their families with their earnings now and then". Several trade union leaders offered the same response. The female cashew workers themselves told quite different stories. When I inquired into their financial situation, I heard them describe themselves over and over again as important breadwinners, just like their mothers had been—or still were.

Four kinds of household situations in which women were the main provider can be identified. First, households characterized by the absence of a resident male head, as in the case of widowhood, divorce, separation, or desertion. Second, households whose male members are absent for prolonged periods while they work far from their homes. Third, instances where the nominal male head-of-household is still living in the house, but has no earning capacity. (Such cases may typically include forced or voluntary unemployment, or disability due to illness.)[118] The fourth situation is when the male residential member has an income, but for various reasons

---

[118] Mayra Buvinic, Nadia Youssef, et al., *Women-Headed Households: The Ignored Factor in Development Planning* (Washington D.C., 1978).

chooses not to support the household. The two last cases are not readily apparent because the household is nominally headed by a male who has power over resources and distribution, although in fact he makes no financial contribution of his own. Joan Mencher has suggested a conceptual distinction between female-headed and female-supported households. In a female-supported household, the main provider is a woman, but her husband or another male member dominates the household in terms of decision making and financial control, whereas in a female-headed household, a woman exercises this power.[119]

There has been continuity among cashew workers in Quilon from the early days of the factories up to present, with many of the workers living year after year in households which are totally or partially female-supported. In some instances a woman is only temporarily the sole provider, but there are many cases where her financial contribution to the household is crucial for the survival of her family. In the early days, a large proportion of the workers were children, but since the 1960s the cashew factories have been dominated by married women.[120] This does not imply that these women live in nuclear families where the husband brings in the major portion of the income. They may very well live in the third or fourth type of household as described above, or in a composite of the four.

It is not possible to obtain much quantitative data for the economic contributions of female cashew workers to their households prior to 1952. The testimony of civil servants who visited the cashew factories in the 1940s suggests that most women who worked there were important providers for their families.[121] Saradamma, a female trade union activist who hid among the cashew workers and worked in several cashew factories between 1949 and 1950 (when the communist trade union was declared illegal) remembered the following:

---

[119] Joan P. Mencher, "Female-Headed, Female-Supported Households in India: Who Are They and What Are Their Survival Strategies?", in Joan P. Mencher and Anne Okongwu (eds), *Where Did All the Men Go? Female-Headed-Supported Households in Cross-Cultural Perspective* (Boulder, 1992), pp. 203-231.
[120] Sarojini, M. "A Study of the Working and Living Conditions of the Women Workers in the Cashew Factories with Special Reference to Chonadam Factory of Messrs Peirce Leslie & Co. Ltd.," (M.Phil., Stella Maris College, University of Madras, 1960); M. Thrivikraman, "Influence of Political Parties on Trade Unions in Jupiter Cashew Factory" (M.Phil., Rajagiri of Social science, Kalamassery, 1969); A. Nair and P.N. Varghese, "Report on Women Workers in the Cashew Industry in Kerala" (Indian Institute of Regional Development Studies, Kottayam 1979); Nair and Thomas, "Socio-Economic Conditions of Working Women in Cashew Industry in Quilon District, Kerala"; Deepa, "Industrial Crisis and Women Workers".
[121] KSA, Development files, No. 341/2093, "Exemption of the Cashew Factories from the Operation of the Factory Act", Note by Director of Industries, E. Chacko, pp. 13-14.

Many—perhaps the majority—of the women whom I met in the cashew factories had the main burden for the survival of the family. Often their unemployed husbands came to the factory on Saturdays when the wages were distributed to collect the women's wages or, at least, to assure that they would get their share for liquor and tobacco. There is no doubt that most of the women had a significant economic burden for the survival of themselves, their children, and to some extent also for their husbands.

—J. Saradamma, female trade union activist[122]

The communist trade union leader, J. Chitharanjan, made similar observations during the early 1950s. He was shocked to see the impoverished women catering to their husbands' needs. Chitharanjan also observed some of these men habitually collecting their wives' wages at the factory gate,[123] further evidence that certain households were headed by males but supported by females.

In surveying the income and consumption of 1,222 households in 1952, the Minimum Wage Committee for Cashew Industry found that women contributed slightly above 40% of a household's total income.[124] Few quantitative studies have addressed the role of women in the household economy of cashew workers. In a 1960 sample of fifty female cashew workers, it was shown that thirty of them (60%) were the only providers for their families.[125] The author of the report stated that most were married, but "uncared [for] by their husbands."[126] Thus, they belonged to the type of household with a male head who contributed little or nothing financially. In addition to factory work, most of these women had other jobs in the informal sector in order to earn enough to maintain their families.[127]

In 1982, 138 cashew workers and their families were polled by means of a structured questionnaire. One of the questions solicited information on the average monthly income of different family members. The study found that the majority lived in nuclear families in which financial contributions to the household income were shared about equally by men and women. On average, women contributed 48% of the total income.[128] Another study of 8,000 female cashew workers some years later came to a

---

[122] Interview 19 November 1997.
[123] Interview 7 August 1998 with J. Chitharanjan, male politician (CPI) and trade union leader for cashew workers in the 1950s and 1960s.
[124] Govt. of Travancore-Cochin, *Kerala Report of Minimum Wages Committee for Cashew Industry 1953*, p. 65.
[125] Sarojini, "A Study of the Working and Living Conditions of the Women Workers in the Cashew Factories", pp. 93.
[126] Ibid., p. 94.
[127] Ibid., p. 95.
[128] Govt. of India, *Report on the Working and Living Conditions of the Workers in the Cashewnut Processing Industry in Kerala* (1982), p. 12.

similar conclusion.[129] Both investigations indicate that women's contribution had increased from its 1952 level, despite the causualization of work in the factories.

In January 1998, I asked the eighty-five women working at the VLC cashew factory to calculate how much money they and other members of their households had contributed during the previous week. Their answers are presented in Table 6.3.[130]

Table 6.3. Estimated contributions of female cashew workers to households in January 1998

Each respondent's estimated share of total income in %	Households headed by males				Households headed by females					
	Nuclear families or joint families		Extended nuclear		Single mothers and children		Single mothers, children, and other adult females			
	Number	%	Number	%	Number	%	Number	%	TOTALS	%
90 -100	15	41%	8	35%	9	75%	10	77%	42	49%
61 - 90	2	5%	3	13%			1	8%	6	7%
51 - 60	11	30%	5	22%	1	8%	1	8%	18	21%
31 - 50	4	11%	3	13%	2	17%	1	8%	10	12%
10 - 30	2	5%	3	13%					5	6%
"don't know"	3	8%	1	4%					4	5%
Total	37	100%	23	100%	12	100%	13	101%	85	100%

By the testimony of these women, forty-two out of eight-five workers were essentially the only wage earners in their households. Only six out of eighty-five corresponded to the ideal: a woman in a nuclear family who only supplements her husband's income. Contrary to the assumption of

---

[129] Nair and Thomas, "Socio-economic Conditions of Working Women in Cashew Industry in Quilon District".

[130] The figures are approximate for several reasons. The women may have miscalculated their income or that of others. They may also have tended to exaggerate their misery and magnify the burden they were carrying. Nevertheless, I ascribed great credence to their testimony. Poverty induced them to recall exactly how much they and others in their household earned and spent. Therefore I believe that miscalculations are negligible. The motive for exaggerating their own misery would be to achieve some kind of benefit from it. It was, however, clearly expressed that the interview was of academic and not social concern. None of the women complained of their situation when being asked about the economic situation of the household. They just reckoned and answered the questions. The reverse situation, i.e., underestimating their own contribution and overestimating their husband's to stress that they lived in a "normal" family with a responsible breadwinning husband in order to raise their own status, is just as plausible a bias as the wish to exaggerate their own misery. Their sincerity cannot be doubted, nor should one deprive them of their say.

the Committee for Minimum Wages, less than half of the female workers
(44 %) lived in nuclear families. Of these, a large majority (76%) contributed more than half of the total household income. It was common, in
both extended nuclear families and joint families, that other income was
brought in by a mother, sister, or mother-in-law. Where females were heads
of households, the other wage earners were invariably daughters, sisters,
mothers and, in only one case, a son.

The transition from joint families to nuclear families has been considered the step from a traditional to a modern social structure.[131] Neither in
1953 nor in 1998 was the nuclear family the reality among most cashew
families, although it seems to have been an *ideal* among all the castes.[132] In
the 1950s, and again in the 1990s, most workers seem to have belonged
neither to a traditional joint family, nor to a nuclear family, but had another
type of living unit due to low level of their earnings.[133] These household
compositions should be seen as survival strategies rather than a residual
cultural phenomenon.

Table 6.3 demonstrates the position of women as family providers. Was
such economic responsibility the norm for these families? How long had
circumstances been that way? Most women answered that this had been the
prevailing situation for a long time. Some had been the main provider for
more than thirty years. They attributed this to the failure of their husbands
to contribute to the household because of unemployment (60%), illness
(25%), or refusal to give money to the household (15%)—the latter often
as a result of alcoholism. Households of this type can typically be defined as
female-supported of the "hidden" category described above. If one divides
those bringing in money to support the family into males and females (in
the same way as the investigators did in 1952), one sees that almost 60% of
all household income was earned by women. It seems as if the female cashew workers' burden in striving to maintain their households has increased
compared to the early 1950s (when this figure came to about 40%)—a
view the workers themselves also expressed.

The women I interviewed unanimously asserted that they were spend-
ing all their income to support their families. The figures in Table 6.3 relate
to their actual contribution. When questioned, these women held that

---

[131] Breman, "The Study of Industrial Labour in Post-colonial India—The Formal Sector",
p. 26.
[132] This statement is based on in-depth interviews with forty-five workers and is supported
by the 1953 investigation of 1,222 cashew families. See Govt. of Travancore-Cochin, *Report of the Minimum Wages for Cashew Industry 1953*, p. 27.
[133] This was pointed out as a general pattern among industrial workers in the 1970s.
Breman, "The Study of Industrial Labour in Post-colonial India—The Formal Sector", p.
27.

their men usually kept some of their money for themselves, and so they did not always know their total earnings.[134]

Since 1961, the number of households in Kerala supported by women has increased dramatically. In 1981, every fifth household—the majority of them composed of agricultural or temporary workers—was officially registered as headed by a woman. This was far above the national average, where the corresponding figure was only 8%. Quilon was one of the districts with the highest proportion of female heads-of-household in Kerala, an increase from 13.5% in 1961 to 22.5 % in 1981.[135] Many of these households were comprised of cashew workers.

---

[134] In the 1930s, the Indian ethnologist, L.A. Krishna Iyer, observed a specific pattern among a group of Pulayas. Male agricultural workers spent more than 60% of their daily wages on private consumption, such as lunch and toddy, before they reached home in the evening. See Iyer, *The Travancore Tribes and Castes*, II, p. 141. Studies from various states in India have shown that the pattern of contribution to the household is unequally divided between men and women; it has been determined that women regularly spend their total income on the survival of their household, while men often withhold part for their personal use. See Bina Agarwal, "Women, Land and Ideology in India", in Haleh Afshar and Bina Agarwal (eds), *Women, Poverty and Ideology in Asia* (London, 1989), pp. 70-98. The same pattern has been observed in Kerala. See Leela Gulati, "Women in the Unorganised Sector with Special Reference to Kerala", in Sharma and Singh (eds), *Women and Work*, pp. 263-265; K. Saradamoni, *Filling the Rice Bowl: Women in Paddy Cultivation* (New Delhi, 1991), p. 56. In the late 1970s it was shown among agricultural households in Kerala that children's nutritional status was linked to the income of the mother to a higher degree than to the father's income. In an extensive study of landless agricultural laborers in a number of villages in Kerala and Tamil Nadu conducted during the period 1979 to 1982, Joan Mencher demonstrated this pattern, stating that women took more responsibility for the reproduction of the family than men. Joan Mencher, "Women's Work and Poverty: Women's Contribution to Household Maintenance in South India", in Daisy Dwyer and Judith Bruce (eds), *A Home Divided: Women and Income in the Third World* (Stanford, 1988), pp. 99-119. See also Leela Gulati, "Profile of a Female Agricultural Labourer", *Economic and Political Weekly*, 13:12 (1978), pp. A27-36; S.K. Kumar, "Role of the Household Economy in Child Nutrition at Low Incomes", Occasional Paper No. 95, Department of Agricultural Economics, Cornell University, December 1978, quoted in Agarwal, "Women, Land and Ideology in India", p. 73. The link between women's incomes and poverty alleviation was stressed by a committee which investigated the cashew sector in 1998. They recommended the government see to it that women in the cashew industry be given regular employment, arguing that if the goal was to improve family welfare, it was more incumbent on the government to ensure regular income for women than for men. Govt. of Kerala, *Cashew Sector and Women Labourers*, Preliminary Report, Department of Industries (Trivandrum, 1998).

[135] Leela Gulati, Ramalingam, and I. S. Gulati, *Gender Profile: Kerala* (New Delhi, 1995), pp. 47-48 and Appendix 29. Female-headed households are therein defined as households in which women have the principal responsibility for the economic maintenance of the family. The *power of controlling consumption* was not considered.

CHAPTER 6

Conclusion

In this chapter we have examined three specific elements of social forma-tion from a historical perspective: a gender ideology based on male bread-winners, institutionalization of this ideology, and the material reality with regard to wages and women's contributions to their households. These components are not all compatible, and living in their midst has created tension—and sometimes paradoxical situations—for the individuals con-cerned. The reality for many of the women we have considered has been as *de facto* providers for their households. But the discrepancy between prac-tice and ideology has widened. The burden of supporting a family has in-creased and, at the same time, the ideology of male breadwinners has be-come institutionalized, encompassing a broad number of classes and castes.

It is indisputable that in the 1940s trade union leaders represented fe-male cashew workers as important providers for their families, a view gov-ernment civil servants also subscribed to (although they emphasized wom-en's domestic responsibilities, as well). Since almost all women in the cash-ew factories belonged to the lowest castes and it was also considered "nor-mal" for low-caste women to support their families, it was quite ordinary to call them workers. But it was emphasized that women were possessed of certain characteristics (docility, fear, need of protection), as well as the dou-ble burden of being factory workers and simultaneously caring for a house-hold.

Employers, on the other hand, took the position best suited to their purposes, balancing between two ideologies. One argument emphasized caste, since lower caste women were expected to provide for themselves. It was touted that work in the cashew factories saved them from starvation, and therefore the Travancore Government should be supportive of employ-ers and refrain from enforcing labor laws. Female cashew workers were at the same time represented as mainly agricultural workers who only did cashew factory work on the side. However, when this strategy failed to convince the government, a more gender-conditioned argument was re-sorted to. Employers denied that these women had responsibilities for the economic maintenance of their families, and insisted that they were pre-dominantly housewives—something which, in actuality, was only true of high-caste women, who were being provided for by men. The poverty of low-caste working women was belittled and their wages declared supple-mentary to their households, since their husbands were repeatedly cited as the breadwinners.

The stricter gender division of labor that was the outcome of the two first Minimum Wage Committees was an attempt to resolve the paradox brought about by the recommendations of the RCFW: on the one hand, men and women should receive equal wages when doing the same type of work; on the other hand, women's wages should not be as high as males because no woman could be presumed to be the sole provider for a family. Through the 1950s, certain trade union leaders seem to have taken an ambivalent stance on this issue. Should a radical communist ideal of gender equality be advocated, or the RCFW's recommendations of gendered wages? The unanimous approval of gendered wages at the 15th Labor Conference in 1957, where radical communist trade union leaders participated, put an end to anyone's doubts.

The call for diminishing the gap between women's and men's wages subsided and, in its place, the notion that women were only supplementary wage earners was accepted. In practice, the wage gap widened, with more and more male workers receiving monthly wages and the right to unemployment compensation. The disparity was not only one of annual income: there was a fundamental difference in the nature of capital-labor relations for men. Monthly male workers were given continuous employment, which meant that their salaries had to cover the costs of reproducing labor. Women, however, were classified as temporary or seasonal workers towards whom their employers had less obligations.

It was natural for trade unions to follow the path of development and modernization set down in the West and consider males alone to be bread-winners. This ideology implied that the normative situation which labor should orient itself by was "a woman equals a housewife". The successful struggle of the unions to obtain monthly wage-earner status for males, as well as the institutionalization of a rigid gender division of labor, must be seen in the light of this Western model, and not as a consequence of Indian tradition. On the institutional level, women have never been a part of discussions about wages.

As discussions of minimum wages continued into the 1980s and 1990s, the RCFW and the 15th Labor Conference continued to be invoked. The principle of gendered wages, although it continued to remain in place, was passed over silently in official reports. The Equal Remuneration Act of 1976 was ignored. The fact that trade union leaders were silent in the last two reports of Minimum Wage Committees with regard to (a) gendered wages, (b) long periods of unemployment, and (c) wages for women below the calculated minimum, may be the expression of a patriarchal culture possessing a strongly polarized, all-encompassing gender ideology. But such silence in connection with discussions of minimum wages may also be seen as a strategy for the survival of KSCDC and CAPEX. A great increase in wages could jeopardize the precarious state-owned factories. One may also understand this all as the process of "taming the trade unions" by the forces of capital with constant threats to close down factories and set up new ones in other jurisdictions. Even male coworkers in the cashew industry have been vulnerable to capitalist forces, contenting themselves with lower wages than most male factory workers in other industries in the region. However, the position of males has become more and more distanced from their female counterparts.

We can trace this historical development not only in actual wages, but even more so in their legitimization in the reports of the Minimum Wage Committees. These reports stand as the expression of a dominant gender ideology encompassing the whole society. The rigid gender division of labor and gendered wages were institutionalized and acknowledged by all parties—including the female cashew workers themselves (see next chapter).

In the foregoing, the ideological, discursive, and material levels have been explored, but we have yet to consider women's own perceptions and construction of their identities on the scale worker-housewife. This overarching question will recur in the chapters which follow.

VII   Trade Unions

The cashew workers are better than most other women. They understand
the capitalist relations a bit better than the majority.
—Male trade union leader, born 1933.[1]

Introduction

Women's activities in Indian trade unions (or their lack thereof) have
not received much attention within mainstream historical or social science. Book after book on the theme "trade unions in India", as Nivedita
Menon points out, have been published with hardly any reference to
women. When they are mentioned at all, it is their low level of trade
union activity, allegedly due to *apathy* and *lack of interest*, which is in
focus.[2] A 1962 publication explained this apathy on the basis of a high
illiteracy rate, female conservatism with regard to religion and social
traditions, and lack of time due to women's domestic responsibilities.[3]
Almost forty years later, some of these same arguments were still being
echoed by researchers who stressed women's higher degree of illiteracy,
lower political consciousness, and heavy household burden—the latter
implying that they had less leisure time than men for the aforementioned union matters.[4] It has also been suggested that women were
largely inactive in trade unions because they were newcomers to the
workplace and lacked knowledge of the potential for organizing.[5] In
1986, when K.B. Pillai found that trade unions in the Kerala cashew
factories were weak and that labor laws were being violated, he pre-

---

[1] Interview 13 August 1998.
[2] Nivedita Menon, "Women in Trade Unions: A Study of AITUC, INTUC and CITU in
the Seventies", in Sujata Gothoskar (ed.), *Struggles of Women at Work* (Delhi, 1992), pp.
187-196.
[3] A.S. Mathur and J.S. Mathur, *Trade Union Movement in India* (Allahabad, 1962), p. 71,
as quoted in Menon, "Women in Trade Unions", p. 187.
[4] Kanchan Sarkar and Sharit K. Bhowmik, "Trade Unions and Women Workers in Tea
Plantations", *Economic and Political Weekly*, 23:52 (1998), pp. L50-52.
[5] Nirmala Banerjee, "Introduction", in Banerjee (ed.), *Indian Women in a Changing Industrial Scenario*, p. 28.

sumed that the reason for this was the illiteracy and ignorance of the female workers.[6]

In the 1930s, literacy among cashew workers, especially Kuravas and Pulayas, was negligible. For women of these two castes the proportion of literate individuals was estimated to be below one percent; for men it was only slightly higher.[7] Gradually the percentage of literacy in Kerala— among cashew workers as well as others—has increased. Literacy among cashew workers, according to various sources, showed an increase from 26% in 1952 to 65% in 1977.[8] Twenty years later, about 70% of all cashew workers were literate.[9]

The rapid improvement in literacy in the quarter century following 1952 shows how individuals below the poverty line have benefited from the expansion of schools in Kerala. The smaller improvement seen since 1977 may be explained by the relatively high proportion of older women in the samples. When divided by caste, it becomes apparent that the higher in the caste hierarchy one looks, the higher the degree of education found. A comprehensive study of 8,000 cashew workers, carried out shortly after Pillai's 1986 study, found that some 64% were literate[11]—a figure far greater than the literacy rate among several groups of radical male workers,[12] contradicting Pillai's presumption of a correlation between illiteracy and weak labor unions.

The studies just cited assume that female trade union activity since Independence has been low, and that this is what is necessary to explain.[13] The implication here is that the failure of women to attain better working

---

[6] Pillai, "Economic Impact", pp. 168, 286.

[7] Govt. of India, *Census of India 1931*, Vol. XXVIII, Travancore, Part I, Report, pp. 287, 291.

[8] Govt. of Travancore-Cochin, *Kerala Report of Minimum Wages Committee for Cashew Workers 1953*, p. 14; Kannan, "Employment, Wages", Appendix, p. 7; Nair and Thomas, "Socio-economic Conditions of Working Women in Cashew Industry", p. 18.

[9] S. Meena, "Changes in the Life Style of Industrial Workers in Kollam District" (Ph.D., Department of Demography and Population Studies, University of Kerala, Trivandrum, 1997), p. 47.

[10] See footnotes 8 and 9. For an account of expansion of schools and literacy in Kerala, see *Poverty, Unemployment and Development Policy: Case Study of Selected Issues with Reference to Kerala*, pp. 121-132; A.C. Kuttykrishnan, "Educational Development in Kerala", in B.A. Prakash (ed.), *Kerala's Economy: Performance, Problems, Prospects* (New Delhi, 1994), pp. 349-367.

[11] Nair and Thomas, "Socio-economic Conditions of Working Women in Cashew Industry", p. 18.

[12] E.A. Ramaswamy, *The Worker and his Union* (Bombay, 1977), p. 189.

[13] For accounts showing female workers active in trade unions in colonial times, see Radha Kumar, "Factory Life: Women Workers in the Bombay Cotton Textile Industry, 1919-1939", in Sujata Gothoskar (ed.), *Struggles of Women* (New Delhi, 1992), pp. 123-131; Saswati Ghosh, "Women Workers and Organisers in the Jute Industry in Bengal, 1920-1950", in Gothoskar (ed.), *Struggles of Women*, pp. 114-122.

conditions is due to their low class-consciousness, as reflected in negligible trade union participation.

Menon discounts the view that this is a consequence of inadequate education. She asserts, instead, that Indian trade unions are embedded in a patriarchal ideology, and that specific women's issues, such as the Equal Remuneration Act, have never been taken seriously by the unions.[14] Two Western feminist researchers, Diane Elson and Ruth Pearson, in a study of women's work in export factories in the Third World, come to similar conclusions, although stressing the nature of production as well.[15]

In 1985, an investigation of coir workers in Kerala over the period 1938-1980 sought to destroy the myth that women were passive and primarily identify themselves as housewives, rather than workers.[16] The author concludes by documenting a high degree of female participation in trade union activities. As suggested in Chapter II, identity is a complex question and cannot be established on the basis of strike activity and demonstrations alone. Nevertheless, belonging to a union and participating in strikes and demonstrations is one of several identity-creating processes to be considered.

In social processes like union activities, the *quality* of participation in collective actions—grass-roots accountability, the relationship with the leaders, and the ability to bring forward issues emanating from one's own experience and problems—all are of prime importance. Such questions have been a main concern for theorists of so-called "new social movements" (i.e., peace, ecology, feminist, and local-autonomy movements).[17] A vast literature exists in this area and is primarily concerned with events which took place during the last twenty-five years. However, one aspect of these movements should be emphasized, viz., the high value given to democracy *within* the movement, and its empowerment for members. Alberto Melucci distinguishes between "traditional labor movements" and "new social

---

[14] Menon, "Women in Trade Unions", pp. 192-195. For a view that Indian trade unions have actively discriminated against women, see Banerjee, "Introduction", p. 28.

[15] Elson and Pearson, "The Subordination of Women ", pp. 144-166. In a study of textile workers in Madras, Uma Kalpagam explains women's failure of organization by the nature of production and capitalist power. See Kalpagam, *Labour and Gender*, pp. 177-187.

[16] Centre for Women's Development Studies, "Workers' Movements in the Coir Industry in Kerala 1938-1980: Women's Role and Participation", in Shimwaayi Muntemba (ed.), *Rural Development and Women: Lesson from the Field, Vol. II,* Sections 1 and 2, International Labour Office (Geneva, 1985), Chapter 13, pp. 223-249. See also V. Meera, "Tradition of Militant Struggle of Women in Coir Industry", *The Voice of the Working Woman,* September 1984, pp. 3-5 and November 1984, pp. 3-5; Meera Velayudhan, "Caste, Class and Political Organisation of Women in Travancore", *Social Scientist* 19:5-6 (1991), pp. 61-79.

[17] For an introduction to theories on new social movements, see *Social Research*, 52:4 (1985).

movements" on the basis of organizational form, the latter being more in-formal, democratic, and self-empowering.[18] A social movement, according to Melucci, should be viewed as a complex, multiple, and antagonist social construction. He stresses the importance of distinguishing the manifest level, i.e., visible actions, from the invisible or latent level, that is, everyday practices and informal networks where identity-creating processes are go-ing on.[19]

Peter Waterman, who has had long experience studying Indian and other trade unions, seeks to establish a connection between new social movements and the labor movement. He emphasizes that, in its early phase, the labor movement had several of the characteristics of new social movements. He introduces the concept of "social-movement unionism" for a new social movement *within* the unions.[20] Waterman's new social unions—a vision for the future—barely resemble traditional trade union-ism based on class struggle and having the capitalist system as its main target.[21] His discussion of integrating domestic work into a union's sphere of interest, and of favoring shop-floor democracy and empowerment for its members, is highly pertinent for any study of women's participation in trade unions.

The concept of the people's participation has also been a major concern for development researchers seeking an understanding of how agencies and planners can best implement various projects in developing countries. In a typology that had been worked out for a totally different purpose by the development researcher, Sarah White, there are four steps on the "partici-pation ladder", ranging from nominal (passive, symbolic participation, meaning that individuals mainly put on a display to show that the agency is doing something) to transformative participation, which actually empow-ers people to make decisions and act for themselves. [22]

Transformative participation has much in common with the way Me-lucci had defined participation in new social movements. A leader's role is not only to identify members' problems, but to actively interact with work-ers and, in the long run, diminish their own importance and power in the movement. The goal of workers' participation is to improve both working

---

[18] Alberto Melucci, *Nomads of the Present: Social Movements and Individual Needs in Con-temporary Society* (Philadelphia, 1989), pp. 205-206.

[19] Ibid., pp. 70-73.

[20] Peter Waterman, "The New Social Unionism: A New Union Model for a New World Order", in Ronaldo Munck and Peter Waterman (eds), *Labour Worldwide in the Era of Globalization: Alternative Union Models in the New World Order* (London, 1999), p. 254.

[21] Others have also predicted that "new social movements" would replace class-based orga-nizations. See, for example, André Gorz, *Farewell to the Working Class* (London, 1982).

[22] Sarah White, "Depoliticising Development: The Uses and Abuses of Participation", *De-velopment in Practice*, 6:1 (1996), pp. 6-15.

and living conditions by exerting pressure through strikes and demonstrations. The movement itself is also a means of empowering members to become less dependent on leaders and more capable of acting for themselves. Means other than those directed towards production may also be used in order to include the reproductive sphere in the social struggle. Such a strategy has been recommended by Amrita Chhachhi and Renée Pittin, who insist that the separation of factory and household, the public and private spheres, must be abolished.[23] Instead of educating for class consciousness alone, the goal is workers' total awareness of their life-situation, including the existence of other oppressive structures which may be based on gender, ethnicity, caste, or generation. Such awareness implies an identification of problems not only related to the workplace, but to the worker's overall life.

The question of the relation between union leadership and the rank-and-file depends on the quality of the participation, as well as the consciousness and identity of the workers. Several studies on Indian trade unions have criticized union leaders for being corrupt, exploitative, and of no use to workers.[24] With regard to the cashew workers in Kerala, Pillai condemns their trade unions for being elitist and undemocratic. Leaders are accused of acting in their own political interest, corruption, neglecting the welfare of members, and even exploitation of workers who, consequently, contribute more money through their dues to the party than to the trade unions themselves.[25] In this picture workers do not understood the processes going on. Such workers are viewed as passive victims who only nominally participate in their unions, and who suffer from false consciousness.

Whether corruption has occurred or not is difficult to ascertain. However, I have been able to explore thoughts among workers with regard to the usefulness of unions, the necessity of political goals, women's power in unions, and the role of the leaders. One aim of my interviews was to inves-

---

[23] Chhachhi and Pittin, "Multiple Identities and Multiple Strategies", pp. 64-82.

[24] The most critical among these authors is probably K. Mamkoottam. See his *Trade Unionism: Myth and Reality: Unionism in the Tata Iron and Steel Company* (New Delhi, 1982). See also Fernandes, *Producing Workers*, pp. 81-82. For a discussion of leadership in Indian trade unions, see Peter Waterman, "Seeing the Straws, Riding the Whirlwind: Reflections on Unions and Popular Movements in India", *Journal of Contemporary Asia* 12:4 (1982), pp. 464-483. With regard to Kerala, K.T. Rammohan has discussed the growth of a trade union bourgeoisie in "Kerala CPI(M): All That is Solid Melts into Air", *Economic and Political Weekly*, 33:40 (1998), pp. 2579-2582. K.K. George has a more generalizing view of Keralite trade unions, labeling them "managerial barons and marauders of public treasury". See his "Historical Roots of the Kerala Model and its Present Crisis", *Bulletin of Concerned Asian Scholars*, 30:4 (1998), pp. 35-40.

[25] Pillai, "Economic Impact", pp. 168, 172, 186-187, 190-193.

tigate whether it is accurate to characterize female cashew workers as having low class and political consciousness, and if this question, which has helped shape the identity of cashew workers, has gone through any historical changes. In previous studies of trade unions (recently referred to as "old social movements"[26]) the aspect of identities other than those of class were not paid much attention to, as class analysis was the prime concern.

The current methodology for finding reasonable answers to questions of consciousness and identity is to integrate printed sources describing the struggles and demands of female workers (achieved and unachieved) with women's own voices and memories and trade union leaders' representation of women workers. How the past is constructed in these stories is essential for understanding the process of identity creation.

Early Mobilizations and Successes: 1937–1954

The 1920s and 1930s were decades of burgeoning mass-mobilization in Travancore. K.C. Govindan was one of the first to organize workers in the state. He had been active in the trade union movement in Alleppey and, in 1937, came to Quilon where he put his experience to good use. He organized tile workers, cotton mill workers, sawmill workers, and ultimately cashew workers as well.[27] The system of discipline (including punishment) in the factories was extremely hard, and workers suspected of being involved in trade union activities were dismissed and subjected to acts of cruelty—even public humiliation.[28] They had no legal right to object, i.e., no grievance procedure, until 1937, when the Travancore Trade Unions Act was introduced.[29] In spite of this act, labor leaders and workers continued to be punished for involvement in trade unions, and activists were constantly watched. As is evident from the police reports, every word of their public utterances was carefully noted by the police, who were under instructions from the government to control and, if necessary, arrest them—something which happened quite often, according to sources from 1939-1949.[30]

Waterman, "The Social Unionism", p. 254.

Govindan, *Memoires*, pp. 49-58.

Ibid., pp. 63-70.

KSA, Development files 189/2052, "Travancore Trade Union Regulation 1112 (1937)".

KSA, Development files 356/600 1946, "Labour Strike in Cashewnut Factories in Quilon"; KSA, Development files 367/1604, 1946, "Confidential Report of Quilon Town Station 26/5 – 46"; KSA, Development file 136, 1946, "Quilon Labour Meeting 5-4-1121"; KSA, Development File No. 866, 1946, "Arrest of Certain Leaders 7-2-1946"; KSA, Confidential Files for the Years 1939–1949, C. S. Nos. 48/238, 49/378, 50/413, 75/321, 88/426, 88/1379, 96/3703, 96/3714-15, 99/740, 110/1953, 132/4248, 132/4258, 174/3156, 174/3638, 174/3854, 132/4248, 133/34399, 143/727, 148/953.

In 1939, although notoriously antagonistic to the unions, the factory owner, Musaliar, registered the first trade union in the cashew industry with the government—the All Travancore Cashewnut Workers Union (ATCWU)—probably to prevent the workers from joining more radical unions.[31] At their second meeting, however, the workers took over the union and selected their own leaders and representatives. One of them was a woman, M.S. Vilasini.[32]

In some factories the workers had objected to the harsh working conditions even before the trade unions started agitating for change, and we have evidence of certain spontaneous strikes in the mid-1930s. As noted in Chapter IV, the proportion of male to female workers varied with the different factories. The India Nut Company, for example, employed female workers almost exclusively, the percentage of adult male workers being very low (between 0% and 6% from 1932 to 1937).[33] It was in this factory that the first known strike by cashew workers occurred. An elderly female worker recalls the India Nut Company in the 1930s:

> I remember the first strike; there was no union at that time. This particular day we had finished our work with shelling, but the owner, Swaminathan (he was in league with W.T. Anderson), wanted us to continue—without payment—grading broken nuts from the whole ones. It was already dark and we wanted to go home. We were fed up with the treatment in that factory. Suddenly a woman—I think it was Lekshmi—shouted: "We won't do it. We are going home and we will not come back until we are being treated better!" This was the first time we had dared to oppose the bosses. All the workers left the factory and went home. We did not go to work for several days, but the owner sent his men to our houses and we decided to go back—after all we had no rice. I am not sure if I correctly remember the names of the leaders in this strike. Several women were leaders; I remember Lekshmi, Chellamma, and Bhargavi. They are all dead and gone now. All the workers went to see Swaminathan and we told him what we wanted. Our main grievance was that we wanted better treatment, especially for our children, and a stop to the severe and humiliating punishments which were imposed upon us, even if we had done nothing wrong. We also wanted to be paid for all our work; we had to do so much unpaid work before, such as sweep, clean, grade, carry baskets, and even work in the owner's house some-

---

[31] Govindan, *Memoires*, p. 81. Musaliar offered a trade union leader, K. Chellappan, a considerable amount of money and a house if he would refrain from organizing the cashew workers. Interview 14 September 1999 with K. Chellappan, trade union leader, born 1914.
[32] Majeed, *The Strike History of the Cashewnut Workers*, p. 24.
[33] The factory was first registered as W.T. Anderson Co. See Govt. of Travancore, *Statistics of Travancore* 1108 ME/1932-1933 AD, p. 135; 1110 ME/1934-35 AD, p. 137; 1113 ME/1937-38 AD, p. 165.

times. We cannot say that our strike was very successful, but nevertheless we were astonished and we felt a little bit strengthened because we had dared to act like this. It had never happened before. We also realized that we had some power; or else why would he come and fetch us in our houses? And we realized that we could do it again, if we only managed to save some rice. There was another strike during this period and the police arrested several women. The manager and his rowdies provided the police with the names of those they suspected to be the leaders. The women I mentioned before were certainly arrested more than once. Shortly after this event we were organized in trade unions with the help of K.C. Govindan and T.K. Divakaran. During the years from then on until we were included in the Factory Act [of 1945], we carried out so many strikes—a behavior that was completely unknown and unthinkable to us only a few years earlier! And then so many people from all factories—men and women—were imprisoned because of this! I can't remember them all.

—Theye, Kurava woman, sheller, born 1922[34]

The two strikes which Theye mentions must have occurred before K.C. Govindan arrived at Quilon in 1937.[35] In his memoirs, Govindan gives an account of a spontaneous strike which was staged in 1937 against the India Nut Company. That may be the second strike Theye describes. After meeting secretly at night for about a week, nearly all the workers in the factory were organized. When this came to attention of management, they dismissed the strike leaders by accusing them of stealing nuts. A series of public meetings followed. Govindan sent for another trade union leader to assist him, but before that person could arrive, the female workers had taken matters into their own hands. Gathering outside the factory at 5:30 in the morning, they successfully prevented the manager and staff from entering.[36] Obviously, they already knew the art of organizing. The leaders, it appears, were all women.

Theye's story, as well as an account included in Govindan's memoirs, indicates that women were already acting collectively in the nascent social struggle of the 1930s, and doing so without the help of outsiders. They were influenced by the turbulence going on among other groups in Quilon.[37] Perhaps male family members were employed in factories where

---

[34] Interview 18 January 1997. In 1962 a similar story was told by a worker to a reporter. See Balakrishnan, "Life and Strikes in the Midst of Smoke and Coal Dust", pp. 2-3.

[35] The trade union activist, Kesavan Nair, interviewed old cashew workers and dates a strike at the India Nut Company to 1933. Kesavan Nair, "Strike History Cashew Labourers , part 1", *CITU Sandesam* 17:5 (1993), pp. 10-18.

[36] Govindan, *Memoires*, pp. 67-71.

[37] Ibid., pp. 57-77.

organizing and strike activity had already begun. There is scant evidence for such collective action prior to the establishment of trade unions by outside organizers. We can only conjecture that there must have been situations in which women were collectively active, revealing an emerging trade union consciousness, although hunger drove them back to work before they could achieve their objectives. Other narratives of the period indicate that caste continued to be a strong barrier against unity in many factories (see Chapter V). According to Theye, only low-caste women worked at the India Nut Company in the 1930s, and this may have facilitated their mobilization as a group.

When Govindan entered on the scene at Quilon in 1937, the complaints of the workers became more organized. His memoirs indicate that it took him several meetings to adequately formulate their demands. In that same year the cashew workers distributed their first leaflet (Table 7.1).

Table 7.1. The cashew workers' earliest leaflet of demands, 1937

1. Provision of bathrooms/latrine facilities
2. Provision of crèches (day-care centers) for children of workers
3. Job security for workers (i.e., abolition of arbitrary dismissal, freedom to organize)
4. Ban on forcible savings for workers
5. Abolition of water charges*
6. Abolition of unpaid labor**
7. Ban on employment of children below the age of fourteen
8. Work beginning at 8 a.m., instead of between 3 a.m. and 5:30 a.m.
9. Payment for broken nuts
10. Maternity benefits for workers
11. Free provision of water
12. Increase of wages for all

*   workers were forced to buy drinking water from their employer
** especially common among peelers, who had to carry baskets to other sections Sources: Govindan, *Memoires*, pp. 67-71.

The strike at the India Nut Company was only partially successful. Of the demands the workers enumerated in their leaflet, only a few were met (i.e., access to latrines, daycare centers for their children, peelers not being asked to do unpaid work, and freedom to join a trade union)—but these were important issues and enough to bolster the spirit of struggle.[38]

As the story of Theye indicates, many strikes took place during the period 1937-1945. The participants in these early actions were mainly

---

[38] Ibid., p. 70.

women and men from the lowest castes, something which the memories of workers (see Chapter V) and contemporary police reports have preserved.[39] By way of example, in 1946 the police in Quilon reported that "about 200 coolies, including men and women, were found assembled near the peeling shed, bawling 'Long live the union!'"[40]

The historian, Robin Jeffrey, characterizes what he calls "old Travancore" as a society in which politics occurred behind closed doors and were a matter for a select few. "New Travancore", on the other hand, Jeffrey describes as an open society in which politics came out into the light and now concerned the majority of the people. Jeffrey places the dividing line between the two political cultures sometime in the 1940s.[41] During a transitional period, both types co-existed, and this dual political culture of the 1940s and early 1950s was reflected in the strategies used by trade unions in the case of cashew workers. We find both mass strikes, such as those in 1939, 1945, and 1951 (each with at least 20,000 participants),[42] and secret negotiations behind closed doors.

On several occasions trade union leaders put pressure on the Travancore Government, threatening to disclose the deplorable working conditions among factory workers in Travancore to the outside world.[43] The first step in combating inhumane working conditions in the cashew industry was to bring all plants under the Factory Act of 1939. This would resolve many of the demands which appeared in the first leaflet, including limited working hours, a ban on child labor (although the Factory Act set the lower limit at age twelve, and not fourteen, as demanded), day-care centers, free drinking water, and latrine facilities.[44]

K.C. Govindan had already begun discussing the inclusion of cashew factories under the Factory Act with the dewan in 1939.[45] According to another trade union leader, M.N. Govindan Nair, the exposure of Travancore's misery to the outside world by union leaders was finally what brought the industry into the Factory Act in 1945. Negative publicity was

---

[39] KSA, Confidential file No. 48/238; Confidential File No. 49-378 1939; Development File No. 356-600.

[40] KSA, Development files, No. 356-600, "Labour Strike in Cashewnut Factory in Quilon", Report from Police Station, Quilon, dated, 31 January 1946, p. 3.

[41] Jeffrey, *Politics, Women, and Well Being*, pp. 1-2.

[42] Majeed, *The Strike History*; P. Kesavan Nair, "A Brief History of Trade Union Movement among Cashew Workers" (Paper presented at the Conference on Development in Kerala, AKG-Centre, Trivandrum 1994).

[43] Obviously, Travancore had been accused of building its industries on "sweated labor". See "Labour Legislation in Travancore", Govt. of Travancore, *Travancore Information and Listener* 6:11(1946), p. 40.

[44] Ibid.

[45] KSA, Confidential file, No. CS 50/455, "Deputation of Quilon Factory Workers Association 1939".

considered a more effective tactic than all the strikes which had been undertaken up to that point.[46]

The same strategy was resorted to in order to obtain maternity compensation. In 1943, the Travancore Government passed the Maternity Benefit Act, but it was unclear whether the cashew factories were covered by the act or not. The law was difficult to interpret and additional clarification was needed.[47] During the early 1940s, cashew workers carried out several strikes for the sake of maternity benefits, but the strategy of disclosing the deplorable factory conditions to outsiders was also used.

K. Subharayan was a prominent woman in the Indian National Congress Party and belonged to the circle of Mahatma Gandhi. Her importance may be illustrated by the fact that she was one of the few Indians who attended the first Round Table Conference in London in 1930 and 1931, when India's political needs and aspirations were discussed with the British government.[48] In 1945, she was invited to chair the annual conference of the Cashewnut Workers' Union in Quilon. The purpose of inviting K. Subharayan was to "show the blistered hands of the labourers to [her] and to the outsiders," and thereby draw the attention of the government to conditions in the factories and to the grievances of the workers.[49]

The actions taken by the Travancore government to prevent K. Subharayan from appearing in Quilon demonstrates their concern that unfavorable aspects of their society not be exposed to outsiders. The director of industries instructed the inspector of factories to "proceed immediately to Quilon and to persuade the Cashewnut Workers' Union to refrain from inviting Mrs. Subharayan".[50] The inspector followed the directive and, in addition, rebuked the trade union leader both for undignified behavior and for showing a lack of self-respect in exhibiting Travancore's shortcomings and complaints to outsiders.[51]

It remains uncertain whether it was really this strategy which gave the cashew workers the right to maternity compensation, but the trade union leader's firm belief that approaching the government rather than the factory

---

[46] KSA, Development files 1946, No. 507, "Memorandum from the Cashewnut Workers", Confidential letter from Chief Inspector of Factories to the Director of Industries, Trivandrum, 1945, p. 47-48.
[47] KSA, Development file No. 316/3898, "Travancore Maternity Benefit Act 1943"; KSA, Development file No. 359/987, "Application of Maternity Benefit Act to Cashew Factories".
[48] Tara Ali Baig (ed.), *Women of India* (New Delhi, 1990), p. 36; Kumar, *The History of Doing*, p. 81.
[49] KSA, Development files 1946, No. 507, "Memorandum from the Cashewnut Workers", Confidential letter from Chief Inspector of Factories to the Director of Industries, Trivandrum, 1945, pp. 47-48.
[50] Ibid.
[51] Ibid., p. 49.

owners would be more fruitful exemplifies not only the closed nature of the Travancore society, but the necessity of achieving labor rights at the legislative level, and the crucial role the leaders had in this struggle.

The earliest unions among cashew workers were not linked to any political parties. Since 1942, the various cashew workers trade unions, like others in the rest of India, have been affiliated with various political parties, and their leaders have been "outsiders"—mainly politicians.[52] In 1939, the Communist Party was formed in Travancore. It emerged from a left-oriented wing of the Congress Party (the Congress Socialist Party). For some years, all cashew workers unions belonged to All-India Trade Union Council (AITUC), the trade union branch of the Communist Party of India (CPI).[53] Since 1947, however, a multiplicity of unions with different political party affiliations has been characteristic of the Indian labor movement.

In October 1946, most unions were banned for a period of about a year as a result of the social and political upheavals which culminated in the so-called Punnapra-Vayalar revolt.[54] Again, after Independence, the AITUC was banned for several periods between 1948 and 1950, and union leaders were either imprisoned or exiled.[55] In order to fill the void left by the shutting down of the AITUC, the Revolutionary Socialist Party, which was not banned, formed a trade union wing, the United Trade Union Congress (UTUC).[56] Its center was in Quilon and the cashew workers constituted the majority of its members. Two male activists, K. Sreekantan Nair and T.K. Divakaran, formed the Quilon Cashewnut Factory Workers Union, and shortly afterwards a central organization named the Travancore Cashewnut Workers Council was constituted under the UTUC.[57]

During the period from 1945 to 1952, several important legal rights were won by cashew workers, who were now included under the labor laws. From this time on, they achieved the right to be designated "factory workers".

The most important labor rights introduced in 1945-1953 are shown in Table 7.2:

---

[52] For an overview of Indian trade unions, see Sohaid Jawaid, *Trade Union Movement in India* (Delhi, 1982). For a discussion of union leaders, see E.A. Ramaswamy, "Indian Trade Unionism: The Crisis of Leadership", in Mark Holmström (ed.), *Work for Wages in South Asia* (New Delhi, 1990), pp. 160-172. By "politician" is meant a person who is actively engaged in a political party. Many trade union leaders held a post in local democratically elected units.

[53] Kannan, "Evolution of Unionisation", pp. 11-12.

[54] Kesavan Nair, "A Brief History", p. 13; For an account of the Punnapra-Vayalar revolt, see P.K.V. Kaimal, *Revolt of the Oppressed: Punnapra-Vayalar 1946* (Delhi, 1994).

[55] Kesavan Nair, "A Brief History", pp. 13-15.

[56] Kannan, "Evolution of Unionisation", p. 13.

[57] Majeed, *The Strike History*, p. 50.

Table 7.2 Labor rights introduced for cashew workers, 1945–1953

Year	Labor law
1945	Factory Act (with certain exemptions regarding child labor)
1945	Maternity Benefit Act
1946	Bonus (to be paid annually as a percentage of a worker's total wage)
1947	Factory Act (child labor banned)
1953	Minimum Wages Act

The agenda for labor during this period primarily emanated from the workers themselves, although it was solicited, formulated, and debated by outside leaders. Older workers, in recalling the struggles and achievements of those years, remember them as the golden age of the labor movement. In the words of Sujatha:

> The 1950s were glorious times for us! We were quite happy at that time. We felt that the state, through the labor commissioner and factory inspector, was on our side. We were on the march—men, women, trade union leaders, and politicians. We had a firm belief that we would continue to be successful. We had won so much—not only such things as labor rights and abolition of child labor, but political issues, too. First Independence, then some of our leaders became ministers, and then the communists came to power in 1957. We felt that nothing could go wrong and nothing could stop us. Never had this country witnessed so many women being so determined!
> —Sujatha, Ezhava woman, born 1925, peeler, trade union convener[58]

Institutionalization of Trade Unions: ca. 1955–ca. 1975

The earliest phase of this period was characterized by a generally left-oriented, radical climate in Kerala. The middle years were one of the most turbulent periods of recent history in the state.[59] It was a time when Kerala became known for its leftist policy.[60]

This was also a period when trade unions matured in their organizational form. The collective bargaining system became institutionalized, and splits in trade unions created competition among leaders and a struggle

[58] Interview 15 August 1998.
[59] E.M.S. Namboodiripad, *The Communist Party in Kerala: Six Decades of Struggle and Advance* (New Delhi, 1994); T. J. Nossiter, *Communism in Kerala: A Study in Political Adaptation* (Bombay etc., 1982), pp. 105-178.
[60] D.R. Mankekar, *The Red Riddle of Kerala* (Bombay, 1965).

to win over members. In 1954, the trade union branch of the Indian Congress Party (INC), named the Indian National Trade Union Congress (INTUC), started to organize cashew industry employees—mainly staff and other white collar workers.[61] Gradually INTUC won influence over blue collar workers, too, and in 1960 about 2,000 cashew workers became registered members.[62]

Thus, by the early 1960s, three major political parties and their trade unions were active among cashew workers. However, the proliferation of political parties continued. In 1964, the Communist Party of India (CPI) split into two. A few years later, the new party, the Communist Party of India, Marxist (CPI-M), formed a trade union wing: the Centre of Indian Trade Unions (CITU). The party split had its repercussions among cashew workers and others in Kerala. From 1965 on, CPI-M leaders organized cashew workers into new unions, and in July 1970 a central organization for cashew workers under CITU, the Kerala Cashew Workers Centre, was formed.[63] As a result, three or four trade unions with different political affiliations have had a presence in most of the cashew factories over the last three decades, as evident in an overview of central trade unions among cashew workers (Table 7.3):

Table 7.3. Trade unions among cashew workers in Kerala

Trade Unions	Inception	Union	Affiliation
All Kerala Cashewnut Factory Workers Federation	1950	UTUC	RSP
All Travancore Cashew Workers' Council	1952	AITUC	CPI
Kerala Cashew Workers' Congress	1953	INTUC	INC
Kerala Cashew Workers' Centre	1970	CITU	CPI-M

Indian trade unions are basically organized in the same way. The earliest unions were less formalized in their structure, but since the 1950s unions have became institutionalized with a strict three-layer pyramidal hierarchy. Individual factories are the basic units, under factory workers who are

---

[61] Pillai, "Economic Impact", p. 161; Kannan, "Evolution of Unionisation", p. 13.
[62] Interview 12 March 1997 with Ben Morris, trade union leader, INTUC, Quilon.
[63] Kesavan Nair, "A Brief History", pp. 21-22. See also Kannan, "Evolution of Unionisation", pp.12-14, and Pillai, "Economic Impact", pp. 154-164.

nominated to be so-called factory conveners (local leaders). At the next (regional) level, a trade union leader has responsibility for several cashew factories in a particular area, usually consisting of one *taluk*. The leaders at this level do not work in the factories, but may be full-time trade unionists. Finally, leaders at the state level, most often full-time politicians, deal with industry-wide issues.[64] Women have only been active as union officials at the factory level, with one exception: Bhargavi Thankappan, a woman, became a top-level leader for CITU in 1982. She was not, however, a former factory worker, but came from a middle class family, several of whose male members were in the same political party. Some male cashew workers had managed to rise from ordinary workers to full-time politicians via the trade unions.[65]

In 1945, a tri-partite conference with representatives from SICMA, workers organizations, and Travancore State marked the beginning of a system which expanded in the 1950s.[66] It was responsible for industry-wide negotiations and settlements. Often convened by the Labor Commissioner, the conference was usually attended by the Labor Minister or the Industrial Minister.[67] The state has, thus, played a decisive role in the relations between capital and labor in the cashew factories, even doing so in an institutionalized form.

The trade union movement grew rapidly. In 1953, the author of an official report on the cashew industry in Kerala stated that "the workers are generally organized in trade unions".[68] According to data from trade union leaders, about 70% of all Kerala cashew workers in registered factories belonged to a trade union in 1960. The number of union members has steadily increased, although the proportion of unionized workers (who numbered about 150,000 in 1995) has only grown to about 75% of all cashew workers in 1995. Three-quarters of the organized workers belong to unions with a political affiliation with parties on the left, viz., CPI, CPI-M, or RSP.[69]

Surveying the daily press in Kerala from the early 1950s onwards gives us a picture of cashew workers in almost constant struggle. Demonstrations, *satyagrahas*, strikes, and other job actions appear to have been very

---

[64] For a detailed account of the organizational system of the trade unions, see Pillai, "Economic Impact", pp. 155-175.

[65] Interview 14 September 1999 with K. Chellappan, trade union leader, born 1914.

[66] Govt. of Travancore-Cochin, *Report of Minimum Wages Committee for Cashew Industry 1953*, p. 49.

[67] Pillai, "Economic Impact", p. 204.

[68] Govt. of Travancore-Cochin, *Report of Minimum Wages Committee for Cashew Industry 1953*, p. 11

[69] Sources of figures: AITUC from J. Udaya Bhanu, president, Kerala Cashew Workers Central Council, Quilon. CITU from Kesavan Nair, secretary, CITU, Quilon. UTUC from A.A. Azeez, president, All Kerala Cashewnut Factory Workers Federation, Quilon. INTUC are estimates received from Ben Morris, president, INTUC, Quilon District.

frequent, especially into the mid-1970s. We find leaders, as well as workers, men along with women, frequently arrested and imprisoned.

Trade union activities in terms of participation in strikes confirms a high degree of involvement on the part of women. K.B. Pillai has analyzed work stoppages during the period 1950-1978 by exploring available statistics concerning length of conflict, number of workers involved, and reasons given to the labor department for the work stoppages. He has documented an extremely high number of strikes in the 1950s and 1960s, most of them due to economic issues such as wages and bonuses. For reasons connected with the non-implementation of stipulated wages, the most turbulent period was the 1960s.[70]

After the successful inclusion of cashew workers under the Minimum Wage Act in 1953, labor laws were openly violated and owners closed down their factories because of union activities.[71] As we saw in Chapter III, along with the increase in clandestine factories, this led politicians to press for the nationalization of the factories. The work of implementing this decision took place at the top political level as part of a more general economic policy.

In the factories, meanwhile, the most burning question prompting demonstrations was being paid enough for day-to-day survival. Then an event during a strike in 1957, the so-called "Chandanathoope Firing", in which the police killed two unarmed male cashew workers protesting conditions in the factory, aroused the anger of both workers and union leaders.[72] The increased number of illegal *kudivarappus* was another reason for mass mobilization. The strikes of the 1960s were great manifestations of power, in which the majority of the workers participated. It was frequently reported that between 75,000 and 150,000 workers demonstrated.[73]

During this period, welfare proposals came to the forefront. Such programs often imply a shared economic burden by the state, the employers, and the employees (see Table 7.4).

[70] Pillai, "Economic Impact", p. 233.

[71] RSP Office, Quilon, Thiruvananthapuram Industrial Tribunal, Shri. K. Purushotham Nair. Labor Conflict No. 15/1951 (8772/50 Oct 21 1951).

[72] *Jennajugham*, 2 September 1958, p. 2.

[73] *Jennajugham*, 15 December 1961, p. 2; 23 August 1962, p. 1; 25 July 1964, p. 4; 27 August 1965, p. 1; 22 March 1966, p. 5; 13 July 1967, p. 1; 6 March 1969, p. 1; 13 August 1969, p. 1; 11 May 1972, p.1; 2 August 1972, p. 5; 24 August 1973, p. 1.

Table 7.4. Social welfare schemes for cashew workers, 1963-1975

Name	Year of inception	Brief description
Employees' Provident Fund (PF)	1963	Workers' savings fund administrated by employers consisting of a certain percentage of wages.* The purpose of the fund is to provide financial security to workers upon retirement due to age or incapacity.
Employees State Insurance Scheme (ESI)	1963	Insurance financed by contributions from employers, employees, and the state, mainly meant for sickness and maternity benefits. To be eligible for the benefits the employee must have worked a minimum of thirteen weeks over a period of six months. A factory covered by ESI will not be covered by the Maternity Benefit Act.
Gratuity Fund	1972	Workers' saving fund administrated by employers consisting of a certain percentage of wages.* The purpose of the fund is so a gratuity can be paid as a lump sum to workers for long, uninterrupted service. It can be paid after a minimum of five years of service.
Employees Family Pension	1975	An insurance fund financed in the same way as ESI, meant to provide the worker's family with a monthly pension in case of an employee's death.

* From its inception, it was 6.25%, but then increased to 8.33% in 1999.

** For seasonal factories, the contribution to the fund is to correspond to seven days' wages, and for non-seasonal factories to the wage equivalent of fifteen days.

During 1965-1973, several strikes and demonstrations put the demand for monthly wages for male workers at the top of the agenda.[74] In 1972, for example, when 150,000 workers (most of them women) went on strike, their first demand was that monthly wages for male workers be implemented.[75] Meanwhile, the Equal Wages Bill was passed, representing another, more egalitarian, gender discourse. However, this bill was never discussed when minimum wages were being negotiated.

The financial status of male workers has increasingly been superior to that of women, mainly because the struggle for monthly salaries was successful. How have the female cashew workers reacted to this fact? Women workers never objected to marching or striking for their male coworkers. An Ezhava woman's reply to this may be taken as representative of the forty-five women interviewed, most of whom said that they supported the men's higher wages, or simply that they had never thought about it.

> Why should we object to higher wages for the men? They are our husbands, brothers, fathers, and friends—and besides, they do the heavy work. Moreover, even if we would have objected, they would never have listened and given us equal wages. And the male workers would not have liked it. Men are men, and women are women—that is a true and irreversible fact! I attended several classes on labor laws arranged by our leaders on Sundays, but we never discussed such a thing as the Equal Wages Bill. It had no relevance for us, as men and women do different work. And besides, they must have some privileges. We must keep peace!
> — Gomathi, woman of Ezhava caste, born 1930, sheller, trade union convener[76]

To some extent Gomathi expresses the view that higher and more regular wages for male workers is a *natural* condition. It was never questioned because of another assumption: the gender division of labor. Gomathi, as with other women interviewed, was in solidarity with male workers and seemed almost a bit offended by the question. She clearly expressed class solidarity beyond gender differences, that is, the language of class has overshadowed the articulation of gender hierarchy. On the other hand she also suggested that capitalist and patriarchal structures have hindered women from even *considering* an objection, since the result—i.e., neither factory owners nor male workers would have consented—could have been foreseen. At the level of individual workers, the issue of men's higher wages was

---

[74] *Jennajugham,* 20 December 1965 p. 3; 23 April 1968 p. 3; 3 February 1969, p. 3; 6 March 1969, p. 1; 2 August 1972, p. 5; 20 June 1973, p. 4.
[75] *Jennajugham,* 2 August 1972, p. 5.
[76] Interview 21 February 1999.

seen to benefit all members of a family. On a structural level, the long-term consequences of keeping women as low-paid labor were not considered. Yet it would be wrong to assert that women have suffered from a lack of feminist consciousness.[77] The mental awareness of gender discrimination appears to have been present, but the structures were considered too powerful to challenge. Thus, the strategy chosen was to make an accommodation. Another trade union convener, Thankamoni, expressed this even more clearly: "We cannot afford to struggle against our male family members, and it is a struggle deemed to be lost. So we keep quiet. And they, too, suffer a lot."[78]

Although the question of equal wages was not taken seriously, it would be erroneous to argue that specifically women's issues were neglected. One of the most important questions during this period was maternity compensation. In 1963, when the ESI scheme, whose rules covered all of India, was introduced in cashew factories, it took the place of the old Maternity Benefit Act. It marked a setback for women because the qualifying days needed to obtain benefits were increased, in comparison to the old rules. The issue, therefore, was one of great importance and caused a number of demonstrations and strikes (initiated by male leaders) before the rules finally were equalized. However, a fundamental difference exists between a question of maternity benefits and that of equal wages for men and women, as the latter directly challenges gender power-relations.

During the first period (circa 1937–1953), worker demands could emanate from men or women, and mainly concerned conditions in the factories. During the second period (circa 1954-1975), many questions on the union agenda still resulted from close interaction between leaders and workers, e.g., women's concern with maternity compensation, and the different welfare plans. However, a new tendency appeared: women were being mobilized to express disapproval of the state government.

December 1961 was probably the first occasion when cashew workers acted for political purposes other than those focussing primarily on amelioration of conditions in the factories. Some 15,000 cashew workers, mainly women, demonstrated against the splitting of CPI into two parties.[79] Thankamoni recalls: "Many cashew workers and their families were involved in party politics, so we agreed to march when they asked us. They managed to mobilize most cashew workers".[80] When the split became a

---

[77] For the critique of a view which considers women who are without "feminist consciousness" victims of a patriarchal ideology, see Beechey, "Studies on Women's Employment".

[78] Interview 22 February 1999 with Thankamoni, woman, born 1946, peeler, trade union convener.

[79] *Jennajugham,* 15 December 1961, p. 2.

[80] Interview 22 February 1999 with Thankamoni, woman, born 1946, peeler, trade union convener.

reality in the local unions, cashew workers were again mobilized by their leaders to protest the new communist party, the CPI-M.[81] Protests against the Emergency Act of 1975, which implied a ban on strikes and unions[82], was another occasion when cashew workers outnumbered others. The political leaders in Kerala objected to the suspension of democratic rights that had resulted in their arrest. At this point the cashew workers went to jail for their leaders. A female sheller, Raji, who had recently joined the CPI-M remembers:

> Some of our male comrades in the party asked us to organize a demonstration with cashew workers. We were instructed go to the Collectorate and demand the release of our leaders who were in prison. Women from all other cashew factories came, too. We went in batches of twenty women. We went inside the hall, and all of us were imprisoned. So the leaders fetched a new batch, and a new batch, and a new batch, and finally the prison of Quilon was overflowing. We did not mind supporting the leaders, and we were not afraid, although the police told us that they would take us to Bombay as prostitutes. I don't want the Emergency back, but in a way it was a great time: I was young and full of hope and it was thrilling to be in the middle of this political battlefield! I felt tremendously powerful. I enjoyed it, I felt important, I did something for this country—I wish that time had lasted forever!
> —Raji, woman of Ezhava caste, sheller, born 1957[83]

Raji's statement that women *were not afraid* is in response to the expectation that *they would be afraid*. She proudly recounts that women were not as frightened as people expected them to be. This was in spite of threats (such as sexual violence) made against them—something which male workers had not been subjected to.

She also expressed satisfaction at her *inclusion* in a radical labor movement. Women older than Raji were less prone to eulogize the 1970s, which they considered a loss of ground vis-à-vis the 1950s. The period was marked by a shift of factories to Tamil Nadu. It was, however, considered a great success when many factories were taken over by the state. But the happiness the workers enjoyed was short-lived, for they soon witnessed the first failure of the state-owned factories, whose annual working days, contrary to the high hopes of year-round employment when they had started up, had dwindled to a few months of operation a year.

---

[81] *Jennajugham*, 21 October 1974, p. 1.
[82] For an account of what the period of Emergency meant to Indian workers, see David Selbourne, *An Eye to India: The Unmasking of a Tyranny* (London, 1979).
[83] Interview 7 February 1999.

Although women participated unhesitatingly, Raji's story, as well as Thankamoni's, illustrates the way they were mobilized *from above* for political purposes. This does not imply, however, that women's loyalty to their leaders, rather than their political convictions, was their main motivation in participating in an action they knew would lead to imprisonment. As we shall see, female cashew workers were well aware of the political significance of their action.

It would be incorrect to say that only political questions were on the agenda, because the strikes and demonstrations also involved conditions inside the factories. There was, however, a tendency during this period to shift from questions exclusively concerning working conditions on the job to "bigger" structural questions, such as support for the cashew industry, and issues of a more general political character.

In spite of a tendency towards stricter organization within the unions and a politicizing of the issues on the agenda, the large number of mass actions during the period acted as an inclusive force for women in the radical labor movement, notwithstanding the fact that their mobilizator came from leaders above their station.

Crises and Declined Militancy: ca. 1975–2000

From the mid-1970s onwards there was a sharp reduction in work stoppages in the cashew factories attributable solely to labor conflicts. The number of man-days lost in this way decreased considerably.[84] Pillai finds this due to (a) the development of an improved bargaining system, (b) the threat of moving factories to Tamil Nadu, and (c) a successful wage revision in 1975.[85] The trend toward fewer and fewer work stoppages continued, however, despite the fact that wages were not revised again until 1990. Only two stoppages due to strikes or lock-outs were reported during 1980-1995, as compared to 464 such interruptions in 1960-1979.[86]

The fact that there have generally been fewer and fewer man-days lost in Kerala since about 1980 has been interpreted by Patrick Heller as a sign of a declining political interest in class struggle, and a favoring of class collaboration or corporate alliances.[87] Still, the general economic crisis in Kerala has led to the displacement of power relations between labor and capital to the advantage of the latter. The last quarter of the twentieth century has been especially characterized by a general economic crisis and high unemployment among all workers in the state, including cashew production.

---

[84] Man-days equal the number of workers multiplied by the number of working days.
[85] Pillai, "Economic Impact", p 365.
[86] Govt. of Kerala, *Administration Report for the Labour Department the Years 1960-1995.*

The state-owned cashew factories have fared worse than the private ones.

Keralite trade unions have never had strike funds: every day out on strike means a day's wages lost for each worker. With a dwindling number of annual working days, strikes became counterproductive and a new strategy was resorted to: public demonstrations, fasting, and so-called poverty marches. However, these actions do not generate any statistics, as they do not result in a loss of working days at the factories. As a weapon against capital, they tend to be weak.

Mass-actions, as those from 1950-1975 in which many thousands of workers were mobilized, have been less frequent since the mid-1970s, although a few large demonstrations have occurred. One such occasion was the so-called "jail-filling demonstration" of 1983. It may be seen as political in nature because its target was the ruling Congress Party government, and its organizers were the three left-oriented trade unions. They demanded government intervention and the reintroduction of state-regulated raw nut distribution with the slogan, "We are starving—imprison us! At least we will get food in jail!".[88] Another mass-demonstration occurred in 1986, once again during the rule of the Congress Party. A huge show of power was staged in which 138 cashew factories were picketed. The formal demand on that occasion was an increase in the dearness allowance, but another declared purpose of the leftist unions was to oppose the ruling party.[89]

On June 5th 1993, thousands of cashew workers were mobilized in a demonstration against the ministry of Karunakaran, the Congress leader at the time.[90] Another mass-demonstration occurred in 1994, when thousands of cashew workers gathered to oppose the ruling government, mainly because of its abolition of the monopoly procurement of raw nuts, but also for not having blocked the return of state-owned factories to their former private owners.[91]

A marked change in mass-actions occurring during this period is the prominence of very outspoken political language. Demands remained tied to the cashew industry, although the thrust was mainly towards the government. The close link between politics and the unions was demonstrated by

[87] Patrick Heller, "From Class Struggle to Class Compromise: Redistribution and Growth in a South Indian State", in *Journal of Development Studies* 31:5 (1995), pp. 645-672; Patrick Heller, "Social Capital as a Product of Class Mobilization and State Intervention: Industrial Workers in Kerala, India", in *World Development* 24:6 (1996), pp. 1055-1071.
[88] Kesavan Nair, "Strike History of Cashew Laborers, part 24", *CITU, Sandesam*, 19:6, pp. 7-8.
[89] Kesavan Nair, "Strike History of Cashew Laborers, part 25", *CITU, Sandesam*, 19:7, pp. 11-13; A.A. Azeez, "The Great Organisation"; Majeed, *The Strike History.*
[90] *Jennajugham,* 5 June 1993.
[91] *Deshabimani,* 27 April 1994.

Thankamoni, the sheller and trade union convener, who asserted that "the reason for not demonstrating lately is that the *just* government is now in power".[92]

In recent times, demonstrations have been on a smaller scale—between a few hundred to a thousand workers. Sometimes only the leaders will take action. Leaders of the cashew workers have conducted fasts and hunger strikes in front of public buildings.[93] Another characteristic of the period has been the activities of people other than the cashew workers or their leaders. Numerous planned maneuvers to stop the smuggling of raw nuts to Tamil Nadu were carried out by male activists from political youth organizations who undertook the dangerous mission of climbing onto and halting trucks with illegal cargo.[94] A sheller, Santha, described the demonstrations of the last twenty-five years thus:

> The men use to go in the front and do more dangerous things. Sometimes they climbed the lorries to stop the factory owners from transporting the cashew nuts to clandestine factories. We, the women, did what the comrades instructed us to do. For example, we used to block the gate or just form a crowd.
> — Santha, woman of Kuruva caste, born 1957, sheller and trade union convener since 1971[95]

Santha's words again illustrate how women were routinely mobilized and directed by "the comrades", as the male leaders were commonly addressed.

Raji, who praised the Emergency because it gave her the possibility of being included in the radical labor movement, lamented:

> Those times never came back—I mean the fighting spirit and the cooperation between leaders and workers. Now it is so different! We do not strike any longer, we do not know our leaders as before, and it is difficult to raise our demands. They decide what issues to bring forward. We are not part of the movement as before.
> — Raji, woman of Ezhava caste, sheller, born 1957[96]

---

[92] Interview 22 February 1999 with Thankamoni, woman, born 1946, peeler, trade union convener.
[93] *Deshabhimani*, 22 February 1994, p. 1; 8 October 1994, p. 1.
[94] Kesavan Nair, "Strike History of Cashew Laborers, part 24", *CITU, Sandesam*, 19:6, pp. 7-8.
[95] Interview 5 September 1998.
[96] Interview 7 February 1999.

More than just a feeling of exclusion has disturbed cashew workers during the past few decades. Interviews with female cashew workers in 1977 revealed that some had started to distrust the unions.[97] (We shall return to these feelings of exclusion and distrust later in this chapter).

In summing up the achievements of organized labor during the period 1975-1990, we note that no revision in wages took place. The most important event for the cashew workers was the establishment of a welfare fund. The decision to create such a fund was made in 1979, but was first implemented ten years later! At the outset it was delayed because the central government had to approve it (they did in 1984). Second, the leftist government, which had introduced the bill in 1979, was out of power until 1988. The fund was to supplement other treasury sources when workers who had too few annual working days could not otherwise qualify for benefits.[98] It was thus a means to meet the consequences of capitalist forces—especially the flight of capital, which signified dwindling annual working days for each worker. Efforts to draw the government's attention to the conditions of cashew workers must be seen in the light of the power of capitalism and the free flow of capital.

Labor Laws at the Factory Level

We have seen that cashew workers have achieved considerable legal rights since the early 1940s. Many of these first appeared in 1937 in their first charter of demands. The question of child labor has been mentioned in passing.[99] From a high frequency in the 1940s, when children even as young as six years of age were employed, child labor decreased considerably within a period of about fifteen years. However, when factory owners from Kerala opened cashew factories across the border in Tamil Nadu (after

[97] Kannan, "Employment, Wages", p. 28.
[98] Govt. of Kerala, *The Kerala Cashew Workers' Relief & Welfare Fund Act 1979, The Kerala Cashew Workers' Relief & Welfare Fund Scheme, 1988*; Interview 9 January 2001 with A.A. Azeez, trade union leader, politician (UTUC, RSP), and president of the Kerala Cashew Workers Welfare Organisation.
[99] This subject is explored in detail in Anna Lindberg, "Child Labor in South India: The Case of the Cashew Workers" (Paper presented at Department of History, Lund University, 2000).
[100] According to employers themselves, in 1979 more than 50% of the workers in the Tamil Nadu cashew factories were children or adolescents. SICMA Office, Quilon, "Memorandum Submitted by the South India Cashewnut Manufacturers' Association, Quilon to the Honourable Minister of Labour, Tamil Nadu 3-11-1979", p. 4. See also S. C. Darish Padmathy, "Health Conditions of Women Workers in Cashewnut Industry. A Study of Selected Units in Kaliyakavilai Village of Kanya Kumari Districts" (M.Phil., Department of Economics, Scott Christian College, Nagercoil, 1990), p. 74.

1960), children were employed in large numbers and continued to be for a long time.[100] In contrast to Myron Weiner, who asserted that the expansion of schooling in Kerala has, in the main, led to the abolition of child labor,[101] the case of the cashew workers indicates that it has been social struggle and economic improvement which have been decisive for the rapid decrease in the exploitation of small children. However, it is evident that young girls between fourteen and eighteen often still work illegally in cashew factories in both Kerala and Tamil Nadu.[102]

Wages and other financial benefits

In Chapter III we saw that since 1970 the cashew industry has had two distinct sectors: public (KSCDC and CAPEX) and private. The private sector may be further split into large concerns and small companies. Workers and trade union leaders have declared that, without exception, since the start of the public sector, minimum wages and all other benefits (such as sick leave, vacations, maternity benefits, bonuses, and contributions to welfare funds) have been paid in such factories. Fringe benefits have grown to where they constitute about 45% of basic wages.[103]

In private factories, however, the situation has been entirely different. In 1959, members of the minimum wages committee visited thirty-two cashew factories in order to see how labor legislation was being implemented. They ascertained that the intentions of the previous committee remained largely unrealized, especially in the case of female workers. The payroll records of twenty-eight cashew factories were carefully studied. On average, only about 20% of the shellers, 8% of the peelers, and 65% of the graders received the legal minimum wage.[104]

By calculating the average daily minimum wage required by law during the years 1953-1975, and comparing them with the actual wage paid (according to official statistics), K.P. Kannan drew the conclusion that actual wages were 25% to 50% below the minimum.[105] Although we may be skeptical about official statistics, especially as it is well-known how bad factory owners are at disclosing figures and how often they keep two sets of books, Kannan's calculations were probably not exaggerated. During the same period, many complaints (i.e., of minimum wages not being paid, full

---

[101] Myron Weiner, *The Child and the State in India: Child Labour and Education Policy in Comparative Perspective* (Princeton, 1991), pp. 175-177.
[102] Interviews with cashew workers carried out from 1997-2000 in Lindberg, "Child Labor", p. 10. See also *New Indian Express*, 30 April 2000, p. 4.
[103] Interview 15 August 1998 with Antoni Das, personal secretary, KSCDC, Quilon.
[104] Govt. of Kerala, *Report of the Minimum Wages Advisory Committee for Cashew Industry 1959*, pp. 9-11. See also *Jennajugham*, 11 May 1954, p. 2.
[105] Kannan, "Evolution of Unionisation", p. 54.

dearness allowance and bonuses not being given, maternity benefits denied, and various welfare funds not functioning properly) were delivered to trade union leaders by workers.[106]

We noted that in the 1960s and 1970s, a large number of strikes concerning the implementation of legislated benefits were carried out. Since that time, according to union leaders and workers, a few of the bigger concerns in the private sector have been obeying the labor laws and paying what is required of them; they are the so-called "model-factories". However, even they retain the power to close down factories and shift production to other locations.[107]

Smaller private factories also seem to have constantly circumvented adherence to laws concerning wages. A government committee declared in 1998 that a main feature of the cashew industry was that labor laws were being violated.[108]

A quantitative measure of the extent of these violations is difficult to come by. In 1959, labor laws were openly flaunted, but in later years, more sophisticated tactics of closing down, reopening under a new name, or leasing a factory to others were more common.[109] Yet another strategy was contrived: the creation of an informal sector *within* the formal sector.[110] Under the circumstances, it was difficult to prosecute the owners.

The interviews conducted for this study all point to the fact that questions of wages and fringe benefits greatly occupied union leaders, although their concerns only extended to workers who were properly registered. Many women acknowledged they had received bonuses, remuneration from welfare funds, maternity benefits, and other forms of benefits over the last few decades. But many others testified that these benefits had been withheld after they were told their annual working days were too few, or that they were not registered workers.[111]

---

[106] *Jennajugham*, 8 June 1954, p. 4; 13 July 1956, p. 4; 14 July 1962, p. 4; 8 June 1967, p. 1; 22 November 1967, p. 4; 15 April 1968, p. 3; 16 July 1968, p. 2; 16 March 1972, p. 4.

[107] When new minimum wages were to be implemented in 1998, the number of working days per week in one of these "model factories" immediately decreased to four (it had previously been six), and raw nuts were shipped away from the factory—probably for processing in a *kudivarappu* or Tamil Nadu, where the owner had several other plants in operation. Interview 15 February with Geetha and Santha, shellers at VLC cashew factory in Chandanathoope.

[108] Govt. of Kerala, "Cashew Sector and Women Labourers", Preliminary report submitted to Industrial Minister, Susheela Gopalan, January 1998. Copy received 5 January 2000 from L. Radhakrishnan, Industrial Department.

[109] Govt. of Kerala, *Report of the Minimum Wages Advisory Committee for Cashew Industry 1959*, pp. 9-11; Govt. of Kerala, *The Report of the Delegatory Committee for the Revision of the Minimum Wages of Cashew Workers 1998*, Order No. G.O. (RT) 2473/96 LBR, chapter 6, pp. 18 ff. (in Malayalam). Copy provided by Labour Department, Trivandrum; Govt. of Kerala, "Cashew Sector and Women Labourers".

[110] This will be further discussed in a later section of this chapter.

[111] Statements based on the forty-five in-depth interviews.

Tools, working clothes, and protective measures

In the earliest factories all workers were obliged to bring their own tools, including roasting pans, baskets, and shelling sticks. When machines were introduced for roasting, only shellers, peelers, and graders (predominantly women) continued to supply their own tools. In the late 1940s, workers began to demand that their employers provide all necessary tools. An elderly woman, Kunji, still remembers how this demand was raised in her factory:

> I was a sheller in Moytheen Kunju's factory at Ashraman at the time. We brought T.K. Divakaran to our factory to investigate the conditions and to put forth our demands. This must have been about the time of Independence. We all met him and, among other questions, we asked to be provided with shellingsticks, baskets, and working clothes. The oil from the shells destroyed our clothes, always making them black and smeary. To buy a basket and a shelling stick was not tremendously expensive, but it was not unusual for me to have to choose between buying new tools or rice—and often I could buy neither of them. And it is still like that for some shellers.
> —Kunji, Pulaya woman, born around 1920, sheller [112]

In the mid-1950s, demonstrations occurred in which the same demands were raised.[113] In 1958, as a result of a long dispute, a court ruled that cashew workers should be provided with all needed tools, except shelling sticks. This exemption was granted on the basis of employers' arguments that shellers had different preferences with regard to the kind of shelling stick to use, so it was deemed reasonable to ask shellers to supply their own.[114]

The question of work clothing was agreed to only with regard to the borma workers. Clothing for shellers was discussed, but then dropped because it was argued that the number of shellers was too high.[115] The tools issue remained on the agenda. Finally, in 1969, it was agreed that all workers be provided with tools, including shellers. Male workers would also be given work clothing and shoes, and would receive an extra laundry allowance.[116]

In spite of the agreement of 1969, shellers have never been provided with shelling sticks, neither in the private nor in the state-owned factories. Only older women recalled it once having been an important agenda item.

---

[112] Interview 19 December 1997.
[113] *Jennajugham*, 15 July 1955, p. 2.
[114] RSP Office, Quilon, Thiruvananthapuram Industrial Tribunal, Shri. K. Purushotham [Nair,/Labor Conflict No. 15/1951 (8772/50 Oct 21 1951), paragraphs 6, 7, 19, 20, 25-29.]
[115] Ibid.

Gomathi, the veteran trade union convener, believed the question was forgotten when state-owned factories started to close down in the mid-1970s and *kudivarappus* expanded:

> When registered factories close down, most workers go to *kudivarappus*, where no labor laws exist and they have to bring their own tools. So when other factories open they are already used to bringing their own tools. The question was given up when illegal factories expanded in the 70s. Nobody speaks about this issue any longer.
> — Gomathi, Ezhava woman, born 1930, sheller, trade union convener [117]

When roasting and shelling were declared dangerous tasks in 1957, it was also stipulated that workers performing those operations be provided with safety equipment by their employers. With regard to male workers, the details were carefully regulated, but for shellers, who were predominantly women, the rules were written in a more diffuse way.[118] Workers had long found gloves indispensable due to the cashew shell oil's corrosive and carcinogenic nature. Coconut oil and wet kaolin or wood ash have been considered another means of protection for the skin from the dangers of cashew shell oil. Medical studies of shellers have revealed a high frequency of skin disease caused by the corrosive cashew shell oil, combined with the average worker's minimal diet and vitamin deficiencies.[119] According to legislation incumbent on the factory, coconut oil and kaolin must be provided to shellers, but it was left to the chief inspector of factories to decide whether their employers would also be required to give them other protective equipment, such as gloves.[120] Employers have steadily argued that cashew shell oil is not very harmful, and that gloves reduce a worker's efficiency, and anyway wear out within a short time.[121] In 1969, a European "expert" on cashew processing invoked a racial issue to defend shelling without gloves in India, asserting that pigmented skin was less sensitive to cashew shell oil than white skin![122]

---

[116] NRC, Labour Department, LBR, series MS, No. 32/72, "Memorandum of Settlement in Cashew Industry in Quilon Area", 15 April 1969.
[117] Interview 21 February 1999.
[118] Govt. of Kerala, *The Kerala Factory Rules 1957*, No. 4373/57/L. and L.A.D., Trivandrum 1957, pp. 177-179.
[119] *Kerala Kaumudi*, 9 December 1980, p. 7; *Jennajugham*, 31 July 1983, p. 4.
[120] Govt. of Kerala, *The Kerala Factory Rules 1957*, pp. 177-179.
[121] SICMA, "Memorandum Submitted by the South India Cashewnut Manufacturers Association, Quilon", 3 November 1979, pp. 4-5; D.C. Russell, *Cashew-nut Processing*, Food and Agricultural Organization of the United Nations (Rome, 1969), p. 43.
[122] Russell, *Cashew-nut Processing*, p. 43.

My interviews in the late 1990s revealed that, whether they worked in private, cooperative, or state-owned factories, (female) shellers still had to buy their own gloves, while male workers were provided with all necessary protective gear ever since it was made mandatory in 1957. This fact was also noted by the minimum wage committee of 1998.[123] In certain smaller factories, the shellers even had to buy the baskets in which they put the shelled nuts.[124] One aging sheller, Kunji, told me:

> I think that there is such a law—that they should give us gloves—but they don't provide us with them, so what to do? We should also be given coconut oil and soap. Earlier they used to give them to us, but in the last eight to ten years they have stopped. I work in a private factory now: the owner's name is Sham. The trade unions do not concern themselves with questions like this any longer. Trade unions today are just for negotiating wages, bonuses, preserving peace at work, and other big questions.
> —Kunji, Pulaya woman, born 1920, sheller [125]

Only a few old women among those I interviewed could even remember that work clothing and gloves were once demanded for women. These are now forgotten questions and, as Kunji indicated, trade union leaders now consider them too small to be paid attention to. Her statement also shows she recognizes a change in the role of trade unions, in comparison with the past.

The two forgotten questions—gloves and shelling sticks—amounted to about twenty rupees per worker a month (about US $ .45) according to the prices of 1999.[126] This represents considerable savings for an employer such as KSCDC, where more than 10,000 shellers are employed, or for some of the private factories in Kerala and Tamil Nadu, which have even more shellers in their employ.

Unpaid work

Unpaid work in the cashew factories has mainly been an issue for shellers and peelers, and has taken three forms:

---

[123] Govt. of Kerala, *Report of the Delegatory Committee for Revision of the Minimum Wages of Cashew Workers*, Labour Department, 1998, G.O.(R.T) 2473/96, p. 19.
[124] Information received from the manager and workers at Southern Cashew Export, Kottiyam, 27 December 1999.
[125] Interview 19 December 1997.
[126] In 1999, workers interviewed estimated the price of gloves at ten rupees per month. A shelling stick, which lasted three to four weeks, then cost about eight rupees.

(a) Workers have been obliged to carry out work other than what they are paid for, e.g., carrying cashew nuts to the next section, grading kernels, sweeping the yard, and similar chores

(b) Underweighing shelled and peeled kernels when recording daily output deprives a worker of full payment

(c) Workers are not paid for kernels that happen to break during shelling or peeling, despite the fact that they are readily saleable on the international market, at prices only slightly lower than whole ones

The first kind of unpaid work, using cashew workers to perform unpaid peripheral tasks, mainly took place up to the 1950s and has gradually disappeared. The reason for the trade unions' success in this area was the employers' preference for strict discipline, including a rigid division of labor, in order to make the most of a worker's skill. The older factories were characterized by inhumane punishments. In the new factory organization it became more common to have supervisors, mostly males, who saw to it that women did not move from their work places, but sat shelling and peeling the whole day without a break (except for lunch), and so-called lap-checkers who regularly body-searched the workers.[127] It also meant the introduction of male helpers, such as the bag-carriers.[128] The previously mentioned European specialist in cashew processing argued that the skill of the shellers was of such economic importance that not one second of their time should be wasted; they should do no other work than shelling, not even getting their own raw material from the next room.[129] Ironically, although always declared unskilled in connection with *wage discussions*, female cashew workers in Quilon have been praised for their high skills in all other contexts. The workers of Quilon hone these skills for many years, but the result of this arduous training is considered to only be a natural female characteristic.[130] The concept of skill is highly gendered and is defined out of power relations.[131] However, a sheller's or peeler's skill was the decisive point in abandoning the practice of requiring women do other work than shelling or peeling.

---

[127] Interview 14 September 1999 with K. Chellappan, trade union leader, born 1914. A worker who was interviewed in 1962 remembered the days without supervisors. See *Jennajugham*, 2 August 1962, pp. 2-3. Workers interviewed said they were body-searched at least three times a day. For a written account of the body search at cashew factories, see Pavanen, "Lives that Revolve around the Cashew Factories", in *Mathrubhumi Weekly*, 55:16 (1977), pp. 26-36.

[128] Lindberg, "The Concept of Skill ".

[129] Russell, *Cashew-nut Processing*, p. 41.

[130] Lindberg, "The Concept of Skill".

[131] Ann Phillips and Barbara Taylor, "Sex and Skill: Notes toward a Feminist Economics," *Feminist Review*, 6 (1980) pp. 7-88; Lindberg, "The Concept of Skill".

When recounting conditions in the cashew factories in the late 1930s, K.C. Govindan notes in his memoirs that "it was common for the Maestris or the management to cheat the workers while weighing the nuts....No one dared to question them, for any such act of rebellion would be punished with dismissal".[132] In the conflict of 1951, this became an important issue.[133] Speaking to the Industrial Tribunal on behalf of workers, Divakaran requested that workers be allowed to have one representative in each factory to oversee the weighing. The court concluded that this malpractice was probably widespread and totally exonerated only one factory, Peirce Leslie & Co. from the charge. In the latter factory, a special tin container was used, making it easier to verify that the weighing was accurate. All the other factories used various kinds of baskets. The result of the verdict was a recommendation that all factories adopt the Peirce Leslie system.[134]

None of the workers I interviewed had even seen the "weighing" tins mentioned in any of the factories where they had worked—not even those in the public sector. One worker, Satyabarna, interviewed in 1973 in a state-owned factory in Kottiyam, held that the major advantage of working at her present job (in comparison to the private factory where she had worked earlier) was that she was no longer being cheated when her daily output was weighed.[135] Other workers interviewed twenty-five years later agreed that weighing had always been fair in the state-owned factories, even though the workers did not actually monitor it.[136]

In the 1960s and early 1970s several strikes included a demand of proper weighing.[137] According to interviewees, these actions materialized after female workers complained to union leaders. The struggle finally resulted in a conference in April 1972 with representatives of the workers, employers, and the Kerala Government. The outcome of the conference was that employers accepted the workers' demand to have the opportunity to re-weigh the kernels.[138] Nevertheless, the malpractice continued, and on June 16 of the same year, occasioned a general strike of 150 factories comprising

---

[132] Govindan, *Memoires*, p. 68.
[133] RSP Office, Quilon, Thiruvananthapuram Industrial Tribunal, Shri. K. Purushotham Nair./Labor Conflict No. 15/1951 (8772/50 Oct 21 1951). See especially paragraphs 6, 7, 25, and 26.
[134] Ibid., paragraphs 25 and 26.
[135] *Jennajugham,* 10 June 1973, p. 9.
[136] Interview 27 December 1998 with Seethu, peeler since 1970 at KSCDC; Interview 8 January 1999 with Kali, sheller since 1972 at KSCDC.
[137] Interview 26 December 1998 with Gomathi, female trade union convener since the 1940s; Interview 14 September 1999 with K. Chellappan, trade union leader, born 1914. See also *Jennajugham,* 28 September 1963, p. 3.
[138] *Jennajugham,* 25 April 1972, p. 3.

more than 150,000 cashew workers.[139] After renewed negotiations between representatives of employers and workers in the presence of the labor
minister and the joint labor minister, an agreement was signed by all parties. It not only stated that workers would have the right to control the
weighing, but also that a representative of the workers was entitled to su-
pervise the process.[140] A demand that first surfaced in the 1930s had now
finally been obtained—at least on paper!

When asking workers whether trade union leaders or other labor representatives had actually been supervising the weighing, I was told that such
control by a representative had not been in place continuously. The reasons
given were either lack of time, or that the leaders found other questions
more urgent. An aged sheller explained:

> Shortly after the agreement in 1972, trade union leaders from outside super-
> vised the weighing in our factory; but then the factory closed for a long
> period, and when it reopened, nobody came to control the man in charge.
> We have reminded our leaders, but they do not have the time to spend all
> day in the factories, and it seems as if it is not an urgent question for them.
> Nobody cares about it any longer. The managers do not let us—the women
> workers—control the weighing, saying that we are not educated enough. I
> have been working in eight different factories and I think cheating has been
> widespread among private factories all the time.
>
> —Chakki, woman of Pulaya caste, born 1927, sheller[141]

Despite the agreement, little actual control was effected by representatives
of the workers. The shady practice of underweighing a worker's output
remains fairly prevalent in the private factories, especially in *kudivarappus*.[142] Moreover, this practice even goes on in well-reputed factories. In
1999, in one of the biggest private factories—one which had been labeled a
"model-factory" for obeying labor laws and providing work for more than
200 days a year[143]—workers accidentally discovered an object under the
weighing-machine. This had resulted in an underweighing of 400 grams
for each sheller, corresponding to about 6% of a sheller's daily production.
The fault was adjusted and the supervisor asserted that it was a mistake
which only happened on that particular day and had not been going on for

---

[139] *Jennajugham*, 16 June 1972, p. 1.

[140] *Jennajugham*, 29 June 1972, p. 3.

[141] Interview 6 January 1999.

[142] *Jennajugham*, 28 May 1992, p. 5.

[143] This view was expressed by several trade union leaders and civil servants. Interview 14
January 1998 with Sam Nathaniel, Labour Commissioner, Quilon; Interview 7 August
1998 with J. Chitharanjan, trade union leader, politician.

a long time—something workers interviewed had ample reason to disbelieve, but wrongdoing was impossible to prove.[144]

Trade union leaders, when being asked about the faulty weighing and the lack of oversight, responded that they did their best to carry out spot checks but that resources were not sufficient for designating one employee in each factory to do this. The women themselves, the leaders objected, were ignorant and not educated for the task.[145] Once again, one hears from both owners and union leaders the argument that women lack education—an argument which has, as its consequence, the fact that women continue to be deprived of power and a sphere of action.

The third form of unpaid work, i.e., not paying workers for kernels which break during processing, was defended from the outset by employers who said that workers would be careless if they were paid for broken pieces. As noted earlier, the question of payment for broken kernels was already raised by workers in 1937. About fifteen years later the same demand had still gone unanswered.[146] The proportion of broken kernels varies with a worker's skill and the quality of the raw nuts. The latter circumstance is obviously beyond a worker's control.[147] According to managers interviewed in 1952, neither shellers nor peelers were paid *anything at all* for broken kernels, which could come to 10%-15% of a worker's total output for indigenous nuts, or 25%-40% for imported nuts. It was estimated that more than 60% of all nuts coming through the plants were imported,[148] yielding a figure of approximately 25% of each worker's daily production going unpaid—assuming that this output was not underweighed as well![149]

The primary complaint among workers in Quilon who were interviewed by civil servants in 1954 was, in fact, about not getting paid for broken kernels, in contrast to the situation in Mangalore (see Chapter III). Workers themselves suggested different rates to prevent them from "getting careless".[150] It must be reiterated that broken kernels have always been sold on the international market, although at slightly lower prices. By way of example, the prices for these kernels amounted on average to 76% of whole kernels during the period 1965 to 1975.[151] This unpaid work is thus creating an extraordi-

---

[144] Interview 15 February 1999 with Geetha and Sumathai, shellers at VLC cashew factory.
[145] Interview 13 August 1998 with R.S. Unni (UTUC); Interview February 1998 with N. Padmalochanen (CITU).
[146] Govt. of India, *Report on an Enquiry into Conditions of Labour in the Cashewnut Processing Industry in India*, p. 23.
[147] Ibid., p. 23.
[148] Ibid., p. 26.
[149] This was calculated in the following way: 40 x (10% + 15%)/2 + 60 x (25% + 40%)/2 = 24.5%
[150] Govt. of India, *Report on an Enquiry into Conditions of Labour in the Cashewnut Processing Industry in India*, p. 26.
[151] CEPC, *Cashew Statistics* (Cochin, 1977), p. 56. Official statistics for other periods were not forthcoming.

nary surplus value for the factory owners at a cost of production of zero.[152]

In the 1950s, trade union leaders raised their voices to seek a change in the existing system and implement payment for broken kernels, but without success.[153] Since 1959, when the trade union leaders, T.K. Divakaran and M.N. Govindan, tried to drive through a new payment system, the question has no longer been on the agenda during top level negotiations. Trade union leaders appear to have bought into the logic of factory management, echoing their claim that "women will not work carefully if they are being paid for broken kernels, and so the profit will be smaller, which will affect the wages."[154] Female shellers and peelers continue to do about one-fourth of their daily work as unpaid labor, while males who are part of the production process get paid full value for all the nuts they handle.

First raised in 1937, this demand, more than six decades later, has still not been met. Gomathi, sheller and trade union convener since 1946, summarized it as follows:

> It was a big question in the 1940s and 50s. We tried to raise the question again in the 1960s, but our leaders told us that other issues were more urgent. Since then everybody has accepted it. Of course, it is wrong, but nobody is prepared to fight for it. It is a forgotten issue nowadays. We have only been able to bring forward questions for which we had full support from our leaders.
> —Gomathi, Ezhava woman, born 1930, sheller, trade union convener[155]

Kavitha, the sheller said:

> Yes, we felt that it was a very urgent question in the 1940s. M.N. Govindan tried to help us, but when he failed, the subject was dropped. We raised the question in my factory once through our factory convener—maybe it was in the late 1960s—but the owner laughed at us and the trade union leader from outside told us to spend our energy campaigning for a public sector instead. It was not seen as an important question, so we felt quite helpless. Besides, the factory closed down now and then, so our fighting spirit was lost.
> —Kavitha, Kurava woman, born around 1920, sheller[156]

---

[152] As these lines were being readied for printing in August 2001, one pound of whole cashews was retailing for nearly US$ 6.00 in a gourmet supermarket in the US, whereas one pound of "cashew pieces" on the same shelf sold for only 76 cents less!

[153] Govt. of Kerala, *Report of the Minimum Wages Advisory Committee for Cashew Industry 1959*, pp. 16-17.

[154] Interview 13 September 1999 with P. Bhaskaran, trade union activist (AITUC) since 1950; A similar view was expressed by A.A. Azeez, trade union leader, politician (UTUC, RSP), and president of the Kerala Cashew Workers Welfare Organisation (interview 9 January 2001).

[155] Interview 12 February 1999.

[156] Interview 7 February 1999.

The women's negative opinion of their union leaders' power to dismiss or put forward a question is evident. Most interviewees belonging to the younger generation had never heard of the broken cashew issue, and simply took it for granted that no payment should be given for broken kernels.[157] It is apparent that women still perform a great deal of unpaid work in shelling and peeling. Faulty weighing and broken kernels may in some cases amount to as much as one-third of their daily output. It is also obvious that the question of such unpaid work is a neglected union issue and that women themselves have been unsuccessful in returning it to the table. During the last few decades they seem to have accepted the reality that setting the agenda is a privilege of union leaders.

Kudivarappus, Class Consciousness, and Trade Union Loyalty

Kudivarappus, unregistered and unlicensed cashew processing operations, expanded after the introduction of minimum wages in 1953. The increase of such processing units, where daily wages were only about half of the government's stipulated minimum, and where workers were denied fringe benefits, led to more stringent legislation. In 1967, a bill was proposed declaring cashew processing in places other than registered factories illegal.[158] In July 1967, 125,000 workers went out on strike to have the law implemented. However, after the bill was passed and the strike was over, the factories reopened, as did the *kudivarappus*. In one village, Kilikolloor, twenty-five *kudivarappus* were functioning in August 1967,[159] and eighteen months later it was reported that "more and more *kudivarappus* [had] sprouted up."[160] During the fifteen years that followed, several demonstrations against these illegal factories were organized.[161] When I visited a *kudivarappu* in February 1999, the owner told me:

> I have about twenty women in this "factory". I need ten workers to make a reasonable profit. Sometimes it is a bit difficult to get enough workers here in this district, so I have started a similar factory in Alleppey with about 100

---

[157] Interviews with Geetha (sheller, born 1978), Prasantha (sheller, born 1980), Sunitha (sheller, born 1978), Sandhya (peeler, born 1978), and Indira (peeler, born 1980).
[158] Kannan, "Employment, Wages", pp. 7-20.
[159] *Jennajugham*, 19 August 1967, p. 4.
[160] *Jennajugham*, 12 February 1969, p. 3.
[161] See, for example, *Jennajugham*, 6 March 1969, p. 1; 4 July 1970, p. 3; 18 June 1972, p. 1; 10 June 1982, p. 2.

women. We should be under the Factory Act when we have more than ten
workers, but the trade unions and labor commissioner know that we work
like this. They do not interfere with us. There are many units like this. The
workers get 35 rupees a day—it is a little bit more than half of the daily
wages in the registered factories.
—Gopala Krishna Pillai, owner of M.G. Enterprises, Kilikolloor[162]

It is difficult to estimate the size of illegal cashew processing. A trade union
leader commented that in 1969 about 60% of all cashew kernel production
in Kerala was carried out in *kudivarappus*.[163] It has been asserted that their
number decreased when the strategy of shifting factories to Tamil Nadu
was resorted to in the late 1960s and 1970s.[164] According to workers interviewed, the number of such illegal production units has never been as high
as in the 1990s; this was also stated in the Kerala daily newspaper, *Jennajugham*[165] and by trade union leaders.[166]

Politicians of the left and union representatives explain the widespread
prevalence of *kudivarappus* in the mid-1990s with the discontinuation of
state-controlled distribution of raw nuts in 1993.[167] Spokesmen of the left
have indicated that *kudivarappus* were more frequent during the period
when the UDF was in power (1983–1987), which was also the time when
the state monopoly procurement of raw nuts was given up.[168] The increase
of *kudivarappus* in recent years may, thus, be partly a result of the new
liberal economy of the 1990s at an all-India level.

As a result of liberalization, with its concomitant elimination of trade
restrictions, a new phenomenon emerged in Kerala after 1990. Foreign
trade companies (often the major importers and distributors of cashew kernels in consumer packages) now import huge quantities of raw nuts and
contract the shelling out to agents by the eighty kilo sack, just as was done
in the 1930s and 1940s.[169]

According to a civil servant, the procedure described has had the effect
of increasing the number of *kudivarappus* enormously, with each one engaged in underbidding the other to obtain contracts. Wages have gone

---

[162] Interview 20 February 1999.
[163] *Jennajugham,* 13 August 1969, p. 1.
[164] Kannan, "Employment, Wages", p. 9.
[165] *Jennajugham,* 14 April 1993, p. 6.
[166] Interview 13 August 1998 with Kesavan Nair; Interview 4 February 1999 with T.M.
Majeed.
[167] Interview 22 September 1999 with Industrial Minister, Susheela Gopalan; Interview
13 August 1998 with Kesavan Nair (CITU); See also *Jennajugham,* 14 April 1993, p. 6.
[168] *Jennajugham,* 28 May 1992, p. 5.
[169] *Kerala Kaumudi,* 19 April 1997, p. 11; See also *Jennajugham,* 6 May 1993, p. 2; *Cashew Bulletin,* 30:4-5 (1993), p. 2.

down as a result, making the economic burden due to competition among the manufacturers fall on the shoulders of the workers. In 1999, it was estimated that an eighty kilo sack of raw nuts cost 1,200 rupees to process in the public sector, but only 600 rupees was paid by foreign companies to the contractors.[170] The range of influence exerted by foreign companies over the cashew market in the 1990s would be a matter for a thorough investigation. It seems apparent, however, that when the restrictions on cashew trade and distribution of raw nuts were lifted, two changes occurred.[171] First, there was a return to the old system of decentralized and uncontrolled production; and second, foreign dominance, which had not been seen since the 1940s, began to characterize the industry.

In 1986, B.K. Pillai concluded that two classes of workers could be distinguished in the cashew factories of Kerala: one which enjoyed their legal rights and the minimum wage, and another which was denied those rights—the workers in the *kudivarappus*.[172] Pillai draws a dividing line between the formal and informal sectors, both with regard to workers and to factory owners. His view, however, may be contested. In 1976, such a duality in the Indian economy had been stressed by Mark Holmström[173], who later reversed himself and denied the existence of two distinct sectors on the grounds that many workers in the formal sector do have legal rights and security, although they may be seldom implemented. Others enjoy fairly reasonable security in the informal sector without the benefit of legislation. Moreover, the individuals concerned do not see themselves as belonging to one or another sector. To them, the major distinction at work was having a permanent job or not.[174]

The *kudivarappus* have existed in various forms. Although, as we have noted, the term literally means "cottage processing", the work is generally carried out in factory buildings. These facilities are often registered factories which formally close for a period, but soon reopen without notifying the

---

[170] Interview 5 January 2000 with L. Radhakrishna, managing director of KSCDC 1996-1999.

[171] Restrictions on imports were lifted in 1984 and the state monopoly on distribution of raw nuts was abandoned in 1993. Judgement, "The Kerala Raw Cashew Nuts (Procurement and Distribution) Act 1981 Declared as Ultra Vires the Constitution of India", reproduced in *Cashew Bulletin*, Vol. XXXIII No. 11, Nov 1996.

[172] Pillai, "Economic Impact", p. 175.

[173] Holmström, *South Indian Factory Workers*.

[174] Holmström, *Industry and Inequality*, pp. 310-313. See also Jan Breman, "A Dualistic Labour System? A Critique of the 'Informal Sector' Concept, part I, II and III", *Economic and Political Weekly*, 11 (1976), pp.1870-1876, 1905-1908, 1939-1944. For a later discussion on the concepts of formal and informal sector, see Jan Breman, "The Study of Industrial Labour in Post-colonial India—The Formal Sector. An Introductory Review", and "The Study of Industrial Labour in Post-colonial India—The Informal Sector", in Parry, Breman, and Kapadia (eds), *The Worlds of Indian Industrial Labour*, pp. 1-41, 407-432.

authorities. Genuine cottage production, i.e., raw nuts distributed to workers in their homes for processing, has always been going on as well. The practice of leasing out factories for certain periods of time to friends, relatives, or those fronting for the owner is part of the scheme of evading the law. According to trade union leaders, even highly-reputed factory owners in the formal sector may run *kudivarappus* through front-men to disguise their involvement in the informal sector.[175] When registered factories close down, workers are dismissed, then soon rehired to work in the same factory with a new owner and a new name, but with no labor rights. This phenomenon seems common,[176] and was admitted by factory owners themselves (see Chapter III). [177]

Several workers interviewed testified to this practice and also remarked that such factories have even changed names every three months in order to confuse authorities, trade unions, and workers, and to circumvent management's legal obligations.

> My sister and I work in a cashew factory in Kilikolloor. You asked me the name of the factory? Honestly [laughing]—— I don't know, because the factory changes names every third month, so we never know. But everything is the same, and it is the same owner. We certainly understand why, but what can we do? Hunger and crying children drive us to accept the circumstances.
> —Sunitha, Kuruva woman, born 1978, sheller[178]

The reason such "three-month factories" exist is that most social welfare programs have rules requiring workers be employed for a minimum of three months in the same factory to be eligible for compensation.

Another link between the formal and the informal sectors has been the buying of processed cashew kernels in large quantities from *kudivarappus* by the registered factories, a practice which indirectly supports the former.[179] The *kudivarappus* clearly belong to the informal sector. Neither their workers nor the factories themselves are registered, no trade unions are active there, and labor laws are disregarded.

There is yet another method of evading labor laws that has long been customary in some of the registered cashew factories: workers are not given

---

[175] Interview 11 March 1997 with Kesavan Nair (CITU); Interview 12 January 1998 with J. Chitharanjan (AITUC); Interview 13 September 1999 with P. Bhaskaran (AITUC).
[176] *Kerala Kaumudi*, 11 April 1981, p. 5; *Jennajugham*, 28 May 1992, p. 5. See also NRC, "Special Officer of Cashew", File No. G.O 43/85/LBR Ms-series.
[177] SICMA Office, Quilon, Memorandum Submitted by Tamil Nadu Manufacturers Association. "Before the Honourable Minister for Labour, Govt. of Tamil Nadu". Dated 18th March 1983.
[178] Interview 10 February 2000. Similar stories were told by Gomathi, sheller, trade union convener, born in 1930 (Interview 26 December 1998), and Thankamoni, sheller, trade union convener, born in 1946 (Interview 14 August 1998).
[179] Interview 5 January 2000 with L. Radhakrishna, managing director of KSCDC 1996-1999.

time cards. Consequently, they work under conditions similar those in the *kudivarappus*. Employers have also been accused of keeping two sets of books: one for the authorities and the trade unions, and one for themselves. Several documented cases of factories have been exposed in which not all of the workers were registered. In 1966, for example, it was noted in a factory with 750 workers, only 150 were on their rolls.[180] A woman who was interviewed in 1969 asserted there were about 1,000 workers at the factory where she was employed, but that fewer than 200 were registered.[181]

The practice of not registering every worker appears to continue.[182] In the interviews, workers estimated the proportion of unregistered workers at about 20%. From their statements it was clear that most of them had waited a long time—from four months to ten years—to get their attendance cards. Meanwhile, they were regarded as apprentices, outside the pale of labor rights. To a great extent this unregistered workforce consists of very young women or adolescents, but it was apparent that older workers have been exposed to the same exploitation. Between the ages of fifty-eight to sixty, a worker may confront the alternative of being dismissed, or remaining in the work force as an unregistered employee—getting paid by piece work, but lacking the dearness allowance or other fringe benefits. These people are, in effect, being *displaced into the informal sector*. As a result, workers who are untrained, or who have lost some of their capacity due to age, constitute an underground of second-class workers without benefits.

In the Kerala cashew factories, contrary to Pillai's finding, the so-called formal and informal sectors are closely interconnected.[183] However, we can neither obtain reliable data regarding the size of this unregistered workforce *inside* the registered factories, nor can we get information about the workforce in *kudivarappus*. One way to calculate the size of illegal processing in Kerala would be to closely analyze the cultivating and importation of raw nuts relative to the production of kernels; but as neither domestic consumption nor domestic growing of cashew nuts are well-documented, adequate figures cannot be determined.[184]

---

[180] *Jennajugham,* 4 August 1966, p. 4.

[181] *Jennajugham,* 12 February 1969, p. 3.

[182] *Jennajugham,* 12 October 1989, p. 3.

[183] Jan Breman has expressed such a view based on other empirical data. See Breman, "The Study of Industrial Labour in Post-colonial India—The Informal Sector: A Concluding Review", p. 426.

[184] A scholar in Trivandrum, G.L. Deepa, compared the statistics of cashew factories, analyzing the number of factories, number of workers, and average number of working days, for the period 1974-1988. Her conclusion was that cashew nut production in the informal sector has increased, while it has decreased in the formal sector. See Deepa, "Industrial Crises and Women Workers". Although her conclusion may be correct, the data she bases her findings on may be inadequate, as the informal sector (the *kudivarappus*) do not submit any statistics to the authorities.

What we do know for sure, however, is that *kudivarappus* have long been phenomena well-known to politicians, civil servants, and trade union leaders. The latter even called the labor minister's attention to it in 1983.[185] The question has also been continuously discussed publically.[186] The relation between cashew production in the formal and informal sectors is illustrated in Figure 7.1.

Figure 7.1 Structure of the formal and informal sector of the Kerala cashew industry

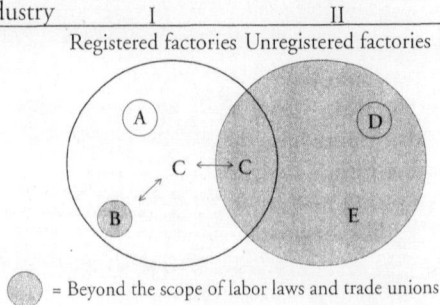

Registered factories Unregistered factories

= Beyond the scope of labor laws and trade unions

A: Permanent male workers in registered factories

B. Female workers in registered factories with no attendance cards working for lower wages without fringe benefits. Young women may become registered workers after some time (four months to several years). Old women may be pushed from C into B at the age of retirement

C. Female seasonal workers in registered factories. Many, dismissed when factories in the formal sector close down, enter the informal sector during such periods

D. Male workers (often seasonal) in the informal sector, who are often compensated for lost fringe benefits and for their "loyalty" with slightly higher daily wages than they would have received in the formal sector

E. Female workers (often seasonal) who work only in *kudivarappus*

Forty of the forty-five women I was able to interview in depth had worked in *kudivarappus* during periods when their regular factory was closed down. Securing such work was especially necessary for women who were employed at KSCDC or CAPEX, where annual working days were extremely

---

[185] NRC, File No. G.O 43/85/LBR Ms-series, "Special Officer of Cashew".

[186] See, for example, *Jennajugham,* 22 May 1967, p. 4; 15 April 1968, p. 3; 31 August 1970, p. 1; 29 June 1972, p. 3; 14 September 1985, p. 3; 20 March 1989, p 2; 5 May 1992, p. 3; 28 May 1992, p. 5; 6 May 1993, p 2; *Kerala Kaumudi,* 22 May 1967, p. 1; 9 June 1967, p. 3; 28 February 1971, p. 3; 21 February 1972, p. 3.

low. Women who began working in private factories were generally not registered during an initial period.

Should one say that these women, accepting employment in *kudivarappus*, lack class consciousness or a radical spirit? In 1977, the well-known Keralite journalist and author, Pavanen, interviewed a family of cashew workers he had visited twenty years earlier. His conclusion was that, in spite of all they may have achieved (minimum wages, bonuses, welfare fund, gratuity, maternity leave, etc.,), their living conditions were as bad as they had been in the mid-1950s. They still lived in a small hut without electricity, water, or kitchen facilities, and with very limited space. The women he spoke with related that where their factory had had 100 workers twenty years ago, it now had 6,000. Twenty years earlier they had worked the year round; in the late 1970s they only worked a couple of months a year—an illustration of the casualization of work. Pavanen was interested in the women's loyalty to the trade unions and their inclination to work in illegal factories. His conversation with three female workers, a young woman (Chandika), an older woman who is probably her mother (Alima Umana), and an elderly lady who is perhaps Chandika's grandmother (Kurumbi), is revealing:

> *Pavanen*: Do you go for Kudivarappu?
> *Alima Umana*: What can we do other than go there?
> *Pavanen*: Is it not an act of betrayal?
> *Alima Umana*: Yes it is, but how can people judge what is right and wrong when we are starving? That job is done privately and not in registered factories. We receive only small wages and yet we do it. What shall we do for survival?
> *Pavanen*: Does the union permit this?
> *Alima Umana*: What can the union do, sir? Can they do something to alleviate the pains of hunger and poverty? If ever the union activists oppose, they will receive severe blows.

Kurumbi, who had been a sheller since 1935 added:

> *Kurumbi*: Only if we conduct a strike we can improve the industry!

At this remark, the others laughed. The young woman, Chandika, said:

> *Chandika*: For the industry to improve, there is a need for more raw nuts. In all places there should be cashew nut trees.
> *Kurumbi*: That is true. What that girl told is true, but for that, too, a strike is necessary![187]

---

[187] Pavanen, "Lives that Revolve around the Cashew Factories", *Mathrubhumi Weekly*, 55:16 (1977), pp. 26-36.

We note a marked difference between the words of the older woman and those of the younger two. Alima Umana clearly showed resignation, as well as dejection about the possibility of the trade unions improving her situation, and she stressed the power of factory owners. The young woman, Chandika, was of the opinion that the problem lay outside the sphere of trade union activity. The grandmother seemed to have more faith in the trade unions, probably as a result of her own experience of successful trade union actions in the 1940s and 1950s and the sacrifices of the leaders at that time. She also lived through the inhumane working conditions of the 1930s and 1940s, and has seen the improvements which had come about since then. In her view, all of these questions—even providing raw nuts to the factories—belonged to the sphere of the trade unions. Her experiences had shaped her consciousness.

The laughter Kurumbi caused with her remark about needing to strike was certainly ironic, in view of the conceived powerlessness of the trade unions. In 1977, workers had witnessed a massive shift of cashew factories to Tamil Nadu. The younger women, too, were guided by *their* experiences.

Between 1997 and 2000, I met several families which were quite similar to those whom Pavanen described. Like Pavanen, I was interested in the question of the *kudivarappus*. The following conversation took place in 1999 at the home of three shellers, Santha (born 1957), her daughter, Meena (born 1982), and Santha's mother, Velumbi (born 1930), a former sheller.[188]

> *Santha*: I work in a state-owned cashew factory, but now it is closed.
> *Interviewer*: How do you survive when the factory is closed?
> *Santha*: I go to a kudivarappu. I have to—otherwise there will be no rice in the house.
> *Interviewer*: How often do you go there, and how much do you earn?
> *Santha*: I go six days a week and I get thirty rupees a day.[189] I work about eight hours a day.
> *Interviewer*: Isn't that betraying the trade unions—going to a kudivarappu?
> *Santha*: It is a betrayal of the *idea* of trade unions—not the trade unions.
> *Interviewer:* Can you explain what you mean?
> *Santha*: There is no trade union in the kudivarappus and we can't start one, because then we will no longer have any work. The trade union leaders from outside know about this, but they don't do anything. It is not in their interest—some of them are even involved in kudivarappus themselves. That is also betraying the *idea* of trade unions. This illegal processing could not have continued without their consensus. But, on the other hand, we need them.

---

[188] Interview in the village of Kilikolloor on the 21th February 1999 with Velumbi, Santha, and Meena, women of Kurava caste, shellers.

[189] In 1999, Thirty rupees corresponded to about $.67 US (One US$ = 45 rupees).

When the state-owned factory is open—last year it was only about one month, but before it has been a little bit better—I get d.a., bonus for *Onam*, and some days off with wages. We would not have achieved those rights without trade unions.

The older woman and her granddaughter now entered the conversation.

Velumbi: That is what people say today, that the unions are involved in businesses behind our backs. I can't believe it, but if it is true we should object loudly. We should not hide when there is a problem like this. And without unions we would never have reached at this stage.

Santha: But, Amma, what to do? There is no rice in the house, *kudivarappu* owners have their own laws and rules, and the unions only care for registered factories. We are caught in a trap.

Velumbi: I am old, but you must never give up like this. Go out and shout!

Meena: Grandmother is so full of trust in unions, but things are not like they were when she was young. Unions are not for us, they are beyond our spheres of life.

Santha: No, Meena, not like that, we need the unions, but it is difficult to make them engage with the *kudivarappus*. They should—but I do not know how.

We changed the subject and started to talk about supporting a family.

Interviewer: How many are working for wages in this family?

Santha: My daughter and I, and sometimes my husband. The other children are too young—they are still at school.

Interviewer: What about your husband? What kind of work does he do?

Santha: He is a casual laborer in agriculture and construction work, but only a few days a week.

Interviewer: How much does he earn a day?

Santha: One hundred rupees is the minimum, but if it is hard work he earns 150 rupees. Normally he gets a job two or three days a week and usually he gives me 50 or 75 rupees for food after one day's work

Interviewer: Is he a trade union member?

Santha: No, we felt that it was too much to pay the fees for two memberships, so we paid only for me.

Interviewer: Can your husband get more work if he accepted lower wages?

Santha: Nobody would do that among the men! And nobody asks them to do it!

Interviewer: Why do you do it?

Santha: What would you do if your children were starving? I will do *anything* for my children. I will even kill myself if that would help them! Last week I had a fever, so I could not go to work. My daughter

fainted of hunger. I borrowed 100 rupees from a moneylender. Now I have to pay it back, but every day my debt will increase by one rupee.[190]
Interviewer: Is not your husband prepared to do *anything* for his children, as you are?
Santha: You see, the responsibility for the children has always lain on my shoulders. My husband is often out and he does not hear their cries of hunger. Men just don't understand these things. They take for granted that there is food in the house. I can't change him. I suppose that he does his best and, besides, what would people think of him if *he* started to work for half wages?

It is remarkable that in 1999, as in the 1940s, factory owners still have the power to dismiss workers or close factories when union activities begin. As was the case with those interviewed by Pavanen, the oldest woman seemed to be the one with the greatest trust in the capacity of trade unions. Conspicuous in this conversation was the fact that a male was able to earn a reasonable wage, even without being a member of a trade union. Of the eighty-five workers interviewed at the VLC cashew factory in January 1998, and the forty-five women interviewed in-depth in 1997-2000, I found a total of sixty-five women (forty-three plus twenty-two) who lived with their husbands in nuclear families (or extended nuclear families) and nevertheless were the main providers (i.e., contributed over 50% of the household income). These women all gave similar accounts of the situation regarding the men in their families. Their husbands and other males in the family were usually day laborers working in agriculture or construction. In 1999 these men refused to work below a daily wage of 100 rupees and, in fact, could often get 150 rupees a day. On the other hand, they could only get work one or two days a week—at least at those wages. Their wives worked in registered cashew factories, sometimes only a few months out of the year, earning a legal daily wage of about 60 rupees. Whenever the factory closed, many of them went to work in unregistered factories for 30 or 35 rupees a day, six days a week.

A paradoxical situation has developed in the last few decades concerning unemployment and a shortage of labor in rural Kerala. A survey of 241 labor households found that about one-third of all male agricultural laborers were willing to work for lower wages, but had not done so because of pressure from trade unions and fellow workers.[191] The same kind of pressure was reported by men in the cashew families interviewed. Women, on the other hand, felt obligated to secure food for their children at any price.

---

[190] Note that this corresponds to the exorbitant interest rate of 365%!
[191] M.K. Sukumaran Nair, "Labour Shortage in a Labour Surplus Economy? A Study of the Rural Labour Market in Kerala", in Oommen (ed.), *Kerala's Development Experience*, I, p. 267.

As a result, men in families of cashew workers have come to consider themselves *true radical members of the labor movement* with the right to demand minimum wages, although for many of them their class and trade union loyalty presupposed that it was a woman's responsibility to securing food for the family—often by working in the informal sector. Santha did not worry about what people would say if *she* worked for half wages—but found it inconceivable for a man to do so.

These women were loving mothers, very close to their children, and dutifully bearing the responsibility for their support. Yet the dominant gender discourse within their culture holds men up to be the breadwinners of their families. Thus, there is a paradox between ideal (or at least prescription) and reality. The same prevailing discourse also assigns men the role of radical worker, loyal unionist, and party member. The strength of these identifications overshadows the breadwinner role, leaving men to pursue their political aims, even to the detriment of their family roles, and yet not be looked down upon as anomalies.

Male workers have entered the *kudivarappus*, too. However, whereas women receive about 50% of their female co-workers' daily wages in registered factories, the difference in daily wages made by male workers in the *kudivarappus* and male workers in registered factories is much smaller. In 1975, workers in *kudivarappus* earned between 90% to 107% of men doing the same work in a registered factory, the most conspicuous difference being that some male workers (e.g., roasters) actually received *higher* daily wages in the *kudivarappus* than in the registered factories. The reason given for this was that "the male workers need to be kept in good humor...lest they create problems for the employers because of the legal ban."[192] The same wage differences still existed in the late 1990s.

Poverty has not only driven women but some men as well to be "disloyal" to the trade unions. The difference between women and men in the *kudivarappus* is that it is considered necessary to bribe male workers to make sure of their loyalty to the factory owners.[193] The gender discourse which has developed defines *all* men as radical and potential trouble-makers, whereas women, by nature, are defined as docile.

The women interviewed were not unaware of the nature of capitalist exploitation or the need to express class demands by taking concerted ac-

---

[192] Kannan, "Evolution of Unionisation", pp. 24, 37. For a similiar result a few years earlier, see Oommen, *Inter State Shifting*, p. 107.

[193] This may be compared to Heidi Hartmann's view that through trade unions male workers in the West have allied themselves with employers in order to secure better paid work for themselves and make sure that women continue doing unpaid work for them in the reproductive sphere. Heidi Hartmann, "The Unhappy Marriage of Marxism and Feminism".

tion; in that sense, they all expressed *class consciousness*. However, material conditions and power structures hampered them from acting as *radical workers*.

Lalitha, a radical trade union convener and member of the communist party, CPI-M, told me that, if it became necessary, she would go to the *kudivarappu*.

> I would go there if I had to. If my children were starving I would go, but with me there is another problem. The owners don't let me inside the *kudivarappus* because they know that I am a party member and that I am prepared to fight for our rights. I have become almost like a man—just like some of the old militant cashew women in the 40s! We are a few like that.
> —Lalitha, Pulaya woman, born 1958, sheller[194]

Lalitha clearly expresses her radicalism in terms of gender. She considers herself unusual—even anomalous—in that she is a radical party member. Lalitha knew of radical female cashew workers in the 1940s through her mother, who had told her stories about them. "Some women of those days were extremely militant and acted as men. They went to the toddy-shop at evenings, they shouted to the supervisors—they were more aggressive than modern women".[195]

Old Pulaya and Kurava women related that it was quite common in the 1930s and 1940s for women of their castes, just as Lalitha's mother had recollected, to occasionally go out to a toddy shop in the evenings (usually with their husbands) and drink some liquor—a behavior which shocked many who considered themselves higher in the social hierarchy.[196] They also told me that women would often go out at night—mostly to work, but also to visit relatives or friends. An old Pulaya woman mused:

> Yes, nowadays, women are so much *women*. We were not like that when I was young. We worked so hard and often we had to work in the evenings. We had to go and fetch water, cow dung, wood, and perform all other kinds of work. Well, I don't say that women don't work today. They do, they do. We tried to enjoy life sometimes and it happened that we went to drink

---

[194] Interview 8 February 1999.

[195] Interview 8 February 1999 with Lalitha, Pulaya woman, born 1958.

[196] Interview 10 January 1999 with Kotha, Pulaya woman, born 1919; Interview 18 January 1999 with Kavitha, Kurava woman, born around 1920; Interview 19 August 1998 with Ponni, Kurava woman, born around 1920. In the early twentieth century, the anthropologist Edgar Thurston noted that it was common to see men, women, and children of Pulaya sitting together drinking toddy (although he observed that they rarely got intoxicated or committed crimes). Edgar Thurston, *Castes and Tribes of Southern India*, 9 vols (Madras, 1909), II, p. 54 and VII, p. 26.

toddy—not as much as the men—but anyhow…Today no woman would ever go to the toddy shop. It is a domain for our men. Still women have to go and fetch water and things like that, but now there are more wells and people don't have to walk for hours like in the past. Many young women today are afraid of going out at night. There are so many drunken men and so much violence—it was not there in the old days. If we were afraid, it was of the *goondas*[197]—they were like the factory owner's private army and they harassed women to make them refrain from joining the union.
—Kotha, Pulaya women, born 1919, sheller[198]

The younger women of these castes were adamantly of the opinion (as were Nair and Ezhava women of all ages) that women should never drink alcohol and should not go out at night unless it was absolutely necessary. Geetha, a young Pulaya woman, said:

A woman should never, never drink toddy and things like that. I know that some old Pulaya women do. They are very special—not like women of today. To drink toddy is unthinkable for modern women. We laugh a little bit at these women. They did and still do all kind of male things, like going out at nights. It is not exactly because I am afraid that makes me stay home after dark. If you go out alone at night people may start to gossip. They may not respect you and start talking about lovers and things like that. And once such a rumor has begun, men may start to disturb you. That is why I stay here. I want peace and I want to be respected.
—Geetha, Pulaya woman, born 1973, sheller[199]

In contrasting the views of women born fifty years apart, my intention is not to romanticize the past or eulogize the habit of poor, low-caste women in joining men in the toddy shop. I merely want to point out the less rigid gender barriers which existed among these castes when a woman like Kotha was young. Her feeling that women are much more *womenlike* today than was the case in her youth, and Geetha's search for peace and respect[200], are issues which will be revisited in Chapter VIII.

During the last twelve years, Lalitha's husband has only had work now and then. Moreover, for long periods of time, he left her and their three children without giving them any support, and so her life has been marked by severe difficulties. It was always very hard to get in touch with Lalitha, as

[197] This may be the origin of the British colloquialism "goon", a thug hired as a union-buster.
[198] Interview 10 January 1999.
[199] Interview 18 January 1998.
[200] For an account of the struggle of British working class women for respectability, see Beverly Skeggs, *Formations of Class and Gender: Becoming Respectable* (London, 1997).

CHAPTER 7

she was constantly "on the move", trying to find a source of income for her family. She grew and sold vegetables, she bought clothing wholesale, fruit and vegetables at the farmer's market, and sold them in the housing areas—her inventiveness seemed to have no bounds. She had almost gotten herself the reputation of a man. However, she was the one responsible for the children. Lalitha's situation, seeking extra income in the informal economy, was not unique. Most women interviewed had tried to find other sources of income during periods when even the *kudivarappus* were closed.[201] Several women told of having to take outside jobs in the evenings or on Sundays to supplement their income. Some sold fruit and vegetables, and some became domestic servants in middle-class households. Such behavior emerged out of necessity after the casualization of work in the factories over the last three or four decades.

It would be beyond the scope of this study to delve into matters such as prostitution, into which, according to my informants, some female cashew workers were driven by dire economic necessity. A former trade union convener and sheller summarized the issue of prostitution thus:

> Long time ago there was prostitution in the houses of some cashew workers in this village. Today, there are special places in the city of Quilon where women go for prostitution, and we can witness that such "trade" increases when the cashew factories close down. It's nothing women do if they are not forced to—it's the last instance to save their children from starvation!
> —Gomathi, Ezhava woman, born 1930, sheller[202]

Women have resorted to all sorts of survival strategies. One surprising move was to switch over to another trade union. A study of a cashew factory in the 1970s concluded that the owner employed more Nairs and Christians because they often belonged to unions affiliated with the Congress-party rather than with communist trade unions.[203] A common opinion among cashew workers interviewed was that the Congress unions are on the side of the employers, and it is reported that a prominent union leader from Congress owns a cashew factory himself, although through a frontman.

Trade unions do not register caste affiliations among members, so it has not been possible to determine whether a correlation exists between caste and trade union affiliation, but my informants claimed

---

[201] For an account of different survival strategies among cashew workers, see Deepa, "Industrial Crises and Women Workers", pp. 60-81.
[202] Interview 21 February 1999.
[203] G. Ramachandra Raj, "Industrial Conflict and Relations in Larger Society: A Case Study", *Journal of Kerala Studies,* Parts 3-4 (December 1978), pp. 585-612.

that such a connection was obvious a few decades ago—a phenomenon noted by a researcher in Kerala in 1989.[204] My interviews do not
show such a correlation at present: different castes were found in all
trade unions.

A sheller at the VLC factory, Geetha, told me she used to be a member
of the communist trade union, but had recéntly changed to the Congress-
affiliated union:

> I belonged to the communist trade union before, but some time ago the
> supervisor told me, as he did several other women, too, that we were going
> to be better paid if we belonged to Congress. The owner is a Congress man.
> I did not like it, but it gave me a little bit better daily income, so I joined
> Congress. You know, every single rupee is important for me and my two
> children. There is nobody else to care for them. But I still vote for CPI-M.
> —Geetha, Pulaya woman, born 1973, sheller[205]

"So", Geetha added with a laugh, "I cheat them in a way", showing that she
at least retained some power—however small.

Illiterate and Ignorant—Exploited for Political Purposes?

There seems to be a widespread opinion in Kerala that female cashew
workers are illiterate, ignorant, and exploited by trade union leaders for
political purposes.[206] Academics have also described them as such.[207]
Women in the cashew factories have also been called "vote-banks".[208] A
civil servant who was experienced in the cashew industry likened the social
struggle among cashew workers to a well-staged drama: trade union leaders
agree with factory owners to organize a demonstration or strike in order to
calm frustrated workers, but arrange it for a time when neither delivery nor
production will be disturbed![209] The underlying presumption of such state-

---

[204] Mathew, *Communal Road to a Secular Kerala*, p. 170.

[205] Interview 18 January 1998

[206] Interview 5 January 2000 with L. Radhakrishna, managing director of KSCDC 1996-
1999. For a discussion of corruption and egoism among trade union leaders in India, see
Jan Breman, "Industrial Labour in Post-Colonial India I: Industrializing the Economy
and Formalizing Labour", *International Review of Social History*, 44 (1999), pp. 249-300,
292-299.

[207] Pillai, "The Economic Impact", p. 168.

[208] Interview 11 September 1999 with Paravadi Devi, journalist, Trivandrum.

[209] Interview 5 January 2000 with L. Radhakrishna, managing director of KSCDC 1996-
1999.

ments is that workers have suffered from *false consciousness* in not knowing their own interests, i.e., they have been duped and deceived. A union leader's ability to mobilize workers and command their loyalty suggests relations similar to those characterized by Chakrabarty with regard to the jute industry in Calcutta earlier in the twentieth century. He calls it a *babu-coolie* relation, meaning by that a traditional bond of hierarchical loyalty, such as those in the caste-system.[210]

In the introduction to this thesis, we have seen the old, illiterate Kurava woman, Kavitha, refer twice to the political system. She said that she joined the communist union when C.P. Ramaswamy Ayyar was in power, and that she shifted to another factory in the year of the dismissal of E.M.S. She did not know the years she or her children were born. Nevertheless, she had a fairly good idea of the chronology of her life. It is obvious that this illiterate woman structured her past around who was governing the country at the time.

It was astonishing to find that this was quite a common way of referring to the past among cashew workers, in particular by older or middle-aged women with little or no education. A few of them could specify a year according to the old Travancore calendar, although most could not. Instead, they used political events if asked when something occurred. The particular dewan ruling at the time, the year when the Punnapra-Vayalar revolt occurred, the CPI-M politician E.M.S.'s first or second ministry, the Emergency period, or the Congress politician Karunakaran's various ministries, were, for many women, important landmarks by which they dated personal events. Several women determined when they joined the union, shifted to another factory, got married, gave birth to a child, became a widow, moved to another dwelling, or became unemployed by referring to political events like the ones cited above. This may be illustrated by the following extracts from interviews:[211]

> I can't tell you which year I started to work in a factory, but it was about a year before E.M.S. won the election. I worked in Musaliar's factory. It closed down after some years, and I started in a *Kudivarappu*....At that time I was not a union member, but during the first presidential rule I became a member in RSP's union.
> —Velamma, Kurava woman, born in 1940, sheller[212]

---

[210] Chakrabarty, *Rethinking*, p. 150.
[211] Several examples are also given in the next chapter, where women reflect on marriage and dowry.
[212] Interview 30 December 1998.

My youngest daughter was born when the Punnapra revolt was going on. I am not sure about the year, but according to our Malayalee calendar, I think it was in the year 1121.
—Ponni, Kurava woman, born in 1920, sheller[213]

I used to live in Kilikolloor, but a few years after my first husband's death I moved to my sister in Kottiyam. This happened during the time when E.M.S. was prime minister for the second time. Later on I got my own house from the government.
—Masis Ally, Pulaya woman, born in 1935[214]

I don't know in exactly which year my daughter was married, but it was in the time of Emergency. We were unhappy because of this political disaster, but at least we had a wedding to celebrate. Her husband is a good man.
—Chakki, Pulaya woman, born in 1927[215]

I was fired from my factory when Karunakaran had become a minister—so I was doubly sorry. Soon, I got a job in the KSCDC factory, but I also work in a small, private factory, because working days are few in the state-owned factory.
—Kunjukutty, Ezahava woman, born in 1923[216]

Without exception, women of the middle or older generation were well aware of the difference between the Left United Front and the United Democratic Front, and could place them on the political map as well as on a chronological time axis.

Younger women were much less prone to refer to political events in order to structure the past. They were also less versed in the political land-scape and less knowledgeable about names of ministers and politicians, although many of them had an opinion about the difference between Left United Front and United Democratic Front.

Several explanations may be given for the marked contrast between the generations. Younger women were more literate and could easily use "modern" ways of describing the past by relating to the Christian calendar. Also, political interest may grow with age and experience, and perhaps the tendency among younger women to be less versed in the political landscape had more to do with their youth than with other factors. Although it is often believed that adolescents and young adults are more engaged in rad-

[213] Interview 22 November 1997.
[214] Interview 2 December 1997.
[215] Interview 6 January 1999.
[216] Interview 11 January 1998.

ical activism, in comparison to the situation when their mothers and grandmothers were their age, the young women of the 1990s seem to have a diminishing interest in politics. Younger women spend less time in the factory than their mothers and grandmothers because their work has mainly been seasonal. This diminished contact with their peers may in part account for their lessened interest in politics and trade union activities.[217]

The older women, most have of whom were less than thirty years old when memorable political events took place, must have avidly followed those events when they occurred. They associated such temporal landmarks with things happening in their own private lives. It is difficult to imagine otherwise, as it is hardly possible for individuals to date their lives as a reconstruction after the fact. The varying degrees of knowledge about politics among different groups of women may be attributed to their generation, rather than to their biological age.

The fact that women of the two oldest generations used political events to structure the past indicates the important role politics must have played in their lives. The aged trade union convener, Gomathi, described how she became aware of politics and government:

> Since the day I listened to M.N. Govindan, I have been interested in politics. It is very natural that we know and remember who was in power because only the Left has helped the cashew workers. They revise the minimum wages and implement welfare schemes. During other ministries nothing ever happens. The Left politicians may sometimes be bad and crave power, but the alternative is worse. Next month are the elections and I can assure you that the KSCDC factories will remain open until the election is over—otherwise they fear that we will not vote for Rajeendran, a CPI-M politician who is on the board. After the election, but not before, they will probably close the factory due to lack of raw nuts—as usual. Most cashew workers have always supported the Left. We are important voters to them. They need us to maintain their power, and we support them. After all, they have done so much for us, but it is not our world, as it was in the past.
>
> —Gomathi, Ezhava woman, born 1930, sheller, trade union convener[218]

The expression "not our world" was used by several cashew workers—especially those of the younger generation—to describe their relation to the unions. Like Gomathi, most workers interviewed declared that only

---

[217] Lars Olsson found that, among typographers, experiences at work when they were young led to radicalism in later life. Lars Olsson, *Gamla typer och nya produktionsförhållanden* (Lund, 1986), p. 192.

[218] Interview 29 January 1999.

the Left had done something for them. Comparing ruling governments with dates for revision of minimum wages and introduction of welfare reforms shows that Gomathi and her co-workers had good reasons for their views. It has principally been governments of the Left which have implemented minimum wages and welfare systems (although they often failed to revise wages within the stipulated time). Most workers, whether they are literate or not, are well aware of what the Left has done. Many workers expressed pride in being responsible for the political shift after the election 1987, when the Left came back to power after five years as the opposition party.[219] In the words of Raji, a CPI-M member and sheller:

> We have almost always supported our leaders. The cashew workers were important in the election of 1986. We dismissed the old government and helped the Left come to power. Why shouldn't we? They are the only ones who have revised the minimum wage or implemented other labor benefits, so trade unionism is also politics!
> —Raji, Ezhava woman, born 1957, sheller, trade union convener[220]

Listening to these women, I found it hard to believe that they were merely "vote-banks" or people exploited solely for political purposes. Cashew workers seem to have been well-aware of their actions, and many considered themselves important historical agents for the advancement of labor rights in Kerala.

Jan Breman has argued that, in spite of little progress, trade unions have played an emancipatory role in India.[221] The Kerala cashew workers' trade unions bear this out when it comes to economic achievement and class awareness. The power structure *within* trade unions, however, has not changed in favor of women. Nevertheless, to believe that trade unions have functioned only to support the interests of labor leaders or the political parties with which they are affiliated would be to underestimate the ability of the workers to know what is in their own interest.[222] Trade unions continue to increase their membership due to the advantages which they provide. The economic gains they have brought are especially visible if we contrast the working conditions in Kerala's

---

[219] In the Quilon district, the Left Democratic Front won 11 out of 12 constituencies, which politicians of the Left have accredited to the cashew workers. See, for example, Kesavan Nair, "Strike History of Cashew Workers", Part 26, *CITU Sandesam*, 19:8 (1995), pp. 31-32.

[220] Interview 7 February 1999.

[221] Breman, "Industrial Labour in Post-Colonial India, I", p. 294.

[222] For a similar conclusion, see Ramaswamy, *The Worker and his Union*, p. 189.

cashew factories with those in Tamil Nadu, where trade unions are rarely found.[223]

If, however, we compare the wages and living conditions of cashew workers with other groups in Kerala, a number of differences become evident. An example is the situation of the beedi-workers.[224] They constitute a group that has had problems similar to those of cashew workers. Continuous violations of labor laws and deplorable working conditions formerly characterized their factories. They, too, suffered in the 1960s from the steady threat of factory closings and jobs being shifted to other states.[225] A workers cooperative, Kerala Dinesh Beedi (KDB), was formed in 1969 in order to "save" the workers. The story of KDB is one of success, involving a unique "shop floor democracy" where workers are empowered and are represented on KDB's board of directors, although most of them have only received a primary education. KDB employs both male and female workers, but only men are found on the board. Nevertheless, the women working in KDB have enjoyed increased wages and secure employment.[226] As discussed in Chapter III, such cooperatives were started in the early 1980s in the cashew sector as well (CAPEX), but the vast difference between those and the beedi-cooperatives was that cooperatives in the cashew sector were formed and run "from above" by politicians. Workers were set aside and never asked to participate in the decision-making process because it was argued that they were illiterate.[227] With regard to working conditions, CAPEX stands in contrast to the success story of KDB in that it has not managed to keep the factories running continuously. Many workers at CAPEX are compelled to seek their livelihood in *kudivarappus*. CAPEX has also been accused of violating labor laws and neglecting to pay bonuses. One of my informants, a sheller born in 1957, and worn out after thirty-five years of work, managed to change her job at the CAPEX factory to overseeing children at the day-care center. In 1999, in spite of industry-wide agreements that such *ayahs* should be paid monthly, she found herself still being treated like a cashew sheller, unemployed for long periods of time without compensation. Differences between the conditions of employment at KDB and CAPEX are to be explained principally in terms of gender.

[223] B.R. Patil, "Cashew Workers of Kanya Kumari" (Indian Institutes of Management, Bangalore, 1984); K.P. Vincent, "The Socio-Economic Conditions of Cashew Workers: A Study Conducted in Kanyakumari District" (M.Phil., Department of Sociology, University of Kerala, Trivandrum, 1983); Padmathy, "Health Conditions of Women Workers in Cashewnut Industry".
[224] Beedis are small hand-rolled Indian cigarettes.
[225] Oommen, *Inter State Shifting*, pp. 108-136.
[226] T.M. Thomas Isaac, Richard W. Franke, and Pyaralal Raghavan, *Democracy at Work in an Indian Industrial Cooperative* (London, 1998).
[227] Interview 15 September 1999 with V.N. Giri, managing director, CAPEX, Quilon.

Relationship to the Leaders

We have seen that the first demands on behalf of cashew workers emanated from those workers themselves. Although the early unions may not be described as democratic or grassroots-oriented (at best they can be considered *less formalized*), older workers were of the opinion that is was easier to approach union leaders in the past.

During periods when trade unions were banned, their leaders hid among the cashew families—a circumstance which probably created feelings of importance and solidarity among the workers. In addition, those leaders who were not imprisoned frequently visited workers where they lived in order to agitate, or organize inter-caste dining. Most older workers prided themselves in having met such revered leaders as K.C. Govindan, M.N. Govindan Nair, Sreekantan Nair, or T.K. Divakaran personally, even having received them in their homes. In 1973, a pioneering communist, N.E. Balaram, described those in the forefront of the unions during the 1930s and 1940s as follows: "The labour leaders of those days were youths who starved, smoked beedi-butts, slept on benches in the shop verandas, and led lives of charming sacrifice. It was thanks to the efforts of those youths, who never bothered to think of their house, family, and life, that trade unions could take root in our land."[228] In contrast to this picture, there is a widespread opinion in Kerala today that union leaders have extravagant lifestyles.[229]

Cashew workers, together with their families, number more than 500,000 individuals. For decades they have been extremely important voters—something most of them seem to be aware of. They also constitute a group which can stage huge demonstrations and manifestations of power for the political parties to which the trade unions belong. "They need us to maintain their political power", Gomathi explained. This is not to say that the trade unions have grown totally corrupt and useless to the workers, as one scholar in Kerala has argued.[230] Gomathi, along with many of her co-workers, asserted that "the trade unions have done so much *for us*!" The expression is an illustration of the power structure in the trade unions and the lack of grass-roots involvement. The leaders at the top level, who are mainly politicians, have resorted to hunger strikes lasting several days, marched many miles, and blocked buildings and roads with their bodies;

---

[228] N.E. Balaram, *Communist Movement in Kerala: The Early Days* (in Malayalam), Vol. I (Trivandrum, 1973), p. 71, cited in K.T. Rammohan, "Kerala CPI(M): All That is Solid", p. 2583, n. 9.
[229] Pillai, "The Economic Impact"; George, "Historical Roots".
[230] Pillai, "The Economic Impact".

they have given greatly of themselves and are often portrayed as heroes.[231] Still, female workers no longer feel they have the power to set the agenda, as they earlier did. It is not "our world", as many women expressed it. The dependence of workers on male leaders is extremely pronounced, and specific issues related to women have been neglected. As cited earlier, women have not been able to advance certain "small" questions (gloves, broken kernels, etc.) to a place on the union's agenda.

When workers were asked of their relation to their leaders, their replies often cited more *militant women* in the past and *other types* of leaders. In 1962, a reporter for *Jennajugham* interviewed a female cashew worker who was treasurer of the trade union at her factory. She expressed disappointment in women being less militant and less independent than in the old days (by which she probably meant the 1930s and 1940s), and she recounted the story of a confrontational strike led by women in those years.[232] Kurumbi, the elderly, illiterate woman interviewed in 1977 (see previous section) seems to represent this older, pro-active generation of women. She, along with others like her, held the view that women were more forthcoming in the 1940s. Gomathi, the trade union convener born in 1930, reflected:

> Definitely, women were more active and militant in the 40s and early 50s than ever since. Now we are so much in the hands of the leaders. Only when *they* think a question is relevant can we demonstrate or bring forward an issue. Leaders in the old days were more honest and only worked with the laborers. Today they are more into politics and there is a marked change in their life style—they have almost become like capitalists. Workers and leaders belong to different classes—they are at different levels. Leaders nowadays have the mentality of power and ruling. But we cannot be without them—after all, they have taught us everything and we are better off with them than without them. We have no chance to act on our own; we are tied hand and foot.
> —Gomathi, Ezhava woman, born 1930, trade union convener[233]

The question of corruption and the collaboration of trade union leaders with factory owners has been a burning issue for some decades. Many rumors circulated about both civil servants and union leaders being corrupt, and sometimes such accusations have been made in court or in the local

---

[231] Dipesh Chakrabarty depicts leaders in Bengal in the early twentieth century as heroes who sacrificed themselves and formed organizations based on loyalty. Chakrabarty, *Rethinking*, pp. 151-154.
[232] Balakrishnan, "Life and Strikes in the Midst of Smoke and Coal Dust", pp. 2 ff.
[233] Interview 26 December 1999.

newspapers.[234] "How can *kudivarappus* go on, how can these factories thrive like never before, if unions and civil servants are not involved in dirty business?" was a frequent comment heard from women of all ages.

Workers commonly accuse trade unions other than their own of corruption. Many trade union leaders have made similar denouncements, occasionally in the newspapers.[235] Only two trade union leaders among thirteen interviewed conceded that corruption might have occurred in their own unions. We noted Santha saying that union leaders themselves were involved in illegal cashew production. Some interviewees believed that union leaders had a share in the profits generated by false weighing. These rumors have seriously damaged the faith that workers may have had in trade unions—especially younger workers who never experienced the struggles of the old days. Contrary to Kannan, who asserted that women have lost faith in unions because those organizations have mainly benefited male workers,[236] the skepticism of my informants can better be attributed to the question of class, as union leaders, in their view, do not represent the working class. In fact, some former male cashew workers have managed to rise above the working class by becoming union leaders and politicians.

Exceptions in the Labor Movement: "the Others"

The few existing accounts of cashew workers', trade unions and their strike history that we have are written by male trade union leaders and activists in the Malayalam language. To rewrite the same history in English would be the work of a translator. On the other hand, one may usefully analyze how such authors have represented female cashew workers, and thereby explore their perception of gender. One way of doing this is to find instances when female cashew workers are mentioned in ways and contexts other than just as "bodies" in a demonstration or participants in a strike.

The Quilon daily newspaper, *Jennajugham*, which ceased publication in 1993, has probably written more about cashew workers than any other newspaper. The paper had ties to the Communist Party of India (CPI) and so its perspective on female workers may be said to represent a general leftist discourse. Its journalists, according to the editorial staff, were active members of the party and, in many cases, the communist trade union, AITUC, as well. Complementing such articles are historical accounts of cashew workers written by trade union leaders during the 1990s. These reflect memories and stories of the past that have survived over the years. A

[234] *Jennajugham*, 7 July 1967, p. 1; NRC, "Sales Tax Officer Accused of Receiving Illegal Gratification", File No. 830/87/LBR (Rt).
[235] *Deshabhimani*, 12 April 1994, p. 2.

common feature of these accounts is that *they rarely mention workers at all,* presenting the history of social struggle in the cashew industry as if it were solely the leaders' fight!

When the *gender* of cashew workers is mentioned in the daily newspaper in connection with strikes and demonstrations, the newspaper's formulation has been quite homogenous for the last four decades. The following excerpts may be taken by way of example:

> Today about 5,000 cashew nut workers, including women, took part in a protest march.[237]

> Twelve hundred cashew workers, including 700 women, picketed the secretariat.[238]

> Cashew workers, including 200 women, carried out a *satyagraha* [protest, demonstration] in front of the owner's house.[239]

> Many workers, including women, participated in a fasting strike.[240]

> Many hundreds of [cashew] workers, including women, assembled at the railway grounds carrying red flags.[241]

> Among the thousands who took part in the picketing, 600 were female workers.[242]

> The female [cashew] workers, too, participated in the strike.[243]

> Disregarding police threats, the women workers raised their slogans![244]

In a 1946 description of one of the earliest demonstrations, we noted the police reporting that 300 coolies, *including men and women,* participated. At the time it was considered remarkable that *not only women,* but *also men* of the lower castes challenged the establishment. Twenty years later, accounts of collective labor actions singled out *women's* participation as remarkable. We get the impression from the newspaper citations that

---

[236] Kannan, "Evolution of Unionisation", pp. 29-30.
[237] *Jennajugham,* 4 August 1967, p. 1.
[238] *Jennajugham,* 1 August 1969, p. 1.
[239] *Jennajugham,* 19 August 1970, p. 2.
[240] *Jennajugham,* 12 June 1975, p. 1.
[241] *Jennajugham,* 21 July1981, p. 1.
[242] *Jennajugham,* 6 April 1982, p. 3.
[243] *Jennajugham,* 23 April 1988, p. 1.
[244] *Deshabhimani,* 29 April 1994, p 5.

women had come to be considered exceptions in labor movement activities and needed to be remarked upon. It appears from these accounts that, in spite of the greater numerical presence of women in the factories, they had become less prone to take an active role in trade unions as time went on. To continually stress that "women, too, participated" is to express the uniqueness of this occurrence. The fact of the matter is, however, that, in most demonstrations of cashew workers, a large number (most often the majority) of the participants were women.[245]

When we consider that since about 1960, more than 90% of all cashew workers have been women, it is rather curious to find that so many men participated in the demonstrations at all! If the newspaper is correct, there were often as many men as women (and sometimes more) in evidence. Who were these men, and why did the reporters not comment on *their* participation? I asked Gomathi, a trade union convener since the mid-1940s, who had participated in hundreds of strikes and demonstrations, and had been imprisoned several times, about the men in question:

> In the old days, many of the men in the demonstrations were cashew workers. I cannot tell you in each and every case who the men and women were, but usually when we staged a *satyagraha* or picketed a road, a factory gate, or a building, most female workers in the shelling and peeling sections participated, and also most male workers. The graders—mainly Nairs—have been a little bit reluctant to participate, but it is better now than, let's say, thirty or forty years ago. The male participants you read about in the paper are, apart from cashew workers, made up of two groups. The first consists of our husbands, brothers, sons, fathers, and uncles. Whenever they had the opportunity—and they often had, as many of them frequently were unemployed—they joined us to help us to create a big crowd. The other category may have been more professional activists from student organizations, youth groups, other trade unions, or political parties. They, too, have shown their solidarity with us. That is why you read about so many men joining the women's struggle.
>
> —Gomathi, Ezhava woman, born 1930, sheller, trade union convener[246]

Gomathi's view was shared by many other of my informants. All of them were women who had participated in a number of strikes, demonstrations, marches, picket lines, and other trade union activities during the last four

---

[245] This statement is based not only on interviews with cashew workers themselves, but on pictures and articles in *Jennajugham* over a forty year period (1953-1993).
[246] Interview 21 February 1999.

or five decades.[247] Their stories suggest that there has been a joint struggle against capitalism in their families. Numerous instances of women mal-treated by their husbands (or other male family members) may be encountered, and yet capitalist exploitation was considered stronger and more important to combat. Male family members were also exposed to capitalist exploitation, and class conflict among men and women were always seen as more important than gender conflicts. The family was considered a joint unit for taking a stand against capitalist forces.[248] However, in reports of demonstrations and other trade union activities, the *true* activists, the women, have been portrayed as the exceptions, the Others. Males—in most instances not even cashew workers—have been regarded as the *true* activists.

A vivid history of another "exception" has been preserved among trade union leaders. It appears that this happened in the early 1960s. A cashew factory near Quilon had suddenly withdrawn all welfare benefits, causing the enraged workers to strike and surround the factory. The manager called the police, who tried to disperse the crowd and send the demonstrators home. Suddenly a young woman jumped in front of the armed police, tore off her blouse, and challenged the police to shoot her through the breast. The story has survived for about four decades and it has been characterized as, on the one hand, *amusing*, and on the other as *unnatural*.[249]

In having the audacity to venture her femininity by tearing her blouse off and exposing her naked breasts to the police, the woman, although perhaps acting intemperately, took a stand as a *true worker* and *true radical member* of the labor movement. This kind of behavior had long been common in Kerala among men, the intent being to shame the police and show them as cowards and traitors for attacking poor, unarmed workers. But when a woman did the same thing, it was considered so remarkable that it engendered a long-lived story among male activists and found its way into the trade unions' historical accounts as an amusing rarity. What made the event remarkable was not only that she exposed her body, but that *she behaved like a man* and was seen to be possessed of the true spirit of radicalism. Such behavior and mentality were not expected of a woman, as women were stereotypically supposed to be frightened and in need of male protection.

---

[247] Interview 25 August 1998 with Seethu, Ezhava woman, born 1938, peeler; Interview 26 August 1998 with Velumbi, Kuruva woman, born 1930, sheller; Interview 12 February 1999 with Thankamoni, Ezhava woman, born 1946, sheller, trade union convener.

[248] For the view that the family has been a place for resistance among black Americans against capitalist forces and racist domination, see bell hooks, *Yearning: Race, Gender, and Cultural Politics* (London, 1991), pp. 41-49.

[249] Kesavan Nair, "Strike History of the Cashew Workers, part 18", *CITU Sandesam*, 18:11 (1995), pp. 13-14.

It is curious to reflect that thirty years *earlier*, the same woman might have had no blouse to tear off. The reason would not only have been poverty, but tradition, which did not then condemn as immoral women who went bare-breasted.[250] Most low-caste women wore only loin-cloths in the 1930s and 1940s; in some rural regions this was common among old women until about as late as 1960.[251] In addition, at that time challenging the police would have been considered remarkable for *any* low-caste person, male or female.

The dress question is an oddity in Travancore. Up to 1859, women in Travancore were actually not allowed to cover their breasts in front of higher caste persons, as a symbol of respect.[252] Gradually women of higher castes started to wear blouses. In the beginning, women were ashamed of covering their breasts; it was even considered an act of sexual enticement, and women have recounted how they only wore a blouse in the bedroom with their husbands.[253] The higher in the caste hierarchy, the earlier women "got civilized" and started to cover their bodies. Old shellers recalled that in the 1940s most women in their department worked bare-breasted, wearing only a short *dhoti* not covering their knees, just like most men of the lower castes did. The tendency for women has been to cover the body more and more: first with a blouse, than with a longer *dhoti*, later with a blouse with a small shawl hanging over the shoulder, and finally a sari with a shawl hiding all female curves. Thus there has been a rapid development towards a way of dressing which increasingly covers the female body, leading towards a widening gender-difference with regard to attire.

In a few of the accounts of the cashew workers' struggles, it is maintained that a characteristic specific to women is *fear*. By way of example, the secretary of an early trade union asserted that "the frightened women" were difficult to organize, as they were afraid they would be dismissed.[254] Another writer stated that "the fear-ridden female workers deserted the union one by one".[255] It is not possible to verify or quantify statements saying that

---

[250] B. Rajeevan, "From Caste to Sex: A Study on Sexuality and the Formation of Modern Subject in Kerala", in Oommen, *Kerala's Development Experience, I*, pp. 45-59.

[251] Interview with Kavitha, Kurava woman, born around 1920; Interview with Kotha, Pulaya woman, born 1919; Interview with Ponni, Kurava woman, born around 1920; Interview with Kunji, Pulaya woman, born 1920. K.C. Alexander found Pulaya women bare-breasted in 1968 and considered this a sign that they were primitive and lacking culture. See Alexander, *Social Mobility in Kerala*, p. 185. The manager of Peirce Leslie in Kundara, A.D. Bolland, asserted that low-caste women in the shelling section worked bare-breasted until the 1960s. Interview with A.D. Bolland, 12 June 1998.

[252] Christian women were permitted to cover their breasts since 1812. Christian missionaries agitated for women's right to be dressed in a decent way. See Robert L. Hardgrave Jr, *Essays in the Political Sociology of South India* (New Delhi, 1993), pp. 146-163.

[253] Rajeevan, "From Caste to Sex ", pp. 45-59.

[254] Quoted in Kannan, "Evolution of Unionisation", pp. 8-9.

[255] Majeed, *The Strike History*, p. 24.

women were more prone to abandon unions than men, but people living in abject poverty are probably not able to be the most radical political activists, because it can cause them their jobs. This can be illustrated in Europe, where skilled craftsmen—a kind of elite among workers—were the first to organize into trade unions.[256] If women were more reluctant to enter into trade union activism, it may also be because of their greater responsibility in providing for their children. In a totally different context, it was reported that among Swedish workers in the late 1920s women were the first to organize, as they did *not* have the responsibility for maintaining the family. On the other hand, their husbands, the main family providers, could not afford to be victimized and lose their source of income.[257]

In May 1954 there was a demonstration in Quilon at which a journalist reported the presence of "female workers carrying babies in their arms and laps".[258] A common way of representing female demonstrators in *Jennajugham*[259] and in the trade union leaders' historical accounts[260] was to persistently link them with the household sphere. Some women may have brought their children with them, but according to Gomathi, the veteran trade union convener, it was not a general phenomenon.

> Most of the women tried to find baby sitters, as a demonstration was very tiresome to small children. Of course, not all the workers had small children. Perhaps, in some factories the workers are younger, but wherever I have worked the majority have not carried babies in their arms when demonstrating, although there have always been some who did.
> —Gomathi, Ezhava woman, born 1930, sheller, trade union convener[261]

Even if only a minority brought children, pictures would be taken of these individuals and stories in the press would focus on them and their poor children. Susie Tharu and Tejaswini Niranjana have noted similar descriptions of women in accounts of demonstrations in other parts of India. They interpret such representations as ways of obscuring women's political aspirations by emphasizing their familial responsibilities instead.[262] The politi-

---

[256] See, for example, Lars Olsson, "Labour Movements, History of", *International Encyclopaedia of Social and Behavioural Sciences* (Oxford, 2001).
[257] *Bohusläns samhälls- och näringslivs 4. Konservindustrin* (Uddevalla, 1982), p. 44.
[258] *Jennajugham*, 13 May 1954, p. 4. .
[259] See, for example, *Jennajugham*, 15 July 1969, p. 2; 8 June 1969, p.1; 1 August 1969, p. 1; 22 July 1970, p. 5; 31 August 1970, p.1; 11 February 1973, p. 1; 11 February 1974 , p. 1.
[260] Azeez, "The Great Organisation of Cashew Workers", p. 108.
[261] Interview 21 February 1999.
[262] Susie Tharu and Tejaswini Niranjana, "Problems for a Contemporary Theory of Gender", in Shahid Amin and Dipesh Chakrabarty (eds), *Subaltern Studies IX: Writing on South Asian History and Society* (New Delhi, 1996), pp. 254-257.

cal demands of the cashew workers were clearly articulated in the material I have examined. Portraying women primarily as mothers was probably not intended to obscure these demands. Rather, it bespeaks another agenda: the presence of *mothers* in demonstrations suggests that women were only temporarily out in the street, and soon would be back in their homes to attend to domestic chores. Whether true or not, it reinforced the "otherness" of women.

It is likely that picturing women with small, often half-starving, children was an attempt to win the sympathy of the public. Such accounts gave the appearance that demonstrating women were not *really* radical workers but, rather, angry mothers protesting in the streets in the name of their children's welfare. Invoking a strong link to the domestic sphere has been a way of expressing the presumably weak class consciousness and home-orientation of women. One trade union leader even urged women to "come out from the kitchens and demand their rights."[263]

E.P. Thompson, in his account of British women of the working class being imprisoned, declared that they were in jail for reasons of *loyalty* to their leaders, rather than out of political conviction.[264] The same term was used by Keralite trade union leaders in describing the imprisonment of female cashew workers. More than one union leader emphatically stated that "the cashew workers have been very *loyal*",[265] thereby underscoring the notion that these women struggled without having understood the politics behind their actions; they were simply following male leadership.

The representation of female cashew workers by trade unionists or left-oriented journalists, although couched in a discourse of masculinity and femininity which may be derogatory for female workers, can, however, also be read as an appreciation of their character. In many accounts, bad weather conditions during marches and demonstrations—heavy rain, for example, or a hot and burning sun—have been stressed. *Jennajugham* and trade union accounts over and over depict female cashew workers in such terms as the following: "In spite of heavy rain, even the women workers took part in the demonstration",[266] or "they braved the heat of the mid-day sun and the cold of the night to demand their rights".[267] The intention of these images may have been an effort to *praise* the cashew workers, who were considered, in the words of one of the trade union leaders, "better than

---

[263] *Jennajugham*, 10 November 1970, p. 4.

[264] Noted by Joan W. Scott in *Gender and the Politics of History*, p. 73.

[265] Interview 12 January 1998 with J. Chitharanjan, trade union leader, politician; Interview 13 September 1999 with P. Bhaskaran, trade union leader, politician.

[266] *Jennajugham*, 19 August 1970, p. 2.

[267] *Jennajugham*, 31 August 1970, p. 1; See also *Jennajugham*, 13 May 1953, p. 1; 1 August 1969, p. 1; 11 February 1973, p. 1; Majeed, *The Strike History*, pp. 127-128.

most other women."[268] The account of Kesavan Nair which introduces Chapter V also views female cashew workers as differing from other women: "The success that social reformers had dreamed of, these cashew workers themselves had achieved". We get the impression it was unexpected that women would be so actively engaged in the labor movement. The aforementioned newspaper accounts let us sample the dominant gender discourse relating to those characteristics that a woman—cashew worker or not—was thought to possess.

The source material contains recurring themes of women's fear, domestic concerns, loyalty, and exceptionality in radical actions. We learned in Chapter IV of other epithets which were given to women: patience, frailty, technical incompetence, and dexterity. Taken together, these form a structure of thoughts or discourse which explains what a woman—in contrast to a man—was considered to be. Such a gender discourse has a decisive impact on an individual's formation of self-identity.

Conclusion

We have seen that, in the late 1930s, the workers at the India Nut Company became members of a trade union within one week. They chose their own leaders, and these leaders were able to organize the workers to picket the factory entrance the next morning, in spite of being illiterate women of the lowest castes. The workers also formulated their own demands, even though trade union leaders from the outside were of paramount importance in later having those demands voiced.

Three distinct periods relating to the overall development of Travancore, Travancore-Cochin, and Kerala society in regard to trade union activities can be distinguished:

The first period, which lasted up to the mid-1950s, was characterized by a break with the past. Travancore went from a society in which trade union leaders negotiated with civil servants behind closed doors for a more open society with radical trade unions, although the latter had not yet become institutionalized. The questions on the union's agenda mainly concerned achieving legal status as workers. The earliest collective actions were for the most part carried out jointly by male and female cashew workers belonging to the lowest castes. The collective memories of older women recount this period as "glorious" because of the achievement of several labor rights. A large number of militant women participated in this early union struggle.

---

[268] Interview 13 August 1998 with N. Madhavan, former trade union leader (UTUC, RSP).

The second period, which may be termed "the radical era", lasted into the mid-1970s. Huge political manifestations were common. It was a time characterized by the growth of competitive unions which became institutionalized into hierarchical organizations. The primary goal of nationalizing the cashew factories (closely related to socialist politics) was achieved during this period. The most important questions of the day concerned upholding those rights which had been achieved for factory workers, and implementing various social welfare programs. In spite of the radicalism of the period and the huge manifestations of solidarity and power (militant struggles in which women also participated), some women began to feel that it was becoming harder to put certain issues on the agenda. A decrease in the number of annual working days and continual violations of labor laws contributed to the material difficulties of women. Rumors of corruption, tendencies to distrust leaders, and the increasing aloofness of union representatives led women to feel excluded from the labor movement.

The third period, from the mid-1970s to the present, witnessed a severe economic crisis. In spite of the prohibition of *kudivarappus*, most women tended to seek employment in such factories when the registered factories closed. Many questions vital to a woman's daily survival, although having been on the agenda since the 1930s, were now relinquished by trade union leaders. As a result, women started to experience powerlessness with regard to setting their union's agenda. Unresolved questions concerned women working up to about 25% of the time without payment, and having to spend a portion of their already meager wages to buy tools and protective clothing. The inability of the trade unions as well as factory inspectors to stop *kudivarappus* was seen as treachery. Constant violations of various labor laws, and women's inability to put forward any questions other than those approved by male leaders, acted to exclude women from considering themselves *radical* union members.

On the positive side, the continuous struggle of cashew workers through their trade unions has led to several achievements—primary among them the *right* to demand certain labor benefits. However, involvement in unions has not empowered female workers by giving them a voice and strengthening their ability to act for themselves.

Although there have been tendencies for nominal participation, it would be erroneous to term cashew workers' activities in their unions as such. Cashew workers have understood the actions which have led to several of their gains, and so can hardly be labeled ignorant. To the workers, their progress, with the help of the unions, has been a matter of life and death; to criticize the unions too severely would be to deny that their struggle has, in fact, led them away from starvation and total deprivation. Some considered it arrogant to criticize the labor movement at all for its shortcomings with regard to participatory democracy, or for neglecting such gender issues as equal wages. Class solidarity has obscured or set aside structural gender conflicts.

E.A. Ramaswamy points out that "illiteracy does not prevent a person from knowing what is in his interest". Ramaswamy's concern, however, was for a group of male workers. With regard to Kerala's female cashew workers, the presumption that women are illiterate has been used as an argument to exclude them from achieving power—not only in trade unions, but in such cooperative cashew factories such as those under CAPEX. However, in Kerala, the women have largely been *literate*. The paradox is that with growing literacy, cashew workers seem to have actually *lost* influence in trade unions. Among three generations of workers, I have noticed a dwindling interest in politics and a more marked distance from trade union leaders. Younger women particularly expressed the view that leaders belonged to "another world". This distance has created alienation within the trade unions in general. Alberto Melucci located identity-creating processes in the daily experience and informal social networks (the latent level) of members in new social movements. In the case of the female cashew workers this level has not led to empowerment. Their trade unions have not given them the impetus to act independently.

For their part, trade union leaders, in spite of touting the cashew workers as "better than most other women", have continued to portray them as *the Others*, part of a more general discourse on women, retaining such epithets as "in need of protection", "patient", "weak", "fearful", and "home-oriented". In reaction to such definitions, women—even among themselves— have begun to visualize their deeds in terms of masculinity. We recall Raji considering that she had "become like a man" by being a radical trade unionist. Stories about militant women in the 1940s have survived, but in retrospect, these women are often considered "unfeminine", and have not served as models for young women of the 1990s.

Poverty, capitalist economic structures (such as management's power to relocate factories and the ensuing casualization of work), as well as gender discourses, have prevented women from taking action. They have mainly been constrained by material realities such as hunger and the prevailing capitalist system. They have to contend with factory owners who can dismiss or otherwise penalize them at whim and union leaders who determine which issues are given priority. But even their own apprehension of what is expected of a woman (a result of a hegemonic gender discourse) has often hindered them from acting as radical workers, a posture their husbands often assume when refusing to work for less than the minimum wage. Thus, the gender discourse is also part of a power structure.[269] Most of the women I interviewed were extremely well-aware of capitalist relations and power structures, whereas patriarchal structures (although recognized) seemed to be too embedded in their culture to challenge.

In Kerala's radical political climate, impoverished female cashew workers have not been able to exhibit the same radicalism that their husbands and other men have shown, due to the necessity of providing for their children. In fact, as we have seen, the ability of men to reject underpaid work has often been founded on women's financial backing through income derived from the informal sector.

All these experiences and memories have shaped women's identities. The cashew workers' sense of who they are seems to have changed over the course of the last seventy years. Their main identity is no longer that of either "low-caste" or "radical working class member", but rather "woman". Female cashew workers may be characterized as having *class consciousness*, in the sense of understanding the capitalist system of production and realizing that collective action is the means of challenging it. Interviews with these women show that they clearly feel their affiliation with the working class (in contrast to the way they view many of their new union leaders), yet without identifying themselves as *radical workers*—for that is something which denotes only *men*. The trade union movement in Kerala has employed a gendered representation of class, just as, according to Joan Scott, the Chartists had in nineteenth century Britain where, at the symbolic level, the working class was constructed as masculine.[270]

The masculine construction of "radical workers" has also been decisive in determining which questions were brought up for consideration in cashew workers' trade unions. When the veteran trade union convener, Gomathi, and her daughter, Chamally, were asked what they believed an ideal union would be like, they answered:

> A perfect union must be only for the workers, and must take up all kind of issues. Such a union should operate at the factory, engage everyone, and have its own leaders. We should solve most problems on the factory level. Every cashew worker should be involved! It should be an organization to which we could go with *all* our problems. It should let us borrow money, give us loans to repair our houses, help us when our husbands mistreat us, give classes to our children so they can manage at school, and find other work for us if the factory closes for the season.
>
> —Gomathi, Ezhava woman, born 1930, sheller, trade union convener, and Chamally, Ezhava woman, born 1955, sheller [271]

[269] James Scott has argued that, for poor peasants in a Malaysian village in the late 1970s, the main obstacle to resisting oppression was not located at the ideological level, but in material power structures. James Scott, *Weapons of the Weak*.

[270] Scott, *Gender and the Politics*, pp. 53-67.

[271] Interview 21 February 1999.

CHAPTER 7

What they described was, by and large, a transformative model of a trade union with empowering capacities and a holistic approach which would include the reproductive sphere—utopian, perhaps, but formulated out of an awareness of their own problems and the will to ameliorate them.

VIII   Marriage, Caste, and Gender

A life without love and children is no life, is it? And we all want to live—
more than anything else. Am I not right?
—Kavitha, sheller, Kurava woman, born around 1920[1]

Introduction

In early 1997, when I carried out my first tentative interviews, I had a two-
hour-long conversation with Kalyani. She had been working as a sheller
since the early 1940s. When she was seventeen years old, she married. Her
husband died sixteen years later and she was left with two sons and three
daughters. The land reforms of 1970 affected Kalyani and she was assigned
a small plot of land and a simple house where she continued to live with her
second husband, with whom she had another daughter. When he abandoned her after a couple of years, Kalyani sold the property, and together
with two of her daughters, moved into her mother's small house, where
Kalyani's youngest sister and her husband were already living. Soon afterward, due to lack of space, Kalyani moved to her son's house (a simple hut
with thatched roof). Our dialogue centered on questions like the working
process, wages, unemployment, factory discipline, trade unions, relations
with male workers and foremen, and changes she had witnessed during her
years as a cashew worker. I then posed my final question: "What has been
the major problem confronting you in your lifetime?" I could in no way
anticipate her answer, especially since our conversation had almost exclusively concerned factory work.

> All the time poverty…it has been a never ending problem which we are
> almost used to, but it became worse when my husband died and when the
> working days decreased in the cashew factory. Some days we ate once, some
> days twice, and some days not at all. But the difficulties in marrying off my
> daughters have caused me so many problems! You see, nowadays, you can't
> marry unless you pay a large dowry to the bridegroom's family, and what is a
> life without a family and children? My eldest daughter got married to her
> cousin; it was my brother who arranged it and it was no problem at all. But
> to get my other daughters married gave me a lot of trouble. I sold the house

---

[1] Interview 11 March 1998.

and the land to get them married, but it was only enough for one daughter. My other daughters worked in the cashew factory to get some money for their dowries—but how can we save when we are hungry? My two youngest daughters are very unhappy. One is not married, even though she is almost thirty years old, and the other one has a lot of problems with her husband, who treats her very badly. It was a marriage without any dowry and that's the reason for her problem. That is my main problem—to see my children unhappy. One son died with TB, the other one is a roaster at the Corporation [state-owned factory]. When he married he got two cents [2/100 of an acre] of land as a dowry where he built a house, and that's where I am living now with my son, his wife, and their three children. But it is not a good solution. The house is extremely small and I am not on good terms with my daughter-in-law.

—Kalyani, Pulaya woman, born 1933, sheller[2]

Even when I did not explicitly ask about marriage and dowry, but rather questioned the interviewees about their daily lives, their difficulties, joys, dreams, memories, and future expectations, they often raised the issue of marriage and dowry themselves. It became clear that such questions were of the utmost relevance in analyzing the lives and identities of cashew workers over the last seven decades.

A major shift in the mode of marriage payment appears to have taken place among the lower castes (e.g., the Kuravas) in the fifty years between 1920 and 1970, as illustrated by the remarks of two Kurava women who were generations apart. One of them, Kavitha, who was born around 1920, told me:

I got married when I was fifteen years old. It was an arranged marriage. My father was the one who arranged the marriage. We were poor, and so were my husband and his family. We married in our house. I got a dress, but no other gifts, no gold, or anything like that, just some flowers and a *thali* [woman's ornamental marriage symbol] in black thread. In those days nobody among us had a golden chain. Today it is a must for young women. Without gold, girls feel that they are not *women,* but we are too poor to buy gold. But young women, they want so badly to be feminine! Dowry was not the custom in the old days. A long time ago the boy's family would pay a small sum to the girl's family at marriage. That has disappeared; it was a long time ago. My mother would have known about it. She was the one who told me about it. It was paid to her father when she got married. Today it is the other way around, and we pay large sums as dowries to the families of the bridegrooms. Dowry is an evil which did not exist in the past. I don't know the reason for this. I have no idea. But we have to marry off our daughters,

---

[2] Interview 14 January 1997.

haven't we? We must secure their happiness. A life without love and children is no life, is it?

—Kavitha, Kurava woman, born 1920, sheller[3]

The second Kurava woman who was much younger, recounted:

I have been working in this factory for three years now. I live with my parents and a brother. We are much in debt and my mother as well as my brother are sick. My father is an agricultural worker and sometimes he works, sometimes not. We owe a lot because my sister got married a couple of years ago and the dowry we had to pay made us borrow a lot of money. I am working to pay the debt and then I will start to save for my own dowry. I want to get married, but I will marry a man my parents will choose for me.

—Sunitha, Kurava woman, born 1978, sheller[4]

Central Concepts

What do we actually mean when we talk about marriage payments, and how can we explain their existence and transformation? M.N. Srinivas has offered interpretations of the fundamental concepts: *bride-price, kanyadhana, stridhanam*, and *modern dowry*, to which the following discussion is indebted.[5]

Bride-price denotes the transferring of resources from the kin of the groom to the kin of the bride. According to Srinivas, groups among whom bride-price has been prevalent were either poor or of low caste, or both.[6] It may be noted that bride-price, i.e., the sum a bride's family received, tended to be considerably less than the amount given to the groom's family when we speak of a dowry.[7]

Kanyadana literally means "the gift of a virgin", and was often accompanied with *dakshina*, a cash gift to the groom's kin. The *kanyadana* form of marriage is directly related to the customs of the Brahmins and is the ideal form of marriage, according to ancient Hindu texts like the Rigveda.[8]

Stridhanam refers to something presented to a woman upon marriage.[9]

---

[3] Interview 11 March 1998.
[4] Interview 8 February 1997.
[5] Summarized most recently in M.N. Srinivas, *Village, Caste, Gender and Method* (New Delhi, 1996), pp. 158-180.
[6] Ibid., pp. 160, 166.
[7] Ibid., p. 166.
[8] For a thorough account of the ancient roots of *dakshina*, see Ranjana Sheel, *The Political Economy of Dowry: Institutionalization and Expansion in North India* (New Delhi, 1999), pp. 38–46.
[9] Srinivas, *Village, Caste, Gender*, p. 162.

The Sanskrit word *stridhanam* literally means "women's wealth" and the significant feature of *stridhanam* is that it is legally owned and controlled by the woman to whom it is given. *Stridhanam* is often considered a pre-mortem inheritance. In case of divorce, the *stridhanam* is to follow the woman.[10]

In contrast to *stridhanam*, *modern dowry* involves a transfer of resources such as large sums of cash, jewelry, or other items of value from the bride's kin to the groom or his kin.[11] *Modern dowry* has lost its voluntarily character and has come to be demanded by the groom's kin. As pointed out by Srinivas, the two phenomena are often confused.[12] I here use the word "dowry" as a blanket term referring either to *stridhanam*, or to *modern dowry*, or both. Several studies on marriage customs in India highlight the shift from bride-price to dowry among large segments of the population.[13] It is sometimes unclear whether this dowry is a *stridhanam* or a *modern dowry*, i.e., whether the resources are owned and controlled by the bride, or by the groom and his kin.

Srinivas points out that hypergamy was unknown in the Dravidian South, but was only found in the North. The term hypergamy refers to the marriage of a woman with a man of a superior grade or clan, although from the same caste. According to Srinivas, status asymmetry at marriage has not been the custom in the southern part of India, where the tradition has been isogamy, i.e., equality of status between the spouses, further reinforced by cross-cousin marriages.[14] The traditional absence of status asymmetry at marriages in the South was, Srinivas suggests, the reason for the prevalence of bride-price instead of dowry. Srinivas is of the opinion that bride-price has been the custom among all castes in South India until quite recently.[15] *Modern dowry* emerged in North India in the mid-nineteenth century, but

---

[10] I use a simplified definition of *stridhanam*, which may suffice in this context. The complexity of *Stridhanam* and its different interpretations and permutations over time is elaborated by S.J. Tambiah in Jack Goody and S.J. Tambiah, *Bridewealth and Dowry* (Cambridge, 1973), pp. 59-166. See also Sheel, *The Political Economy of Dowry*, pp. 46-52.

[11] Srinivas, *Village, Caste, Gender*, p. 161.

[12] Ibid., p. 162.

[13] See, for example, T.S. Epstein, *South India: Yesterday, Today and Tomorrow* (London, 1973), pp. 94 ff.; den Uyl, *Invisible Barriers*, pp. 206 ff. In a study of a fishing community in South India, Kalpana Ram illustrates a change from *stridhanam* to modern dowry. Ram, *Mukkuvar Women*, pp. 185 ff. See also Sheel, *The Political Economy of Dowry*, pp. 79 ff.

[14] Srinivas, *Village, Caste, Gender*, p. 160. However, the tradition of marriages between Nambuthiri-Brahmins sons (except the oldest brother) with women of the Nair caste must be viewed as a hypergamous marriage, although with the peculiarity that the spouses did not live together and the husband did not have the economic responsibility for his wife/wives.

[15] Srinivas, *Village, Caste, Gender*, pp. 160-161.

in the South it is a phenomenon which arose much later. As we shall see, the practice has taken on devastating proportions all over India since Independence.[16]

Theoretical Approaches

Theories on marriage payment can broadly be divided into two categories: economic and ideological theories—although they often merge. Explanatory models under the first category stress either the nature of women's work, the inheritance system, or both.

Writing about Europe, Marion Kaplan suggests that dowry disappeared mostly as a result of the expectation that a woman would earn a wage during her first years of marriage. Dowry payments were abandoned in many places between the two World Wars, and Kaplan points to the wholesale entrance of women into paid jobs as the main reason for its decline. She sees modernization and the increase of women working outside the home as marking the end of the traditional dowry system.[17]

Ester Boserup, taking a global perspective, links the system of marriage payment to the dominant mode of production. She argues that in societies where women's labor is central (and women consequently enjoy relative economic independence), *bride-price* is common; whereas in societies where women's productive role is lower (and women's dependency on men greater), *dowry* is common at marriage.[18] When different systems exist within one society, various classes or castes may have disparate ideologies with regard to women's contribution in terms of productive work.[19] In this view, a bride-price represents compensation for a loss of the bride's labor to her family, and a dowry is correspondingly a payment for receiving an economic burden, i.e., a dependent woman. In theory, an alteration in women's role in production may cause a shift in the mode of marriage payment. In 1974, such a casual link was also expressed by the authors of the Report of the National Committee on the Status of Women in India. Their con-

---

[16] Ibid., pp. 161-162, 173; Sheel, *The Political Economy of Dowry*, pp. 103 ff.; Kumar, *The History of Doing*, pp. 115 ff. In Bengal, the *modern dowry* system already spread among lower castes at the beginning of the twentieth century. See Sen, *Women and Labour*, p. 87.
[17] Marion A. Kaplan (ed.), *The Marriage Bargaining: Women and Dowries in European History* (New York, 1985), pp. 6-7. For accounts of women in Great Britain going to work to save for their dowry, see Louise A. Tilly and Joan W. Scott, *Women, Work, and Family* (New York, 1978), pp. 95, 109-110, 186.
[18] Boserup, *Women's Role in Economic Development*. See also Goody and Tambiah, *Bridewealth and Dowry*, and G. Rajaraman, "Economics of Bride-price and Dowry", *Economic and Political Weekly* 18:8 (1983), pp. 275-279.
[19] Epstein, *South India*, pp. 194-200.

clusion was that the appearance of women in the statistical tables as paid workers had declined radically in the intervening years between the census of 1921 and that of 1971. The prevalence of dowry payments was reported to have increased in the same period. As a consequence, girls have become an economic liability. Parents, therefore, have had to pay a dowry at marriage for their daughter's maintenance.[20] Indira Rajaraman, too, offers an economic analysis of the spread of dowry, while asserting that a dowry should be seen as a virtual purchase for female leisure.[21] Rajaraman's economic theory has been criticized for being too simplistic.[22]

Several writers have highlighted the importance of the system of inheritance for the explanation of marriage payments. Dowry has been equated with pre-mortem inheritance, i.e., a system which gives the daughter her share of a parental inheritance at her marriage.[23] But, as in the case of dowry vs. bride-price, it has been pointed out that often this pre-mortem inheritance has been much smaller than the shares which sons have received. There has also been no guarantee that the dowry would remain under the control of the woman.[24] Madhu Kishwar has further elaborated the links between inheritance and dowry, asserting that since a woman always inherits her husband's property, the groom's demand for a dowry should be seen as an entrance fee initiating the bride into the property of the groom's kin.[25]

Other scholars have argued against narrow economic interpretations and instead underscored the social prestige and status connected with the marriage payment.[26] A process in which lower castes emulate a cultural behavior (including marriage customs) of the Brahmins or other higher castes has been seen as a strong force for achieving upward mobility in a caste-stratified society. Although acknowledging the system of *modern dowry* to be a Brahmin custom, Srinivas strongly objects to calling the appropriation of this practice "Sanskritization". He asserts that it should rath-

---

[20] Govt. of India, *Towards Equality*, pp. 69-77, 152 ff.

[21] Rajaraman, "Economics of Bride-price and Dowry".

[22] Srinivas, *Village, Caste, Gender*, p. 167; I. Sambrani et al., "The Economics of Bride-price and Dowry", *Economic and Political Weekly* 18:15 (1983), pp. 601-604; Shalini Randeria and Leela Visaria, "Sociology of Bride-price and Dowry", *Economic and Political Weekly*, 19:15 (1984), pp. 648-652.

[23] Goody and Tambiah, *Bridewealth and Dowry*, p. 64.

[24] Madhu Kishwar, "Dowry—to Ensure Her Happiness or to Disinherit Her?", *Manushi*, No. 34 (1986); Madhu Kishwar, "Dowry Calculations: Daughter's Rights in Her Parental Family", *Manushi*, No. 78 (1993), pp. 8-17.

[25] Kishwar, "Dowry Calculations".

[26] Klas Van de Veen, *I Give Thee My Daughter—A Study of Marriage and Hierarchy Among the Anival Brahmins of South Gujarat* (Assen, 1972); Veena Das, "Marriage Among Hindus", in Devaki Jain (ed.), *Indian Women* (New Delhi, 1975); Srinivas, *Village, Caste, Gender*, pp. 158-180.

er be called Westernization, since *"modern dowry* is the product of such forces let loose by British rule as monetarization, education, and the introduction of the 'organised sector'".[27]

Srinivas gives priority to non-economic status raising and explains the spreading of *modern dowry* to lower castes by their wish to obtain a higher social and ritual status through imitation of the Brahmins. He gives the example of a low-caste community in Northern India which has emulated Brahmin customs by giving up their own traditions of bride-price, drinking alcohol, eating meat, and widow remarriage—former cultural habits the community now considers "uncivilized". To further show that non-economic factors are decisive in the shift from bride-price to dowry, he gives examples of communities where dowry is paid, even though the women continue to work for wages. [28]

Den Uyl, in studying a Harijan colony in Kerala, also concluded that a shift from bride-price to dowry had occurred since the mid-twentieth century, a phenomenon she interprets as emulation of Brahmin customs.[29] However, in the material she interprets, there is a steady increase in love-marriages (at least up to 1980)[30], which contradicts her finding of Sanskritization. When den Uyl asserts that much matrilineal culture still exists among the Harijans, she further speaks against a movement toward Brahmanic tradition. The matrilineal Harijans, in keeping their own traditions, appear to resist Sanskritization and prefer their own cultural continuity.

Karin Kapadia, too, in her study of five different castes in central Tamil Nadu, found non-Brahmin castes imitating Brahmin marriage customs, but unlike den Uyl she concludes that this is an effort to become urbanized and modern and, above all, to enhance the *class status* of the non-Brahmins, rather than their ritual status.[31]

---

[27] Srinivas, *Village, Caste, Gender*, p. 163. For a criticism of Srinivas' argument that *kanya-dana* and *dakshina* gave status to the bride's family, and the paradox that the groom's family did not need to enhance its status, see Sheel, *The Political Economy of Dowry*, pp. 22-23.

[28] Srinivas, *Village, Caste, Gender*, p. 171. Sheel agrees about the importance of British rule, but she stresses the institutionalization of Brahmin marriage through the codification of a new law. Sheel, *The Political Economy of Dowry*, pp. 64 ff.

[29] den Uyl asserts that the marriage she found is a commercialized form of dowry, i.e., modern dowry, but in her study it is unclear who in effect controls the marriage payment. den Uyl, *Invisible Barriers*, pp. 206 ff.

[30] Ibid., p. 204.

[31] Kapadia, *Siva and Her Sisters*, pp. 11, 46 ff.

Marriage Payment in Travancore and Kerala

Trivandrum the 2nd January 1945

Sir,

...You are personally aware how many Brahmin families have faced utter ruin on account of the insistence of heavy dowry amounts by the bride-groom-to-be. Strangely this obtains only among the Smartha Brahmins....Would you kindly come to the rescue of the Smartha Brahmins in this matter and ban absolutely the system of dowry from raising its head in this land? You would be doing a real service to the community concerned if dowry system is banned by legislation"[32]

The above is an abstract of a letter sent by a man from the Smartha Brahmin community to the dewan of Travancore. The system of paying dowry at marriage was clearly experienced as extremely burdensome. According to the writer, it seems to have been a custom restricted to the Smartha Brahmins—a community originally from Tamil Nadu[33]—although according to other sources, a marriage dowry had been common in Travancore for a long time among such other communities as the Syrian Christians and Nambuthiri Brahmins.[34] In 1931, the authors of the Census Report of Travancore asserted that the custom of dowry was a late form of "marriage by purchase" which had become universal among Brahmins and Christians and had started to spread to other communities. This *modern dowry* had come into vogue as a means of the bride's parents financing the new husband's education at an Indian or foreign university[35]—a fact which underlines the class aspect of such dowries. This kind of dowry did not provide any material security for the wife, as had been the idea with *stridhanam*.

The family system among the matrilineal castes in Travancore had characteristics which, in many ways, contradicted the ideal Brahmanic family and marriage system: marital instability, a loose bond between the spouses, the possibility of love-marriages, and the existence of divorce. In a Brahmanic marriage, divorce was virtually impossible, and even the remarriage of widows was stigmatized. Among matrilineal castes in Travancore, divorce was both common and easy for men or women to initiate, and widows frequently remarried.[36]

---

[32] KSA, Legislative department 1945, file no. 21, letter to the dewan, C.P. Ramaswamy Aiyar, dated 2/1-45.

[33] Govt. of India, *Census of India 1931*, Vol. XXVIII, Travancore, Part I, Report, p. 371.

[34] Pillai, *Travancore State Manual*, Vol. I, p. 419; Rao, *Social Change in Malabar*, p. 104.

[35] Govt. of India, *Census of India 1931*, Vol. XXVIII, Travancore, Part I, Report, p. 162.

The orthodox way among Nairs was for a girl to marry her cross-cousin—most commonly, the son of her mother's brother. The motive here was economic, so that all property would be kept within the kin. However, lower landless matrilineal castes also practiced cross-cousin marriage. Polyandry was common, and Nair women stayed in their *taravad* even after marriage. A system of visiting husbands existed; men did not have the responsibility of maintaining their biological children, whereas they *were* responsible for their sister's children.[37]

The letter to the dewan cited earlier, in which a man begs for relief from the dowry system on behalf of the Smartha Brahmin community, did not result in the legislation desired. It took until 1961 for a general prohibition banning the dowry system to be promulgated. It has, however, failed to put an end to the practice in Kerala and in the rest of India. On the contrary, an extreme increase in both the range and size of dowries can be witnessed. It must be noted that only *modern dowry* is prohibited, not *stridhanam*—which has led to severe criticism of the "patriarchal state."[38]

As we saw in Chapter II, the abolition of the matrilineal system in Travancore had far-reaching consequences for gender relations. Fidelity and stable nuclear families with a housewife and a male breadwinner became the norm—although not the reality—for all communities in Travancore. As another consequence of the new inheritance rules, *modern dowry* was introduced where it had never been heard of before, but it took some decades until it became the common practice.

In several village studies carried out in Kerala in 1961, dowry was prevalent among most patrilineal communities, and, in a few instances, among Nairs, as well.[39] After extensive field work among the Nairs in the mid-1970s, an Indian researcher concluded that dowry was paid in about one-fourth of all marriages in South Kerala. He traced the custom back to a few communities of Brahmins and Christians, from which he found it was quickly spreading elsewhere.[40]

Bride-price has never been practiced among Nairs and higher castes in

---

[36] Ibid., pp. 171, 175, 185; S.J. Puthenkalam, *Marriage and the Family in Kerala* (New Delhi, 1977), pp. 105 ff.; Alexander, *Social Mobility in Kerala*, p. 130; Iyer, *The Travancore Tribes and Castes*, Vol. II, pp. 151, 177, 188 (with regard to Pulayas). See Thurston, *Castes and Tribes of Southern India*, Vol. II, p. 125, for Kuravas.

[37] See Mencher, "The Nayars of South Malabar"; Alexander, *Social Mobility in Kerala*, pp. 65-69; Saradamoni, *Matriliny Transformed*; Jeffrey, *Politics, Women and Well Being*.

[38] Sheel, *The Political Economy of Dowry*, pp. 148-189. Madhu Kishwar has challenged this opinion and argues that *stridhanam*, after all, gives women some economic power. See Madhu Kishwar, *Off the Beaten Track: Rethinking Gender Justice for Indian Women* (New Delhi, 1999), pp. 11-36.

[39] Govt. of India, *Census of India 1961*, Vol. VIII, pp. 63, 114, 244.

[40] Puthenkalam, *Marriage and the Family in Kerala*, p. 104.

Travancore and Kerala. It was a custom related to lower castes. Among the Ezhavas, Pulayas, and Kuravas, the paying of a bride-price was common in the early twentieth century.[41] It was also paid among Pulayas as recently as in the 1960s.[42] In the Constitution of the Pulaya Caste Association, bride-price was prohibited and giving of a dowry was advocated instead.[43] This shift was seen as part of a general social awakening and modernization among the Pulayas.

In the area where I conducted interviews, it seems as if bride-price was abandoned around the 1930s (or perhaps earlier), as few people had any memory of it. In the Census of 1901, it had been asserted that bride-price was paid among such castes as the Pulayas and Ezhavas[44], but in the Census of 1931, bride-price was only mentioned in connection with what were labeled "primitive tribes".[45] This indicates that the custom had decreased considerably among other communities over the course of thirty years.

Cashew Workers and Marriage Payment

Based on interviews with eighty-five female workers at the VLC Cashew Factory and forty-five workers interviewed in-depth in their homes, tables of dowries paid or received at marriage from 1935 to present date have been constructed.[46]

Only one interviewee mentioned bride-price without being asked about it; when prompted, only a few persons could remember such a tradition at all. Kavitha, the seventy-seven year-old Kurava woman quoted earlier, was one, and the other was an old Pulaya woman. Their memories indicate that bride-price once existed among the Kuravas and Pulayas in this region in a not too distant past. Very few of the persons above the age of

---

[41] Thurston, *Caste and Tribes*, pp. 67,125; Iyer, *The Travancore Tribes and Castes*, Vol. II, p.187; Govt. of India, *Census of India 1901*, Vol. XXVI, Travancore Part I, Report, p. 343 for the case of Pulayas; for Ezhavas, see p. 280. When lower castes, such as Pulayas, were bonded slaves, the bridegroom's master paid bride-price both to the bride's master and to the bride's mother. See Iyer, *The Cochin Tribes and Castes*, Vol. I, p. 100, and Thurston, *Castes and Tribes*, pp. 67 ff.

[42] den Uyl, *Invisible Barriers*, p. 208; Govt. of India, *Census of India 1961*, Vol. VIII, p. 101.

[43] Alexander, *Social Mobility in Kerala*, p. 141, note 19.

[44] Govt. of India, *Census of India 1901*, Vol. XXVI, Travancore Part I, Report, pp. 280, 343.

[45] Govt. of India, *Census of India 1931*, Vol. XXVIII Travancore, Part I, Report, p. 161.

[46] Overlaps, i.e., cases where mothers, sisters, and daughters were interviewed, have been eliminated from the analysis. From 130 interviews, I obtained information on 506 marriages in which respondents had knowledge of marriage payments. I asked about the informant's own marriage, his/her children's, parents', and siblings' marriages.

fifty knew anything at all about their parents' marriages, a fact which would account for their inability to recall matters of bride-price. If bride-price was once a widespread custom among the lower castes, as asserted by Thurston in 1909,[47] it has now become a more or less forgotten phenomenon. Dowries, however, are quite another matter.

Tables 8.1–8.3 show that paying or receiving dowry was not always a widespread custom among the castes in the sample. With few exceptions, the year 1970 seemed to form a watershed in the communities investigated. Since then, the custom has increased tremendously. In the 1990s, dowry was paid in about 75% of all marriages.

Table 8.1. Number of marriages with dowries paid and received among Scheduled Castes, 1940–1999 (based on 43 interviews)*

	Dowry paid	None	Total	Dowry received	None	Total
1990-1999	15 (75%)	5	20	7 (41%)	10	17
1980-1989	12 (52%)	11	23	7 (30%)	16	23
1970-1979	11 (48%)	12	23	4 (19%)	17	21
1960-1969	4 (29%)	10	14	0	19	19
1950-1959	0	15	15	0	6	6
1935-1949	0	14	14	0	7	7
Totals	42	67	109	18	75	93

* Twenty-nine workers were interviewed at the VLC cashew factory and fourteen other workers were interviewed at greater length in their homes. The figures relate to marriage of informants, their daughters and sons and, where forthcoming, their knowledge of parents', sisters', and brothers' marriages.

Table 8.2. Number of marriages with dowries paid and received among Ezhavas and other middle castes, 1940–1999 (based on 28 interviews)*

	Dowry paid	None	Total	Dowry received	None	Total
1990-1999	14 (78%)	4	18	6 (43%)	8	14
1980-1989	9 (64%)	5	14	3 (23%)	10	13
1970-1979	6 (55%)	5	11	1 (7%)	13	14
1960-1969	3 (33%)	6	9	0	7	7
1950-1959	1 (10%)	9	10	0	6	6
1935-1949	0	12	12	0	4	4
Totals	33	41	74	10	48	58

* Nineteen workers were interviewed at the VLC factory and nine other workers were interviewed in depth in their homes. Three Muslim and two Christian women are included in the sample. The figures relate to marriage of informants, their daughters and sons and, where forthcoming, their knowledge of parents', sisters', and brothers' marriages.

[47] Thurston, *Castes and Tribes of Southern India*, Vol. II, pp. 67, 125.

Table 8.3. Number of marriages with dowries paid and received among
Nairs, 1940–1999 (based on 33 interviews)[*]

	Dowry paid	None	Total	Dowry received	None	Total
1990-1999	14 (74%)	5	19	9 (64%)	5	14
1980-1989	15 (79%)	4	19	6 (50%)	6	12
1970-1979	9 (64%)	5	14	6 (40%)	9	15
1960-1969	8 (33%)	16	24	2 (13%)	13	15
1950-1959	2 (15%)	11	13	1 (11%)	8	9
1935-1949	1 (10%)	9	10	0	8	8
Totals	49	50	99	24	49	73

[*] Twenty-eight workers were interviewed at the VLC factory and five workers were interviewed in depth in their homes. The figures relate to marriage of informants, their daughters and sons and, where forthcoming, their knowledge of parents', sisters', and brothers' marriages.

The figures for the somewhat earlier introduction of dowries into the Nair community support the view that the custom spread from the higher to the lower castes. However, the Nairs in the cashew factories enjoyed a slightly better economic position than the lower castes and were thus in a position to offer their daughters a *stridhanam*—often a small piece of land—so it may well be that their class rather than their caste accounts for this earlier introduction of dowry.

The majority of those interviewed were registered workers from a private factory which had been run more continuously than most other factories.[48] The resulting large proportion of cashew workers who had reportedly paid dowries may be misleading, as these particular workers may form a kind of "elite" amongst cashew workers. When I visited a Harijan colony of mainly Pulayas and Kuravas, all the women interviewed worked in small, private factories which had been running very irregularly during the past forty years. Dowry was a lesser part of their lives. "No, no", one of these women told me, "we are too poor for paying or receiving dowries! We do not even have money for food—how can we pay a dowry? It has never been the custom among us. It is for rich people. But we try to save, we really try!".[49] The demand for and payment of dowry cannot evolve where there are virtually no resources, and such statements as the above show that, to the women in the Harijan colony, it was a class-based issue—but also a goal to strive for.

Receiving a dowry is less commonly documented in the interviews (and appears later) than *paying* a dowry, although it may seem logical to assume that

[48] Among the remaining forty-five workers, most of them worked in smaller factories or very irregularly in KSCDC or CAPEX factories.
[49] Interview 3 January 1997 with Kali, Pulaya woman, born 1940.

families who pay dowries when their daughters are married would also receive dowries when their sons were married (as illustrated earlier by Kalyani).

Without knowledge of what exactly has been paid and who has been the controlling party, one cannot assess the scope and complexity of the dowry system. As it was not possible to ascertain either the amount or to whom the dowry was actually paid in all 176 instances of dowries paid or received, I had to rely on the limited number of cases (74 of 176 marriages) in which I was able to obtain such information during the in-depth interviews. This revealed that the dowries may have consisted of three components: cash payments, land, or gold. [50] Tables 8.4-8.6 note each marriage involving a dowry and the distribution of the dowry into its three components.

Table 8.4. Amount of dowry paid or received 1960-1999 among Scheduled Castes (cash in Indian rupees, land in acres, gold in grams)

1990-1999			1980-1989			1970-79			1960-69		
Cash	Land	Gold	Cash	Land	Gold	Cash	Land	Gold	Cash	Land	Gold
10,000	0	0	5,000	0	0	1,000	0	16	0	0.04	0
7,000	0	0	5,000	0	0	0	0.04	0			
3,000	0	16	0	0.03	0	0	0.05	16			
2,000	0	16	2,000	0	0	0	0.04	0			
2,000	0	24	2,000	0	0	0	0.05	0			
0	0.03	16	10,000	0	24	0	0.10	0			
15,000	0	24	10,000	0	16						
5,000	0.04	16									
6,000	0.05	40									

Table 8.5. Amount of dowry paid or received 1960-1999 among Ezhavas and other middle castes, (cash in Indian rupees, land in acres, gold in grams)

1990-1999			1980-1989			1970-1979			1960-1969		
Cash	Land	Gold	Cash	Land	Gold	Cash	Land	Gold	Cash	Land	Gold
30,000	0	16	25,000	0	16	0	0.30	0	0	0.20	0
20,000	0	24	10,000	0	40	0	0.25	16	0	0.04	0
25,000	0	56	20,000	0	24	0	0.05	16	0	0.03	16
0	0.05	16	5,000	0.04	16	1,000	0	24	0	0.03	0
5,000	0	24	2,000	0	16	2,000	0	24	0	0	32
3,000	0	16	10,000	0	40	1,000	0.035	24	300	0	0
10,000	0	24	7,000	0	0				1,000	0.035	24
0	0	40	15,000	0	40						
6,000	0.02	40	0	0.05	0						
10,000	0	40	3,000	0	24						

[50] The interviewees counted gold in sovereigns or pavans (1 sovereign = 1 pavan = 8 grams). Land was counted in cents (1 cent = 1/100 acre).

Table 8.6. Amount of dowry paid or received 1940–1999 among Nairs (cash in Indian rupees, land in acres, gold in grams)

1990-1999			1980-1989			1970-1979		
Cash	Land	Gold	Cash	Land	Gold	Cash	Land	Gold
40,000	0	24	0	0.10	0	0	0.10	24
40,000	0	40	35,000	0	40	0	0.12	16
10,000	0.05	16	30,000	0	80	0	0.10	48
15,000	0	16	10,000	0	40	5,000	0.05	16
5,000	0.06	24						

1960-1969			1950-1959			1940-1949		
Cash	Land	Gold	Cash	Land	Gold	Cash	Land	Gold
0	0.07	24	0	0.10	40	0	0.20	0
0	0.15	56	0	0.15	0			

The data demonstrates that from about the 1980s onwards, priority has been given to dowries paid in cash. The practice of making gold part of a dowry has become widespread. It is also apparent that amounts paid by Kuruvas and Pulayas are considerably lower than in other communities, indicating that these castes are still more impoverished than others. The bestowal of land has also been infrequent in this group.

The families interviewed referred to the marriage payment as *stridhanam*, irrespective of what was given and to whom. In order to clarify if the marriage payment should be considered as a *stridhanam* or as a *modern dowry*, it was necessary to examine each case more closely. It became obvious during the interviews that cash payments almost invariably had been given to the groom or to his kin in a way that made it inaccessible to the bride, and also that the giving of cash was a fairly recent phenomenon.[51] Gold, on the other hand, was presented directly to the bride in all communities. The lesser prevalence of gold among the Kuruvas and Pulayas reflects their deep poverty, in the present as well as in the past. Women of all castes told me they had tried to give their daughters some gold when they married, to keep as a reserve for survival in times of hardship and starvation. However, having a bride "covered with gold" has also been a demand of some grooms and their kin. Among the cashew workers, however, the amount of gold involved has hardly been enough to "cover the bride", as it was among higher classes.[52] Gold is not only viewed as a sign of wealth, but

---

[51] In a study of a fishing community in South Tamil Nadu, Kalpana Ram also found that there had been a shift towards a greater amount of cash, but, in contrast to my study, the share of jewelry which women controlled had decreased. Ram, *Mukkuvar Women*, pp. 185 ff.

[52] Most women interviewed had bought gold imitations.

also as an expression of femininity. Three young women of Scheduled Castes had similar attitudes. Sunitha told me the following: "I am sorry, but to us, women like you are a bit masculine because they don't have any gold". "Without jewelry you are not a real woman", Geetha remarked to me. "Gold makes me feel more woman-like, more feminine", said a third woman named Prasantha. Such gold—often only a few grams of it—has frequently been used as something to survive on, for it could be pawned at private money-lenders for usurious loans.[53]

With regard to the question of land, the findings were more complex. Among the Nairs, traditionally a landowning community, a woman's property rights were recognized; transferring land from mother to daughter was common among my interviewees.[54] It was also a common practice among lower castes. Women as property owners had long been a tradition among matrilineal castes. Among all castes in my sample, when land was transferred, it was seen as a pre-mortem inheritance of the daughters. Workers who, irrespective of caste, had given land to their daughters at marriage asserted that any remaining land (commonly the mother's property) would be divided between the sons.

In this instance, the marriage payment must be considered as *stridhanam*, but several cases were reported to me in which the dowry had been paid in cash to the groom, who then used the money to buy land *in his name* or, in some cases, in the name of both spouses. Still, the money was considered by the donors to be a *stridhanam* in the sense of a pre-mortem inheritance, even though it had been secured beyond the reach of the intended heiress.

Geetha, a Pulaya woman born 1973, got a small piece of land from her mother when she was married in 1990. Geetha's brothers will someday inherit the remaining land their mother owns, indicating clearly that Geetha's share is her inheritance from her mother. Her husband, however, has continuously demanded that Geetha's land be transferred to him, as he regards himself the head of the family. The result is incessant conflict, and even violence. Geetha's case does not seem exceptional. During the last two decades, there has been a marked tendency for grooms to assume control of land given as *stridhanam*. In the period 1980-1999, out of eleven cases of marriage payments involving land given as the daughters' *stridhanam*, the land in question was legally owned and controlled by husbands in four cases, by the spouses jointly in three cases, and by the wives in four cases. In my sample, prior to 1980 the land involved in marriage payment was,

---

[53] Between 100% and 600%!
[54] Observations in Kerala in 1991 suggests that dowry has become common among the Nairs, but is given in the bride's name, i.e., a *stridhanam*. Agarwal, *A Field of One's Own*, p. 177.

without exception, owned and controlled by wives. Such land was also more common than cash or gold and should be seen as *stridhanam*—but a *stridhanam* which is currently undergoing a transformation towards the institution of *modern dowry*.[55]

In contrast to den Uyl's study on marriage payment in Kerala, which only found instances of *modern dowry*[56], this investigation shows that *stridhanam* and *modern dowry* occur simultaneously, although the tendency for *stridhanam* to fall into disuse is evident.

Bridegroom price: the legitimacy of dowries

Kalyani's story, which introduced this chapter, illustrates how the demands on the families of the brides to pay a dowry had become more pronounced. Moreover, stories similar to Sunitha's were very common among the cashew workers interviewed. Young women tried to save for their own dowry or their sister's, while mothers and grandmothers worked to earn a dowry for their daughters and granddaughters. Even though most of the women barely earned enough to subsist on, they insisted that "if we don't pay we will not get a *good* husband—so we have to save".[57]

The size of the dowry seems to be dependent on the groom's ability to provide for a family. Education, job-opportunities, wages, home ownership, and health were relevant factors, and some scholars have asserted that it is accurate to call the *modern dowry* a "bridegroom price".[58] As one listens to women speak there appears to be a recurring view of value which legitimizes dowry from the point of view of the donors as well as the receiver.

I married fifteen years ago—in 1982—and my family gave a house and five cents of land as a dowry to my husband. But my husband's family cheated us. After the marriage we realized that he was paralyzed in his legs and, thus, unable to work. Since then I have been the only provider for the family.
—Vasantha, Ezhava woman, born 1964[59]

I married in 1986. My husband had a house and a job driving a rickshaw, so it was all right to pay a dowry. My family gave a house and some land, which is jointly owned by me and my husband. I got some gold. But when I was

---

[55] Madhu Kishwar has pointed out the lack of historical research on the issue of the transformation from *stridhana* to modern dowry. Kishwar, "Dowry Calculations", p. 9.
[56] den Uyl, *Invisible Barriers*, pp. 206-218.
[57] Interview 12 February 1999 with Sandhya, Ezhava woman, born 1978.
[58] Kishwar, "Dowry Calculations ", pp. 8-17; Michael S. Billig, "The Marriage Squeeze on High-Caste Rajasthani Women", *The Journal of Asian Studies*, 50:2 (1991), pp. 341-360.
[59] Interview 14 February 1997.

without a job for a long time in the late 1980s we had to pawn it and we did not redeem it yet.
—Chitra, Nair woman, born 1968[60]

We tried to ask for a dowry when my youngest son was getting married, but we were ridiculed since he had no job and no education. I don't know exactly what year it was, maybe in 1972 or 1973. It was during Achuta Menon's second ministry.
—Kotha, Pulaya woman, born 1919[61]

When my youngest son was married about twenty years ago, we received two cents of land as a dowry. He had a permanent job as a roaster at the Corporation, so we had the right to ask for a dowry.
—Kalyani, Pulaya woman, born 1933[62]

I have been working at the cashew factory for seven years. I was married in 1990. My husband told my brothers that he was a lorry-driver and that he had a job. My family did not inquire about this man. If they would have done that, maybe my life would not have been such a misery. My mother stopped working in order to get her pension for my dowry. We bought this land, which is in my name, but I have a lot of problems with my husband, because he wants us to sell the land and buy some new land in his name. He got a lot of cash when we married, but he wants more. There are so many quarrels and so much violence because of this. In this country people should not live like this, and all this happens because the men are not looking after their obligations. But I will not give the house to him. I have to think of my children.
—Geetha, Pulaya woman, born 1973[63]

I have been working in the grading section for six years. I am not married, because all proposals were cancelled since we did not have money for a dowry. I am trying to save for my dowry, but it is difficult. My parents are sick, so I have to provide for them. Everybody wants to get married, but no dowry, no marriage—at least not with a decent man who provides for his family. That is the truth and my faith.
—Renuka, Nair woman, born 1978[64]

Dowry, as conceived by the women I interviewed, has obviously been legitimized by the prospective husband's ability to provide for his family. How-

---

[60] Interview 23 August 1998.
[61] Interview 16 August 1998.
[62] Interview 19 December 1997.
[63] Interview 18 January 1998.
[64] Interview 14 February 1999.

ever, the opinion was also expressed that a dowry should be a pre-mortem inheritance for women. Obvious confusion and in some cases struggles over resources are still going on.

Marriage dowries have often led to severe conflicts and overt violence; many cases of suicide and murder as a result of dowry conflicts have been reported in India.[65] However, Madhu Kishwar questions whether dowry is the only reason for conflict, violence, and divorce, or if it is not often used to legitimate an argument.[66]

Cross-cousin marriages were prevalent among Nairs, Ezhavas, Pulayas, and Kuravas during the time the interviews were conducted, although marriage within the kinship circle has become less common than in earlier days. According to Srinivas, cross-cousin marriages reinforced the status symmetry between the families and was a motive for not paying a dowry.[67] However, the status asymmetry which is based on gender (with the family of the bride being inferior to the family of the bridegroom) must not be lost sight of, as *modern dowry* has also been demanded in cross-cousin marriages in recent times, as illustrated by the two women below:

> There was no dowry when I got married since he was my cousin, but nowadays boys ask for dowries even when they are your own cousin, at least if they have a job and a house. That was what happened to my granddaughter.
> —Kalyani, Pulaya woman, born 1933[68]

> In 1972, my uncle arranged the marriage for me with his son. He is my cousin, so there was no dowry, but actually my uncle asked for 3,000 Rupees as a dowry—but my grandparents prevented that. They said that cousins should get married without dowries. Today I hear of dowries even when the boy and girl are cousins, and sometimes even in love-marriages.
> —Sarojini, Pulaya woman, born 1954[69]

---

[65] Miranda Davies, "Indian Women Speak Out Against Dowry", in Davies, M. (ed.), *Third World—Second Sex: Women's Struggles and National Liberalism. Third World Women Speak Out* (London, 1983), pp. 201-213; Kumar, *The History of Doing*, pp. 115 ff; Srinivas, *Village, Caste, Gender*, pp. 178 ff.; Julia Leslie, "Dowry, Dowry Deaths and Violence Against Women", in Enrica Garzilli (ed.), *Journal of South Asian Women Studies 1995-1997* (Milano, 1997), pp. 135-143.; Himendra Thakur, "Preface", in Werner Menski (ed.), *South Asians and the Dowry Problem* (New Delhi, 1998), pp. xiii-xxi. See also the on-line *Journal of South Asia Women's Studies*, www.asiatica/org.

[66] Kishwar, *Off the Beaten Track*, p. 15.

[67] Srinivas, *Village, Caste, Gender*, p. 160.

[68] Interview 14 January 1997.

[69] Interview 14 February 1997. .

In the mid-1970s, in a study of Nairs, J. Puthenkalam observed a decline in the custom of cross-cousin marriages and interpreted this as an outcome of the young men's ability to demand a dowry—a demand which was too delicate to bring forward to an uncle.[70] My informants all witnessed the decline of this custom, though it was not totally abandoned.

The question of the legitimization of *modern dowry*, irrespective of caste, among the donor families seems to be connected to survival and economic strategies: even their wish to increase their status is economic, not ritual or cultural. To pay a dowry is an effort to achieve a better economic situation for the daughters, that is to say, it is a question of class mobility. Efforts to rise in the class hierarchy have seldom materialized among the interviewees, but paying a dowry has nonetheless become a conscious strategy and the means of fulfilling a hope for a brighter future for their daughters. This may also explain my having found fewer cases of marriages where a dowry had been received than instances where one was paid. Many of the interviewees were too poor to ask for a dowry when their sons were getting married: just to present oneself as a bridegroom was not enough to occasion the request for a dowry. The ability to provide for a family must be there, too. Thus the status asymmetry between families based on gender is supplemented by that of class.

To call the process of taking over marriage customs from higher castes "Sanskritization" would be misleading because it is not part of a wider cultural emulation of Brahmins or other high castes. Among the women I interviewed, I did not discover cultural borrowings from the Brahmins or other high castes concerning food or drink. Although we may speak of a Sanskritization process in the early years of the twentieth century with regard to religious customs, we cannot do so when it comes to modern dowry.[71]

Neither Pulayas, Kuravas, Ezhavas, nor Nairs have become vegetarians. According to their own words, they have increased their consumption of meat (including beef) compared to 1930 and 1940 levels, in consequence of better economic circumstances. Contrary to their tradition, I found Nairs eating beef, something also observed by Alexander in 1968, a phenomenon which he interpreted as a result of Westernization and secularization.[72]

With regard to drinking habits, being "Sanskritized" would require abstention from alcohol, but the pattern I found was quite different. In every family interviewed, the male members usually drank alcohol, although the

---

[70] Puthenkalam, *Marriage and the Family in Kerala*, p. 93.
[71] For a discussion of this process among Ezhavas, see Rao, *Social Change in Malabar*. For Pulayas, see Alexander, *Social Mobility in Kerala*.
[72] Alexander, *Social Mobility in Kerala*, p. 68.

females had *ceased* to do so. Some old women of the lowest castes would still consume small quantities of liquor, but it was seen as extremely masculine among younger women of Scheduled Castes. Habits taken over from higher castes thus seem to be selective and highly gendered.

The practice of dowry has had great economic implications. Certainly, the introduction of this custom has changed the gender relations of power to the disadvantage of women. The social pressure behind adjusting to a new gender ideology (for men and for women) has shown itself to be extremely hard. This pressure emanates from the strengthening of patriarchal relations, i.e., increased male power over women. The demand for a dowry has been a male strategy for achieving power in the family—either power lost through unemployment, or taking upon oneself a power that was always limited, as in the cases of the lower castes. The emerging gender ideology declared men to have the power of being breadwinners—an ideal which was difficult to actualize.

Since the late 1960s Kerala has suffered from a severe economic crisis. Factories have commonly relocated to neighboring states. The period since 1960 has been characterized by steadily growing unemployment[73], not only among female cashew workers, but equally among male members of their families, most of whom worked in agriculture or did other casual work.[74] Geetha's unemployed husband, who had to ask Geetha for money, and whose job was mainly to look after the small plot Geetha received as a *stridhanam* from her mother, sought to rescue his honor and masculinity by trying to be a land-owner, which was probably his reason for insisting that Geetha's land be either transferred to him, or sold and new land bought in his name.

---

[73] Pillai, *Kerala Economy*, pp. 166 ff.; M.A. Oommen, *Essays on Kerala Economy* (New Delhi, 1993), pp. 106 ff.; E.T. Mathew, *Employment and Unemployment in Kerala: Some Neglected Aspects* (New Delhi, 1997).
[74] The 1960s and 1970s were not only decades of unemployment—they were also the decades when the labor emigration from Kerala to the Gulf countries took on great proportions, and the remittances from those countries grew. It has been estimated that about 500,000 Keralites worked in the Gulf during the 1980s. Most of them were young, uneducated, previously unemployed men from the coastal areas of Kerala. In the late 1990s, this figure rose to more than one million. It is likely that the capital inflow from these workers facilitated both the demand for and the payment of dowries, but it was, of course not, the basic reason for the increasing occurrence of *modern dowry*. See P.R. Gopinathan Nair, "Migration of Keralites to the Arab World", in Prakash (ed.), *Kerala's Economy*, pp. 104-105. In 1998 an estimated 1.17 to 1.55 million Keralites had migrated, of whom 95% were in Gulf countries. K.C. Zachariah, E.T. Mathew, and S. Irudaya Rajan, "Migration in Kerala State India: Dimensions, Determinants and Consequences" (Working Paper I, Centre for Development Studies, Trivandrum, September 1999).

Earned welfare benefits turn into dowries

The dowry system is part of a social system of transferring resources from women to men. Women who were gainfully employed lost the property they had purchased. Property assigned to them through land reforms often slipped out of their hands, as well. During the last two or three decades, it has been the strategy of many female workers to sell such land to finance the marriage of a daughter. Welfare benefits, like the pension from the Gratuity Fund (see Chapter VII) which women receive for having worked a lifetime, have in many cases been turned into a dowry, as illustrated by the stories of the two women below:

> I worked in the cashew factory for many years. I started to work when I was sixteen years old. Two years later I was married, and it was my one and only brother who got me married because my parents were dead. My brother did not have anything to give as a dowry, but there was no custom of dowry at that time, anyhow. My husband died more than twenty years ago, and since then it has been much more difficult for me. He was a casual laborer, and even if he could not get work regularly, his income, just like mine, was necessary for the survival of the family.
>
> I had seven children, six girls and one boy. One daughter died as a child (it was TB) but all my other daughters are working in the cashew factories and all of them are married. My first daughter was married thirty years ago, but no dowry was asked for her, so we did not give anything. The next daughter was married twenty-two years ago and there was no dowry because we did not have anything to give. She suffers so much because of that and her husband treats her very badly. If we don't give dowry now it will cause us so much sorrow. The men will be ridiculed, the girls will be harassed and the parents will feel very bad. My daughter's situation is very pitiable, but I can't give him [the daughter's husband] anything. I don't *have* anything!
>
> My next daughter married in a love-marriage, so there was no dowry. He belonged to the same *jati*, but he left her. He is gone, so she has a lot of problems, just like my other daughter. When my next daughter was going to be married, I had to pay a dowry. To get the money required I retired early and got a lump sum of money as a pension. With that money I got my daughter married. The money was given to her husband and he bought a small piece of land.
>
> When my youngest daughter was going to be married eight years ago, it was difficult. About twenty years ago I got a house and a small plot of land from the government. I sold it to get my last daughter married. Without a

dowry, how can you marry today? The money was given to her husband, but he demanded 2,000 rupees more, so I had to borrow that money. So I was in debt and had nowhere to live, but we must have our children married—I had no choice.

After that I came to live with my son for a while, but he lives with his wife's parents—I was living there against their will, so I had to leave. We wanted to ask for a dowry when my son was getting married, but how could we get something when he has no job and hardly any education? Now I stay in my daughter's house, but it is a big problem with her husband. He doesn't want me there. I don't know what to do. I have no pension, and it is difficult for me to work, but I work in the cottages with shelling whenever I can. The wages are bad in the cottages and I am too sick and too old to work. Sometimes I eat, sometimes not.
—Masis Ally, Pulaya woman born 1935[75]

When my daughter was going to marry, it was difficult. Our relatives brought a proposal and it seemed as if that man was educated and had a job. He demanded so much dowry and I told him that I will give land worth 25,000 rupees, 6,000 rupees in cash, and five sovereigns of gold. This was six years ago. To get the money I resigned from the cashew-nut factory and I got a nice sum as a pension, 2,000 rupees. The rest I borrowed. Now I work in another factory, but I am not a registered worker. The property was bought in my daughter's name, but her husband tried to persuade us to put it in his name. When I die my sons will inherit this property where I live now, but not my daughter, because she had her part already.
—Sarojini, Pulaya woman born 1954[76]

These two stories highlight the common practice of using hard-earned welfare benefits to "marry off" daughters and granddaughters. The famous land reforms of Kerala, in which resources were redistributed to attain a more egalitarian society[77], have only meant a temporary security of owning their own dwelling and some land for Masis Ally and many other cashew workers like her. At her advanced age, Masis Ally still has nowhere to live and no pension to live on. It seems to have become a strategy among poor cashew workers to withdraw from their formal workplace prior to the age of retirement, so that they can collect their

[75] Interview 20 December 1997.
[76] Interview 14 February 1999.
[77] For accounts of the land reforms see, for example, Oommen, *Essays on Kerala Economy*, pp. 1–22; A. Balakrishnan Nair, *The Government and Politics of Kerala* (Trivandrum, 1994), pp. 325 ff.; Franke, *Life is a Little Better*, pp. 121 ff; Jeffrey, *Politics, Women and Well Being*, pp. 160-185.

accumulated savings in the Gratuity Fund and then start working in the informal sector. Thus, the primary aim of the fund, to be a means of support for workers as they grow old, is defeated. Masis Ally and Sarojini were not the only women who had used this fund to finance a dowry, nor was Masis Ally the only one who had sold the land which she had obtained through land reform. We saw that Kalyani, too, sold the house which she had gotten through land reform in order to get her daughter married.[78] Among the forty-five workers interviewed, I found five cases of early retirement, and seven where, within the last two decades, cashew workers had sold the house and land which they had gotten in consequence of land reform. Their purpose was to convert everything they could into cash for dowries.

To "marry off" one's children is a most significant parental duty. For many of the cashew workers, it has been the duty of the mother. Welfare benefits, whether obtained in the form of land, a house from the Government, or from earnings in the Gratuity Fund, were commonly transferred from women to men.[79] Prior to 1970, most poor workers owned neither land nor the houses they lived in—nor did they have any security at work. Many of them, especially among the Scheduled Castes, are still landless and many have never become registered workers. Among those who have, however, it is ironic that when they had finally achieved some resources and a little security, they lost it again.

Not only is their dwelling no longer theirs, but they have also been forced from their formal position at work (as a registered worker) into the informal factories. Thus, in their old age many women loose the little security they have achieved and they continue to work without an attendance card, at lower wages, and without such benefits as sick leave and paid holidays.

In the 1930s the system of joint families was still prevalent among many communities in Travancore. It has gradually lost its significance and, in its place, the ideology of a nuclear family has achieved dominance.[80] During the following two decades the nuclear family seems to have been the ideal, but for economic reasons many parents and married children continued to live together—perhaps with separate finances, but still sharing a house. The joint family system had prevailed in the not too

---

[78] See the introduction to this chapter.
[79] A similar transference of resources from women to men has been observed among fishing communities in Tamil Nadu. See Ram, *Mukkuvar Women*, pp. 192-193.
[80] Joint families have been most prevalent among Nairs and Brahmins. Alexander has stated that Pulayas most often lived in nuclear families. See Alexander, *Social Mobility in Kerala*, pp. 129-130. However, according to my informants, joint families or extended nuclear families were common in the 1930s among Pulayas, Kuravas, and Ezhavas, as well.

distant past, and so it was relatively easy to motivate children to care for their parents. Today the nuclear family may not be a reality for poor people, since they often live in extended nuclear families, although as an ideal it is very strong. It is no longer a matter of course for married children to stay together with their parents, and this seems to be a source of conflict for many poor cashew workers. Very often in-laws eject an old parent from the nuclear family, and several of the old female workers I have interviewed, like Masis Ally, have had to move from one son or daughter to the next several times. The rapid transformation of family ideologies has left people in a state of confusion, something which is reflected in the question of whose responsibility it is to take care of aged parents.[81]

Inter-caste marriages and love-marriages

Today many people in Kerala would call inter-caste marriages, love-marriages[82], and divorces "modern"—or often, in the case of love-marriages and divorces, "Western".[83] It may be noted that a love-marriage is usually looked upon as a marriage without a dowry. Many of my interviewees responded along the following lines: "Nowadays people marry out of love, and inter-caste marriages are very common. Young people go away and marry anyone!". However, this was not what I found, for when I asked mothers if they could imagine their son or daughter marrying a lower caste person, the answer in more than ninety percent of the cases was a resounding "no!". The few inter-caste marriages parents had approved occurred in families closely affiliated with one of the leftist parties. They all claimed that caste was a "pre-modern system" and that only class continued to have relevance in Kerala today:

> I am a communist, and in my opinion caste is nonsense and belongs to the past! Now we concentrate on class struggle. Both my daughters have married into other castes. One girl is married to a Christian, the other to a Pulaya. In a way, they were arranged marriages because I was the one who suggested their husbands, but in both cases I knew that it was their wish.
> —Velu, Kurava man, born 1923[84]

---

[81] See also Leela Gulati, *Economic and Social Aspects of Population Ageing in Kerala, India* (New York, 1992), pp. 35-37.
[82] A love-marriage is defined as a marriage which is initiated by the couple themselves, i.e., not arranged by parents or other relatives.
[83] This statement is based on conversations with a number of different people, mainly from the English-speaking middle class in Trivandrum and Quilon.
[84] Interview 20 December 1997.

With few exceptions, the principle of caste endogamy in marriage has remained in place over the years. I did not find many inter-caste marriages during the entire period from 1930 to the present. It seems as if a language of leftist politics, which denies the importance of caste, has evolved. But it is mainly rhetorical since so few—including political leaders at high levels—seem to live in accordance with it. Among 506 marriages surveyed, I found only eight cases of inter-caste marriage. With only two exceptions, they all were between spouses from Scheduled Castes—mostly between Kuravas and Pulayas. One of the exceptions I found was a love-marriage between a Nair girl and a Pulaya boy. The girl, Nalini, as well as her mother, was a sheller, and her husband, Appu, was, like most other husbands of the cashew workers, a casual laborer who mainly did agricultural work, as did Nalini's father. Thus, there was no decline in economic status in the case of Nalini. They married in 1990. I met the couple several times, and it seemed to be a rather happy marriage, although beset by two major problems: extreme poverty and the fact that Nalini's family refused to accept the marriage. They refused to see the couple or their children, or touch a "dirty Pulaya child". This may have been an extreme case, but many young women held the view that they should marry the person their parents chose or face serious problems. Parents' choices seldom crossed caste barriers.

Another case of inter-caste marriage was a Christian woman, Meera, and a Pulaya man. Meera had problems with her alcoholic husband, but could get no help from her family since, according to them, "she had chosen to disobey and give shame to the family". She was expelled, not only from the circle of her family, but also from the church.

> Sometimes my husband is very violent. I can't get any help, because it was a love-marriage. My parents disapproved of the marriage and so did my other relatives and the church. There is no one to help me. It is difficult, but I must go on. I don't want to think of the future when my daughters are to be married. If I don't pay dowries they will end up like me. I try to save money, but we do not even have rice enough. I pray to God!
> —Meera, Christian woman born 1967[85]

In two other cases of inter-caste marriages which took place against the wishes of the parents, I was told by the parents that they refused to see their daughters at first, but reconciled after some time. "After all, I love my daughter", Chamally explained to me, "so why should I make it even more difficult for her?"[86]

It did not seem as if the women I interviewed insisted on arranging

---

[85] Interview 16 January 1998.
[86] Interview 25 August 1998 with Chamally, woman of Ezhava caste, whose daughter eloped and married a Pulaya man.

their daughters' marriages in order to control them, but to secure their future happiness, as expressed by the Pulaya woman below:

> I want only the best for my daughter, and the best for her is a good husband and a sustainable relationship, but I would never suggest a husband whom she opposed. I cannot go to another caste or community and suggest a marriage between a man there and my daughter. That is just not possible. So she will marry a Pulaya man.
>
> —Lalitha, Pulaya woman, born 1958[87]

Most people I spoke with considered an arranged, inter-caste marriage an impossibility. Different castes working side-by-side (although caste barriers still are visible at the factories), striking and demonstrating together, and helping each other as neighbors, are all situations that have become familiar with time, but when it comes to marriage, caste remains a persistent issue. The essence of caste in contemporary Kerala seems to rest mainly on endogamous families.[88] We recall in Chapter V that most women interviewed described other castes as different from their own. In some cases the dissimilarity was linked to the traditional ritual hierarchy, but often other castes were simply spoken of as having different cultural habits. Such a view has similarities with the way different *ethnic* groups describe each other and refrain from inter-marriages with other ethnic groups.[89]

The specific concept of love-marriage was not commonly used in the early twentieth century, but the loose bonds between spouses and the frequency of divorces and remarriages (especially among the lowest castes) suggest that not all marriages were arranged.[90] This was confirmed by several old Kuravas and Pulayas, who asserted that people in their caste had been quite free to marry whomever they wished. Den Uyl, however, states

---

[87] Interview 31 January 1998.
[88] This view is basically a criticism of Dumont's perspective that the essence of caste lies in the ritual hierarchy ordered in relative purity. For authors who have stressed the importance of endogamous families, see Dipankar Gupta, "Continuous Hierarchies and Discrete Castes", *Economic and Political Weekly*, 19:46-48 (1984), pp. 1955-1958; G.S. Ghurye, *Caste and Class in India* (Bombay, 1957); and G.S. Ghurye, *Caste and Race in India* (Bombay, 1969).
[89] In the 1930s and 1940s, some scholars compared race in United States with caste. André Béteille has later argued that caste identity in contemporary India has several similarities with ethnic identity, especially with regard to stress on cultural diversity. André Béteille, *Society and Politics in India*, pp. 37-56. Béteille has also highlighted the interesting similarity between white men's concern for the purity of their own women while themselves having access to women of color, and high-caste men's like concern for their women and their right to sexual access to women of lower caste. Ibid., pp. 20-26.
[90] Alexander, *Social Mobility in Kerala*, p. 130.

that in the Sakthikulangara colony, near Quilon, "love-marriages were the exception to the rule until the 1960s, after which they became more common. In the 70s, roughly a quarter of the weddings were decided on the basis of individual choice".[91] But in the material which she presents, we find that, prior to 1940, four out of eleven marriages were love-marriages,[92] which is remarkable even if the sample is extremely small. It seems, rather, that between 1940 and 1970, love-marriages were more rare than before and after those years. Unfortunately, den Uyl, gives no information on the prevalence of love-marriages after 1979.

Throughout my interviews, I found that respect for the wishes of the parents was extremely pronounced, but also respect for the wishes of the children. My interviewees mostly defined love-marriage as a marriage in which the couple knew each other previously and themselves initiated the marriage, although it was sometimes difficult to distinguish between arranged marriages and love-marriages. There were love-marriages with the consent of the parents, and arranged marriages with the consent of the bride and the groom—which makes it is difficult to strictly classify such marriages. Madhu Kishwar has argued that many so-called love-marriages in the West are virtually 'self-arranged' marriages. She has also opposed what she calls the Western myth that arranged marriages are a main reason for Indian women's oppression, and that love-marriages are superior because they are built on mutual, romantic love. In the long-run, the differences between the two types of marriage may be less pronounced than one may imagine at the outset.[93]

Within the limitations described above, the data indicates that there has been a decrease in love-marriages among cashew workers since the 1970s.

Table 8.7. Percentage of love-marriages among cashew workers of different communities, 1930-1999

	90-99	80-89	70-79	60-69	50-59	40-49	30-39
SC	12	11	26	8	9	12	16
MC	5	8	15	9	3	4	4
HC	3	6	12	6	4	3	5

SC: Scheduled Castes MC: Middle Castes (mainly Ezhavas) HC: Higher Castes (mainly Nairs)

Due to the difficulties in classifying the marriages, the above figures can only be an approximation. One may with caution conclude that love-marriages peaked among all castes in the 1970s. The lowest castes show a high-

[91] den Uyl, *Invisible Barriers*, p. 204.
[92] Ibid., p. 290, tables 26 and 27.
[93] Kishwar, *Off the Beaten Track*, pp. 192-208.

er degree of love-marriages prior to 1950. The recent decrease in love-marriages may be interpreted as a consequence of the growing demand for *modern dowries*, since a love-marriage does not entitle one to claim a dowry.

Many of the interviewees were of the opinion that women preferred love-marriages, while men favored arranged marriages, but the women interviewed also asserted that they feared love-marriages because they would be left alone in the case of serious marriage problems. Many of the love-marriages had ended in divorce or separation, and it was widely felt that an arranged married guaranteed stability. Stability, i.e., a long-lasting marriage, has become the ideal, although hardly the reality.

The conflicting processes of Sanskritization versus "modernization" or "Westernization" are gender-bound—at least when we speak about marriage. A preference for arranged marriages may reflect the ability to demand a dowry, so that perhaps "modernization" is here curbed by a strengthening of male interests. Anthony Giddens has shown that romantic love in pre-industrial Europe was seen as feminine, and virtually in conflict with the prevailing ideology of masculinity.[94] In Kerala, it seems as if a new ideology of masculinity has emerged—one which rejects love-marriages and puts a price upon a man's capacity to maintain a family. The new masculinity even seems to be strong enough to challenge the view that love-marriages cannot involve dowries. I had been told of such cases, and in den Uyl's study a dowry had, in fact, been given to the groom in eight of eighteen love-marriages.[95]

Unstable marriage patterns and divorces

During the monsoon in Kundara in 1945, just outside the city of Quilon, a twenty-five-year-old Pulaya woman called Nani was fatally injured while working at the cashew factory of Myrtheen Kunju. Nani, who had worked there for the past eleven years, was a sheller. On the 9th of June a cyclone had hit the thatched shed in which she and her friends were shelling cashews, killing Nani and injuring fourteen of her friends. The circumstances entitled Nani's heirs to compensation under the Workmen's Compensation Act. Nani had been the main earner of her family. She lived together with her mother, her younger brother (who was fifteen at the time of the accident), and her second husband, whom she had recently married. A few years before, her child from an earlier marriage had died. The father of the child, Nani's legal (or perhaps illegal) former husband, was not living in Nani's house when the accident occurred. Her present husband, a part-time coolie worker of Pulaya caste, had lived with Nani for only a short

---

[94] Anthony Giddens, *The Transformation of Intimacy* (Cambridge, 1992), p. 43.
[95] den Uyl, *Invisible Barriers*, p. 204, note 8.

time. The civil servant who wrote the official report found the fact of Nani's divorce and remarriage worthy of comment, probably because it contrasted with the norm of stable families and the absence of divorces in his own (higher) caste and class.[96]

Two aspects of Nani's situation deserve special comment. The fact that she lived in her mother's house (or perhaps it was her own) reflects the matrilineal system of the Nairs. The father of her child having left indicates a rather loose marriage tie. Nani and her mother appear to represent the stability in the family. In many parts of India, divorce—and especially the remarriage of a woman—would have been impossible in the 1940s, and so it remains among some communities in India today. Among the lowest castes, however, divorce was common in those days.[97]

The process of Sanskritization would include a development toward stigmatization of divorce and more stable bonds between husband and wife. Several studies highlight this shift among former matrilineal castes during the last half century.[98] Such a process reflects stronger control by men over female sexuality.

It is likely that the proportion of divorced women has been higher among cashew workers than in society in general. Among the cashew workers of Kerala, it has fluctuated between 7% and 13% during the period 1960-1998, a figure which is considerably higher than for the total population.[99] These statistics reflect the status quo at the time when the study was conducted at the factory. If one were to analyze the number of women which had been divorced and remarried in earlier years, the figures might have been even greater.

I found a very high percentage of divorces, remarriages, and also remarriages of widows among the Pulayas and Kuruvas, and less among the Ezhavas and Nairs. During the last sixty years, about 35% of the Pulaya and Kurava women in my sample can be placed in the category "unstable marriages", indicating a carry-over from the past, when divorce and remarriage seem to have been much more prevalent. Family situations similar to that of Nani were still quite common among Pulayas and Kuravas I inter-

---

[96] KSA, Development Files 338/1950. Letter from the Inspector of Factories, Quilon to Director of Industries, dated June 1945.
[97] Govt. of India, *Census of India 1931*, Vol. XXVIII, Travancore, Part I, Report, p. 385.
[98] Alexander, *Social Mobility in Kerala*; Puthenkalam, *Marriage and the Family in Kerala*; den Uyl, *Invisible Barriers*.
[99] Sarojini, "A Study of the Working and Living Conditions of the Women Workers in the Cashew Factories"; Thrivikraman, "Influence of Political Parties on Trade Unions in Jupiter Cashew Factory"; Nair and Varghese, "Report on Women Workers in the Cashew Industry in Kerala"; Nair and Thomas, "Socio-Economic Conditions of Working Women in Cashew Industry in Quilon District, Kerala"; Deepa, "Industrial Crisis and Women Workers".

viewed, although no longer considered "normal". However, the social stigma of divorce was seen as less of a burden today than in the 1950s and 1960s. As in the case of love-marriages, this may be interpreted as a sign of "modernity". But in the early twentieth century, there was no loss of social status with divorce, neither for men nor women of a lower caste, and either party could initiate the divorce.[100] Today, the question of who initiates the divorce seemed of great importance to those I interviewed. All divorces were initiated by the husbands. The reason, according to my informants, had to do with respectability. Geetha, a Pulaya woman, re-counted:

> My husband is hardly ever home. I know that he has mistresses. He treats me badly and even beats me, and he does not contribute financially to my or our children's maintenance. In fact, I provide for him! But I don't want to ask for a divorce, because it will put me in an unfavorable position. People around will put the blame on me. But sooner or later he will leave me. I'll wait for that—then people will not accuse me. It is a matter of respect.
> —Geetha, Pulaya woman, born 1973, sheller[101]

A woman who does not fulfil her obligations as a wife and mother is looked upon with disdain and disrespect, whereas an abandoned woman is pitied. Geetha (and other women in similar situations) chose to remain silent, adapt to the situation, and wait until her husband leaves. The fate of being looked upon as a bad wife and mother is considered worse than silent suffering. The tendency in all cases of divorce that I encountered was for small children to remain with the mother, while of children above the age of twelve, only the daughters stayed with their mothers. In such cases, the mother was left to deal with the problem of "marrying off" her daughter alone, and finding a way to accumulate a dowry for her.

In the early twentieth century, divorces were frequent among lower, formerly matrilineal castes, and were explained in terms of "old (i.e., uncivilized) traditions". As such, they were rejected by social reformers in Travancore. Today, most often among the English-speaking middle class, such practices are explained as "evils of the West". An everlasting marriage was seen as an ideal among my interviewees, and one way to assure such a marriage was considered to be the payment of a dowry. Several women gave similar views on the link between divorce and dowry:

---

[100] Alexander, *Social Mobility*, p. 130.
[101] Interview 20 February 1999.

I was married five years ago and my parents paid 3,000 rupees to my husband. He left after a short while because he said the dowry was not enough. It will be very difficult for me to remarry. How can I ever get money for a dowry? I work every day, but it is hardly even enough for food.
—Sandhya, Ezhava woman, born 1972, peeler[102]

We were married fifteen years ago. It was a love-marriage, but he left me after two years. Suddenly I was alone with two babies. We were happy in the beginning, but since he did not get any dowry, he just left for another woman.
—Meera, Pulaya woman, born 1972, sheller[103]

I work in the grading section and I have been here for the last thirty years. My husband has a tea shop, but his income is not very big. We have four daughters. For the last two, we gave dowries. They got five cents of land and three or four sovereigns of gold each, and some cash. The land was given in the name of the girl and the boy together. The cash, 2,000 rupees, was given to the boys. The other two husbands left my daughters—both of them because they did not get any dowry.
—Asryamma, Nair woman, born 1939, packer[104]

In fact, almost every divorce occurring during the last twenty years that my interviewees told me of was linked by them to the absence of a *modern dowry*. Although this may represent the good reason but not the real reason for the divorce, the intention when paying a dowry to the groom is clear: not only to secure a viable male breadwinner, but also to insure a stable, everlasting marriage.

The importance of marriage, motherhood, and work

Among those I interviewed, I found that being a wife and a mother was an essential part of a woman's identity, irrespective of caste affiliation. The few women I met who were without children were viewed by others to have suffered a very tragic fate. We recall Kavitha's words: "A life with no children is no life at all". Most of the women I spoke with expressed similar attitudes. A very commonly heard expression was: "We must marry off our daughters". The social pressure also seemed to be strong. "If we don't marry, people will make fun of us".[105] For the women interviewed, it seems that life without being married and having children is unthinkable.

---

[102] Interview 23 February 1998.
[103] Interview 21 August 1998.
[104] Interview 13 December 1999.
[105] Interview 29 August 1998 Lalitha, Pulaya woman, born 1958.

Early in the twentieth century, when a woman from among former agricultural slaves got married, it was crucial what kind of conditions her future husband labored under. If her intended's landlord was a good employer, with enough fertile land, she would be able to find work there as well. It was also of importance to find a husband with plenty of job prospects.[106] A man, in turn, sought a woman who was a capable worker, since both of them were then expected to bear the responsibility of maintaining the family. When there was a lack of work for the men, the women were expected to support the children—reinforcing the need to have chosen a strong, healthy spouse.[107] Low-caste men enjoyed a great degree of freedom within their families, in the sense that they could come and go, not being solely responsible for the family's upkeep. This was how girls and boys among the lower castes were socialized; their parents', ideal of finding someone who was a good worker reverberates for many years. But the way their parents acted came into collision with another ideology of what makes a "good husband" and a "good wife", namely, the notion of a male breadwinner who maintains the family unaided by the housewife. "If we don't pay, we will not get a good husband," lamented Sarojini, a Pulaya woman born in 1954. What she meant was a husband who by himself took full responsibility for his family. This meaning of "a good husband", expressed in the 1990s, contrasted with the same expression as used by earlier generations of Pulayas and Kuruvas, who were referring to a husband who could supply good working conditions and work opportunities for his wife.

The new family role imposed on men conflicted with the rather free life they had seen other men of the community live, i.e., the kind of life they had been socialized into from childhood. In the 1930s and 1940s, it was a matter of course for Kavitha's parents and other Kuravas and Pulayas to take for granted that every family member needed to work for survival. The burden on each was extreme, and yet in all of this hardship gender relations were more equal then in later historical settings. Kavitha and her husband held the same ideology as their parents, but gradually the new family norm of a male breadwinner spread and now encompasses the lowest castes as well. Kavitha's granddaughter, Ajitha, is a housewife, even though the material conditions of the family are such that they barely can afford for her to stay at home. She, her husband, and their children live in an illegally-built, small hut without water, outhouse, or electricity on so-

---

[106] Interview 19 December 1997 with K. Bhanu, former journalist in Kilikolloor, born 1913; Interview 31 January 1999 with Kotha, Pulaya woman, born 1919. The same observation was made in 1961 in a village survey which included interviews. See Govt. of India, *Census of India 1961*, Vol. VIII, p. 92.

[107] Alexander, *Social Mobility in Kerala*, p. 133.

called *purampokke land*.[108] For Ajitha, the hegemonic ideology has imposed itself on reality, and she also has been encouraged to stay at home due to her husband's assertion that he was in position to provide for a family. "After marriage, he told me not to work", she stated simply, "and since I married him, I have to listen to what he says".[109]

As we have seen in Chapter VI, the ideal family norm has seldom become a reality among female cashew workers. The majority of women interviewed were not living in a family with a male breadwinner and considered themselves anomalies in their present role. "It ought to be the husband who provides for the family, but in my case it is the other way round", said Geetha. Similar utterances were heard from many young cashew workers.

Several cashew workers strongly preferred to have paid work than be a housewife. I asked if they would change their mind if economic conditions let them, that is, if they had a husband who could provide for them and their children. Of the 130 women interviewed, their answers did not reveal any difference on a caste basis, but a divergence was noted between generations. The preference for factory work was only heard from individuals over thirty-five, but they were quite unanimous, and their reason most commonly had to do with economic freedom. "No, I like to have my own money. I know I can manage." "I don't trust my husband to provide for me. I want the freedom that I get when I receive my wages." "I want more work—not less, because it gives me freedom." These were the most common replies, but a few of the women added that their friendship with co-workers strengthened their will to keep on with their factory work. Some of the women expressed the view that they would feel bored staying at home all the time. In other respects, economic coercion has been decisive. The overwhelming affirmation of factory work held by this group, in spite of their awareness of its exploitative nature, seems to be the expression of some kind of power. Factory work has given them a measure of self-confidence: many of them have been able to provide for themselves and their children, in contrast to the dominant ideology of femininity and the view of women as housewives. The contesting of this ideology coincides with the way lower caste women have been socialized by their mothers and grandmothers, who have worked outside the household all their lives. Strangely enough, the same women, when asked about what they wished for their daughters' or granddaughters' futures, were firm in declaring that the best option for a woman would be to become a housewife. Sumathai's opinion

---

[108] Literally, *purampokke* means "outside land", i.e., land that is not owned by anyone. In practice, state-owned land close to rivers, roads, and railroads use to be labeled *purampokke*. The inhabitants of *purampokke* are well aware of their lack of legal standing, and of the fact that their dwellings may be removed at any time.

[109] Interview 7 February 1999.

regarding her daughter's future may stand for the majority of the women with daughters in their upper teens:

> I have made the best of my position in life. I am a factory worker. I have been able to provide for myself and my children. I do not complain and do not wish to change my life, but this is my destiny, and I wish a better life for my daughter. The most important thing is to have her married properly, and I wish her to become a housewife.
> —Sumathai, Kuruva woman, born 1964, sheller[110]

I also encountered women who had left the factory because they aspired to greater upward social mobility as a housewife. In the case of Kavitha's granddaughter, Ajitha, although she lived in poverty, she preferred being a housewife, declaring that it was unnecessary for her to work since her husband could bring home enough food for her and their two children. She did not have the desire to improve her family's economic status by contributing financially through factory work and, in fact, she had only worked outside the home for a very short period of time prior to her marriage. For her it was a matter of class status and pride that her husband was "a good man, who fulfilled his duties". Her attitude echoes the sentiment of other women I met below the age of thirty who, with very few exceptions, expressed their desire to leave the cashew factories and become housewives. This may be related to their position in the life cycle, i.e., having small children.

On the other hand, a few exceptional women who did not live in abject poverty did keep working in the factory. Gomathi's daughters, in spite of living in a well-equipped house with a telephone, toilet, and items brought back by Gomathi's son-in-law from Saudi Arabia where he had worked for the last eight years, continued at the factory. The difference in attitude between Kavitha's granddaughter and Gomathi's daughter seems to be not only their faith in their husbands' ability to maintain their family, but rests also on their own self-confidence and desire to have an income of their own. To a great extent, their experience as factory workers has made a few women reject the dominant gender ideology and even describe themselves as poor, *but independent and modern.*

Many women showed considerable ability in handling money, cultivating land, building houses, finding alternative sources of income, negotiating marriages, or participating in classes given by political parties on Sundays. The imposition of a gender ideology which posits women as housewives has not totally impacted all women in the cashew factories. Those

---

[110] Interview 12 February 1999.

individuals who were exceptions all described themselves as different from other women, and from the norm of what is considered a "real" woman. One of them even expressed shame for being too masculine and for neglecting her obligations as a mother:

> I would like to be more woman-like, to have soft hands, and not be working hard like this in the factory, and with regard to other things. I like the party work, but sometimes I feel too masculine and people look down upon me—perhaps because my son, who is eleven years old, often stays alone in the house.
> —Sarojini, Pulaya woman, born 1954, sheller[111]

Another woman, Raji, who was politically active and a trade union convener, told me that she felt that she was opposing all of society and that some men may fear her.

> I work, I am a union convener and party member, I provide for my husband and children, I cultivate the soil, I have even made the bricks for this house with my own hands. Some men fear me because I am not like other women, but I must say that I have never felt bad among my male party friends. They accept me.
> —Raji, Ezhava woman, born 1957, sheller[112]

Conclusion

In replacing the bride-price with a dowry payment, a substantial shift in power has taken place with regard to gender relations. It is, however, important to stress that this phenomenon must not be seen purely as a conflict between men and women (women, too, have helped to expand the custom), but as part of patriarchal processes which are constructing masculinity and femininity.

This study of cashew workers supports the view that theories drawing only on women's role in production are not enough to explain the complexity of the dowry system, which has ramifications all over India—including communities and classes where women are the main breadwinners. Purely economic, as well as purely ideological, theories do not satisfactorily explain the widespread custom of *modern dowry*. A dowry is of economic importance in two respects. First, paying *modern dowry* has been an effort to secure upward class mobility for the next generation of daughters. (We

[111] Interview 10 August 1998.
[112] Interview 7 February 1999.

CHAPTER 8

can even assert that it has been a strategy of survival, since the parents often live in such poverty that survival could not be taken for granted.) Second, the phenomenon may also be explained in economic terms, as the size of dowries have been determined by a bridegroom's ability to provide for a family. By contrast, a woman's ability to support a household by her earnings has not figured in the matter of marriage payments, that is, the fact that women have been workers has neither had any impact on the demand for a dowry, nor on the size of the dowry. Most women interviewed have not become housewives, but have continued to work in factories, often as their family's main breadwinner. The new cultural custom of *modern dowries*, is, however, linked to an ideology of a housewife—an ideology which, however, has seldom become reality among the cashew workers.[113]

On the other hand, the appropriation of a custom emanating from a higher caste, in an attempt to raise one's ritual and cultural status in the Hindu caste hierarchy, cannot be accepted as a valid explanation of the dowry system. Although several Brahmin customs (including some pertaining to marriage) have been imitated by the lower castes, most upper caste practices were *not* taken over. Lower castes have neither emulated vegetarianism nor abstention from alcohol. As seen earlier in this chapter, only women abstain from alcohol, and the consumption of meat has gone up. Moreover, the number of love-marriages has increased considerably compared to the 1950s and 1960s, which speaks against a process of Sanskritization, although it could be the outcome of a competing ideology—that of "Westernization" or "modernization". However, love-marriages may be becoming less common because of a patriarchal interest in an arranged marriage with a dowry. A love-marriage has sometimes been labeled "modern", which is quite ironic since early in the twentieth century what was "modern" for a woman living in a matrilineal society in Travancore was to become a housewife in a nuclear family. Today divorces are often seen as "Western" or sometimes as "modern" phenomena, but in the early decades it was part of the cultural tradition of the matrilineal castes, whereas a stable marriage was considered to be "modern", "Western", and "civilized".

In the historical development of *modern dowry*, it may appear as if Brahmin culture has been emulated. However, any such emulation has been limited to an imitation of some Brahmin gender ideology. It is, therefore, not accurate to speak about Sanskritization in this context, as true "emulation" would include many other cultural behaviors. Rather than the diffusion of the Brahmin culture, a new gender ideology seems to have arisen independently.

---

[113] For a contrasting appraisal of the reason for the emergence of *modern dowries*, see Ram, *Mukkuvar Women*, pp. 46 ff. In her study of a fishing community in Tamil Nadu, she found that women actually became housewives and withdrew from paid work. As a result her interpretation is based more on economic theories.

Among cashew workers, the new gender ideology emerged fully in the 1960s and 1970s, at the same time the demand for dowry began. However, dowries in those days were often very small, and part of them were controlled by women, i.e., they were *stridhanams*. Developments since then have been toward stronger male control over the marriage payment—a process which continues up to the present. For many cashew workers, especially those among the lowest castes, the 1970s were the first time they possessed anything of their own, other than a few pots and pans and some clothing. They now owned a piece of property as a result of progressive land reforms. In a slightly later historical setting, some older cashew workers managed to obtain a small amount of capital through the Gratuity Fund, intended to be a source of support after retirement.

Because of demands for dowry, welfare payments to elderly women often wound up in the hands of young men, leaving those women with neither dwelling nor security. The hegemonic ideology of the nuclear family made it difficult for such elderly people to live together with their married children in an extended nuclear family system.

We can trace cultural patterns from a matrilineal society by the fact that houses were often owned by women. The trend points to the decline of such women because of the dowry system, which itself is the economic outcome of a patriarchal gender ideology.

The processes through which gender ideologies became dominant and then shifted from one generation to another are very much embedded in hegemonic discourses, and less so mediated through socialization from mothers to daughters. [114] Diana Mulinari has shown that poor mothers in Nicaragua socialize their daughters not to depend on men for their own or their children's maintenance. Radical, revolutionary women have served as role models for younger women.[115] The cashew workers of Kerala show a contrasting pattern, indicating the importance of forces outside the experiences of individuals. The concerns of the impoverished mothers of Kerala, who give high priority to making good marriages for their daughters by earnestly seeking reliable "breadwinners" for them, must not be taken as a lack of consciousness of the oppressive patriarchal structure under which they live. It is, rather, a survival strategy and the acknowledgement of enormous structural hindrances.[116] In it we see an attempt to plan for their

---

[114] For views that find familial arrangements with regard to production and reproduction decisive for the shaping of gender identity, see Nancy Chodorow, *The Reproduction of Mothering: Psychoanalysis and the Sociology of Gender* (Berkeley, 1978), and Gayle Rubin, "The Traffic in Women: Notes on the 'Political Economy' of Sex", in R.R. Reiter (ed.), *Towards an Anthropology of Women* (New York, 1975), pp. 157-210.

[115] Mulinari, *Motherwork and Politics in Revolutionary Nicaragua*, pp. 118-120.

[116] For the absence of resistance as a recognition of structural constraints, see Pierre Bourdieu, "The Social Space and the Genesis of Groups", *Theory and Society*, 14 (1985), pp. 723-744.

children's future in a rational way, within the limited scope of action available to them. The collective experience of capitalist oppression and failure to radically improve material conditions through class struggles may have contributed to the acceptance of this strategy. Like the cashew workers, many poor people in Kerala found the 1970s to be the first decade in which they could set aside something for the future, and many saw in the provision of a dowry for their daughters an investment in their child's future happiness.

The dowry system has provided women with an inferior identity. The new pattern of dowries has further effeminized poor female cashew workers by defining them as dependent in a very tangible way. Despite its illegality, the dowry system has been acknowledged to some extent by the trade unions. In the statutes of the Kerala Cashew Workers' Relief & Welfare Fund Board, which began functioning in 1988, and where male trade union leaders occupy the board, it is stated that cash advances can be given to workers when their daughters (not their sons) are about to be married.[117] This clause legitimizes the dowry system and the practice of having all wedding expenses borne by the family of the bride.

Kerala has long prided itself on being the only state in India with a unique sex ratio, i.e., a surplus of women over men.[118] This has been credited for the high status of women, perhaps a result of education and the echoes of a matrilineal system which once valued girls even higher than boys. Phenomena like female infanticide and the abortion of female fetuses, which have been widely reported in many other parts of India[119], are unknown in Kerala. The large majority of the women interviewed said that newborn girls have always been as welcome as newborn boys. Nevertheless, a few confessed that, "Nowadays everyone wants a boy. They cause us less trouble than girls because they are not expensive to marry off." Although contested, a group of researchers in Kerala have highlighted the fact that, in the 1991 census of Kerala, the demographic figures concerning boys and girls ages 0-4 years indicate sex-selective abortions or an excess of female child mortality.[120]

---

[117] "Note on the Activities of the Kerala Cashew Workers' Relief & Welfare Fund Board, Kollam, Kerala"; copy received from the chairman, A.A. Azeez.
[118] William M. Alexander, "Normal Kerala within Abnormal India: Reflections on Gender and Sustainability", in Parayil (ed.), *Kerala: The Development Experience* pp. 139-157.
[119] Elisabeth Bumiller, *May You Be the Mother of a Hundred Sons: A Journey among the Women of India* (New Delhi, 1990); Kishwar, *Off the Beaten Track*, pp. 78-92; Thakur, "Preface", p. xv.
[120] S. Irudaya Rajan, S. Sudha, and P. Mohanachandran, "Fertility Decline and Worsening Gender Bias in India: Is Kerala No Longer an Exception?", *Development and Change*, 31:5 (2000), pp. 1085-1092. For criticism, see Alaka, M. Basu, "Fertility Decline and Worsening Gender Bias in India: A Response to S. Irudaya Rajan et al.", *Development and Change*, 31:5 (2000), pp. 1093-1095.

IX   Conclusion

Main Themes

The preceding pages have concerned several generations of women workers in the cashew factories of Kerala during the period 1930-2000. The topic was chosen because these women did not seem to fit the stereotypical view of Third World women as not organized into unions, working in the informal sector, illiterate, and submissive. For the past six decades, cashew workers constituted a major proportion of the working class in Kerala. Today registered cashew workers number about 200,000—most of them women, and the majority members of trade unions. The "Kerala Model", i.e., the political context of a state known for its radicalism, redistribution of resources, and high social indicators for citizens (men as well as women), served as an inspiring background. But the Kerala cashew workers, who suffer a higher degree of poverty, deprivation, and starvation than the average Keralite, have partly been left behind in the positive historical development of Kerala.

This study has been built upon interviews and archival sources, encompassing the analysis of material "realities" as well as discourses and ideologies. Work organization in the factories, wages, trade unions, marriage, and—weaving through all of these—the ever-present issue of class, caste, and gender, were among the main themes studied. Each chapter has a twofold approach: materiality and meaning. Different levels of analysis are used in an attempt to reach the center of women's experience and identity.

To understand the arena in which cashew workers have lived and worked, the structure of the cashew factories has been analyzed from a historical perspective. Powerful capitalist forces have determined this arena. The global nature of capital brought the factories to Quilon more than seven decades ago, when international companies searched for profitable export products, cheap labor, and an absence of restrictive labor laws. Although cashew factories were later owned by indigenous men, the same forces were responsible for the factories leaving Quilon and Kerala in the past three decades. Since around 1950, three main strategies have been employed by cashew factory owners to minimize labor costs: seasonalization (decreasing the number of annual working days), decentralization (locating production in non-registered "factories"), and playing the two states,

Kerala and Tamil Nadu, against each other—even by resorts to threats and corruption. The result was an acceptance of low wages and subminimal labor conditions in both states. However, trade union activity and a more labor-friendly policy in Kerala, in contradistinction to its neighbor, Tamil Nadu, have resulted in progressive labor legislation, even though it is not always enforced.

It has always been important for politicians and trade union leaders to attract and keep cashew factories within their respective states. Kerala, despite nationalizing the first cashew factory in 1970 and gradually bringing more factories under state control, has not been able to combat the flow of jobs to competing states. Moreover, even state-owned factories, as we have seen, have discriminated against women, in spite of their publically-announced labor-friendly policy.

The limitations imposed upon female laborers by poverty, and the extremely unequal power relations between capital and labor, cannot adequately account for the more pronounced exploitation of female workers over males. Neither can women's lack of class consciousness or their ignorance of their rights serve as a justification. Although women had the potential for collective power, they continued to be maltreated by their employers, and were to some extent also excluded from setting the agenda in the trade unions. The story of the Kerala cashew workers chronicles not only shameless, brutal capitalist exploitation, but also demonstrates that we have to go beyond economic structures to explain oppression and lack of empowerment: cultural and ideological factors must be incorporated in the analysis. In particular, gender ideologies and gender discourses have been strong forces in promoting the continual subordination of cashew workers.

The issue of identity and consciousness among female cashew factory workers has been a major concern of this study, i.e., the way in which production and reproduction, social struggle, ideologies, and the cultural and social construction of gender identities are closely bound together. A decisive theoretical point of departure has been the view that identities are shaped and constructed in the middle ground in which social practice, ideologies, and discourses intersect. Thus, experiences and events have been explored from several perspectives, with priority given to gender relations.

I have argued for a conceptualizing of ideologies and discourses as related, instead of seeing them as belonging to incompatible theoretical positions. Ideology is here given a discursive understanding, with ideas and social forces linked, and conveyed through language and representation. Discourses may be ideological and work to create, sustain, and transform power-relations, but always as an integral part of other social practices. Hence, discourses may be studied critically and with the integration of everyday experiences. Discourses and ideologies, however,

Table 9.1. Schematic overview of important results

Period	Social practice	Gender discourse	Gender ideology	Identity
1930–1950	- unfixed gender division of labor, but moving towards being more rigid - extremely poor working conditions - men and women paid by piece rate - women important providers in their families extreme poverty- bride price sometimes paid at marriage, but no dowries	- lower castes excluded from a dichotomized gender discourse (exists among higher castes) - women in cashew factories mainly represented as 'workers'	- low-caste women supposed to care for themselves and their children - low-caste women supposed to do hard work - low-caste women can be out at night and mingle with men - low-caste women and men dress similarly, but women start to cover upper body more and more - marriages often unstable	Caste: active and politicized, but moving to a more passive identity Class: moving to an active and politicized identity Gender: passive, but moving to a more active identity (i.e., constantly visible)
1950–1970	- radical era with regard to class struggle- strict gender division of labor is institutionalized- important achievements with regard to labor laws- seasonalization of factory work, excluding many workers from labor laws- women continue to be important family providers - poverty still widespread but economic conditions slightly improved	- gender discourse becoming more dichotomized and widespread - women increasingly represented with epithets such as weak, patient, docile (see table 9.2)	- gender relations built on nuclear families and male breadwinners becoming increasingly the hegemonic ideology - women's wages to be lower than men's - women supposed to be protected by men - women only to do certain kind of work - marriages should be stable with faithful spouses	Caste: passive, but activate in caste division at work, and in marriage Class: active and politicized, but gap between male and female members of working class widening Gender: more active than earlier (one's gender is a greater determinant of wages, work tasks, and general behavior)
1970–2000	- women continue to be seasonal workers with even fewer annual working days in registered factories, whereas men often become monthly employees. - women work in the informal sector in great numbers - poverty still widespread - women continue to be breadwinners - dowry payment to the bridegroom's family becomes growing problem	- dichotomized gender discourse is strengthened (see table 9.2) - women linked to children's welfare, whereas men represented as radical workers and trade union activists	- conflicting gender ideologies: "modern" society with equal wages for men and women (based on individualism) versus ideology of male breadwinners - women's work to be only supplementary - women should be "feminine" in appearance, behavior, and dress "properly" - marriages should be stable	Caste: passive, but activate in caste division at work and in marriage Class: active and politicized, but women only peripheral. Only men are "true" radical members of working class (i.e., have a central, politicized identity) Gender: active, encompassing all aspects of life

may also be conflicting and contradictory. Ideologies are normative and more consciously formulated, whereas discourses operate on a more subtle level; they are not necessarily viewed as value-laden, but appear to be "true". A strict distinction between them is necessary at the analytical and theoretical levels. In the empirical analysis, however, the two concepts are often comingled, illustrating their connection.

The main results of this investigation are presented in a schematic form in Table 9.1. The periods are approximations. Discourses and ideologies are interpretations of printed sources, as well as of interviews. With regard to identities, what are given here are tendencies which emerged from the interpretations of the forty-five in-depth interviews carried out. Thus they must not be seen as reflections of the "truth" for every cashew worker in Kerala. The table reminds us that social practices have often conflicted with discourses and ideologies. In the middle-period, for example (1950-1970), the fact that women were main breadwinners conflicted with the hegemonic gender ideology, as well as with the gender discourse that had started to encompass low-caste women. During the past thirty years the same tension has been prevalent, but competing gender ideologies have also appeared, one official, "modern", and individualist, and the other more silent, based on the male breadwinner/female housewife model. The "modern" gender ideology has conflicted greatly with the hegemonic gender discourse and has not become dominant.

Gender Division of Labor

This study has found that workers' everyday experiences in the factories have undergone a transformation with regard to gender relations. In the early cashew factories, the gender code for certain tasks was less rigid than it came to be in later times. Although the majority of the shellers were women, still low-caste men and women shelled cashew nuts side by side (in some factories as much as half of the shellers being male), and some women worked with roasting—a task which later became totally male-dominated.

Among the lower castes, a rigid division of labor cannot be assumed to be a cultural inheritance from traditional society. It was, rather, a phenomenon which appeared around 1950. Women were forbidden to work as *roasters* in 1957, but these same women had ceased working in that section years earlier, because they were subject to abuse for doing men's work. Cultural gender codes made women choose other occupations, rather than being excluded (and protected) from roasting by law (a law which probably would have been easy to violate, as so many other laws were).

Low-caste male *shellers* were similarly abused for not being "real men".

This may have been the reason some of them searched for other jobs. Many who chose to continue this work (often out of poverty and a lack of other options) were dismissed. Factory owners were interested in creating female-dominated work-places, as wages could thereby be kept lower. All labor-intensive departments were soon characterized by the absence of male workers. However, if a rational goal had been to reduce wage expenditures by recruiting solely women, factory owners would have done so even in the roasting division. They did not because of the gender discourse which they supported and spread by stressing different female and male characteristics. It was in the financial interests of factory owners to promote and reinforce a dichotomous construction of masculinity and femininity, thereby fostering unequal gender relations such as had not previously affected lower as much as higher castes.

A less rigid division of labor in the past was denied by many interviewees who were not involved in cashew production during the time in question. They saw non-gender specified work as incompatible with certain attributes assigned to men and women. People who had not actually witnessed such a past were influenced by a gender discourse which only took hold later, and they found it inconceivable that a gender division of labor had not always been this way. Those men who did such "women's work" were defined as "not able-bodied men", that is, they were viewed more as women. Male and female attributes were seen as essential and even "natural", i.e., the gender discourse was powerful since it appeared to be "true". Today, only women are found in all labor-intensive departments, working at a piece rate and employed only seasonally, whereas male workers are often employed on a monthly basis.

The rigid gender division of labor is overtly related to a gender ideology based on male breadwinners. However, the model of male breadwinners did not belong to the traditional gender ideology among the lowest castes, where every woman was supposed to provide for herself and her children. This was reflected in public communications between factory owners, trade union leaders, and civil servants in 1945 and 1946. At that time, female cashew workers were represented as *workers* dependent on their wages for survival, although employers used strategies to avoid labeling them as factory workers. They were defined instead as agricultural workers with factory jobs on the side. Later, the same women were recast as housewives who (it was alleged) were living in families with male breadwinners. Both strategies served to define women as not fully proletarianized, a way to avoid paying higher wages and certain fringe benefits.

As an outcome of the first two minimum wages committees of 1953 and 1959, a rigid gender division of labor was established as the only logical solution in accord with the recommendations of an influential national

committee, the Fair Wages Committee. In their report, that committee
stated that that men and women doing the same type of work should receive equal wages, but also that women should get only about two-thirds of
a man's wage, since women were not considered to bear as much of a burden as men in providing for a family. Since then, such a gendered and
conflicting way of reasoning has been common when fixing minimum
wages for cashew workers. The concept of the male breadwinner, imported
from the West via the international labor movement, was now institutionalized and supported by union leaders, as well as by the state. Nuclear families with male breadwinners have subsequently been held up as "modern"
and a model to emulate.

When one considers only the legislated minimum daily wage paid to
cashew workers, it appears as if the wage gap between males and females
has diminished between 1953 to 1998. In fact, it has actually widened.
From a beginning in which wage conditions for males and females were on
an equal footing, most male workers have gradually gotten paid monthly.
Many of them are permanent employees who continue to receive salaries or
unemployment compensation when the factories close down. They have
achieved a better position than female workers, although this is not to deny
that they, too, have been exploited by capitalist forces. During the entire
period studied, wages in cashew factories have also been low for male workers, although women, who have in addition suffered from insecure working
conditions (i.e., continuous dismissals and violations of labor laws) have
been paid less.

At the minimum wage committee meeting in 1953, male trade union
leaders opposed the difference between male and female wages—probably
on the grounds of a communist ideology of gender equality. When the
same issue was raised again in 1959, it was not given much attention. Since
then, the gendered wage gap has hardly been contested by union leaders. It
may be argued that the relative silence of union leaders on this question
should be seen in light of unequal power relations between labor and capital, along with the constant threat of closing factories and reopening them
either in another name or in another jurisdiction. Union leaders may also
be concerned about the survival of the public sector of the cashew industry,
and about the political power of the parties to which unions are affiliated.

However, these arguments do not suffice to explain such a silence.
Trade union leaders' failure to deal with issues such as gendered wages and
female unemployment reflects a patriarchal culture possessing a strongly
polarized, all-encompassing gender ideology.

Women, in spite of their skill at a variety of work tasks, have been considered as a single category of worker with the same wage. Other studies
have shown that male workers who have been caste-segregated at work also

have received caste-related wages. As workers, women in the cashew factories have been differentiated along caste-lines for the different processing operation, but not with regard to payment. The work tasks have not been evaluated according to skill or danger, which means that their economic value as workers are the same, whatever kind of work they do. Men, on the other hand, have been differentiated by education and skill in the tasks they perform. To be stereotyped as part of an anonymous mass spells a loss of power for the individual. The variations in male job descriptions indicate that each person is considered an individual capable of advancing in the company hierarchy.

Trade Unions Participation

Women's lack of trade union participation, which has been explained by their lower degree of literacy and presumed ignorance, has often been mentioned. The fact of the matter is that most cashew workers of the 1940s were not literate, yet this decade produced several militant women workers, as well as union actions initiated by women themselves. Stories related by, an older generation of female workers suggest that they were very conscious of the political situation surrounding them, and often associated the past and their own life history with important political episodes or events.

Because of unacceptable working conditions in the factories, the workers formulated a charter of demands in 1937. Although a union leader drew it up, the points were formulated by the workers themselves. Several of these demands were obtained (at least on paper) in 1945, with the incorporation of cashew factories in the Factory Act. From that time up to the mid-1970s, cashew workers have been extremely militant, especially as measured by man-days lost due to strikes.

The early unions in the cashew sector appear not have been hindered by a traditional, hierarchical culture, as Chakrabarty described the situation in Bengal (see Chapter II). Although there were some initial difficulties in organizing higher castes, workers were unionized across caste barriers in collective struggles before Independence in 1947, and they felt their leaders very near to them then.

The period from around 1950 to the mid-1970s may be characterized as a radical era with huge political manifestations. Out of the turbulence emerged the goal of nationalizing the cashew factories as a top priority. The period from the mid-1970 and up to 2000 has seen crises for cashew workers in growing unemployment, diminishing annual working days, and weakening trade unions.

Many women interviewed held the view that it has become harder to put certain issues on the agenda in the last two or three decades. Matters of vital importance for women's daily survival, unresolved since 1937, have been forgotten or given up on by trade union leaders. Without male support, women have not been able to advance these questions.

Women have always been dependent on male leaders. However, their own stories describe a widening gap between male leaders and themselves from the time of the early mass actions to present day trade union participation. As the politicization and institutionalization of the trade unions progressed in the 1950s, more hierarchical organizations evolved, and the distance between workers and leaders was felt to increase. Workers were directed from above, rather than having the power to set their own agenda.[1] However, it would be false to characterize female workers solely as having been exploited by leaders for their own political purposes, for such a view would assume that "the led" have not understood their situation, or suffer from a lack of class consciousness (or even false consciousness). In spite of certain drawbacks, the positive aspects of trade union affiliation have overshadowed the negative, and the women interviewed have shown themselves well-aware of both aspects.

Women have increasingly come to distrust their leaders. The reasons for this may be attributed to questions of class and alienation from the unions. Trade unions have become new power bases which are totally male-dominated. Their leaders are full-time male politicians. Most of the workers interviewed believed that such leaders were no longer part of the working class. Instances of corruption and collaboration with factory owners are given as grounds for popular distrust of union leaders. Caste seems less relevant in accounting for a distance between the leaders and the rank and file, and several low-caste male cashew workers have advanced to careers as trade union leaders and politicians. Significantly, however, not a single female worker has risen in the same way.

Through the struggle of trade unions, the cashew workers of Kerala have achieved such benefits as bonuses, maternity leave, pensions, and welfare. Unfortunately, far from all cashew factory workers enjoy these rights, since a minimum number of annual working days is required in order to be covered by certain labor laws. Regulations continue to be violated in private factories.

The number of unregistered factories (*kudivarappus*) were considerable during the period from 1946 up to the present, and many workers were of the opinion that clandestine factories became even more prevalent in the

---

[1] There seems to have been a lack of the kind of empowering everyday practice and participation that Alberto Melucci finds important for identity-creating processes (see Chapter VII).

1990s—a phenomenon that may be linked to deregulation of imports which made it easier for *kudivarappus* to obtain raw nuts from abroad. In *kudivarappus*, workers are paid one-third to one-half the legal minimum wage and receive no fringe benefits. By preference, these same workers would rather seek employment in registered factories when these are in operation. In fact, unregistered factories are sometimes owned or leased out by owners of registered factories, and so one cannot really speak of a dualism of formal versus informal sectors with regard to either workers or factory owners.

Young girls commonly begin to work in unregistered factories when they are thirteen or fourteen, so that when they later enter the registered factories they are already skilled. A large number of elderly women also work in the cashew industry. It has long been the custom—even in the registered factories—to keep many workers off the rolls in order to pay them less than the stipulated minimum wage, and give them no fringe benefits. Such an "informal sector" exists *within* the registered factories. Those paid off the books are often the very young or those above the official retirement age. As a result, many women who are either as yet untrained, or who have lost some of their former agility due to age, constitute an underground of second-class workers receiving lower wages and fewer benefits.

Some male workers have also been drawn to the *kudivarappus*, but in contrast to the female workers, often they are actually paid *higher* daily wages than they make in registered factories to compensate for their lost fringe benefits and "to keep them in a good mood".

Class Consciousness and Class Identity

Because females work in the informal sector at underpaid jobs and have no labor rights does not mean they have a lower degree of class consciousness than men. The difference in kinds of employment should be attributed to people's identities, which have been constructed in the realm of experiences, ideologies, and discourses. As Santha, the trade union convener, said of her husband, "What would people think of him if *he* started to work for half wages?"

The concept of *breadwinner* is central to any understanding of gender identity. Although for the last forty or fifty years it has generally been taken for granted that husbands are the main breadwinners, a considerable number of female cashew workers occupy that role. Still, these women have not been *recognized* as breadwinners. Because women bear the overwhelming responsibility for the maintenance of their children, they are compelled by necessity to work for whatever they can get, since the absence of work means starvation. This is in spite of the fact that they are said to be only supplementary wage earners. "I was the one responsible for the children. Their bellies were crying—so what should I do?" was the explanation many female cashew workers gave for their decision to work in a clandestine, unregistered cashew factory. The daily struggle for survival in the midst of such poverty as is unimaginable for most people in the West has left women no choice. The "luxury" of their male family members demanding minimum wages and rejecting low-paid work (i.e., proudly declaring themselves uncompromising radical members of the working class) is predicated on women's work and women's assumption of responsibility in providing for *their* children. A man is expected to show loyalty to his class, even if his family is on the verge of starvation—a view in agonizing conflict with his titular role as provider for the family. Thus there is a structural link between men's success in trade union activities and the ideology of women as mere supplementary providers. The radicalism of such males has to a great degree been built upon the backs of women supporting their families—a reality which severely clashes with hegemonic gender discourses and confuses gender identities.

In the 1930s and 1940s, it was seen as a matter of course among the lower castes that all family members should work and contribute to the household. People saw their own poverty first and foremost in terms of caste affiliation, and then, as the labor movement grew stronger, in terms of class exploitation as well. Although we may speak about an emerging *class consciousness*, the fact remains that a central, politicized *class identity* never obtained a firm hold on female workers. They believe they belong to the working class—and their identity as such has been politicized because they are engaged in collective class actions—but their activities have not been empowering; rather than lead, they have been led. They seem to be have been quite cognizant of the capitalist forces behind their exploitation, and also aware of the necessity of the trade union struggle; yet, surprisingly, impoverished female cashew workers have begun explaining their poverty as a consequence of their marriage.

The explanations for poverty that are commonly heard have a familiar ring: "My husband is dead [or sick, alcoholic, disabled, unwilling, unemployed, or has disappeared] and can't provide for me." "My parents chose the wrong husband for me." "I have just had bad luck in my marriage." At the individual level such women have started to identify themselves as anomalies. Several women said that the gender roles in their families were reversed and not "normal". This may be the result of their constructing gender identity through a perception of femininity and masculinity which has been nourished in the factories, the trade unions, and in society at large.

The dichotomic language of femininity and masculinity results in the erection of differences that create meaning for specific behaviors and give people their identities. Certain behavioral dichotomies appear related to gender, and represent a discourse which has been expressed in reports, newspapers, trade unions accounts, and interviews (see Table 9.2).

Table 9.2 Various attributes related to gender

Femininity	Masculinity
1. Bodily attributes significant for work: Weakness Dexterity Untechnical	1. Bodily attributes significant for work: Strength Awkwardness Technically-minded
2. Mental attributes of consequence in relations: Patient Docile Loyal Home-oriented Timid	2. Mental attributes of consequence in relations: Impatient Unruly Rebellious/faithless Outgoing Fearless, brave
3. Resultant attributes: Dependent (housewife) Helpless Nurturing/emotional	3. Resultant attributes: Supportive (breadwinner) Protecting Political/rational

These attributes are neither universal nor timeless, but culturally specific and related to a historical context. The discourse of femininity and masculinity among low-caste women and men does not appear to have been as dichotomized in the first half of the twentieth century as it became after Independence. Up to about the mid-1940s, women, like men, were expected to do hard manual labor, be able to go out at night, provide for themselves, and dress only in a loincloth. Correspondingly, many low-caste men did not assert their masculinity and performed work which later was characterized as "female". All this was also an outcome of one's material circumstances, and there was no space for being "feminine" or "masculine".

In weighing narratives of the past, we must beware of the tendency to idealize the "good old days". In point of fact, however, many of my informants made disparaging references to bygone times. It was a period when, according to them, men were less masculine and women less feminine, and some even referred to it as a *shameful past*. Significantly, this "shameful past" was not a topic they advanced themselves. When stories about militant female trade union activists of the older generation were recounted, most of my informants did not consider such women heroines to emulate. Rather, they ridiculed them somewhat as backward, masculine women. In that "shameful past", low-caste women went to drink alcohol after work together with men, and did not cover their upper bodies. Such behavior was later censured as masculine. A new expression of femininity among the younger generation is manifest in their wearing jewelry (although most of them can only afford gold imitations) and in covering their bodies more and more. The female body has become sexualized and controlled in a way it was not in the 1930s and 1940s.

With a more rigid gender division of labor, the introduction of male breadwinner-wages, and the emergence of a male power base in the trade unions, the gender discourse described above has become more pronounced. For poor women, the improvement of material conditions, however slight, acted as an incentive to nourish their dream of the right to be *feminine*.

Caste Identities

A common method of exploring the question of workers' identity has been to examine their class or caste solidarity under exceptional circumstances, such as strikes and riots. This analysis has tried to consider not only workers' loyalty in those situations (i.e., moments when caste identities may have been weakened—or strengthened—temporarily), but also acknowledge the importance of caste in daily life. One way of approaching the connection of everyday activities and caste is to explore caste relations at the factory.

Caste was a very strong form of identity in the 1930s and 1940s. The first workers in the cashew factories were mainly from the lowest castes, as the work was considered *infra dig* to others. Such workers were recruited from rural areas and accommodated in sheds near the factories. Soon, however, proletarianized women of higher castes entered the workforce, and then, with the advent of employees of mixed castes, a caste division of labor (kept up both by workers and factory management) was created. It was extremely difficult for the higher castes to adjust to the fact that they were in a similar position as "untouchable" women. As a result, higher-caste women were the last to join the unions. However, the continuing agitation of trade union leaders in the 1940s and 1950s caused women and men of different castes to join in strikes and demonstrations, marking a development from *caste* to *class* identity. This description, however, must be modified when we come to analyze actual social life and daily experiences. In the workplace, caste segregation continued and is to a large extent still prevalent.

The caste division of labor in the cashew factories is unrelated to meritocratic principles and wage differences, although several studies have shown that this is not true of factories in other parts of India. The position a caste occupies within the cashew factory's operations is linked to the old Hindu ritual hierarchy of pollution (by the degree of cleanliness or uncleanliness in the work task). In the early phase, factory owners were interested in keeping the caste division in order to split the work force and prevent unionization, but later it was preserved because mothers would teach their daughters their own skilled task to secure the same factory job for them. Widespread unemployment has contributed to preserve the caste division of labor. However, traditional ideas of a correspondence between certain formerly untouchable castes and unclean work are still common among people of higher castes, although the radical class discourse which has long since evolved denies that caste has any importance.

Low and middle caste women interviewed showed a very materialist view of the origin of caste as being a result of a struggle for power and resources (especially food). Such views have been passed down to them through the generations. According to these women, the caste system was not based on consensus nor on any unquestioned view of caste hierarchies being natural, but on oppression and the lack of opportunity to challenge such oppression.

Following Gramsci, Chatterjee has argued that subaltern people in India have a "common sense" whose existence is divided in a contradictory consciousness: the one is experienced in daily activities (e.g., working together with others) and the other, uncritically inherited from the past, accepting and affirming the caste system, while realizing their class position. The women interviewed here have not uncritically accepted the caste system—at least they do not believe that the hierarchy is based on *dharma*. However, they have viewed the caste system as "natural" in one aspect: different castes are considered essential groups with distinct cultural habits. There seems to be no desire to dissolve such distinctions by agreeing to inter-caste marriages, although some do take place. Trade union leaders stopped agitating against the caste system after different castes joined the same union and participated in a joint class struggle. For whatever reasons, the unions have never taken it upon themselves to try and dissolve the caste division of labor in the factories or encourage inter-caste marriages.

The identity of caste was only temporarily weakened as a result of class struggles. Caste is still an important part of one's identity, with its primary significance in the reproductive sphere. Caste identities have changed from something politicized to a more passive identity which comes to the fore and becomes activated on certain occasions (e.g., marriage).

In the early twentieth century, there were diverse gender codes for various castes. It meant something entirely different to be a woman of low caste than to be a high-caste woman who rarely left her house and seldom mixed with men. The higher the rank a caste was assigned in the social hierarchy, the more regulations it imposed upon women. Any inability on the part of low-caste men to control their women was part of a circle of behavior that rendered the whole caste impure. A new loss of freedom by women became conspicuous when a caste tried to rise in the social hierarchy. However, there was also a material basis for the relationship between caste and gender: the more property involved, the more important the restrictions on a woman's sexuality. To introduce restrictions on women also served to increase the class status of men.

The upward mobility of low-caste women interviewed is reflected in the way they have started to cover their bodies, stay home after dark, and cease to mingle with men at liquor or teashops. The complex relationship between caste and gender needs to be accounted for more comprehensively than on a material basis alone. Hegemonic gender discourses and ideologies are equally decisive in the process of making women more feminine and widening the gap of appropriate behavior for women and men.

The process of emulating higher castes has been termed Sanskritization. However, to label the process we have witnessed among the women in this study by that term would be misleading, as what they have done is not part of a wider cultural emulation of Brahmins or other high castes. What emulation there is has been limited to parts of the Brahmanic gender ideology, whereas true emulation would include many other cultural behaviors. Although the "elevation" of lower castes (led by social reformers such as Sree Naryana Guru and Aiyappan) in the early twentieth century may rightly be termed Sanskritization, the process which has implied a new femininity among low-caste women has less to do with caste than with class status and patriarchal forces. As we have seen, parts of the gender ideology emanate from the West and the international labor movement, part coincides with an age-old Brahmanic gender ideology, and part has arisen independently.

Dowry and the Male Breadwinner

The dependency of women upon men manifested itself during the 1970s in the growth of a system of dowry payments made to the bridegroom at marriage—something which had not previously existed among the lower castes in Kerala. Since then, it is common practice for parents (often single mothers) to arrange marriages for their daughters by offering a dowry so as to secure a "good" husband, i.e., one who can provide for a wife and keep her far from factory work, so that hopefully she may have a better life than her mother.

Equity accumulated by women in their capacity as workers, including pensions and bonuses, or real estate distributed to them through land reforms, has come to be transferred to men at marriage. For many female cashew workers this has meant that they have been forced to leave a registered factory and retire prematurely in order to obtain their pension savings in a lump sum. They then begin working in the informal sector.

Many of the women interviewed owned houses, which may be a holdover from the time when a matrilineal society existed. The trend, however, seems to be that this tradition has dwindled, in part as a result of the dowry system: houses are sold to get cash for dowries; in some cases the house is given as a dowry to the bridegroom.

The dowry system is very much a part of a gender ideology which defines women as dependent. It is built upon the presumption of a "happy nuclear family" centered around a male breadwinner—something which seems unshakably rooted in the minds of cashew workers. Trade unions, while ostensibly condemning dowry payments, have actually supported and encouraged them by establishing funds for poor workers to be used for their daughters' marriages. This in turn has further strengthened the view that the dowry system is "natural". From a Western point of view, the phenomenon of dowry stands out as the practice of a traditional society, and a thing that will disappear with "modernization". Among my interviewees, dowry has been considered a "modern" habit, firmly linked to the nuclear family and to men's presumed role as breadwinners.

The majority of female cashew workers, especially the "middle generation" which has worked for ten to thirty years, asserts that in spite of their poverty and misery, working in the cashew factory has given them the ability to survive, the possibility of feeding their children, and some power in the household. "I want to continue the work in the cashew factory. It gives me security, since I don't trust my husband's willingness or capacity to maintain the family—but I want my daughters to be *housewives*." This is the general opinion. A common aspiration for the next generation is to help them escape direct capitalist exploitation.

Several scholars have questioned the link between empowerment and wage labor for Third World women.[2] My findings point towards a correlation between women's earnings from wage labor and their power in the

---

[2] See, for example, Ruth Pearson, "Gender Relations, Capitalism and Third World Industrialization", in L. Sklair (ed.), *Capitalism and Development* (London, 1994), pp. 339-358.

household. This is not to subscribe to Engels' view that by women entering the wage labor market an end will be put to gender discrimination. However, what little power these women have achieved in the household, they stand prepared to exchange for a better material life for their daughters. They are well aware that a "woman's wage" is not enough to feed a family. A woman has to work up to five times longer than a man to achieve the same income, a fact of life that motivates efforts to spare their daughters such drudgery and secure for them the prospect of having a "normal" nuclear family.

The Process of Effeminization

The women studied here have gone through a process which may be termed *effeminization*, i.e., the representation of women with the kinds of epithets relating to femininity (such as weakness and dexterity) alluded to earlier; and the consequences of this, which include stereotyping as housewives. Maria Mies coined the term *housewifization* to designate "a process in which women are socially defined as housewives, dependent for their sustenance on the income of a husband, irrespective of whether they are de facto housewives or not".[3]

For the lowest castes, who were not included in totally polarized gender ideology in the 1930s and 1940s, it was evident that men *and* women were workers. This is not at all to romanticize that era, which was in fact characterized by extreme poverty and starvation for both men and women belonging to families of cashew workers. *Housewifization* among cashew workers has been solely ideological, lacking any material ground and leaving women in the paradoxical situation of being looked upon as economic liabilities, while functioning on a day-to-day basis as factory workers and breadwinners. For cashew workers, the situation is more subtle than Mies' *housewifization*, since here women have not been relegated to working in their homes, nor have they been officially defined as housewives. It is a more invisible, insidious, and inaccessible process, but also a more pervasive one.

Effeminization includes Mies's *housewifization*, but carries a broader meaning: it encompasses perceptions of a woman's way of dressing, behaving, and acting in different spaces—in the factory, in union participation, in the household, and out in society at large. The way such ideologies become dominant and vary from one generation to the next is attributable more to hegemonic discourses, and less so to socialization from mothers to daughters.

---

[3] Mies, *The Lace Makers of Narsapur*, p. 180.

A person's childhood and familial arrangements with regard to production and reproduction are often seen as decisive for the shaping of gender identity. We might expect a girl whose mother is a factory worker (on top of bearing the primary responsibility for maintaining her family) to identify herself with such a role. Most female cashew workers have witnessed their mothers working in the same kind of factories, and the majority have also seen them contribute substantially to the income of the household. Their experiences as workers and principal family breadwinners did not result in their being considered "working class " as their dominant identity. They have developed a politicized class identity, but a peripheral one. The concept of experience, so central for E.P. Thompson, can be expanded to include experiences other than class that have proven more important in the shaping of their identities. The experience of being a "temporary guest" in the labor movement, the steady victim of labor law violations and unemployment; of being defined as *the Other*, feeling alienated from the trade unions, but thoroughly dependent on men (on an ideological and a discursive level) have all exerted very strong influences on their sense of who they are. Daughters of female cashew workers tend to see themselves as anomalies if they become workers, too.

The story of the Kerala cashew workers illustrates the importance of forces outside the experiences of individuals. Women workers' tendency to plan for their daughter's future by seeking reliable "breadwinners" must not be viewed as a lack of consciousness of the oppressive patriarchal structure under which they live. It is, rather, a survival strategy and a rational rejection of direct capitalist oppression. Most interviewees recognized both capitalist and patriarchal structures, but seemed to choose the best possible "contract" they could under prevailing circumstances. Their experiences in the cashew factories, and their collective memories of capitalist oppression, made them try to find ways to escape such a situation— although the solution available to them included another kind of structural oppression (i.e., patriarchal), which, however, has been seen as a greater possibility of escape.

Whereas class has been characterized as a passive identity in Western post-industrial society and as having largely "lost its voice"[4], class is a very active identity in Kerala. The language of class has been very pronounced, as has oppression based on class—factors which have contributed to obscure gender inequalities. However, what exists is a gendered definition of class, with men holding the central politicized identity. The identity of the women interviewed in this study seem to have moved in a direction stressing gender, which has become a overarching, active identity, but one not at

---

[4] Bradley, *Fractured Identities*, pp. 72-73.

all politicized. The widened gap in the construction of femininity and masculinity has served to activate the identity of being a "woman" among the low-caste women interviewed. The forces behind the Kerala Model, radical though they have been in promoting class and caste emancipation, have to some extent neglected the question of gender. Condoning the exploitation of women in the workplace, while the exploitation of men has been more contested, has unfortunately resulted in a situation where laboring women have failed to be identified as true workers and true radical members of the labor movement.

Hegemonic gender ideologies and dominating gender discourses, when applied to the cashew workers of Kerala, contrast their experiences, and a strong tension between the two has evolved. By perpetrating gender stereotypes in which active, politicized workers are automatically equated with *male* identities (the same males who often must ask their wives for financial support), while the multiple role of nurturer, caregiver, and supporter of the family remains inextricably linked with the *female* (although these same women are driven by necessity to go out and become the breadwinners), such discourses confound gender identities among men and women.

Another tension can be discovered between the official Kerala history of success and the personal narratives of the women interviewed. Although having integrated "the big story" in their life stories by asserting that "things are much better now", "people are educated and live much better today", or "trade unions have done so much for us", the narratives also include opinions such as "union leaders were closer to us before", "with regard to trade unionism, the 1950s were golden times", "dowry is an evil which did not exist in the past" and "we are still starving ". This should not be interpreted to mean that women have uncritically absorbed a "story of success" and are victims of manipulation. The two aspects, inclusion in and exclusion from the Kerala successes, were experiences interviewees saw as part of their ambiguous reality. The inclusion was based on class and caste, whereas the exclusion to a great extent was based on gender.

Theoretical Implications

The present study suggests that understanding the identity and rational agency of individuals requires that one complement the analysis of economic forces by the inclusion of discourses and ideologies. The historical development we have traced shows a widening gap between femininity and masculinity, with a more dichotomized gender ideology visible among low-caste cashew workers. While it does not mean to imply a deterioration of living conditions for women, nor should it be taken as romanticizing a better and more gender-equal past, it does seek to highlight the complexity of historical developments. It has striven to show that, once one takes a gender perspective, a polarization such as "traditional" or "modern" is seen as flawed. The foregoing becomes especially visible when taking the reproductive sphere into account. What are generally known as *traditional* phenomena may, in fact, turn out to be the most *modern*—an insight which may not only apply in the case of Kerala, but may have applications in other contexts as well.

The strategy of capital to support and be part of the creation of a dichotomized gender discourse, which was, in fact, *not* a traditional one among the lowest castes, illustrates its active role in promoting a patriarchal gender ideology. To say that capital supported a traditional culture is not entirely to the point, because that culture did not encompass the communities where cashew workers were recruited. Rather, capitalist forces were active in spreading a high-caste gender ideology among lower castes, who were seen to "modernize" their gender relations by introducing male breadwinners and dependent housewives as the ideal. Union leaders also "modernized" gender relations by supporting an internationally acknowledged wage system which was institutionalized by the minimum wages committees in 1953 and 1959. Thus, with regard to gender relations, traditional high-caste values coincided with "modern" Western gender ideologies that included male breadwinners and female dependents.

The present study has attempted to contribute to the body of theory in two academic fields: labor history and feminist studies. In dialogue with Marxism, feminism, and postmodernism, an attempt has been made to add new perspectives and to extend the traditional concern of labor history (i.e., the analysis of class formation and class consciousness, and the relationship between capital and labor) to include issues of people's identities other than those based on class. As we have seen, a point of departure which assume that these identities are both multiple and fragmented, and have been constructed at the intersection of experience, ideology, and discourse, has both theoretical and empirical consequences.

This study exists in the intersection of several different disciplines in an attempt to position the analysis at the center of women's lives. The advantages of such an interdisciplinary approach may extend its utility beyond the purview of the Kerala cashew workers to any feminist study. To probe the depths of women's experience and identity, it has been necessary to engage a variety of methods and theoretical approaches, and in so doing, two epistemological traditions have been combined—one primarily employing the concept of discourse and the other that of ideology. Hopefully, it has been shown that they are not contradictory but related, and possible to integrate in the same analysis. Discourses affect ideologies in a dialectic relationship and vice-versa, and both of them are interwoven in social practice. Working conditions, the shifting gender division of labor, gender relations at work and in other spaces of social importance, gender ideologies, and gender discourses are interconnected fields. All of these become necessary to embrace in our analysis if we are to not only grasp at, but understand the actions of women and the rationality for their strategies.

Epilogue

Few things are static in a society, and that holds true for the cashew factories of Kerala as well. In 2014, I revisited some of those factories in the vicinity of Kollam and Alappuzha, where I had a chance to interview workers, owners, and union leaders. I noticed one remarkable change that had taken place: there was a new division of labor based on ethnicity, the result of shifting migration patterns.

The director of CAPEX, a government-run cashew factory, told me that there were three million migrant workers in Kerala, mostly Bengali men, many of whom worked in the cashew industry. In order to see what kind of work those men actually did and under what conditions they labored, I visited three factories. One man I met, who owned a few private cashew factories, said that he employed about fifty such men in his plants. They all operated tools called cutters. Cutting is another way to split raw cashew nuts instead of shelling them by hand with a mallet. I had seen women working with similar semi-mechanized cutting tools in the late 1990s. When I asked him why only migrant men from the north did that job, he answered, "It is hard work, not suitable for women, and Malayalee men refuse to do it. They only want white-collar jobs." I recalled that at the time of my fieldwork in the 1990s, the recently-introduced cutting tools were considered the exclusive domain of women. Cutting, like shelling, is highly labor intensive, and the idea of engaging men to do this was unheard of in the 1990s. That all changed, however, once the so-called Bengali men entered the Kerala labor market.

As I visited the factories, I realized that those who were referred to as Bengali men included male workers from other places in northern India, especially Assam, but also from Bangladesh and Nepal. Some said they had been hired by recruiters at home; others were offered jobs when they got off the train in Kerala.

The migrant cutting workers, who were mostly young men, told me they were paid by piecework. By contrast, the few Malayalee men who worked in another section of the factory received monthly salaries. While the piece rate for migrant men was the same as for female Malayalee workers in the manual shelling section, the men could earn more per hour because the cutting tools they used were faster. As a result, migrant men were making about 30% more than female workers in the factory, and at least twice as much as they could have made back home. In addition, foreign workers were provided with meals and free accommodations in a side room of the factory. On the other hand, they received no fringe benefits, such as overtime or pensions, and had no medical insurance. One man, for example, who had injured his hand with a cutting tool, had to quit and return home.

The migrant men worked six days a week, and since their hours were unregulated by labor laws, they put in as many as twelve hours a day and hardly ever left the factory. When I questioned one of the union leaders about this, I was assured that the "Bengali" men did not want to be organized, but "only wanted to make fast money and go home." However, when I asked the migrant workers themselves, they said that the factory owners did not allow them to unionize. Factory owners, for their part, insisted that union leaders had no objection to the "Bengali" men remaining unorganized.

As to why they were trying to accumulate money, the migrant men generally replied that they wanted to buy some land or go into business when they returned home. This would allow them to get married and start a nuclear family. As one man stated, "Where I come from, if you work in agriculture, you have to give all your earnings to your father and it goes into the joint family, so you never get any money of your own. But I want to have my own family." This is reminiscent of the many generational disputes in early twentieth century Kerala, where young men wanted to be independent and dissolve their allegiance to joint families—something that facilitated the capitalist development of the state.

Ironically, globalization and extended migration has brought labor conditions in the cashew factories back to the pre-union era for migrant men. What drives these men seems to be a desire to create their own nuclear families. The same may be said for the millions of Malayalee men who go to the Gulf countries to earn higher wages. The wish for independence from joint families or parents, and the determination to establish a nuclear family is related to masculinity. Thus, in an analysis of labor conditions, it is relevant to include the reproductive sphere: dominant ideologies and discourses about families also have an impact on working conditions and migration patterns.

If I would have written a similar book about cashew workers in 2014, I might have entitled it "Class, Caste, Ethnicity, and Gender in the Cashew Factories of Kerala" and used the concept of intersectionality to examine the prevailing power relations, such as how a formerly women's occupation like cutting has been transformed into a job for migrant men who constitute a new category of laborers. However, writing today, in 2021, there might have been yet another title because the pandemic of 2020 and 2021 has cut off the migration streams both to and from Kerala.

June 2021   ANNA LINDBERG
Stockholm, Sweden

Appendix: Subjects Interviewed and Factories Visited

A. Cashew workers interviewed in-depth by gender, caste, year of birth, and occupation

Name	Caste	Year of birth	Occupation
Women: 45			
1. Chirutha	Kurava	1919	sheller
2. Ponni	Kurava	1920	sheller
3. Kavitha	Kurava	1920	sheller
4. Theye	Kurava	1922	sheller
5. Velumbi	Kurava	1930	sheller
6. Velamma	Kurava	1940	sheller
7. Santha	Kurava	1957	sheller
8. Sumathai	Kurava	1964	sheller
9. Sunitha	Kurava	1978	sheller
10. Ajitha	Kurava	1980	sheller
11. Meena	Kurava	1982	sheller
12. Kotha	Pulaya	1919	sheller
13. Kunji	Pulaya	1920	sheller
14. Chakki	Pulaya	1927	sheller
15. Kalyani	Pulaya	1933	sheller
16. Masis Ally	Pulaya	1935	sheller
17. Kali	Pulaya	1940	sheller
18. Sarojini	Pulaya	1954	sheller
19. Lalitha	Pulaya	1958	sheller
20. Meera	Pulaya	1972	sheller
21. Geetha	Pulaya	1973	sheller
22. Prasantha	Pulaya	1980	sheller
23. Devaki	Ezhava	1918	sheller
24. Kunjukutty	Ezhava	1923	grader
25. Sarasu	Ezhava	1925	sheller

26. Sujatha	Ezhava	1925	peeler
27. Gomathi	Ezhava	1930	sheller
28. Seethu	Ezhava	1938	peeler
29. Thankamoni	Ezhava	1946	sheller
30. Chamally	Ezhava	1955	peeler
31. Raji	Ezhava	1957	sheller
32. Vasantha	Ezhava	1964	peeler
33. Sandhya	Ezhava	1978	peeler
34. Indira	Ezhava	1980	peeler
35. Bharathiamma	Nair	1912	peeler
36. Vijayamma	Nair	1920	peeler, grader
37. Bhaggerathi	Nair	1926	grader
38. Kousalya	Nair	1928	grader
39. Asryamma	Nair	1939	packer
40. Leela	Nair	1950	grader, sheller
41. Chitra	Nair	1968	peeler
42. Gisiya	Nair	1970	grader
43. Nalini	Nair	1974	sheller
44. Renuka	Nair	1978	grader
45. Meera	Christian	1967	peeler

Men: 7

1. Velu	Kurava	1923	sheller
2. Kuttan	Kurava	1928	sheller
3. Venu	Kurava	1930	sheller, roaster
4. Aiyyan	Pulaya	1930	sheller
5. Arangan	Pulaya	1931	sheller, roaster
6. K. Bhaskaran	Ezhava	1924	tinfiller
7. Prabhakaran	Ezhava	1950	sheller, roaster

B. Trade union leaders and politicians

Women: 2
1. Gopalan, Susheela, industrial minister, Govt. of Kerala
2. Sarademma, J., trade union activist, AITUC, CPI

Men: 14
1. Azeez, A.A., UTUC, RSP
2. Chellappan, K., AITUC, CPI
3. Chitraranjan, J., AITUC, CPI
4. John, D., CITU, CPI-M
5. Madhavan, N., UTUC, RSP
6. Majeed, T.M., AITUC, CPI
7. Morris, Ben, INTUC, Congress
8. Nair, Kesavan, CITU, CPI-M
9. Nold, A.S., INTUC, Congress
10. Padmalochanan, N., CITU, CPI-M
11. Prakaran, Perumpuzha, INTUC, Congress
12. Prakash, P., UTUC, RSP
13. Udayabhanu, J., AITUC, CPI
14. Unni, R.S., UTUC, RSP

C. Supervisors, managers, staff

Women: 1
1. Santhamma, J., managing director, Southern Cashew Factory, Kottiyam

Men: 17
1. Anirudhan, K., clerk, KSCDC, Kottiyam
2. Balasubramaniam, D., former manager, Peirce Leslie & Co., Calicut
3. Basu, J., clerk, KSCDC, Kottiyam
4. Bolland, A.D., former manager, Peirce Leslie & Co., 1946-1978
5. Chandy, Thomas, former manager, Peirce Leslie & Co., Kundara
6. Das, Antoni, personnel secretary, KSCDC, main office, Quilon
7. Giri, V.N., managing director, CAPEX
8. Nair, K. Gopinathan, managing director, K. Gopinathan Nair, Quilon
9. Nair, Ramachandran K.P., general manager, Lakshman & Co., Kilikolloor

10. Nair, Ravidranathan, owner of the VLC group of companies in South India
11. Pillai, Gopala Krishna, owner of M.G. Enterprises, Kilikolloor
12. Pillai, Gopinathan, production chief, KSCDC, main office, Quilon
13. Pillai, Ramachandran, managing director, VLC, Kanyakumari
14. Pillai, Sreedharan, former clerk in a cashew factory in Kilikolloor
15. Pillai, Vijayanandan, managing director, VLC, Chandanathoope
16. Rahim, P., owner of Southern Cashew Factory, Kottiyam
17. Rajeendran, P., chairman, KSCDC, Quilon

D. Civil servants and journalists

Women: 1
1. Devi, Paravadi, journalist, Trivandrum

Men: 6
1. Bhanu, K., retired journalist, Quilon
2. Madhavan, P., retired joint district labor commissioner 1951-1983, chairman of the Minimum Wage Committee in 1997-98
3. Nathaniel, Sam, labor commissioner, Quilon
4. Radhakrishna, L., managing director of KSCDC 1996-1999
5. Ravikumar, S., inspector of factories, Quilon
6. Udayabhanu, A.P., retired advocate, chairman of the Minimum Wage Committee in 1953

E. Factories which were visited 1997-2000

State-owned: 1
1. KSCDC No. 1, Kottiyam

Private, large companies: 4
1. KPP Cashew Factory, Kilikolloor
2. Peirce Leslie India, Ltd., Calicut
3. VLC, Chandanathoope
4. VLC, Kanyakumari, Tamil Nadu

Private, small entities: 6
1. Cashew Industries, Puthoor
2. Lourdmatha Cashew Industry, Puthoor

3. MEK Cashew Factory, Peroor
4. Popular Cashew Exports, Peroor
5. Sai Exports Enterprise, Kunnuthur
6. Southern Cashew Factory, Kottiyam

Unregistered: 1
1. MG Enterprises, Kilikolloor

F. Short interviews of female workers in VLC factory, Chandanathoope (January 1998)

Shellers, cutters	37
Peelers	34
Graders	10
Packers	4
Total	85

Bibliography

A. Archives

1) Kerala State Archive (KSA), Nalanda, Trivandrum
    Confidential files 1920-1955
    Development files 1920-1955
    General files 1920–1955
    Judicial Department files 1920-1950
    Legislative Department files 1920-1950

2) Kerala Government South Record Cellar (SRC),
    Secretariat, Trivandrum
    Labor Department files 1955-1960
    Health and Labor Department files 1955-1960

3) Kerala Government North Record Cellar (NRC),
    Secretariat, Trivandrum
    Labor Department files 1961-1997

4) School of Oriental and African Studies (SOAS) Archive, London
    Council for World Mission (CWM) Archives, Indian Correspondence 1951-60

5) Arbetarrörelsens arkiv (ARA), Stockholm.
    International Conference of Women Trade Unionists, July 7, 1936, London

B. Published Government Records

Government of India

Annual Survey of Industries (ASI) 1964, Vol. II
Annual Survey of Industries 1969, census sector, Vol. II
Annual Survey of Industries 1978-79, factory sector, Vol. II
Annual Survey of Industries 1983-84, factory sector, Vol. II

Annual Survey of Industries 1989-90, factory sector, Vol. III
Annual Survey of Industries 1993-94, factory sector, Vol. III
Census of India 1901, Vol. XXVI, Travancore, Part I, Report
Census of India 1931, Vol. XXVIII, Travancore, Part I, Report
Census of India 1961, Vol. VII, Part VI E, Kerala, Village Survey Monographs, Quilon District (New Delhi, 1966)
Census of India 1961, Vol. VIII, Kerala Village Survey Monographs, Kottayam District (New Delhi, 1966)
Indian Labour Investigation Committee, Main Report 1946
Large Industrial Establishments in India, Labour Bureau, 1931-1947 (Simla, 1933-1951)
Report of the Committee on Fair Wages, Ministry of Labour (Simla, 1954)
Report on an Enquiry into Conditions of Labour in the Cashewnut Processing Industry in India, Labour Bureau (Simla, 1954)
Report on Survey of Labour Conditions in Cashewnut Factories in India 1965-66, Labour Bureau (Simla, 1969)
Report on the Cashew Industry, The Cashew Corporation of India (New Delhi, 1983)
Report on the Marketing of Cashew Nuts in India, Agricultural Marketing in India, Marketing Series No. 47 (Calcutta, 1944)
Report of the Royal Commission on Labour in India (Calcutta, 1931)
Report on the Working of the Minimum Wages Act of 1948 (Simla, 1955)
Report on the Working of the Minimum Wages Act, 1948, during the Years 1968 and 1969 (Simla, 1973)
Report on the Working and Living Conditions of Workers in the Cashewnut Processing Industry in Kerala 1982, Labour bureau (Chandigarh, 1983)
Statistical Profile on Women Labor 1983 (Simla, 1985)
Statistical Profile on Women Labor 1998 (Simla, 1999)
Towards Equality: Report of the National Committee on the Status of Women in India (New Delhi, 1974)

Government of Mysore

Report of the Administration of Mysore for the Year 1921-22 (Bangalore, 1924)
Report of the Administration of Mysore for the Year 1925-26 (Bangalore, 1928)
Report of the Administration of Mysore for the Year 1927-28 (Bangalore, 1930)
Report of the Administration of Mysore for the Year 1928-29 (Bangalore, 1931)

Government of Kerala

Administration Report for the Labour Department for the Years 1960-1995
Cashew Industry in Kerala, State Planning Board (Trivandrum, 1969)
Cashew Sector and Women Labourers, Preliminary Report, Department of
　　Industries (Trivandrum, 1998); copy received from L. Radhakrish-
　　nan, Department of Industries, Trivandrum
Economic Review, 1960-1998
The Kerala Cashew Workers' Relief and Welfare Fund Act 1979
The Kerala Cashew Workers' Relief and Welfare Fund Scheme 1988
The Kerala Factories Rules, 1957 (Ernakulam, 1989)
Proceedings of the Kerala Legislative Assembly, First Session 1964, 13
　　March 1964, XVIII, No. 25, "Resolution 3, Women Workers in Ker-
　　ala", pp. 2211-2225 (Trivandrum, 1964) (in Malayalam)
Report on Annual Survey of Industries, various issues 1963-85, Department
　　of Economics and Statistics (Trivandrum, 1964-1986)
*Report of the Delegation Committee for the Revision of the Minimum Wages
　　of Cashew Workers 1998,* G.O. (R.T) 2473/96, Labour Department
　　(Trivandrum, 1998) (in Malayalam); copy received from the chair-
　　man, P. Madhavan
*Report of the Minimum Wages Advisory Committee for Cashew Industry
　　1959,* Labor Department (Trivandrum, 1959)
*Report of the Minimum Wages Committee for Employment in Fish Canning,
　　Freezing, Peeling and Exporting Seafood and Frogs Legs in Kerala State
　　1970-73* (Ernakulam, 1973)
*Report of the Survey on Socio-Economic Conditions of Agricultural and other
　　Rural Labourers in Kerala 1983-1984,* Department of Economic and
　　Statistics (Trivandrum, 1985)

Government of Travancore

Report of the Banking Enquiry Committee Travancore 1929
　　(Trivandrum, 1931)
Report of the Economic Depression Enquiry Committee 1931
　　(Trivandrum, 1932)
Statistics of Travancore, 8ᵗʰ issue, 1102 ME/1926-27 AD
　　(Trivandrum, 1928)
Statistics of Travancore, 14ᵗʰ issue, 1108 ME/1932-1933 AD
　　(Trivandrum, 1934)
Statistics of Travancore, 16ᵗʰ issue, 1110 ME/1934-1935 AD
　　(Trivandrum, 1936)

Statistics of Travancore, 18th issue, 1112 ME/1936-1937 AD
(Trivandrum, 1938)
Statistics of Travancore, 19th issue, 1113 ME/1937-1938 AD
(Trivandrum, 1939)
Statistics of Travancore, 20th issue, 1114 ME/1938-1939 AD
(Trivandrum, 1940)
Travancore Administration Report 1102 ME/1926-27 AD
(Trivandrum, 1929)
Travancore Administration Report 1103 ME/1927-28 AD
(Trivandrum, 1930)
Travancore Administration Report 1104 ME/1928-29 AD
(Trivandrum, 1931)
Travancore Administration Report 1105 ME/1929-30 AD
(Trivandrum, 1932)
Travancore Administration Report 1113 ME/1937-38 AD
(Trivandrum, 1939)
Travancore Administration Report 1114 ME/1938-39 AD
(Trivandrum, 1940)
Travancore Administration Report 1115 ME/1939-40 AD
(Trivandrum, 1941)
Travancore Administration Report 1120 ME/1944-45 AD
(Trivandrum, 1946)
Travancore Information and Listener 4:12
(Trivandrum, 1944)
Travancore Information and Listener, 6:11
(Trivandrum, 1946)

Government of Travancore-Cochin

Report of the Minimum Wages Committee for Cashew Industry 1953
(Trivandrum, 1953)
Report of the Minimum Wages Committee for the Manufacture of Coir 1952
(Trivandrum, 1959)

C. Publications of Organizations

1) Cashew Export Promotion Council (CEPC), Cochin
     Leaflet: "Indian Cashews"
     Cashew Statistics (Cochin, 1977)
     Indian Cashews: Facts and Figures (Cochin, 1994)
     Indian Cashew Statistics 1991-1996 (Cochin, 1996)

2) The World Bank, Washington D.C.
   The World Bank, *India Staff Appraisal Report Cashewnut Project*, Confidential Report No. 2437-IN, 1979 (available at CDS library, Trivandrum)

3) South Indian Cashew Manufacturers Association, Quilon (SICMA)
   SICMA Souvenir 1967, South Indian Cashew Manufacturers Association (Quilon, 1968). Correspondence and settlements

4) Revolutionary Socialist Party (RSP), Quilon
   Thrivananthapuram Industrial Tribunal, Labour Conflict No. 15/1951
   Confidential Report of the Central Team on Cashew Industry in Kerala State, Decisions taken at the meeting of the all-party delegation from Kerala and the Prime-Minister of India on 13th May 1971, Chairman R.V. Raman, 13 May 1971
   Pamphlets
   Correspondence and settlements
   Annual Reports
   A.A. Azeez, "The Great Organisation of Cashew Workers", *RSP Golden Jubilee* (Quilon, 1990)

6) Kerala State Cashew Development Corporation (KSCDC), Quilon.
   Personal Department: settlements and wage scales 1970-1999

7) Peirce Leslie India Ltd., Calicut
   "Random thoughts from a Century and a Half in Malabar of a British firm" (Calicut, 1997)
   Various Annual Reports, Peirce Leslie India, 1980-1995

D. Unpublished Papers and Thesis

Beevi, A.J. Eman. "Impact of Minimum Wage Legislation on Cashew Industry" (M.Phil., Jawaharlal Nehru University, New Delhi, 1978).

Buvinic, Mayra, Youssef, Nadia H., and von Elm, Barbara. "Women-Headed Households: The Ignored Factor in Development Planning" (Working Paper, International Center for Research on Women, Washington D.C., 1978).

Deepa, G.L. "Industrial Crisis and Women Workers, A Study of Cashew Processing Industry in Kerala" (M.Phil., Centre for Development Studies, Trivandrum, 1994).

Engels, Dagmar. "The Changing Role of Women in Bengal, c.1890-c.1930, with Special Reference to British and Bengali Discourse on Gender" (Ph.D., SOAS, University of London, 1987).

Erwér, Monica. "Development Beyond the Status of Women: The Kerala Model from a Gender Perspective" (M.Phil., Department of Peace and Development Research, Göteborg University, 1998).

Faria, S.H. "A Study of the Socio-economic Conditions of the Cashew Labourers with Special Reference to the Women Workers at Dhanalakshmi Vilasam, Quilon" (M.Phil., Rajagiri College of Social Sciences, Kalamassery, Cochin, 1958).

Göransson, Anita. "Meaning and Materiality: An Attempt to Synthesize or a Reconciliation of Realist and Poststructuralist Positions?" (Paper presented at the Nordic Thought Conference at the University of Oslo, March 1994).

Isaac, Thomas. "Class Struggle and Structural Changes in the Coir Industry in Kerala" (Ph.D., University of Kerala, Trivandrum, 1983).

Jain, Devaki. "Displacement of Women Workers in Traditional Industries—Three examples: Cotton Handlooms, Wollen Cottage Industry and Handblock Printing" (Paper submitted to the Second National Conference on Women's Studies, Trivandrum, 1984).

Kannan, K.P. "Employment, Wages and Conditions of Work in the Cashew Processing Industry" (Working Paper No. 77, Centre for Development Studies, Trivandrum, 1978).

—. "Evolution of Unionisation and Changes in Labor Process under Lower Forms of Capitalist Production" (Working Paper No. 128, Centre for Development Studies, Trivandrum, 1981).

Krishnakumar, S. "Women in Workforce–The Cashewnut Labourers in the State of Kerala" (Report, Centre for Education and Communication, New Delhi, 1998).

Kumar, S.K. "Role of the Household Economy in Child Nutrition at Low Incomes" (Occasional Paper No. 95, Department of Agricultural Economics, Cornell University, December, 1978).

Lindberg, Anna. "Class-collaboration and Gender Struggle" (Paper presented at Department of History, Lund University, 1996).

—. "The Concept of Skill and the Kerala Cashew Workers" (Paper presented at Department of History, Lund University, 1999).

—. "Child Labor in South India: The Case of the Cashew Workers" (Paper presented at Department of History, Lund University, 2000).

Meena, S. "Changes in the Life Style of Industrial Workers in Kollam District" (Ph.D., Department of Demography and Population Studies, University of Kerala, Trivandrum, 1997).

Nair, N.K. Aravindakshan and Varghese, P.N. "Women Workers in the

Cashew Industry in Kerala" (Indian Institute for Regional Development Studies, Kottayam, 1979).

Nair, P. Kesavan. "A Brief History of Trade Union Movement among Cashew Workers" (Paper presented at the Conference on Development in Kerala, AKG-Centre, Trivandrum, 1994).

Nair, R. Gopalakrishnan and Thomas, T.S. "Socio-economic Conditions of Working Women in Cashew Industry in Quilon District, Kerala" (Report, Loyola College of Social Sciences, Trivandrum, 1989).

Padmathy, S. C. Darish. "Health Conditions of Women Workers in Cashewnut Industry. A Study of Selected Units in Kaliyakavilai Village of Kanya Kumari Districts" (M.Phil., Department of Economics, Scott Christian College, Nagercoil, 1990).

Patil, B.R. "Cashew Workers of Kanya Kumari" (Indian Institutes of Management, Bangalore, 1984).

Pillai, K. Balan. "The Economic Impact of Collective Bargaining on Cashew Industry in Kerala" (Ph.D.,Department of Economics, University of Kerala, Trivandrum, 1986).

Rammohan, K.T. "Material Processes and Developmentalism: Interpreting Economic Change in Colonial Tiruvitamkur, 1800 to 1945" (Ph.D., Centre for Development Studies, Trivandrum, 1996).

Sarojini, M. "A Study of the Working and Living Conditions of the Women Workers in the Cashew Factories with Special Reference to Chonadam Factory of Messrs Peirce Leslie & Co., Ltd.," (M.Phil., Stella Maris College, University of Madras, 1960).

Sen, Samita. "Women Workers in the Bengal Jute Industry, 1890-1940: Migration, Motherhood and Militancy" (Ph.D., Cambridge University, 1992).

Sundaresan, R. "State Intervention in Support of Traditional Industries— the Case of the Kerala State Cashew Development Corporation" (M.Phil., University of Kerala, Centre F.M.N. College, Quilon, 1994).

Tharakan, Michael and Isaac, Thomas. "Historical Roots of Industrial Backwardness of Kerala" (Working Paper No. 215, Centre for Development Studies, Trivandrum, 1986).

Thrivikraman, M. "Influence of Political Parties on Trade Unions in Jupiter Cashew Factory" (M.Phil., Rajagiri College of Social Science, Kalamassery, 1969).

Véron, René. "State Interventions in the Cashew Sector in Kerala, India" (Paper presented at the 14th European Conference on Modern South Asian Studies, Copenhagen, 21-25 August 1996).

—. "Markets Environment and Development in South India. Cultivating and Marketing of Pineapple and Cashew in Kerala" (Ph.D., University of Zurich, 1997).

Vincent, K.P. "The Socio-Economic Conditions of Cashew Workers: A Study Conducted in Kanyakumari District" (M.Phil., Department of Sociology, University of Kerala, Trivandrum, 1983).

Zachariah, K.C. and Mathew, E.T. and Rajan, S. Irudaya. "Migration in Kerala State India: Dimensions, Determinants and Consequences" (Working Paper I, Centre for Development Studies, Trivandrum, 1999).

E. Newspapers and Periodicals

Bulletin of Concerned Asian Scholars 1998 (Charlemont, MA)
Cashew Bulletin 1995 (Cochin)
CITU Sandesam 1993-1996 (Quilon) (in Malayalam)
Deshabhimani 1994-1999 (Trivandrum) (in Malayalam)
Economic and Political Weekly 1990 (Bombay)
The Hindu 1995, 2000 (Trivandrum)
Indian Express 1995 (Trivandrum)
Jennajugham 1950-1993 (Quilon) (in Malayalam)
Kerala Kaumudi 1960-1999 (Trivandrum) (in Malayalam)
Mathrubhumi Weekly 1977 (Trivandrum) (in Malayalam)
New Indian Express 2000 (Trivandrum)
The Times 1991 (London)

F. Books and Articles

Acker, Joan, Barry, Kate, and Essevald, Johanna (eds). "Objectivity and Truth. Problems in Doing Feminist Research", *Women's Studies International Forum*, 6:4 (1983), pp. 423-435.

Afshar, Haleh (ed.). *Women, Work, and Ideology in the Third World* (New York, 1985).

Afshar, Haleh and Agarwal, Bina (eds). *Women, Poverty and Ideology in Asia* (London, 1989).

Afshar, Haleh and Maynard, Mary (eds). *The Dynamics of 'Race' and Gender: Some Feminist Interventions* (London, 1994).

Agarwal, Bina. "Women, Land and Ideology in India", in Afshar and Agarwal (eds), *Women, Poverty and Ideology in Asia* pp. 70-98.

—. *A Field of One's Own: Gender and Land Rights in South Asia* (Cambridge, 1994).

Alex, George. "Social and Economic Aspect of Attached Labourers in Kuttanad Agriculture", *Economic and Political Weekly*, 22:5 (1987), pp. A141-150.

Alexander, K.C. *Social Mobility in Kerala* (Poona, 1968).

Alexander, William M. "Normal Kerala within Abnormal India: Reflections on Gender and Sustainability", in Parayil (ed.), *Kerala: The Development Experience* pp. 139-156

Allen, Sheila. "Race, Ethnicity and Nationality: Some Questions of Identity", in Afshar and Maynard (eds), *The Dynamics of 'Race' and Gender* pp. 85-105.

Althusser, Louis. *Lenin and Philosophy and Other Essays* (London, 1977).

Anthias, F. and Yuval-Davis, N. "Contextualizing Feminism: Gender, Ethnic, and Class Divisions", *Feminist Review*, 15 (1983), pp. 62-75.

Antony, M.J. *Women's Rights* (New Delhi, 1989).

Avineri, Shlomo (ed.). *Karl Marx on Colonialism and Modernisation, his Dispatches and Other Writings on China, India, Mexico, the Middle East and North Africa* (New York, 1968).

Baaz-Ericson, Maria. "Bortom likhet och särart", *Feministiskt Perspektiv*, No. 4 (1998), pp. 7-11.

Bahl, Vinay. *The Making of the Indian Working Class: A Case Study of the Tata Iron Steel Company* (London, 1995).

—. "Relevance (or Irrelevance) of Subaltern Studies", *Economic and Political Weekly*, 32:23 (1997), pp. 1333-1345.

Bagchi, Amiya Kumar. "Working Class Consciousness", *Economic and Political Weekly*, 25:30 (1990), pp. PE54-60.

Baig, Tara Ali (ed.). *Women of India* (New Delhi, 1990).

Balakrishnan, Thengamam. "Life and Strikes in the Middle of Smoke and Coal Dust", *Jennajugham*, Aug 2 1962, pp. 2, 3 (in Malayalam).

Balaram, N.E. *Communist Movement in Kerala: The Early Days*, Vol. I (Trivandrum, 1973) (in Malayalam).

Banerjee, Nirmala. "Introduction", in Banerjee (ed.), *Indian Women*, pp. 11-32.

Banerjee, Nirmala (ed.). *Indian Women in a Changing Industrial Scenario* (New Delhi, 1991).

Bannerji, Himani. "Projects of Hegemony: Towards a Critique of Subaltern Studies' 'Resolution of the Women's Question'", *Economic and Political Weekly*, 35:11 (2000), pp. 902-920.

Barnett, Stephen A. "Approaches to Changes in Caste Ideology in South India", in Burton Stein (ed.), *Essays on South India* (New Delhi, 1975).

Baron, Ava (ed.). *Work Engendered: Toward a New History of American Labor* (New York, 1991).

Barrett, Michèle. "Words and Things: Materialism and Method in Contemporary Feminist Analysis", in Barrett and Phillips, *Destabilizing Theory*, pp. 201-219.

Barrett, Michèle and Phillips, Anne. *Destabilizing Theory: Contemporary Feminist Debates* (Cambridge, 1992).

Basham, A.L. "Hinduism", in R.C. Zaehner (ed.), *The Concise Encyclopedia of Living Faiths* (Boston, 1959), pp. 225-260.

Basu, Alaka, M. "Fertility Decline and Worsening Gender Bias in India: A Response to S. Irudaya Rajan et al.", *Development and Change*, 31:5 (2000), pp. 1093-1095.

Beechey, Veronica. "Studies on Women's Employment", in *Waged Work: A Reader* (London, 1986), pp. 130-159.

Benhabib, Seyla. "Epistemologies of Postmodernism: A Rejoinder to Jean-Francois Lyotard", in Linda J. Nicholson (ed.), *Feminism/Postmodernism*, pp. 107-130.

Bennholdt-Thomsen, Veronika. "Subsistence Reproduction and Extended Production: A Contribution to the Discussion about Modes of Production", in K. Young, Carol Wolkowitz and Roslyn Mc Cullagh (eds), *Of Marriage and the Market* (London, 1981), pp. 16-29.

—. "Why do Housewives Continue to be Created in the Third World too?', in Mies et al. (eds), *Women: The Last Colony*, pp. 159-167.

Berlanstein, Lenard, R. (ed.), *Rethinking Labor History: Essays on Discourse and Class Analysis* (Urbana, 1993).

Berreman, Gerald D. "The Brahmanical View of Caste", *Contributions to Indian Sociology*, No. 5 (1971), pp. 16-25.

—. *Caste and Other Inequities: Essays on Inequality* (Meerut, 1979).

Béteille, André. *Caste, Class and Power: Changing Patterns of Stratification in a Tanjore Village* (Berkeley, 1965).

—. *Social Inequality: Selected Writings* (Harmondsworth, 1970).

—. *Society and Politics in India. Essays in Comparative Perspective* (London, 1991).

Bhai, L. Thara. "Caste Stratification in South Travancore Region", *Journal of Kerala Studies*, 5, Parts III and IV (December 1978), pp. 493-511.

Bhatt, Anil. *Caste, Class and Politics* (New Delhi, 1975).

Bhattacharya, S. "Capital and Labour in Bombay City, 1928-29", *Economic and Political Weekly*, 16: 42-43 (1981), pp. PE35-44.

Bhavnani, Kum-Kum and Phoenix, Ann (eds). *Shifting Identities. Shifting Racisms: A Feminism and Psychology Reader* (London, 1994).

Billig, Michael S. "The Marriage Squeeze on High-Caste Rajasthani Women", *The Journal of Asian Studies*, 50:2 (1991), pp. 341-360.

Billings, Martin, H. and Singh, Arjan. "Mechanisation and the Wheat Revolution—Effects on Female Labour in Punjab", *Economic and Political Weekly*, 5:52 (1970), pp. A169-174.

Bohusläns samhälls- och näringslivs 4. Konservindustrin (Uddevalla, 1982).

Bordo, Susan. "Feminism, Postmodernism, and Gender-Skepticism", in Nicholson (ed.), *Feminism/Postmodernism*, pp. 133-156.

Borland, Katherine. "That's Not What I Said: Interpretative Conflict in Oral Narrative Research", in Perks and Thomson (eds), *The Oral History Reader*, pp. 320-332.

Boserup, Ester. *Women's Role in Economic Development* (New York, 1970).

Bourdieu, Pierre. "The Social Space and the Genesis of Groups", *Theory and Society*, 14 (1985), pp. 723-744.

Bozzoli, Belinda. *Women of Phokeng: Consciousness, Life Strategy and Migrancy in South Africa 1900-1983* (London, 1991).

Bradley, Harriet. *Men's Work, Women's Work: A Sociological History of the Sexual Division of Labor in Employment* (Cambridge, 1989).

—. *Fractured Identities: Changing Patterns of Inequality* (Cambridge, 1997).

Brandell, Inga (ed.). *Workers in Third-World Industrialization* (London, 1991).

Braudel, Fernand. *La Méditerranée sous la régime de Philippe* (Paris, 1947).

Breman, Jan. "A Dualistic Labour System? A Critique of the 'Informal Sector' Concept, parts I, II, and III", *Economic and Political Weekly*, 11 (1976), pp.1870-1876, 1905-1908, 1939-1944.

—. "The Study of Industrial Labour in Post-colonial India–The Formal Sector: An Introductory Review", in Parry, Breman, and Kapadia (eds), *The Worlds of Indian Industrial Labour*, pp. 1-41.

—. "The Study of Industrial Labour in Post-colonial India—The Informal Sector: A Concluding Review", in Parry, Breman, and Kapadia (eds), *The World of Indian Industrial Labour*, pp. 407-432.

—. "Industrial Labour in Post-Colonial India I: Industrializing the Economy and Formalizing Labour", *International Review of Social History*, 44 (1999), pp. 249-300.

Brook, Ezriel. *Cashew Nuts: Review and Outlook,* Economic Analysis and Projections Department, World Bank, Commodity Notes No. 5 (Washington D.C., 1978).

Bryceson, D.F. and Vuorela, U. "Outside the Domestic Labour Debate: Towards a Materialist Theory of Modes of Human Reproduction", *Review of Radical Political Economics*, 16: 2-3 (1984), pp. 137-166.

Bumiller, Elisabeth. *May You Be the Mother of a Hundred Sons: A Journey Among the Women of India* (New Delhi, 1990).

Carby, H. "White Woman Listen! Black Feminism and the Boundaries of Sisterhood", in Centre for Contemporary Cultural Studies (eds), *The Empire Strikes Back* (London, 1982).

Carlsson, Christina. *Kvinnosyn och Kvinnopolitik: En studie av svensk socialdemokrati 1880-1910* (Lund, 1986).

Cashew Marketing, International Trade Centre, Unctad, Gatt (Geneva, 1968).

Centre for Women's Development Studies, "Workers' Movements in the Coir Industry in Kerala 1938-1980: Women's Role and Participation", in Shimwaayi Muntemba (ed.), *Rural Development and Women: Lesson from the Field*, Vol. II, Sections 1 and 2, International Labour Office (Geneva, 1985), pp. 223-248.

Chakrabarty, Dipesh. *Rethinking Working-Class History* (New Delhi, 1989).

—. "Marx after Marxism: History, Subalternity and Difference", *Meanjin* 52:3 (1993), pp. 421-434.

—. "Marx after Marxism: A Subaltern Historian's Perspective", *Economic and Political Weekly*, 28 (1993), pp. 1094-1096.

—. "Radical Histories and Questions of Enlightenment Rationalism", *Economic and Political Weekly*, 30:14 (1995), pp. 751-759.

Chakravarty, Uma. "Conceptualising Brahmanical Patriarchy in Early India: Gender, Caste, Class and State", *Economic and Political Weekly*, 28:14 (1993), pp. 579-586.

—. "Gender, Caste and Labour: Ideological and Material Structure of Widowhood", *Economic and Political Weekly*, 30:36 (1995), pp. 2248-2256.

Chatterjee, Partha. "Caste and Subaltern Consciousness", in Ranajit Guha (ed.), *Subaltern Studies VI: Writings on South Asian History and Society* (Oxford, 1989), pp. 169-209.

Chhachhi, Amrita and Pittin, Renée. "Multiple Identities and Multiple Strategies: Confronting State, Capital and Patriarchy", in Ronaldo Munck and Peter Waterman (eds), *Labour Worldwide in the Era of Globalization: Alternative Union Models in the New World Order* (New York, 1999), pp. 64-79.

Chirayath, John Thomas. *A Study on the Cashew Industry in Kerala*, Labour and Industrial Bureau (Trivandrum, 1965).

Chodorow, Nancy. *The Reproduction of Mothering: Psychoanalysis and the Sociology of Gender* (Berkeley, 1978).

Clark, Alice. *Working Life of Women in the Seventeenth Century* (London, 1919).

Cockburn, Cynthia. *Brothers: Male Dominance and Technological Change* (London, 1983).

—. *Machinery of Dominance: Women, Men and Technical Know-How* (London, 1985).

Crompton, Rosemary (ed.). *Restructuring Gender Relations and Employment: The Decline of the Male Breadwinner* (Oxford, 1999).

Das, Arvind, Nilakant, V., and Dubey, P.S. (eds). *Worker and the Working Class* (New Delhi, 1984).

Das Gupta, Ranajith. "Indian Working Class and Some Recent Historiographical Issues", *Economic and Political Weekly,* 31:8 (1996), pp. L27-31.

Das, Jayadeva, D. "Genesis of Trade Union Movement in Travancore", *Journal of Kerala Studies* 7:1-4 (1980), pp. 99-133.

Das, Veena. "Marriage Among Hindus", in Devaki Jain (ed.), *Indian Women* (New Delhi, 1975).

Datar, Chhaya. *Waging Change: Women Tobacco Workers in Nipani Organize* (New Delhi, 1989).

Datta, Satya Brata. *Capital Accumulation and Workers' Struggle in Indian Industrialisation: The Case of Tata Iron and Steel Company 1910-1970* (Stockholm, 1986).

Davies, Miranda. "Indian Women Speak Out Against Dowry", in M. Davies (ed.), *Third World—Second Sex: Women's Struggles and National Liberalism. Third World Women Speak Out* (London, 1983).

Deliège, Robert. "Caste without a System: a Study of South Indian Harijans", in Searle-Chatterjee and Sharma (eds), *Contextualising Caste:* pp. 122-145.

D'Souza, Radha Iyer. "Industrialization, Labour Policies, and the Labour Movement", in T.V. Sathyamurthy (ed.), *Class Formation and Political Transformation in Post-colonial India* (New Delhi, 1996), pp. 105-126.

Dumont, Luis. *Homo Hierarchus* (Chicago, 1970).

Eaton, Richard M. "(Re)imag(in)ing Otherness: A Postmortem for the Postmodern in India", *Journal of World History,* 11:1 (2000), pp. 57-78.

Elson, Diane and Pearson, Ruth. "The Subordination of Women and the Internationalisation of Factory Production", in Kate Young, Carol Wolkowitz, and Roslyn McCullagh (eds), *Of Market and the Market: Women's Subordination in International Perspective* (London, 1981), pp. 144-166.

—. "'Nimble Fingers Make Cheap Workers': An Analysis of Women's Employment in Third World Export Manufacturing", *Feminist Review,* No. 7 (1981), pp. 87-107.

Engels, Dagmar. "The Myth of the Family Unit: *Adivasi* Women in Coal-Mines and Tea Plantations in Early Twentieth-Century Bengal", in Peter Robb (ed.), *Dalit Movements and the Meanings of Labour in India* (New Delhi, 1993), pp. 225-244.

Engels, Friedrich. *The Origin of the Family, Private Property and the State* (London, 1972) [1884].

Enloe, Cynthia. *Bananas, Bases and Beaches: Making Feminist Sense of International Politics* (London, 1990).

—. "Silicon Tricks and the Two Dollar Woman", *New Internationalist*, January (1992), pp. 12-14.

Epstein, T.S. *South India: Yesterday, Today and Tomorrow* (London, 1973).

Evans, Barbara. "Constructing a Plantation Labour Force: The Plantation-village Nexus in South India", *The Indian Economic and Social History Review*, 32: 2 (1995), pp. 155-176.

Evans, Richard J. "Politics and the Family: Social Democracy and the Working Class Family in Theory and Practice before 1914", in Richard J. Evans and W.R. Lee (eds), *The German Family: Essays on the Social History of the Family in the Nineteenth and Twentieth-century Germany* (London, 1981), pp. 256-280.

Fairclough, Norman. *Discourse and Social Change* (Cambridge, 1992).

—. *Critical Discourse Analysis* (London, 1995).

Fernandes, Leela. *Producing Workers: The Politics of Gender, Class, and Culture in the Calcutta Jute Mills* (Chicago, 1997).

Foreman, Ann. *Femininity and Alienation: Women and the Family in Marxism and Psychoanalysis* (London, 1977).

Foucault, Michel. *The Archeology of Knowledge* (London, 1989).

—. *Diskursens ordning* (Stockholm, 1993).

Frank, Andre Gunder. *Capitalism and Underdevelopment in Latin America* (New York, 1969).

Franke, Richard. *Life is a Little Better: Redistribution as a Development Strategy in Nadur Village, Kerala* (New Delhi, 1996).

Franke, Richard and Chasin, Barbara. *Kerala: Radical Reform As Development in an Indian State* (San Francisco, 1989).

—. "Is the Kerala Model Sustainable? Lessons from the Past, Prospects for the Future", in G. Parayil (ed.), *Kerala: The Development Experience*, pp. 16-39.

Fröbel, F., Kreye, J. and Heinrich, O. *The New International Division of Labour* (Cambridge, 1980).

Fuller, C.J. *The Nayars Today* (Cambridge, 1976).

—. "Kerala Christians and the Caste System", in Gupta (ed.), *Social Stratification*, pp. 195-212.

—. *Caste Today* (Bombay, 1996).

Garzilli, Enrica (ed.). *Journal of South Asian Women Studies 1995-1997* (Milano, 1997).

Geertz, Clifford. *The Interpretation of Cultures* (New York, 1973).

—. "On the Nature of Anthropological Understanding", *American Scientist*, 63:1 (1975), pp. 47-53.

—. *Works and Lives: The Anthropologist as Author* (Cambridge, 1988).

Geiger, S. "What's so Feminist about Women's Oral History?", *Journal of Women's History*, 2:1 (1990), pp. 169-170.

George, K.K. "Historical Roots of the Kerala Model and its Present Crisis", *Bulletin of Concerned Asian Scholars*, 30:4 (1998), pp. 35-40.

Ghosh, Saswati. "Women Workers and Organisers in the Jute Industry in Bengal, 1920-1950", in Gothoskar (ed.), *Struggles of Women*, pp. 114-122.

Ghurye, G.S. *Caste and Class in India* (Bombay, 1957).

—. *Caste and Race in India* (Bombay, 1969).

Giddens, Anthony. *The Transformation of Intimacy* (Cambridge, 1992).

Glucksmann, Miriam. *Women Assemble: Women Workers and the New Industries in Inter-War Britain* (London, 1990).

Goodman, Sara and Mulinari, Diana (eds). *Feminist Interventions in Discourses on Gender and Development* (Lund, 1999).

Goody, Jack and Tambiah, S.J. *Bridewealth and Dowry* (Cambridge, 1973).

Gorz, André. *Farewell to the Working Class* (London, 1982).

Gothoskar, Sujatha (ed.). *Struggles of Women at Work* (New Delhi, 1992)

Gough, Kathleen. "Nayar: North Kerala", "Nayar: Central Kerala", "Tiyyar: North Kerala", in D. Schneider and K. Gough (eds), *Matrilineal Kinship* (Berkeley, 1961), pp. 298-442.

—. "Palakkara: Social and Religious Change in Central Kerala", in K. Ishwaran (ed.), *Change and Continuity in India's Villages* (New York, 1970), pp. 129-164.

—. "Changing Households in Kerala", in D. Narain (ed.), *Explorations in the Family and Other Essays* (Bombay, 1973), pp. 218-276.

Govindan, K.C. *Memoires of an Early Trade Unionist* (Trivandrum, 1986).

Govindan Nair, M.N. *Autobiography of M.N., Part II* (Trivandrum, 1988) (in Malayalam).

Grele, R. *Envelopes of Sound* (Chicago, 1975).

Guha, Ramachandra. "Subaltern and Bhadralok Studies", *Economic and Political Weekly,* 30:33 (1995), pp. 2056-2058.

Guha, Ranajith. "On Some Aspects of the Historiography of Colonial India", in Ranajith Guha (ed.), *Subaltern Studies I: Writings on South Asian History and Society* (New Delhi, 1982), pp. 1-8.

Gulati, Leela. "Profile of a Female Agricultural Labourer", *Economic and Political Weekly,* 13:12 (1978), pp. A27–36.

—. *Economic and Social Aspects of Population Ageing in Kerala, India* (New York, 1992).

—. "Women in the Unorganised Sector with Special Reference to Kerala", in Sharma and Singh (eds), *Women and Work*, pp. 263-265.

Gulati, Leela, Ramalingam, and Gulati, I.S. *Gender Profile: Kerala* (New Delhi, 1995).

Gupta, Dipankar. "Continuous Hierarchies and Discrete Castes", *Eco-*

nomic and Political Weekly, 19:46-48 (1984), pp. 1955-1958.

— (ed.). *Social Stratification* (New Delhi, 1996).

Haan, Arjan de. *Unsettled Settlers: Migrant Workers and Industrial Capitalism in Calcutta* (Rotterdam, 1994).

Hall, John R. (ed.). *Reworking Class* (New York, 1997).

Hall, Stuart. "The Toad in the Garden: Thatcherism among the Theorists", in Cary Nelson and Lawrence Grossberg (eds), *Marxism and the Interpretation of Culture* (Houndmills, 1988).

—. "The West and the Rest: Discourse and Power", in S. Hall and B. Gieben (eds), *Formations of Modernity* (Cambridge, 1993), pp. 276-320.

—. "The Problem of Ideology: Marxism without Guarantees", in Morley and Chen (eds), *Stuart Hall* pp. 25-46.

Haraway, Donna. "Situated Knowledge: The Science Question in Feminism and the Privilege of Partial Perspective", *Feminist Studies*, 14:3 (1988), pp. 575-597.

Hardgrave Jr, Robert L. *Essays in the Political Sociology of South India* (New Delhi, 1993).

Harding, Sandra. "Feminism, Science, and the Anti-Enlightenment Critiques", in Nicholson (ed.), *Feminism/Postmodernism*, pp. 83-106.

—. *Whose Science? Whose Knowledge? Thinking from Women's Lives* (Buckingham, 1991).

Hartmann, Heidi. "The Unhappy Marriage of Marxism and Feminism: Towards a More Progressive Union", in Lydia Sargent (ed.), *The Unhappy Marriage of Marxism and Feminism: A Debate on Class and Patriarchy* (London, 1981), pp. 1-41.

Hartsock, Nancy. "Foucault on Power: A Theory for Women?", in Nicholson (ed.), *Feminism/Postmodernism*, pp. 157-175.

Heller, Patrick. "From Class Struggle to Class Compromise: Redistribution and Growth in a South Indian State", in *Journal of Development Studies*, 31:5 (1995), pp. 645-672.

—. "Social Capital as a Product of Class Mobilization and State Intervention: Industrial Workers in Kerala, India", in *World Development*, 24:6 (1996), pp. 1055-1071.

Hennessy, Rosemary. *Materialist Feminism and the Politics of Discourse* (New York, 1993).

Hennessy, Rosemary and Ingaham, Chrys (eds). *Materialist Feminism: A Reader in Class, Difference an Women's Lives* (London, 1997).

Hexter, Jack, H. *On Historians: Reappraisals of Some of the Makers of Modern History* (Cambridge, 1979).

Hoare, Quintin and Nowell Smith, Geoffrey (eds). *Antonio Gramsci: Selections from the Prison Notebooks* (Chennai, 2000).

Hobsbawn, Eric. "From Social History to the History of Society", in Eric Hobsbawn, *On History* (London, 1997), pp. 71-93. [Originally published in *Daedalus*, Vol. 100 (1971)].

Holmström, Mark. "Caste and Status in an Indian City", *Economic and Political Weekly*, 7:15 (1972), pp. 769-774.

—. *South Indian Factory Workers: Their Life and Their World* (Cambridge, 1976).

—. *Industry and Inequality: The Social Anthropology of Indian labour* (Cambridge, 1984).

hooks, bell. *Ain't I a Woman? Black Women and Feminism* (London, 1982).

—. *Yearning: Race, Gender, and Cultural Politics* (London, 1991).

Hopkins, Terence K, and Wallerstein, Immanual (eds). *World-systems Analysis* (Beverly Hills, 1982).

Humphries, Jane. "Class Struggle and the Persistence of the Working-Class Family", in Alice Amsden (ed.), *The Economics of Women and Work* (New York, 1980), pp. 140-165.

Hutton, J.H. *Caste in India: Its Nature, Function and Origins* (Bombay, 1963).

Internationella Arbetsorganisationen II: Arbetskonferensens första-femte sammanträden 1919-1923 (Stockholm, 1930).

Isaac, Thomas. "The Trend and Pattern of External Trade of Kerala", in Prakash (ed.), *Kerala's Economy* pp. 368-393.

Isaac, T.M. Thomas and Franke, Richard W. and Raghavan, Pyaralal. *Democracy at Work in an Indian Industrial Cooperative* (London, 1998).

Iyer, L.A.K. *The Cochin Tribes and Castes*, Vol. I (Madras, 1909).

—. *The Travancore Tribes and Castes,* Vol. II (Trivandrum, 1939).

Jacob, Georg. *Religious Life of the Ilavas of Kerala: Change and Continuity* (New Delhi, 1995).

Jain, D.P. *Industrial and Labour Laws* (New Delhi, 1996).

Janssens, Angélique. "The Rise and Decline of the Male Breadwinner Family? An Overview of the Debate", in Angélique Janssens (ed.), *The Rise and Decline of the Male Breadwinner Family?* (New York, 1998), pp. 1-23.

Jawaid, Sohaid. *Trade Union Movement in India* (New Delhi, 1982).

Jeffrey, Robin. *The Decline of Nair Dominance* (New Delhi, 1976).

—. *Politics, Women and Well Being: How Kerala Became "A Model"* (New Delhi, 1993).

Jenkins, Keith. (ed.), *The Postmodern History Reader* (London, 1997).

Joyce, Patrick. *Visions of the People-Industrial England and the Question of Class 1848-1914* (Cambridge, 1991).

—. "The End of Social History", *Social History*, 20:1 (1995), pp. 73-91.

Kabeer, Naila. *Reversed Realities: Gender Hierarchies in Development Thought* (London, 1994).

Kaimal, P.K.V. *Revolt of the Oppressed: Punnapra-Vayalar 1946* (New Delhi, 1994).

Kalpagam, Uma. *Labour and Gender: Survival in Urban India* (New Delhi, 1994).

Kannan, K.P. *Cashew Development in India, Potentialities and Constraints* (Trivandrum, 1981).

—. "Evolution of Unionisation and Changes in Labour Processes under Lower Forms of Capitalist Production", in Das et al. (ed.), *Worker and the Working Class*, pp. 45-61.

—. *Of Rural Proletarian Struggles: Mobilization and Organization of Rural Workers in South-West India* (Bombay, 1988).

—. "Poverty Alleviation as Advancing Basic Human Capabilities", in Parayil (ed.), *Kerala: The Development Experience*, pp. 40-65.

Kapadia, Karin. *Siva and Her Sisters: Gender, Caste and Class in Rural South India* (Boulder, 1995).

—. "Gender Ideologies and the Formation of Rural Industrial Classes in South India Today", in Parry, Breman, and Kapadia (eds), *The Worlds of Indian Industrial Labour*, pp. 329-352.

Kaplan, A. Marion (ed.). *The Marriage Bargaining: Women and Dowries in European History* (New York, 1985).

Karlsson, Lynn and Wikander, Ulla. *Kvinnoarbete och könssegregering i svensk industri 1870-1950: Tre uppsatser*, Uppsala Papers in Economic History, Research Report No. 9 (Uppsala, 1985).

Kayamkulam, Yoonus. *Thangal Kunju Musaliar Biography* (Quilon, 1997) (in Malayalam).

Kessler-Harris, Alice. *A Woman's Wage: Historical Meanings and Social Consequences* (Lexington, KY, 1990).

Kishwar, Madhu. "Dowry—to Ensure Her Happiness or to Disinherit Her?", *Manushi*, No. 34 (1986), pp. 8-17.

—. "Why I Do Not Call Myself a Feminist", *Manushi,* No. 61 (1990), pp. 2-8.

—. "Dowry Calculations: Daughter's Rights in Her Parental Family", *Manushi*, No. 78 (1993), pp. 8-17.

—. *Off the Beaten Track: Rethinking Gender Justice for Indian Women* (New Delhi, 1999).

Kolenda, Pauline Mahar. "Religious Anxiety and Hindu Fate", *Journal of Asian Studies*, 23 (1964), pp. 71-82.

Krishnamurty, J. (ed.). *Women in Colonial India: Essays on Survival, Work and the State* (New Delhi, 1989).

Kumar, Radha. "Family and Factory: Women in the Bombay Cotton

Textile Industry, 1919-1939", in Krishnamurty (ed.), *Women in Colonial India*, pp. 133-162.

—. "Factory Life: Women Workers in the Bombay Cotton Textile Industry, 1919-1939", in Gothoskar (ed.), *Struggles of Women at Work*, pp. 123-131.

—. *The History of Doing* (New Delhi, 1993).

Kuttykrishnan, A.C. "Educational Development in Kerala", in Prakash (ed.), *Kerala's Economy*, pp. 349-367.

Laclau, Ernesto and Mouffe, Chantal. "Post-Marxism without Apologies", in Ernesto Laclau, *New Reflections on the Revolution of Our Time* (London, 1990), pp. 97-132.

Laduries, Le Roy. *Les Paysans de Languedoc* (Paris, 1966).

Lal, Jayati. "Situating Locations: The Politics of Self, Identity, and 'Other' in Living and Writing the Text", in Dianne Wolf (ed.), *Feminist Dilemmas in Field Work* (New York, 1996), pp. 185-214.

Langley, W.K.M. *Century in Malabar, The History of Peirce Leslie & Co., Ltd. 1862-1962* (Madras, 1962).

Larrain, Jorge. *The Concept of Ideology* (London, 1979).

—. "Stuart Hall and the Marxist Concept of Ideology", in Morley and Chen (eds), *Stuart Hall*, pp. 47-70.

Leffler, Marion. *Böcker, bildning, makt: Arbetare, borgare och bildningens roll i klassformeringen i Lund och Helsingborg 1860-1901* (Malmö, 1999).

Lemercinier, Genevieve. *Religion and Ideology in Kerala* (Trivandrum, 1994).

Leslie, Julia. "Dowry, Dowry Deaths and Violence Against Women", in Garzilli (ed.), *Journal of South Asian Women Studies 1995-1997* pp. 135-143.

Lewis, Jane. *Women in England 1870-1950* (Brighton, 1984).

Liddle, Joanna and Joshi, Rama. *Daughters of Independence* (London, 1986).

Lim, Linda. "Women's Work in Export Factories: The Politics of a Cause", in Irene Tinker (ed.), *Persistent Inequalities: Women and World Development* (New York, 1990), pp. 101-119.

Lindberg, Staffan. "Farmers' Movements and Agricultural Development in India", in Staffan Lindberg and Árni Sverrisson (eds), *Social Movements in Development: The Challenge of Globalization and Democratization* (Basinstoke, 1997), pp. 101-125.

Lovibond, Sabina. "Feminism and Postmodernism", *New Left Review*, 178 (1989), pp. 5-28.

Lugones, Maria C. and Spelman, Elizabeth. "Have We Got a Theory for You! Feminist Theory, Cultural Imperialism and the Demand for 'The Woman's Voice'", *Women Studies International Forum*, 6:6 (1983), pp. 573-581.

Luxemburg, Rosa. *Die Akkumulation des Kapital, Ein Beitrag zur ökonomischen Erklärung des Kapitalismus* (Berlin, 1923).

Lyotard, Jean-Francois. *The Postmodern Condition* (Manchester, 1984).

Mahadevan, Raman. "Industrial Entrepreneurship in Princely Travancore: 1930-47", in Sabyasachi Bhattacharya et al. (ed.), *The South Indian Economy: Agrarian Change, Industrial Structure, and State Policy c.1914-1947* (New Delhi, 1991).

Majeed, T.M. *The Strike History of the Cashewnut Workers* (Kollam, 2000) (in Malayalam).

Mamkoottam, K. *Trade Unionism: Myth and Reality; Unionism in the Tata Iron and Steel Company* (New Delhi, 1982).

Mandal, R.C. *Cashew Production and Processing Technology* (New Delhi, 1992).

Mankekar, D.R. *The Red Riddle of Kerala* (Bombay, 1965).

Mann, M. "The Social Cohesion of Liberal Democracy", *American Sociological Review*, 35 (1970), pp. 423-439.

Marriot, McKim. *Caste Ranking and Community Structure in Five Regions of India and Pakistan* (Poona, 1960).

Marshall, Barbara L. *Engendering Modernity: Feminism, Social Theory and Social Change* (Cambridge, 1994).

Marx, Karl, and Engels, Friedrich. *The German Ideology* (London, 1965).

—. *On Colonialism* (Moscow, 1968).

Mathew, E.T. *Employment and Unemployment in Kerala: Some Neglected Aspects* (New Delhi, 1997).

Mathew, Joseph. *Ideology, Protest and Social Mobility: Case Study of Mahars and Pulayas* (New Delhi, 1986).

Mathur, A.S. and Mathur, J. S. *Trade Union Movement in India* (Allahabad, 1962).

Matthen, C.P. *I Have Borne Much* (Madras, 1951).

Matthew, George. *Communal Road to a Secular Kerala* (New Delhi, 1989).

May, Martha. "Bread before Roses", in Milkman (ed.), *Women, Work, and Protest* pp. 1-22.

Meera, V. "Tradition of Militant Struggle of Women in Coir Industry", *The Voice of the Working Woman,* September 1984, pp. 3-5 and November 1984, pp. 3, 5.

Melucci, Alberto. *Nomads of the Present: Social Movements and Individual Needs in Contemporary Society* (Philadelphia, 1989).

Mencher, Joan. "The Nairs of South Malabar", in M.N. Nimkoff (ed.), *Comparative Family Systems* (Boston, 1965), pp. 162-191.

—. "The Caste System Upside Down ", in Gupta (ed.), *Social Stratification* (Oxford, 1996), pp. 93-109. [Excerpted from Joan P. Mencher, "The Caste System Upside Down or the Not-So-Mysterious East", *Current Anthropology*, 15:4 (1974)].

—. "On Being an Untouchable in India: A Materialist Perspective", in Eric B. Ross (ed.), *Beyond the Myths of Culture. Essays in Cultural Materialism* (New York, 1980), pp. 261-294.

—. "The Lessons and Non-Lessons of Kerala: Agricultural Labourers and Poverty", *Economic and Political Weekly*, 15 (1980), pp. 1781-1802.

—. "Women's Work and Poverty: Women's Contribution to Household Maintenance in South India", in Daisy Dwyer and Judith Bruce (eds), *A Home Divided: Women and Income in the Third World* (Stanford, 1988), pp. 99-119.

—. "Female-Headed, Female-Supported Households in India: Who Are They and What Are Their Survival Strategies?", in Joan P. Mencher and Anne Okongwu (eds), *Where Did All the Men Go? Female-Headed-Supported Households in Cross-Cultural Perspective* (Boulder, 1992), pp. 203-231.

Mendelsohn, Oliver and Vicziany, Marika. *The Untouchables: Subordination, Poverty and the State in Modern India* (Cambridge, 1998).

Menon, A. Sreedhara. *Social and Cultural History of Kerala* (New Delhi, 1979).

—. *A Survey of Kerala History* (Madras, 1984).

—. *Cultural Heritage of Kerala* (Madras, 1996).

—. *Kerala and Freedom Struggle* (Kottayam, 1997).

Menon, Dilip M. "Review of Subaltern Studies III", *The Indian Economic and Social History Review*, 32:3 (1995), pp. 392-394.

Menon, Nivedita. "Women in Trade Unions: A Study of AITUC, IN-TUC and CITU in the Seventies", in Gothoskar (ed.), *Struggles of Women at Work*, pp. 187-196.

Merton, R. "Insiders and Outsiders: A Chapter in the Sociology of Knowledge", *American Journal of Sociology*, 78:1 (1972), pp. 9-47.

Mies, Maria. *The Lace Makers of Narsapur: Indian Housewives Produce for the World Market* (London, 1982).

—. "Towards a Methodology for Feminist Research", in Gloria Bowles and Renate Duelli Klein (eds), *Theories of Women's Studies* (London, 1983), pp. 117-139.

—. *Patriarchy and Accumulation on a World Scale. Women in the International Division of Labour* (London, 1986).

—. "Capitalist Development Production", in Mies et al. (eds), *Women: The Last Colony*, pp. 27-63.

Mies, Maria, Bennholdt-Thomsen, Veronika, and von Werlhof, Claudia. *Women: The Last Colony* (New Delhi, 1988).

Mies, Maria, and Bennholdt-Thomsen, Veronika. *The Subsistence Perspective Beyond the Globalised Economy* (London, 1999).

Milkman, Ruth. *Gender at Work: The Dynamics of Job Segregation by Sex during World War* II (Urbana, 1987).

Milkman, Ruth (ed.). *Women, Work, and Protest: A Century of U.S. Women's Labor History* (London, 1991).

Mills, Sara. *Discourse* (London, 1997).

Mitter, Swasti. *Common Fate, Common Bond: Women in the Global Economy* (London, 1986).

—. "On Organising Women in Casualised Work: A Global Overview", in Rowbotham and Mitter, *Dignity and Daily Bread*, pp. 14-52.

Modleski, Tania. *Feminism Without Women: Culture and Criticism in a 'Postfeminist' Age* (New York, 1991).

Mohandas, M. "Poverty in Kerala", in Prakash (ed.), *Kerala's Economy*, pp. 78-94.

Mohanty, Chandra Talpade. "Under Western Eyes: Feminist Scholarship and Colonial Discourse", in Chandra Talpade Mohanty, Ann Russo, and Lourdes Torres (eds), *Third World Women and the Politics of Feminism* (Bloomington, 1991), pp. 51-80.

Momsen Henshall, Janet. *Women and Development in The Third World* (London, 1991).

Morley, David, and Chen, Kuan-Hsin (eds). *Stuart Hall: Critical Dialogues in Cultural Studies* (London and New York, 1996).

Morris D. Morris, *The Emergence of an Industrial Labour Force in India: A Study of the Bombay Cotton Mills, 1854-1957* (Bombay, 1965).

—. *Measuring the Condition of the World's Poor: The Physical Quality of Life Index* (New York, 1979).

Mukherjee, Mukul. "Impact of Modernisation on Women's Occupations: A Case Study of the Rice Husking Industry of Bengal", in Krishnamurty ed.), *Women in Colonial India*, pp. 180-198.

Mulinari, Diana. *Motherwork and Politics in Revolutionary Nicaragua* (Lund, 1995).

Mulinari, Diana, and Sandell, Kerstin. "Exploring the Notion of Experience in Feminist Though", *Acta Sociologica*, 42 (1999), pp. 57-75.

Nair, Balakrishnan. *The Government and Politics of Kerala* (Trivandrum, 1994).

Nair, Janaki. *Women and Law in Colonial India: A Social History* (New Delhi, 1996).

—. *Miners and Millhands: Work, Culture and Politics in Princely Mysore* (New Delhi, 1998).

Nair, Kesavan. "The Strike History of the Cashew Workers, part 1- 29", *CITU Sandesam*, Vol. 17-19, 1993-1996 (in Malayalam).

Nair, M.K. Sukumaran. "Labour Shortage in a Labour Surplus Economy? A Study of the Rural Labour Market in Kerala", in Oommen (ed.), *Kerala's Development Experience*, Vol. II, pp. 247-268.

Nair, P.R. Gopinathan. "Migration of Keralites to the Arab World", in

Prakash (ed.), *Kerala's Economy*, pp. 95-117.

Namboodiripad, E.M.S. *The Communist Party in Kerala: Six Decades of Struggle and Advance* (New Delhi, 1994).

Narayan, Kirin. "How Native is a 'Native' Anthropologist?", in Louise Lamphere, Helena Ragoné, and Patricia Zavella (eds), *Situated Lives: Gender and Culture in Everyday Life* (New York, 1997), pp. 23-39.

Nicholson, Linda, J. (ed.), *Feminism/Postmodernism* (New York, 1990).

Nossiter, T. J. *Communism in Kerala: A Study in Political Adaptation* (Bombay, 1982).

Nyström, Per. *Stadsindustrins arbetare före 1800-talet* (Stockholm, 1955).

Oakley, Ann. "Interviewing Women: A Contradiction in Terms", in H. Roberts (ed.), *Doing Feminist Research* (London, 1981), pp. 30-61.

O'Hanlon, Rosalind. *Caste, Conflict and Ideology* (Cambridge, 1985).

O'Hanlon, Rosalind and Washbrook, David. "After Orientalism: Culture, Criticism, and Politics in the Third World", *Contemporary Studies in Society and History*, 34:1 (1992), pp. 141-167.

Ohler, J.G. *Cashew*, Department of Agricultural Research (Amsterdam, 1979).

Olsson, Lars. *Gamla typer och nya produktionsförhållanden* (Lund, 1986).

—. "Labour Movements, History of", in *International Encyclopaedia of Social and Behavioural Sciences* (Oxford, 2001).

Olsson, Torvald. *Folkökning, fattigdom, religion* (Lund, 1988).

Omvedt, Gail. "Class, Caste and Land in India: An Introductory Essay", in Gail Omvedt (ed.), *Land, Caste, and Politics in Indian States* (New Delhi, 1982), pp. 9-50.

Oommen, M.A. *Inter State Shifting of Industries: A Case Study of Selected Industries in Kerala, Tamil Nadu and Karnataka* (Trichur, 1979).

—. *Essays on Kerala Economy* (New Delhi, 1993).

— (ed.). *Kerala's Development Experience*, 2 vols (New Delhi, 2000).

Open the Social Sciences. Report of the Gulbenkian Commission on the Restructuring of the Social Sciences (Stanford, 1996).

Ouwerkerk, Louise. *No Elephants for the Maharaja* (New Delhi, 1994).

Pannikar, K. M. *Hindu Society at the Cross Roads* (Bombay, 1956).

—. *A History of Kerala* (Annamalai, 1960).

Parameswaran, M.P. "Kerala 'Model'—What Does It Signify?", *Bulletin of Concerned Asian Scholars*, 30:4 (1998), pp. 35-52.

Parayil, Govindan (ed.). *Kerala: The Development Experience: Reflections on Sustainability and Replicability* (New York, 2000).

Parry, Jonathan P., Breman, Jan, and Kapadia, Karin (eds). *The Worlds of Indian Industrial Labour* (New Delhi, 1999).

Pavanen (pseud). "Lives that Revolve around the Cashew Factories", in *Mathrubhumi Weekly*, 55:16 (1977), pp. 26-36 (in Malayalam).

Pearson, Ruth. "Industrialization and Women's Subordination: A Reappraisal", in Valentine M. Moghadam (ed.), *Patriarchy and Economic Development. Women's Positions at the End of the Twentieth Century* (New York, 1996), pp. 169-183.

Perks, Robert and Thomson, Alistar (eds). *The Oral History Reader* (London and New York, 1998).

Personal Narratives Group (eds). *Interpreting Women's Lives: Feminist Theory and Personal Narratives* (Bloomington, 1989).

Phillips, Ann and Taylor, Barbara. "Sex and Skill: Notes toward a Feminist Economics," *Feminist Review*, No. 6 (1980), pp. 79-88.

Pillai, K. Raman. "Coalition Politics: The Kerala Experience", in Oommen (ed.), *Kerala's Development Experience*, Vol. I, pp. 99-110,

Pillai, P. Mohanen. "Performance of State Sector Enterprises in Kerala", in Prakash (ed.), *Kerala's Economy*, pp. 259-278.

Pillai, P.P. *Kerala Economy: Four Decades of Development* (Thrissur, 1994).

Pillai, T.K. Velu. *Travancore State Manual*, 4 vols (Trivandrum, 1940).

Pocock, David F. "Sociologies: Urban and Rural", *Contributions to Indian Sociology*, 4 (1960), pp. 63-81.

Poverty, Unemployment and Development Policy: Case Study of Selected Issues with Reference to Kerala, United Nations (New York, 1975).

Prakash, B.A. "Kerala's Economy: An Overview", in Prakash (ed.), *Kerala's Economy*, pp. 15-39

— (ed.). *Kerala's Economy: Performance, Problems, Prospects* (New Delhi, 1994).

Preston, P.W. *Development Theory: An Introduction* (Oxford, 1996).

Puthenkalam, S.J. *Marriage and the Family in Kerala with Special Reference to Matrilineal Castes* (New Delhi, 1977).

Quigley, Declan. "Is a Theory of Caste Still Possible?", in Searle-Chatterjee and Sharma (eds), *Contextualising Caste*, pp. 25-48.

Raj, G. Ramachandra. "Industrial Conflict and Relations in Larger Society: A Case Study", *Journal of Kerala Studies,* Parts 3-4 (December 1978), pp. 585-612.

Rajan, S. Irudaya, and Sudha, S. and Mohanachandran, P. "Fertility Decline and Worsening Gender Bias in India: Is Kerala No Longer an Exception?", *Development and Change*, 31:5 (2000), pp. 1085-1092.

Rajaraman, G. "Economics of Bride-price and Dowry", *Economic and Political Weekly,* 18:8 (1983), pp. 275-279.

Rajeevan, B. "From Caste to Sex: A Study on Sexuality and the Formation of Modern Subject in Kerala", in Oommen, *Kerala's Development Experience*, Vol. I, pp. 45-59.

Ram, Ahuja. *Indian Social System* (Jaipur, 1993).

Ram, Kalpana. *Mukkuvar Women: Gender, Hegemony and Capitalist Transformation in a South Indian Fishing Community* (New Delhi, 1992).

Ramachandran, V.K. "On Kerala's Development Achievements", in Jean Drèze and Amartya Sen (eds), *Indian Development: Selected Regional Perspectives* (Oxford, 1996), pp. 205-356.

Raman, Unni. "Sources of Agricultural Labour in Kerala: Some Social Perspectives", in Balakrishna Nair (ed.), *Culture and Society: A Festschrift to Dr. A. Aiyappan* (New Delhi, 1975), pp. 216-239.

Ramanujam, G. *Indian Labour Movement* (New Delhi, 1990).

Ramaswamy, E.A. *The Worker and his Union* (Bombay, 1977).

—. "Indian Trade Unionism: The Crisis of Leadership", in Mark Holmström (ed.), *Work for Wages in South Asia* (New Delhi, 1990) , pp. 160-172.

Ramaswamy, Uma. *Work, Union and Community. Industrial Man in South India* (New Delhi, 1983).

—. "Women and Development", in Sharma and Singh (eds.), *Women and Work*, pp. 323-337.

Rammohan, K.T. "Kerala CPI(M): All That is Solid Melts into Air", *Economic and Political Weekly,* 33:40 (1998), pp. 2579-2582.

Randeria, Shalini and Visaria, Leela. "Sociology of Bride-price and Dowry", *Economic and Political Weekly*, 19:15 (1984), pp. 648-652.

Rao, M.S.A. *Social Change in Malabar* (Bombay, 1957).

Reinharz, Shulamit. *Feminist Methods in Social Research* (Oxford, 1992).

Renjini, D. *Nayar Women Today: Disintegration of Matrilineal System and the Status of Nayar Women in Kerala* (New Delhi, 2000).

Revri, C. *Indian Trade Union Movement: An Outline History 1880-1947* (New Delhi, 1972).

Riley, Denise. *'Am I that Name?': Feminism and the Category of 'Women' in History* (London, 1988).

Ringgren, Helmer and Ström, Åke V. *Religions of Mankind: Today and Yesterday* (Philadelphia, 1967).

Robertson, A.F. *Beyond the Family: The Social Organization of Human Reproduction* (Cambridge, 1991).

Rogers, Barbara. *The Domestication of Women: Discrimination in Developing Countries* (London, 1980).

Rose, Hilary. *Love, Power and Knowledge: Towards a Feminist Transformation of the Sciences* (Cambridge, 1994).

Rowbotham, Sheila and Mitter, Swasti (eds). *Dignity and Daily Bread. New Forms of Economic Organising among Poor Women in the Third World and the First* (London, 1994).

Rubin, Gayle. "The Traffic in Women: Notes on the 'Political Economy' of Sex", in R.R. Reiter (ed.), *Towards an Anthropology of Women* (New York, 1975), pp. 157-210.

Russell, D.C. *Cashew Nut Processing*, Food and Agriculture Organization of the United Nations (Rome, 1969).

Safa, Helen I. *The Myth of the Male Breadwinner: Women and Industrialization in the Caribbean* (Boulder, 1995).

Saha, Panchanan. *History of the Working Class Movement in Bengal* (New Delhi, 1978).

Said, Edward. *Orientalism* (New York, 1978).

Sambrani, I. et al. "The Economics of Brideprice and Dowry", *Economic and Political Weekly,* 18:15 (1983), pp. 601-604.

Sangster, Joan. "Telling our Stories: Feminist Debates and the Use of Oral History", in Perks and Thomson (eds), *The Oral History Reader,* pp. 87-100.

Saradamoni. K. *Emergence of a Slave Caste* (New Delhi, 1977).

—. *Filling the Rice Bowl: Women in Paddy Cultivation* (New Delhi, 1991).

—. *Matriliny Transformed* (New Delhi, 1999).

Sargeant, Lydia, (ed.). *Women and Revolution: A Discussion of the Unhappy Marriage of Marxism and Feminism* (Boston, 1981).

Sarkar, Kanchan and Bhowmik, Sharit K. "Trade Unions and Women Workers in Tea Plantations", *Economic and Political Weekly,* 23: 52 (1998), pp. L50-52.

Sarkar, Sumit. *Writing Social History* (New Delhi, 1999).

Scott, James C. *Weapons of the Weak: Everyday Form of Peasant Resistance* (New Haven, 1985).

Scott, Joan W. *Gender and the Politics of History* (New York, 1988).

—. "Experience", in Judith Butler and Joan W. Scott (eds), *Feminists Theorize the Political* (New York, 1992), pp. 22-40.

Searle-Chatterjee, Mary. "Caste, Religion and Other Identities", in Searle-Chatterjee and Sharma (eds), *Contextualising Caste,* pp. 147-168.

Searle-Chatterjee, Mary and Sharma, Ursula (eds). *Contextualising Caste: Post-Dumontian Approaches* (Oxford, 1994).

Seccombe, Wally. *Weathering the Storm: Working Class Families from the Industrial Revolution to the Fertility Decline* (London, 1993).

Selbourne, David. *An Eye to India: The Unmasking of a Tyranny* (London, 1979).

Sen, Amartya. *Development as Freedom* (New Delhi, 2000).

Sen, Samita. *Women and Labour in Late Colonial India: The Bengal Jute Industry* (Cambridge, 1999).

—. "Women Workers in the Bengal Jute Industry", in Parry, Breman, and Kapadia (eds), *The Worlds of Indian Industrial Labour,* pp. 239-269.

Sen, Sukumal. *Working Class in India: History of Emergence and Movement, 1830-1970* (Calcutta, 1977).

Sewell, William H. Jr. "Towards a Post-materialist Rhetoric for Labour History", in Lenard R. Berlanstein (ed.), *Rethinking Labor History: Essays on Discourse and Class Analysis* (Urbana, 1993), pp. 15-38.

Sharma, Alakh N. and Singh, Seema (eds). *Women and Work: Changing Scenario in India* (New Delhi, 1992).

Sharma, G.K. *Labour Movement in India* (New Delhi, 1963).

Sheel, Ranjana. *The Political Economy of Dowry: Institutionalization and Expansion in North India* (New Delhi, 1999).

Sheth, N.R. *The Social Frame Work of an Indian Factory* (New Delhi, 1981).

Shorter, Edward. "Women's Work: What Difference did Capitalism Make?", *Theory and Society*, Vol. 3, 4 (1976), pp. 513-527.

Sinha, S.P. "Technological Change in Agriculture and Women Workers in Rural Bihar: A Case Study", in Sharma and Singh (eds.), *Women and Work*, pp. 209-218.

Sivanandan, P. "Caste, Class and Economic Opportunity in Kerala: An Empirical Analysis", *Economic and Political Weekly*, 14:7-8 (1979), pp. 475-480.

Skeggs, Beverly. *Formations of Class and Gender: Becoming Respectable* (London, 1997).

Somers, Margaret. "Deconstructing and Reconstructing Class Formation Theory: Narrativity, Relational Analysis, and Social Theory", in John R. Hall (ed.), *Reworking Class* (New York, 1997), pp. 73-105.

Spivak, Gayatri Chakravorty. "Can the Subaltern Speak?", in Patrick Williams and Laura Chrisman (eds), *Colonial Discourse and Post-Colonial Theory* (New York, 1993), pp. 66-111.

—. "The Politics of Translation", in Barrett and Phillips (eds), *Destabilizing Theory*, pp. 177-200.

Sreekantan Nair, N. *Memories of the Past* (Kottayam, 1976) (in Malayalam).

Srinivas, M.N. *Caste in Modern India and Other Essays* (London, 1962).

—. *Social Change in Modern India* (Berkeley, 1966).

—. "Varna and Caste", in Gupta (ed.), *Social Stratification*, pp. 28-34.

—. *Village, Caste, Gender and Method: Essays in Indian Social Anthropology* (New Delhi, 1996).

Stacey, J. "Can there be a Feminist Ethnography?", *Women's Studies International Forum*, 11:1 (1991), pp. 21-27.

Standing, Guy. "Global Feminization through Flexible Labor", *World Development*, 17:7 (1989), pp. 1077-1096.

Standing, Hilary. "Employment", in Lise Östergaard (ed.), *Gender and Development: A Practical Guide* (London, 1992), 57-75.

Talle, Aud. *Women at a Loss: Changes in Maasai Pastoralism and Their Effects on Gender* (Stockholm, 1988).

Tanner, Clare L. "Class, Caste and Gender in Collective Action: Agricultural Labour Unions in Two Indian Villages", *The Journal of Peasant Studies*, 22:4 (1995), pp. 672-698.

Thakur, Himendra. "Preface", in Werner Menski (ed.), *South Asians and the Dowry Problem* (New Delhi, 1998), pp. xiii-xxi.

Tharakan, P.K.M. "Socio-Economic Factors in Educational Development: Case of Nineteenth Century Travancore", *Economic and Political Weekly,* 20:46 (1985), pp. 1959-1967.

Tharamangalam, Joseph. *Agrarian Class Conflict: The Political Mobilization of Agricultural Labourers in Kuttanad, South India* (Vancouver, 1981).

—. "The Perils of Social Development without Economic Growth: The Development Debacle of Kerala, India", *Bulletin of Concerned Asian Scholars*, 30:1 (1998), pp. 23-34.

Tharu, Susie and Niranjana, Tejaswini. "Problems for a Contemporary Theory of Gender", in Shahid Amin and Dipesh Chakrabarty (eds), *Subaltern Studies IX: Writing on South Asian History and Society* (New Delhi, 1996), pp. 232-260.

Thompson, E.P. *The Making of the English Working Class* (London, 1963).

Thompson, John B. *Studies in the Theory of Ideology* (Berkeley, 1984).

Thompson, Paul. *The Voice of the Past* (Oxford, 1978).

Thorner, Daniel. "Marx on India and the Asiatic Mode of Production", *Contributions to Indian Sociology*, No. 9 (1966), pp. 33-66.

Thurston, Edgar. *Castes and Tribes of Southern India,* Vol. II (Madras, 1909).

—. *Castes and Tribes of Southern India*, Vol. VII (Madras, 1909).

Tilly, Louise and Scott, Joan. *Women, Work, and Family* (New York and London, 1987).

Tosh, John. *The Pursuit of History: Aims, Methods and New Directions in the Study of Modern History* (London, 1999).

Törnquist, Olle. *The Next Left? Democratization and Attempts to Renew the Radical Political Development Project. The Case of Kerala* (Copenhagen, 1995).

—. "The New Popular Politics of Development: Kerala's Experience", in Parayil (ed.), *Kerala: The Development Experience*, pp. 116-138.

Uyl, Marion den. *Invisible Barriers: Gender, Caste and Kinship in a Southern Indian Village* (Utrecht, 1995).

Valestrand, Halldis. "Housewifization of Peasant Women in Costa Rica", in Kristi Stölen and Mariken Vaa (eds), *Gender and Change in Developing Countries* (Drammen, 1991), pp. 165-196.

Veen, Klas Van de. *I Give Thee My Daughter—A Study of Marriage and Hierarchy Among the Anival Brahmins of South Gujarat* (Assen, 1972).

Velayudhan, Meera. "Caste, Class and Political Organisation of Women in Travancore", *Social Scientist*, 19:5-6, (1991), pp. 61-79.

Walby, Sylvia. *Theorizing Patriarchy* (Oxford, 1990).

—. "Post-Post-Modernism? Theorizing Social Complexity", in Barrett and Phillips (eds), *Destabilizing Theory* (Cambridge, 1992), pp. 31-52.

Wallerstein, Immanuel. *A Capitalist Agriculture and the Origins of the European World-Economy in the Sixteenth Century* (New York, 1974).

—. *Historical Capitalism* (New York, 1974).

—. "World-Systems Analysis", in A. Giddens and J.H. Turner, (eds.), *Social Theory Today* (Cambridge, 1987), pp. 309-324.

Waterman, Peter. "Seeing the Straws, Riding the Whirlwind: Reflections on Unions and Popular Movements in India", *Journal of Contemporary Asia*, 12:4 (1982), pp. 464-483.

—. "The New Social Unionism: A New Union Model for a New World Order", in Ronaldo Munck and Peter Waterman (eds), *Labour Worldwide in the Era of Globalization. Alternative Union Models in the New World Order* (London, 1999), pp. 247-264.

Webb, Beatrice and Sidney. *Industrial Democracy* (London, 1920).

Weber, Max. *The Religion of India* (Glencoe, 1958).

Weiner, Myron. *The Child and the State in India: Child Labour and Education Policy in Comparative Perspective* (Princeton, 1991).

Weitz, Eric D. "The Heroic Man and the Ever-Changing Woman: Gender and Politics in European Communism, 1917-1950", in Laura L. Farder and Sonya O. Rose (eds), *Gender and Class in Modern Europe* (New York, 1996).

White, Sarah. "Depoliticising Development: the Uses and Abuses of Participation", *Development in Practice*, 6:1 (1996), pp. 6-15.

Williams, Raymond. *Problems in Materialism and Culture* (New York, 1980).

Wilson, Roger J. *The Market for Cashew-nut Kernels and Cashew-nut Shell Liquid,* Tropical Products Institute (London 1975).

Winther-Jörgensen, Marianne and Phillips, Louise. *Diskursanalys som teori och metod* (Lund, 2000).

Wood, Ellen Meiksins and Foster, John Bellamy (eds). *In Defense of History: Marxism and the Postmodern Agenda* (New York, 1997).

Woodward, Kathryn (ed.). *Identity and Difference* (London, 1997).

Worsley, Peter. *The Three Worlds: Culture and World Development* (London, 1984).

Studia Historica Lundensia

Birgitta Odén *Rikets uppbörd och utgift. Statsfinanser och finansförvaltning under senare 1500-talet.* 1955 (BHL 1). Diss.

Åke Ljungfors *Bidrag till svensk diplomatik före 1350.* 1955 (US). Diss.

Per Nyström *Stadsindustrins arbetare före 1800-talet. Bidrag till kännedomen om den svenska manufakturindustrin och dess sociala förhållanden.* 1955 (US). Diss.

Göran Rystad *Johan Gyllenstierna, rådet och kungamakten.* 1955 (BHL 2). Diss.

Kjell-Gunnar Lundholm *Sten Sture den äldre och stormännen.* 1956 (BHL 3). Diss.

Ola Lindquist *Jakob Gyllenborg och reduktionen.* 1956 (BHL 4). Diss.

Åke Sällström *Bologna och Norden intill Avignonpåvedömets tid.* 1957 (BHL 5). Diss.

Jörgen Weibull *Carl Johan och Norge 1810–1814.* 1957 (BHL 6). Diss.

Lars-Arne Norborg *Storföretaget Vadstena kloster. Studier i senmedeltida godspolitik och ekonomiförvaltning.* 1958 (BHL 7). Diss.

Allan Mohlin *Kristoffer II av Danmark. 1. Välmaktstiden.* 1960 (US). Diss.

Helle Stiegung *Ludvig XV:s hemliga diplomati och Sverige 1752–1774.* 1961 (BHL 8)

Sven Tägil *Valdemar Atterdag och Europa.* 1962 (BHL 9). Diss.

Ingvar Elmroth *Nyrekryteringen till de högre ämbetena 1720–1809. En socialhistorisk studie.* 1962 (BHL 10). Diss.

Kerstin Strömberg-Back *Lagen – Rätten – Läran. Politisk och kyrklig idédebatt i Sverige under Johan III: s tid.* 1963 (BHL 11). Diss.

Lars-Olof Larsson *Det medeltida Värend. Studier i det småländska gränslandets historia fram till 1500-talets mitt.* 1964 (BHL 12). Diss.

Olafia Einarsdottir *Studier i kronologisk metode i tidlig islandsk historieskrivning.* 1964 (BHL 13). Diss.

Sten Körner *The Battle of Hastings: England and Europe 1035–1066.* 1964 (BHL 14). Diss.

Tore Nyberg *Birgittinische Klostergründungen des Mittelalters.* 1965 (BHL 15). Diss.

Carl-Axel Gemzell *Raeder Hitler und Skandinavien. Der Kampf für einen maritimen Operationsplan.* 1965 (BHL 16). Diss.

Ulf Sjödell *Kungamakt och högaristokrati. En studie i Sveriges inre historia under Karl XI.* 1966 (BHL17). Diss.

Alf Erlandsson *Skånska generalguvernementet 1658–1693 och dess arkiv. Förvaltnings- och arkivhistoriska undersökningar.* 1967 (BHL 18). Diss.

Ann Christina Meurling *Den svenska domstolsförvaltningen i Livland 1634–1700.* 1967 (BHL 19). Diss.

Arne Remgärd *Carl Gustaf Tessin och 1746–1747 års riksdag.* 1968 (BHL 20). Diss.

Sven Anders Söderpalm *Storföretagarna och det demokratiska genombrottet. Ett perspektiv på första världskrigets svenska historia.* 1969 (BHL 21). Diss.

H. Bertil A. Petersson *Anglo-Saxon Currency. King Edgar's Reform to the Norman Conquest.* 1969 (BHL 22). Diss.

Lars Linge *Gränshandeln i svensk politik under äldre Vasatid.* 1969 (BHL 23). Diss.

Sverker Oredsson *Järnvägarna och det allmänna. Svensk järnvägspolitik fram till 1890.* 1969 (BHL 24). Diss.

Sven Tägil *Deutschland und die deutsche Minderheit in Nordschleswig.* 1970 (LSIH 1)

Sven Tägil *Probleme deutscher Zeitgeschichte.* 1970 (LSIH 2)

Kerstin Malcus *Maktpolitik och länsrättslig förvaltning. Den regelrättsliga doktrinen i Sverige under 1560-talet.* 1971 (BHL 25). Diss.

Eva Österberg *Gränsbygd under krig. Ekonomiska, demografiska och administrativa förhållanden i sydvästra Sverige under och efter det nordiska sjuårskriget.* 1971 (BHL 26). Diss.

Bengt Ankarloo *Trolldomsprocesserna i Sverige.* 1971 (US). Diss.

Erik Sandstedt *Studier rörande Jöran Nordbergs Konung Carl XII:s historia.* 1972 (US). Diss.

Lars-Olof Larsson *Kolonisation och befolkningsutveckling i det svenska agrarsamhället 1500–1640.* 1972 (BHL 27)

STUDIA HISTORICA LUNDENSIA

Conny Blom *Förbindelsedikten och de medeltida rimkrönikorna.* Studier kring omarbetningen av Erikskrönikan och tillkomsten av Förbindelsedikten samt dessa krönikedelars plats i den medeltida rimkröniketraditionen. 1972 (BHL 28). Diss.

Steven Koblik *Sweden: The Neutral Victor.* Sweden and the Western Powers 1917–1918. 1972 (LSIH 3)

Nordal Åkerman *On the Doctrine of Limited War.* 1973 (US). Diss.

Hans Petersson *Morgongåvoinstitutet i Sverige under tiden fram till omkring 1734 års lag.* 1973 (US). Diss.

Göran Wensheim *Studier kring freden i Nystad.* 1973 (BHL 29). Diss.

Carl-Axel Gemzell *Organization, Conflict and Innovation. A study of German Naval Strategic Planning 1888–1940.* 1973 (LSIH 4)

Lars Lundgren *Vattenförorening. Debatten i Sverige 1890–1921.* 1974 (BHL 30). Diss.

Sveinbjörn Raffisson *Studier i Landnamabok. Kritiska bidrag till den isländska fristatstidens historia.* 1974 (BHL 31). Diss.

Göte Paulsson *Annales Suecici mediiaevi. Svensk medeltidsannalistik kommenterad och utgiven.* 1974 (BHL 32). Diss.

Bo Huldt *Sweden, the United Nations and Decolonization: A study of Swedish Participation in the Fourth Commitee of the General Assembly, 1946–69.* 1974 (LSIH 5). Diss.

Lars H. Niléhn *Nyhumanism och medborgarfostran. Åsikter om läroverkets målsättning 1820–1880.* 1975 (BHL 33). Diss.

Agnes Wirén *Uppbrott från örtagård. Utvandring från Blekinge till och med år 1870.* 1975 (BHL 34). Diss.

Roland Persson *Rustningar i Sverige under det stora nordiska kriget. Studier rörande makten över krigsfinansieringen i det karolinska samhället 1700–1709.* 1975 (BHL 35). Diss.

Erland Alexandersson *Bondeståndet i riksdagen 1760–1772.* 1975 (BHL 36). Diss.

Leokadia Posten *De polska emigranternas agentverksamhet i Sverige 1862–1863.* 1975 (BHL 37). Diss.

Ulf Sjödell *Riksråd och kungliga råd. Rådskarriären 1602–1718.* 1975 (BHL 38)

Birgitta Odén *Lauritz Weibull och forskarsamhället.* 1975 (BHL 39)

Göran Rystad *Ambigious Imperialism: American Foreign Policy and Domestic Politics at the turn of the Century.* 1975 (LSIH 6)

Sven G. Trulsson *British and Swedish Policies and Strategies in the Baltic after the Peace of Tilsit in 1807.* 1976 (BHL 40). Diss.

Eva Block *Amerikabilden i svensk dagspress 1948–1968.* 1976 (BHL 41). Diss.

Sven Rubensson *The Survival of Ethiopian Independence.* 1976 (LSIH 7). Diss.

Rune Ivarsson *Jordförvärvslagen, socialdemokratin och bönderna. En studie över jordförvärvslagstiftningen i svensk politik 1945–1965.* 1977 (BHL 42). Diss.

Eva Österberg *Kolonisation och kriser. Bebyggelse, skattetryck, odling och agrarstruktur i västra Värmland ca 1300–1600.* 1977 (BHL 43)

Lars-Erik Nyman *Great Britain and Chinese Russian and Japanese Interests in Sinkiang 1918–1934.* 1977 (LSIH 8). Diss.

Sven Tägil (coordinator) *Studying Boundary Conflicts: A Theoretical Framwork.* 1977 (LSIH 9)

Anita Diehl *E. V. Ramaswami Naicker-Periyar: A Study of the Influence of a Personality in Contemporary South India.* 1977 (LSIH 10). Diss.

Gunnel Rikardsson *The Middle East Conflict in the Swedish Press: A Content Analysis of Three Daily Newspapers, 1948–1973.* 1978 (LSIH 11). Diss.

Birgitta Eimer *Cavour and Swedish Politics.* 1978 (LSIH 12). Diss.

Bo Blomkvist *International i miniatyr. Studier i skånsk arbetarrörelse före 1880 och dess internationella kontakter.* 1979 (BHL 44). Diss.

Kim Salomon *Konflikt i Grænseland. Sociale og nationale modsætninger i Sønderjylland 1920–33.* 1980 (US). Diss.

Lars Olsson *Då barn var lönsamma. Om arbetsdelning barnarbete och teknologiska förändringar i några svenska industrier under 1800- och början av 1900-talet.* 1980 (US). Diss.

Pau Puig i Scotoni *Att förstå revolutionen. En kritisk undersökning om historisk stabilitet och förändring.* 1980 (US). Diss.

Jan Brunius *Bondebygd i förändring. Bebyggelse och befolkning i västra Närke ca 1300–1600.* 1980 (BHL 45). Diss.

Anna-Brita Lövgren *Handläggning och inflytande. Beredning föredragning och kontrasignering under Karl XI:s envälde.* 1980 (BHL 46). Diss.

Hans-Albin Larsson *Partireformationen från bondeförbund till centerparti.* 1980 (BHL 47). Diss.

Kjell Emanuelsson *Den svensk-norska utrikesförvaltningen 1870–1905. Dess organisations och verksamhetsförändring.* 1980 (BHL 48). Diss.

Eva Queckfeldt *Vietnam. Tre svenska tidningars syn på Vietnamfrågan 1963–1968.* 1981 (BHL 49). Diss.

Ingvar Elmroth *För kung och fosterland. Studier i den svenska adelns demografi och offentliga funktioner 1600–1900.* 1981 (BHL 50)

Göran Rystad (ed.) *Congress and American Foreign Policy.* 1981 (LSIH 13)

Reda Mowafi *Slavery, Slave Trade and Abolition Attempts in Egypt and the Sudan, 1820–1882.* 1981 (LSIH 14). Diss.

Joseph Zitomersky (ed.) *On Making Use of History.* 1982 (LSIH 15)

Christer Olsson *Congress and the Executive: The Making of United States Foreign Policy 1933–1940.* 1982 (LSIH 16). Diss.

Sten Skansjö *Söderslätt genom 600 år. Bebyggelse och odling under äldre historisk tid.* 1983 (US). Diss.

Käthe Bååth *Öde sedan stora döden var... Bebyggelse och befolkning i Norra Vedbo under senmedeltid och 1500-tal.* 1983 (BHL 51). Diss.

Imants Alksnis *Den marxistiska publicistiken i Lettland 1912–1914. En studie i effektiv propaganda.* 1983 (BHL 52). Diss.

Christer Strahl *Nationalism och socialism. Fosterlandet i den politiska idédebatten i Sverige 1890–1914.* 1983 (BHL 53). Diss.

Lars Niléhn *Peregrinatio Academica. Det svenska samhället och de utrikes studieresorna under 1600-talet.* 1983 (BHL 54)

Anders Lindberg *Småstat mot stormakt. Beslutssystemet vid tillkomsten av 1911 års svensk-tyska handels- och sjöfartstraktat.* 1983 (BHL 55). Diss.

Carl Gustaf Stenkula *Gammal i Lund. Utvecklingstendenser inom kommunal kyrklig och enskild åldringsvård i Lund 1900–1918.* 1983 (BHL 56). Diss.

Ingemar Norrlid *Demokrati, skatterättvisa och ideologisk förändring. Den kommunala självstyrelsen och demokratins genombrott i Sverige.* 1983 (BHL 57). Diss.

Bengt Nilsson *Handelspolitik och skärpt konkurrens. England och Sverige 1929–1939.* 1983 (BHL 58). Diss.

Wilhelm Agrell and Bo Huldt (eds.) *Clio Goes Spying: Eight Essays on the History of Intelligence.* 1983 (LSIH 17)

Göran Rystad (ed.) *Europe and Scandinavia. Aspects of the Process of Integration in the 17th Century.* 1983 (LSIH 18)

Terence Graham *The "Interests of Civilization"? Reaction in the United States Against the "Seizure" of the Panama Canal Zone 1903–1904.* 1983 (LSIH 19). Diss.

Olof Åhlander *Staat, Wirtschaft und Handelspolitik. Schweden und Deutschland, 1918–1921.* 1983 (LSIH 20). Diss.

Hans Sundström *Bönder bryter bygd. Studier i övre Norrlands äldre bebyggelsehistoria.* 1984 (US). Diss.

Kristian Gerner *The Soviet Union and Central Europe in the Post-War Era: A Study in Precarious Security.* 1984 (LSIH 21). Diss.

Sven Tägil (ed.) *Regions in Upheaval: Ethnic Conflict and Political Mobilization.* 1984 (LSIH 22)

Wilhelm Agrell *Alliansfrihet och atombomber. Kontinuitet och förändring i den svenska försvarsdoktrinen från 1945 till 1982.* 1985 (US). Diss.

Göran V. Johansson *Kristen demokrati på svenska. Studier om KDS tillkomst och utveckling 1964–1982.* 1985 (BHL 59). Diss.

Bengt Sandin *Hemmet, gatan, fabriken eller skolan. Folkundervisning och barnuppfostran i svenska städer 1600–1850.* 1986 (US). Diss.

Christina Carlsson *Kvinnosyn och kvinnopolitik. En studie av svensk socialdemokrati 1880–1910.* 1986 (US). Diss.

Lars J. Larsson *Sören Norby och Östersjöpolitiken 1523–1525.* 1986 (BHL 60). Diss.

Ingemar Ottosson *Krig i fredens intresse eller neutralitet till varje pris? Sverige, NF och frågan om kollektiv säkerhet 1935–1936.* 1986 (BHL 61). Diss.

Monica Braw *The Atomic Bomb Suppressed: American Censorship in Japan 1945–1949.* 1986 (LSIH 23). Diss.

Marie Nordström *Pojkskola, flickskola, samskola. Samundervisningens utveckling i svenskt skolväsen 1866–1962.* 1987 (BHL 62). Diss.

Hans-Olof Ericson *Vanmakt och styrka. Studier av arbetarrörelsens tillkomst och förutsättningar i Jönköping, Huskvarna och Norrahammar 1880–1909.* 1987 (US). Diss.

Lars Edgren *Lärling gesäll mästare. Hantverk*

och hantverkare i Malmö 1750–1847. 1987 (US). Diss.

Klas-Göran Karlsson *Historieundervisning i klassisk ram. En didaktisk studie av historieämnets målfrågor i den ryska och sovjetiska skolan 1900–1940.* 1987 (US). Diss.

Désirée Haraldsson *Skydda vår natur! Svenska Naturskyddsföreningens framväxt och tidiga utveckling.* 1987 (BHL 63). Diss.

Bernt Ralfnert *Kvinnoprästdebatten i Sverige i perspektivet kyrka-stat.* 1988 (US). Diss.

Karl Johan Krantz *Garnisonsstadens politik och ekonomi. Växjö, Jönköping och Eksjö inför bygderegementenas kasernering.* 1988 (US). Diss.

Rune Johansson *Small State in Boundary Conflict. Belgium and the Belgian-German Border 1914–1949.* 1988 (LSIH 24). Diss.

Per Jonsson *Finntorparna i Mången. Jord, människor och rättsuppfattning i förprolётär bergslagsmiljö.* 1989 (US). Diss.

Stefan Håkansson *Konsulerna och exporten 1905–1921. Ett " Government failure"?.* 1989 (BHL 64). Diss.

Yvonne M. Werner *Svensk-tyska förbindelser kring sekelskiftet 1900. Politik och ekonomi vid tillkomsten av 1906 års svensk-tyska handels- och sjöfartstraktat.* 1989 (BHL 65). Diss.

Per Bolin-Hort *Work, Family and the State: Child Labour and the Organization of Production in the British Cotton Industry, 1780–1920.* 1989 (BHL 66). Diss.

Rune Johansson & Hans-Åke Persson (ed) *Nordisk flyktingpolitik i världskrigens epok.* 1989 (CESIC 1)

Björn Fryklund & Tomas Peterson *Vi mot dom. Det dubbla främlingskapet i Sjöbo.* 1989 (CESIC 2)

Thorlcifur Fridriksson *Den Gyldne Flue. De skandinaviske socialdemokratiers relationer til den islandske arbejderbevægelse 1916–56. Internationalisme eller inblandning?* 1990 (US). Diss.

Ingrid Millbourn *"Rätt till maklighet". Om den svenska socialdemokratins lärprocess 1885–1902.* 1990 (US). Diss.

Ralf Rönnquist *Historia och Nationalitet. Skotsk etno-territorialitet i ett historiskt perspektiv.* 1990 (BHL 67). Diss.

Göran Göransson *Virtus Militaris: Officersideal i Sverige 1560–1718.* 1990 (BHL 68). Diss.

Göran Rystad (ed.) *The Uprooted: Forced Migration as an International Problem in the Post-War Era.* 1990 (LSIH 25)

Gunnar Alsmark & Paula Uddman *Att möta främlingar. Vision och vardag.* 1990 (CESIC 3)

Göran Rystad (ed.) *Looking inward – Looking outward: Aspects of American Foreign Policy in an Age of Uncertainty.* 1990 (CESIC 4)

Lars Berggren *Ångvisslans och brickornas värld. Om arbete och facklig organisering vid Kockums mekaniska verkstad och Carl Lunds fabrik i Malmö 1840–1905.* 1991 (US). Diss.

Birgitta Odén *Forskarutbildningens förändringar 1890–1975.* 1991 (BHL 69)

Tommie Sjöberg *The Powers and the Persecuted: The Refugee Problem and the Intergovemmental Committe on Refugees (IGCR)1938–1947.* 1991 (LSIH 26). Diss.

Kim Salomon *Refugees in the Cold War: Toward a New International Refugee Regime in the Early Modem Postwar Era.* 1991 (LSIH 27)

Eva Österberg *Mentalities and Other Realities: Essays in Medieval and Early Modern Scandinavian History.* 1991 (LSIH 28)

Kerstin Nyström (ed.) *Judarna i det svenska samhället. Identitet, integration etniska relationer.* 1991 (CESIC 5)

Thomas Söderblom *Horan och batongen. Prostitution och repression i folkhemmet.* 1992 (US). Diss.

Mats Greiff *Kontoristen. Från chefens högra hand till proletär.* 1992 (US). Diss.

Sverker Oredsson *Gustav Adolf, Sverige och Trettioåriga kriget. Historieskrivning och kult.* 1992 (BHL 70)

Göran Blomquist *Elfenbenstorn eller statsskepp? Stat, universitet och akademisk frihet i vardag och vision från Agardh till Schück.* 1992 (BHL 71). Diss.

Peter Aronsson *Bönder gör politik. Det lokala självstyret som social arena i tre Smålandssocknar, 1680–1850.* 1992 (BHL 72). Diss.

Conny Blom *Tiggare, tidstjuvar, lättingar och landstrykare. Studier av attityder och värderingar i skrån, stadgar, ordningar och lagförslag gällande den offentliga vården 1533–1664.* 1992 (BHL 73)

Lars Edgren & Eva Österberg (red.) *Ut med historien! Sju historiker om historieundervisningens uppgifter idag.* 1992 (BHL 74)

Göran Rystad (ed.) *Encounter with Strangers: Refugees and Cultural Confrontation in Sweden.* 1992 (CESIC 6)

Anders Svensson *Ungrare i folkhemmet: svensk flyktingpolitik i det kalla krigets skugga.* 1992 (CESIC 7). Diss.

Sven Tägil (ed.) *Konflikt och samarbete vid Persiska viken.* 1992 (CESIC 8)

Karin Helmer *Arrendatorer och professorer. Lunds universitets jordegendomar under 325 år.* 1993 (BHL 75)

Kerstin Sundberg *Resurser och sociala relationer. Studier av ett lokalsamhälle i förändring 1600–1800: Österhaninge och Västerhaninge socknar.* 1993 (BHL 76). Diss.

Jan Samuelson *Aristokrat eller förädlad bonde? Det svenska frälsets ekonomi, politik och sociala förbindelser under tiden 1523–1611.* 1993 (BHL 77). Diss.

Dick Harrison *The Early State and the Towns: Forms of Integration in Lombard Italy AD 568–774.* 1993 (LSIH 29). Diss.

Cecilia Ruthström-Ruin *Beyond Europe: The Globalization of Refugee Aid.* 1993 (LSIH 30). Diss.

Hans-Åke Persson *Retorik och realpolitik. Storbritannien och de fördrivna tyskarna efter andra världskriget.* 1993 (CESIC 9). Diss.

Sven Tägil (ed.) *Den problematiska etniciteten – nationalism, migration och samhällsomvandling.* 1993 (CESIC 10)

Rudolf Thunander *Hovrätt i funktion. Göta Hovrätt och brottmålen 1635–1699.* 1994 (US). Diss.

Peter Billing (med Mikael Stigendal) *Hegemonins decennier. Lärdomar från Malmö om den svenska modellen.* 1994 (US). Diss.

Monika Edgren *Tradition och förändring. Könsrelationer, omsorgsarbete och försörjning inom Norrköpings underklass under 1800-talet.* 1994 (BHL 78). Diss.

Ulla Rosén *Himlajord och handelsvara. Ägobyten av egendom i Kumla socken 1780–1880.* 1994 (BHL 79). Diss.

Mikael af Malmborg *Den ståndaktiga nationalstaten. Sverige och den västeuropeiska integrationen 1945–1959.* 1994 (BHL 80). Diss.

Joseph Zitomersky *French Americans – Native Americans in Eighteenth Century French Colonial Louisiana: The Population Geography of the Illinois Indians, 1670–1760s. The Form and Function of French – Native Settlement Relations in the Eighteenth-Century Louisiana.* 1994 (LSIH 31). Diss.

Kenneth Nyström (ed.) *Encounter with Strangers: The Nordic Experience.* 1994 (CESIC 11)

David Edgerton, Björn Fryklund & Tomas Peterson *"Until the Lamb of God Appears …" The 1991 Parliamentary Election: Sweden Chooses a New Political System.* 1994 (CESIC 12)

Bo Bjurulf & Björn Fryklund (red.) *Det politiska missnöjets Sverige. Statsvetare och sociologer ser på valet 1991* 1994 (CESIC 13)

Göran Rystad (ed.) *Encounter with Strangers: Aspects of the American Experience.* 1995 (CESIC 14)

Hans Wallengren *Hyresvärlden. Maktrelationer på hyresmarknaden i Malmö ca 1880–1925.* 1995 (US). Diss.

Per Bauhn, Christer Lindberg & Svante Lundberg *Multiculturalism and Nationhood in Canada.* 1995 (CESIC 15)

Rune Bokholm *Städernas handlingsfrihet. En studie av expansionsskedet 1900–1930.* 1995 (BHL 81). Diss.

Lars I. Andersson *Kommunalskattefrågan under mellankrigstiden. Skatterättvisa i och mellan kommuner.* 1995 (BHL 82). Diss.

Bengt Åhsberg *Studenter och storpolitik. Sverige och det internationella studentsamarbetet 1919–1931.* 1995 (BHL 83). Diss.

Anders Olsson *Borgmästare, bastioner och tullbommar. Göteborg och Halmstad under statligt inflytande 1630–1660.* 1995 (BHL 84). Diss.

Marcos Cantera Carlomagno *Ett folk av mänsklig granit. Sverige i den italienska utrikespolitiken 1932–1936.* 1995 (US). Diss.

Ulf Bergman *Från bondelots till yrkesman. Lotsning i Östergötland 1537–1914.* 1995 (BHL 85). Diss.

Lennart Johansson *Systemet lagom. Rusdrycker, intresseorganisationer och politisk kultur under förbudsdebattens tidevarv 1900–1922.* 1995 (BHL 86). Diss.

Borhanedin A. Yassin *Vision or Reality? The Kurds in the Policy of the Great Powers 1941–1947.* 1995 (LSIH 32). Diss.

Göran Rystad (ed.) *Encountering Strangers: Responses and Consequences.* 1996 (CESIC 16)

Hans Hägerdal *Väst om öst. Kinaforskning och kinasyn under 1800- och 1900-talen.* 1996 (BHL 87). Diss.

Jasmine Aimaq *For Europe or Empire?:*

French Colonial Ambitions and the European Army Plan. 1996 (LSIH 33). Diss.

Eva Helen Ulvros *Fruar och mamseller. Kvinnor inom sydsvensk borgerlighet 1790–1870.* 1996 (US). Diss.

Dick Harrison *Medieval Space: The Extent of Microspatial Knowledge in Western Europe during the Middle Ages.* 1996 (LSIH 34)

Marie Lindstedt – Cronberg *Synd och skam. Ogifta mödrar på svensk landsbygd 1680–1880.* 1997 (US). Diss.

Hans-Åke Persson (ed.) *Encounter with Strangers: The European Experience.* 1997 (CESIC 17)

Åke Sundell *Patriarkalism och föreningsrätt. Om produktion och facklig kamp inom trädgårdsnäringen i Malmö med omnejd fram till 1936.* 1997 (BHL 88). Diss.

Eric Carlsson *Sverige och tysk motståndsrörelse under andra världskriget.* 1998 (BHL 89). Diss.

Yngve Tidman *Spräng Amalthea! Arbete, facklig kamp och strejkbryteri i nordvästeuropeiska hamnar 1870–1914.* 1998 (BHL 90). Diss.

Magnus Persson *Great Britain, the United States, and the Security of the Middle East: The Formation of the Baghdad Pact.* 1998 (LSIH 35). Diss. .

Gunnar Dahl *Trade, Trust and Networks: Commercial Culture in Late Medieval Italy.* 1998 (US). Diss.

Thomas Sörensen *Det blänkande eländet. En bok om Kronprinsens husarer i sekelskiftets Malmö.* 1998 (US). Diss.

Magnus Perlestam *Den rotfaste bonden – myt eller verklighet? Brukaransvar i Ramkvilla socken 1620–1820.* 1998 (US). Diss.

Olle Larsson *Biskopen visiterar. Den kyrkliga överhetens möte med lokalsamhället 1650–1760.* 1999 (US). Diss.

Göran Rystad *Dream and Reality: The United States in Search of a Role in the Twentieth Century World.* 1999 (CESIC onumrerad)

Marion Leffler *Böcker, bildning, makt. Arbe-* tare borgare och bildningens roll i klassformeringen i Lund och Helsingborg 1860–1901. 1999 (BHL 91). Diss.

Malin Lennartsson *I säng och säte. Relationer mellan kvinnor och män i 1600-talets Småland.* 1999 (BHL 92) Diss.

Roddy Nilsson *En välbyggd maskin, en mardröm för själen. Det svenska fängelsesystemet under 1800-talet.* 1999 (BHL 93) Diss.

Fabian Persson *Servants of Fortune: The Swedish Court between 1598 and 1721.* 1999 (US). Diss.

Mikael Ottosson *Sohlberg och surdegen. Sociala relationer på Kosta glasbruk 1820–1880.* 1999 (US). Diss.

Sanimir Resic *American Warriors in Vietnam: Warrior Values and the Myth of the War Experience during the Vietnam War 1965–1973.* 1999 (US). Diss.

Agneta Ljungh *Sedd, eller osedd? Kvinnoskildringar i svensk historieforskning, mellan åren 1890 till 1995.* 1999 (US). Diss.

Inger Hammar *Emancipation och religion: den svenska kvinnorörelsens pionjärer i debatt om kvinnans kallelse ca 1860–1900.* 1999 (US). Diss.

Mark Davies *A Perambulating Paradox: British Travel Literature and the Image of Sweden c. 1770–1865.* 2000 (US). Diss.

Lars M Andersson *"En jude är en jude är en jude…". Representationer av "juden" i svensk skämtpress omkring 1900–1930.* 2000 (US). Diss.

Mats Hellstenius *Krigen som inte blev av. Sveriges fredliga officerskår vid 1800-talets mitt* 2000 (US). Diss.

Irene Andersson *Kvinnor mot krig. Aktioner och nätverk för fred 1914–1940.* 2001 (LUS). Diss.

Elisabeth Reuterswärd *Ett massmedium för folket. Studier i de allmänna kungörelsernas funktion i 1700-talets samhälle.* 2001 (LUS). Diss.

Anna Lindberg *Experience and Identity: A Historical Account of Class, Caste, and Gender among the Cashew Workers of Kerala, 1930–2000.* 2001 (LUS). Diss.